Lancashire

A SOCIAL HISTORY, 1558 – 1939

For my parents, Eric and Nora Walton,
and in memory of my maternal grandparents,
Alec Kimmons, who died before I could enjoy his company,
and Emma Kimmons, who taught me to read

John K. Walton

LANCASHIRE

A SOCIAL HISTORY,
1558 – 1939

Manchester University Press

Copyright © John Walton 1987

Published by Manchester University Press
Oxford Road, Manchester, M13 9PL
and 27 South Main Street, Wolfeboro, NH 03894-2069, U.S.A.

British Library cataloguing in publication data
Walton, John K.
  A social history of Lancashire. 1558–1939.
  1. Lancashire — Social conditions
  I. Title
  942.7'6   HN398.L3

Library of Congress cataloging in publication data
Walton, John K.
  A social history of Lancashire, 1558–1939.
  Includes index.
  1. Lancashire — Social conditions. 2. Great Britain —
History — Modern period, 1485–   . I. Title.
HN398.L3W35   1986   942.7'6   86-21659

ISBN 0-7190-1820-X
hardback

Typeset in Baskerville
by Williams Graphics, Abergele, Clwyd, North Wales

Printed in Great Britain
by Robert Hartnoll (1985) Ltd, Bodmin, Cornwall

Contents

[v]

Maps and plates

Credits   *CJ* – Maps drawn by *Claire Jarvis*   *JS – Jenny Smith*   *HM – Harris Museum*, Preston, with special thanks to Frank Carpenter   *MM – Mike Mullett*   *MS – Manchester Studies*, Manchester Polytechnic, with special thanks to Audrey Linkman   *HCM – Halton Chemical Museum*, Widnes, with special thanks to Mike Greatbatch   Thanks also to Nigel Morgan for advice and guidance

Preface

In a sense, this book began life in 1974, when I began to teach a course on 'The Regional History of North-West England, 1750–1900' (as it then was) at the University of Lancaster. In the following year I also introduced a course on 'Pre-industrial Society in England, 1600–1750, with special reference to the North-West'. These courses are still running, though they have changed a great deal in the intervening years. What follows is a development of the lectures and seminar notes for those courses; but it is also much more than that. It represents nearly four years of research, writing and revision, building on what I had believed to be a useful working knowledge of the main themes and issues in the social history of Lancashire. It also represents a daunting accumulation of academic and personal debts. I acknowledge them with pleasure and gratitude.

At Lancaster, in the first place, Harold Perkin suggested that a course on pre-industrial English history, with a local dimension, would be a useful addition to the History Department's repertoire; and I was appointed, in part, to teach it. Without that initiative, this book would certainly never have been written. My ideas and approach were also influenced in a formative way by John Marshall, and I hope that some at least of his stimulating approach to regional history will have made its mark on what follows. More generally, my colleagues in Lancaster's excellent History Department have provided an ideal academic environment. If I single out Mike Winstanley and Eric Evans, it is because their work is closest to my own; but Mike Mullett and Sandy Grant have also been particularly helpful on occasions, and Bob Bliss's conversation remains as essential a stimulant as his coffee. But this book is also the product of innumerable discussions, formal and informal, with students. The contribution of the MA course in Modern Social History is hinted at in the footnotes; but many undergraduates have also made their mark on this book, if only by failing to prepare for seminars and forcing me to desperate expedients in an effort to provoke discussion. In very different vein, I am glad to have the opportunity to thank Martin Blinkhorn for being such a friendly and supportive head of department.

This book stands on the shoulders of many previous researchers and interpreters. At times, no doubt, it falls off them. To make an invidious selection, I am conscious of èspecial debts to Christopher Haigh, B. G. Blackwood, G. H. Tupling, A. P. Wadsworth and J. de L. Mann, Alan Booth, Douglas Farnie, Robert Sykes, Patrick Joyce, Nev Kirk, Jill Liddington and the late Jill Norris, Elizabeth Roberts, Joseph White, and Peter Clarke. I have disagreed with several of them, and with many others, in the text; but their work has stimulated argument and made it possible to attempt to pull threads together over wide areas and long periods. I hope I have treated other people's work with the respect it deserves. The book could not have been attempted without them.

[vii]

Many friends have helped the book on its way, directly or indirectly. Bill Fuge, Bob Poole, Lyn Murfin, Phil Ingram, Meg Whittle, Cliff O'Neill and Sylvia Walby fall into both categories. I hope that Bernice Walton knows how important she was to the early stages of the book, and especially to its formative years. Zena Haigh helped more than she may think; and the De Pols in Preston, and the Winstanleys in Lancaster, have provided valued moral support. Nigel Morgan drew my attention to unsuspected wonders, and Jonathan Ratter was also kind enough to share his expertise. Frank Carpenter of the Harris Museum, Preston, and Audrey Linkman of Manchester Studies at Manchester Polytechnic, were helpful beyond the call of duty in advising on illustrations. Claire Jarvis drew the maps, and Peter Mingins contributed excellent practical carto-graphical advice. John Banks at Manchester University Press waited patiently for a delayed manuscript, and Cath Annabel and Juanita Griffiths applied the thumbscrews with amazing delicacy. Jenny Smith commented on some of the chapters, took some of the photographs, encouraged me through the difficult bits and made it all seem fun: I thank her especially.

J.W.
Preston, Easter Sunday, 1986

Map 1 Lancashire in the sixteenth century: towns, topography and administrative boundaries.

[ix]

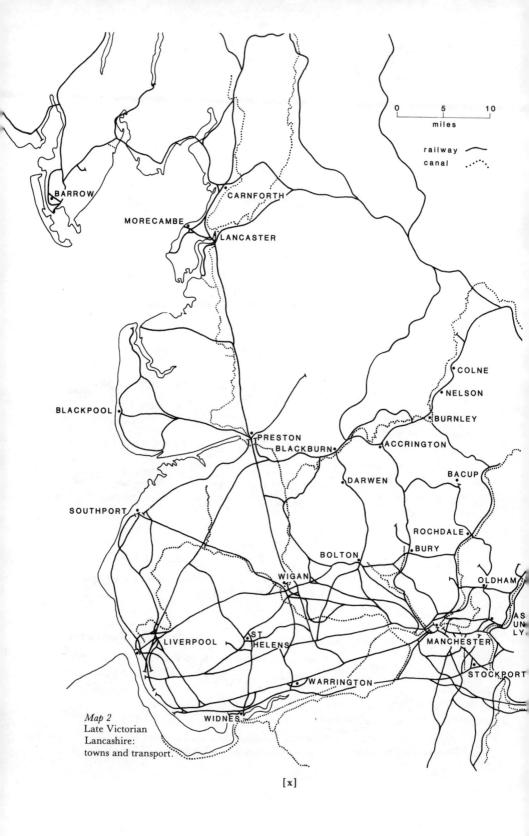

0   5   10
miles

railway ———
canal ....

BARROW

CARNFORTH

MORECAMBE

LANCASTER

COLNE

NELSON

BLACKPOOL

BURNLEY

PRESTON

ACCRINGTON

BLACKBURN

BACUP

DARWEN

SOUTHPORT

ROCHDALE

BURY

BOLTON

OLDHAM

WIGAN

AS
UN
LY

LIVERPOOL

ST
HELENS

MANCHESTER

STOCKPORT

WARRINGTON

WIDNES

Map 2
Late Victorian
Lancashire:
towns and transport.

[x]

Introduction

The Lancashire of this book was officially abolished in 1974; and was not resuscitated by the demise of the metropolitan counties of Greater Manchester and Merseyside in April 1986. The historic county was much more extensive than the truncated remnant which retains the label at the time of writing. It extended from the Mersey in the south to the coppices and rounded hills of Furness and Cartmel, north of the sands of Morecambe Bay; from the docks of Liverpool to the shipyard cranes of Barrow. It also stretched out south-eastwards to the commercial metropolis of Manchester and its satellite industrial towns, and stitched together an untidy frontier with similarly remote corners of Derbyshire, Cheshire and the West Riding of Yorkshire, high in the inhospitable moorlands and welcoming upland settlements of the Pennines. It is all, I suspect, still 'Lancashire' to most of its inhabitants, who share more than just an allegiance to the proud traditions and faltering current fortunes of the county cricket club which still preserves its territorial integrity. What precisely it is that they share is difficult to define, for these broad and sprawling acres are more a geographical expression than a cultural unity. We shall see that the differences between Liverpool and Manchester, Barrow and Blackpool, Oldham and St. Helens, and even between neighbours like Blackburn and Burnley, Bolton and Wigan, have deep historical roots. The farming systems and rural societies of Furness and the Fylde, west Lancashire and the Pennine uplands, also present sharp and arresting contrasts. This gives variety and interest to the social history of a county which is too often written off by outsiders as an unlovely jumble of derelict mills, inky rivers and Victorian urban nostalgia. The prevailing picture is derived from Coronation Street and *Hard Times*, and from Orwell's Wigan Pier rather than the tourist board's revised version. Despite the best efforts of romantic topographers like Jessica Lofthouse, Lancashire's 'fair face' of water meadow and moorland stream, stately homes and Roman remains, is known to relatively few outside the North-West. But the contrasts are vivid and inescapable. It is easier to describe the divisions in the county, than to say what unites it. Customs, accents and tricks of speech vary not only from one end of the county to the other, but also from town to neighbouring town. What unity there is, perhaps, flows from a dim but real consciousness of a historical identity which demands allegiance to the Red Rose, if only in opposition to the pallid symbol of a neighbouring county. Administrative boundaries have an almost inevitable artificiality: they rarely coincide with, or keep in step with, the social and economic relationships which matter to people, although they usually define the political ones. Thus the cotton industry spilled over from Lancashire into Cheshire and Derbyshire, and the Liverpool and Manchester suburbs marched across the Mersey and into the Cheshire plain. As a result, this book cannot shelter behind the Lancashire boundary: its basic terms of reference must range a little more widely. But Lancastrians know that they live in Lancashire, and that this makes them different from Yorkshire or Derbyshire people; and this sense of identity, though elusive to the scientific measurer, provides a rationale for what follows.

Academic historians will require a more academic justification for this book. Why a county history? Why Lancashire? And why this particular time-span? In the first place, the county as an administrative unit has deep enough historical roots for it to be an essential focus of traditional loyalty, at a comprehensible intermediate level between the locality and the nation, throughout the period covered by this book. Always, of course, there were administrative and economic divisions within the county. Already in the seventeenth century, and with sharpening clarity from the late eighteenth century, two distinctive economic and cultural regions were cohering within Lancashire, and extending into adjoining counties: the one centred on Manchester, which will often be referred to by the convenient shorthand of 'cotton Lancashire'; and the one which owed allegiance to Liverpool, which will often be labelled 'Merseyside'.[1] North of the Ribble and in Furness, identities of this kind remained less clear-cut; and the two industrial Lancashires met in a confusion of overlapping characteristics somewhere around Wigan and Leigh. These differences within Lancashire constitute a real advantage to the social historian of the county. Under the umbrella of a recognisable area which was intelligible to contemporaries, and important to them, we can trace, assess and seek to explain the emergence and development of visibly differing regional economic and social systems. Such an enterprise has an importance of its own, as we draw up comparisons and contrasts within a framework which allows deep and satisfying analysis. It should also form a contribution to the new social history of Britain which must eventually emerge, taking full account of the diversity of regional experiences which went to make up the national whole.

Regional variations are so pervasive and enduring in British society that national generalisations which fail to take full account of them, and to use them as an essential basis for analysis, must remain abstract and unsatisfactory. Moreover, although the nature of these variations certainly changed in important ways in response to industrialisation, transport innovation, administrative changes and the rise of mass entertainment, among many other things, the essential significance of regional differences remains un-impaired. British history is a jigsaw puzzle with ever-changing pieces, rather than a smooth, easily generalisable unity. John Langton's argument that 'there were important regional as well as local differences in pre-industrial England, and that ... far from eradicating them, the process of industrialization both intensified them and heightened people's consciousness of their existence', is brilliantly expressed and highly apposite. One might take issue with his accusation than historians have neglected or played down regional differences: it depends which ones you read, and how you read them. The existence of this book, too, constitutes a rebuke to the geographical imperialism which allows Langton to write that it 'is our job, not [historians'], to write the regional geography of early industrial England'. It reminds me irresistibly of Sellar and Yeatman's discovery, in their sequel to *1066 and All That*, of Geography's ambition to become Top Subject, and hold the academic world in thrall.[2] In fact, of course, historians and geographers offer interrelated approaches to cognate problems, and they share a lot of territory. We shall severely constrict the advancement of our understanding of the rise and decline of industrial Britain if we regard this territory as debatable land to be fought over by raiding parties from the stockaded encampments of rival disciplines, rather than cultivating it in common or in amicable collaboration. I hope that this book, which depends heavily in places on excellent work by historical geographers (Langton included), has been written in just such an unsectarian spirit.

Why Lancashire? Quite simply, because the county's history is of world historical importance in its own right. It contains within its boundaries the area which became the cradle of the world's first industrial revolution. There are other contenders, perhaps: the Ironbridge area might have its partisans; so in a different idiom, might the North-Eastern coalfield, or Clydeside.[3] What gives south, and especially south-east Lancashire its overwhelming claim to pre-eminence is the early combination of large towns and factory industries alongside mining and heavy industry of various kinds, and the mid-Victorian coalescence of the Manchester and Liverpool conurbations. Contemporaries were well aware of this uniqueness, as the comments of a procession of visitors, sometimes awed, sometimes appalled, always profoundly affected by the experience, bore eloquent witness; and it is highly significant that so many of them were published, and that some have become classics of their kind. Historians have been well aware of it too, as the Lancashire experience has been tested by researchers of every conceivable political colour, from evangelists of world-wide economic growth seeking in Lancashire a model for the industrialisation of 'undeveloped' countries, to Marxists seeking to understand why the world's first industrial society so signally failed to produce the world's first proletarian revolution. Cotton Lancashire, especially, has its place in imaginative literature, from Dickens and Mrs Gaskell to Walter Greenwood and Howard Spring; and a flourishing Victorian dialect literature

[3]

coexisted with the rich variety of outpourings for the wider public. It has generated a powerful and distinctive artistic imagery, especially in the work of Lowry, although (Sir Thomas Beecham apart) its musical culture has depended heavily on imported genius.

Persuasive historical simplifications and myths have grown up and been perpetuated alongside these artistic images. The eighteenth-century innovators in the cotton industry have become household names, and garbled versions of their heroic exploits have been inflicted on generations of schoolchildren. The horrors of the slave trade have been placed at the core of a brilliant and widely influential polemic which gives Liverpool's exploitation of the Africans a central explanatory role in the genesis of the 'Industrial Revolution' in Lancashire and, by extension, in Britain as a whole.[4] The myth of the self-made, rags-to-riches industrialist, steeped in a Nonconformist Protestant work ethic, has been undermined by academics but not in the outside world. Many people still believe that the agricultural population of southern and eastern England, dispossessed by enclosures, limped northwards in their millions to work in Lancashire's factories: a belief which was exploded by the late Arthur Redford as long ago as 1926.[5] I could go on at length; but I hope to undermine and complicate a lot of the mythology of Lancashire in the main body of the book. However, it is also worth noting the possible emergence of a new mythology about Lancashire among academics. It arises from calculations which suggest that the principal stimulus to Victorian economic growth came from the service sector, which responded to consumer demand generated by industrial trade and finance and the lavish lifestyles of landed society. The great plutocrats, too, were bankers and financiers rather than industrialists; and the key to national prosperity was London as opposed to the industrial centres of the provinces. This is salutary and useful: the danger is that it may generate a presumption that manufacturing industry was of secondary importance in British economic and social history. This is to be resisted: social history is ultimately about the experiences, relationships and values of all sorts and conditions of people, and the importance of the Lancashire industrial complex as an employer of labour and a concentration of population, and as a crucible for social and political change, remains intact even if we accept the still debatable contention that the main impetus to economic growth in nineteenth-century Britain came from the metropolis and high finance, the Home Counties and the landed wealth of shires.[6]

Lancashire's historical importance has been recognised by the appearance of a vast and proliferating cornucopia of studies, usually concentrating on particular themes and places within the county, and often explicitly testing theories in the context of what the writers regard as self-evidently an important kind of setting. The result of all this is a daunting volume of material which confronts the would-be county historian like a mountain range. Two illustrations must suffice. Terry Wyke's 'preliminary', 'select list of the secondary literature' on Manchester alone contains 1200 items; and Douglas Farnie's bibliography (also 'select') of printed sources on the cotton industry between 1815 and 1896 runs to 45 pages of annotated listings.[7] But modern studies of the county as a whole, or even of the cotton district or Merseyside, over extended periods are few and usually lightweight. The best recent short history is probably J. D. Marshall's *Lancashire*, which compresses some interesting original research into its brief but lively chapters, and suffers severely from the publishers' constraints on length and format. Philip Gooderson's survey of the county tries to cover almost everything within a limited compass, and the results are readable but sometimes idiosyncratic. The contributions by Aspin and Bagley also have their virtues; and Sheila Marriner packs a lot of economic material into her more substantial work on the economic and social develop- ment of Merseyside.[8] Still very useful is the survey of the county's economic history in Freeman, Rogers and Kinvig's historical geography of Lancashire, Cheshire and the Isle of Man.[9] Most of the old county political histories are of little use to the modern social historian, but contemporary surveys and descriptions like those of Aikin and Baines can be quarried with enjoyment.[10] But there has been no attempt to produce a substantial survey of the social history of Lancashire as a whole over the period of its economic rise and decline, making use of the enormous range of often conflicting local and thematic case studies and pulling them together into an overall interpretation. This is an important gap in the literature; and this book is an attempt to fill it.

But why start in 1558 and finish in 1939? The first date is, in many respects, arbitrary; but it expresses my belief that the middle years of the sixteenth century saw the beginning of a wide range of important and interrelated changes which mark the years around the beginning of Elizabeth I's reign as a watershed in the history of the county. By 1939, on the other hand, the first 'Industrial Revolution', the product of the chain of events which began in earnest in Elizabethan times, had run its course, and the demise of the set of economic, social and political arrangements which had emerged in the Victorian heyday of industrial Lancashire was far enough advanced to be clearly terminal. The period covered by this book thus has a kind of dramatic unity. It might have been possible to take the story into the false dawn of post-1945 revival and the subsequent collapse of the remains of the old system; but the secondary literature on this period is only just beginning to emerge, and it would be very difficult to sit back and set these very recent years in perspective. Within the period 1558–1939, the book is quite heavily weighted in its coverage to the developments after 1770 or so. This is not because the earlier centuries are somehow unimportant: it reflects the magnitude and complexity of changes in the classic 'Industrial Revolution' period and afterwards, and the need to do justice to a vast array of sometimes furious historical debates. A study based mainly (though never entirely) on secondary

[5]

sources has to respond to the interests and priorities of those who have gone before, although that should not preclude, and has not precluded, due attention being given to important themes which have been little discussed in a Lancashire context. There is room for book-length studies of several shorter periods of Lancashire social history, and I hope this book will not inhibit their appearance. Meanwhile, I offer what follows as an interim assessment of the main themes in the social history of a part of Britain whose central place in world history is secure, but deserves to be more fully and subtly understood.

1

LANCASHIRE IN THE MIDDLE
OF THE SIXTEENTH CENTURY

Mid-Tudor Lancashire was an obscure, remote, insular and backward corner of England.[1] The population density was low, towns were small and under-developed, long-distance trade was very limited in its scope and range, and wide areas of the county were given over to moss and moorland. Local magnates retained considerable autonomy; some still exercised feudal rights of wardship and marriage over their tenants, and labour dues and payments in kind were widespread elements in the relationships between small farmers and their landlords. Many gentlemen maintained armed bands of liveried retainers, whose presence helped to ensure a low threshold of violence in an infamously unruly society. The machinery of national government, whether ecclesiastical or secular, creaked protestingly or failed to work at all; indeed, the first loyalty of many was to the Earl of Derby, or to some lesser local landowner, rather than to a distant monarch. Substantial gentry were thin on the ground, and only a narrow élite among them looked beyond the county for marriage partners, education or political preferment. Churches and schools were in short supply, and Lancashire's reputation for poverty and barbarism remained widespread in Elizabethan times and beyond. Heralds, antiquarians and topographers throughout the century approached the county with some trepidation: William Camden, for example, experienced 'a kind of dread: may it forebode no ill!'[2]

Camden's fears were inspired more by the remoter and more mountainous parts of the county than by the southern and western plains, however, and by the time of his visit in 1585 momentous changes were beginning to take place, though their impact was patchy and localised as yet. The roots of these changes can already be discerned in the second quarter of the sixteenth century, when

[7]

modest but significant innovations in economy, society and administration were making themselves felt. It was at this time that the spread of encroachment and enclosure began in earnest on the upland wastes of the Pennine foothills, especially in the old forest areas. The Lancashire textile industries began to reach out to distant markets and sources of supply, and evidence of the growth of coal mining and other industries becomes increasingly noticeable. In association with these trends, there was probably a sharp upturn in population growth, although satisfactory figures seem impossible to come by. The gentry were brought increasingly into contact with external educational and cultural influences, and their manners and morals were regulated a little more closely by the new ecclesiastical administrative machinery of the diocese of Chester, founded in 1541 and significantly less remote than the previous régime which had been based in Lichfield, although we shall see that the new arrangements remained decidedly ramshackle. County administration was also tightened up, as quarter sessions met more regularly and systematically. In the favourable climate of Edward VI's reign, moreover, a sprinkling of earnest religious reformers appeared, almost all of them based in the Manchester area, although the county at large long remained a bastion of traditional Catholicism.[3]

Emphasis on the feudal backwardness of mid-Tudor Lancashire thus requires some qualification. In any case, Elizabethan feudal and Catholic survivals were far from being confined to the north of England. B. W. Beckingsale provides a wide range of examples from the Midlands and South to show that great territorial magnates with liveried retainers, feudal tenurial survivals, forest areas where the influence of official religion and the law was slender and ineffectual, and a propensity to violence, rebellion and determined allegiance to local custom, were far from being the sole prerogative of the northern shires.[4] There is an element of special pleading about his impressionistic case, but at least it reminds us that in comparing regions we are dealing with differences of emphasis and degree rather than talking about stark and absolute contrasts. The evidence of incipient change in Lancashire in the second quarter of the sixteenth century can only reinforce this point, and as we explore the condition of mid-Tudor Lancashire a little further, we shall need to bear it constantly in mind.

In the first place, however, we must admit that by all available measures Lancashire was one of the poorest of English counties in the early sixteenth century. Indeed, it had long been so, and was to remain so for well over a century. In the tax assessments for the lay subsidy of 1515, Lancashire came last of the 38 English counties assessed in terms of pounds levied per thousand acres, although four of the poorest counties, Cumberland, Westmorland, Northumberland and Durham, were exempted. Lancashire's assessment per thousand acres, at £3.8, compares very unfavourably with Northern and Midland neighbours like Staffordshire and the West Riding of Yorkshire, and more so with figures of £102 for Essex, £100.5 for Kent and £238.1 for metropolitan Middlesex. Even when the assessments are adjusted to take account of wealth in ecclesiastical hands, Lancashire lags far behind the rest, to an extent which seems clearly to reflect variations in the distribution of real wealth rather than differences in assessment policy. Lancashire was, admittedly, a thinly populated pastoral county with few population concentrations, and its comparative per capita wealth was probably much healthier than its wealth per acre. But the county came at or near the bottom of a series of rankings compiled from less satisfactory taxation evidence at various points between the early fourteenth and mid seventeenth century, and its assessed wealth shows very little growth in real or comparative terms between the fourteenth century and the early sixteenth, although Lancashire's population may well have risen over two-and-a-half times between 1377 and 1563.[5]

Before we can discuss the implications of this apparent relative poverty, we need to say a little more about the economic activities on which the people of Lancashire depended. In the first place, the absolute predominance of agriculture stands out, in Lancashire as almost everywhere in mid-sixteenth-century England. Farming practices varied considerably within the country, however. Climate and soil conspired to ensure that the eastern uplands would be predominantly pastoral, with vast expanses of common and waste for rough grazing, and a very limited cultivation of oats to meet the basic needs of the occupiers of increasingly small and subdivided parcels of enclosed land. Cattle raising had dominated the economy of these Pennine foothills since the major landowners had developed dairy farms in the forest areas during the thirteenth century. During the first half of the sixteenth century, however, sheep were becoming increasingly important in Pendle and Rossendale, at least, though probate inventories suggest that they were less in evidence elsewhere.[6] The south-western lowlands were mainly pastoral, cattle-rearing areas, with a high proportion of undrained moss and marshland. Where soil type and relief permitted, however, there were islands of more prosperous arable farming, with wheat and barley being grown as well as oats; but the main area of arable formed a crescent stretching from the Manchester district in the south-east to Preston, with outlying fingers extending into parts of the Fylde and along the Ribble valley. Even in this central Lancashire plain, arable land made up only between 55 and 62 per cent of the cultivated area, on evidence which spans the period from 1450 to 1558; and even here, apparently, 'almost half the land stood idle'.[7] Mixed farming prevailed, with small herds of cattle and sometimes sheep. Oats was the main grain crop, being used for bread and malt as well as fodder, although a wider range of grain and fodder crops was possible than on the uplands.[8]

Significant changes were taking place in Lancashire agriculture during the first half of the sixteenth century. On the Pennine foothills, the long process of population growth, subdivision of holdings and squatter encroachment on the extensive commons and wastes was beginning in earnest, aided by the Crown's lack of interest in the old royal forests as hunting preserves, and by its eagerness to maximise revenues from its broad acres of Lancashire uplands by ratifying the tenure of squatters to bring in rents and entry fines. Deer and woodlands were in rapid retreat by the 1550s, when common land was beginning to be parcelled out by commissioners on a substantial scale in the Forests of Bowland and Rossendale. The small copyhold tenants who benefited from these developments were often eager recruits to domestic industry, and the growing importance of sheep rearing in Rossendale may well have been connected with the early stages of the domestic woollen industry there.[9] Further north, commons were being improved and partitioned by tenants on the Dacre estate at Halton and Aughton in the Lune valley.[10] In south-west Lancashire, according to Walker, the early sixteenth century was a period of transition, as new areas of pasture were brought into use to supplement existing arable and meadow land and tilt the balance of specialisation towards cattle. Walker's account, published in 1939, is difficult to fit into more recent analyses of Lancashire's farming areas, as he lumps together the south-western district with part of the central Lancashire plain; and the picture is complicated still further by Thirsk's suggestion that social problems in central Lancashire arose from a rapid transition in the opposite direction, from pasture to arable, which was also being experienced in a more gradual and less traumatic way in the south-west of the county. These accounts and speculations are very difficult to reconcile, and only a systematic programme of research in primary sources will provide an answer.[11] What does seem clear is that despite wide areas of unproductive mosses and marshes, the south-western hundreds of Leyland and West Derby, the former including a substantial wedge of central Lancashire arable, were wealthier and more densely populated in the mid sixteenth century than the rest of the county, so far as can be judged from military levies and tax assessments. But the main centres of economic activity were already beginning to shift eastwards with the colonisation of the Pennine uplands, a trend which was to accelerate over the next century.[12]

Certain distinctive Lancashire features stand out among the cross-currents and occasional contradictions in the secondary sources. Like much of the northern and western half of England, this was an area of late settlement in which most of the cultivated land had been enclosed as it was cleared, a process which was still continuing in most of the county. This produced a landscape of scattered settlement and small pastoral farms with many little meadows and arable closes, and limited control of farming practices by manorial overlords and manor courts. Enclosure took the form of parcelling out extensive common land and waste, rather than the conversion of open-field arable to pasture which had such disruptive effects in parts of the Midlands during a period when the terms of trade were moving in favour of cattle and sheep. Lancashire enclosures, indeed, tended to encourage population growth, in-migration and the proliferation of small farms. Common arable fields and meadows formed only a small proportion of the cultivated area by the later sixteenth century in those townships where they survived, and Youd, at least, finds little evidence of even the most unsophisticated of crop rotation systems on them, though others are more sanguine.[13] Indeed, apart from the breeding and rearing of longhorn cattle on the plain, which helped to improve or at least maintain the quality of stock in other parts of the country, it is hard to find significant sectors of innovation or advancement in Lancashire agriculture at this time.[14] Small farmers with limited access to capital, new ideas or major markets eked out an often precarious existence on land which was often difficult and sometimes downright inhospitable.

An economy of this sort was well suited to the development of rural industries, especially as the availability of land and (in some areas, at least) the practice of partible inheritance encouraged population growth and a supply of under-employed labour on the uplands.[15] Significantly, the Lancashire textile indus-tries really began to develop in earnest in the second quarter of the sixteenth century, especially in the east of the county. Coarse woollen cloth had long been manufactured here: there were fulling mills at Manchester, Burnley and Colne in the late thirteenth and early fourteenth centuries, and cloth exports to the Low Countries via Hull may already have been under way in the late fourteenth century.[16] In the 1530s and 1540s, however, a spate of evidence suggests a rapid expansion of regular trade and employment. Manchester, especially, became a thriving centre for the manufacture and marketing of coarse woollens and linen, and Bolton, Bury, Burnley, Rochdale and Colne developed as small but important organising centres for the woollen manufacture of their surrounding countrysides, while Eccles, Wigan and Ormskirk served the linen industry in similar ways. Linen yarn and wool were being imported from Ireland in significant quantities by this time, and wool was also brought in from Yorkshire and the Midlands to supplement the coarse local product. Markets were also expanding, as occasional ventures to London, Hereford and Southampton in the 1530s (and, perhaps, earlier) developed to such an extent that the early 1560s saw a separate hall set aside for Lancashire woollens at Blackwell Hall in London. From here much of the cloth was exported by London merchants, mainly at this stage to France. Lancashire's woollen cloths were of low quality, but they were increasingly finding a ready sale, and this was reflected in the growing concern of central government to regulate the county's cloth trade in the 1550s.[17] The linen industry remained more locally orientated in its marketing.

Several other important industries were developing noticeably towards mid-century. Coal was being dug commercially in several places: on the Bradshaw estate at Haigh, near Wigan, and elsewhere in south-west Lancashire by the 1530s; in the Bolton area at about the same time; and in Pendle and Rossendale, where disputes were arising between copyholders and manorial overlords about the right to dig for coal on the waste. At Prescot, in particular, mining operations began early, with the Earl of Derby leasing out coal mines at Whiston in 1521; by 1564 coal from this area was being exported through Liverpool to Ireland. Significantly, after 1550 the Duchy and Palatinate of Lancaster began to take a keen interest in surveying their estates for coal.[18] The uses of coal were still mainly domestic, and Lancashire was anyway well supplied with peat for household purposes; but the increased exploitation of this resource is a significant straw in the wind. So are stray pieces of evidence about the rise of a variety of manufactures, from pewter to felt hats, which suggest incipient, if small-scale and localised, industrial advance on a broad front.[19]

These economic stirrings were concentrated in the south and east of the county, although a long-established charcoal iron industry was in desultory operation in Furness as well as Rossendale at around mid-century.[20] As yet, little urban development had resulted from what were essentially rural industries based on a 'dual economy' which mainly involved agriculture and textiles. Manchester seems to have been the largest and most prosperous Lancashire town at mid-century: Leland thought well of it, and the built-up area seems to have had between 1500 and 2000 inhabitants at this time.[21] Liverpool's population is even harder to assess: a household listing of 1565 puts it as low as 700, but around 1000 is probably a more accurate figure.[22] Preston, with its administrative functions and expanding market area, may have been slightly larger, and so may Warrington ('of a prety bygnes ... a better market then Manchestre', according to Leland), and Wigan ('as bigge as Warington and better buildid').[23] Lancaster itself was sadly decayed, and nowhere outside Manchester was there much evidence of urban prosperity or political autonomy.[24] Below this level Lancashire was quite well endowed with little market towns, though the word 'town' is misleadingly grandiose in this context. Over the period 1500–1640 Lancashire's markets were as thick on the ground as those of Staffordshire, Leicestershire and Wiltshire, and their density was greater than in any of Lancashire's neighbours, including Cheshire, Derbyshire, Nottinghamshire and Lincolnshire.[25] Some of the old-established markets were ailing or extinct by Leland's time, while several in the textile district were only just becoming established, with more to come later in the century; so the mid-Tudor position may not have been as favourable as figures spanning 1500–1640 make it look. Moreover, even the largest towns of mid-Tudor Lancashire came a long way down the contemporary urban hierarchy. On Hoskins's reckoning there were up to fifteen provincial towns with populations over 5000 in 1524, and 'a considerable number' with three or four thousand; but none were in Lancashire.[26] The five largest towns in the county, small as they were, can have accounted for little more than one in seventeen or eighteen of a Lancashire population estimated by Haigh at 95,000 in 1563.[27] Even Manchester (like many much larger towns) had a strong rural element in its mid-Tudor economy,[28] and the low level of urbanisation in the county reminds us that economic development and specialisation was still very limited, despite the evidence for growth and change in certain sectors and areas.

Social structure and living standards reinforce the overall impression of agrarian domination and mitigated, but real, backwardness. The Stanleys, Earls of Derby, dominated the county to a remarkable extent, after a rapid but not embarrassingly meteoric rise from obscure Cheshire gentry origins since the fourteenth century. Despite the limited abilities of the third Earl, his wealth and territorial influence were such that his support became indispensable to Thomas Cromwell during the Pilgrimage of Grace in 1536. The government paid a high price for Derby's aid against the rebels, for he was granted full governmental powers within the county, delegated from the Crown, and henceforth, as Haigh says, 'The Earl of Derby and his council ... formed the link between central and local government. The Earl was too important to be bypassed, and the Crown ruled Lancashire through him ...' Derby obtained the county lieutenancy, with its important military powers, at its inception in 1551, and contrary to the usual practice of regular rotation, it remained in the Stanley family for ninety years with only one short break. This combination of territorial and political predominance was already unique in mid-Tudor England, and after the 1530s the role of the Stanleys in Lancashire came to look increasingly anachronistic; but their power was none the less real for that.[29] Their position was buttressed by broad acres, enormous wealth, and an ostentatiously numerous and hospitable household which cost over £1500 per year in food in 1561, and provided jobs for large numbers of gentry and their sons, as well as many more menial servants. In the same year £81 was apparently spent on wine, at a time when it was still an unusual luxury in Lancashire, and over £131 on 'Spices and ffrutes' bought in London as well as Lancashire.[30] Apart from a household of well over a hundred, an unusually large establishment at this time, the third Earl could command the loyalty of hundreds or even thousands of tenants and retainers, and in 1557 he was responsible for 800 of the 2000 soldiers mustered in Lancashire for a Scottish campaign.[31]

The Stanleys were not alone in keeping liveried retainers in what was still a notoriously violent county, where the peculiar legal system of the Duchy and Palatinate made the machinery of justice particularly intractable. No other family could approach the Stanleys in sheer breadth of resources and political clout, however. Immediately below them in the county hierarchy lay a wider élite of knights and esquires, who provided the manpower for subordinate administrative posts, from deputy lieutenants and sheriffs to forest officials and Justices of the Peace. Among this group, ten or a dozen families stood out as particularly wealthy and active in major offices, although very few made any impact at all beyond the county.[32] Below this small band of county leaders stretched an uncertain number of lesser and parochial gentry, shading off across an ill-defined and shadowy frontier into the upper yeomanry.

The dividing line between the gentry and the lower orders is rightly regarded as very important by social historians of pre-industrial England, but in practice the circumstances of mid-Tudor Lancashire make it very difficult to locate. Haigh accepts the verdicts of the Heralds, who made their way gingerly into the county to investigate claims to gentility in 1533 and 1567, and suggests on this basis that in Lancashire the gentry 'formed a much smaller proportion of the total population than in most other areas', with a ratio in the 1560s of one gentleman to every 800 people.[33] His attempt to compare Lancashire with Yorkshire, Essex and Kent comes to grief, however, because the figures he cites for those counties come from between 40 and 75 years later, after an 'inflation of honours' in which the Heralds' criteria for gentility had been considerably relaxed.[34] In any case, there was more to the making of a gentleman than lineage and armorial bearings: wealth, acreage, lifestyle, education, conduct and acceptance of responsibility counted for at least as much in determining the attitudes of peers and neighbours which alone made the title meaningful.[35] If we were to compare the number of Lancashire gentry in 1567, on Haigh's definition, with the total for 1600 arrived at by B. G. Blackwood on the less demanding basis of description as a gentleman in the freeholders' list of that year, we would find a sevenfold increase, or very nearly so, from 112 to 763.[36] This is, to say the least, implausible, and it seems certain that Haigh has seriously understated the number of people regarded by their neighbours as gentlemen in the Lancashire of the 1560s, though we cannot say how great his shortfall was, and nor can we be sure how many of Blackwood's Lancashire gentry would have been accepted as such in other counties. What does emerge quite clearly, however, is that Lancashire was very short of really substantial gentry families, and that a large number of middling landowners were poised uncertainly between the parish gentry and the upper yeomanry.

The limited number of substantial gentry families was reflected in the paucity of Justices of the Peace – only 24 for the whole county in 1564, despite administrative problems – and in the prevailing tendency to inter-marriage within a narrow cousinhood of leading families.[37] Even this county élite had an unenviable reputation for violence, parochialism and sexual laxity. Disputes were still being settled by pitched battles between bands of armed retainers, probably to a greater extent than in the rest of England (excepting the northern borders and not including Wales), and a surviving tradition of child marriages, with property and territorial considerations uppermost, no doubt helped to encourage the proliferation of mistresses, concubines and bastard children which reduced some households to utter confusion.[38] Most members of the Lancashire élite married within the county, and few of them were educated or sought office beyond its bounds, a state of affairs which bolstered the pre-eminence of the Earl of Derby, with his wider contacts, still further. As in so many other respects, the pattern was beginning to change in the 1530s and 1540s, as more Lancastrians attended the universities and Inns of Court, or took apprenticeships with London companies; but many of these were younger sons who never returned to the county. The wilder excesses of the resident gentry were beginning to be curbed a little by the church courts and by royal commissions against adulterers in the middle decades of the sixteenth century, and the law was already becoming more attractive than brute force as a means of solving disputes. Haigh cites the case of the Rishton family, whose response to a dispute over seating arrangements (and therefore family prestige) in the chapel at Church in 1536 was to wreck the contested pews and fight a pitched battle with their opponents. In 1555, however, they took a similar quarrel to the Bishop of Chester's consistory court.[39] This particular example may well give an unduly optimistic impression, however, and we should remember the persistent delinquency of office-holding gentlemen like Sir John Atherton, who before his death in 1573 was involved in 'over twenty court cases, in most of which he was a defendant, for violence, theft, conspiracy to cheat, debt and abuse of his wife'.[40] Recourse to the law did not preclude the persistence of a low threshold of violence, especially when those who administered the law were themselves visibly disreputable. The Tudor quest for order and control was making headway, but its realisation in mid-sixteenth-century Lancashire was very incomplete.

The limited financial and cultural resources of the Lancashire gentry found expression in their houses and material possessions. In this respect as in others, the vivid opulence of the Earl of Derby's calculatingly ostentatious lifestyle was brought into even sharper relief by the lack of local competition. Castles were thin on the ground in Lancashire, and the mid-Tudor survivors were either decayed or in the hands of the Crown. Most gentry families still lived in unpretentious timber-framed houses with wattle-and-daub infill, and the use of brick and stone crept in only gradually during Elizabeth's reign, as did the more spectacular and elaborate manifestations of timber-framed construction on the grand scale.[41] There were a few ostentatious late medieval houses, as at Rufford and Ordsall, and some extensions and rebuilding in brick or stone took place at Hornby in the early sixteenth century, and at Samlesbury (probably the first use of brick walling in the county) in 1545. The new architectural fashions of the south and east took a long time to make an impact on the conservative and culturally isolated Lancashire gentry, who also failed to take up the fashion for elaborate funerary monuments.[42] Nor do household inventories suggest much attention to the trappings of wealth and status. Bedding and cushions are plentifully documented for the mid sixteenth century, and the assets of gentry families included silver spoons, brass candlesticks and at least one clock. Some inventories include impressive lists of satin, damask and velvet gowns, and Dame Anne Radcliffe left eight gold rings and various other jewellery, as well as three 'borders for french howds of goldsmythe work' valued at £50, at her death in 1551. But the overall impression is of a relatively limited interest in, or capacity for, conspicuous consumption or the expression of wealth through material possessions.[43] This may well reflect insecurity as well as insularity; but it also suggests a relative lack of cultural distance between most of the gentry and many of the yeomanry and tenant farmers.

Mid-Tudor Lancashire had a large and growing population of small freeholders, manorial copyholders and tenant leaseholders, often heavily dependent on access to communal grazing land as they scraped a modest living with a few acres of arable and anything between a dozen and fifty cattle and sheep.[44]

[15]

On the mixed farming lowlands, a minority of substantial freeholders had farms of 60 acres and more, but most occupiers of land, especially the majority made up of holders by manorial custom and tenants-at-will, had between 5 and 20 acres. Very small farms also predominated in the pastoral areas, especially perhaps in the south-west but increasingly also on the Pennine uplands, where copyholders had generous common rights and were allowed practically a free hand to organise and dispose of their holdings, which were already becoming steadily subdivided during the first half of the sixteenth century.[45] Farmhouses were very basic indeed,[46] but customary rents for copyholders were already firmly established, and were to prove difficult to alter in line with inflation when landlords began to feel the need for increased income later in the century. Labour services were still demanded by gentry landlords on many estates in the mid sixteenth century and long afterwards, but they seem to have been acceptable to tenants who had little cash and plenty of scope for independent action in other ways. Haigh is probably right to argue that 'social relationships in rural Lancashire were relatively tranquil ... there is no sign that the small farmer was suffering in Tudor Lancashire at this time'.[47] The 1530s and 1540s may have seen an increasing volume of disputes between gentry and copyholders over common encroachments, peat-cutting and quarrying rights on mossland and waste, and manorial mill monopolies, and after the Dissolution of the Monasteries the attempts of lay impropriators to increase their tithe exactions helped to bring about additional conflict in this sphere.[48] But the twin pressures of inflation and over-population were largely problems of the future.

At mid-century, then, we are dealing with a changing but still essentially stable rural social system, based on the small family farmer, who coexisted in reasonable harmony with bucolic and unassuming squirearchical landowners who could be violent when crossed, but still espoused a paternalistic mode of relationship with tenantry and dependants. Even where the Crown was landlord, its estates were administered by stewards drawn from the local gentry, who were often eager to attract the loyalty of the tenants, although the occasional exactions of forest officials modify this picture somewhat.[49] There was still plenty of available land, and the emergence of a landless agricultural proletariat was largely a thing of the future, although incipient pressures in the uplands are hinted at by the growing concern in Marsden, for example, for the discouragement of sturdy beggars in the 1540s.[50] Wages seem to have been comparatively low, but so were prices, and although poor cottagers and labourers were not absent from the county, most wage labour was probably undertaken by youthful farm servants awaiting the opportunity to marry and set up on a holding of their own.[51] Lancashire was a poor county, but its resources were spread fairly evenly through a wide middling spectrum of lesser gentry, yeomanry and small farmers.

By the 1530s and 1540s Lancashire's overwhelmingly agrarian society was becoming more complex. The rise of the textile industries enabled many yeomen and smaller farmers, especially in the south-east of the county, to augment their family incomes by participating in some or all of the manufacturing processes, preparing raw material, spinning and weaving, although the finishing of the cloth remained in the hands of specialist fullers and dyers. Farming still dominated most of these family economies, especially in the linen industry, and at this stage, and for long afterwards, the country manufacturers kept their independence from suppliers of raw materials and vendors of finished products. Itinerant dealers provided the necessary organisational lifeline, and legislative attempts to suppress them as parasites and threats to public order in 1552 were successfully evaded. A few urban merchants were beginning to prosper through a mixture of manufacturing and dealing, especially in Manchester; but in contrast with developments in Wiltshire, for example, capital and control were widely diffused through the Lancashire textile industries.[52] Liverpool had its successful merchants, too, but its battle for supremacy with Chester was far from being resolved, and the port's trade was still very limited at mid-century. Manchester apart, indeed, the towns of Lancashire still provided limited opportunities for tradesmen and manufacturers, whose main role was to serve their agricultural hinterlands. Centres like Wigan, Preston and Liverpool were subordinate to their surrounding gentry, and an alternative social hierarchy based on trade and industrial wealth was still a long way from emergence.[53]

Trade was already acceptable enough to attract the younger sons of Lancashire gentry, however, although we know little of the extent and nature of their participation.[54] The transition from violence to the law for settling disputes, and the remarkable litigiousness of propertied Lancastrians, brought about a growing demand for lawyers by the 1530s and 1540s, and this, too, proved an expanding outlet for younger sons, as the more prosperous gentry families sent their offspring to the Inns of Court.[55] Younger sons could also go into the church, of course, and the large Lancashire parishes provided substantial incomes for their rectors. By 1560 half the livings were in the gift of local gentry families, and the most lucrative places were often filled by their relatives and friends. Many of these were absentees, and the bulk of the work was done by ill-paid vicars, curates, chaplains and (until their suppression) chantry priests of humble origins and very limited education. Most were so poorly paid that they had to supplement their income by a variety of expedients, from running schools to keeping alehouses. The church provided a good living for a minority, but a precarious existence for most of the small proportion of Lancashire ordinands who stayed in the county.[56]

The implications of Lancashire's limited church and school provision, and the repercussions of the religious changes around mid-century, will be explored in Chapter 3; but it is worth noting here that church building, rebuilding and embellishment, especially through the endowment of chantries, was proceeding apace in the early sixteenth century, well after such activity had passed its peak in other parts of the country. It took not only the Henrician Reformation but also the confusion of the two succeeding reigns and the unwilling local acceptance of the Elizabethan settlement to discourage this religious investment in Lancashire. Wills and charities aimed at religious objectives rather than school provision or poor relief, and this says a great deal about the priorities of the Lancashire propertied classes, and their perceptions of their own needs and those of the society in which they lived.[57] This evidence reinforces the impression that we are dealing with a conservative, traditionalist society in which resources were limited but increasing, and so distributed as to minimise extremes of wealth and poverty. The dissolution of the Lancashire monasteries probably made little difference to this picture, as the limited impact of the Pilgrimage of Grace in the county suggests. The church was unable to exert a positive and sustained influence on the manners and morals of most Lancastrians, despite all the expenditure on churches and chantries; and the apparent ineffectiveness of the coercive apparatus of organised religion is symptomatic of the county's general impermeability to outside forces. It was equally difficult to make the writ of central government run when its demands ran counter to the interests of the locals, and opposition to initiatives from central government forms a recurring theme in the county's history. In this period the failure of attempts to regulate the Lancashire woollen industry is perhaps the most obvious case in point.[58] With its peculiar judicial system and lack of reliable agents of central government Lancashire was a difficult county to govern from without, and from this perspective the role of the Earl of Derby was at best ambivalent. These problems helped to confirm the county's contemporary reputation for backwardness, insularity, ignorance and evildoing.

How far was this reputation justified at mid-century? Increasingly it applied much more convincingly to some parts of the county than to others. In the west and north, mosses and rivers posed transport problems which made many areas difficult to reach from the outside world. In the absence of a well-frequented port north of Liverpool, and given the hazards of the Morecambe Bay crossing, this was especially true of Furness, which defeated Camden and left him with the second-hand conviction that 'there is nothing to be seen, but the ruins of *Forness-Abbey*'.[59] Under such conditions, whole populations could be particularly inward-looking and self-contained. It was in these areas that traditional Catholicism or (in the absence of committed Catholic landowners) religious ignorance and indifference were to survive longest. But only parts of the county qualified as full-scale 'dark corners of the land', to use the Puritan terminology made famous by Christopher Hill.[60] The Pennine foothills north and east of Manchester were already attracting migrants in search of land and work, and the needs of the emergent woollen industry ensured a measure of outside contact for the yeomen clothiers, although the cultural impact of such mobility and accessibility might be quite limited, as we shall see. The growth of Manchester's trade with London, and with distant parts of provincial England, as well as with Ireland and (through Liverpool and Chester) parts of continental Europe, was bringing new influences to bear by the 1540s; and Liverpool's own growing overseas trade was making it an island of relative sophistication, with merchants who travelled long distances for trading purposes.[61] The gentry, too, were coming more into contact with London and the universities, and losing some of their provincial insularity, although it may be significant that where people had the resources to seek advancement or preferment elsewhere, they seldom returned to Lancashire. The county also exported poorer migrants, who bulked disproportionately large among the recipients of poor relief in places as distant as Norwich and Kent;[62] but Haigh is wrong to infer from this that overall 'migration was away from rather than towards the county'. The influx of squatters into the Pennine foothills shows that Lancashire had its attractions, although it is impossible to tell how far its population was growing by natural increase, and how far by migration. Manchester and Liverpool apart, perhaps, it was a poor county for ambitious people with resources – 'betterment migrants', in Peter Clark's terminology – but its unimproved commons and forest areas were a haven for the poor and landless.[63]

By the mid sixteenth century much of south Lancashire, including the cattle-rearing central Lancashire plain, was already being affected significantly by external forces making for economic specialisation and national integration. Their pull was slight as yet, but it was noticeable enough to force the historian to qualify simplistic views of mid-Tudor Lancashire as backward and barbaric. It was a divided county, but important areas of it were visibly in transition by the eve of Elizabeth's reign. Persisting divisions and continuing transition will bulk large in our analysis of the ensuing century.

2

ECONOMIC CHANGE AND POPULATION CRISIS, 1558 – 1660

In Lancashire, the most important economic changes of the century after Elizabeth's accession involved the textile industries. Growth in the output and employment capacity of woollen and linen manufacturing was considerable, though it defies accurate quantitative measurement; and early in the seventeenth century the momentous rise of the cotton industry began. Technological innovations and changes in industrial organisation were still very limited; but textile growth was closely intertwined with increasing population, agricultural change, the emergence and growth of towns, and the closer integration of parts of Lancashire into a national economy and culture. These changes were most obvious, and most influential, in the Manchester area and in the Pennine foothills immediately to the north, where important religious and political changes accompanied economic development. On the other hand, extensive areas of the western half of the county became distinctive as strongholds of Roman Catholic survival and revival. Economic, religious and political developments were clearly interrelated in this period; and the historian's problem is to disentangle the mechanisms of cause and effect, and to try to establish the directions in which the causal relationships operated. The first essential is to grasp the extent and nature of the rise of the textile industries.

The Lancashire woollen and linen manufactures continued to expand through the later sixteenth century. The prevailing system of small holdings and mainly pastoral farming ensured that many families had the time, and felt the need, to augment their income through work which required little capital outlay and imposed limited risks on small independent manufacturers.[1] Textile growth was particularly pronounced in areas like Rossendale, where arable farming was at a minimum and partible inheritance conspired with encroachment on the moorland waste to encourage the multiplication of small holdings;[2] but the woollen industry continued its steady expansion over a wide area of east Lancashire. In the late sixteenth century wartime disruption of overseas markets brought a widespread switch to the security of linen, which relied almost entirely on home demand; but in many cases this was temporary, and Willan's research does not confirm suggestions that Manchester, in particular, was beginning to specialise in linen at the expense of wool in Elizabethan times. In any case, the output of the Lancashire woollen industry was also adjusted to cater for home demand in these difficult years.[3]

The late sixteenth and early seventeenth centuries were a transitional period in more lasting ways. Lancashire began to diversify its output of woollens, producing its own versions of some of the new, lighter fabrics which were being introduced further south. The Manchester linen industry moved into smallware manufacture, producing tapes, garters and assorted fripperies for the widening consumer market of the period.[4] Most important of all was the introduction of cotton through the manufacture of fustians, a mixed fabric which combined cotton and linen.[5]

There are stray hints of a small-scale fustian industry in Lancashire as early as the 1560s,[6] but the growth of specialized production began in earnest in the first years of the seventeenth century. The industry expanded rapidly from small beginnings, especially in the Blackburn and Bolton areas, and by 1620 it was well established. Its subsequent development is poorly documented until the late seventeenth century, but Wadsworth and Mann have some justification for speaking of a 'minor industrial revolution' at the turn of the sixteenth and seventeenth centuries.[7]

The changes hardly extended to the organisation of the textile industries. Production was carried out by small independent manufacturers who bought their raw material and sold their finished products in the open market. Willan finds 'no evidence' of a putting-out system in Elizabethan Manchester, despite its prevalence at this time in parts of East Anglia and the West Country. Merchants and middlemen supplied materials to manufacturers on credit as a matter of course, and as the fustian manufacture developed there was a growing tendency for the supply of raw cotton to be channelled through a small number of very substantial capitalists. But well into the seventeenth century there was no systematic shift from a system which regularly placed small producers in debt to their suppliers, without completely undermining their independence, to one in which the supplier was able to demand the resale of the finished product to himself at a prearranged price which amounted to a piece-rate wage. Such a transition to dependency and control was becoming widespread during the last quarter of the seventeenth century, but there is little evidence of such developments during the early and middle decades of the century.[8]

The extensive use of wage labour and the coalescence of large units of production were still things of the future in Lancashire textiles at the Restoration. A few substantial clothiers, especially in Manchester, might employ up to a dozen journeymen, even as early as the turn of the century; but carding, spinning and weaving were dominated by small family-based domestic workshops which were distributed through an increasingly densely populated countryside.[9] The great fortunes were amassed by merchants rather than manufacturers. The Mosleys in the late sixteenth century, and the Chethams a generation later, used their mercantile success to amass landed estates and rise to offices of dignity and power in the county. Sir Nicholas Mosley, who managed the London end of the family business, also became Lord Mayor of London, and made controversial efforts to exploit his purchase of the lordship of the manor of Manchester. A few other families achieved social promotion by a similar route.[10] But most cloth merchants were unable or unwilling to set themselves up as landed families in this way, although like the Mosleys and Chethams many prospered by lending money at interest, over and above their textile-related activities. Willan finds Manchester linen dealers leaving personal estate worth over £1500 and £2344 in 1598 and 1609, but even in Manchester such wealth was exceptional, and even successful merchants and manufacturers normally left a fraction of these amounts.[11] The Lancashire textile industries were carried on predominantly by small businessmen with precarious finances, operating in the countryside and in the small emergent urban centres around Manchester.

Even at the Restoration, indeed, relatively few family economies depended exclusively on the textile trades. Many merchants, even in Manchester itself, were also engaged in agriculture; and domestic manufacture in the countryside was often a sideline, employing the surplus labour of large families in areas of small-scale pastoral farming with a limited demand for agricultural labour.[12] The importance of textiles to local economies declined approximately in direct proportion to the distance from Manchester and its satellite market towns. At Rochdale in the 1650s nearly one-third of the bridegrooms whose occupations were recorded in the parish register were in textiles, in a parish which was dominated by an extensive rural area. The figure for Middleton was similar, and at Radcliffe textiles accounted for 30 of the 61 recorded fathers, while only 14 returned agricultural occupations.[13] Most if not all of these people would in practice have divided their energies between textiles and farming, but the balance of priorities was tilting increasingly towards the former. Further to the northwest, the impact of textiles on the predominantly pastoral Forest of Pendle was much less pronounced. Ninety-three of Mary Brigg's 123 seventeenth-century inventories listed 'cards, combs and wheels' for spinning, and 45 also contained one or two hand-looms; but only five people described themselves as textile manufacturers or dealers, and all of these were also farmers. Here, the woollen industry was pervasive, but of secondary importance to family economies.[14] Beyond Pendle, the woollen industry seems to have been negligible in the Forest of Bowland, despite pastoral agriculture and a rising population; and the linen manufacture of west Lancashire catered mainly for local and domestic needs, although there were centres of more sophisticated commercial activity at Preston, Ormskirk and Liverpool.[15] The northern outposts of Lancashire in north Lonsdale and Furness formed part of the declining Westmorland woollen district, and the experience of this area contrasted sharply with the south-east of the county.[16] The impact of the textile industries was thus far from uniform; and even where their growth and influence were strongest, they remain difficult to disentangle from the other elements of complex local economies.

Textiles were not the only source of growth and diversification in the Lancashire economy. Coal mining was particularly important, although Nef's estimate of a fifteenfold increase in output between the 1550s and 1700 has been challenged by Langton, who argues for a 60 per cent rise over the century after 1590 in the important central and south-western areas, including Wigan, St. Helens and Prescot.[17] But there was rapid expansion here during Elizabeth's reign, and if we allow for the later starting point of Langton's comparison the gap between these assessments may not be quite as wide as it appears at first glance. We have less information on developments elsewhere in Lancashire, but there was clearly considerable extension of mining in north-east Lancashire over a similar period, while the Manchester and Bolton areas saw activity on a much larger scale, with gentry involvement and some bitter lawsuits.[18] But Langton is surely right to draw attention to the small scale, limited capital and intermittent activity of most colliery enterprises, and his evidence for limited development and relative backwardness in central and south-west Lancashire during the seventeenth century probably holds good for the rest of the coalfields.[19]

The larger collieries, especially in the Wigan area, enabled and probably stimulated the growth of a variety of metalworking trades, including nail-making in the Chowbent area to the east of Wigan, and pewter, brass, copper and church bell manufacture in Wigan itself. All these trades lacked local raw materials, coal excepted; and the Wigan foundries may have benefited from the favourable characteristics of the local cannel and 'smiths' coal, with their low sulphur content. Further south, the coalfield also helped to nurture the seventeenth-century appearance of wire, glass and pottery manufacture.[20] A diverse industrial economy was thus developing here, generating employment for whole families and stimulating the accumulation of substantial merchant capitals in a manner similar to the textile industries further east.

Apart from Furness iron mining, and the intermittent operation of charcoal ironworks there, industrial development was hardly in evidence elsewhere in Lancashire. Even on the Wigan coalfield and in the textile heartland around Manchester, moreover, agriculture remained an essential component of the local economy; and elsewhere its predominance remained complete. But there were few significant innovations in this period. The most important trend was already strongly marked in mid-Tudor times: the enclosure of waste land and the fragmentation of holdings continued over wide areas of the county. These developments were particularly conspicuous in the old royal forests of the northern and eastern uplands, from Bowland to Rossendale. Here, the piece-meal encroachment of small farmers into adjoining areas of moorland and scrub, augmented by occasional large-scale partitions of the waste under the auspices of Crown commissioners, brought about a cumulative trans-formation of landscape and ecology. Porter calculates that one-third of the whole land area of south-eastern Bowland was reclaimed from the waste between 1550 and 1630, when several new settlements were founded. The population of western Bowland probably more than doubled between 1527 and 1664.[21] Similar trends were apparent in Pendle, where the population may have trebled between the early sixteenth century and the Restoration, and in Rossendale, where the number of separately rented parcels of land increased by 50 per cent between 1608 and 1662, as the sixteenth-century processes of encroachment on the waste and subdivision of existing holdings continued unabated and in tandem.[22] Elsewhere in the county, similar processes were at work, though their impact was less dramatic. At Lytham in the Fylde and Wray in the Lune valley manorial overlords encouraged their tenants to enclose tracts of the extensive commons, and extensions of the productive area were a general Lancashire theme. Only the mosses of south-west Lancashire, which posed intractable drainage problems, escaped almost completely, although even here there were one or two small schemes.[23]

Changes in agricultural practice were less in evidence. Arable farming became more important in parts of the Fylde and the central Lancashire plain, and the use of marl and lime may have become more general and systematic; but Lancashire agriculture remained relatively unsophisticated in its techniques.[24] Cattle remained the most important livestock, and dairy production for the market was being intensified in some areas by the 1630s; but in Rossendale, at least, sheep flocks were increasing in number and value during the seventeenth century, and challenging cattle for supremacy in the local farming economy. This was exceptional, and what stands out over the period is the general continuity of agricultural practices and preoccupations. Despite an impressive expansion of the cultivated area, Lancashire's agriculture remained decidedly backward by comparison with most of the Southern and Midland counties.[25]

Economic development was sufficient, even so, to sustain a considerable level of population growth and urban expansion, although we shall see that increased numbers put a dangerous strain on the county's resources in time of bad harvest and trade depression. If we assume that the mean household size remained the same between the Bishop of Chester's survey in 1563 and the Hearth Tax returns of 1664, Lancashire's population increased by 76.2 per cent over the century: a misleadingly precise figure which probably con-veys a reasonably accurate general impression.[26] As Table 1 shows, this increase was spread unevenly through the county. Salford Hundred, the south-eastern

Table 1   *Population change in Lancashire, 1563–1664*

	No. of households in 1563	1664	% increase 1563–1664	No. of households as % of all households in the county: 1563	1664
Salford Hundred	4719	10767	128.2	24.8	32.2
West Derby Hundred	4032	6935	72.0	21.2	20.7
Blackburn Hundred	2657	4740	78.4	14.0	14.2
Leyland Hundred	2058	2368	15.1	10.8	7.1
Rest of Lancashire	5534	8672	56.7	29.2	25.8
Lancashire total	19000	33482	76.2	100	100

Sources: B. L. Harleian Mss. 594, fol. 101–8, for 1563; the Rest of Lancashire figure is found by subtracting the figures for Warrington, Manchester, Leyland and Blackburn deaneries from Haigh's overall total of 19,000 for the whole county. For 1664, Blackwood, *Lancashire Gentry*, 7. The 1563 figures are based on deaneries rather than hundreds, but south of the Ribble the boundaries of the religious and secular administrative divisions were almost identical. C. D. Rogers, 'The Development of a Teaching Profession in England 1547–1700', Ph.D. thesis, Univ. of Manchester, 1975, 12–13, offers parish-by-parish population figures for Lancashire in 1620, but his method assumes a uniform and arbitrarily derived birth-rate, and his findings are out of line with those from the household listings. His estimates have therefore been discarded.

administrative division which contained the core of the fastest-growing textile district, more than doubled its population, and increased its share of the county total from a quarter to nearly one-third. Blackburn Hundred, where textiles were also developing, was second in the growth league table, while population expansion in the south-western West Derby Hundred, traditionally the wealthiest and most populous, seems to have slowed down markedly in the seventeenth century. If we assume an average household size of 4.75, in conformity with recent findings by historical demographers, Lancashire's population grew from just over 90,000 in 1563 to nearly 160,000 in 1664.

The pattern of urban growth confirms that the county's economic centre of gravity was shifting towards the south-east. If we count Manchester and Salford separately, there were nine and probably ten towns with over 1000 inhabitants at the Restoration. Manchester had almost doubled its population to about 4000, and was firmly established as an important regional centre with several dependent market towns and villages, although it was still a long way down the national urban hierarchy. Wigan and Preston hovered around the 2000 mark, and in the woollen and fustian textile districts Bolton, Bury and Blackburn entered the list, with Rochdale not far behind. Warrington and Liverpool had grown more slowly, Lancaster was stagnating, and there was little evidence of authentic urbanisation elsewhere.[27] By 1664 town-dwellers accounted for one in nine of

Lancashire's inhabitants, and in Salford Hundred the figure was one in six. A national calculation for the late seventeenth century estimates that 20 per cent of English people lived in towns, on the same definition; so urbanisation in Lancashire, and especially in the textile district, was catching up with the nation at large, although outside Manchester the scale of urban living remained small even by the standards of the time.[28]

At this stage the textile towns were developing as centres of trade rather than manufacture. Even Manchester, with its dyers, shearmen and tanners, was pre-eminently a market centre, with grocers, butchers, mercers and various shop-keepers bulking large in its economic life alongside the textile merchants.[29] The lesser textile centres serviced manufacturing hinterlands which depended heavily on wool from outside the county, and linen yarn from Ireland, to supplement the meagre local production. They also needed access to grain supplies over and above the harvest from the small acreages of oats which must have been insufficient for the subsistence of many upland exponents of the 'dual economy' of textiles and pastoral farming. Further west, Preston served a prosperous agricultural area and benefited from its growing administrative functions, while the modest but signifi-cant growth of Wigan and Warrington was boosted by the coalfield and its industries. Liverpool took an ever-increasing share of the Irish trade, as Chester's harbour silted up and her claims to administrative pre-eminence became unten-able. But ships from more distant parts were rare arrivals, and Liverpool's dependence on Ireland was cruelly exposed by the collapse of the Irish economy after 1641, which ended a brief period of growth and relative prosperity in the town. In national terms Liverpool was a sleepy backwater at the Restoration, with little indication of the rapid expansion that was to come.[30]

Most of Lancashire's towns remained small and unprepossessing. They suffered regular economic setbacks, and devastating epidemics were frequent visitors. Plague killed more than half Preston's inhabitants in 1630 – 1, leaving only 887 survivors; and this was the best-documented of many such disasters.[31] The Civil War brought an added dimension of calamity, as sieges and disrupted trade were accompanied by food shortages and further epidemics. The siege of Bolton in 1644 may have killed half the population, and Liverpool also suffered in the same year. Manchester was to avoid the worst of the fighting, but it had long-term problems of its own. Provision for the poor was being pushed upwards, though modestly, in the late sixteenth century, and in the 1620s the town's leading citizens began to complain of 'multitudes of poor strangers' who 'pestered and overburthened' the propertied and deprived 'the native Poore' of 'that provision wch was intended onely for them'.[32] Such intimations of urban crisis were not peculiar to Lancashire, and we shall see that within the county they were far from being the sole preserve of the towns; but Lancashire's urban economies were shaky enough, and its urban governments were weak enough, to suggest that problems here may have been unusually acute by the second quarter of the seventeenth century.[33]

Some sectors of Lancashire society were undoubtedly prospering, however. The surviving probate inventories suggest that Elizabethan Manchester already had a relatively wealthy élite: the median value of personal property listed in them was £101, much higher than the equivalent figures for the much larger towns of Leicester and Worcester.[34] This pattern probably persisted in the seventeenth century. We lack similar calculations for other Lancashire towns, but we can also show that the lifestyle of some of the gentry and substantial yeomanry were increasing in opulence and comfort. Nearly half of those upper gentry families, from whose ranks the county magistrates were recruited, rebuilt or substantially extended their houses between 1575 and 1635, and there was similar activity slightly lower down the social scale. Some gentlemen were building town houses, in Ormskirk and Lancaster as well as Preston, for their regular visits on legal and administrative business, and for the associated social round. Meanwhile, the sturdy stone farmhouses of the upper yeomanry proliferated in Pendle and Bowland.[35] This apart, however, levels of consumption and display were relatively unassuming, apart from a handful of particularly powerful or wealthy families. Prodigious new houses like Gawthorpe and Stonyhurst expressed the ostentation of the remarkably successful, and most of the rebuilding was altogether more modest in scope. Sir John Radcliffe of Ordsall kept a coach and sent his son on the Grand Tour before 1590, but he seems to have stimulated few imitators in the county before the Restoration. In 1613 Sir Thomas Walmesley of Dunkenhalgh allocated £622 14s 6d of his fortune, which had been greatly enhanced by a lucrative legal career, to an ostentatious funeral and an alabaster tomb; but here again, there were few imitators. Sir Richard Molyneux of Sefton aspired to a town house at Chiswick, and the Earl of Derby's unique position in county society was expressed in such exotic possessions as a huge silver candelabrum, twelve pillows covered with yellow damask, and a 'red velvett close stool', as well as more orthodox status symbols. Long remarks on a 'rising standard of comfort and elegance, in some cases luxury', among the magistracy before the Civil War; but most of it was concentrated into a few families with particularly extensive estates, provident marriages or sources of non-landed income from commerce or the law. Otherwise, the limits even to magisterial ostentation were expressed by the low valuations given to clothing in their inventories, and by their attachment to hunting and other outdoor sports rather than the softer enjoyments of courtly society.[36] In similar vein, the evidence for yeoman prosperity comes mainly from the upland areas of former royal forest, where copyhold rents were pegged throughout the long inflation of the sixteenth and early seventeenth centuries, to the considerable benefit of tenants who were also able to involve themselves profitably in the organisation of the textile industries.[37]

Lancashire as a whole remained a relatively poor county, from the gentry downwards. It remained at or near the bottom of the tax assessment league, although Quintrell points out that the ease with which taxes were collected, even in the contentious 1630s, suggests that Lancastrians knew that their assessments were disproportionately low, and sought to remain in that happy state. In this respect as in others, remoteness from central government had its advantages.[38] But the gentry at large were less affluent than those of the Southern and Midland counties, and indeed than those of Yorkshire. In Kent or Leicestershire most of the Lancashire Justices of the Peace would have had the incomes and lifestyles of wealthy yeomen rather than gentlemen; and the magistrates were drawn mainly from the upper levels of the Lancashire gentry. Blackwood finds only 24 of his 774 gentry families in 1642 enjoying an annual landed income of more than £1000, with another 89 receiving between £250 and £999. This amounts to fewer than 15 per cent of the Lancashire gentry, compared with nearly 47 per cent of their Yorkshire counterparts. The Lancashire figure is understated, but probably not by much; and additional incomes from minerals, office, commerce, religious revenues and the law made a significant difference only to a few families, most of whom were already relatively affluent and well connected.[39] Overall, indeed, the incomes and property of the Lancashire gentry may actually have declined during the generally inflationary years between 1600 and 1642, although the evidence is less than convincing, and their numbers remained stagnant in a period of population growth. The Civil War and its aftermath made surprisingly little difference to the economic fortunes of most families, as the penalties against Royalists were evaded and mitigated by a variety of subterfuges, often with the connivance of sympathetic neighbours. The most conspicuous losers were the Earls of Derby. There was little economic mobility within the gentry's ranks, but a busy toing and froing into and out of the lower levels.[40] But the suspicion remains that this extensive interchange between the lesser gentry and greater yeomanry tells us little about real changes in wealth and status. It is more likely to indicate the difficulties that contemporaries experienced in differentiating between these imprecisely delineated social groupings, in a county where small and middling landowners continued to predominate and the really wealthy were thin on the ground.

The upper and middle strata of Lancashire society probably remained relatively stable over the century after Elizabeth's accession. The major changes took place among the lower orders, as smallholders and wage-labourers proliferated to account for most if not all of the county's population increase. These people are elusive to the historian. They were too poor to leave inventories, their property transactions were small-scale and limited, and most of the surviving evidence is impressionistic. Even so, a disturbing picture of widespread poverty and insecurity emerges in the seventeenth century, especially in the areas where industry was beginning to develop. Keith Wrightson is quite sure that Lancashire was developing 'a very large agricultural proletariat of landless and virtually landless labourers' by this time, and where the textile industries had taken root large populations were at the mercy of the trade cycle by the 1620s and 1630s.[41] For Rossendale, Tupling calculates that by 1660 nearly two-thirds of the heads of household were 'maintaining their domestic establishments on farms or plots of land which were either very small or of very inferior fertility', making ends meet through domestic textile manufacture.[42] In 1634 the magistrates of Blackburn Hundred reported that within 'these two years in this little Hundred we have bound 200 apprentices or thereabouts, poor boys and girls which before have begged'. A similar policy was adopted on a large scale in Rochdale parish.[43] Even on the central Lancashire plain, very small land-holdings were multiplying through 'the subletting and dividing of freeholds and customary holdings', and these practices also prevailed on the coalfield, helping to increase the labour supply for the mineowners. At mid-century the local vicar described his Prescot parishioners as 'very poore, a greate parte of them liveing in summer tyme by digginge and windinge coals, and in the winter by beggeinge'.[44] In 1664 extensive areas of south-east and central Lancashire, and much of Furness, had more than 40 per cent of their house-holders exempted from the Hearth Tax on the plea of poverty: their cottages were assessed at less than 20s per year, or their property was worth less than £10.[45] Even allowing for tax evasion, this is a grim picture, and it confirms the other indications that by the second quarter of the seventeenth century large numbers of Lancashire smallholders and wage-earners were living in grinding poverty, on the very margin of subsistence. The growing numbers of the poor and near-destitute posed a potential threat to the social and economic stability of the county.

The vulnerability of cottagers and labouring poor was painfully demonstrated by a series of subsistence crises. The best-documented is that of 1623, when depression in textiles coincided with harvest failure to produce a catastrophic increase in mortality. In Lancashire as a whole, the burial rate was three times the average for a normal year, and the crisis probably killed 5 per cent of the county's population. Mortality was especially severe in the upland textile areas, from the south-east to Furness, and in some of the remoter agricultural parishes. High mortality coexisted with a sharp decline in marriages and conceptions to delineate a classic crisis of subsistence, no doubt exacerbated by the limited purchasing power and grain-growing capacity of the upland smallholders. Bad communications must also have played a part, as the crisis reached its peak in the bleak moorland winter.[46] Outbreaks of high mortality in the late sixteenth century may also have had a subsistence element, for this was a difficult period for the woollen industry, and there were subsistence crises in the Lake District at this time.[47] The threat of starvation was still real enough in the 1630s and 1640s. At Rochdale in 1638 a 'slightly deficient harvest brought hunger to over two hundred families', and the dislocations and military exactions of the Civil War and its aftermath made the 1640s particularly troubled years, in Manchester and Wigan as well as Bolton and Liverpool.[48] Times were especially hard between 1647 and 1650, and a heart-rending plea for aid came from the Wigan area in May 1649:

The hand of God is evidently seen stretched out upon the county, chastening it with a three-corded scourge of sword, pestilence and famine, all at once afflicting it. They have borne the heat and burden of a first and second war in an especial manner... In this county hath the plague of pestilence been ranging these three years and upwards, occasioned chiefly by the wars. There is a very great scarcity and dearth of all provisions, especially of all sorts of grain, particularly that kind by which that country is most sustained, which is full six-fold the price that of late it hath been. All trade, by which they have been much supported, is utterly decayed; it would melt any good heart to see the numerous swarms of begging poore, and the many families that pine away at home, not having faces to beg.[49]

Lancashire's poor may well have suffered as much in these years as in the crisis of 1623. In the Wigan area and parts of south-west Lancashire the poor relief system broke down, and in Liverpool and Manchester the strain on resources led to increasingly harsh and discriminatory policies.[50]

Civil War and plague combined to exacerbate existing problems during the 1640s; but there was a further crisis in south-east Lancashire in 1654, and 1662 was another bad year.[51] Even if we adjust for the special circumstances of the Civil War period, in the longer term the evidence strongly suggests that parts of Lancashire were experiencing a pattern of events which closely resembled a Malthusian crisis. The subdivision of holdings, the availability of poor-quality common land and the employment opportunities in domestic industry encouraged the population to grow well beyond medieval levels, and beyond the capacity of the area to sustain it in time of bad harvest and reduced purchasing power; so continuing population increase was punctuated by periodic subsistence crises. Recent optimistic interpretations of the century after 1540 have challenged views of this kind at national level; but whatever may have been the case further south, the evidence for Lancashire (and Cumbria) looks convincing.[52] There could be no more dramatic indicator of the transition to endemic poverty and insecurity among the emergent lower orders of the Lancashire uplands, though the evidence for central Lancashire, the coalfield and the south-west is less compelling, as the worst distress here was so strongly influenced by plague and civil war.

The economic pressures of this period generated surprisingly little overt conflict between rich and poor, landlord and tenant. Walter and Wrightson remark on the apparent absence of grain riots in Lancashire, although here as elsewhere the number of prosecutions for theft increased in bad harvest years.[53] This sheds more light on the attitudes of prosecutors than on the level of actual crime, and contemporary fears of a sustained and systematic threat to property and order in time of dearth were unfounded.

The responses of landlords to the long Elizabethan and early Stuart inflation did generate sporadic and sometimes bitter conflicts with their tenantry, although the disputes remained localised and were almost always contained within official legal channels. The power of custom was strong, and few Lancashire landlords were willing to prejudice the goodwill of their tenants by trying to maximise their incomes from agricultural rents and dues. Long leases, for two or three lives or 99 years, remained the norm on most Lancashire estates, and this limited the scope for raising rents in line with inflation. Even James Bankes of Winstanley, newly risen into the gentry after a lucrative metropolitan career as goldsmith and moneylender, drew back from exploiting his tenants to the full. He introduced short leases in the interests of discipline, but kept his rents low for deserving tenants, and his advice to his son expresses the motivation and social expectations of many older-established gentry families: 'Be kind and loving unto your tenants, and so they will love you – both you and your house shall live in worship and credit'. The expectation that tenancies should be passed on from father to son, and that long-established tenant families should receive preferential treatment, persisted on the Blundell estate at Little Crosby, and no doubt elsewhere.[54] The belief that substantial landowners had duties towards their tenants as well as rights over them, and that honour and respect should be pursued alongside financial gain, remained strong among the Lancashire gentry into the Civil War era and beyond.

Most Lancashire landlords did try to raise rents when leases fell in, and to increase the yield of entry fines levied at the succession of a new landlord or tenant. In some cases they went further and pursued an apparent policy of maximising income on all fronts, overturning the constraints of custom and ignoring the outrage of their tenantry. Several Royalist landlords in the Lonsdale and Furness areas of north Lancashire were behaving in this manner at the outbreak of the Civil War. The Middletons of Leighton Hall were particularly pushing. They tried to overturn customary levels of rents and entry fines, insisting on their right to increase them as they saw fit; they denied the right of succession to tenancies; they claimed food rents and labour services whose validity their tenants denied; they overstocked their deer park, enclosed part of the commons, and denied customary rights to timber from the woodlands.[55] This was an unusually extensive catalogue of misdeeds, and it was fiercely resisted by the tenants. Further south, there seems to have been less conflict, although several families tried to introduce or revive rents in kind or labour services, clung to feudal mill monopolies and even asserted the right of wardship over their tenants.[56] The revival of payments in kind and the assertion of feudal obligations represented a useful hedge against inflation, and this patchy but significant 'seigneurial reaction' constitutes an attempt by some of the gentry to increase their share of the product of the soil without additional investment or the encouragement of new techniques which marked the more acceptable face of the new capitalist landownership further south. In general, estate management in Lancashire remained 'conservative and, on the whole, backward'. There was little sign of the willingness to invest and innovate which was emerging closer to London.[57]

The Crown itself made a sustained effort to increase revenue from its Lancashire estates, as its financial difficulties deepened in the reign of James I.

The customary tenants of the Honor of Clitheroe paid low rents and minimal entry fines, but from 1607 onwards royal lawyers systematically challenged their legal title to their holdings. They were required to pay considerable lump sums to retain possession, and the slow progress of the legal proceedings resulted in prolonged unease and uncertainty, which was not fully removed until 1662. Tupling argues that this lucrative and long-drawn-out exploitation of legal loopholes by the Crown may help to explain the widespread and enthusiastic support for Parliament during the Civil War in the affected area, which covered extensive tracts of small upland holdings from the Ribble valley to Rossendale.[58]

But disputes of this kind did not always reduce the relationship between landlord and tenant to mere economic calculation. Expectations of personal loyalty and mutual obligation were deep-rooted. The 'sturdy churles' of Rossendale and Pendle who fought for Parliament in 1642 'rather than their Beefe and fatt Bacon shall be taken from them' were only part of the story: the victorious Parliamentarians drew up a long list of actively Royalist yeomen from the same areas in 1655.[59] Even Sir George Middleton of Leighton Hall was able to lead his Yealand tenants into battle against the Roundheads, although it is difficult in such cases to establish the relative importance of loyalty to the cause and loyalty to a seemingly unpopular landlord. In strongly Parliamentarian areas, tenants were more likely to repudiate their obligations to Royalist landlords; but on the whole it seems likely that in Lancashire 'the tenants of the overwhelming bulk of aristocrats (*i.e.* substantial gentry) were loyal, or at least not disloyal'.[60] The Civil War provides a useful touchstone for the nature of landlord/tenant relations, and it brings out the limited extent and impact of economic conflict in this sphere. We shall see that conflict between Puritan gentry and the unregenerate poor was becoming increasingly bitter in the seventeenth century, as the former attempted to reform the manners and enjoyments of the latter; but even so, the widening gap between the poor and the comfortably-off was less dangerous to the social system than in more economically advanced counties like Essex or Wiltshire. Lancashire retained an extensive middling group of yeomanry and lesser gentry who continued to mix socially, and the claim by an Elizabethan MP that in Lancashire it was 'a common and usual thing ... for gentlemen as they go a-hawking to ... take a repast at an alehouse' remained true of all but the more zealous of the Puritans.[61] In many respects Lancashire remained a relatively stable county.

By the Restoration, however, Lancashire was gradually moving closer to the mainstream of national life. Transport and administrative links with London had been improving, steadily if unobtrusively, and the gentry, at least, were beginning to experience the world beyond the locality and the region. Education at the universities and Inns of Court was becoming more common, although until after the Restoration Lancashire's record still compared unfavourably with other counties. Between 1590 and 1640 fewer than 30 per cent of Lancashire's magistrates had been to university, a lower proportion than in Yorkshire or Somerset.[62] Growing numbers of Lancastrians were apprenticed in London, but many never returned to the county, although they proved generous in the endowment of schools in their native parishes.[63] The persisting cultural distinctiveness of Lancashire was in some ways rather emphasised than undermined by increasing contact with the metropolis: Rogers suggests that among London playwrights in the seventeenth century 'the most abused county was Lancashire because of its witches, its accents, its recusancy and peculiar customs'.[64] Most gentry lacked the wealth or range of personal contacts to marry outside the county, and in 70 per cent of gentry marriages in Lancashire towards the mid seventeenth century both partners came from within the county, a higher incidence of endogamy than was usual.[65]

The continuing limits to the real impact of outside influences are well expressed by Lancashire's educational condition. W. K. Jordan was immensely impressed by the rate and extent of grammar school endowment in Lancashire during this period, when the proportion of Lancashire charities directed to education was much higher than in any other county. Lancashire's record was 'amazing', 'incredible', and showed 'almost fanatical zeal ... for the extension of educational opportunities'. The rsources came hardly at all from the upper gentry, but from yeomen, village élites, and above all London merchants of Lancashire origins. The main impetus (apart from the Manchester merchants Mosley and Chetham) came from Lancashire exiles, who were no doubt eager to amend the perceived backwardness of their native county.[66] But the fruits of their investment, within Lancashire at least, were rather limited. Illiteracy remained relatively high: Wrightson's analysis of Lancashire sessions depositions towards the mid seventeenth century suggests that 9 per cent even of the gentlemen (in a very small sample) were unable to write their names, and this test was failed by 43 per cent of the yeomen, 64 per cent of the tradesmen, 86 per cent of the husbandmen, 94 per cent of labourers and male servants, and 98 per cent of women. This compares unfavourably with similarly derived figures for the North-East at the same time. The ability to read was almost certainly much more widespread, but cannot be measured; and this evidence suggests a very widespread dependence on face-to-face contacts and a localised, oral culture. The diarist Roger Lowe lightens the gloom somewhat: he was in demand to write letters for his neighbours, who were thus not without their outside contacts, and his alehouse conversations on theology and Aesop's fables show that even Ashton-in-Makerfield had its coterie of the literate, thoughtful and aware.[67] But most people must have had very narrow educational horizons. Even the schoolteachers generally had little knowledge of the outside world. Their numbers were growing steadily until the 1620s, when a plateau was reached; and most of the increase was accounted for by graduates. Their impact on attitudes and outlooks was probably even less than their impact on literacy. The teachers themselves were deeply attached to their localities, whether by inclination or necessity.

Over three-quarters of the Lancashire and Cheshire graduates in C. D. Rogers's survey found jobs within ten miles of their home town or village, and only 1 per cent even of the graduate teachers came from beyond Lancashire, Cheshire and the adjoining counties. Once in post, the vast majority stayed put, unless they secured clerical preferment.[68] So the great educational expansion of the century after Elizabeth must have had limited results in overcoming Lancastrian isolation and insularity: it was probably more effective at propelling successful scholars beyond the county than at changing society within it. In this respect as in others, Lancashire was still resisting full integration into the development of English culture.

New ideas and external influences were diffused most effectively among the upper gentry, who were much more likely to send sons to university or Inns of Court and to marry outside the county,[69] and in the emergent textile district around Manchester. They were less in evidence in central and south-west Lancashire, despite the trading links of Liverpool and the coalfield, and least pervasive in the agricultural north and west, although even Furness was acquiring local concentrations of religious Nonconformity by the 1650s.[70]

Religious innovation was, indeed, the most effective indicator of permeability to external influences. Puritanism and Protestant Nonconformity were most conspicuous and influential in south-east Lancashire, especially where the textile industries were strongest. The nature of the connection between these phenomena is still a matter for argument, but Puritanism clearly did not straightforwardly 'cause' economic development in Lancashire in this period. The rise of Lancashire textiles had altogether more complex roots. As in other areas with poor soil, pastoral agriculture, divided landownership and extensive common land, the population growth and new settlement of the sixteenth century and after created a pool of potential cheap labour which was obviously attractive to entrepreneurs. The lack of corporations and guilds with power to restrict the establishment of new businesses and to control the supply of labour was probably a significant advantage to Manchester and its satellite settlements in the early stages, enabling a symbiotic relationship to develop between towns and their manufacturing hinterlands. Wigan and Preston, which tried to use their corporate privileges against developments which seemed to threaten the interests of established traders, fared less well in this period.[71] The absence of enforceable central government intervention was an added bonus. The adaptability of an existing linen industry to the introduction of cotton, at a time when links with London were already well established through the wool trade, was an enormous asset. Radical Protestantism, indeed, was brought in along the existing traderoutes of the woollen industry, from London and from Yorkshire; and its consolidation in south-east Lancashire was due in large part to its appeal among influential gentry families, especially in the Manchester area.[72] Puritan habits of thrift, industry, discipline and accumulation, in so far as these were recognisably Puritan traits, may have helped to stimulate the further growth of established industries; but the more important causal links ran in the opposite direction. Economic development generated Puritanism: it was successful in this area because the nature of the economic and social system provided fertile soil for its development, with a multiplicity of small landowners and independent traders and a shortage of strong Catholic gentry or pre-existing religious influences of any kind. But we need to explore the nature and extent of Puritan influence, and the significance of Roman Catholic survival elsewhere, at greater length; and we shall do so in the next chapter, which also looks more generally at the nature of political and religious authority in Lancashire.

3

—————

RELIGION AND AUTHORITY,
1558 – 1660

—————

The religious complexion of Lancashire posed persisting and intractable problems of order and control for monarchs and their ministers in Elizabethan and early Stuart England. Above all, there was the strong survival and revival of Roman Catholicism in west Lancashire, which was perceived as a threat to the authority and stability of the state, but defied or evaded religious and secular pressure for conformity to the Church of England as defined by the Elizabethan settlement. At the other extreme, radical Protestantism became strong and assertive in the textile district, with outposts of support cohering around embattled ministers and sympathetic gentry elsewhere. At best, these Puritans (a convenient generic term which is as useful – and potentially as misleading – for historians as for contemporaries) were tolerated uneasily, or even cautiously encouraged as a vanguard movement against the Catholics, by central government and the established church, within which they formed a radical wing of controversial activists. At worst, they were pursued through the ecclesiastical courts for their failure to conform to prescribed usages and doctrines. In the aftermath of the Civil War, the Puritan ascendancy brought about an apparent revolution in the organisation and government of the church, which was carried into effect more determinedly in Lancashire than in almost any other part of the country, although its effective impact outside the south-east of the county was probably very limited. After the Restoration, on the other hand, the Act of Uniformity was to push many Puritans, along with other dissenting groups, outside the bounds of the established church as redefined in 1662. Protestant Nonconformity thus became an important force in Lancashire at an early stage.

Lancashire thus gained, and retained, a reputation for intransigent and enduring religious extremism and conflict. There is much truth in this portrayal, but it is far from being the whole story. Over much of the county the effective influence of organised religion remained very limited, and there were frequent complaints about the ignorance, apathy and ungodliness of the general population. Lancashire remained short of churches and adequately trained clergy, as its limited medieval provision failed to increase in step with rising population. It was part of the enormous and administratively cumbersome diocese of Chester, whose bishops and archdeacons found it very difficult to oversee their clergy at the level of the parish. Most of the parishes themselves were very extensive compared with the rest of England, and some were very large indeed. Whalley parish occupied 106,000 acres, and several others contained over 30,000 acres. Under these conditions, attendance at the parish church was difficult, public worship was often neglected, and even conscientious clergy found it impossible to keep in touch with their scattered but numerous parishioners.[1] Parish boundaries sometimes took no account of natural obstacles. At Croston, a large parish but not one of the largest, the River Douglas made churchgoing very difficult for people living in some of the outlying townships:

There is a greate river called Astlon, over wch the Inhabitants of the said townes of Tarleton, Holmes Sollome, Hesketh and Becconsall cannot pass into Croston Church wthout a boate, neither can they passe wth a boate in some seasons of the yeare by reason of the greate Inundacon of the said waters there, And alsoe by reason of the greate river of Duglas, the ffinney poole, and the river of Yarrowe overflowinge the way for all the most pte of the winter tyme.[2]

This was an unusually graphic account of a common Lancashire problem, exacerbated by bad roads and a paucity of bridges which could turn small rivers into major obstacles. Even the Puritan commissioners who made this report in 1650 accepted that the length and hazardous nature of the journey made absence from church understandable under such conditions.

The problems arising from vast parishes and inaccessible churches were mitigated by the building of chapels of ease in strategic places. A surge of chapel building formed an important part of the impressive spurt of religious investment in Lancashire during the first half of the sixteenth century. Between 1470 and 1548 about 46 new chapels were built, almost doubling the total. After this, however, the rate of increase in provision slackened off: in the mid sixteenth century there were 58 parish churches and about 100 chapels in the county, and the 1650 survey found 63 churches (to which we should add North Meols, which the commissioners forgot) and 118 chapels, to which 10 more should probably be added. As the Croston example illustrates, this level of provision was still too thinly spread to encourage regular churchgoing among a large proportion of Lancashire's population.[3]

To make matters worse, even in 1650, 38 of the chapels listed in the survey had no minister; and this reflected a persistent and intractable problem of low clergy incomes and quality, which was especially apparent in the chapelries. The mid sixteenth century pattern of substantial revenues from large parishes being siphoned off by laymen, or pocketed by well-connected absentee rectors, persisted through this period; and most of the services and pastoral work fell to curates and chaplains, who were paid small, fixed stipends which were vulnerable to inflation and often left them hard-pressed to make ends meet. Some depended entirely on the goodwill offerings of the people who attended their services. In 1642 the Long Parliament prescribed a minimum income of £60 per annum for clergy; but eight years later the incumbents of 17 Lancashire parishes were still receiving £40 or less, and 51 curates had annual incomes of £15 or less.[4]

Most resident Lancashire clergy were thus very ill-paid, both relative to clergy elsewhere and in many cases absolutely. As a result, wide areas of the county became a last resort for ministers who were unable to obtain positions elsewhere. Widespread ignorance, incapacity and occasional scandal ensued. Elizabethan clergy were regularly accused of adultery, fornication and drunkenness. George Dobson, vicar of Whalley, was described as 'a common drunkard, and such an ale-knight as the like is not in our parish ... he will, when he cannot discern black from blue, dance with a full cup on his head, far passing all the rest'. George Hesketh, at Halsall, was pointed out by a parishioner with the words, 'This is he that corrupteth all the women in the county'.[5] More or less dubious expedients to eke out exiguous stipends, or to augment more adequate ones, included alehouse keeping, wool dealing, coal mining, weaving and possibly sorcery as well as the more orthodox resources of farming and schoolteaching. Graduates, and clergy licensed to preach, long remained in very short supply, and the catechising of the young was widely neglected.

There was a distinct improvement in the educational background of the Lancashire clergy, and an apparent decline of scandalous behaviour, in the late sixteenth and early seventeenth centuries, as Bishops of Chester became more demanding in their ordination policy and supervision became less ineffective. The Puritan search for godly, preaching ministers bore fruit during the first half of the seventeenth century, especially in the south-east of the county. But the basic structural problems remained, and the impressive augmentations of clergy incomes, at the state's behest, in many Lancashire parishes and chapelries between 1645 and 1660 failed to solve them, though they made a considerable difference in the short run.[6] Over much of Lancashire the clergy were too few, too scattered and often too ineffective to have much influence on a recalcitrant or apathetic laity.

Under these conditions, the complaints of contemporaries about the religious deficiencies of the Lancashire laity become readily understandable, even when we adjust for the demanding expectations of Puritan reformers. Both Richardson and Haigh provide examples of popular ignorance of and even hostility to organised religion, and both cite the entertaining example of the old man of Cartmel who was reported by a Puritan minister in 1644 as having heard of Jesus

Christ only once, at a Corpus Christi play at Kendal. This area of north Lancashire was particularly isolated and lacking in religious provision, as Haigh remarks; and even here, as he acknowledges, 'It is dangerous to try to sum up the religious history of almost a quarter of a county in one example'. The old man of Cartmel may have been teasing his earnest interrogator, or pretending ignorance for reasons of his own; and other specific examples are also vulnerable to allegations of misinterpretation or untypicality. Much stronger evidence is provided by widespread complaints of general absenteeism from church, and by the difficulties experienced by the church courts in bringing to book even that minority of offenders who were summoned before them. Puritans complained that alehouses were better-frequented than churches in service time, and church attenders themselves were often inattentive, noisy, sleepy or unruly. Wrightson remarks that in Lancashire churchgoing was seen more as 'a gathering of neighbours than ... a religious exercise'. Even excommunication was ineffective as a penalty, except for a minority of the propertied who suffered from the resultant legal disabilities.[7]

Between the broad acres of Roman Catholic survival in the west, and the emergent area of Puritan strength in the south-east, much of Lancashire's population, especially in the north, was little affected by religious influences of any kind. We shall see that even in the Puritan strongholds which developed in the seventeenth century, most of the population remained unresponsive or hostile to the threats and blandishments of the godly. Apathy, ignorance and even overt scepticism were not peculiar to Lancashire or to the North, as Keith Thomas shows; but he suggests that 'religious ignorance was probably particularly common in the heath and forest areas, where society was less rigid and disciplined than in the stable, nucleated villages of the fielden communities'.[8] Upland Lancashire, especially, had many such areas; and much of the county continued to match up to the contemporary Puritan stereotype of a 'dark corner of the land', steeped in ignorance, superstition and idolatry which were compounded and exacerbated in places by Roman Catholic survival. Other regions shared some of these characteristics, but they seem to have been particularly pronounced in Elizabethan and early Stuart Lancashire.

The influence of secular government and administration was also constrained by limited resources and geographical and cultural isolation. Leading Lancastrians, with their metropolitan contacts, knew much more about central government and the Court than central government knew about Lancashire. Successive Privy Councils were administratively weak and lacked the cohesion, continuity and local influence to make their policies effective in a county which lay beyond their visiting range and outside their aura of awe. Apart from a brief period when the fourth Earl of Derby was an active Privy Councillor in 1586-9, central government's perceptions of Lancashire depended heavily on reports from the assize judges, whose fleeting visits rarely took them far beyond the courtroom. In the 1630s the county Justices of the Peace began to make regular reports to the assize judges, but this probably gave a veneer of administrative coherence to a system which still left very extensive practical autonomy to the Justices.[9]

Successive governments continued to rely heavily on the goodwill of the Earls of Derby, whose power in Lancashire was not seriously undermined until the Civil War, the execution of the seventh earl at Bolton in 1651, and the forfeiture and reduction of the family's estates, which ultimately resulted in 'quite considerable' losses of Lancashire property, especially in the south-east.[10] An earlier crisis, involving an expensive inheritance dispute after the death of the fifth Earl in 1594, had been successfully overcome. Admittedly, Coward draws our attention to the limits of the family's power even in its heyday. The Stanleys' position depended increasingly on careful management and skilful political manoeuvring, as they had to placate central government without committing themselves to policies within Lancashire which would have identified them with a particular segment or faction in an increasingly divided county. Above all, of course, religious divisions were contentious, and the Stanley method of coping with ultimately irreconcilable differences is well illustrated by the activities of the fourth earl in the later sixteenth century. He was a patron of strongly Protestant preachers but maintained close social ties with his Catholic relatives and neighbours, provided ready support for plays and players, and kept a mistress. Circumstances might constrain the Earls of Derby to seem to be all things to all men, but the significant point is that they were able to sustain this position for nearly a century. Central government needed them, and could not afford to call their bluff; while the county gentry accepted their predominance and did not overtly challenge their authority. In practice, that authority was becoming more symbolic, and less effective, outside the corner of south-west Lancashire where the Stanleys' territorial influence was most strongly concentrated; but the family's continuing social and political predominance remained impressive, and had few parallels elsewhere.[11]

The persisting but qualified importance of the Earls of Derby as mediators between the centre and the county still left an extensive field open to the initiative of Justices of the Peace whose activities remained difficult to oversee from the centre. Although their numbers increased, Justices remained in short supply when Lancashire is compared with most other counties. Different sources give conflicting figures, but the number of Justices may have more than doubled to 56 between Elizabeth's accession and 1592, rising again to 75 in 1618. In 1620, however, a more demanding definition gives the number of resident lay gentry with JP status as 56, and despite a continuing increase in demands, responsibilities and administrative needs this figure declined to 39 in 1640.[12] Numbers were kept down by the persisting importance of Roman Catholicism among the gentry, as central government became increasingly unwilling to countenance JPs with Catholic connections. Hence, especially, the purge of the 1620s and 1630s, when new families had to be introduced to the bench to prevent the system from collapsing altogether. But there were limits to the scope for such initiatives, especially in western Catholic strongholds like the Fylde, for the established magisterial families resented and resisted the introduction of obviously inferior newcomers, and central government depended on their goodwill. The result was that county administration in Lancashire remained thinly populated, except perhaps in Protestant Salford Hundred, and magisterial supervision over the localities inevitably suffered.[13]

Secular authority at the level of the village or hamlet was thus left largely in the hands of unpaid local officials who were elected or appointed through the manorial courts and the parish vestry. The maintenance of order, the relief of poverty and the enforcement of religious orthodoxy were conducted in the first instance at local level, with recourse to Quarter Sessions and Assizes only when disputes were so intractable, offenders so brazen or persistent, or offences so heinous as to demand recourse to higher authority. We shall see that Justices, especially in south-east Lancashire, were making efforts from the late sixteenth century to coerce local officials into the stricter regulation of behaviour according to an externally imposed code of legal and moral expectations; but this was not widely or systematically sustained outside the Manchester area until after 1640, and especially after 1646. This apart, county government might intervene to enforce local obligations to maintain roads and bridges, for example, but the JPs rarely attempted to probe more deeply into the workings of local society. Before the 1640s, at least, Lancashire's villages and hamlets were largely self-regulating.[14]

Lancashire's part-time local officials were numerous, and drawn from a wide cross-section of the community, with regular rotation of office. Prescot's Court Leet regularly appointed at least 21 officials, including 2 constables, 2 clerks of the market, 2 aletasters, 4 affeerors who assessed how much offenders should be fined, and 2 streetlookers who dealt with obstructions and encroachments. Manchester, in keeping with its size and importance, regularly appointed over a hundred officials. These were unusually sophisticated bodies, but everywhere the constables, the churchwardens and (by the early seventeenth century) the overseers of the poor embodied (not always very impressively) the authority of the local community, or at least of the property-owning householders within it.[15]

Keith Wrightson remarks that the petty constables who had local charge of law and order were 'ordinary members of their communities, subject to the prejudices, the strengths and weaknesses of their societies'. Their role could be unenviable when they were caught up between the countervailing expectations of external authority, concerned to uphold the letter of the law, and local community, concerned to preserve a fragile ideal of harmony and good neighbourliness and to settle conflicts quietly and informally. The office could also be expensive in time, trouble and cash, as constables often experienced difficulty and delay in obtaining expenses for attending higher courts and conveying prisoners. Attempts were sometimes made to impose the office of constable on the poor and powerless, as substantial members of the community used their influence to evade their responsibilities. Paid substitutes were also employed by men of substance when their turn for office came, and in 1632 two such men were put in the stocks themselves for drunkenness. But appeals to the Justices sometimes prevented the worst abuses, and in many Lancashire villages the custom was to choose the constable in rotation from among the householders, ensuring that the responsibility was widely shared among the heads of families. The constable's main aim was usually to resolve disputes and grievances locally and informally, passing on to higher authority only those offenders who had 'scandalized, threatened or alienated the greater part of the community' by their misdeeds, and otherwise preferring to mediate or compromise an informal settlement. Failing this, prosecutions were often presented in such a way as to fit them for a local court. These attitudes and expectations help to explain the relatively low proportion of cases handled by south Lancashire JPs. In seven sample years between 1626 and 1638 they dealt with only 33 cases per 10,000 population, on Wrightson's calculation, compared wtih 51 in Essex, where ideals of village consensus and harmony were already breaking down as wealthy Puritans became culturally and economically divided from poor and unregenerate cottagers and labourers. Lancashire village society was less sharply polarised, and here the thin scattering of Justices usually responded to complaints arising from specific disputes in the localities, rather than looking to regulate behaviour in any positive or systematic way. In any case, the administrative and judicial systems were riddled with loopholes, and even when offenders were brought before local courts a high proportion seem to have evaded punishment by failing to appear or neglecting to pay fines.[16] Lancashire was perhaps becoming an increasingly law-abiding society, in the sense that the legal process was steadily superseding brute force during the century after Elizabeth's accession; and in normal times it may also have become a less violent society, although an apparent decline in prosecutions for assault is susceptible of more than one explanation; but a more secure conclusion is that neighbourly mediation and intercession at the local level remained the preferred and most effective way of defusing conflict.

The relief of poverty likewise remained a local matter, except in time of major crisis or insoluble disagreement. The formal Poor Law machinery of overseers and churchwardens, as prescribed in the 1601 Act, was introduced at parish and sometimes township level in the early seventeenth century, and by the 1620s unsuccessful petitioners for aid at the local level were applying to Justices of the Peace for redress, sometimes successfully. By this time the aged and infirm, the widowed and orphaned were increasingly being supported by doles from the poor-rates.[17] This innovation spread rapidly not only in response to the pressures of economic dislocation and over-population, but also because large-scale, formally organised charitable endowments for poor relief in Lancashire were remarkably limited. The poor, as such, attracted only 22 per cent of all the charitable benefactions traced by Jordan in the county for the years between 1480 and 1640: 'by far the lowest percentage thus provided in all the counties we have studied and very possibly, save for Cumberland and Westmorland, in England as a whole'. In the early decades of the seventeenth century poor relief did account for over 40 per cent of Lancashire's charitable donations, but Jordan comments that this was still 'grossly inadequate in fact, and, in relation to other counties ... still very low indeed'.[18]

How do we explain the comparatively low level of formal charitable provision for the poor? The emphasis on educational funding as opposed to poor relief in Lancashire's charities might suggest a preference for the encouragement of individual advancement through the kind of upward social mobility which education could sustain, coupled with the dissemination of godly learning for the salvation of souls: the 'Protestant ethic' in action. But this is probably an anachronistic judgement, and Manchester merchants of Puritan leanings were prominent among the most willing benefactors of the poor through bequests and foundations, as well as investing in education.[19] More to the point, perhaps, is Lancashire's distinctive social structure, with its shortage of really substantial gentry and its extensive middle ranks, many of whom might have some spare resources but lacked the financial muscle to endow major charities on a sufficient scale to generate the surviving documentation upon which Jordan's enquiry depends. Personal charity to the poor was much more important in Lancashire than Jordan's work would suggest: but what predominated was the *ad hoc*, informal dispensation of assistance to neighbours and dependants in need, nurtured by ethics of paternalism and neighbourly mutual aid. Those who sought assistance from the Poor Law in the 1620s and 1630s often did so after several months of depending on the charity of their neighbours, or on begging. Only when their continuing needs became intolerably burdensome was the formal administrative machinery brought into play, to spread the load among the ratepayers at large.[20] Many of the numerous Lancashire alehouses were kept by poor people, labourers and widows who might otherwise, it was thought, have become a burden on the poor-rates or the charitable; and unlicensed alehouses were tolerated by local communities and officials, at least until the 1640s, unless their frequenters indulged in persistently scandalous behaviour of a visibly lewd and disorderly kind. Alehouse keeping was viewed in many places as an unofficial but legitimate extension of the informal approach to poor relief through neighbouring and mutual aid.[21] Harsh treatment for the poor was reserved for vagrants, and for the mothers of illegitimate children who could not be supported by the woman's family or by the putative father; and as we saw in Chapter 2, there were occasions when the strain of famine and trade depression was such that effective relief became impossible. On the whole, however, as with law and order, the relief of poverty was conducted, as far as possible, locally and informally, in what was still a face-to-face, insular society.

The self-regulating and mutually supportive aspects of Lancashire society were sustained by the persisting, and in some cases increasing, importance of the small and middling landowner and the independence provided by domestic industry before the spread of the putting-out system. But we must not romanticise this way of life. The systematic concern to sustain harmony and defuse conflict was a defensive reaction against built-in tendencies towards bitter disagreement and violence in small-scale societies with limited resources. Disputes over the ownership of land, over access to and use of commons, and the taking of turf and timber, were endemic and sometimes violent, although it is impossible to say whether they were increasing in frequency. Changes in the law gave an added dimension of danger to the malicious gossip which flourished in inward-looking settlements where many residents were better known by nick-names than surnames. As the penalties for religious and sexual nonconformity, and for witchcraft, increased, and as the courts began to pay more attention to them, there was a rapid upsurge in prosecutions for slander in the church courts, as people sought formally to clear their names from threatening allegations.[22] The famous Lancashire witch-trials of 1612 and 1633 also furnish evidence of sustained social tensions in the form of family feuds and disputes over the informal relief of poverty. Most of the Pendle witches regularly sought alms from their better-off neighbours, and accusations of witchcraft came when the 'victims' suffered ill-health, misfortune or death after refusing a request for aid or otherwise slighting or threatening the alleged witch.[23] This evidence calls to mind Alan Macfarlane's suggestions about the roots of Essex witch-trials. He argues that those who refused alms knew themselves to be rejecting the consensus values of a community in which the poor had a legitimate right to expect relief from their neighbours. The resulting burden of guilt made them expect retribution, and when misfortune came they were eager to blame the aggrieved alms-seeker, who may in turn have cultivated a reputation for witchcraft as her only bargaining-counter in an inhospitable world.[24] Chattox, Demdike and their families in Pendle Forest were perhaps especially likely to be refused alms, as unattractive and unsympathetic characters with reputations for dishonesty and unneighbourly conduct. Probably the local poor relief system was usually capable of sustaining the 'deserving' poor, those with a reputation for hard work, honesty and good neighbouring; but it ran into difficulties when confronted with the needs and machinations of the deviant and disreputable. The actual witch-trials, which were brought to court largely through the obsessive interest of one particular magistrate, are isolated markers denoting the more general presence of potentially violent social tensions, which are normally hidden from historians but also reached the surface in the form of small assaults, 'tussles', property disputes and slander actions.[25]

Despite the subsequent notoriety of the Pendle witches, full-scale witch-trials involving accusations of systematic malevolence and compacts with the devil seem to have been unusual in Lancashire, although there was a 'minor witch-craze' in the late 1590s. More generally, however, popular magical beliefs persisted tenaciously, and charmers and folk-healers remained much in demand, perhaps especially in the areas of strongest Roman Catholic survival in the west and south. Outside this area, the content of one of Chattox's charms for mending soured drink suggests a close relationship between traditional religious and magical beliefs in Pendle Forest: it invoked the Trinity and the 'five wounds of our Lord', and included five paternosters and five aves.[26] But the main preoccupation of reformers was with the control and discouragement of Roman Catholicism as such, and witchcraft and popular magic were usually seen as a subordinate problem within the wider spiritual and cultural pathology of interrelated papistry, ignorance and vice.

Lancashire's reputation as the strongest bastion of Roman Catholicism in England was established early in Elizabeth's reign. Despite mounting legal and administrative pressure, Lancashire's Catholics became, if anything, increasingly visible and confident towards the end of the sixteenth century, and under the early Stuarts they went from strength to strength. In so doing they overcame or evaded penal legislation which looked formidable on paper but proved very difficult to enforce on the ground in the peculiar social setting of Lancashire, with the conspicuous exception of the south-eastern administrative division of Salford Hundred, as we shall see.[27]

It is very difficult to assess the numerical strength of Lancashire Catholicism during this period. It expressed itself in two visible ways: there were recusants, who cut themselves off from the religious life of the reformed Church of England altogether, and church-papists, who made the minimum number of church attendances necessary to escape prosecution, but took no active part in the services and refused Communion. In many gentry families the head conformed in this token fashion, while his wife and children stayed away. Beyond this, there were those who conformed on the surface but were eager to hear Catholic masses when opportunity arose, and in Elizabethan times there remained a significant, if declining, number of 'conservative' clergy within the Church of England, who kept up as many Catholic practices as they could. Such clergy were unlikely to report the recusants and non-communicants in their parishes to the authorities.

Legislation at the beginning of Elizabeth's reign laid down heavy penalties, in the form of crippling fines and imprisonment, for absence from church on Sundays and holy days, and especially for hearing Mass. Catholic priests, of course, risked execution if caught. In 1581 the penalties were increased, certain legal loopholes were tightened, and the machinery of detection was formalised, with offenders reported at episcopal visitations being referred to secular authority and dealt with at Quarter Sessions or Assizes.[28] In spite of all this, the number of recusants and non-communicants reported to the bishop in Lancashire increased steadily in Elizabeth's later years, from 304 and 29 in 1578 to 754 and 349 in 1601. Hopes of a more tolerant régime under James I brought many more Catholics into the open: in 1604 the figures were 3516 and 521, and the number of recusants held firm thereafter until the even of the Civil War. This is, of course, the tip of an iceberg of uncertain size; but even on these minimum figures, it is clear that Lancashire as a Catholic stronghold was matched elsewhere in England and Wales only by Monmouthshire.

To speak of 'Lancashire' in this vein is, of course, to over-simplify. Recusants were thickest on the ground in the southern and western deaneries of Warrington and Amounderness, and very thinly scattered in the emergent textile district around Manchester. In 1604 recorded recusants accounted for as many as 1 in 9 of the *total population* of Amounderness, and the Warrington figure was 1 in 13, compared with 1 in 2479 for Manchester deanery, where the large numbers of Puritan clergy must have ensured that returns were more assiduously compiled. Gentry Catholicism was particularly conspicuous in the south and west, and also in the Ribble Valley.[29] In extensive areas of the south and west, the recusancy returns probably conceal an almost universal adhesion to, or at least strong sympathy for, the Catholic faith. We need to enquire further into the reasons for this patchy but remarkable Catholic resilience, and into the implications for the nature of Lancashire society.

There is some dispute as to whether this Lancashire Catholicism was a matter of survival or revival. As Haigh points out, existing priests who refused to conform to the Elizabethan settlement, or who subsequently repudiated it, were especially numerous in Lancashire, and recusancy there was already beginning to worry central government during the 1560s, long before the missionary priests from Douai and elsewhere were capable of making a significant impact. There was clearly a strong vein of continuity and traditional attachment in Lancashire Catholicism, on which the seminary priests of the late sixteenth century were able to build.[30] This point is highly relevant to the nature of Lancashire Catholicism. Although it was nourished by the patronage and protection offered by the gentry, it kept much firmer roots among the lesser landowners and farmers than was the case in most areas. It was not exclusively dependent on seminary priests with new theological ideas, operating from great houses and ministering mainly to their occupants, but it retained the services of many non-conforming priests from pre-Reformation days.[31] Lancashire's traditional Catholicism never quite lost touch with the needs and aspirations of the people in its strongholds in the Fylde and the south-west, and this gave added fuel to its capacity for survival.

But why *did* Catholicism persist and revive so strongly in these areas? Bossy rightly warns us against the perils of geographical determinism, of 'treating types of religious belief as if they were types of vegetation';[32] and the Catholic areas of Elizabethan and early Stuart Lancashire were no more remote or primitive than the uplands of Cumbria and the Borders, where recusants were in very short supply, while their boundaries do not correspond convincingly with any distinctive area of agriculture or other economic activity, except in the negative sense that Catholics were almost absent from the south-eastern textile district. Nor do the efforts of individuals take us much further towards a satisfying explanation. Admittedly, the failure of the early Protestant preachers to penetrate beyond the Manchester area, and the influence of Catholic organisers and preachers such as Allen, Vaux and Campion, clearly contributed to the emergence of the Catholic strongholds, although Haigh argues that Campion's role in Lancashire has been greatly exaggerated.[33] But we really need to explain why these areas were so much more receptive to some kinds of religious influences than to others. More to the point here, perhaps, were economic, political and institutional factors which were related to geographical features without being determined by them, and which provided the necessary framework for the operation of individual influences. In the first place, these were relatively isolated and backward areas, despite the stirrings of new economic activity on the coalfield around Prescot and Wigan. Outsiders needed local guides, and it was easy to hide priests and other wanted persons from external authority. Most economic activity was locally orientated, and outside influences made little impact unless they worked with the grain of local culture. A conservative gentry protected and sustained the old religious ways among tenants and dependants. There was much social mixing between the classes, and a common attachment to hunting and traditional enjoyments. The ecclesiastical system reinforced conservatism. The pre-Reformation church had been just sufficiently effective, in contrast with wilder areas further north, to claim the loyalties of the locals, but the leakage of clergy from the Elizabethan church to the Catholics was particularly pronounced here, and the failure of Bishop Downham of Chester and the Earl of Derby to act decisively against incipient recusancy in the early 1560s helped the recusants to gain a firm foothold, especially as the Church of England as such had little of its own to offer. Above all, most of the secular office-holders in the relevant districts were themselves Catholics, or willing to protect the interests of Catholic relatives and neighbours. Successive Earls of Derby were themselves equivocal, and in 1564, 19 of Lancashire's 25 JPs were said to be 'unfavourable' towards the Elizabethan church. As late as 1598, 14 of the working justices were church-papists, and 10 more had close relatives who were recusants; and even the newly purged Ecclesiastical Commission for the Diocese of Chester still contained several 'crypto-Catholics', despite its supposed role as enforcer of conformity. It was, and remained, particularly difficult to find firmly Protestant JPs of adequate social standing in the south-western and western hundreds of West Derby and Amounderness.[34] The churchwardens who were supposed to inform on recusants and non-attenders at the local level likewise came under the influence of Catholic gentry, relatives and neighbours. Seminary priests were increasingly attracted to a promising area (and many were Lancastrians anyway); and their survival rate was relatively high. There seems to have been no shortage of Catholic clergy. A few prominent gentry were harshly treated, with repeated imprisonment and heavy fines, especially in Elizabeth's middle years; but generally the social and administrative barriers against effective persecution were remarkably effective. The active Puritans were at a safe distance, apart from a few parish clergy and their isolated and embattled allies; and in general the Catholics could be seen to pose no real threat to their conforming neighbours. By the turn of the century many Catholics were becoming increasingly public in their religious activities, and assertive in each other's defence. Their survival offers another reminder of the importance of close-knit, mutually supportive local communities, and the defence of Catholicism shows that whatever the internal tensions might be, it remained possible to preserve a remarkably effective common front against external threat in these generally traditionalist and economically backward parts of Lancashire.

Where Catholic survival tended to unite communities, or to respond to existing social solidarities, Puritanism divided them, or perhaps underlined existing or emergent divisions. Even in their south-east Lancashire strongholds, the Puritans conspicuously failed to win the hearts and minds of the vast majority of the population. But attempts to chart the extent of their influence are hampered by problems of definition. As Richardson and Haigh point out, not all of those who might be seen as Puritans fell foul of Elizabethan or early Stuart church discipline; but the ones who did are the most visible and accessible to subsequent historians. The label 'Puritan' could be affixed to Nicholas Assheton of Downham, who combined regular and attentive sermon-hearing with a lifestyle in which hunting, gaming, dancing and heavy drinking all bulked large, as well as to earnest abstinent Sabbatarians who regularly deviated from prescribed Prayer Book usages in a strongly Protestant direction, and who sought to suppress the amusements Assheton enjoyed. 'Puritans' embraced a wide spectrum of attitudes to theology, ceremonial, service content and church government. The most visible and straightforward examples were those radical Protestants who refused to wear the surplice or to make the sign of the cross in baptism, who administered communion in unorthodox and informal ways, opposed episcopacy, sought to rewrite the Prayer Book and tinkered around with the order of service, usually in order to allocate extra time to the sermon. Clergy of this sort were tolerated much more readily by the ecclesiastical hierarchy in Elizabethan Lancashire than elsewhere; they were even encouraged as an antidote to popery, especially in the 1580s, when preaching exercises under Puritan management were made compulsory for clergy and schoolmasters. Of the four Queen's Preachers appointed to strengthen the preaching ministry in Lancashire in 1599, at least three had marked Puritan leanings. The climate of official opinion became less benign in the early seventeenth century, but there was no sustained campaign against Lancashire Puritans until 1633, and even then only a handful of deprivations resulted from a visitation by the Archbishop of York. For the most part Lancashire Puritanism was allowed a free hand to develop unmolested, to a remarkable and perhaps unique extent.[35]

The impact of effective Puritan influence was limited, however, both geographically and socially. Puritan ministers were already concentrated disproportionately into the south-eastern textile district by 1590, and in 1595 ten of the thirteen benefices in Manchester and Blackburn deaneries were held by recognisable Puritans. Evidence of Puritanism among the laity begins to appear in the early seventeenth century, and popular preachers like John Angier of Denton and Richard Midgeley of Rochdale developed devoted local followings. Local congregations subscribed endowments for additional sermons and ensured the appointment of Puritans to outlying chapels where the minister's payment depended on the goodwill of his congregation. In this area at least, seventeenth-century Puritanism was taking root and spreading. Elsewhere in the county, however, the Puritans enjoyed very limited success. Liverpool's Corporation promoted sermons and paid for a Puritan lecturer, and nearby Toxteth was settled by Puritans, apparently from the Bolton area; but otherwise the sprinkling of Puritan clergy who were presented to livings by outside patrons seem to have made little headway. The market towns of the south and west sometimes had Puritan incumbents, but their local allies were few, embattled and sometimes intimidated. Their precarious position is suggested by a particularly revealing passage in a lament from Lancashire's Puritan clergy in 1590:

The disturbance of the divine service most offensive to everie good conscience ...

4. By the greate tumultes of the people remaininge in the Churchyarde, stretes and alehouses, in time of divine service. ffrom whence stones ar often times throwen uppon the leades of the Churche, and many a clamorowse noise and showte geven owte to the disquietinge of the Congregation.[36]

Outside the Manchester area and mercantile Liverpool, the Puritan message fell on very stony ground.

How should we explain the geographical distribution of Puritan support? As we have seen, the south-east had trading links with London and the West Riding of Yorkshire, which brought it into contact with innovatory religious ideas; and the Manchester area had a Protestant tradition on which the Elizabethan reformers were able to build. Lancashire-born London merchants invested in schools, scholarships, sermons and chapels, and Lancashire scholars in growing numbers were confirmed in a Puritan cast of mind at Oxford and Cambridge before returning as ministers to the county. Once a core of Puritan clergy and congregations had become established, a feedback process was set in motion, and the attractions of south-east Lancashire for Puritans in search of cures were enhanced by the unusual extent of official toleration and by the effectiveness of the secular arm in suppressing local Catholic recusancy. The strength of Protestant support among the gentry and Justices of Salford Hundred helped to create an environment in which Puritans could work unmolested.[37] Whether their teachings had a special appeal for an emergent stratum of proto-capitalist entrepreneurs in search of a work ethic, is a more difficult question. The sermons delivered by John Angier of Denton, near Manchester, in 1638 should warn us against facile conclusions about Puritans and the promotion of a work ethic:

We bestow too much pains and labour about our callings, too much spend the vigour and strength of our bodies, that they become unfit to serve our souls in the worship of God. What means our sleepy praiers every night in our families, but the over-wearying of our bodies? What means our sleepy Sabbaths, but the overtiring of our bodies on the week daies?[38]

Angier's sermons also reinforce suggestions that Lancashire's Puritans preached successfully only to a godly minority. His comments on the sleepy inattention of his congregations, and their propensity to whisper, laugh or gaze vacantly into space during the service, indicate considerable consumer resistance to Puritan practices and doctrines even among church attenders. At one point he even divides the sleepers into categories, from those who 'sleep from the beginning to the end, as if they come for no other purpose but to sleep', to those whose 'heads are so leaden and weighty, that they cannot hold them up, and their eies so heavy, that they cannot hold them open'.[39]

Angier seems to have been a conscientious and well-liked minister, with a concern to present his sermons in plain, direct language; and his difficulties are doubly significant if we remember that not all Puritan ministes were cast in this mould.[40] Haigh has pointed out some of their deficiencies in Elizabethan times, when 23 of the 40 Puritan clergy in Lancashire were accused of some form of pastoral neglect, including failure to catechise in 19 cases and even neglect of preaching. Perhaps not surprisingly, absenteeism was rife among Puritan clergy in heavily recusant parishes. Even Manchester and Bolton were neglected by their Puritan clergy, and moral offences and excommunications were rife in both places. Even in their south-east Lancashire stronghold, 'the Puritan clergy could not overcome the paucity of their own numbers, economic pressures, difficult parochial conditions, a general hostility towards sermons and the competition of Sunday entertainments'.[41] There are strong indications that the emergence of a godly laity in the seventeenth century involved a small minority of the population, and that most of the poor and many of the middling sort remained almost untouched by Puritan teaching. The long-term failure of the Puritan campaign for a reformation of manners, which reached its peak in the 1640s and 1650s, suggests a lack of social depth to the effective influence of the movement, as we shall see. Lancashire may have had its godly poor, but all the indications are that its convinced Puritans were recruited disproportionately from the ranks of the literate and the propertied.[42]

The polarisation between Catholics and Puritans left relatively little middle ground for moderate Anglicans to occupy; and the strife between the two extremes grew angrier and more strident during the 1630s. Whatever it may have been elsewhere, indeed, the Civil War in Lancashire was dominated by the dimension of religious conflict. Blackwood finds that economic distinctions between supporters of King and Parliament were minor and marginal; as J. S. Morrill remarks, his painstaking work on the part played by the gentry in the conflict 'offers very little comfort to those who want to see the Civil War as being a social revolution in its causes'.[43] We cannot identify the Royalists with feudalism, backwardness or reaction, or the Parliamentarians with capitalism and 'progress', through any convincing economic analysis of gentry families. Over 60 per cent, indeed, were apparently neutral. Of the rest, the Royalists recruited a slightly higher proportion of their support from older-established families, from esquires rather than plain gentlemen, and from families with substantial rent-rolls; they also had a higher proportion of families in financial difficulties, although these accounted for only one-sixth of their number. The Parliamentarians had a slightly larger share of those families which had acquired considerable property in the seventeenth century, and they attracted substantially more of the mercantile and legal gentry. But the differences were so marginal, or the numbers involved so small, that no grand theories of economic causation can be supported from this evidence.

At the level of the gentry, indeed, three main differences between the two sides emerge most obviously. The first is geographical: only in Salford Hundred were the Parliamentarian gentry in the majority among those who took sides, and even here there were 39 Royalists to set against the 46 Parliamentarians. The latter were heavily concentrated into the Bolton and Manchester districts. Elsewhere the Royalist majority was strong, and in the south and west it was overwhelming. Secondly, a larger minority of the Parliamentarian gentry had experienced some form of higher education: 30 per cent in total, as against 20 per cent of the Royalists. But the really remarkable contrast was in religious adherence. On Blackwood's calculation 63 per cent of Lancashire's Parliamentarian gentry were Puritan, and although Morrill suggests that on Blackwood's definition 'his "Puritan" gentry ... include men with a wide variety of beliefs, and many who would not have seen themselves, or been seen by their contemporaries, as Puritans', the evidence remains arresting.[44] On the other side, 57 per cent of Blackwood's Royalists were Roman Catholics, and a high proportion of these actually fought in the war. They accounted for more than three-quarters of those of the King's field officers from Lancashire whose religion can be traced, and they were much in evidence at other levels in the army.[45] In all 116 Catholic families can be identified as Royalist, while none supported Parliament; while 67 Puritan families were Parliamentarian, and only 7 supported the King. The extent of this polarisation was probably unique to Lancashire, and the impression of a high level of commitment is reinforced by evidence that very few families changed sides between 1642 and 1648, or were divided among themselves.

The gentry are, of course, only part of the story. Brian Manning has pointed out 'the inadequacy of seeing the English Revolution as merely a conflict within the ruling class', and he argues that independent small producers were capable of thinking and acting for themselves in defence of their own interests, rather than blindly following the major landowners.[46] Parliament's cause in Lancashire was materially helped by the appearance of large numbers of the 'middling sort', especially smallholders who doubled as domestic manufacturers or nailmakers, at crucial points in the campaign, from the siege of Manchester onwards. As we saw in Chapter 2, some of these people were led into battle by gentlemen from their localities, and Manning acknowledges that 'the defence of Manchester [against the Royalists] ... depended heavily on the local gentry and their influence over their tenants and neighbours'. But he also argues for the importance of independent small producers in their own right, fearing for the security of their lands and businesses, and resenting the attempts of Lord Strange, the Earl of Derby's heir, to press the sons of yeomen and tradesmen into the Royalist armies. Many such people declared for Parliament on their own account, and played a significant part in some of the fighting. Puritanism, again, was often influential in helping them to make up their minds. The problem is to disentangle the deferential from the independent among these 'middling' people, and to assess the relative importance of religious, economic and other motives in their decision to participate. These difficulties remain intractable; but Manning's independent smallholder/craftsmen were undoubtedly present in the conflict. Their eagerness and numerical strength sometimes worried those in authority on the Parliamentarian side, who feared a possible threat to the hierarchical social order if these enthusiastic middling men were given too much encouragement. We must not exaggerate the importance of the independent 'middling sort', especially as Parliament did not monopolise their allegiance: many were undoubtedly traditionalist or neutral. But the 'middling sort' were particularly numerous in Lancashire, and their activities cannot be ignored. The Civil War in this county, as elsewhere, was far from being a class war; but nor was it simply an internecine struggle between the gentry. The lower levels of propertied society had their own part to play in the conflict, although its exact nature must remain obscure.[47]

Above all, the Civil War in Lancashire was fuelled by local issues and tensions, which were ignited by events on the national stage. Charles I's new taxation was endured with unusual tolerance in Lancashire. Serious difficulties in collecting Ship Money did not appear until 1638–9, in striking contrast with many counties; and resistance was strongest, paradoxically, in the Wigan area and the hundreds of Amounderness and Lonsdale, which were predominantly Royalist in the ensuing conflict. But this apart, the really divisive issues in the early 1640s lay closer to home: fear among Puritans of a Catholic uprising after the pattern of recent events in Ireland, which were near enough to be particularly frightening in Lancashire; Catholic fears of the possible consequences of this alarm; growing Puritan worries about persecution as the machinery of ecclesiastical discipline was used against them with increasing frequency after 1633; anger at the attempts by Lord Strange to exercise authority in parts of the county where the rule of the Earls of Derby was no longer automatically accepted; and the continuing threat to the security of tenure of copyholders in the old royal forests, as the Crown's legal officers procrastinated.[48] As the conflict developed, local feuds and local pressures drew moderates out of neutrality and attached them to one side or the other, although active participants remained a minority. Attempts to organise a formal pact of neutrality within the county, and to keep the war at arm's length, were doomed to failure from the beginning: the interests and fears of the extreme partisans were beyond reconciliation in a context of national conflict.

The result of the war in Lancashire, with its sustained Parliamentarian ascendancy damaged only by the occasional incursions of Royalist armies, may seem surprising in the light of the pattern of gentry allegiance. But the Parliamentarians, though outnumbered, were more committed and pertinacious than the Royalists, and they could count on more willing support from their tenantry and from the population at large, especially in the strategically important south-east. The leading Royalists, moreover, were drawn away to campaigns in other parts of the country, which drained Lancashire of effective resources. Ultimately, the Parliamentarian stranglehold on the county was remarkably complete.[49]

The most clear-cut divisions, then, were along religious lines. It was from Catholics and Puritans, above all, that the keenest activists were recruited. But we must remember that in the county as a whole, these religious divisions also had a geographical and an economic expression. The economically backward areas *were* Catholic and Royalist; the main area of textile development *was* a Puritan and Parliamentarian stronghold. Admittedly, the Catholic area included the coalfield around Wigan and Prescot, while Manchester itself was thought to contain a substantial majority of potential Royalists and supporters of the Earl of Derby in 1642; but these examples do not invalidate the general argument. So the failure of Blackwood's research to find significant economic differences between Royalist and Parliamentarian gentry may be misleading. An analysis of the hard-core activists on both sides, leaving out the moderates and the reluctant campaigners, might lay bare more striking differences between the two sides in wealth, social standing and economic experience. There may also have been significant differences in economic outlook and social attitudes. Blackwood looked for evidence of this sort, but failed to find enough material on economic attitudes and estate management to substantiate any convincing generalisations, except, importantly, that the Royalists included every kind of landowner from the benevolent paternalist to the enterprising developer and the ruthless rack-renter.[50] This leaves little encouragement for stereotypes about feudal backwardness. But we cannot write off the possibility that further research might show that economic differences in experience or outlook might have had a stronger causal influence on both the religious and the political aspects of the Civil War in Lancashire than the current orthodoxy allows. The evidence is not yet conclusive either way.

The impact of the Civil War on Lancashire landed society was quite limited. Admittedly, the social composition of the county magistracy changed markedly after the renewal of hostilities in 1648 and the subsequent execution of the King. Between 1648 and 1652 the greater gentry lost their traditionally overwhelming preponderance among the active magistrates, and until the Restoration they were outnumbered by the lesser gentry and a fluctuating handful of plebeians. A similar change in the balance of power took place at about the same time on the county committees which were set up by Parliament in 1643 to supplement the existing administrative system. Militia officers were also increasingly recruited from the minor gentry and yeomanry. But the changes in Lancashire came later and were less far-reaching than in many other counties, and they were probably due mainly to the withdrawal or exclusion of moderate or Royalist gentry, and the resultant lack of traditionally qualified administrators, rather than to any policy of exalting the 'middling sort'. The changes in the county's power structure were matters of emphasis, falling a long way short of social revolution, and they were to be reversed at the Restoration.[51]

The aftermath of the Civil War brought no lasting or spectacular redistribution of land. Blackwood tells us that '71 per cent of the Lancashire Royalist gentry were victims of Parliamentary sequestrations, composition fines and forfeitures. But few of these declined socially or economically as a result.' Most of the Royalists contrived to hold on to their estates, or to buy them back after forced sale, and only the Earls of Derby seem to have suffered serious permanent losses, especially to purchases by yeomen and sitting tenants in south-east Lancashire. Nor were the Parliamentarian gentry conspicuous beneficiaries from the purchase of confiscated Royalist, royal or episcopal land. Between 1642 and 1664, 318 families dropped out of the Lancashire gentry, as defined rather generously by Blackwood, and only 171 newcomers replaced them; but 80 per cent of the disappearing gentry 'had apparently played no part in the Civil War'. We shall see that families continued to drop out of the gentry in large numbers after the Restoration; but the influence of the Civil War cannot be isolated as a significant cause of this trend. Indeed, the conflict and its aftermath seem to have made very little long-term difference to the structure of Lancashire society.[52] The county's underlying social stability was such that even the Earl of Derby's rising in 1651 failed to attract more than a handful of former Parliamentarian gentry, despite the recent threat to patriarchal and hierarchical order posed by the execution of Charles I. Fear of royalism remained more potent than fear of disruption from below, although attitudes were changing sharply by the eve of the Restoration, as central government became more unstable and Charles II made attractive promises. In 1659 a perceived threat to the established social and political order in Lancashire induced ministers and substantial gentry to rally to the support of Sir George Booth's rising. Fear of Quakers and other sectarian fringe groups coalesced with alarm at a recent shift in the social composition of county government, as only 30 per cent of those nominated to the militia committee were greater gentry. Booth failed to obtain support outside Lancashire and Cheshire for his attempt to obtain a conditional restoration, but after his defeat he and his supporters went effectively unpunished, and the widespread and influential support for the rising (among Presbyterians as well

Evidence of yeoman prosperity: part of the impressive cluster of stone houses and barns at Hurstwood, in the hills above Burnley. We need to know more about the origins and significance of places like this. (See p. 27.)

[*Right*] St Mary's church, Newchurch-in-Pendle, with its mid-sixteenth-century tower and eighteenth-century nave. This was one of Lancashire's ill-served upland chapels-of-ease. (See Chapter 3.)

[*Below*] John Kay, inventor of the fly-shuttle. (See p. 64.)

An engraver's impression of Liverpool in 1680. (See p. 68.) [*Below*] Solid evidence of rural landowning prosperity in the Pennine foothills in the seventeenth century: Extwistle Hall. (See Chapter 2.)

as Episcopalians) presaged the ready acceptance in the county of Charles II's return in 1660.[53]

Just as the most obvious reasons for taking sides in the Civil War in Lancashire were religious, so the most important short-term repercussions of Parliament's victory affected ecclesiastical authority and administration. Halley tells us that 'the presbyterian discipline' was 'organised and established ... in Lancashire more completely and firmly than ... in any other county of England'; and this suggestion still carries conviction. In 1646 authority over Lancashire's parishes and chapelries was formally vested in congregational assemblies, in which the minister was joined by elders elected from the congregation. Each assembly sent minister and delegates to a classis, a federation of congregations with disciplinary authority over its constituent parts. Lancashire contained nine classes, each of which sent delegates to an annual provincial assembly or synod in Preston. On paper, this way of replacing the old ecclesiastical hierarchy seems a potentially formidable instrument of religious discipline, with considerable power vested in local notables to discipline the recalcitrant and enforce godly living, and with sanctions from above readily available against neglectful clergy as well as errant parishioners.[54]

The system seems to have worked quite effectively for the first two or three years in the south-eastern classes of Manchester and Bury, for which minutes have survived; but it is hard to imagine it ever being more than an empty shell in Furness or the Catholic strongholds of the south and west. Even in the southeast, problems soon became overwhelming. The Presbyterians were unable, in practice, to prevent clergy of Episcopalian or Independent opinions from going their own way in their own parishes, if the consensus of opinion among leading laymen was in their favour; and attendance at classis meetings declined rapidly in the 1650s, as their lack of power to impose any religious orthodoxy or common discipline became apparent when their bluff was called. The legal basis for the Presbyterian system was so insecure that its advocates were unwilling to test it in the courts, and when this was discovered its authority was undermined. Individual parishes might be kept on a tight rein by exacting ministers with powerful lay support, but at best this meant stricter controls on the admission of parishioners to the sacraments, with no effective means of requiring religious attendance or obedience from the unregenerate majority. The provincial assembly continued to meet until 1660, and in 1657 the Manchester Presbyterians made a final effort to secure the general catechising of all the laity, godly and ungodly alike, and the punishment of absentees from church. But this initiative, like the previous ones, petered out, and ecclesiastical discipline continued to be effective only against those who already believed, or found it useful to seem to believe.[55]

Attempts to impose a reformation of manners in public behaviour were less unsuccessful, though still very limited. Here, the secular arm of the law could be invoked, and the disobedient could be punished more effectively. Negative and restrictive social regulation was easier to enforce than the positive acceptance of religious beliefs and duties. Whatever their views on church government, theology and the content of services, moreover, Puritans of all shades of opinion, whether Episcopal, Presbyterian or Independent, could agree on the need to repress certain kinds of ungodly behaviour, if only to prevent God from intervening directly to punish an erring people through pestilence and war. As Puritan influence grew in parts of Lancashire from the late sixteenth century, so campaigns against alehouses and drunkenness, illicit sex and bastardy, Sabbath-breaking and traditional festivities, all gathered momentum. They reached a climax in the late 1640s, and persisted strongly through the following decade, as the Puritan magistrates of the Interregnum sought to enforce increasingly fierce prohibitive and regulatory legislation. The reformers encountered determined opposition in some places, and passive resistance in others, and their successes were patchy and limited, although some apparent headway was made in the curbing of unlicensed alehouses and the reduction of illegitimate births.

Alehouses were particularly thick on the ground in Lancashire. In 1647 thirty south-western townships had an approximate ratio of 1 alehouse to 57 inhabitants, which can be compared with an Essex figure of 1:81 in 1644. Manchester's ratio in 1651 was approximately 1:70, and Liverpool in 1646 had 1:46, compared with 1:76 in London in 1641 and 1:52 in Cambridge in the 1620s. Small market towns in Lancashire could show particularly spectacular figures: 1 alehouse to between 15 and 20 inhabitants for Prescot in the early seventeenth century, and 1:15 for Clitheroe in 1645. These figures include unlicensed alehouses as well as licensed ones, and most of the Lancashire figures come from years in which the main campaign of regulation and suppression was already well under way. Alehouses catered for travellers and market visitors as well as locals, of course, and some alehouse keepers brewed only on special occasions; but by any standards, drink outlets in Lancashire were remarkably ubiquitous.[56]

In Lancashire as elsewhere, alehouses catered mainly for the lower orders: craftsmen, husbandmen and labourers. But gentlemen, and even some Puritan ministers, were not above frequenting them on occasion, though no doubt such custom was mainly reserved for the more opulent and respectable establishments. Above all, however, the alehouse was the hub of a convivial, tolerant popular culture, the embodiment of an ideal of good neighbourliness which was often damaged by drunkenness and violence, but which remained resilient and pervasive nevertheless. As dancing and games on Sundays and festivals were banished from the precincts of the church, the alehouse became increasingly important as the main focus for communal festivities.

Lancashire's Puritans viewed alehouses with scant sympathy, especially when they opened during service time on Sundays and provided seductive alternatives to the sermon. As a distinctive, privatised, morally restrictive culture of the godly emerged, mainly among the 'better sort', the alehouse came to be viewed as a dangerous repository of sin and sedition. Alehouses were held to promote drunkenness (which both encouraged sin and anaesthetised guilt) and sexual misdemeanours, to threaten household discipline by promoting idleness and misbehaviour among servants and dependent relatives, and to provide refuges for papist defenders of old religious festivals such as Wakes, with their associated piping and dancing. But serious and sustained attempts at regulation and suppression came later in Lancashire than in such southern counties as Essex and Somerset, even though the population crises of the early seventeenth century also drew attention to the alehouse as consumer of grain which might otherwise make bread. Puritan pressure on Sunday games and dancing after church was already apparent early in the seventeenth century, prompting James I to defend local customs by issuing the famous Book of Sports during his visit to Lancashire in 1617; but systematic efforts to reduce the number of alehouses did not begin in south Lancashire until the late 1630s. The real peak of activity came between 1647 and the late 1650s, as the Puritan magistrates who predominated after the end of the Civil War put pressure on village constables to prosecute unlicensed alesellers who had hitherto been ignored, or tolerated on payment of a token annual fine. Petitions from local Puritan worthies, and from other interested parties who sometimes included rival alesellers, were regularly presented to the magistrates, and in 1647 a memorial against alehouses was signed by over 800 ministers and godly laymen. In 1656–7 over 400 alehouses in Salford and Blackburn Hundreds were officially suppressed, although the authorities may subsequently have had second thoughts in view of the likely loss of tax revenue, and this was the climax of a sustained campaign which must have had a perceptible effect on lifestyles and popular culture in the county.[57]

We must not exaggerate the success of these endeavours. Alehouses which had officially been abolished were prone to reappear in subsequent listings, and widespread poverty and insecurity continued to make the trade attractive to the poor, the aged and the infirm. Moreover, wakes and other celebrations did not disappear, even in the difficult years of the late 1640s. Attachment to custom was strong enough to resist the ramshackle machinery of law enforcement, and even its worst enemies admitted that the alehouse could be a necessary aid to travellers and a provider of essential goods and services to the local poor. Not all Puritans abjured the alehouse altogether. Mr Gilbody, minister of Holcombe and sometime moderator of the Bury classis, was suspended because, among other misdemeanours, 'he did sit tipling in an ale house where was fiddling'; and the Manchester minister Henry Newcome was addicted to billiards in alehouses. Horse-racing, cock-fighting and other earthy entertainments were also tempting to many of the less stringent Puritans, and only a small minority set their faces against all amusement. Under the circumstances it is not surprising that the campaign against alehouses, in particular, and popular festivities in general, had limited and transitory success: as Wrightson says, a 'superficial social discipline' might have been achieved, but there was no lasting 'transformation of the texture of popular life'.[58] Halley's entertaining description of the Restoration in Lancashire underlines the truth of this comment: 'The morris-dancers, the pipers and fiddlers, the bear-wards, the wrestlers, the rush-bearers, and the players, came forth in extraordinary gaiety and strength', and maypoles sprouted everywhere, while Manchester's conduit ran with claret, 'which was freely drunk by all that could'. Restraint had indeed been superficial: a vibrant and resilient popular culture must have been bubbling close to the surface throughout the Puritan ascendancy.[59]

The Puritan campaign against illicit sex and bastardy had similarly ambiguous results. Illegitimacy was both a moral and (potentially) an economic offence, and it was prosecutable in both ecclesiastical and secular courts. The economic dimension arose if the child was likely to become a charge on the parish, and in time of hardship, economic uncertainty and population pressure sanctions against offending couples were often severe. The Puritans merely added an additional weight of moral disapproval to a set of laws and attitudes which were already condemnatory, although most illegitimacy seems to have arisen from frustrated marriage plans rather than from promiscuity. In south Lancashire, at least, illegitimacy rates were relatively high from the late sixteenth century to the Civil War. In the 1630s illegitimate births ranged from 3 per cent of registered births in Standish, through 6.6 per cent in Eccles, to 10 per cent in Sefton, as against an average of 2.4 per cent for England as a whole. But over the following decade the Lancashire rates (Eccles excepted) fell below a national average which had itself fallen to 2.1 per cent, and in the 1650s Lancashire, like the nation at large, had reached 'the nadir of illegitimacy', with derisory figures below 1 per cent. Even Eccles had almost fallen into line.[60]

Does this fall in bastardy rates indicate a successfully imposed Puritan reformation of manners? Wrightson thinks not. The parents of potentially chargeable bastards were sometimes severely punished long before the 1640s, quite apart from being required to fix sureties and pay maintenance. Whipping was a frequent punishment, but increasingly after the opening of Lancashire's House of Correction in 1619, parents were incarcerated for several months at a time, although this punishment was used more readily against women than men. But many escaped punishment, and Wrightson tells us that 'real severity was reserved for repetitive bastard-bearers, who were almost invariably committed to the House of Correction'. From the late 1640s similar policies were administered with greater rigour; but Justices of the Peace did not actively pursue bastard-bearers, continuing to wait for prosecutions to be initiated at local level. Many illegitimate births thus no doubt continued to go unpunished, and Wrightson argues that the apparent decline in illegitimacy is an optical illusion, caused by an increasing reluctance to register illegitimate births. Fear of severe punishment, especially under the new legislation of the Interregnum against fornication, coupled with the administrative chaos resulting from the decline of the classis system in the sprawling and unwieldy Lancashire parishes, provide motive and opportunity for such a response, which may have been further encouraged by growing uncertainty as to what constituted a valid marriage, as custom and statute law came into conflict.[61]

For Wrightson, variations in the economic circumstances and expectations of the poorer and middling sort of people were far more important as influences on the incidence of illegitimacy than campaigns of repression which operated with inadequate administrative support. Bastardy itself is a surprisingly difficult concept to define in the context of this period, and its incidence may tell us very little about sexual mores and behaviour more generally. The Lancashire practice of unsupervised courting, with couples meeting in alehouses or 'sitting up' by the parlour fire, seems to have continued unscathed, as did the popular sentiment that fornication was merely 'a tricke of youth'. Bridal pregnancy remained a frequent occurrence.[62] The church courts and their successors dealt with some sexual offenders, but many escaped their notice, and punishments were rarely severe. The disapprobation of neighbours was much more telling than the censure of ecclesiastical authority. As in the case of alehouses and popular festivals, the Puritan repression may well have induced more evasive action than real conformity, and a distinctive popular culture survived the Interregnum almost unimpaired in most of Lancashire.

These findings bear out the general drift of this chapter. I have argued that Lancashire's distinctive social structure and weak administrative systems left room for a great deal of local autonomy, and made the enforcement of directives from central and county government very difficult except when they worked with the grain of local custom and expectation. The rulers of church and state might initiate ambitious programmes of reform, repression and control, but they were liable to be confounded by passive resistance in the localities. Apart from an active Puritan minority, Lancashire society retained a remarkable cultural homogeneity, and despite the growing numbers of cottagers and landless poor, social divisions remained less stark and polarised than they were becoming in counties closer to the economic pull of London. Traditional attitudes and beliefs remained strong and resilient among most of the population at the Restoration; and one of the aims of the next two chapters will be to assess the impact of subsequent accelerating economic and demographic change on the county's lively and distinctive popular culture.

4

TOWARDS INDUSTRIAL REVOLUTION: ECONOMY AND SOCIETY IN TRANSITION, 1660 – 1770

The century or so after the Restoration saw gradual and unobtrusive but cumulative economic and social changes in Lancashire. The domestic textile industries expanded and intensified their influence, especially in the south and east, as Manchester grew rapidly in size and importance; and the organisation of production changed significantly as the putting-out system became general. Liverpool transformed itself into one of the leading provincial ports and commercial centres, stimulating the extractive and manufacturing industries of its immediate hinterland and spreading its influence further east and south, to the textile districts of south-east Lancashire and the West Riding and to the manufacturing centres of the West Midlands. Important innovations in road and water transport were introduced, and population growth began to accelerate impressively. These developments were concentrated in the southern half of the county; north of the Ribble, and wherever agriculture still dominated local economies, change was much less in evidence. But where trade and textiles flourished, they gathered momentum rapidly during the eighteenth century, with profound implications for the lifestyles and expectations of many of the county's inhabitants. By the third quarter of the eighteenth century, a further transition to a new kind of industrial society was beginning, as technological innovations and new ways of organising production ushered in the age of the factory in the cotton industry. Despite the importance of transport improvements and the rise of Liverpool in stimulating economic and social change in Lancashire, our analysis must again begin with the textile industries, which constituted the most dynamic sector of the county's economy in these crucial formative years.

The main changes in Lancashire's textile output took place in the Manchester and Bolton areas. The cotton-using fustian manufacture spread outwards from its original Bolton base in the later seventeenth century, predominating as far north as Blackburn and as far east as Oldham by the turn of the century. Cotton was also introduced into the Manchester linen industry in the form of cotton-linens, mixed checked and striped cloths which were incorporating an increasing admixture of cotton from the 1690s. Smallwares remained usually a mixture of linen and worsted, and Manchester long remained important as a centre for the organisation of the Lancashire woollen industry; but the use of cotton grew steadily more prevalent during the first half of the eighteenth century and pure cotton cloths were increasingly in evidence by the 1750s, though their production was to be greatly expanded by the advent of machine spinning.[1]

The cotton-using textile manufactures made very limited inroads into the established woollen district to the north of Manchester, which stretched from the Bury and Rochdale area through Rossendale and Colne and into the West Riding of Yorkshire, until well into the eighteenth century. The change from woollens to worsteds here was well advanced by the end of the seventeenth century. Subsequently 'in the Bury, Middleton, Oldham and Ashton districts cotton encroached steadily', and outposts of the worsted industry in southern and central Lancashire had disappeared by the later eighteenth century, but 'there was virtually no cotton manufacture at Rochdale or in Rossendale until the coming of the spinning factories'. The old Lancashire linen industry was ailing by the turn of the century, however, as it suffered severely from foreign competition. By the 1760s it was rapidly giving way to the newer cotton-using fabrics, or disappearing without replacement, over most of the county.[2] Around Kirkham, in the Fylde, and at Warrington the development of specialisation in sailcloth enabled the linen industry to survive and prosper, using imported Russian flax, during the eighteenth century; but this was exceptional.[3] By 1770 cotton-using cloths of various kinds and qualities had long dominated the output of the Lancashire textile industry, especially in the areas of rapid growth and concentration in the south-east of the county.

Home demand accounted for much of the early expansion of Lancashire's cotton-using textile manufactures, but from 1730 onwards overseas markets steadily increased in importance. Ireland had long been a substantial importer of fustians, but the main growth-areas were the American colonies and West Indian plantations, where cotton-linen checks made successful inroads in the 1750s and 1760s, and the African market, where Manchester manufacturers stepped in to fill the gap when supplies of Indian cottons were interrupted by wars and disturbances between 1749 and 1763. But these gains were not permanent, and the industry remained vulnerable to high raw material costs, price fluctuations and foreign competition. It took the acquisition of new markets in Europe during the 1760s to guarantee continuing growth on a firm basis.[4]

The fact of sustained and accelerating expansion with a growing emphasis on exports and a strongly accentuated upward trend from the 1720s and 1730s, is clear enough. It is much more difficult to assess the scale of output and employment, and the importance of textiles to local economies. Retained raw cotton imports rose steadily from an annual average of just over one million pounds in 1698–1710, to well over two million in 1741–50. After this the growth-rate accelerated, and the annual average from 1761–70 was 3,681,904 pounds, rising sharply to 5,127,689 in the following decade. A growing proportion of this cotton was being worked in Lancashire, as the industry became concentrated here and in the Glasgow area. Most of the raw material came from the West Indies, but the Levant often accounted for between one-third and half of the annual totals. The figures provide only the broadest indication of trends, especially as the cotton was used in conjunction with varying amounts of linen; but the overall outline carries conviction.[5]

Employment levels are difficult to measure, and problems are exacerbated by the persistence of a symbiotic relationship between small-scale agriculture and domestic industry, which makes it difficult to fix satisfactory occupational labels to individuals. But evidence from parish registers suggests that in some parishes in south-east Lancashire well over half the adult males drew most of their income from textiles by the 1740s and 1750s. Textile occupations were recorded for 54 per cent of Oldham fathers in the 1720s, rising to 59 per cent in the 1770s, and at nearby Middleton the figure for sample years in the 1740s was nearly 72 per cent. The woollen industry in Rossendale accounted for about two-thirds of Haslingden fathers in the 1740s and 1750s, while Wild's calculations for Saddleworth record an astonishing total of 88 per cent in 1760. In Manchester itself a census of 1751 found 4674 looms in the parish, or roughly one to every household. This level of specialisation in textiles was not sustained further west, although at Walton-le-Dale, near Preston, half the fathers had textile occupations in the 1720s and 1730s, and the figures for Upholland and Penwortham were far from negligible. Substantial population growth, as we shall see, was occurring in the south-east Lancashire countryside and beginning to coalesce in towns; and by the early eighteenth century the local economy depended very heavily on the fortunes of the rapidly expanding textile industries, which were themselves undergoing major organisational and technological changes.[6]

The putting-out system was firmly established in the cotton-using textile industries by the 1680s and the Rochdale woollen and worsted industries were not far behind, although in Rossendale and perhaps elsewhere in the east Lancashire woollen district the transition was delayed until well into the new century.[7] The small independent manufacturer did not disappear, but the industries were increasingly dominated by large merchant capitalists who distributed work, often through middlemen, at what amounted to piece-rate wages.

At the top of the scale in the late seventeenth century were the Manchester linen drapers, employers (especially in bleaching, dyeing and the other finishing trades) and organisers of production over a wide area, who were beginning to accumulate very substantial capitals and to engage in credit transactions involving several thousands of pounds. They were attracting the younger sons of the gentry as apprentices, and charging premiums of up to £50 or £60 despite the menial nature of much of the work. Their successors, the leading merchants and manufacturers of Manchester in the mid eighteenth century (by which time the term 'linen draper' was no longer current), included men of much greater weight. The home market had been greatly stimulated since 1730 or so as 'riders-out' took orders from provincial towns throughout the country, and the competitive assertiveness of a rising generation of merchants, often from humble origins, was expressed in rapid upward social mobility. The Manchester of the 1750s was capable of nurturing Samuel Touchet, who moved on from extensive dealings in linen yarn and cotton imports to become involved in the slave trade, in loans to the aristocracy, and in government finance and contracting. His eventual fall was greeted with grim enjoyment by his more cautious compatriots whose horizons stopped short at an opulent town house and carriage or, at best, the foundation of a landed dynasty in the nearby countryside. Such aspirations were becoming realistic for a widening circle of the Manchester élite at mid-century, as the most expensive apprenticeship premiums ran to several hundred pounds (£500 in one case in 1769) and lifestyles became more openly opulent. The leading Rochdale woollen merchants were similarly prospering, accumulating capital and beginning to move into the ranks of the gentry.[8]

Manchester's dominance was far from complete even in the cotton-using manufactures. Many merchants in the surrounding district traded direct with London as well as putting work out in their own localities, and below this stratum came a large number of middlemen who put out work for Manchester merchants as well as trading on their own account. The system was complex: the different levels of the trading hierarchy overlapped, and all participants were vulnerable to the vagaries of an increasingly sophisticated maze of credit transactions which as yet stopped short of developing into a formalised banking system. But during the eighteenth century an ever-growing proportion of the small rural manufacturers fell under the influence and control of merchant capitalists, though often at one or two removes, as dependence on a single source of renewable credit shaded over into full-time employment. This transition was not complete by 1770, but it was well advanced: wage labour was the norm for most participants in the Lancashire textile industries long before the rise of the factory system.[9]

The growing importance of wage labour was accompanied by a further tilting of the balance of family economies towards dependence on textiles rather than agriculture, as the fragmentation of landholdings continued and a new stratum of landless cottagers emerged in the country districts of south-east Lancashire. In Haslingden, for example, the number of landowners increased from 182 in 1650 to 421 in 1782. Admittedly, there was continuing enclosure and encroachment on common and waste land, and few farmers were owner-occupiers: only 19 per cent in Rossendale in 1782. So we need to know more about trends in farm sizes, on which the evidence remains inconclusive; but the apparent tendency towards shorter leases and rising rents, coupled with widespread evidence that most farms ranged from under 10 acres to 30 or so in the upland areas, suggest high levels of demand and probable pressure to subdivide. Such plots were only viable if most of the family's energy and output was directed into textiles; and the rash of landless cottages, already well in evidence by the 1750s, confirmed the strong trend towards specialisation in domestic industry. Manchester, of course, had long had large numbers of landless weavers, and the lower strata of the textile industries were becoming visibly divided between the smallholders who usually worked for putters-out, employing family members and perhaps the odd apprentice, and cottagers who depended completely on textiles for their living.[10] The significance of this division will become apparent later.

These changes in the organisation of textile manufacture were accompanied, and in some respects encouraged, by technological innovations. The complex and expensive Dutch smallware loom was introduced into Manchester soon after the Restoration and was used in small groups by men of moderate capital who employed journeymen on contract work for the leading merchants. By 1750 there were at least 1500 of these looms and units of production were gradually increasing in size. At this time, too, a more sophisticated variant, the swivel loom, was being introduced, and during the 1750s attempts were made to apply water power to its operation in a substantial building which was recognisably a precursor of the factory. Sailcloth making at Warrington and Prescot was also being concentrated into larger production units in the 1750s.[11] Bleaching and dyeing, which had always come under the aegis of the merchant capitalists, increased in scale and complexity at the same time, and the newer technology of printing migrated from London to the Lancashire manufacturing districts, especially after 1760, in search of economies of scale, cheaper labour and lower rents. Units of production were growing rapidly, far beyond a domestic scale, in all these processes by the third quarter of the eighteenth century, further enhancing the power of substantial capitalists.[12] In spinning, weaving and the preparatory processes, which dominated the employment structure of the textile industries, the domestic system still prevailed in 1770, although its days were numbered on the spinning side; but here, too, innovations were beginning to make a significant difference at mid-century. Above all, Lancashire weavers were quick to adopt Kay's fly shuttle, which proved capable of increasing their productivity considerably. It was already being widely used in the Rossendale woollen industry by the late 1730s, as was demonstrated by Kay's unavailing attempts to enforce his patent; and it seems to have spread rapidly in the cotton-using industries from the 1750s.[13] This helped to tilt the balance of productivity between spinning and weaving, and weavers found it increasingly difficult to sustain an adequate supply of yarn from the spinners within their own households and neighbourhoods. Spinners' labour was in great demand, and the industry was extending into new areas, while efforts to improve the technology of spinning were eagerly pursued through the middle decades of the eighteenth century. The ultimate success of these endeavours will be discussed in Chapter 6; but meanwhile we should note that Lancashire textiles in the mid eighteenth century were by no means stagnant in organisation or technology. The pace of change was already quickening on the eve of the transition to the various factory systems which were to proliferate so rapidly from the 1770s.

The growth of the textile industries was not yet giving rise to substantial urbanisation. Manchester is the obvious exception: its population grew more than fivefold between the Restoration and 1773, when a house-to-house enumeration found 22,481 inhabitants. This expansion propelled Manchester firmly on to the highest rung of the national hierarchy of provincial towns. Most of the increase was concentrated into the eighteenth century, and this is true of the other emergent towns of the textile district. But none of Manchester's satellites was remarkably large by the early 1770s. Urban enumerations found 4765 people in Salford in 1773, and 4568 in Bolton's urban area: Rochdale, Blackburn, Preston and Stockport were of similar size. Bury had 2090 inhabitants in 1773, and two years later a similar count found 2859 people living in Ashton-under-Lyne. Outside Manchester towns were beginning to cohere and grow, but the bulk of the textile district's population increase was spread thickly through the countryside, as the populations of many parishes multiplied three or fourfold between the early eighteenth century and the 1770s or 1780s. This was increasingly an industrial society but, Manchester apart, it was not yet an urban one.[14]

Despite the limited scale of urbanisation, changes in the social structure accelerated as the textile industries developed. Population growth expanded the lower ranks of wage-earners and smallholders, but at the same time opportunities increased for putters-out and middlemen. The distance was widening between the great Manchester capitalists, with their metropolitan connections, and the growing number of weavers who eked out a precarious wage-dependent existence in their landless cottages; but there were many intermediate stages to bridge the gulf. As Wadsworth and Mann remark, 'The system was not a closed one ... it provided a ladder up which the energetic man could climb. It was a short step from weaver to putter-out, and from putting-out agent to manufacturer.'[15] This may be too sanguine: as the same authors remind us, credit was the essential fuel for social mobility, and we know too little about how it was allocated to the aspiring, in an ingenious but still very imperfect capital market. Moreover, the eminence accorded by successful credit-finance dealings could be precarious, especially in the early stages of a career, and a large proportion of business ventures came to grief. Social mobility prevailed, but in both directions; security was at a premium; and the dice were loaded most obviously against the growing ranks of the wage-earning and property-less.

Can the label 'proto-industrial' be attached with profit to the Lancashire textile district in the mid eighteenth century? Was the development of domestic handicraft production, in symbiosis with small-scale agriculture organised on a putting-out system and selling its output in distant markets through merchant capitalists, visibly preparing the ground for a more thoroughgoing transition to factory-based industrialisation? Was the rise of domestic industry stimulating population growth beyond the capacity of the region's agriculture to supply its workforce, providing additional pressures for integration into national and international economies? Was capital accumulating in the hands of merchants who were led by diminishing returns in domestic industry to seek more centralised, disciplined and controlled outlets for their industrial investment? As we have seen and shall see (in the case of population), the nature and mechanisms of social and economic change in south-east Lancashire correspond closely with these aspects of the 'proto-industrial' model, in broad outline at least.[16] But this does not mean that conditions in the 1750s and 1760s were such as to make an 'industrial revolution' somehow inevitable, as exponents of 'proto-industrialisation' are well aware.

Many regional economies elsewhere in Europe reached a similar position, without crossing the threshold to a new era of factory industry and large-scale urbanisation; and the circumstances of south-east Lancashire's transition were governed by the peculiar characteristics of the region itself.[17] This casts some doubt on the utility of the concept of 'proto-industrialisation' as a tool for explanation, but it does at least provide a set of descriptive generalisations within which the Lancashire experience can be set with profit. At this stage, Lancashire's condition was remarkable but not unique. During the last two decades of the century its uniqueness was to become apparent.

By the middle quarters of the eighteenth century Lancashire's textile economy, and especially its cotton-using sector, was beginning to develop with remarkable speed and intensity. Even if we set aside hindsight and deny the inevitability of industrial revolution, there is something here to explain. Why south-east Lancashire, and why now?

Explanations involving natural advantages carry little weight at this stage. The presence of accessible coal measures became essential to sustained growth through urbanisation and the steam-powered factory from the end of the eighteenth century, but at this stage local coal was a minor fringe benefit. The humid climate may well have given the area a genuine advantage in the working of cotton, although the climatic differential between south-east Lancashire and other upland areas with high rainfall and established textile industries may not have been sufficient to be critical.[18] Nor, as we have seen, can religion be shown to have initiated or stimulated economic development. The heyday of Protestant Dissent among the local manufacturers was probably the second half of the seventeenth century, and the major economic expansion of the eighteenth century took place largely under more moderate Anglican auspices.[19]

More to the point is the nature of economy and society at the beginning of the eighteenth century. The social structure with its wide spread of limited but useful capital resources through an extensive middling stratum of yeomen clothiers, provided scope for upward social mobility and encouragement for enterprise; and the poor quality of much agricultural land, especially in relation to the range of available improvement techniques helped to push investment in industrial directions. The relationship between poor land, small holdings, subdivided plots and the rise of domestic industry is also highly relevant, of course; but in this respect south-east Lancashire was part of a much wider pattern of development.[20] Moreover, the established textile industries over most of the area were linen-based, and south-east Lancashire thus had expertise in working a material which could readily be combined with the cotton which was to have such spectacular growth potential in world markets. The linen industry eased the path for cotton; and the woollen industry, with its London contacts and access to capital, provided further advantages which could be brought together through the Manchester mercantile community. South-east Lancashire's fortunate factor endowments lay in the pre-existing economic and social arrangements rather than in mineral or climatic resources.

Political advantages were also very important. The lack of restraint on rural trade and industry from incorporated towns and guilds remained a major asset, as contemporaries were aware. James Ogden averred in 1783 that Manchester's business success owed much to the openness of its trade: 'Nothing could be more fatal to its trading interest, if it should be incorporated, and have representatives in Parliament.'[21] Historians of various persuasions have agreed with the first part of his assertion, if not with the second; and the interdependence of town and country continued to provide an environment conducive to unfettered expansion. The weakness of trading organisations and vested interests meant that innovatory machinery was already being adopted and accepted with an ease unusual elsewhere: the ready adoption of the Dutch loom for tapes and ribbons, soon after the Restoration, is an early case in point.[22] Not that the workforce was, or remained, cowed or pliable, as we shall see; but it lacked an organisational focus for effective resistance to innovation of this sort. On the other hand, Lancashire benefited from national legislation restricting imports of Indian calicoes, culminating in the prohibitory Act of 1721; and the combination of local free trade and national protection was particularly useful during the formative and transitional years.[23]

The proximity of Liverpool, another much-canvassed 'cause' of the rise of the textile district, was as yet of limited importance. Cotton was being imported through Liverpool in the later seventeenth century, and we have seen that Africa and the West Indies provided important markets for certain Lancashire textile products around the middle of the eighteenth century; but most cotton imports continued to be channelled through London until the 1790s, although by 1770 Liverpool's export returns included a rich and bewildering variety of textile goods. Long before this dealers were paying regular weekly visits to Liverpool to buy cotton, but the port and its services were far from being essential to the growth of the textile district. The rise of the slave trade opened out new markets for Lancashire cloth, and the complex credit transactions associated with the triangular trade between Liverpool, Africa and the West Indies or America engendered increasingly sophisticated financial arrangements from which textile merchants and manufacturers benefited; but here again it is difficult to see these developments as sufficient to give south-east Lancashire a clear competitive advantage. The profits of Liverpool merchants were ploughed back into their businesses, enjoyed through gracious living and invested in the transport systems and emergent industries of south-west Lancashire and north-west Cheshire, rather than providing capital for the textile industries. As yet, Liverpool's fortunes and those of Lancashire's textile heartland showed surprisingly little mutual interdependence.[24] Eric Williams's assertions that 'It was only the capital accumulation of Liverpool which called the population of Lancashire into existence and stimulated the manufacturers of Manchester', and that 'The first stimulus to the growth of Cottonopolis came from the African and West Indian markets' are not borne out by the available evidence.[25]

The main causes of Liverpool's spectacular growth during the century after the Restoration lie in trades other than textiles. Its population at the Restoration was well under 2000; by the turn of the century it hovered around 5000; and thereafter the rate of increase accelerated steadily, until an enumeration in 1773 found 34,407 inhabitants, excluding the 4000 seamen who were away on voyages.[26] The expansion of overseas trade was responsible for this population explosion, although the development of associated manufacturing activities was not negligible. The key commodities in an increasingly diverse and wide-ranging trading pattern were salt, tobacco and sugar, with the slave trade becoming important during the second quarter of the eighteenth century. The salt trade was one of Liverpool's oldest commercial activities; but as entrepreneurs from Liverpool and Cheshire responded to rising world demand by investing in extraction, processing and transport in the port's hinterland exports increased seventyfold between the 1660s and the 1720s, from 6000 bushels per annum to 428,000; and the upward trend continued, as exports more than trebled between 1732 and 1770 to reach 48,000 tons by the latter year. The fuel needs of the salt-boilers, coupled with domestic demand in Liverpool, also stimulated the coal industry, and by 1770 coal exports to Ireland and America were reaching significant levels.[27] These mundane staples of the export trade were augmented by a widening range of manufactured goods, from the port itself as well as its hinterland: in addition to shipyards, saltworks and sugar refineries, pottery, glass and metalworking became established during the eighteenth century, including copper and ironworks and the manufacture of clocks and watches.[28]

But the main driving force behind Liverpool's growth, stimulating demand for its emergent industries, was its successful entry into the lucrative African, West Indian and American trades, especially tobacco and sugar. Tobacco imports from Chesapeake Bay began in earnest during the 1660s, weighing in at over a million pounds per year by the early 1690s, enjoying a rapid surge of growth to top six million pounds in the 1740s, and standing at nearly nine million pounds in 1770. Sugar imports from the West Indies grew even faster, from 35 tons per annum in the late 1660s to 580 at the turn of the century, about 5000 in the 1740s and 8250 in 1770.[29] As the rate of expansion in these early mainstays of Liverpool's growth began to level off towards mid-century, the slave trade took up the running. Liverpool's West Africa trade was insignificant in the early eighteenth century, but by the 1730s, 21 ships were leaving the port annually for this destination, rising to 49 in the 1750s and 107 in 1771. By the 1750s Liverpool's activity in this sector outweighed that of London and Bristol combined, and this position was maintained during the subsequent period of rapid expansion.[30]

The slave trade, and the African and West Indian or American triangular trade of which it formed a component, became an important but not essential element in a Liverpool mercantile economy which was already growing impressively in the early eighteenth century. Ships did not always carry cargoes on all three sides of the triangle; indeed, this seems to have been unusual. The slave trade increasingly used purpose-built ships which often returned in ballast, leaving the carriage of sugar and tobacco to vessels trading directly with the colonies. Slaving brought spectacular windfall profits on occasion, and thus attracted the participation of a large but uncertain proportion of the Liverpool merchant community; but the risks were also high and the market fiercely competitive. The rate of return in the long run was probably about 8 per cent, much more alluring in purely financial terms than investment in government stock, but less than the probable return on slum housing. Specialists in the slave trade, like the infamous William Davenport, were unusual: it formed part of a much wider pattern of trading, encouraging the opening out of new markets (though not the most lucrative ones in the long run), helping to provide ample supplies of working capital, and playing its part in the creation of sophisticated credit and financial networks. The Liverpool slave trade had yet to reach its peak in 1770, and the full extent of its local importance is impossible to disentangle from a maze of related and unrelated activities. But distinctive and controversial though it was, it was only one among several contributors to the port's remarkable economic development.[31]

The African and colonial trades were only part of the story. The early eighteenth century also saw a marked expansion of trade with Ireland, which supplied the sugar plantations with agricultural produce, and with northern Europe, where Merseyside salt was exchanged for iron and timber. Salt also went to Rotterdam and various ports in southern Europe, and the return cargoes added additional variety to the colonial export pattern. In 1665, 4 ships imported goods to Liverpool from continental Europe; in 1722, admittedly an outstanding year, the total was 53.[32] The exotic and cosmopolitan range of Liverpool's imports can be sampled in a return of 1770: 6855 'elephants' teeth' brought from West

Africa via the West Indies; a 'seahorse' from Greenland; aniseed from Malaga; and sturgeon from Danzig.[33] In the century or so after the Restoration, a provincial backwater had transformed itself into the nation's leading provincial port, outstripping even Bristol.[34] Why did this transformation occur, what was the social context, and what were the implications for the rest of Lancashire?

In the first place, Liverpool was conveniently situated to benefit from the rapid rise of the Atlantic and colonial trades in this period, and its northern location reduced the threat from privateers and enemy action during the numerous wars. But these geographical advantages were not peculiar to Liverpool, and would have been unavailing without the willingness of the town's merchants to invest heavily in a difficult and expensive but sustained programme of dock building, which overcame the natural disadvantages of the harbour. The first dock was promoted in 1709 and opened in 1715, and extensions and additions soon followed. Hyde calculates that at least £50,000 was spent on docks and warehouses between 1710 and 1750.[35] Merchant enterprise went further than this: the tobacco trade was greatly stimulated by the widespread evasion of duty, especially through the inflation of allowances for damage, and these practices were strenuously protected by Liverpool MPs in the early eighteenth century.[36] More reputably, Liverpool merchants increasingly invested in improved transport links with the port's south Lancashire and north Cheshire hinterland, as well as in coal, salt and agriculture, as we shall see.

Mercantile enterprise, partly channelled through the Corporation, was at the core of Liverpool's expansion. We need to know more about Liverpool's merchants in this period, but they seem to have exhibited a telling combination of wealth and openness to upward social mobility. Hyde points up the importance of a few substantial established landowning families who 'invested surplus income in commercial ventures' when opportunity arose; and Liverpool's success began to attract capitalists from elsewhere, 'professional businessmen', from the early eighteenth century.[37] But some contemporaries offered a different emphasis. A satirist in 1706 alleged that most Liverpool merchants had humble and uncouth origins:

> When Business call'd me first to Change,
> I cou'd not chuse but think it Strange
> To see so many rough hewn faces,
> The Saylor's Hitch in all their Paces:
> Each Merchant like Tarpaulin moves,
> As if he had no Use of Gloves:
> Hands hugging Hose, with Head in Neck,
> Like Seaman traversing the Deck.
> Belike they most of them were so,
> From Cabin-Boys, tho' Merchants now.[32]

James Boardman's commentary on the Liverpool directory of 1766 provides specific instances of rags-to-riches mobility at a later stage of the port's development. Thus we find William Boats, who began life as 'a waif, found in a boat' but became 'most remarkably prosperous' as a merchant, exclaiming on the Pierhead on the occasion of one spectacular coup, 'Billy Boats – born a beggar, die a lord!' Intimations of social unease are provided by the success of a fake herald in selling bogus coats-of-arms to Liverpool merchants, and by the fame which accrued to Caryl Fleetwood for his expertise at dancing the minuet, 'at that time a test of breeding'. The social acceptability of the highest echelons of Liverpool merchants was indicated by Nicholas Ashton's service as High Sheriff of Lancashire in 1770, but many wealthy commercial men were far less secure in their status, and no doubt in their fortune, than this rarefied distinction might suggest.[39] In a competitive and insecure society such as this, there was little room for economic complacency, and the drive for social advancement must have made an important contribution to the rapidity of Liverpool's growth.

The extent of Liverpool's influence on the south-east Lancashire textile district was limited in this period; but Liverpool investment, and the stimulus of demand arising from its growth as town and port, gave a considerable boost to the economy of south-west and central south Lancashire, to the west of Wigan and the Warrington area. Road and river improvements linking Liverpool with the mineral resources of this hinterland, and cutting the cost of taking Lancashire coal to Cheshire salt, were gathering momentum in the 1720s and 1730s. The Common Council of Liverpool Corporation took the initiative in promoting the turnpiking of the road to Prescot in 1725, rendering the town's coal supply less precarious, and in the late 1740s and early 1750s the road improvement was extended to St. Helens, Ashton-in-Makerfield and Warrington. This was the prelude to a more general spread of road improvements in the 1750s and 1760s. Their quality was debatable, but their influence on the quickening of economic growth in Liverpool's widening sphere of influence should not be ignored.[40]

More spectacular, and more important to the pace and pattern of development in staple industries, were the improvements in water transport. Here initiatives from Liverpool merchants were often of secondary or minor importance. The improvement of the Mersey as far as Warrington in the 1690s was carried out at the behest of a Warrington merchant, and the eventual completion of the Mersey and Irwell Navigation through to Manchester in the mid-1730s was overwhelmingly a Manchester project, though it used Liverpool expertise in the person of Thomas Steers. Steers was also involved in the Weaver Navigation, which promoted Liverpool interest in the salt trade and opened in 1732; but here again most of the active support came from Cheshire salt producers. Further north, the Douglas Navigation, which was finding coastwise outlets for Wigan coal, especially in north Lancashire, by 1740, showed a stronger Liverpool presence among its active promoters, but local landowners and coalmasters seem to have been mainly responsible for the project's completion. Where Liverpool capital and influence did play the leading part was in the successful construction of the Sankey Brook Navigation, 'the first English canal', which opened in 1757. It was promoted by Liverpool Corporation, with a view to solving persisting coal supply problems. Most of its shares were held by Liverpool merchants, and the work was planned and supervised by the Liverpool dock engineer. The canal's initial impact on coal transport costs was not sustained, but it succeeded in opening out the St. Helens coalfield, and provided a major stimulus to the wider Merseyside economy, especially the salt industry. Elsewhere, Liverpool's active role in transport innovation was less obtrusive, although persisting problems in the Mersey estuary led the Corporation to give financial support to the preliminary stages of further canal schemes, including the Trent and Mersey. As Dottie remarks, 'The Council was willing to assist canal projects, but its preoccupation with coal supplies caused it to be concerned with their efficiency in carrying coal over short distances, rather than as long-distance hauliers.'[41]

The development of longer-distance transport schemes bears out this assertion, although Liverpool's trade and traffic flows often bulked large in promoters' calculations. Turnpike roads came relatively late to Lancashire; the Liverpool – Prescot road, authorised in 1725 and completed in 1732, was the earliest in the county. It was followed almost immediately by the Wigan – Preston road, which was bringing coal to Preston by the early 1730s, and by the Buxton – Manchester section of the London – Manchester road, which was much used by textile manufacturers. The main burst of improvement came in the early 1750s, when turnpike trusts were established on several trans-Pennine routes between Manchester, Rochdale and the West Riding, and a network of turnpikes was created on the coalfield between Manchester and Wigan, while at the same time the main route northwards between Warrington and the Westmorland border was completed. The roads from Liverpool fed into this expanding system, and by 1760 a regular stage-coach service linked Liverpool with Manchester. Wagons from Liverpool could now reach London in five days. But we have no way of knowing the source of the subscriptions which underwrote these ventures, and the real extent of the improvements remains uncertain. The roads before their advent were notoriously bad, although there were outspoken complaints about them in their improved state in the later eighteenth century; but turnpikes did clearly reduce the cost of coal in Liverpool, while making possible long-distance coach and wagon services throughout the year. Liverpool's trade was certainly facilitated by the rise of the turnpike system, but its direct administrative and financial role in the process in Lancashire at large was uncertain and probably quite limited.[42]

The more ambitious canal schemes which were being planned in the 1760s and completed in the mid-1770s, and which extended and consolidated Liverpool's hinterland, form a much more clear-cut case. The extension of the Bridgewater Canal, which so spectacularly cut the cost of coal in Manchester, to Runcorn and the Mersey, was funded almost entirely by the Duke of Bridgewater's estate. Liverpool merchants took some interest in developments at the western end, but the initiative for this great expansion in transport capacity was not theirs. Similarly, the Trent and Mersey Canal, which linked Liverpool with an extensive and productive area of the Potteries and West Midlands, was a Staffordshire enterprise in its origins and its funding; and here again, landed investment predominated. The Leeds and Liverpool, a much more ambitious and capital-hungry scheme, took much longer to complete. The initiative came from Bradford, and the West Riding supplied most of the capital. The substantial Liverpool contingent among the subscribers showed most interest in the rapid construction of the link between Liverpool and the Wigan coalfield, which in 1774 became one of the earliest sections of the canal to open. The Lancashire canal system was still in its infancy at this stage, but Liverpool was probably its greatest early beneficiary, despite the limited range of vision of many of the Liverpool merchants themselves.[43]

Liverpool's quest for a reliable coal supply increasingly ensured that its merchants would become aware of investment opportunities in the south-west and central Lancashire coalfield; and the third quarter of the eighteenth century saw a growing willingness to participate in risky but potentially lucrative mining speculations, which were especially attractive to those who also had interests in salt. Langton's figures suggest a steady rise in the coalfield's output over the half-century after 1690, from 28,000 tons per annum to 78,000. Explosive growth followed over the next two decades, as transport innovations coincided with accelerating population growth and the rise of new industries; and by 1760 the annual output was nearly 200,000 tons. This strong overall trend masks wide fluctuations in the fortunes of individual collieries and different sections of the coalfield, especially as transport improvements changed the relative cost and convenience of coal supplies from different areas; but the rise in output was accompanied by a growth in the number of large and long-lived collieries, especially close to the canals and river navigations. Capital requirements increased, as steam pumping engines and deeper shafts became more widely used; and the social background of mining entrepreneurs began to change. The lesser gentry became less active, preferring to lease their coal-bearing land to speculative partnerships which were often drawn from the local yeomanry. Only a few substantial landed families, led by the Earls of Derby and Balcarres, persisted in sustained and extensive mining operations on their own account; and as the navigations spread, Liverpool merchants began to invest in the largest and most lucrative pits, a process which began in the Prescot area in the 1720s and became more widespread during the third quarter of the century. Most pits remained small, and few employed more than ten or twelve miners; but the ground had been prepared for the massive expansion which was to follow from the 1770s onwards.[44] Further east, the coal industry was also expanding . The Bridgewater mines at Worsley were only the most famous of several major operations, and small-scale working was widespread; but we lack a satisfactory study of the pace and nature of development in this area and period.

Liverpool's growth, and the associated transport changes, helped to cause a shift in the centre of gravity of the south-west Lancashire industrial belt in the middle decades of the eighteenth century. The older metalworking industries of the Wigan area declined. The pewterers, who had been very important in the economic and political life of the town in the late seventeenth century, faded away as the demand for their product waned; the bellfounders, who had traded over a wide area of northern England, the Midlands and north Wales, lost out to competitors elsewhere after mid-century; and even the nailmakers of Chowbent and the nearby villages were less in evidence. The growth of large ironworks, especially the Earl of Balcarres's enormous Haigh complex, redressed the balance a little; and so did the expansion of watch, clock and file manufacture on the putting-out system, especially in the Prescot area. By the 1750s and 1760s, however, a clear tendency was emerging for large-scale new industries to concentrate in Liverpool and close to the Mersey and its associated waterways. Brass, copper, salt and sugar boiling, brewing, pottery and glassmaking all followed this pattern, and the initiatives of mid-century were to provide the basis for a new heavy industrial economy in the classic 'Industrial Revolution' years, although ultimately this lucrative harvest was reaped in St. Helens, Warrington and the surrounding area rather than in Liverpool itself. But the growth of large-scale, capital-intensive industry in the area, in symbiotic relationship with the coalfield and fuelled by investment from Liverpool and further afield, was beginning in earnest by the 1760s.[45]

By this time Liverpool's growth was also making an impact on agriculture, at least in its immediate hinterland. Farmers on both sides of the Mersey were competing in the 1760s to supply the earliest new potatoes for the tables of the affluent citizenry, and by 1773 this competition had extended to gooseberries and asparagus. More plebeian vegetables, such as cabbages, were in demand for ships' stores, and dried herbs were exported to Africa. Farmers around Liverpool also began to specialise in cowkeeping, to supply the townspeople with milk and butter, and in return Liverpool itself provided a remarkable variety of manures, including blubber dregs and soap ashes as well as street and stable dung and nightsoil. Mutual assistance of this kind between port and rural hinterland was to increase rapidly in importance in the late eighteenth century, as Liverpool merchants began to invest in drainage and other agricultural improvements, and the canals gave further encouragement to vegetable cultivation and market gardening.[46]

After mid-century Manchester began to have a similar effect on its surrounding countryside, as the balance of agriculture in Prestwich parish, for example, tilted away from tillage towards dairying for the urban market, while vegetables came from north Cheshire and the Warrington area.[47] But significant changes in agricultural practice were more widespread than this. Reclamation from the waste continued steadily on the eastern uplands, and by 1772 much Furness upland was being enclosed to grow wood for the charcoal iron industry and timber for the mines.[48] Enclosure of the few remaining common fields under tillage, especially in Furness, was almost completed, usually by agreement among the proprietors; but common pasture remained extensive, and many depended for their living on access to it. Drainage schemes for the mosses and meres which occupied so much of the south and west began to be pursued in earnest by the large landowners, with some success in the Fylde, although further south Martin Mere and its mossland continued to resist the efforts to the improvers.[49]

Perhaps the most important innovation was potato cultivation, in which Lancashire took the lead. It was introduced towards the middle of the seventeenth century, and by 1680 it was well-established on the south-western mosslands, with a specialised market at Wigan. Potato cultivation subsequently spread eastwards, but a century later potatoes from south-west Lancashire were making a significant contribution to feeding the swelling population of the south-eastern textile district, through the markets of Oldham and Rochdale as well as Manchester. Agricultural improvers at this time held up Lancashire practice as an example to other areas, in this respect if in few others.[50]

Turnips, the main stock-in-trade of improvers further south, were adopted much more sparingly in Lancashire, where the soils seldom suited them; and vetches and lucerne were even more unusual, though clover was more widely grown, especially as feed for horses.[51] Sheep also remained unusual, and were largely confined to the upland commons, forming no part of any programme of improved husbandry in arable areas. Even on the hills of Rossendale and Furness the number of sheep declined during the eighteenth century, as the enclosure of waste proceeded and timber provided a more lucrative investment in the latter area.[52]

Away from the influence of a few large landowners, especially in the south-west, Lancashire agriculture remained conservative in practices and products. Cattle and oats remained the staple products, although wheat output was not negligible on the central Lancashire plain. South-east Lancashire, in particular, saw a switch from fatstock to dairying in response to demand from a growing population; but the emergent science of selective breeding was neglected, and it was alleged that the quality of the county's longhorn cattle was declining.[53] Most farms were small, even on the plain: holdings of less than 50 acres were the norm, and Rossendale was not the only area in which little plots of less than 10 acres began to multiply in the eighteenth century. Inventories suggest an average of only 9 cattle per farm in the later seventeenth century, falling to 7 in the early decades of the eighteenth. The old three-life lease, which was thought to inhibit improvement, was giving way only gradually to shorter leases for fixed terms in the second half of the eighteenth century; and occasional labour services had still not completely disappeared in the 1790s. The limited number of substantial landowners, few of whom took an active interest in improvement, and the shortage of capital and incentive among the multitude of freeholders and small farmers, ensured that advocates of new farming systems would find much to criticise, especially where agriculture became a by-employment for small-holder/craftsmen and industrial workers. Comments on crop rotations were particularly savage, as land was exhausted by continuous cultivation of the same crop, and then left wastefully to fallow. But more generally, Lancashire farming was more effectively attuned to local climatic, geological and market conditions than outside observers allowed, and in the south-west, especially, major changes were appearing by the mid eighteenth century. But over wide areas of the county manufacturing and mining increasingly competed with agriculture for attention and investment in the eyes of landowners, farmers and their families, and this in turn ensured that cheap labour for labour-intensive forms of husbandry became less readily obtainable than in parts of southern and eastern England.[54]

Agriculture still dominated the economy of most of Lancashire in 1770, however, especially north of the Ribble. Lancaster itself was treated dismissively by Defoe in the early eighteenth century; but its port was never as decayed and deserted as he suggested, and the quickening of its trade with the West Indies and the Baltic in the second quarter of the eighteenth century was further stimulated by harbour improvements, while a flourishing merchant community invested in sugar-boiling and dabbled extensively in the slave trade. Further north, the Furness charcoal iron industry grew steadily for much of the eighteenth century, making its own contribution to Lancaster's exports. Quarrying and domestic textiles were also important locally; but these were urban and industrial outposts in an essentially agricultural landscape, although even in Furness the predominance of agriculture as an employer was much less marked by 1770 than it had been at the turn of the century.[55]

Almost everywhere in Lancashire there was a perceptible quickening in economic growth around the middle of the eighteenth century; and this was accompanied by a general resumption of substantial and sustained population increase. Between 1664 and 1801 Lancashire's population grew more than fourfold to approach 700,000. In the south-eastern Salford Hundred the rise was more than fivefold, while in West Derby, including Liverpool and the coalfield around Wigan, Prescot and St. Helens, growth was nearly as rapid. In the northern and western hundreds of Lonsdale and Amounderness, where the advance of industry and urbanisation was much patchier and more limited, the population doubled.[56] But much of this increase was concentrated into the last quarter of the eighteenth century, and it is difficult to chart the course of population change before then. The work of the Cambridge Group of historical demographers has produced convincing new estimates of national population trends and the reasons behind them, but its data are not amenable to the reconstruction of regional experiences, and the new interpretations have undermined and perhaps destroyed the credibility of existing estimates of eighteenth-century population change in the counties, without putting anything in their place.[57]

We do have two imperfect but usable intermediate markers from which to make a tentative assessment of the pace of population change. The episcopal visitations of 1717 and 1778 involved the collection of returns of the number of households in each parish, and although these returns are incomplete and sometimes clearly unreliable, some broad conclusions can be drawn from them. The 1717 return covers Lancashire south of the Ribble, and suggests that population growth was very limited indeed over most of the county between 1664 and 1717. Even in the south-eastern textile area there was, at best, stagnation, and the only evidence of marked expansion comes from the south-west, where the population of Warrington deanery was perhaps 75 per cent higher in 1717 than that of the corresponding West Derby Hundred in 1664.[58] The gaps in the 1778 returns are more randomly distributed, and there are no entries for Lancaster, Preston, Blackburn or Wigan. Moreover, several clergymen complained of the impossibility of their task: counting households was 'rather difficult and a work of time' to the vicar of Middleton, who made no return, and the curate at Ardwick declared that the number was 'impossible to ascertain'. Others resorted to obvious guesswork: 'something more than 2000' at Colne, and three rival Liverpool estimates ranging between 7000 and 8000 from different parishes in the town. But if we use this evidence to obtain rough orders of magnitude, it seems that the population of Manchester and Blackburn deaneries more than doubled between 1717 and 1778, while outside the textile district Warrington deanery grew nearly as rapidly, with a slower rise of uncertain magnitude north of the Ribble.[59] The turning point came in the middle decades of the eighteenth century, and we shall see that population growth continued to accelerate thereafter.

Detailed studies of smaller areas support these overall impressions. The surprising findings for the textile district before 1717 are corroborated by King's work on Rossendale, and further north Marshall suggests that the turning-point in Furness came in about 1740.[60] The long period of stagnation and even decline after the Restoration, and the subsequent upturn, both require explanation, although they run closely parallel to trends in the nation at large. We should also note that, Liverpool and Manchester apart, the scale and pace of urbanisation remained quite limited. This was the case in the textile district, as we saw earlier; and elsewhere, too, the largest towns had yet to record five-figure populations in the 1770s. Preston and Wigan, with their restrictive corporations and limited textile development, had little more than five or six thousand inhabitants each at this time, and were outpaced by Warrington and Lancaster, where local enumerations found 8791 and 8584 people respectively in the early 1780s. Ulverston, the largest town of Furness, grew from about 1100 people in 1710 to 3000 in 1772.[61] Below the highest level of the urban hierarchy, population growth in the countryside was still outpacing that of the towns.

But why, in most of Lancashire, was a long period of post-Restoration stagnation followed by steadily accelerating growth from the 1740s onwards? There is an urgent need for research in this field, especially in the textile district; but some basic arguments can be developed. First, we should note the exceptional case of south-west Lancashire, where steady and cumulatively impressive population growth was sustained throughout the period. Here, an expanding economy generated a wide range of job opportunities which, no doubt, boosted the marriage rate, encouraged earlier marriage and additional children, and attracted migrants from elsewhere. Marriage need no longer be delayed until an agricultural holding became available.

We lack hard evidence in support of these conjectures, but they are plausible in the light of experience elsewhere, and Langton does demonstrate that St. Helens mining families showed high fertility rates in the early eighteenth century.[62] But in any case, we need to ask why economic growth took longer to stimulate, or at least permit, population expansion in the textile district itself. In domestic textiles, after all, the ease of setting up in business with very limited capital and the scope for maximising output by involving the whole family could remove the most important constraints on population growth by permitting early marriage and encouraging procreation.[63] The delayed emergence of this pattern in south-east Lancashire may well be connected with the relationship between agriculture and domestic industry. While textiles provided an essential but unreliable supplement to the incomes of small farmers, a cautious agrarian pattern of late marriage and demographic restraint may have prevailed, especially after the disastrous mortality crises of the second quarter of the seventeenth century. When the balance of most domestic economies tilted in favour of textiles, however, with a proliferation of smallholdings and landless cottages, renewed population growth began rapidly. In Rossendale this change took place quite early in the eighteenth century. Birth-rates rose from less than 30 per thousand in 1716 to nearly 41 per thousand in 1731, and then stabilised at or near the higher figure; marriage-rates performed a similar evolution between 1706 and 1721; and the intervals between births fell from an average of 27.8 months in the early 1720s to 22.3 months in the early 1780s. In nearby Saddleworth the median age at first marriage also fell significantly.[64]

Similar changes almost certainly took place at some point in the early to mid eighteenth century throughout the textile district, although the timing probably varied from place to place. In the early stages of this transition, the minor population crises which had persisted sporadically through the later seventeenth century became temporarily endemic in Rossendale, and no doubt elsewhere. Burials regularly rose to 20 per cent above the average for the three pre-crisis years, but the rhythm quickened sharply afte 1720, with periods of high mortality on this definition falling in 1722, 1726–8, 1736–7 and 1740–5. After 1750, however, years of this sort became occasional. At their worst, these were minor setbacks when compared with the first half of the seventeenth century, and they required a combination of bad trade, but harvests and disease to set them off. Some, indeed, were part of a much wider geographical pattern of high mortality, and none after 1720 inhibited the long-run upward trend in population. The threat of serious and sustained population crisis may have flickered in the 1730s and 1740s, but it was overcome by the growing strength of the textile industries and the diversification of their markets, coupled with improved links with the outside world, easier access to imported foodstuffs and increased purchasing power.[65]

Mortality levels may well have declined more generally, but changes in the birth and marriage rates were the most important influences on population growth, in the textile district as elsewhere.[66] Migration into the area may well have supplemented locally generated surpluses of births over deaths, but, Manchester apart, most of it was short-range, now as later, and population growth was essentially locally generated. One further caveat remains. The proliferation of very small holdings and landless cottages which tipped the economic balance in favour of textiles must itself have been, in part, the *result* of population growth; so the peculiar demographic circumstances of textiles explain not so much the *existence* of an upward population trend, but its unusual strength and sustained nature in south-east Lancashire. In this context we should emphasise that the agrarian north of the county also experienced a sustained rise in population, of a less spectacular nature, after 1740, as evidence from Warton and Furness demonstrates. Here again, by-employments in mining, quarrying, metalworking and woodland industries no doubt helped to sustain larger families, while the scope for migration to nearby areas of rapid economic growth provided a safety-valve for the rural demographic system.[67] But the most powerful and effective stimuli for sustained population growth developed in the emergent industrial areas of south-east Lancashire and Merseyside; and we shall see that subsequently this trend became even more strongly marked.

Changes in the social structure accompanied these developments. As before, and as we have seen for the textile district, they involved a disproportionate expansion of the smallholding and wage-earning strata, with a less marked increase in the ranks of the entrepreneurial and agricultural 'middling sort'. The gentry, meanwhile, declined as a proportion of the population, if not in influence or prosperity. Blackwood's figures suggest that the numerical decline of the Civil War and Interregnum was arrested in the late seventeenth century: he finds 627 gentry families in 1664 and 662 in 1695. But this apparent stability masks accelerated mobility into and out of the ranks of the gentry: 381 of the 662 families were newcomers since 1664, while 346 of the 627 families of 1664 had fallen from grace by 1695.[68] The reasons for this mobility are complicated and uncertain. The demarcation line between lower gentry and upper yeomanry was still blurred, and some families, especially the active Parliamentarians, lost gentility through ceasing to hold office rather than as a result of economic decline. The failure of families to produce male heirs also played a significant part. There is disagreement over the impact of the Civil War and of continuing legal discrimination against property-owning Catholics: Blackwood and Galgano discount these influences, but Langton argues that Catholic coal-owning gentry in south-west Lancashire suffered severely from capital shortages arising from the long-term effects of sequestrations and fines, which were exacerbated in some cases by punishments for supporting the Jacobites in 1715.[69] We lack systematic evidence on the gentry's fortunes in the eighteenth century, although the indications of rising entry fines and (less frequently) increased rents suggest that landed incomes were improving even without the benefit of mining royalties or urban development. The social structure changed little at this level, despite the rapidity of turnover into and out of the ranks of the acknowledged gentry. A handful of aristocrats, with the Earls of Derby still at their head, and a limited number of really substantial gentry, concentrated especially into the south and west of the county, were best placed to profit from mineral exploitation, urbanisation and agricultural improvement. They presided over a landed society which was dominated numerically by the lesser gentry and greater yeomanry, whose ranks were continuously being swelled by industrial and commercial wealth, a trend which was already apparent before the Civil War, and depleted by loss of office, financial stringency and demographic failure. Below the level of the magnates and old-established gentry with broad acres, the line between landed and industrial or commercial wealth remained ill-defined. By the middle years of the eighteenth century, the leading Liverpool and Manchester merchants were moving into a new world of conspicuous consumption and competitive display which had already been foreshadowed by the rise of Preston as the fashionable meeting-place for the leading county gentry; but at this level, despite intermarriage and the recruitment of merchants' apprentices from the younger sons of gentry, similarity of leisure activities and consumption patterns did not necessarily betoken a common culture, especially as the gentry retained attachments to hunting, hawking and fishing which their urban counterparts found it difficult to share.

Preston was not yet a major textile centre, although the linen industry was important there; and its central position and administrative convenience enabled it to outshine Lancaster as the centre of polite society in post-Restoration Lancashire. This encouraged a concern for urban amenities which responded to the rising expectations of the affluent and temporary residents. Town houses for gentry and lawyers proliferated, following new national fashions for order, symmetry, classical detail and the use of brick: already in the 1680s Preston had 'handsome buildings ... here and there interwoven with stately fabricks of brick-building after the modish manner, extraordinarily adorning the streets which they belong unto'. In the late seventeenth and early eighteenth centuries the Corporation became actively involved in road-widening, the limited but early provision of street lamps, and the promotion and patronage of leisure activities for polite society. Avenham Walk, a formal promenade above the river, was laid out in the late seventeenth century and regularly refurbished thereafter. By 1728 the Town Hall was being used for formal assemblies and balls, and every twenty years the Preston Guild celebrations brought especially fashionable gatherings and elaborate festivities to the town. In 1726 the Corporation granted an annual subscription to encourage horse-racing on Preston Common, which was well established by this time, and from at least the 1690s a town hunt was maintained, in response to another emergent preoccupation of the leisured and genteel. All this helped to stimulate luxury and service trades, such as barbers, innkeepers, gardeners, confectioners, tobacconists, booksellers and goldsmiths, while the town's administrative functions attracted lawyers and other professionals. Preston compared favourably with county towns and emergent resorts in other parts of the country in terms of the services and amenities it provided. The extent and nature of its success brings out the extent to which Lancashire landed society was prospering during this period. Wealthy Lancastrians were clearly being firmly assimilated into a national polite culture of the affluent leisured, taking their cue from London. Preston's experience demonstrates that for a widening circle of the better-off, post-Restoration Lancashire was rapidly ceasing to be a remote cultural backwater.[70]

Preston was pioneering and pre-eminent in its role as centre for polite society, but during the eighteenth century several other Lancashire towns developed similar amenities and institutions. As commerce prospered in Liverpool and Manchester, so the lifestyles of the leading merchants became less abstemious. Architectural display became more assertive: by the mid-1720s these towns were among the first seven in the English provinces to develop formal squares of substantial terraced houses. Liverpool earned lavish praise more generally for the impressive new streets and wide roads of its new residential districts, although subsequent commentators were to bemoan the lack of overall planning on the extensive Corporation estate.[71] New churches and other public buildings began to appear in both towns, and merchants and their families begun to keep carriages, to drink tea (and in Liverpool's case rum) instead of home-made wine, to frequent dancing assemblies and race meetings, and to pursue and patronise literature and the arts. These developments came later than in Preston, and the landed and commercial élites may have continued to move mainly in separate social spheres; but they were well advanced by mid-century, expressing the growing opulence, self-confidence and social aspirations of commercial Lancashire.[72] In some of the smaller towns, too, there were similar stirrings on a more limited scale: even Ulverston had its Book Club, formed in 1756.[73]

Lower down the social scale, there is also evidence of improving living standards among the yeomanry, farmers, husbandmen and rural craftsmen, which is open to debate in the later seventeenth century but becomes unequivocal towards the middle of the eighteenth. In Furness, especially, we can see a steady increase in the value of probate inventories among these middling groups between the 1660s and the 1740s. Marshall's sample shows the average gross value of goods and credits left at death by the Furness yeomanry more than doubling between 1661–90 and 1721–50. Savings and credits accounted for most of the increase: here and at this social level, conspicuous consumption was still having a very limited impact on a cautious and thrifty peasantry. The most obvious and important improvements were in the size and quality of farmhouses, as the rural 'Great Rebuilding' of the late seventeenth and early eighteenth centuries proceeded alongside the dramatic changes in urban housing and planning. A more tightly focused study of Hawkshead suggests that a growing and prospering group of 'upper peasantry' gained disproportionately from improved economic conditions and more sophisticated trading activity. Here at least, rural society was becoming increasingly highly stratified, with the more established families among the comfortably-off being joined by large numbers of the upwardly socially mobile.[74]

The Furness experience reflects a gradual but cumulative improvement in farming practices and marketing, coupled with the growth of crafts and rural industries to provide additional and alternative employment. As such it was probably duplicated, in outline at least, over much of rural Lancashire, although much of this limited affluence was precarious, and farmers remained very vulnerable to bad weather and cattle disease.[75] In Rossendale, the inventory evidence suggests that a clear rise in wealth levels among the 'middling sort' was delayed until well into the eighteenth century, when there was also a 'widening in the structure of local wealth distribution', and an increase in the number of substantial houses, as the relatively well-off improved their condition still further.[76] Here, however, the rise of the textile industries and the associated increase in the number of smallholders and landless cottagers, people with little property who rarely needed to leave inventories, makes the sample much less representative of the population at large; and we need to consider how the changes of this period affected the numbers and fortunes of the smallholding and wage-earning poor.

Lancashire's lower orders continued to grow rapidly in numbers and as a proportion of the population, especially in Liverpool, Manchester and the textile district. As we shall see, the gulf between the poor wage-earner and the increasingly gentrified large employer was widening sharply during the eighteenth century, and bitter and sustained conflicts between capital and labour began to occur in several guises. Meanwhile, however, poverty became less abject and threatening even as the poor became more numerous, and as poor relief expenditure increased in time of slump. The danger of subsistence crises receded, and the official poor relief machinery became firmly established, though not without complaints from the master manufacturers, who alleged that thrift, forethought and sustained industry among the workforce were being undermined by the expensive security provided by the Poor Law. The perceived dangers from hard times in the eighteenth century involved hunger, anger and disorder, but not mass starvation.[77] Miners, it seems, were relatively well paid, and textile workers were often able to indulge their leisure preference by spending Mondays in the alehouse.[78] But specialisation in one occupation and wage-dependence were becoming more widespread, although the 'dual economy' of industry and small-scale agriculture survived tenaciously among miners, nailmakers and watchmakers as well as in the textile industries, in the 1770s and beyond. Some of the other social costs of economic growth and urbanisation were also becoming apparent, as medical men began to notice the prevalence of disease and premature death among the inhabitants of the insanitary slums and cellar dwellings which were proliferating in Liverpool and Manchester.[79] The short working life of miners, who were unlikely to survive far beyond the age of 40, may have been less obvious to contemporaries than it has become to historians.[80] But the emergent Lancashire working class was having to adjust to new kinds of poverty and to new patterns of industrial relations. It was aided in this task by deep local and familial roots, for despite much short-distance migration, Lancashire's industrial population was recruited mainly by natural increase in ways which enabled local customs and practices to be endorsed and perpetuated, and permitted kinship ties to remain strong and effective.[81] This made it more difficult for those in authority to control the lower orders and mould them in a chosen image, and they became increasingly worried about the scope for social insubordination and threats to property and order. In the next chapter we shall look at how the problems of order, discipline and control, which arose from widening social and cultural divisions, were tackled, and with what success.

5

AUTHORITY AND CONFLICT,
1660 – 1770

The accelerating economic and social changes of this transitional period brought several kinds of response from those who were concerned with, and interested in, the protection of property and the exercise of authority. The power of central government remained very limited in practice at the local level, where the institutions which mattered most were often voluntary and informal. The maintenance of order was pursued not only through the official machinery of the civil and criminal law, and the increasingly complex administration of the Poor Law, but also through religious institutions and private charity. Attempts to influence the wage-earning and smallholding classes in ways conducive to social stability were fuelled by humanitarian and religious motives as well as by coercive authoritarianism and fear of disorder; and the drive to order and control was complicated and impeded by divisions within the ruling and propertied groups, especially where religious issues became entangled with national politics. When challenged from below, however, Lancashire's leaders remained well capable of closing ranks and defending their interests, and threats to authority remained sporadic, geographically isolated and, for the most part, easily contained, except, perhaps, where disturbances were themselves encouraged by sections by the propertied class and directed against their political opponents.

Who were Lancashire's rulers? At the very top, the social and political leadership exercised by the Earls of Derby came under challenge during the Civil War and its aftermath, and the family never fully or securely recovered its predominant position. The seventh Earl had failed to heal the conflicts of the early 1640s in county society, and came under fire from both extremes as the Civil War polarised opinions. His eventual isolation, loss of property and execution left his successors with an uphill task, and the eighth Earl may have made matters more difficult by his abandonment of the family policy of attempting to mediate between contending local factions and the Crown. Instead, the early Restoration years saw him espousing a militant and intolerant Anglicanism, attacking religious dissenters of all kinds, and falling foul of Charles II as well as stirring up powerful opposition among leading gentry families. At the eighth Earl's death in 1672, a measure of harmony had been restored, and financial recovery was also well under way; but the days of unchallenged pre-eminence were over, and it was no longer possible to bridge the gulf between the contending factions in a divided county. The ninth Earl tried to sustain the role of mediator and minimiser of conflict, but this left him sitting on the fence at the Revolution of 1688, when he lost the Lord Lieutenancy of Cheshire and reacted to this slight by giving up the equivalent office in Lancashire. This loss of office was more than just symbolic: Coward suggests that 'In the period immediately after the Glorious Revolution the Earls of Derby became merely one of a number of people challenging for the rule of Lancashire and Cheshire'.[1] The ninth Earl was reinstated in 1702, and between 1706 and 1710 his successor combined the offices of Lord Lieutenant and Chancellor of the Duchy of Lancaster, thus nominating his deputies and having the strongest voice in choosing county magistrates. But this potentially formidable power base proved temporary: by this time the Earls of Derby were no longer strong enough in the county to hold the lieutenancy as of right, but became subjected to the changing political complexion of central government. They remained the richest and most powerful landowners in Lancashire, but they could no longer claim to represent its interests or to dominate the workings of its local government. More work is needed on their role in the middle and later eighteenth century, but their eclipse, though far from total, was a long-term and significant change in the pattern of authority in the county.[2]

The lieutenancy was important partly because the Lord Lieutenant controlled the militia, which as reconstituted at the Restoration became a citizen army whose main role involved 'animating the well-disposed and aweing the disaffected mobile'. It was used especially to police the potentially subversive activities of Catholics, a persisting preoccupation in Lancashire; and despite its alleged inefficiency it was of considerable significance as a protector of property and pillar of the social order.[3] Its failure to act effectively against the Jacobites in 1745 was due to legal problems as well as to poor quality and lack of training, and the Lancashire militia was said to have fought creditably alongside the regulars at Preston in 1715.[4] The persisting importance of the militia should not be underrated, if only as a deterrent to riot and social upheaval, and its direction was a weighty enough matter to ensure that the deputy lieutenancies were filled from gentry families of wealth and substance, as well as political reliability.[5]

But the prestige – and burden – of day-to-day administration, in Lancashire as elsewhere, remained with the county Justices of the Peace. As in other counties, their numbers increased steadily after the Restoration: they had fluctuated in the fifties and low sixties in the 1630s, and fallen as low as 26 during the Interregnum, but by 1675 there were 71 on the list, rising to 117 in 1714 and falling back again to 95 in 1720.[6] Not all were active, of course, and we need research on the Lancashire magistracy of the middle and later eighteenth century. What stands out, however, is the rapid turnover of Justices after the reign of Charles II, as central government sought to control the political composition of the bench. Purges took place regularly as monarchs and governments changed, and there was remarkably little continuity of service. Like the lieutenancy, the position of county magistrate was becoming a party political appointment. In 1700 nearly two-thirds of the Lancashire Justices had been recruited since 1689; and after the spectacular purge on the eve of the Jacobite rising of 1715, only a single magistrate had seen continuous service since the Glorious Revolution.[7]

Glassey believes that a period of stability followed during the long Whig ascendancy; but the decades of flux must have reduced the experience and efficiency of the county's governors. But there was an important mitigating feature. Whatever the composition of the bench at a given moment, the vast majority of the magistrates were drawn from a recognisable pool of socially acceptable upper gentry families. When people of insufficient status were nominated by politicians, the opposition among the established justices was sufficient to ensure that their tenure of office was insecure and brief. When Roger Kenyon, clerk of the peace, described six of the new nominations of 1696–7 as a collier's son, an apothecary, a shopkeeper, two traders and a former preacher at conventicles, it is not surprising to find them disappearing in the reshuffle of 1698. All six were also Protestant Dissenters, which did not ease their reception, and Roman Catholics were decidedly unacceptable to many of their potential colleagues, although a distinguished reservoir of old Catholic gentry families was available in which James II and his advisers were able to fish in 1687.[8] But these social demarcation lines effectively restricted entry, and ensured that, at any given time, enough Justices had accumulated sufficient administrative experience to keep the wheels of county government turning, however insecure their tenure of office as individuals in the short run. The attitudes in question certainly persisted far beyond 1720: Wadsworth and Mann remark of Thomas Percival, a Royton Justice in the late 1750s, that 'although the son of a Manchester tradesman, he had all the squire's contempt for the new trading rich'. Substantial commercial or mineowning wealth, allied to landownership, was acceptable, and several south-west Lancashire Justices fell into this category; but those who still depended mainly on trade and manufacture were excluded from the county bench until the second quarter of the nineteenth century. Wealth did not immediately purchase status and acceptability, especially if its beneficiaries were visibly uncultivated and lacked a suitable landed background.[9] These social constraints ensured that the intervention of central

John Horrocks of Preston, one of the most successful of the first generation of Lancashire factory masters. (See p. 108.) [*Below*] 'Rational recreation' in the home: Joseph Livesey, the Preston teetotaller, and his family engaged in very sedate enjoyment on a Sunday afternoon. (See p. 190.)

Mid-Victorian church-building: Hansom's magnificent St Walburge's, a Roman Catholic response to Church of England initiatives. (See p. 246.)

[*Left*] The sixteenth Earl of Derby as Preston's Guild Mayor in 1902. (See p. 223.)

government had a more limited impact in practice than might have been expected from the bare figures.

More generally, central government's pretensions to control were still far less effective in actuality than they might appear on paper; and this will remain a recurrent theme. It is illustrated further, from a different angle, by the very low Land Tax assessment which was allotted to Lancashire, in common with other Northern and Western counties, and by the limited impact of the efforts of the later Stuart monarchs to control the internal affairs of the Lancashire boroughs.[10]

Local government in the boroughs established or confirmed the power and status of those leading citizens who were sufficiently well-connected to enter the urban governing élite of mayors and aldermen. In Liverpool, Preston, Lancaster and Wigan, the major Lancashire boroughs, the power was real enough: there was extensive corporate property to administer and patronage to allocate, there was largesse to distribute and ceremony to organise, there was justice to dispense and controls over trading and markets to exercise, and the Corporations' rulers had a strong, if not always dominant, voice in the selection of the towns' MPs.[11] Three related themes dominate the post-Restoration history of these towns: the drive to emancipation from the tutelage of the surrounding landed gentry; the struggle to minimise the impact of central government intervention in borough affairs, which sometimes favoured the gentry; and the gathering trend towards oligarchy in borough government, as the influence of the ordinary freemen, the small traders and journeymen, was eroded.

These trends were particularly marked in Liverpool, where the Corporation's successful defence of the town's economic interests and political autonomy against the claims of the nearby landowning Moore and Molyneux families has been described as an example of 'open class conflict' between merchants and aristocracy.[12] At this time, too, soon after the Restoration, central government was periodically seeking to remodel the borough corporations, like the county magistracy, in a chosen image, and new charters in 1677, 1685 and 1695 saw the battle between local autonomy and external county influence ebb and flow, complicated by internal faction-fighting, until the charter of 1695 left the Corporation in command of its own destiny. But a drive to oligarchy was already well advanced, and during most of the eighteenth century municipal influence was concentrated into the hands of a small group of established, Anglican mercantile families, a state of affairs which was regularly but unavailingly challenged from below in the courts. This opposition movement was supported by the tenth Earl of Derby, who retained a strong presence in Liverpool politics until his death in 1735, after which the earldom passed to a different branch of the family and its Liverpool connection was severed. Liverpool's oligarchic Corporation was highly successful in promoting economic expansion, positively through the dock estate and negatively through its willingness to allow immigrant traders to settle and set up in business with the minimum of molestation.

These attitudes contrasted with more restrictive policies at Preston and Wigan, and in this respect Liverpool's experience resembled Manchester's more closely than might have been expected.[13]

In Preston and Lancaster, as in Liverpool, royal initiatives in the later seventeenth century made little or no long-term difference to the effective autonomy of increasingly oligarchical corporations; but in these centres of county administration the leading landed families exerted more influence for a longer period, especially the Earls of Derby in Preston, where a battle for supremacy between the Stanley family and the Corporation was approaching its climax in the later eighteenth century.[14] Towns without corporations were governed through the manorial court, the Court Leet, which looked after policing, markets, tolls and the removal of nuisances, and by the parish vestries, which administered the Poor Law. Even Manchester still operated in this way in 1770, although important changes were soon to begin.[15] The Lord of the Manor might thus retain considerable potential influence, but it was being eroded in practice; and in all of Lancashire's larger towns, recognisable urban élites of merchants, professionals and opulent tradesmen were becoming visibly masters of their own destinies during the eighteenth century. The county's power structure was acquiring a distinctive and independent urban dimension which could no longer be ignored or despised by central government or landed society. Urban leaders were expected to confine themselves to their own sphere of activity, and within that sphere the corporate oligarchies were frequently and sometimes riotously challenged by the humbler citizens who were losing their voice in decision-making; but the emergence of these prosperous and self-confident urban élites constitutes an important theme on which further research is urgently needed.

The bottom tier of administration, manorial and parochial government in the villages and hamlets, is even less adequately documented. Constables, manorial officials, churchwardens and overseers of the poor must still have been drawn mainly from the yeomanry, farmers and village craftsmen, open to pressure from their relatives and neighbours, and with widely varying levels of literacy and competence. There was some gentry involvement: the Townleys of Royle near Burnley served as churchwardens, overseers and surveyors of highways as well as acting as county magistrates and bearing the title 'Esquire'.[16] But this was probably unusual: surviving evidence is patchy and difficult to use. It is easy to sympathise with Barker and Harris's enthusiasm for Leigh Leaf, overseer at Parr in the late 1760s, 'whose beautiful handwriting is a welcome change after the vile hands of his Parr contemporaries'.[17]

We know more about the workings of the Poor Law than any other aspect of the exercise of authority at village level. It was the most expensive and potentially contentious aspect of local government, and it is no surprise to find even small villages beginning to employ regular, if part-time, paid overseers in the 1750s.[18] Throughout Lancashire, the cost of poor relief began to rise noticeably around the middle of the eighteenth century. There had, of course, been short sharp rises in difficult years throughout the later seventeenth century: the early 1660s, in particular, saw a spate of complaints to the county magistrates about the burden of the poor-rate and its unfair distribution. In 1662, Burnley's property-owners petitioned to complain that they were 'overcharged with poor, consisting of 300 poor and impotent'. If true, this would amount to about a quarter of the population; and even allowing for special pleading, it suggests serious, if temporary, pressure on local resources. Fessler alleges a more general and lasting post-Restoration trend towards the cutting of allowances in face of rising costs, with frequent conflict between overseers, claimants and magistrates intervening on the claimants' behalf; but this suggestion needs fuller documentation than it has yet received, and the clearest evidence of sustained and significant growth in poor relief expenditure comes from the mid eighteenth century.[19] In the St. Helens area it becomes apparent in the 1750s; in Rossendale poor relief expenditure trebled during the crisis of 1740–1, and then showed a 'dramatic' increase in the 1750s, which was maintained through the third quarter of the eighteenth century; something similar occurred in Burnley; and in Furness relief expenditure rose temporarily in the 1730s, followed by a more sustained upward trend from about 1770.[20] These widespread developments arose from changes in the social structure, especially the growing importance of wage labour, which accompanied population increase; they were perhaps also connected with increasing longevity and reduced infant mortality, for most pauperism arose from age, infirmity or a temporary surplus of dependent children. Such an interpretation would help to overcome the apparent paradox of increasing pauperism marching in step with declining vulnerability to mortality crises, as a ramshackle, decentralised, essentially amateur Poor Law organisation found it difficult to control expenditure.[21]

Changes in poor relief policy were beginning before the upturn in spending. Workhouses were opened all over Lancashire in the 1730s and 1740s, as townships adopted the general enabling legislation of 1723. In many cases they were originally intended to house and (where possible) set to work all of the local poor, ending outdoor relief and testing the extent to which applicants were really destitute. But such policies were invariably short-lived. Many individual townships found workhouses expensive and difficult to administer, and most such ventures were short-lived, although when several parishes or townships banded together to set up jointly run workhouses the economies of scale brought more satisfactory and lasting results. Even under these conditions, however, workhouses became repositories for the aged, ill, infirm, and unmarried mothers with young children: the long-term poor who always predominated among the recipients of relief. Almost always, the vast majority of paupers were relieved at home. It was cheaper to provide outdoor relief, whether rent, fuel, food or money payments, than to spend large amounts on workhouse building and upkeep; and workhouses remained small and unassuming, with few pretensions to deterrence or industrial efficiency. In the

[89]

villages and smaller towns they seldom made much difference to the overall direction of relief policy.[22]

From time to time rising poor-rates brought attempts to curb expenditure by reducing relief scales or introducing deterrent or regulatory measures, such as requiring paupers to wear distinctive badges; but Fessler's assertion that attitudes towards the poor were hardening cannot be sustained by the available evidence.[23] At Parr, part of the future St. Helens, tobacco and sugar were provided for workhouse inmates in the mid eighteenth century, when pauper burials involved spending on candles, wine, tobacco and invitations to mourners, as well as a coffin. Barker and Harris comment that there was little evidence of 'stinginess' or 'moral disapproval', and 'the boundary ... between pauperism and independence was less strict, and the stigma less cruel' than in later years. 'It was possible for a labouring man's wife, during hard times, to have a new gown from the overseer without any serious diminution of self-respect'; and although this optimistic comment is difficult to verify, we should remember that the magistrate could be a sympathetic court of appeal when matters were less cosy.[24] The hard-nosed, *laissez-faire* attitudes of some of the spokesmen for the emergent manufacturing interest were not yet permeating Poor Law policy over most of Lancashire; and some of the pressure on the ratepayers was eased by a modest but useful flow of charitable endowments, and by a persisting expectation of neighbourly assistance in time of illness or unemployment.

In Liverpool and Manchester, the problems were on a different scale altogether, as urban growth generated visible concentrations of poverty, and the cost of relief began to rise rapidly at an early stage. Liverpool's experience is particularly striking. In 1681 only 20 adults received weekly doles from the overseers, and the annual cost of relief, including support for destitute strangers, was £40. By 1691 it had reached £135, in 1719 it was £520, and three years later it had topped £1000. Under these circumstances the overseers were eager to introduce a supervised housing scheme in the early 1720s, and when the poor-rate rose again by one-third between 1727 and 1729 an attempt was made to decant all the town's paupers into a new workhouse, opened in 1733. This brought a short-term fall in expenditure; but despite enlargements in 1757 and 1762, and the opening of a large new workhouse in 1769, it was never possible to abolish outdoor relief in an urban economy which offered only fluctuating and insecure employment to the majority of its labour force. Along with its early and sustained commitment to the workhouse, Liverpool's Poor Law administration developed administrative innovations, with an early and extensive use of salaried officials and the development of a supervisory committee elected annually by the ratepayers, which set it apart from the rest of the county.[25] Manchester is less clearly documented, but its Poor Law authorities were also struggling with rising costs from the late seventeenth century, and an obsessive interest was taken in the supervision and control of lodgers and poor immigrants. Workhouse schemes were slower to be adopted here, however: in 1730–1 a proposal foundered when the political divisions in the town made it impossible for Whigs and Tories, Low and High Churchmen to agree on the composition of the board of management. The building was designed to set the poor to work, mainly at weaving, and to hold up to 140 inmates; but its opponents argued that 'the variety of manufactures carried on in the town, affords a constant supply of work to the Poor of both sexes, of what Age soever', rendering a workhouse unnecessary. This was disingenuous; but despite strictures from other quarters on the alleged idleness and improvidence of Manchester's poor, no workhouse seems to have been provided until 1754, and for long afterwards outdoor relief was granted to the vast majority of paupers, although the scales were alleged to be low. Even so, although the rhetoric of commentators on poverty was becoming harsher in Liverpool and Manchester than elsewhere in Lancashire, and the pressures to economise and control were stronger, the end results were less effectively coercive and socially divisive than might have been expected.[26]

The Manchester workhouse dispute of 1730 – 1 reminds us that the ruling and propertied classes in Manchester particularly, and in Lancashire more generally, remained deeply divided on religious and political issues. Until the mid eighteenth century, and indeed beyond, the dissensions and hatreds between Tories and Whigs, Jacobites and Hanoverians, Roman Catholics, High Anglicans and Protestant Dissenters, mattered more to the upper and middle ranks of Lancashire society than the relationship between propertied and poor, employer and wage-earner: it was both more fraught and more threatening. Indeed, these preoccupations were not solely the preserve of the literate and comfortably-off: they reached down through the social hierarchy to engage the loyalties of tradesmen and labourers as well as merchants and gentlemen. Except where special and temporary circumstances prevailed, the most visible and disruptive fault-lines in Lancashire society during this period were derived from religious and political conflicts which cut across the new divisions of an emergent class society.

Lancashire remained the most Catholic county in England, and Irish immigrants were beginning to join the locals in noticeable quantities by the mid eighteenth century, especially in Manchester.[27] The eager pursuit of recusants on the eve of the Civil War had netted 9000 convictions in 1641: perhaps 12,000 or so if children are included. In 1778, Bishop Porteus's visitation found well over 20,000 Roman Catholics in the county: so their numbers had increased considerably, without keeping pace with population growth in the county as a whole. Throughout the period, Lancashire alone accounted for perhaps a quarter of all the Catholics in England and Wales. Moreover, they remained heavily concentrated into the south and west of the county, and in the Ribble valley, with Preston, Wigan, the Fylde, Prescot and the countryside around Liverpool retaining their established reputations as Catholic strongholds.[28] This persistence owed much to the influence and commitment of Catholic gentry families such as the Blundells and Cliftons: on Magee's calculations (which Bossy

treats with some reverse), 35 per cent of Lancashire landed property was owned by Catholics in about 1715.[29]

Geographical concentration encouraged a measure of social segregation,
which reinforced Protestant suspicions about political loyalties. At gentry level,
Galgano suggests that, 'The high degree of intermarriage [between Catholics
and within the North-West] established a network of Catholic connections which
were particularly strong and made the Catholic families of the north-west practically a society unto themselves'.[30] The sons, and sometimes the daughters, of
Catholic gentry were educated abroad, and Catholic landlords were likely to have
large numbers of Catholic tenants and labourers on their estates, although complete uniformity was rare. But we must not exaggerate this separateness:
Catholics rarely suffered severely under the penal legislation
against recusants, and although they mixed mainly with other Catholic families,
their way of life was not markedly dissimilar to that of their neighbours. The
Walmesleys of Dunkenhalgh, for example, patronised pipers and tumblers, and
went hunting and hawking with other Catholic squires in the 1660s in a manner perpetuated by the Blundells and Tyldesleys in the early eighteenth century;
but this attachment to customary enjoyments was not solely a Catholic preserve,
and the Walmesleys, like the Blundells, were also assiduous followers of London fashions in everything from toys to tobacco. Catholics were rarely prominent in mercantile or other entrepreneurial activity outside agriculture; but the
unfavourable location of their estates was significant here, and Catholic gentry
involvement in coal mining in south-west Lancashire was quite extensive.
Galgano argues that, 'Socially, culturally and intellectually the Catholic community ... was not radically different from its Protestant counterpart.'[31] But
Catholics were distinctive and identifiable enough to be marked out as suspect
and potentially disaffected by their Protestant neighbours, and by more distant
authorities. The bitter legacy of the Civil War was lasting; and we shall see that
on occasion some of the suspicions were amply justified.

At the opposite end of the spectrum, Lancashire also became a stronghold
of Protestant Nonconformity, as defined by refusal to accept the religious and
political orthodoxies prescribed by the Act of Uniformity in 1662. The Puritan
ascendancy had always been a thin veneer in most of Lancashire, and it evaporated almost overnight when the political climate changed at the Restoration; but
congregations of Presbyterians, Independents, Baptists and Quakers became influential, and locally numerous, in parts of the county during the later seventeenth century; and by the early eighteenth century south Lancashire was
second only to Essex in the size of its Dissenting population.[32] Subsequently,
the emergence of the Unitarians and the rise of Methodism added further complexities to the pattern.

Williams calculates that 78 ministers were permanently ejected from their
parishes or chapelries when the Act of Uniformity took effect. Fourteen of them
were based in the Manchester area, and fifteen more in the surrounding textile

district which had also been a centre for Puritan activity and organisation.[33] Organised Dissent cohered around these deprived clergymen, whose numbers were augmented by several recalcitrant Puritans who stayed on, defiant but unmolested, in chapels whose revenues were so slender, or so dependent on the goodwill of conscientious Puritan families, that no conforming minister could be found. Thus John Angier of Denton ignored the Act of Uniformity and yet remained in post until his death in 1677; and elsewhere successive Nonconforming ministers held on to chapels for much longer. In twenty cases, chapels were not returned to the effective possession of the Church of England until various dates between 1678 and 1729; and at Toxteth and Elswick, too, Nonconformists kept control until well into the eighteenth century.[34] The disciplinary and financial resources of the Church of England were still insufficient for it to control events in the outlying chapelries of the Diocese of Chester, even with the support of the coercive machinery of secular law and order, and especially where the leading local property-owners supported Nonconformity or at least protected Nonconforming ministers.

The commitment to Presbyterianism or Independency, the prevailing forms of Protestant Dissent, was strong enough to sustain deprived ministers in some comfort and to keep congregations together through the decades of threatening but arbitrary and only occasionally effective persecution which followed the Act of Uniformity. Ministers were given financial support by their congregations, and molestation from Justices of the Peace was seldom sustained to the point of imprisonment or other legal penalties, although preachers were regularly silenced or forced to go to ground for short periods. At Chowbent, Tockholes, Birch near Manchester, and Greenacres near Oldham, Dissent was patronised and protected by leading local gentry families; and everywhere it evaded the full rigour of the law, meeting in barns and private houses where nothing better was available.[35] But we cannot assess the numerical strength and distribution of Lancashire Nonconformity with any confidence, still less its social structure, until the aftermath of the Toleration Act of 1689, when a more secure environment encouraged chapel building and record keeping.

Our most reliable source seems to be a return of 1715, made to promote a fair distribution of 'the monies collected by the London churches for the benefit of country ministers'. This found 42 congregations of Presbyterians and Independents in Lancashire, with 18,000 'regular hearers'; and Halley reminds us that since 1688 'commodious meeting-houses' had been built in 'almost all the towns and ... many of the larger villages'.[36] Bishop Gastrell's diocesan survey a few years later suggests that numbers were smaller, but it is not always clear whether his returns of Dissenters represent individuals or families, and the figures for important centres such as Bolton and Leigh are clearly too low.[37] If we take Baptists and Quakers into account, Protestant Dissenters were at least as numerous as Catholics in the Lancashire of 1715; but their geographical distribution was very different. The Manchester area had the largest congregations, with perhaps 3000 regular attenders in the town and its immediate area, and over 1000 at Bolton. Dissent prospered elsewhere in the textile district, too, with substantial congregations in the Bury and Rochdale areas, and Gastrell was told that at Todmorden, Ainsworth and Horwich more than half the population were Protestant Nonconformists. Dissent was also strong in Liverpool, with well over 1000 adherents, and the third largest single congregation, also in four figures, was at the nailmaking settlement of Chowbent, which had been so belligerently Parliamentarian in the Civil War. Every sizeable town had its Nonconformists, and village congregations were scattered around the whole county, Furness and the Fylde included; but the main strength of Dissent still lay in Manchester and the textile district.[38] Most of it was still nominally Presbyterian, although it was becoming harder to distinguish Presbyterians from Independents in the absence of a centralised system of church government; and in Lancaster and Furness, where the Puritan tradition was weak, and at Todmorden the Quakers had a firm foothold.[39] But the old Puritan centres of the textile district had become the main bastions of eighteenth-century Nonconformity.

But we should not exaggerate the strength of Nonconformity in this area; and its influence was already waning by the second quarter of the eighteenth century. Quakers were comparatively 'particularly numerous' in parts of Lancashire, and prominent as entrepreneurs in the Furness iron industry and as merchants in Lancaster and elsewhere; but Marshall suggests that even in their Furness stronghold, where the memory of George Fox was most potent, their numbers in the eighteenth century 'can never have exceeded three hundred'. Moreover, their influence on the wider world was reduced by their inward-looking, defensive concentration on internal regulation and mutual assistance, although several held minor public offices in Lancaster despite their refusal to swear the oaths which were nominally essential.[40] Like the Quakers, the more numerous Presbyterians and Independents were probably becoming more narrowly drawn from the middle ranks of merchants, tradesmen and substantial farmers, although these groups had always predominated anyway. Dissenting worship set a premium on literacy and the ability to concentrate on long sermons, while most of the seating in the chapels was appropriated by families who paid pew-rents as their contribution to the minister's stipend and other expenses. The poor were therefore never much in evidence, domestic servants excepted; and during the eighteenth century the Dissenting landed gentry made a gradual and piece-meal return to the Church of England. Indeed, the middle-class backbone of Dissenting support weakened noticeably after 1715. The vicar of Bolton in 1778 noted a widespread transformation: 'The Trade was for many years principally in the hands of the Dissenters, but they are lately much sunk in number, Credit and Fortune.' Nonconformist sources bear this out: Joseph Priestley 'reckoned that in the reigns of the first two Georges the Dissenters had diminished by nearly a third of their original numbers'. Only Manchester, where Bishop Porteus's visitation found 5000 Nonconformists, mostly Presbyterians, in 1778, and Cross Street chapel kept an imposing presence of magistrates and prosperous merchants, was apparently exempt from this trend.[41]

Why this decline? Subsequent Nonconformist commentators have blamed lack of charismatic preaching and evangelical zeal, coupled with increasingly heterodox theology, as many hearers were alienated by the appearance of Unitarians in erstwhile Presbyterian pulpits. There was a cumulative loss through seepage between one generation and the next, and the losses were not made good by new converts. Some returned to the Church of England, others founded new independent congregations of their own.[42] Still others, no doubt, joined the Methodists, whose enthusiastic evangelism made them the only religious grouping to show significant advances in the middle decades of the eighteenth century. The riots which had regularly greeted John Wesley and his allies in Manchester at around mid-century were stilled by 1756, although in Bolton, Rochdale and other towns toleration took rather longer, and at Oldham mobs led by churchwardens and constables still assailed Methodist preachers in the 1770s. But preaching-houses were taking root in the cotton towns, with important outposts at Liverpool and Warrington, from the 1750s. By 1770 the movement was well established, and it was already demonstrating a unique capacity to reach out successfully to the emergent industrial working classes.[43]

Meanwhile, the problems of the Church of England remained unresolved. Large parishes, neglected and inaccessible churches, badly paid and ill-qualified clergy, pluralism and non-residence, all remained intractable, and little was done to bring the Church's resources into step with the growth and changing distribution of population. Between 1660 and 1717 only nine new churches were consecrated in the whole of the Diocese of Chester; and most of the new building thereafter was a belated and inadequate response to the growth of the larger towns, especially Liverpool and Manchester.[44] At Todmorden in Gastrell's time 'the clerk beggs Wooll through ye Chappelry for his maintenance'; and the 1778 visitation found that most Lancashire curates received between £40 and £50 per year, a low enough figure by contemporary standards, while the going rate in Furness was no more than the annual wage of a ploughman or shepherd. At this time about 200 of the clergy in the diocese were non-graduates, and 98 were non-resident.[45] Wesley was full of praise for sermons given by some of the Lancashire clergy, but all the evidence suggests that they were a virtuous, learned or fluent minority.[46]

The Church of England itself came to be divided between warring factions, the High Church and Low Church parties, expressing widely divergent theological and political attitudes: the former closer to the traditions of Archbishop Laud, to the Tories and sometimes to the Jacobites, and usually intolerant towards Dissenters; the latter showing more sympathy with the Puritan tradition and the Whigs. Manchester was riven particularly deeply in the late seventeenth century and for much of the eighteenth. Its collegiate church became a bastion

[95]

of High Church Toryism, although the Wardens of the college after 1718 were staunch Hanoverian Whigs, the Peploes, son succeeding father, whose authority was resented and sometimes resisted by the rest of the clergy. But the new church of St. Ann's, which was consecrated in 1709, provided a different style of worship for a different clientele. Halley expresses the contrast vividly:

Ladies in plaid petticoats, and gentlemen in plaid waistcoats, representing Stuart preferences, frequented the collegiate church except when the warden preached, while other ladies with orange ribands, and other gentlemen with orange handkerchiefs, worshipped in St. Ann's or in the Cross Street meeting-house. In the collegiate church, when the prayer for King George was mumbled over, the people rose from their knees: in St. Ann's that prayer was repeated with emphasis and fervour.[47]

The divisions between Manchester's substantial citizenry, amounting to political polarisation, were uniquely deep and bitter. The balance of power had changed sharply since the Restoration, too, as the Puritans lost their uneasy ascendancy and the initiative passed to keen Royalists who were succeeded by a generation of Tories, strongly tinged with Jacobitism. Here is Halley again, lamenting the early stages of a transition which needs further exploration, and which further emphasises the wide spectrum of attitudes and behaviour which prevailed in the society which was to spawn the first industrial revolution:

[In 1673] a reaction was commencing against puritanism, which proceeded until it produced a complete change in the political and religious character of the town. Manchester, having been ... distinguished ... for its love of puritanism and constitutional liberty, became ... the stronghold of intolerance and arbitrary power ... the austerities, and I fear the good morals, of puritanism had become unwelcome to the new generation ... [who fell] into shameless irreligion, intemperance and profligacy ... despised the virtues which their fathers honoured, and indulged in the vices which their fathers abhorred. In the next generation Manchester became one of the most prelatical and Jacobitical towns in England.[48]

Halley exaggerates the contrast, of course: Royalism had been strong in Manchester during the Civil War, and the town's Puritan tradition was far from disappearing. The number of Dissenters actually increased, as we have seen, but their social and political influence collapsed at the very time when the town's economic development was gathering momentum. Elsewhere in Lancashire the divisions on partisan and religious grounds were less bitter, though we shall see that they could be violent; but everywhere in the county, the propertied élite was deeply riven on religious and political issues. The attention lavished by the Lancashire ruling class on its internecine conflicts suggests that the grievances and organisations of the lower orders were seen to pose little or no serious threat to the social order, despite the rapidity of economic change in parts of the county; and this is borne out by the lack of investment in the Church of England, despite its persisting failure to exert a restraining influence over the manners and morals of the poor. Wesley was scathing about the ignorance and intemperance of many of his Lancashire hearers, in town and country alike, at mid-century. Even Chowbent, with its flourishing Nonconformist congregation, was 'a den of lions' and 'the roughest place in all the neighbourhood': a reminder that even the most successful religious initiatives made a lasting impact only on a minority drawn mainly from the middle and upper ranks.[49] The complaints which surfaced at Bishop Porteus's visitation in 1778 reflected a very long-standing state of affairs, as the clergy tried to explain the large numbers of non-attenders in terms of competition from alehouses or successful attacks from scoffers.[50] Outside the Catholic strongholds of south-west Lancashire and the Fylde, the effective influence of organised religion on the minds of the lower orders was still very limited indeed.

Educational provision increased much more rapidly than the number of churches, clergy or services; and most schooling was provided under religious auspices, especially those of the Church of England. After an apparent hiatus in the later seventeenth century, school endowments and foundations expanded and multiplied apace in the early eighteenth century, as grammar school numbers continued to grow alongside a rapid proliferation of parish schools which aimed at teaching basic literacy and religious dogma to the children of the lower orders. We know of 92 new school foundations based on charitable endowments in Lancashire between 1700 and 1779; and between 1700 and 1750 the number of such schools grew from 67 to 129, widely spread through the county. There clearly was a definite charity school movement in Lancashire, reaching its peak in the 1720s; and this expanded provision had a visible impact on literacy levels, as measured by the unsatisfactory but inescapable method of counting signatures and marks in marriage registers. In Bury, Eccleston (St. Helens), Deane, Kirkham and Preston, five parishes with a wide geographical spread and covering a variety of economic experiences, percentage literacy on this basis reached a peak in the 1750s or 1760s before declining in face of population pressure and economic change; and in Chorley the high point came in the 1770s. The peak figures varied from 59 per cent in Preston to just over 40 per cent in Deane, although in the Blackburn area they seem to have been rather lower; and the percentages mask marked differences between male and female literacy, as in the best decades between 61 and 76 per cent of men signed the registers, while the corresponding figures for women ranged between 15 and 44 per cent. This was a distinct improvement on the mid-seventeenth-century figures, but what it all means in terms of functional literacy must remain an open question. If most people learned reading before writing, as seems likely, the signatories to marriage registers probably express the approximate diffusion of basic competence in reading.[51] We cannot know how far the Church of England succeeded in imparting stabilising notions about religion and the social order along with the transmission of basic skills; and in any case, even in the best decades a substantial proportion of Lancashire's children did not remain in school for long enough to acquire more than the merest rudiments of literacy. Moreover, not all of these skills were acquired in endowed schools or under Church of England control: Mrs Raffald's second Manchester directory in 1773 listed 22 private and commercially run educational establishments in the town, and many back-street dame schools were certainly omitted.[52] The Church of England probably reached a wider public through its schools than through its services, but the extent and nature of its influence on attitudes and values remains at best problematic.

We lack evidence on the literacy levels of different occupational or status groups for Lancashire in this period, but we can safely assume that the main beneficiaries of the educational expansion were the middling ranks of farmers and tradespeople, whose children were more likely to attend school with few interruptions, to continue long enough to go beyond the rudiments, and to be able to indulge in the more expensive and sophisticated curriculum of the endowed grammar or commercial school. The gap may well have been widening not only between the polite society of the gentry, the Preston season, and the Liverpool and Manchester mercantile élites, with its increasingly metropolitan orientation, and a more rustic and provincial mainstream Lancashire society, but also between the lettered middle ranks and the unlettered or semi-literate husbandmen, wage-earners and poor. Some of the remarks on the lifestyles of the lower orders which emerged from large employers and their allies in the later eighteenth century suggest that a yawning cultural divide had opened. In Manchester in 1755 the Revd John Clayton could describe the town's poor as having 'an abject Mind, which entails their Miseries upon them; a mean sordid Spirit, which prevents all attempts at bettering their condition'. They were idle, feckless, drunken, dirty, dissolute and took no thought for the morrow. In 1787 a Bolton magistrate complained of the luxurious habits of the local labourers, as they allegedly demanded tea, ale and 'the finest wheaten bread'. The observance of wakes and 'St. Monday' was also a target for regular complaints. These were indeed 'threadbare commonplaces of eighteenth century thought', as Wadsworth and Mann remark; but they are all the more revealing for that. An increasingly important strand of opinion among the educated and propertied was outspokenly out of sympathy with the preferred lifestyle of many of the poor.[53]

But these attitudes were far from universal; and the critics of social morality did not confine their attacks to the lower orders. Lancashire's rulers were themselves divided, on these issues as on others. In 1733, for example, a diatribe against Manchester Races complained that gentry patronage was encouraging 'Oaths and Blasphemy, Drunkenness and Debauchery, and all kinds of Wickedness' among the poor, and accused the county's social leaders of setting a bad example while neglecting their duty to provide hospitality and charity to their social inferiors.[54] Such conflicts were not new: the Puritan frame of mind had not become extinct, as we have seen, but its advocates faced a difficult struggle in an uncongenial moral climate. Gentry patronage of cock-fighting, bull-baiting, wakes and morris dancing remained widespread until the late eighteenth and early nineteenth centuries, and moral reformers made little headway until the advent of the Evangelical revival. Many of the gentry, and indeed the industrial employers, combined an awareness of metropolitan fashions with an amused tolerance of traditional enjoyments, and in many parts of Lancashire the use of impenetrable dialect and nicknames instead of surnames persisted into the railway age alongside a cocktail of beliefs involving witchcraft, magic and super-natural beings.[55] The worlds of the fashionable gentleman, the newly literate tradesman and the rustic labourer still overlapped to a remarkable extent on the eve of the 'Industrial Revolution', even though they were beginning to move apart; and even the Nonconformist minister was not yet divorced from the society of the alehouse, of billiards, rum and water, and good fellowship.[56] The inconsistencies of individuals are endearingly illustrated by the activities of the Ashton-in-Makerfield shopkeeper Roger Lowe and the Manchester wigmaker Thomas Harrold, both of whom combined earnest attendance at sermons with regular heavy drinking, gaming and repentance. When a successor to the famous Dissenting academy at Warrington was established in Manchester in 1786, one of the reasons for the choice of venue was said to be 'the regularity of [Manchester's] police', and worries were expressed about the Nonconformist students' propensities for frequenting taverns and affecting unduly fashionable attire.[57] Thoroughgoing advocates of the suppression of popular enjoyments and the remodelling of traditional culture were now, and long remained, thin on the ground, and initiatives from above and new influences from without were as yet making little difference to the attitudes and way of life of Lancashire's lower orders.

This emphasis on religious and political divisions, and on a measure of persisting cultural homogeneity, is not intended to suggest that Lancashire society was free from conflicts which pitted employer against employee, propertied against poor, in ways which hinted at the formation of the horizontal solidarities of class. In fact, such conflicts seem to have been erupting with increasing frequency by the middle of the eighteenth century, although this may be partly an optical illusion arising from improvements in the quality and coverage of the sources. But the 1750s saw a spate of industrial disputes in the textile trades of the Manchester area, which revealed the existence of well-established organisations among the journeyman weavers, which collected subscriptions and sought to regulate the supply of labour and conditions of work. They were particularly concerned to protect wage levels by excluding interlopers from other trades, and by controlling apprenticeship; but in 1757–8 the smallware and check weavers showed themselves able and willing to strike in pursuit of higher wages and recognition of their society by the employers. The check weavers' strike was protracted and bitter, and the employers were eventually victorious. The strike leaders were successfully prosecuted, and their organisations were proscribed; but from this point onwards workers' combinations were endemic in the textile industries, organising resistance every time rising prices, falling wages or an influx of unapprenticed labour appeared to threaten the interests of the journeyman weavers. Similar developments were becoming visible in other Lancashire trades at about the same time, in Liverpool as well as Manchester, as tailors, shoemakers, cabinet-makers, sawyers, seamen and others began to combine against their employers in a period of rising prices and sharp fluctuations in the trade cycle.[58]

The activities of these journeymen were too narrow and sectional in their concerns to merit the label 'class-conscious', however; and they were directed against fellow workers who threatened the privileges of the trade or the protective autonomy of the local labour market, almost as much as against the employers. Something resembling class solidarity was exhibited more convincingly by the employers themselves, who took concerted action against embezzlers of yarn and organisers of combinations, sought to push wages downwards and tried to enforce stricter labour discipline on their scattered and recalcitrant workforces.[59] Disturbances of other kinds were also beginning to worry the authorities during the 1750s and 1760s, involving conflict over prices rather than wages, and pitting the purchasers and consumers of food against producers, vendors and speculators. South Lancashire was already dependent on grain shipments from outside in the late seventeenth century, and the area was visibly vulnerable to bad harvests and disrupted supplies by the 1750s. In 1757 a series of riots took place in Manchester, where the coal miners and weavers from the surrounding district tried to enforce 'fair' prices for potatoes and oatmeal, and were met in June by the threat of force from the High Sheriff's hastily organised 'small civilian army' of gentlemen and their allies, armed with muskets, swords and sticks. A further riot in November was put down by the militia with the loss of several lives, and disturbances in Prescot worried the Corporation of Liverpool sufficiently for the citizens to be issued with muskets and bayonets. But these were isolated occurrences, and in the present imperfect state of research what stands out at this stage is the occasional and limited occurrence of food riots in Lancashire as compared with other parts of the country, despite the problems of supply and the fluctuating wages of miners and textile workers.[60]

Much more threatening in the eyes of contemporaries were the activities of the Jacobites; and much more damage to property was done by the mobs which destroyed Dissenting and Catholic chapels as part of the recurrent pattern of religious and political faction-fighting which also helped to inflame election riots. The Jacobites were notoriously able to call on support from Lancashire's Catholic gentry and from some of the powerful and vociferous High Church party in Manchester; and the suspicions of the authorities were manifested in the years immediately after the Revolution of 1688. Rumours and accusations were rife, as Lancashire gentlemen were alleged to be importing Irish soldiers and arms; but when eight prominent Catholics were brought before a Manchester jury in 1694 on the evidence of a professional informer, they were acquitted. The informer's testimony was certainly suspect, but the rights and wrongs of the case are still a matter for conjecture.[61] There was no doubt, however, about the response to the Jacobite invasion of 1715. Catholic gentry and their tenants joined the Pretender's army in substantial numbers at Lancaster and Preston, although the High Church Anglicans who had also identified themselves with 'the King over the water' proved more forward in drinking toasts than in military campaigning. Events proved this to be sensible, if less than heroic; and Catholic gentry were prominent among the victims of the judicial blood-letting which followed the defeat of the rising. Thirty years on, the Catholics were more reticent, and the strongest show of support for the Jacobites came from Manchester, where three hundred volunteers joined the Pretender's Manchester Regiment, although many of them quickly repented their indiscretion. As McLynn comments, 'Of all the urban areas of England, Manchester was the most obvious hotbed of Jacobite feelings.' The reaction against Puritanism had been augmented by an influx of younger sons of Catholic gentry, and the High Church party included the separate congregation led by Dr Deacon, who had refused the oath to the Hanoverian succession. These were particularly eager Jacobites, supplying many recruits to the Pretender's army; and the cause was further helped by Manchester's lack of the restraining powers of a borough corporation, which permitted the unfettered growth of Jacobitism as well as trade and industry.[62]

Manchester was indeed unique, and this was reflected in the nature and extent of the subsequent repression. The Manchester Regiment was 'the only English unit raised for the service of Prince Charles', and so its members were 'pursued with relentless severity regardless of social rank'. Twenty-four were executed, and others were acquitted in spite of determined efforts by the Crown to secure convictions. The scars took a long time to heal, and street disturbances were endemic in the town for several years afterwards.[63] Elsewhere in Lancashire there was little overt support for the Pretender in 1745; and a public subscription in Liverpool confirmed the town's Whiggery by raising enough money to equip a regiment of eight hundred men, although the protection of the town from plunder may have been as strong an initial motive as loyalty to the House of Hanover.[64]

Violent conflict along these religious and political fault-lines was not confined to Manchester, however, nor to the invasions themselves. In June 1715, several months before the arrival of the Jacobite army, mobs destroyed Dissenting meeting-houses over a wide area of south Lancashire, with no effective discouragement from the magistrates. This campaign seems to have been orchestrated by Manchester Jacobites, but it had powerful support elsewhere, especially in Warrington; and this very recent memory no doubt fuelled the martial ardour of James Woods, the Presbyterian minister of Chowbent, who armed his congregation with scythes and pitchforks as well as swords and muskets and led them into battle against the invaders at Preston.[65] In 1746 two Catholic chapels, one in a private house, were destroyed in Liverpool by 'a mob of ship-carpenters, sailors and others', in spite of the reading of the Riot Act.[66]

On occasions such as these, and at the regular election disturbances, popular grievances overlapped with, and were stimulated by, the concerns and attachments of branches of the propertied élite. Such disturbances never got out of hand to the extent of threatening life and property indiscriminately: indeed, the elements of threat and ritual display were probably as significant as the actual violence. Popular disturbances were abnormal, occasional events, and they usually united master and man, landlord and tenant, against rival groups or factions, rather than being the product of nascent class divisions. What stands out, indeed, is the remarkable social stability of a county in which economic change was rapidly gathering momentum: the security of life and property which made it possible to build up a commerce in valuable and readily portable goods, which were manufactured in remote places, without recourse to a formal, professional policing system. The networks of coiners, clippers and counterfeiters which operated in Westmorland in the 1680s and around Halifax in the 1760s certainly extended their tentacles into Lancashire; but these united gentlemen and clothiers with wage-earners against the Crown and the enforcers of its laws, and posed little threat to local social solidarities.[67] Violence might be endemic, but it wa limited and contained; and crime, like riot, constituted no major or persistent threat to the social order and the economic system, although we need to know much more about these matters. Disruptive social polarisations on class lines were just beginning to emerge in the 1750s, but Lancashire on the eve of the 'Industrial Revolution' was a relatively orderly, self-policing society, bucolic and uncultivated though many of its denizens might be. The rapid economic growth which began in earnest in the 1770s and 1780s was aided significantly by these characteristics; and in the next four chapters we shall analyse Lancashire's 'Industrial Revolution' at some length, and explore its social and political implications.

6

THE ACCELERATION OF ECONOMIC GROWTH, 1770 – 1850

In the late eighteenth century, the Lancashire economy moved into a higher gear: to use a metaphor more appropriate to the times, the pace of change altered from a brisk walk to a businesslike trot, and by the early decades of the nineteenth century it was at full gallop, leaving contemporary observers and participants alarmed and exhilarated by turns at the novelty and danger of its headlong progress. The cotton industry was the prime mover in this acceleration; and whatever may be thought of its role in the development of the national economy, whether as leading sector or prominent but over-publicised element in a more balanced process of growth, its significance in Lancashire's changing fortunes was very evident indeed. But even here, we must not over-simplify. The rise of the cotton industry transformed economy and society over an extensive area of south-east and central Lancashire, from Preston and Wigan in the west to the Pennines in the east, spilling over into north-west Derbyshire around Glossop and north-east Cheshire around Stockport. But we shall see that Merseyside's economy developed in very different ways, with contrasting social implications and limited linkages with the cotton district, if we leave aside the increasingly important role of the port of Liverpool. North of the Ribble, too, the direct impact of the cotton industry on a mainly agricultural economy remained very limited, although the indirect implications of proximity to an industrialising area were often highly significant. Even in Lancashire, cotton's position as 'leading sector' in economic development and social change was far from obvious outside its distinctive Manchester-centred heartland. But it was in the cotton industry that the most spectacular and far-reaching changes occurred during the classic 'Industrial Revolution' period between the 1770s and the 1840s; it was cotton, above all, which transformed Lancashire in the eyes of the outside world from provincial backwater to herald of a new economic system and social order; and it is with these themes and in this area that this chapter must begin.

The rise of Lancashire cotton, as a factory-centred industry which generated a distinctive pattern of rapid urban growth and associated social problems, took place in three stages. The last decades of the eighteenth century saw the mechanisation of cotton spinning in water-powered factories, many of which were widely dispersed through remote upland areas in search of an adequate and reliable power source.[1] Domestic spinning disappeared very quickly, but increased yarn output created an enormous demand for hand-loom weavers which gave a further impetus to rural cottage industry. From the 1790s onwards, however, the steam engine began to augment, and then to displace, the water-wheel, while the process of dispersal was sharply reversed, and the cotton industry began to concentrate in urban locations on the coalfield, especially along the canals which provided water for condensing purposes as well as ready access to coal. This transition, which was accompanied by accelerating growth in output, labour force and associated population, was almost complete by 1840, although outlying water-powered factories in favourable locations were able to survive and prosper for many years.[2] It was in the 1790s, too, that Liverpool began to dominate the import – export trade in raw cotton and finished goods, most of which had hitherto travelled through London; and the close, even symbiotic, relationship which developed between the cotton industry and aspects of the Liverpool economy was essentially a product of the early decades of the nineteenth century.[3] Finally, the invention and widespread adoption of a commercially attractive power-loom from the mid-1820s enabled the factory system to spread to weaving, although the transition took much longer than in spinning, and numerous hand-loom weavers still plied their trade, especially in central Lancashire, even in the early 1850s.[4] These were complicated processes, and before we try to explain them and assess their social and political implications, we need to chart their progress at somewhat greater length.

The rising level of retained raw cotton imports continues to provide a useful guide to the extent and timing of the industry's growth, although a declining but not negligible proportion of the imported cotton was used elsewhere in Britain. From 4.2 million pounds in 1772, the total increased to 24.7 million in 1789 and 41.8 million in 1800. This was impressive enough, but in the new century the pace of growth was transformed: 65 million pounds in 1811, 141 in 1821, 249 in 1831 and 452 in 1841.[5] Even when we allow for reductions in wastage and a shift in emphasis towards a higher quality of finished product, the magnitude of this expansion was clearly dramatic; and it was accompanied by important changes in the organisation of production and the location of industry, which had far-reaching social consequences.[6]

As we saw in Chapter 4, the shortage of spinning capacity in the mid eighteenth century encouraged a widespread and assiduous search for effective ways of mechanising the process; and between the late 1760s and the early 1780s a series of successful inventions transformed the productivity of spinning and the preparatory processes. The spinning jenny came first, and rapidly showed a capacity for expansion of output beyond the original handful of spindles: by 1780 machines with 120 spindles were not uncommon. The greatly increased potential for yarn output led to a bottleneck in the supply of cotton prepared for the machine; and innovations in carding and other ancillary activities came thick and fast. This early machinery was inexpensive, and capable of assimilation into the domestic system; but during the 1770s collections of hand-, horse- and water-powered machinery began to accumulate in substantial workshops, taking these operations out of the home. This challenge to existing arrangements was well advanced by 1779, when widespread riots in Lancashire were directed against large establishments using jennies with more than 24 spindles, which were deemed to provide unfair competition for the domestic manufacturers who used family labour and had limited resources.[7]

By this time the water-frame had also made its appearance in Lancashire, and a factory on this principle at Birkacre, near Chorley, fell victim to the rioters on 4 October, two years after it opened. But the widespread adoption of the water-frame was delayed until after the cancellation of Arkwright's patent in 1785. This was a more capital-hungry innovation, although it did not necessarily require the imposing purpose-built premises, earthworks and factory housing of Cromford or Styal. Cheap conversions of corn and other mills were common enough, labour forces could be drawn from the surrounding countryside, and even the newly built water-frame factories were rarely remarkably large: the standard size was three or four storeys, with a rectangular ground plan measuring 70–80 feet by 25–30 feet. Rural sites were not essential either, though often preferred: Manchester in the 1780s could still provide adequate water power for substantial factories on the Arkwright principle. Where it was adopted, the water-frame marked a more decisive break with domestic industry, and imposed the strict labour discipline of a continuous process on a labour force predominantly composed of women and children; but we must not exaggerate its impact, especially as the large isolated country mill with several hundred operatives and associated housing remained conspicuous but exceptional.[8]

The third of the famous trinity of spinning innovations, the mule, had a crucial advantage over its precursors. It was capable of producing the finest yarns, which could be used for muslins and other fashionable fabrics. It began life in the early 1780s as a hand-operated machine which required strength, stamina and skill, and 'remained an integral part of the domestic system' until the 1790s, when the cumulative effects of a series of piecemeal improvements made it possible to harness the mule to water and steam operation, to increase the number of spindles per machine, and to go over to factory production in earnest. It was the steam-powered mule, an almost unrecognisable beast when compared with Crompton's wooden contraption of a few years earlier, which provided the technological basis for the great acceleration of the cotton industry's growth which began towards the turn of the century.[9]

We ought to emphasise the limited extent of the transition to the factory before the early 1790s. Cotton spinning was already a factory industry by this time, although many of the units of production were small and unassuming, especially where the jenny still prevailed. Large units of production were appearing by the 1780s in the finishing processes of bleaching and calico printing, and major technological advances followed in the next decade.[10] But the domestic system still flourished in weaving, and the number of hand-loom weavers was expanding rapidly as the growth of yarn output increased the demand for their labour. Here and there, collections of twenty or more looms were being assembled in workshops, as employers sought to tighten discipline by exercising closer control over the labour process; but this was exceptional.[11] We shall see that the industrial population remained widely scattered through the countryside: Manchester apart, large-scale urbanisation was a thing of the future in the cotton district. The developments of the later eighteenth century laid the necessary groundwork for what followed, but the really spectacular changes began in the 1790s rather than the 1770s.

The number of cotton factories in south-east Lancashire increased very rapidly from the 1780s; but the upward trend was punctuated by periods of over-capacity and retrenchment, and convincing figures are impossible to obtain. Early estimates are highly suspect, and clouded by the difficulty of defining a factory in an industry containing many small accumulations of assorted machinery using converted premises and lacking a continuous power source. Colquohoun's figures for 1787 and 1790 suggest that 143 and 155 water-frame factories were then in operation, but the source does not command universal confidence, and it is not clear how many of these mills were in Lancashire. Samuel Crompton claimed in 1811 that there were more than 650 cotton mills within a 60-mile radius of Bolton; and in 1841 the factory inspector Leonard Horner found 871 spinning firms in Lancashire, 321 of which were also engaged in weaving. By this time there were also 104 firms specialising in power-loom weaving, and Horner also listed 141 woollen, 19 flax, 13 worsted and 28 silk firms. These sets of figures are not strictly comparable, due to variations in source reliability and definition of terms; and they all exclude the finishing processes of bleaching, dyeing and printing.[12] Moreover, they convey a misleading impression of continuous growth: evidence for Manchester suggests that the number of firms in factory spinning more than doubled from 50 in 1795 to 111 at the height of the boom at the Peace of Amiens in 1802, fluctuating downwards thereafter to reach 56 in 1820. But the assessed rateable value of these firms showed a different trend, quadrupling to more than £9000 between 1795 and 1802, and subsequently following a wavering upward path to a total of £14,461 in 1820.[13] The figures for factory numbers nevertheless give a useful indication of orders of magnitude and underlying trends in the growth of the Lancashire cotton industry; but for a fuller understanding of developments, we must try to take account of changes in factory size and productive capacity.

Improvements in productivity within the factory system were associated with two sets of innovations: the transition to steam power and the sustained increases in scale, speed and reliability which were made possible by the continuing development of the mule. Steam made rapid headway from the 1790s, especially in the towns, but it did not triumph overnight. Many of the early engines were small and temperamental, and supplemented water-wheels rather than displacing them: the average output of all the Boulton and Watt engines constructed before 1800 was only 15 horsepower. By 1841, however, nearly two-thirds of Horner's 871 spinning and combined spinning and weaving mills employed more than 20 horsepower, and more than a quarter had over 50, with 21 leading firms topping 200 horsepower. Almost all of this came from steam engines, and the average steam-generated horsepower per firm was as high as 38.7.[14] The balance of power output had probably tilted from water to steam during the 1820s; but water power remained important to many smaller firms for a long time, especially in Rossendale, with its excellent water supplies and relatively expensive coal, but also, for example, in the hills around Bolton. In favoured locations, as at Calder Vale near Garstang, new water-powered factories might still be constructed on remote sites, and thrive, as late as the mid-1830s.[15] In the cotton industry nationally, 21.7 per cent of horsepower was still derived from water-wheels in 1838, and as late as 1850 the figure was 14 per cent. Cotton spinning was far ahead of other manufacturing industries in its adoption of the steam engine, and even in 1870 it accounted for over 30 per cent of the steam power used in British manufacturing industry; but even so it should be emphasised that the transition in cotton was gradual and cumulative rather than sudden and traumatic.[16]

Steam power helped to make possible the great increases in the speed and capacity of the spinning mule in the early nineteenth century. Crompton's first mule operated 48 spindles, but its capacity was soon doubled and then trebled, and by 1795 McConnell and Kennedy in Manchester were making mules with up to 288 spindles. As power became applied to more of the processes, one spinner could be made responsible for a pair of mules, and by the late 1830s mules with up to 1000 spindles were being introduced. The speed of spindle rotation also increased, from 1700 revolutions per minute on Crompton's machine to about 3000 on the latest mules of 1825. A few years later the introduction of the self-acting mule increased productivity still further while reducing the labour and skill inputs required of the mule-spinner. Further innovations continued through the later nineteenth century, and it was many years before the older pattern of mule was ousted from the spinning of the highest qualities of yarn; but the most important changes were well advanced by the 1840s. Expressed in OHP (the number of operative hours required to process 100 lb. of cotton), productivity had improved from the 2000 needed using Crompton's original mule to 300 with the power-assisted mules of 1795 and 135 with the self-acting mules which were appearing in large numbers in the 1830s. It will be clear that the invention of the mule was only the first instalment in a long story; and we shall return to the implications of this pattern of development later in the book.[17]

These innovations were accompanied by, and probably helped to cause, changes in the size of firms and factories, although in this respect as in others they were less sudden and dramatic than has sometimes been assumed. The few giant firms which emerged in the early days of the factory system did not tighten their grip on the industry in the early decades of the nineteenth century, and their numbers showed no significant increase. In 1841 only 25 Lancashire cotton firms had labour forces over a thousand strong, and 85 employed more than 500 each. Most of the biggest firms divided their operations between two or more factory sites. The representative firm employed nearer 100 than 200 people, and small firms remained numerous and fiercely competitive, though their failure rate was high. In Manchester, and perhaps elsewhere, there was a shift towards larger units of production in the middle of the size range, and in Lancashire as a whole 77 per cent of the factory labour force worked for firms employing more than 150 people. Even so, many factory workers clearly experienced working units which might be daunting compared to their previous experience, but whose size was more manageable than expectations based on the predominance of the giant firm might have led one to believe.[18]

Who invested in these cotton mills? How much capital did they need, and where did they get it from? Why did the large firms not swallow up their smaller competitors, as machinery and buildings became more expensive, widening cyclical fluctuations worsened cash-flow problems, and economies of scale appeared to be shifting the terms of trade in favour of the big battalions?

In the first place, few of the large millowners came from humble origins. At the top end of the scale, 'their origins in non-manual and often substantially wealthy backgrounds' have been clearly demonstrated, and many were recruited from the younger branches of established gentry families.[19] This apart, most of the successful entrepreneurs of the late eighteenth century were firmly grounded in established mercantile and putting-out textile businesses, and this pattern persisted among recruits to the upper levels of the industry. Lower down the scale, early factories were often set up in converted corn mills and even private houses, and the initial fixed capital outlay posed few obstacles to men with moderate capital, appropriate contacts and a reputation for competence. Machinery could be rented, bought second-hand or gradually accumulated, factory space could be hired out to other aspiring entrepreneurs until capital could be raised to equip it, and loans could be raised from relatives, neighbours and sleeping partners seeking outlets for their capital, while bank loans steadily became more readily available. Except at the level of the smallest firms, where documentation is thinnest, the early cotton factory masters were drawn almost entirely from the middle and upper ranks of established industrial, commercial and landed society in the emergent cotton district itself.[20] But the small spinning firms remained numerous, and proliferated in every boom, often working on commission for the big establishments. Although they lacked the access to working capital which enabled the larger producers to compete in an ever-widening circle of overseas markets, a freedom which sometimes led them into liquidity crises and bankruptcy, the smaller firms were more flexible in their output and employment commitments, and had no more difficulty than the giants in adopting the latest technical improvements. The scale of production and employment achieved by the largest spinning and integrated spinning/weaving firms was itself limited by cautious credit policies for most of the period on the part of banks and mercantile houses, who were only too aware of the cash-flow problems generated by selling in distant markets, and by the reluctance of the millowners themselves, aware of their vulnerability and the limited convertibility of their assets, to push their fixed capital investment beyond a certain level. Cotton spinning remained a highly volatile industry in which bankruptcy was an ever-present risk at all levels; but despite a high rate of mobility into and out of the industry, the overall distribution of firm sizes stayed surprisingly similar through the turbulent first half of the nineteenth century.[21]

The transition to the factory came much later in weaving. It was retarded not only by the difficulty experienced in creating a cost-effective and reliable power-loom, but also by the ample and elastic supply of labour in hand-loom weaving, whose productivity had been enhanced by technological improvements in the early nineteenth century. The labour supply was augmented by the collapse of apprenticeship restrictions and the ease of learning the rudiments of the trade, while in times of peak demand yarn was exported in increasing quantities to be woven cheaply on the Continent. As hand-loom weavers' piece-rates fell in a glutted labour market from the mid-1820s onwards, exacerbated by the introduction of power-looms in significant numbers, they fell into a vicious spiral of working ever-longer hours at ever-lower wages, thereby compounding the over-supply of labour and increasing the tendency to over-production and cyclical depression.[22] The existence of this reservoir of ever-cheapening labour further delayed the advance of the power-loom, despite the persistent problems of embezzlement of yarn and unreliable deliveries of finished products; and many employers installed only sufficient machinery to cope with normal demand, using hand-loom weavers as a reserve army of labour in good times. The rise and fall of the cotton hand-loom weavers, with their distinctive culture and political outlook, must be seen against this background. Their numbers probably trebled to about 225,000 between 1795 and 1811, when relative prosperity was already being punctuated by severe depressions, and stabilised for a decade from the mid-1820s at about a quarter of a million, though these are at best well-informed guesses, and weaving often supplied only part of a personal or household income. But at its peak hand-loom weaving dominated the economy of an extensive and thickly populated upland district of north-east Lancashire, and was important over a much wider area. Timmins's figures for the percentage of bridegrooms returned as hand-loom weavers, in those Lancashire marriage registers which recorded occupations, show a very interesting distribution, despite the lack of evidence for Preston and several north-east Lancashire parishes. At Newchurch-in-Pendle about 80 per cent of the bridegrooms were weavers, and the rural areas around Blackburn would probably show similar figures if they could be isolated from the more complex economy of the town itself. Even so, Blackburn parish had well over 50 per cent in this category, as did two large parishes south of Preston. Oldham, Rochdale and Bolton hovered around 50 per cent and in a wide area of central and eastern Lancashire between one-third and half of the grooms were hand-loom weavers, but they were already a small minority in Manchester itself, and they quickly dwindled into insignificance west of Wigan and north of the Ribble valley.[23]

These figures come from the years 1813 – 22, which were the high water mark of hand-loom weaving, as it recruited its last full generation of young men; but its decline was protracted. Until the 1820s family incomes remained buoyant at most stages of the trade cycle, and children's contributions compared favourably with factory wages; but as power-looms began to spread in earnest after the 1826 slump, factory work became a more attractive option for weavers' children, whose parents often remained at their looms, kept afloat by the better-paid labour of their offspring. In the 1830s adolescents began to migrate in a swelling flood from weaving villages to industrial towns, and the population of the specialised weaving settlements fell into decline. But domestic weaving remained profitable into the 1840s for the putters-out, with their limited overheads, and some hand-loom weaving settlements in central Lancashire were still recruiting the young in 1851. The 'dual economy' of farming and hand-loom weaving survived strongly in Ribble valley villages like Samlesbury at this time. But the triumph of the power-loom was largely completed over most of Lancashire during the 1830s and 1840s.[24]

Factory weaving provided even more openings for the small entrepreneur than factory spinning. Many of the power-loom pioneers were large integrated spinning and weaving firms in south-east Lancashire and north Cheshire, who had also brought concentrations of hand-loom weavers together on their premises to eliminate embezzlement of yarn and unreliability of delivery; but by 1850 the industry was becoming concentrated into north-east Lancashire, and the average number of employees per firm was less than 100, with many small firms hiring room and power. In 1841, 65 of the 104 specialised power-loom weaving firms in Lancashire employed fewer than 100 people, and 27 of these employed fewer than 50. As in spinning, the weaving-shed was a highly personalised, even socially claustrophobic working environment; but we shall see that it engendered a very different pattern of workplace relationships from those of the spinning factory.[25]

We saw in Chapter 4 that textiles already dominated the employment structure of a wide area of south-east Lancashire in the mid eighteenth century; and

Timmins's figures for hand-loom weaving show that specialisation in cotton could be just as strong in the early nineteenth century. Farnie estimates that the penetration of the cotton industry as employer reached a peak in the heyday of hand-loom weaving, involving nearly 37 per cent of Lancashire's population in 1811 and declining to 18.7 per cent by 1851.[26] By the latter year the dominance of the factory system had identified work in the cotton industry with adolescence and early adulthood for most people: in 1851 nearly 40 per cent of girls aged between 15 and 19 in Lancashire worked in cotton manufacture, and about one in every four boys. This suggests that factory work was almost a universal experience for female teenagers, and very much the norm for males, in the cotton towns themselves. The age participation rate dropped sharply thereafter, as young men who failed to make the grade as mule-spinners sought better-paid jobs in other industries, and women married and started families. The overall percentage of the population over 20 years old working in cotton, including the surviving non-factory sector, ranged in 1851 from 38.3 in Blackburn through 34.7 in Ashton and 29.5 in Preston to 16.5 in Wigan, with its important coal industry, and 16 in Manchester itself, where the cotton industry coexisted with a wide range of commercial and city-centre casual employments. As with hand-loom weaving, the figures for Merseyside and Lancashire north of the Ribble valley were negligible, with the exception of Lancaster itself.[27]

By 1850 the Lancashire cotton industry had reached maturity. We shall explore the social consequences of its remarkable rise in later chapters; but meanwhile a few words of explanation are in order. Why did this exotic industry, with its distant sources of raw material and its increasing dependence on foreign markets, take root and flourish so luxuriantly in this hitherto obscure corner of provincial England? A convincing set of answers must take account of the two phases of the industry's early development. The innovations and expansion of the later eighteenth century helped to ensure the development of a sufficient infrastructure to support accelerated growth on a much larger scale beyond the turn of the century. As we saw in Chapter 4, the social structure, landholding pattern and agricultural system were all conducive to the rise of domestic textiles; but what set Lancashire apart was its specialisation in cotton-using cloths. Cotton's elasticity of supply, especially when the invention of the cotton gin removed a crucial bottleneck in the preparation processes, its flexibility of use, enabling the various grades of cloth to satisfy an almost infinite range of social and geographical markets, and its ready adaptability to machine production, made it the vehicle for stimulating and satisfying a rapid increase in world textile demand; and the Lancashire of the 1770s was uniquely equipped to take advantage. Cotton required expertise in the purchasing, for there were complex and subtle variations in price, quality and characteristics.[28] It required experience in the manufacture, especially for the higher qualities of yarn and cloth; and it also required a wide-ranging and intimate knowledge of world markets if the right goods were to be sent to the right locations. The emergent

Lancashire textile district, with its merchants, manufacturers and labour force already accustomed to the peculiarities of cotton, and its established links with the London merchant houses, had a long start over its potential competitors. As machinery became more sophisticated, the proximity of watchmaking and related precision engineering industries in the Prescot area, not far away, was a further bonus; and it is significant that Hargreaves and Arkwright, the most famous of the early inventors, tried to bring their innovations to fruition outside Lancashire only to find that the county's gravitational pull was strong enough to ensure their full development within its boundaries.[29] Lancashire had generated capital, expertise and skills in sufficient quantities to enable it to build on its other advantages and outdistance all of its competitors in the race to capitalise on the peculiar opportunities afforded by the cotton manufacture.

The new century brought new advantages into play. The local coal supply was abundant, and transport improvements made it more readily available for the new steam engines, as well as assuring new urban dwellers of adequate supplies of food, domestic fuel and building materials after the dangerous food shortages of 1795 – 6 and 1798 – 1800. By that time the cotton district was already attracting investment in a dense network of turnpike roads and canals, in which capital from the cotton interest supported investments by landowners and coal-owners. This linked up with a western transport system constructed for coal-owners and Liverpool merchants, and enabled Liverpool, with its variety of existing trading connections, to take over cotton exports and imports from London. The balance here tipped irrevocably at the turn of the century, as the main source of cotton supply shifted to the United States.[30] The expertise of Liverpool merchants, who also grew in importance as providers of working capital, became a vital asset to an industry which depended increasingly on exports to distant markets for sustained expansion, and whose credit had always depended on knowledgeable support. The railways after 1830 consolidated these locational advantages for south-east Lancashire, which were reinforced by the high birth-rate, abundant labour supply and growing reservoir of relevant skills and disciplines, while Manchester's role as the commercial hub of the cotton industry began to generate additional external economies. But although the cotton industry gained by, and even depended on these developments for its accelerating growth, it did not bring them about purely by its own efforts and influence. We must now look more closely at the other key sectors of the Lancashire economy, and examine the extent and nature of the relationship between them and the cotton industry.

The trade of the port of Liverpool grew very rapidly indeed while the cotton industry was transforming the economy of south-east Lancashire. The figures assembled by Edwin Butterworth in 1841 offer some telling indices: the number of ships trading at Liverpool grew from 1704 in 1767 to 15,998 in 1840; the customs duties collected in 1839 stood at over £4,000,000 compared with £85,000 in 1770; and the dock duties rose over a similar period from £4142 to £197,477.[31]

Between 1801 and 1855, according to another source, the tonnage of shipping entering Liverpool docks increased from 450,000 to well over four million.[32] Cotton played an increasingly important part in all this after the turn of the century. Between 1785 and 1810 cotton imports grew twentyfold to 40,000 tons, and over the next forty years this substantial base figure was multiplied by nine.[33] By this time Liverpool's status as Britain's busiest port outside London owed a great deal to the cotton trade. Raw cotton became the port's largest single import during the 1820s, when it also began to take the lion's share of the export trades in yarn and finished goods. Between 1820 and 1850 Liverpool 'never handled less than 80% of the UK's imports' of raw cotton, while in 1857 cotton goods accounted for 42 per cent of the value of the port's export trade.[34]

But we must not over-simplify the relationship between the 'Industrial Revolution' in cotton and the apotheosis of the port of Liverpool. Cotton played a very limited role in the vital formative years of Liverpool's development in the later eighteenth century, when the main impetus to growth came from other sources; and it was this phase of development which enabled the cotton towns to call upon the services of a well-established port, with its extensive docks and mercantile expertise, after 1800. Before the turn of the century, Liverpool's prosperity remained firmly grounded in its established staples of salt, sugar, rum, tobacco and coal, though these were woven into an increasingly complicated pattern of diversified and proliferating trades. The slave trade also continued its upward trend, especially when the increasing capacity of ships is taken into account. Sailings to West Africa were cut severely during the War of American Independence and at the start of the French wars in 1793, but growth was accelerating rapidly towards the turn of the century as planters stocked up in anticipation of abolition.[35] As Klein and Engerman remark, however, 'Though Liverpool's contribution was of outstanding importance for the slave trade, the slave trade was considerably less important for Liverpool.' In 1785–7 ships to Africa accounted for 'less than 10 per cent of the outbound tonnage from Liverpool', and this proportion must have declined thereafter as growth in other sectors outpaced the slave trade.[36]

In any case, Liverpool's problems of adjustment after abolition in 1807 were short-lived and far from severe: growth continued with scarcely a hiccup, and in 1814 a petition against the reintroduction of the slave trade at the end of the French wars attracted tens of thousands of signatures and little or no dissent.[37] This underlines the diversity of the ingredients for Liverpool's growth in the late eighteenth century, and drives home the point that the great expansion of fixed capital investment in dock and harbour work, and of mercantile capital and financial expertise, was only marginally influenced at this stage either by cotton or the slave trade.

Cotton took a leading role in Liverpool's economy just as the slave trade was leaving the stage, although these events were not causally connected in any direct or straightforward way. In any case, trading patterns were changing more generally at this time, and the growth of the port was fuelled by the rise of several other major commodities in addition to cotton. Sugar and rum imports showed very limited growth between 1810 and 1850, and tobacco actually declined; while the continuing expansion of the salt and coal export trades was eclipsed by newer developments. Wheat and flour imports rose spectacularly, and hardware, woollens and other textile goods took a prominent place among the exports alongside cotton yarn and cloth, while new markets were exploited in South America, India and China as trading restrictions and monopolies were abolished.[38] Cotton became the single most important influence on Liverpool's growth in these years, but it was supported by less spectacular advances and consolidations in a wide range of import and export trades.

As its overseas trade – and indeed its coastal shipping – expanded, the role of manufacturing industry in Liverpool's economy became less conspicuous. Dock building programmes were major employers of capital and labour: between 1796 and 1841 the dock acreage increased from 28 to 111. Of the fourteen docks operating at the latter date, Prince's alone had cost £650,000 to build, and Butterworth informs us with relish that the total frontage extended to 2 miles 820 yards. The monumental architectural styles favoured by successive dock engineers made this achievement all the more impressive in the eyes of contemporaries.[39] But manufacturing industry failed to fulfil the promise of the late eighteenth century. Liverpool had twenty potteries by 1760, and other industries which took root in the town included iron foundries, soapboiling, watchmaking, glass, copper and salt works, as well as import processing activities such as sugar baking and snuff manufacture. Shipbuilding was also expanding in these years, and attempts were made to start a cotton manufacture. We must not exaggerate the extent of these developments: Aikin in 1795 commented that 'Liverpool is less of a manufacturing town than Bristol, nor does it supply so many articles for the use of the West India islands'.[40] In any case, the rise of the manufacturing and processing sectors was not sustained. Shipbuilding fell foul of competition from Canada and the United States, with their superior timber supplies. Its output fluctuated wildly in the early nineteenth century, although in 1835 Liverpool was still capable of producing over 5 per cent of the United Kingdom's output of ships. By this time, too, Lairds of Birkenhead were starting to make iron steamships, and laying the foundations for a major new industry.[41] Watchmaking and the manufacture of iron chain cables continued to flourish, but most of the other manufactures languished or stagnated. The soapboilers did well in the early nineteenth century, and in 1822 James Muspratt's soda works brought the heavy chemical industry into Liverpool. But Muspratt's operations emitted noxious hydrochloric acid gas, and complaints from residents and pressure from the Corporation soon led him to move inland. In the early 1830s the soapboilers followed him along the Mersey to sites closer to their fuel and raw materials.[42]

The increasingly commercial rather than industrial bases of Liverpool's economy were expressed in its social structure. Dockers, transport workers and seamen dominated its occupations, and the building industry was the most important manufacturing sector. Otherwise, there were relatively few skilled workers, and factory operatives were conspicuous by their absence. Regular employment for women and children was in very short supply. Few individuals employed numerous workforces on a regular, long-term basis: this was an economy dominated by causal labour and fluidity of employment. As we shall see, Liverpool offered a marked contrast to the cotton towns in these respects as in others.[43]

Liverpool's influence on the Lancashire cotton industry grew in importance during the first half of the nineteenth century. It was never a significant provider of fixed capital for mills and machinery: this was generated within the cotton district itself, and the factory spinning and weaving processes were too risky and too unfamiliar to attract mercantile capital which had plenty of other outlets. In 1815 the Liverpool cotton merchant Alexander Brown was firm in dissuading his son from putting any of the partnership's money into cotton spinning:

However profitable the business may be now, *we know of none subject to more reverses* than the cotton spinning trade ... your capital, credit and resources would be called into action for the use of that establishment whenever it would be required; and when once it is known or suspected that you are in any way interested in such an establishment, it would do injury to the credit of our House.[44]

In themselves, such obviously widespread and firmly held perceptions would go far to refute the suggestion that the profits of the slave trade, limited as they were even in its heyday at around the turn of the century, could have supplied the necessary investment basis for the 'Industrial Revolution' in cotton.[45] But the access to markets, expertise and credit provided by the proximity of Liverpool was increasingly valuable to the cotton industry in the nineteenth century, as Liverpool's exports surpassed London's from the 1820s, while its economies of scale and cheap freight rates made it 'the universal depot for all the cotton crops of the world ... [it] made available to spinners a wider range of choice than that possessed by lands confined to the use of home-grown cotton'.[46]

The rise of Liverpool, which had owed little to the cotton industry until it had reached a prosperous and well-equipped maturity, thus brought the world's resources and markets almost to the doorstep of south-east Lancashire just as its drive to predominance reached a climax. The distance was shortened still further by continuing transport improvements. The continuing expansion of the canal network provided further alternative routes and increasing carrying capacity between Liverpool and the Manchester area, and more of the growing industrial towns were put into direct touch with supplies and markets by water-ways. Several new routes opened at around the turn of the century, and in 1804 the first trans-Pennine canal linked Manchester with Rochdale and the West Riding. In 1816 the Leeds and Liverpool canal, with its northerly route through

Blackburn and Burnley, was at last opened throughout, and in 1821 a branch from it met the Bridgewater canal at Leigh, opening out a third waterway between Manchester and Liverpool.[47]

The initiative and investment for the new canals came almost entirely from local landowners, especially coalowners, and from employers in the textile industries. Their traffic tonnages were dominated by coal, grain and building materials, although textile goods were always important to their finances, and the continuing expansion and intensification of the network removed constraints which would otherwise have limited the scale of the region's population and industrial growth. The Rochdale canal, in particular, reduced the cotton district's dependence on Liverpool by bringing corn westwards from the Gainsborough and Lincoln areas, as well as opening out a through route from Hull. Canals could provide a powerful short-term stimulus to local economies: it is no coincidence that the rate of population growth in Blackburn, Burnley and Colne accelerated rapidly after the opening and completion of the Leeds and Liverpool canal through the district. But even in their heyday, in the 1820s and 1830s, Lancashire's waterways never held sway unchallenged. Road transport was itself innovative and competitive, and its flexibility ensured that it continued to offer more than just feeder services to canal basins. In 1833, 120,000 of the 584,950 tons of coal consumed in Liverpool came by road from the Prescot area; and even more impressively, 316,258 of Manchester's coal supply of 913,991 tons in 1836 came in by road. Cotton goods were even more likely to use road transport, and the millowners along the proposed Rochdale canal route in 1792 were more worried about the prospect of interference with their water supplies than about any problems with their existing transport arrangements.[48]

The impact of the railways, though eventually considerable, was also less immediate and overwhelming than some of the literature might lead one to expect. As is well known, steam-operated public railways came early to Lancashire. The pioneer line was the Bolton and Leigh, which opened in 1828 and was soon able to link up with its famous neighbour, the Liverpool and Manchester, which began operations in 1830 with a fanfare of publicity which has never really died away. After a short pause, the Lancashire network developed apace, accelerating rapidly during the 1840s. By 1850 it was almost complete in outline, as the West Coast main line between London, Birmingham and Scotland passed through Warrington, Wigan, Preston and Lancaster, while the first of the trans-Pennine lines were open, and all the major cotton towns were connected to the system. Even the infant seaside resorts of Southport, Lytham, Blackpool and Morecambe already had their branch lines.[49]

The initial stimulus and financial support for the Bolton and Leigh came mainly from local industrial interests, especially coalowners; and these sources of investment remained important for most subsequent Lancashire railways. In sharp contrast with most of the canals, however, Liverpool investment soon came to dominate Lancashire's railway capital market. The Liverpool and

Manchester line itself was 'pressed from Liverpool for the supply of the inland market with foodstuffs and raw materials, rather than from Manchester for the export of Manchester goods less in bulk and greater in value'.[50] Manchester opinion was at best lukewarm about the whole idea, and in 1829 only 2 per cent of the shares were held in Manchester, compared with over half in Liverpool. Almost all of the Lancashire railway promotions of the 1830s and 1840s derived at least two-thirds of their capital from sources within the county, and Liverpool investors were invariably prominent alongside local industrialists, while landed society as such was of minor importance. After the early success of the Liverpool and Manchester, indeed, Liverpool's role in railway finance extended far beyond the confines of the county, including important schemes as far away as Scotland and East Anglia.[51]

Farnie has neatly summarised the commercial impact of the spread of the railway network. The Liverpool and Manchester line

decisively centralized the raw cotton market in Liverpool ... separated it physically from the market for manufactured cotton in Manchester, and ... made possible the weekly visit by Lancashire spinners to buy cotton in a market where they enjoyed the widest possible range of choice, the services of highly skilled brokers, and the facilities for rapid shipment to the mill ...

In the cotton district the railways accentuated the commercial and cultural predominance of Manchester, reduced overheads by cutting transit times and providing warehouse space, increased carrying capacity and opened out additional resources in minerals and food supplies.[52] We shall see that they also offered important new opportunities in the development of popular enjoyment and mass entertainment. But this does not mean that they revolutionised the transport system at a stroke. The canals competed successfully for most kinds of traffic, and retained their prosperity well into the early railway age. Important waterways like the Bridgewater and Leeds and Liverpool canals carried increasing tonnages into the 1840s, and for a time the Bridgewater and Lancaster canals even attracted a growing share of the passenger traffic. Competition between canals and railways was mitigated by compromise, rate adjustment and even pooling arrangements, and it was not until mid-century that a fast-maturing railway network really began to undermine the prosperity of the larger concerns. The Leeds and Liverpool's dividend rose from 20 per cent in 1831 to a sustained peak of 34 per cent in the mid-1840s, and a rapid decline did not set in until 1848. Shortly afterwards the railways at last captured the majority share of the Liverpool – Manchester traffic, and the decline of the waterways began in earnest. But it was still to be a protracted process, and the persisting importance of road transport, especially for cotton goods in the Manchester area, should also be borne in mind.[53]

Liverpool investment in the improvement of Lancashire's transport systems was patchy outside the port itself and its immediate hinterland; but industrial growth in a wide area of south-west and south central Lancashire owed much to Liverpool entrepreneurs. The continuing development of the coalfield and its industries attracted increasing involvement from Liverpool mercantile capital, operating alongside the landed estates and yeoman coalmasters. As coal output in south-west Lancashire grew from about 221,000 tons in 1773 to 680,000 tons in 1799, Liverpool merchants dominated the mining syndicates which stepped in to provide the capital which most of the gentry were unwilling to risk and the lesser local entrepreneurs were unable to raise. This trend was especially apparent in the establishment of new long-life pits along the Leeds and Liverpool canal, west of Wigan, where Bradford investment was also important, and along the Sankey Navigation in the St. Helens area. This district supplied the Cheshire saltworks, which were themselves being taken over by Liverpool capitalists in the late eighteenth century; and Liverpool investment in the mines, after a period in which small independent adventurers held sway, formed part of a wider search for control over the output and raw materials of lucrative export commodities. By 1799 only six collieries in south-west Lancashire were still run by gentry families, and the smaller local proprietors proved unwilling or unable to make the transition to a larger scale of operations. This was, after all, a high-risk business, as frequent bankruptcies showed, and extensive capital reserves were needed to ride out depressions and geological problems. Moreover, the rate of profit was falling in the later eighteenth century. But this did not deter investment on the same pattern, which expanded even more rapidly during the first half of the nineteenth century, as overall output and colliery sizes grew impressively. A handful of the largest collieries each produced between 35,000 and perhaps 60,000 tons per year, and employed up to a hundred people, at the end of the eighteenth century.[54] Fifty years later, the *average* colliery output for Lancashire as a whole was over 27,000 tons per year, and the south-western figure was certainly substantially higher. The most extensive collieries might employ over 400 men. The giants of 1799 would have been representative establishments half a century later.[55] At the local level, growth could be explosive in the short run, especially after 1830. Liverpool's pioneering role in the growth of seagoing steam navigation, and the simultaneous emergence of export opportunities in the Irish market, helped to boost the output of the St. Helens coalfield from 400,000 tons in 1830 to between 800,000 and a million tons in 1846.[56] Given the obvious strength of the stimuli to growth further east, it is not surprising that Pollard finds Lancashire's coal output growth to be the fastest in Great Britain over the century after 1750. South-west Lancashire accounted for nearly half the county's production in the early 1800s, when the average annual figure is computed at 1.4 million tons. In 1854 the official returns give a total of more than 9.8 million. By this time Lancashire and Cheshire contributed 15.3 per cent of the nation's coal, compared with 10.1 per cent in 1801–10 and 5.1 per cent in 1771–80. Liverpool markets, capital and entrepreneurial drive fuelled much of this spectacular expansion, directly and indirectly; but we must remember that growth east of Wigan, under the different auspices of a Manchester-centred economy, was just as dramatic, if less well-documented.[57]

An increasing proportion of the expanding coal output of south-western and south central Lancashire was being consumed by local industries. The triangle bounded by Wigan, Prescot and Warrington was already well stocked with furnaces and coal-using workshops by the early 1770s, but the scale and pace of subsequent growth was altogether novel, as new kinds of activity emerged alongside the old, and outside capital was attracted by the opportunities afforded by natural resources, transport systems and access to markets. Within the triangle, the main focus of activity shifted southwards, as Wigan's non-ferrous metal industries continued their decline, while the really spectacular growth took place in and around the congeries of industrial villages which coalesced towards the mid nineteenth century to form the town of St. Helens. Here the rise of the copper, glass and chemical industries called into existence a complex of smelting plants and furnaces which had few parallels elsewhere in the Britain of the 1840s.

The later eighteenth century saw the development of ironworks at several points on the coalfield, especially near the canals. The established trades of watchmaking and the manufacture of nails and precision tools continued to expand their output, especially in the Prescot area, where a putting-out system was becoming more tightly organised, while at the turn of the century Peter Stubs in Warrington was beginning to centralise the production of his famous files under one roof in a substantial workshop, although here, too, domestic outwork long continued to predominate.[58] But the major innovations came in copper, chemicals and glass. Copper smelting came and went in south-west Lancashire according to the state of supplies and markets. It had been introduced to Warrington in 1717, and expanded after mid-century in response to a growing demand for bangles and other items for the African slave trade, which encouraged a Macclesfield firm to set up a Liverpool smelting works in 1767, refining copper ore from recently discovered mines in Anglesey. The Sankey Canal enabled copper smelting to migrate to the St. Helens coalfield during the 1770s, as ore could be brought direct from Anglesey and the refined copper shipped out to manufacturing plants in Flintshire or to Liverpool for export. The industry was an important formative influence on the growth of St. Helens, although it had passed its peak by the early nineteenth century and the works were closed in 1815, as their owners decided to concentrate production in South Wales when the output of the Anglesey mines declined. In 1830, however, the availability of imported copper ore through Liverpool brought copper smelting back to St. Helens, attracting investment from London as well as from Liverpool merchants connected with the carrying trade.[59]

Glass and chemicals were more important in the long run. Glass became a speciality of St. Helens, and eventually dominated the town's economy. In 1773 a London company was incorporated with an initial capital of £40,000, a vast sum for the time, to manufacture plate glass, a luxury product which was used especially for ostentatious mirrors in fashionable houses. Its factory was established on the St. Helens coalfield at Ravenhead, using coal from mines belonging to one of the promoters, a well-connected London-based Scot called John Mackay, and taking advantage of the Sankey Canal. Production began in 1776; and this novel and expensive undertaking, which captured the imagination of contemporaries, overcame early managerial problems to prosper spectacularly at the turn of the century and afterwards. Smaller glassworks also made use of the local raw materials and transport advantages, and flint, bottle and window glass were all manufactured in the area by the end of the eighteenth century. In 1826 the second major enterprise was launched, as the surgeon, distiller and landowner William Pilkington and his brother-in-law Peter Greenall, the leading local brewer, joined forces with other local businessmen to form the window-glass manufacturing firm which eventually became Pilkington Brothers. Here, too, there were early managerial and financial difficulties; but the sustained rise in demand for window glass, especially in Lancashire itself, the convenient collapse of rivals both locally and on Tyneside, the original home of the industry, and the firm's crucial willingness to embrace the new technology of sheet glass manufacture, all ensured rapid growth and the attainment of financial security during the potentially difficult 1840s.[60]

The alkali industry came to Merseyside in response to the changing needs of the soap manufacturers. Soap output on Merseyside expanded rapidly in the early nineteenth century because of the ready availability of coal and imported raw materials, including tallow, kelp ashes and vegetable oils, including palm oil and pine resin. Population growth in the North-West ensured a buoyant local demand for hard domestic soap, especially as consumption per head doubled nationally between 1801 and 1851; and the textile industries generated a subsidiary but very important demand for soft soap, which was used in the finishing processes. Where Merseyside's hard soap manufacturers used Scottish kelp, their London rivals imported barilla, the ashes of plants of the goosefoot family, from the Mediterranean; and when the excise duties on kelp and barilla were adjusted in favour of the latter in 1822, the Merseyside soapboilers were induced to look elsewhere for their alkali. They turned to an alternative technology, the use of soda ash derived from common salt by the Leblanc process, which used one of Merseyside's most abundant raw materials. Hence the arrival of James Muspratt in Liverpool from Dublin; and when the seaport's suburbs became inhospitable, he transferred his business to St. Helens, where the glass industry provided additional markets for his products. Muspratt himself soon moved again, a few miles along the Sankey Canal; and he was joined in the area by several other soda manufacturers, with a variety of local and distant origins, who collectively provided a firm basis for the industry in the area during the 1830s. Meanwhile, the soap firms themselves were becoming established in Runcorn and Warrington, and some were setting up their own alkali works, foreshadowing the future development of Widnes as the main centre of the Merseyside heavy chemical industry in the railway age. Warrington itself remained a 'town of many trades', with the soap industry developing alongside wiredrawing, watch-making, toolmaking, brewing, tanning and several other activities; and Runcorn was a canal port with shipbuilding and even, for most of the period, health resort functions. But growth was concentrated disproportionately into the St. Helens area, with its alluring combination of raw materials and transport facilities.[61]

The nature of south-west Lancashire's industrial economy, as it developed between the 1770s and the 1840s, thus contrasted sharply with that of the cotton district. There were one or two outposts of the textile industries: the odd short-lived cotton mill, silk around Southport and Ormskirk, linen and sailcloth around Warrington; but increasingly coal and heavy industry predominated. Manchester and the cotton district exercised little direct influence in this area, apart from helping to boost the regional demand for window glass and hard soap, and providing a more specialised market for soft soap. Liverpool was the hub of the south-west Lancashire economy, with its port providing essential raw materials and access to markets, and its merchants investing eagerly in coal, salt and inland transport, although they were less in evidence as promoters of the new heavy industries of the St. Helens coalfield. This was an economy which offered plenty of heavy work for men with youth, strength and endurance on their side; but little of it was skilled, and even the élite of craftsmen among the glassmakers were insecure in time of depression. Arduous, dangerous work prevailed, with little scope for women and children to contribute to family economies, although mines and even glassworks offered some openings of this kind for most of the period. The gulf between capital and labour was wider, and the opportunities for personal advancement were more limited than in the cotton industry. The upper working and lower middle strata were more thinly populated than further east. The 'Industrial Revolution' in south Lancashire gave rise to two contrasting kinds of economy and society, east and west of Wigan, with surprisingly little mutual contact or common experience.

Despite the growth of mining, manufacturing and commerce in Lancashire, agriculture remained important to the county's economy, especially north of the Ribble. In 1851 it accounted for 10.7 per cent of Lancashire's adult males, and the figure for the rural districts of the county was obviously much higher than this. More impressive still is the evidence that at this time 29.6 adult males per square mile in Lancashire worked in agriculture, compared with 22 for England and Wales as a whole; and over 1200 square miles of industrial south Lancashire and north Cheshire the average was 38.3 per square mile, considerably more than the highest figure for any English county.[62] The persisting predominance of small farmers helps to explain these remarkable figures, though a tendency to engrossment was appearing on some of the larger estates by the 1830s. But in 1851 three-quarters of Lancashire's farms occupied fewer than 50 acres each. Owner-occupiers were still relatively numerous, despite an accelerated decline after 1815, and extensive landed estates were in short supply away from the western and south-western plains and the Ribble valley. Much of the labour was provided by the farmers and their families, although in 1851 agricultural day-labourers and living-in farm servants averaged more than two per farm. But major changes were beginning in the late eighteenth century, and accelerating by the 1830s and 1840s, especially close to canals and population centres and on the larger landed estates. South-west Lancashire saw the most impressive early improvements, as Liverpool merchants joined established landowners in draining mossland for cultivation during the French wars, and the use of town and industrial manures, and later imported guano, encouraged new crops and more intensive arable production. On the eastern uplands, meanwhile, the growth of urban markets intensified the specialisation of small farmers in milk and butter production, and the already limited grain acreages declined still further. Elsewhere in the county a change of emphasis occurred within the prevailing pattern of mixed farming, with more attention being paid to cattle and fodder crops, while wheat-growing declined after the artificial demand conditions of the early nineteenth century, when wartime trade disruption brought high prices and encouraged the cultivation of grain crops in improbable places. By the 1790s, if not before, Lancashire was quite unable to feed its own population even in good years, and depended heavily on imports through Liverpool and on the produce of neighbouring agricultural counties, especially Cheshire. Some contemporaries blamed the unwillingness of farmers to adopt, and landowners to impose, the orthodox Norfolk system of improved husbandry; but others were aware that it was unsuited to the prevailing climate, soil types and demand conditions. The enclosure movement in Lancashire, moreover, was confined to upland commons and wastes and lowland mosses, and drainage was the panacea, especially on the clays which predominated over most of the county. But it was not until the 1830s and especially the 1840s, with the emergence of a consensus about technology and methods, and the availability of cheap government loans after 1846, that the major landed estates really began to make headway in this respect. Moss improvement accelerated at this time, too, alongside farm engrossment and the widespread adoption of leases prescribing improved farming methods. Even so, agriculture remained labour-intensive, farming units small-scale and the acceptance of innovation patchy over most of Lancashire in 1850, although competition for labour ensured that wage-rates were consistently higher than in the South and Midlands. There was little serious rural poverty, but there was little farming prosperity either. The agricultural system was kept in uneasy equilibrium by the availability of urban and industrial employment, which creamed off potential labour surpluses and reduced competition for holdings through migration, while generating demand for the dairy produce of the small family farms which still dominated the rural economy over most of the county.[63]

Lancashire north of the Ribble was not unaffected by developments further south. Convenient sites attracted water-powered cotton mills in the late eighteenth and early nineteenth centuries, and there were outposts of the silk and worsted industries at Galgate and Dolphinholme; but these factory villages were already declining by the 1830s and 1840s, with few exceptions, as the pull of the coalfield grew stronger. The growth of mining and quarrying in the later eighteenth century was not sustained subsequently, although the iron industry was to be revitalised in Furness in the 1840s and afterwards. The port of Lancaster, whose West India merchants had invested some of their trading profits in the textile industries of the surrounding area, lending some credence to a localised and miniature version of the Williams thesis about the influence of the slave trade on economic development, failed to sustain its prosperity in the nine-teenth century despite its new canal and the opening of an estuarine outport at Glasson Dock. It fell victim to silting and the increasing optimum size of ocean-going ships, and Liverpool took over its long-distance trade. By the 1830s, if not before, south Lancashire, instead of acting as a positive stimulus to economic growth and social change north of the Ribble, had become a successful competitor for its fruits, enticing the natural increase of the countryside southwards in the process.[64]

Population growth and urbanisation matched the pattern of economic development. By 1851 the county's population was over two million, having nearly trebled over the past fifty years; and this unprecedented growth was particularly marked in the cotton district. Over an extensive area of southern and eastern Lancashire and north-east Cheshire, which was already densely populated in 1801, the population trebled. In south-west Lancashire, including Liverpool, it more than quadrupled, but from a much lower base figure. The rural north saw a much more modest increase of 55 per cent, on Danson and Welton's definition.[65] Over the same period, the population of England and Wales doubled. Urbanisation on the grand scale began in earnest at the turn of the century, and gathered momentum to reach a spectacular peak during the 1820s. Between 1801 and 1851 Manchester more than quadrupled its population to over 300,000, while in 1851 four other towns in the cotton district (including Salford) counted more than 50,000 inhabitants, and five more (including Wigan) topped 20,000. Liverpool's growth easily outstripped Manchester if development in West Derby is taken into account, although the towns of its immediate hinter-land were much less numerous and prolific. On Danson and Welton's contem-porary definition of a town (2000 or more people per 180 acres) nearly two-thirds of the inhabitants of the cotton district lived in its thirty towns by mid-century.[66] This was urbanisation on an altogether novel scale and pattern, although it was to be dwarfed by subsequent developments; and although the towns outside Manchester and Liverpool were tightly packed and therefore compact, facilitating social contacts and encouraging the development of neighbourhood and work-place solidarities, the impact of these changes in the scale of living on attitudes, ways of life and social relationships will bear extended examination. These themes will be taken up in later chapters. Meanwhile, we need to consider the mechanisms which enabled this extraordinary population growth and redistri-bution to occur. What stands out above all is the great and sustained increase in birth-rates and fertility ratios, which reached a peak in the 1810s and 1820s, more than counterbalancing the county's very high death-rates. Even in the depressed years of 1837 – 41 the Lancashire birth-rate was the highest in England. Migration, on the other hand, was of limited importance: the towns recruited mainly from their surrounding countryside, although Liverpool and Manchester had much wider catchment areas, and the Irish were making a serious impact here, and in Wigan and Preston, by 1851. Otherwise, migration from beyond the county and its immediate surroundings was disproportionately the preserve of such skilled and specialised minorities as the St. Helens glassblowers and the Furness ironworkers. Lancashire supplied most of its own population increase, and Fleischmann sums up the nature of the process effectively. His comment is directed at the 1830s but holds good for most or even all of the period: 'Lancashire had higher birth, death and marriage rates, shorter life expectancy and a younger population than any other county in the nation'.[67] The opportunities for early marriage and employment far outweighed the problems of bad health and high mortality which were engendered by the concomitant changes in working and living conditions.

We shall explore the social and political consequences of these major economic and demographic changes in the next three chapters. Meanwhile, we should remember that the twin transitions to the factory and the town took place over several generations, and that it was rare for individuals to make both transitions at the same time. Much industry was rural, especially in the early stages, and most urban work, especially for adult males, was outside the factory. Moreover, many of the key changes we associate with the 'Industrial Revolution' were still not far advanced by the mid nineteenth century. Important changes had occurred on an unprecedented scale, but they coexisted with significant continuities of attitude and behaviour. This applied to the upper and middle strata of Lancashire society, as well as to the emergent working class; and this will become clearer as we examine the fortunes of the county's landed, industrial and professional classes in Chapter 7.

7

LANDED SOCIETY AND INDUSTRIAL WEALTH: THE CHANGING DISTRIBUTION OF POWER AND INFLUENCE, 1770–1850

The economic innovations of the classic 'Industrial Revolution' period not only brought far-reaching changes in the relationships between employer and employee, landlord and tenant, but also in the distribution of wealth, prestige and authority among the upper and middle strata of society. The established dominance of the landed aristocracy and gentry, and of a commercial middle class which shared their cultural assumptions, was challenged by a new, thrusting, competitive, entrepreneurial, industrial middle class, some of whose members took pride in their humble origins, self-made status and Dissenting religion. This new and powerful social and political grouping espoused a distinctive ideology based on competitive individualism, *laissez-faire*, free trade and the dismantling of aristocratic privileges and patronage. It sought to oust the older élites from positions of power in local government, and even attacked their dominant position in national politics. The campaign against aristocratic rule at Westminster reached its apotheosis in the repeal of the Corn Laws in 1846; but this was a concession to circumstances rather than an abdication of power, and the new middle class made little effective impact in Parliament more generally. At this level, landed influence proved to be remarkably resilient in the long run, though this owed much more to adaptability and receptivity to new ideas and new sources of wealth, than to obdurate resistance to the forces of change. The 'old society' of ascribed status, lineage, traditional sources of wealth, patronage, deference and vertical ties of interest linking rich and poor, was still very much alive in England as a whole at mid-century and beyond. Where its assumptions and institutions came under real and sustained challenge was at local rather than national level; and the pressures for change developed a particularly powerful momentum in industrial Lancashire. The Anti-Corn Law League, after all, had its headquarters in Manchester, and the factory masters of the cotton district included many of the most outspoken and vituperative advocates of the new industrial order. The institutions of county and municipal government were besieged by the new bourgeoisie, and so were the parliamentary constituencies, especially the new urban seats which were created in 1832. There is much truth in this conventional picture; but we shall see that in important respects it is over-simplified and even misleading. Before we can explore the development of popular radicalism and emergent working-class institutions, we need to know more about the attitudes, institutions and activities of their rulers and employers; and in this chapter we shall pursue this theme by looking at the economic, political, religious and cultural activities of Lancashire's overlapping but rival and often conflicting ruling classes.

Derek Fraser remarks that for the great Manchester middle-class radical Richard Cobden, 'The great political issue of his day was the class struggle between bourgeoisie and aristocracy, between town and county, for the soul of England'; and this battle was particularly fierce and compelling in the Lancashire cotton district itself.[1] V. A. C. Gatrell agrees that, in Manchester at least, conflict within the propertied classes was more important to the leading citizens than conflict between middle class and working class, rich and poor, employer and employee: 'Indeed, viewed from the middle class perspective, Manchester's political life in the first half of the nineteenth century was dominated less by overt class conflict than by the competitive pursuit of power by groupings within the middle class community.'[2] The apparent difference in emphasis between the commentators is really a matter of terminology, for in many respects the Tory, Anglican, gentry-connected wing of the Manchester middle class stands in for Fraser's 'aristocracy' in the context of local politics. We shall see that this was a widespread feature of political conflict in Lancashire's industrial and commercial towns. But Gatrell's analysis draws our attention to complexities and cross-currents: we must remember that the urban middle class in Lancashire was far from being monolithic and united; and the same applies to the cotton factory masters who formed an important and vociferous part of the middle class, but who should not be treated as representative of the experiences and opinions of the whole. Merchants, manufacturers and professional men included Tories as well as reformers of various hues, Anglicans as well as a broad spectrum of Dissenters, and men who came from landed backgrounds and aspired to assimilation or readmission into county society as well as angry opponents of landed hegemony and privilege. Many factory masters, moreover, displayed the characteristics of industrial squires, presiding over their factory villages with pride and paternal authority, and expecting deferential acquiescence from their dependent workpeople: so paternalism was far from being the sole preserve of the landed aristocracy and gentry. On the other hand, of course, many landed families invested heavily in transport, towns and industry, especially but not exclusively in coal mining; and some were aggressively competitive entrepreneurs in their own right. Some, like the Earls of Wilton, were as detached from the practice of squirearchical paternalism as Nonconformist, abrasively anti-aristocratic millowners like Henry Ashworth were immersed in it.[3] We are not dealing with straightforward polarities, but with nuances and subtleties of emphasis; and our further analysis of the powerful and propertied in the Lancashire of the 'Industrial Revolution' will give additional emphasis to this point, although the cross-currents will not be so strong and confusing as to inhibit qualified but confident generalisations.

Lancashire was not short of aristocratic landowners, although the proprietors of several substantial estates were normally resident elsewhere, and the distribution of aristocratic holdings within the county was very uneven. In the early 1870s, 24 per cent of Lancashire's agricultural land was held by 'great landowners' with over 10,000 acres. This matched the national average; but below this level substantial gentry were relatively thin on the ground, as were the squirearchy and greater yeomanry; and 18 per cent of the land in Lancashire, compared with 12 per cent in England as a whole, was held in units of between one and a hundred acres. Large estates were concentrated disproportionately into the low-lying and generally relatively fertile south and west: the Earl of Derby's 47,269 acres were mainly gathered here, as were the Earl of Sefton's 18,769 acres and the 15,802 which belonged to the Cliftons of Lytham. South-west Lancashire, the Preston area and the Fylde accounted for more than half of the three dozen or so resident landowners with estates of more than 3000 acres; and there were smaller but noticeable concentrations in the Burnley area and the upper Lune valley, while the Cavendishes owned more than 12,000 acres in Furness. The heartland of the cotton industry in south-east Lancashire was almost bereft of resident gentry.[4]

We lack similarly systematic evidence for earlier periods, and these mid-Victorian patterns partly resulted from changes over the previous century. The exodus of the older landed gentry families from the Manchester area, for example, was largely completed by the early nineteenth century, although elsewhere in south-east Lancashire the greater gentry had always been conspicuous by their absence.[5] Moreover, three-quarters of those recruits to the Lancashire gentry of the 1870s who had risen during the previous century, had done so through commerce and industry. But the overall structure of Lancashire landownership had probably remained intact, despite many changes among the individual members, especially at the level of the squirearchy and greater yeomanry which was most open to, and attractive to, aspiring merchants and industrialists. The great estates of the south and west, from the Stanleys downwards, prospered from steadily rising rent-rolls, especially during the French Wars, with only occasional interruptions thereafter, especially in the early 1820s and late 1840s. Mining and urbanisation could bring windfall profits, with spectacular results in some cases: Bateman shows Lord Gerard of Garswood as receiving £42,487 per annum from his 6192 acres, mainly in the south-west Lancashire heavy industrial belt, at a time when £2 per acre was a very good return on agricultural land over most of the country. Urban ground-rents in Southport brought even more spectacular returns to several landed families, mainly in mid-Victorian times; and the Earls of Derby, Wilton and Bradford made similar gains in Manchester and the cotton towns. Handsome incomes could be obtained by a fortunate few from small estates which sustained neither residence nor territorial influence, such as the £10,144 which the Welsh baronet Sir Edmund Buckley received from 91 Lancashire acres, or the £2263 from a single acre which almost outweighed John Robert Shaw's annual income from over 9000 acres in Cheshire and Ross. But Lancashire agriculture paid well in its own right; and for most landed families, other sources of income, where they existed, were the icing on an already rich and appetising cake, as landowners reaped the benefits of population growth and began to invest in agricultural improvements.[6]

As Graham Rogers points out, the aristocracy and gentry responded to the opportunities of the time in a wide variety of ways.[7] At one extreme was the aggressive entrepreneurial activity of Charles Scarisbrick, an ambitious younger son who lifted his annual income from about £5000 in the early 1820s to at least £56,000 in 1856. He achieved this by pursuing ruthless lawsuits against his sisters, and by investing in coal mining, brick making and stone quarrying, land speculation on the grand scale in Paris, urban estate development in Southport and even speculation in the art market. By these diverse routes he acquired an aristocratic income, but refused to acknowledge any associated social responsibilities, whether to his peers or to his social inferiors. Instead he concentrated on securing the interests of his three illegitimate children, and 'lived the life of a somewhat eccentric recluse, never involved himself in county society, and steadfastly refused to take part in county or national politics', never writing or answering a single letter except on business matters.[8] More orthodox was a combination of eagerness to make the most of assets alongside a concern to retain the goodwill and respect of tenants and dependants, which might extend into the industrial sphere where landowners became involved in mining and related enterprises. At Worsley, for example, Lord Francis Egerton ended a long period of absentee landownership in 1837 by settling on the estate and exhibiting a sustained concern for the morals and welfare of his miners, which involved investment in schools and churches, and intervention against beerhouses and Sabbath profanation. This patriarchal régime was sometimes used to undermine strikes and the threat of strikes, but it fitted in with a widespread code of authoritarian paternalism and *noblesse oblige* which was often carried over from large landowners' agricultural estates into their industrial activities.[9] For many large landowners, however, the profits derived from mineral exploitation, railways and urban development were accepted happily enough without being pursued aggressively or wholeheartedly for their own sake. The landed estate as such, and the power and prestige that went with it, dominated their perspectives and expectations, and investment or speculation elsewhere was usually aimed at providing a more secure basis for the expansion, improvement and consolidation of their agricultural acres. A few families, like the Braddylls of Samlesbury, overstretched themselves and burned their fingers; but most used the opportunities provided by the rise of towns and industries to augment their incomes without exhibiting a marked change in their wider view of how society ought to work.[10] It should be stressed that the landlords themselves prospered as a result of the economic forces which also generated the challenge, and the challengers, to their political and social dominance.

With a few Whig exceptions, as we shall see, Lancashire's aristocracy and gentry were Tory; and with a few Roman Catholic exceptions, declining in numbers and importance through the period, they were members of the Church of England. The senior branches of the substantial gentry families had little direct involvement in industry apart from mining and transport, although Thomas Eccleston of Scarisbrick was a partner in the first St. Helens cotton mill in 1784, and the Earl of Derby himself had a brief flirtation with a mismanaged cotton mill in Preston.[11] But the cotton trade continued to be an acceptable outlet for younger sons, and a network of connections and relationships developed between merchants and putting-out manufacturers, some of whom were becoming factory masters in the late eighteenth and early nineteenth centuries, and the gentry families from whose ranks they sprang or into whose cousinhoods they married.

The Hornby and Birley families of Kirkham, Preston, Manchester and Blackburn were at the core of the most prominent and best-documented of these kinship systems, ramifying as they did across the whole of south Lancashire; but at a less exalted and more local level, the 'amphibian nature' of this important stratum of gentry-industrialists was much in evidence, accounting for a small proportion of the firms but a substantial segment of the really wealthy industrial élite. This was the case in Oldham, for example, where the hatting and of course the coal mining industries were dominated by families of similar background; and of course it was especially significant in mercantile Manchester, with its tradition of recruiting the gentry's younger sons.[12] Manchester's leading Tory families also intermarried with Liverpool mercantile wealth, and their institutions brought cotton spinners, calico printers, dyers, fustian manufacturers, professionals and merchants with long-established businesses and links with middling landed estates and rural industry into contact with the gentry-related groups. The membership of John Shaw's punch club epitomised the interests and activities of the Manchester Tory élite in 1825: many of them held office in local government as police commissioners or at the Manchester or Salford Court Leet, or at the Collegiate Church as sidesmen or churchwardens; several had cultural interests, though their expression was seldom intellectually demanding, as members of the Literary and Philosophical Society, the Portico Library and the Natural History Society; some were in the Yeomanry, and several had been involved on the side of repression at Peterloo; and a large proportion were Manchester-born and educated at Manchester Grammar School.[13] Such was the resident Tory middle class of Manchester as the town matured into the commercial capital of south-east Lancashire, at a time when most of its businessmen still lived within a mile or so of the town centre and participated actively in its cultural and political institutions; although the pinnacle of the Tory élite was less town-bound than this, living further afield and mixing on easy terms with county society. Liverpool had a similarly well-established mercantile and professional Tory élite by the late eighteenth century, which maintained exclusive control over the town's Corporation until the advent of municipal reform in 1835; and here again the wealthiest merchants were moving out to country estates in the early nineteenth century, mixing in the more elevated circles of county society.[14]

This comfortable, established, often dynastic Tory middle class was and remained more numerous and more powerful than historians have sometimes suggested; and even when we look at the rival élite of radical Nonconformist opponents of aristocratic government and landed privilege, we find few abrasive self-made men in the idiom of Gradgrind or Bounderby. This group was generally represented by smaller firms of more recent origins, whose principals or partners came from the yeomen clothiers rather than the orbit of the gentry; but we are dealing with gradations in status and background here, rather than sharp polarities. This is especially true of Manchester, where Cross Street and Mosley Street chapels became the social centres of a Unitarian business and professional élite, self-consciously intellectual, rational and questioning, cohesive in the face of the outside world's suspicion of their religious heterodoxy, much intermarried, and every bit as deeply rooted in mercantile Manchester society as their Tory counterparts. Similar Unitarian cousinhoods were prominent in other Lancashire towns, especially Liverpool, where as in Manchester they were at the core of the political and religious reform movements of the 1790s, and Bolton.[15] The Unitarians were a small and élitist grouping, whose members passed the necessary privileges of wealth and education from one generation to the next; but alongside them, usually at a less elevated social level but also better integrated into the surrounding community, other Dissenting groups formed an influential counterpoise to the Anglican Tories and their landed connections. Rising industrialists of humbler yeomanry or artisan origins, who were becoming increasingly numerous from the 1780s, probably tended to attach themselves to one or other of these established groups rather than forming a distinctive cultural and political entity in themselves; and this evidence should deter us from too facile an equation between new wealth, rapid upward social mobility and fierce opposition to the institutions of landed society.[16] The reality was altogether more complex.

Howe's study of 351 Lancashire textile masters and partners who were active between 1830 and 1860 reminds us that even this most visible and controversial segment of Lancashire's industrial middle class was drawn largely from substantial propertied families, with very little rags-to-riches mobility; and this is borne out by the work of Chapman and Honeyman on the pioneers of the industry. Even in the 1820s, when many firms were moving into the second generation of family ownership, most new recruits to cotton spinning and manufacture still came from relatively affluent landed, mercantile and professional backgrounds. Only 5 per cent of Howe's sample definitely 'rose from the ranks of shopkeepers, artisans and operatives' between the late eighteenth century and the 1840s, although a further 21 per cent had untraceable origins whose obscurity may indicate lowliness. At the other end of the rags-to-riches scale, the fortunes made in cotton were substantial by provincial standards, but could not compare with the opulence of the richest metropolitan bankers and merchants.[17] Such upward social mobility as the cotton industry encouraged was usually limited and gradual. Howe undermines further stereotypes. The relative importance of religious Dissent is put in perspective: 45 per cent of the sample were Anglicans, and the only Nonconformists to be over-represented were the Unitarians and the equally heterodox and affluent Quakers. The archetypal Methodist factory master is seriously downgraded in importance by this evidence. Nor were textile masters, as a group, notably abstemious, by 1851 if not before: more than 60 per cent of a smaller sample kept three or more resident domestics, and only 3 per cent managed without a resident servant. The substantial cotton masters were not a race apart: they expressed the characteristics and divisions of the society which spawned them, and remained well integrated into its life and institutions. They might be to some extent 'prisoners of their firms', unable to sell up and step off the business treadmill; but a significant number aimed at, and achieved, partial or complete emancipation from business and a degree of ostentatious leisure. By 1872, 39 of Howe's sample (or their direct descendants) owned landed estates of more than 1000 acres, in the softer climes of the Midlands and South as well as in Lancashire itself; and many more had a smaller stake in the land, reinforcing the point that aspiration to landed status could be just as potent a force among cotton masters as opposition to landed privilege.[18]

One or two caveats are necessary. Howe's sample is dominated by the larger, longer-lasting and more successful firms, and leans towards families which were well established by the 1820 and 1830s. Generalisations across a long period may conceal many transitions in lifestyle and religious affiliation. The 'Puritan' abstemiousness with which some of the industrial pioneers accumulated and ploughed back capital, as epitomised by Foster's description of the employers in the small manufacturing settlements around Oldham,[19] might give way in the second generation, or even within an individual lifetime, to a more carefree and even ostentatious affluence. The frugal, cautious and abstemious Unitarian Bolton quilting manufacturer John Heywood, for example, was succeeded in the 1820s by his son Robert, who indulged interests in fishing, travel and gardening on the grand scale, eventually building an impressive new house in

extensive grounds on the outskirts of the town.[20] Nor did Dissent itself necessarily connote frugality: Manchester's Unitarians, especially, were noted for
enjoying the good things of this world, and the Quaker Henry Ashworth kept
a large wine cellar and an excellent billiard table for his many guests at the Oaks,
where there were numerous servants and much conviviality. In the 1850s he
began to hire shooting lodges and estates in Scotland for up to £500 a year, and
on occasion he enjoyed the enthusiastic company of John Bright for part of
the season. These activities were quite capable of coexisting with a principled
opposition to the 'Citadel of Monopoly' which was backed by 'Aristocratic and
Sacerdotal power'.[21] The many Methodist newcomers to the cotton élite in the
1820s and 1830s may well have been more attached to 'Puritan' virtues of thrift
and abstemiousness than their older-established and more secure Dissenting
counterparts.

Just as some of Lancashire's industrialists pursued and enjoyed aspects of a
landed lifestyle, so their ranks also included large, and perhaps growing, numbers
of active and concerned paternalists who sought to translate the deferential
relationships of the 'close' agricultural village into an industrial setting, taking
on a quasi-squirearchical role. This was especially the case in the smaller, outlying
factory villages or 'industrial colonies', where the factory master might house,
feed and educate his employees, as well as seeking to supply their religious and
recreational needs; but similar communities were conspicuous in some of the
growing towns, especially Blackburn and Ashton-under-Lyne. Provision of this
all-embracing kind readily shaded into authoritarianism, and sometimes into
an industrial despotism which sought to regulate, control and exploit every aspect
of the workers' lives; and even at its most benign, this paternalist frame of mind
was entirely compatible with unbending, principled opposition to state intervention in the regulation of working hours, conditions, child labour and
education. Henry Ashworth was not alone in believing that this was a matter
for each individual firm to decide, and there was widespread resentment at any
attempt to restrict the autonomy of the entrepreneur in dealing with 'his' workpeople. We shall see that similar attitudes generated angry opposition to trade
unions. Even so, many factory masters presented themselves as benevolent
paternalists, to the gratification of those who sought to heal the conflicts of
industrial society by reverting to an idealised system of feudal relations, when
property admitted its responsibilities as well as asserting its rights; and the
squirearchical industrialist, watching over the morals as well as the health and
education of his workpeople, was a pervasive phenomenon. Patrick Joyce argues
that such attitudes were spreading in the 1830s and 1840s, as economic calculations about the benefits of cordial industrial relations were reinforced by fears
of social unrest and political upheaval; and Dickens's portrayal of the Grants
of Ramsbottom as the Cheeryble brothers in *Nicholas Nickleby* was a product of
these years, although their sphere of operations was transferred to London.
But the former radical Samuel Bamford was equally capable of propagating a

paternalist ideal, with his presentation of the benevolent millowner Mr Staidley and approving descriptions of factory villages in the Bury area. Joyce even ventures to suggest that 'industrial rather than rural society may have been the chief seat of paternalism in nineteenth-century England'; and the practices and attitudes he describes were evident in factory villages from the earliest years of the water-frame. By the 1840s, industrial Lancashire was certainly capable of supplying plenty of examples to support Joyce's assertion at the local level, if for 'rural' we read 'agricultural', sweeping thought it may be in the context of England as a whole. The squirearchical millowners may have been a minority, but they were a conspicuous and well-publicised group drawn from all points on the political and religious spectrum, and their wider importance goes beyond their numbers and the sum of their local influence.[22]

All this drives home the difficulty of constructing an identikit cotton factory master; and similar problems arise with other industries and other sectors of the Lancashire middle class. Foster's work on Oldham provides a framework for analysis at the local level, which takes account of the economic, religious, political and cultural dimensions of divisions within the industrial middle class while helping us to make sense of the whole.[23] His division of the Oldham employers into an affluent 'big bourgeoisie' embracing coal, hatting and later engineering as well as cotton, and an insecure petty bourgeoisie of immigrant Nonconformist tradesmen and unpretentious small employers, has wider validity; and this fault-line has considerable social and political significance. We shall see that shop-keepers and people of uncertain status on the fringes of the professions were prominent among the leaders and activists of the radical reform movements which culminated in Chartism; but the numerous tradesmen and small employers were also courted assiduously by the more affluent middle classes on both sides of the political and religious divide, as Gatrell shows for the Manchester of the 1830s.[24] But Foster also splits his 'big bourgeoisie' three ways, identifying an abstinent, 'traditional' employer group in the industrial settlements on Oldham's fringe, which reinforced its workplace discipline by religious and housing controls in a face-to-face village society; a Manchester-oriented, affluent, conspicuously consuming town centre élite; and an even more prosperous stratum of well-connected families whose reference group was the county gentry rather than the Manchester Exchange. These alignments could cut across denominational divisions, as each group moulded its religious institutions to suit its chosen lifestyle; and here Oldham may have been unusual, although in the case of Henry Ashworth's children, for example, money and status talked louder than Quakerism when marriage prospects were being considered.[25] Religious and political divisions within the middle class sometimes did run very deep, however, as we shall see. But the 'big bourgeoisie' was well capable of closing ranks and uniting against any serious threat from below; and as a social formation the middle class in general, and the cotton masters in particular, came to convey a similar appearance of unity when viewed from above, however socially acceptable individual cotton magnates might appear in the eyes of the established landed families whose power and prestige came to be challenged by these representatives of new economic forces.

During the 1830s and 1840s such a challenge became apparent on several fronts, especially in the cotton district. The landed gentry lost their traditional control of county administration. In 1831, 60 of the 105 active county magistrates were landed gentry; by 1851 the figure was 144 out of 400. Industry, banking and commerce accounted for 28 JPs in 1831 (including 7 cotton magnates) and 187 (109 cotton magnates) in 1851, as the millocracy took over judicial and administrative control of the industrial parts of the county, in the absence of a sufficient number of traditionally qualified gentry to cope with the pressure of business arising from the explosive growth of population and economy and a frightening rise in recorded crime and civil disorder. Lancashire's parliamentary representation was transformed even more remarkably. Between 1800 and 1831 only 4 of its 59 MPs had been cotton masters, and landed influence predominated, especially that of the Earls of Derby; but between 1832 and 1852 textile employers accounted for 24 of the 85 MPs, and landed society claimed only 23 of them, with the balance drawn mainly from commerce, other industrial interests and the professions. As well as the boroughs, whose numbers were considerably increased by the 1832 Reform Act, industrial and commercial interests invaded the southern division of the county, and had to be conciliated by the Stanleys and Cavendishes even in the mainly agricultural northern division. They made little impact at Westminster, and many were quickly disillusioned by its ways; but the implications for Lancashire's power structure, social order and image in the outside world were real enough.[26] Meanwhile, urban local government was passing to new institutions which were dominated by the middle classes to the exclusion of the landed interest, as exemplified by the declining influence of the manorial Court Leet, in Manchester and Preston among other places, and the rise of improvement or police commissioners, usually elected by substantial ratepayers and deriving their powers from special private Acts of Parliament.[27] Moreover, the advent of reformed Corporations in Liverpool (1835) and Manchester (1838), and lower down the urban hierarchy in such important industrial centres as Preston and Bolton, outflanked and defeated the established Tory élites there, with their landed connections.[28] These groups proved strong and resilient, as we shall see, and recovered during the 1840s; but the growing unease of many of the landed gentry at this time was understandable. It was easy to equate the outpourings of the Anti-Corn Law League and other anti-landlord pressure groups with the collective voice of an alien, threatening new class of thrusting industrialists. Such perceptions were capable of provoking expressions of generalised hostility in return. Thus Thomas Clifton of Lytham, complaining to his steward in 1848: 'I must confess to some prejudices against the class to which Mr Hornby belongs – viz. cotton spinners and persons who have the constant habit of driving bargains are always attempting to overreach themselves.'

Lady Clifton, twenty years later, expressed a heightened sense of vulnerability: 'We have the misfortune to belong to a county where merchants and wealth are for above, in their own opinion, the aristocracy and the old landed gentry.'[29]

The Cliftons were close to the top of Lancashire's landed hierarchy, and most of the gentry, most of the time, must have been aware that most of the reality of the middle-class challenge was less novel and less disturbing. Many of the manufacturer recruits to the county bench, and even some millowner MPs, were Tory protectionists who were anxious to become assimilated into county society by a well-trodden route, through the purchase of an estate and the adoption of an appropriate lifestyle. The suggestion that the dominant issue was 'the class struggle between bourgeoisie and aristocracy' is an accurate enough expression of the great divide between a vociferous segment of the entrepreneurial middle class on one hand, and the rural landed interest on the other; but it leaves out of account the extensive middle ground of industrialists with landed connections and aspirations, and of landowners with industrial interests, which accounted for a large proportion of the county's substantial employers and property-owners. Moreover, it sidesteps an important dimension of conflict within the middle class, which dominated the politics of municipal government from the 1790s onwards, especially in the emergent regional capitals of Manchester and Liverpool.

The divisions within Manchester's middle class were particularly deep and angry. The scars left by the Jacobite invasion of 1745 seemed to have healed in the following generation, as the mercantile and manufacturing élite was greatly augmented by new arrivals. As Bohstedt remarks, by the 1770s and 1780s 'commercial unity outweighed political differences', as Manchester's leading citizens 'formed committees to suppress embezzlement and workers' combinations, to oppose Arkwright's patents, and to promote the cotton trade'. They could also combine effectively against threats from above, as the successful campaign against Pitt's fustian tax in 1784–5 revealed. But there were serious disagreements over economic policy in the later 1780s, and at the end of the decade the old antagonisms between Whig and Tory, Church of England and Dissent, reappeared in new and dangerous guise.[30] The Tories had lost their Jacobite affiliations, and were conspicuous by their loyalist attachment to the House of Hanover, while the Whigs were no longer aligned with the ascendant party at Westminster. But Tory identification with quasi-Divine Right monarchy, and with the defence of Church of England privileges, continued to define their position as one of intolerant opposition to the causes of limited monarchy and political rights for Dissenters which the Whigs espoused. These tensions came to the surface during the crisis over George III's 'madness' in 1788–9, when Pitt's refusal to declare a regency, which would have brought the Whigs into office, generated petition and counter-petition from the rival factions in Manchester, keeping closely to party lines and religious allegiances; and within a year the bitter conflict over the unsuccessful Nonconformist campaign for the repeal of the Test and Corporation Acts exacerbated the divisions and generated open and lasting enmities between the two groupings.[31]

Reactions to the French Revolution converted bitterness into hatred. Two new political societies were formed in 1790, and partisan opinions and prejudices crystallised around them. The Church and King Club was formed in March to celebrate the successful defence of the Test and Corporation Acts; and it subsequently became the focus for increasingly virulent campaigns against all kinds of constitutional reformers. Its motto and toast of 'Church and King, and down with the Rump', harked back overtly to earlier struggles within the Manchester middle class. Meanwhile, the democratic principles of the French Revolution were attracting the eager support of many of the Manchester Whigs, who already predominated among the questing intellectuals of the flourishing Literary and Philosophical Society, and in October they formed the Manchester Constitutional Society. As events in France began to seem more violent and more threatening, the rival societies became vehicles for the institutionalisation and exacerbation of conflict; but as activists in the Constitutional Society became more vociferously involved in the French revolutionary cause, it lost the active support of moderate reformers, who preferred to keep a low profile or to concentrate more narrowly on the grievances of Nonconformity, while elements within the Church and King Club began to stir up violence against the reformers. As war with France approached, while threatening stirrings began among the lower orders, and the pamphlet war over Paine's *Rights of Man* intensified, the reformers were driven to the margins of Manchester middle-class society. When the existing newspaper press became closed to them, they founded their own *Manchester Herald* in March 1792, aiming at the political arousal of 'tailors, farmers, butchers and blacksmiths'; but from June 1792 onwards an increasingly confident Church and King faction, which now controlled the town's law and order and local government institutions, began a campaign of orchestrated riots and legal harassment. This focused especially on Thomas Walker, a prominent merchant who had been the hero of the Fustian Tax campaign in 1785, and had held the town's leading office of boroughreeve as recently as 1790. As the war lent justification to intensified repression, the middle-class reformers fled or were silenced by prosecutions, espionage and violence. Even after Walker and several others were tried for sedition in 1794, however, reformers continued to skirmish with the ruling group. They joined in the long campaign against corruption in Manchester's Poor Law administration; they petitioned for peace in 1795, when their document attracted more signatures than the Tory counter-petition; they petitioned against repressive legislation on the freedom of speech and assembly in 1796, with equal success in the local context; and they formed a Society for Constitutional Thinking, which held silent meetings to demonstrate the absurdity of the curbs on freedom of speech and assembly.[32]

At this point, the stamina and courage of the middle-class reformers were exhausted, and organised opposition passed into the hands of men of lower status.

Most of the Unitarian radicals, indeed, gave in to the war fever at the turn of the century, making visible and substantial donations to the Volunteers and the General Defence Fund. Meanwhile, Manchester's Tories established a stranglehold over the town's institutions which they retained until the 1830s. They were able to exclude the reformers from local office, and they dominated the police commissioners which were established in 1792 and soon became Manchester's most powerful local government body. The 'Lit. and Phil.' also changed its character, as it 'no longer speculated in political philosophy, but ceded primacy to scientific investigations' and to antiquarianism, as a steady influx of High Church Tory dilettanti altered the complexion of the membership. But the currents of thought which Walker and his allies represented were not extinguished. They continued to bubble beneath the surface, to reappear when constitutional reform again became a live issue in the next generation.[33]

Manchester's middle-class reformers began to emerge from the shadows in 1812, when they opposed a vote of thanks to the Prince Regent for retaining his father's ministers in office. This was the cautious beginning to a new challenge to Tory dominance, in which Unitarian veterans of the 1790s were joined by a new generation of rising merchants, manufacturers and journalists, the Potter brothers and their allies, drawn from a wide range of Dissenting religious backgrounds. This group provided money for the defence of prosecuted working-class radicals in 1816, gave moral support to the Blanketeers and sought redress for their wrongful imprisonment, and spoke up angrily against the magistrates' version of the Peterloo massacre. On this issue they secured extensive support: as Gatrell remarks, 'Peterloo polarized middle-class opinion for the first time in twenty years'. Once again, battle was joined in earnest; and this time, in the long run, the Tories were to be the losers.[34]

The balance of power in Manchester politics began to change on several fronts after 1820. The middle-class Dissenting reformers succeeded in mobilising the support of the numerically important and rapidly expanding strata of small employers and shopkeepers. They campaigned against church-rates, securing their effective abolition in Manchester in 1835; they encouraged vociferous and disorderly mass participation by tradesmen and shopkeepers in the deliberations of the police commissioners, culminating in a reform of the commissioners' constitution in which the Tories were obliged to make concessions; and in 1838 Cobden's campaign for municipal incorporation bore fruit, as a new corporation was founded, elected on a wider franchise, outflanking and superseding the older, Tory-dominated local government bodies and placing the liberal reformers firmly in the saddle. They were also active in pursuit of parliamentary reform; and while even the Tories were generally in favour of Manchester's enfranchisement by the late 1820s, the Potter coterie went further and supported a ratepayer franchise, though they stopped short of endorsing the more radical demands of the shopkeeper-dominated Manchester Political Union. Manchester's first MPs in 1832 were Liberal reformers, and they soon made their priorities clear: the pursuit of free trade and the repeal of the Corn Laws. The stage was set for the Anti-Corn Law League, with its vituperative attacks on the landed interest, and its strong identification with Manchester; and the league's immensely effective propaganda campaign completed the process of convincing contemporaries, and historians, that Manchester middle-class opinion was firmly on the side of economic and political liberalism and Free Trade as a panacea. As Gatrell shows, this view is over-simplified. Just as the Tory hegemony of the early nineteenth century was more fragile than it looked, sustained as much by bluster and intimidation as by numerical or ideological predominance, so the facade of Mancunian unity presented to the outside world by the Liberal reformers and the Anti-Corn Law League in the next generation masked a strong continuity of Church-and-King Tory traditions among the town's professional men and the most prosperous of the merchants and manufacturers. The balance of power had tilted, and the nature of the town's institutions had changed, but the Manchester middle class remained deeply divided into mutually antagonistic camps. Appearances to the contrary were merely superficial.[35]

A similar divergence of opinion and outlook developed among the merchants and professional men of Liverpool, where Dissenters and relative newcomers, however prosperous and reputable, were systematically excluded from the town's closed Corporation, whose oligarchical privileges and alleged corruption and mismanagement provided further grievances. As in Manchester, Unitarians and other Dissenters were prominent among the political reformers, and the campaigners of the 1790s had served their apprenticeship in the struggle against the Test and Corporation Acts. The Liverpool Literary Society played a similar part to Manchester's 'Lit. and Phil.' in providing a forum for idealistic and principled discussion; and in Liverpool especially, opposition to the slave trade nurtured more general attachment to the Rights of Man and constitutional liberties, fuelling reformers' ardour while isolating them from the economic interests and defensive ideologies of the hostile mainstream of Liverpool mercantile opinion. The Liverpool reformers also came out in favour of free trade with the Indies, as well as urging the reform of the Corporation; but the potential popularity of these causes was more than outweighed by the local unpopularity of opposition to the slave trade. But in any case the nationally orchestrated campaign against the 'Jacobin' reformers in late 1792 and early 1793 was as effective in Liverpool as in Manchester, although the local context of conflict was marginally less violent and vindictive. The reformers lost access to the local press and were intimidated into silence, apart from the occasional pamphlet of protest against war and repression. Here again, they reappeared in the new century, and William Roscoe, Unitarian merchant, biographer of Lorenzo de Medici and idealistic advocate of a cultural renaissance on Merseyside, briefly became an MP for Liverpool in 1806 – 7 under Whig auspices, taking the opportunity to speak against the slave trade in the Commons. But Liverpool's Dissenting middle-class reformers remained in the wilderness until the coming of municipal reform in

1835, when they almost swept the board at the ensuing elections, and a change took place in the public face of the town's governing élite; but again as in Manchester, the Tory Churchmen remained numerous and powerful, and soon began to reassert their influence in the 1840s.[36]

In the smaller Lancashire towns, too, existing religious, political and cultural divisions within the middle class were exacerbated and perpetuated by the traumas of the early 1790s. Loyalist associations to defend Church, King and Constitution against 'levellers and Jacobins' were founded in at least thirty north-western towns in and after December 1792, and Church-and-King mobs appeared in smaller settlements like Failsworth, Chowbent, Chorley and Royton as well as in Manchester and Liverpool. Radical Dissenting congregations were prime targets; and the balance of power between the rival élites was generally sustained in favour of the Tory Churchmen until the 1820s and especially the 1830s. When the pendulum began to swing the other way, it gathered momentum from the 1832 Reform Act and, in the corporate boroughs, from the municipal reform legislation of 1835; but the extent and nature of the transition varied widely from place to place. At Darwen, for example, the manufacturing élite which crystallised as the town grew was uncompromisingly liberal and predominantly Congregationalist, leaving little room for rival claims to predominance. In Rochdale, Liberal Nonconformist manufacturing influence outweighed the landed and clerical local Tories and their professional allies; at Bolton the rival élites were more evenly matched, each with its own institutional strongholds; and in Blackburn the Anglican Tories retained a very strong position in the 1840s and beyond.[37] Darwen, indeed, was exceptional in the homogeneity of its employing class; and over most of Lancashire the substantial merchant, manufacturing and professional middle class remained more or less bitterly divided along lines which had been defined, in many important respects, during the early years of the French wars.

Religious differentiation was, and remained, a particularly important touchstone of political allegiance. Some moderate reformers came within the pale of the Church of England, but that body was overwhelmingly Tory in its political outlook, which predominated among the leading citizens of greater Merseyside and much of north Lancashire, including parts of the emergent weaving district. Unitarians, Quakers and the Old Dissent of Congregationalists and Baptists, on the other hand, had distinctive reformist political traditions and, often, distinctive cultural institutions of their own; while the various Methodist groupings ran the gamut by the 1830s and 1840s from the well-established hierarchical constitutional loyalism of the original Wesleyans to the democratic sectarian Liberalism of the emergent Free Methodists.[38] This intertwining of religion and politics gave wider meaning to the struggles for office and influence which engrossed the substantial and prospering middle classes of the rapidly growing Lancashire towns of the first half of the nineteenth century; and it provided an ideological component which emphasised and sustained the divisions which prevented the propertied classes from presenting a united front in their responses to the accelerating changes of these important transitional decades.[39] These divisions, indeed, help to explain some of the complexities which arise in interpreting the rise of a more thoroughgoing radical politics, and a flickering and intermittent but sometimes threatening perception of common interests among Lancashire's artisans, lesser tradesmen, weavers, factory workers, miners and even small farmers in the late eighteenth and early nineteenth centuries. We shall examine these important developments in the next chapter.

8

RADICALS AND TRADE UNIONS:
POPULAR PROTEST AND WORKING-CLASS
ORGANISATION FROM THE JACOBINS
TO THE CHARTISTS

We saw in Chapter 5 that, by the 1750s and 1760s, groups within the rapidly growing wage-earning strata of Lancashire society were beginning to combine in defence of their living standards. Trade societies were forming, especially in the textile district; strikes were beginning to occur; and on a different but related plane of conflict, food riots were becoming endemic. As the expansion of industries and towns proceeded on its wayward but accelerating course in the late eighteenth and early nineteenth centuries, these conflicts became more frequent, and their implications became more disturbing to those in authority. Their worries were compounded in the 1790s by the emergence of organised and principled support for radical political reform among artisans, weavers and petty tradesmen, which emerged later than the middle-class movement discussed in Chapter 7 but showed greater stamina and tenacity of purpose. The food riots declined, in Lancashire as elsewhere, in the early years of the nineteenth century; but trade union activity spread and intensified, improving in organisation and extending in range whenever opportunity arose, though remaining vulnerable to the regular cyclical depressions of the developing industrial economy. The political reformers also went from strength to strength in the long run, despite short-term setbacks when prosperity distracted their mass support or when repression deprived them of their leaders and drove their activities underground. Sometimes industrial and political concerns overlapped to give additional weight and determination to campaigns for economic amelioration and parliamentary reform; and the challenge to the established order reached a climax in the years of disillusionment after the first Reform Act, as parts of Lancashire acquired national significance in the late 1830s and early 1840s as hotbeds of Chartism.

Most of this activity was concentrated into the textile district, and this will itself require explanation; but the main purpose of this chapter is to trace the development of trade unionism and radical politics among Lancashire's wage-earners and petty tradesmen, and to assess the validity of the suggestion that their mobilisation added up to the making of a united and class conscious working class, which identified itself with national struggles against a corrupt and uncaring government in distant London as well as engaging in more localised battles with substantial employers and property-owners.

The discussion of these themes is complicated by the varying aims, tactics and fortunes of trade unions in Lancashire, by the fluctuating nature of their relationship with radical political movements which had complexities and internal divisions of their own, and by the complex and controversial nature of many of the events which must be analysed if the broader arguments are to carry conviction. We shall begin by following the fortunes of the trade unions in Lancashire's major industries from the late eighteenth century to the early 1830s, in conjunction with an examination of the riots and popular disturbances which frequently erupted in parts of the county in times of economic hardship. We shall then trace the growth of popular radical political activity over the same period, assessing the extent and significance of its points of contact with the trade unions; and the concluding section will analyse the contribution of working-class and more broadly 'popular' commitment to Chartism in Lancashire, and provide a critical review of the important and sometimes acrimonious debate on the nature and meaning of Chartism in the cotton district.

Wage-earners in many crafts were organising on what seems to have been a permanent basis, though often informally and usually locally, by the middle and later years of the eighteenth century; but the best-documented, and in many ways the most important, of Lancashire's early trade unions developed in the cotton industry. But the cotton hand-loom weavers and the factory spinners were utterly different, in their organisation, methods and aspirations and in the nature and extent of their impact, as befitted their contrasting origins, workplace organisation and systems of production.[1] The preparatory processes seem not to have been fertile soil for trade union growth, despite their employment of adult males supervising women and children at a potentially strategic initial stage of production where disruption could have had knock-on effects on the rest of the industry. There is some evidence of ephemeral attempts at organisation in the card-room, especially in the early 1830s, but not very much came of this in the short run, and it was to be another fifty years before permanent and effective organisations began to cohere in this sector of the industry.[2] We shall concentrate in the first instance on weaving and spinning, before moving across to look at developments in other industries and at the extent of collaboration beyond the boundaries of individual trades.

The economic and institutional context of trade union activity must be borne in mind. This was a period of rapid economic growth in Lancashire, of course;

but it was punctuated by sharp cyclical fluctuations, and on the downswing of the trade cycle it was very difficult indeed for unions to protect their members against wage cuts, especially when cyclical unemployment created a desperate surplus labour pool of potential strike-breakers. Moreover, the legal position of trade unions was always very insecure: the Combination Acts of 1799–1824 were only the most explicit of several pieces of legislation under which labour organisations could be outlawed and their leaders arrested and imprisoned. Most Justices of the Peace increasingly adopted a belligerent attitude to strikers and union organisers, and strikes were sometimes brought to an untimely end by the arrest of leaders and committee members, while publicans' licences and livelihoods were often at risk if they harboured union meetings. We shall see that the majesty of the law was not always effective in face of defensive local solidarities; but the legal environment for trade unions nevertheless ranged from the unsympathetic to the inimical. The continuity and administrative effectiveness of trade unions, in Lancashire as elsewhere, remained vulnerable to trade depression and legal repression throughout the period.[3]

The cotton hand-loom weavers found it particularly difficult to organise and sustain trade union activity. United action was hampered by their wide dispersal across extensive tracts of industrial countryside, and by the putting-out system, which left individual weavers to deal with individual masters whose influence over them was strengthened by ties of debt, and by the practical inconveniences of seeking an alternative employer. We must not exaggerate these difficulties: weavers were able to exchange gossip and compare notes about the trade when they made their weekly visit to the employer's warehouse, and in the alehouses where their friendly societies met, and solidarity through shared grievances might be engendered where a single master employed most of the families in a single village or hamlet. In any case, the wages and practices of different employers were rarely out of step for very long. But the putting-out system also reduced the employers' fixed capital overheads, rendering them less vulnerable to strikes; and the long-run terms of trade were shifting inexorably against the weavers from the mid-1790s onwards. As we saw in Chapter 6, the occupation became overstocked with newcomers, and each successive depression exposed a deeper pool of surplus labour, while extended working hours and more intensive exploitation of family labour, as weavers defended basic living standards against falling piece-rate wages, compounded the problem and accelerated a decline in bargaining power which was further exacerbated by the spread of the power-loom from the 1820s onwards. Under these conditions, it was increasingly difficult for overworked and preoccupied weavers to combine in their own defence; and it is remarkable that they were able to mount sustained strikes in pursuit of wage advances across a wide area of Lancashire in 1808 and 1818, although their subsequent trade union activities were desultory, localised and altogether less sophisticated as they began their decline into poverty, marginality and eventual extinction.[4]

[143]

Trade societies were already in evidence in specific branches of hand-loom weaving by the 1750s, and there are suggestive examples in succeeding decades of the negotiation of agreed piece-rate wage lists, of the organised defence of apprenticeship, and of combination in pursuit of wage increases. Most of this activity was locally based, although several weavers' societies combined in the depression of 1779 to petition for legal enforcement of minimum wage-rates. At the local level, indeed, organisation was probably endemic, finding formal and visible expression at times of stress and conflict; and even if the influx of new workers into the less-skilled branches of the trade in the 1780s and 1790s made the existing societies less representative and less able to defend their interests, events at the turn of the century showed that the vastly expanded body of hand-loom weavers was capable of organising across a wide area in an attempt to arrest a sustained fall in living standards.[5] In 1799, as Booth remarks, 'As if by magic a general Association of Weavers emerged representing a broad spectrum of cotton towns' in response to a combination of fuller employment and rising prices after several years of sharp wage cuts. Delegates converged on Bolton from towns as far apart as Warrington and Oldham, Blackburn and Stockport.[6] This was the beginning of a sustained campaign, although the Association itself was short-lived; and whether or not the local magistrates' fears of political motivation were well-grounded, the organisers must have built upon a well-established, if usually inconspicuous, network of local societies.

The weavers' campaigns of the early nineteenth century sought the legal reassertion and local enforcement of legislation for the protection of wages, reinforced by the regulation of labour supply through compulsory apprenticeship. They also asked for restrictions on the export of yarn to be woven at a cheaper rate on the Continent. They proceeded as far as possible within the letter of the law, petitioning Parliament for redress of grievances; and even in the immediate aftermath of the Combination Act of 1799, which was partly occasioned by fear of the weavers' new organisation, Pitt's government was sufficiently responsive to the lobbying of the Association of Weavers to pass an Arbitration Act in 1800. This followed the presentation of a petition of 23,000 signatures, which was accompanied by ostentatious declarations of constitutional loyalism, against a backcloth of unrest and deepening distress. The Act provided that disputes over piecework should go before two arbitrators, one chosen by either side, before being referred to a magistrate (the practice hitherto) in case of disagreement. Not surprisingly, the Act soon proved unsatisfactory to both sides: most of the masters campaigned for its repeal, while the weavers continued to agitate for a fairer and stricter system of enforcement. A new Act in 1804 gave wider powers to the magistrates, but this did not allay the discontent on both sides: the masters complained about its restrictive character while systematically evading its provisions, while the weavers' demands for effective legal protection became angrier as petitions were ignored and piece-rates continued to fall. The 1800 Act, indeed, was the last real concession the weavers gained by parliamentary petitioning.

Their frustration came to a head in the great strike of 1808. A petition of 130,000 signatures in support of wage regulation had made no headway in 1807, but as conditions continued to worsen, and as political reformers pressed for peace, a minimum wage bill was debated in Parliament in May 1808, with some support from master manufacturers. Its rejection sparked off a well-organised, widespread and lasting strike for a substantial wage increase, which gained a temporary improvement of 20 per cent in piece-rate wages, when 33 per cent had been the target. A mass meeting in Manchester was dispersed by the cavalry, and one death resulted; but otherwise there was little overt violence on either side. The strike ended untidily, with disagreement over whether to accept the masters' offer; but despite the dissension and the transitory nature of the gains, it was a major and remarkable victory. Bohstedt calls it 'the culmination of nearly a decade of impressive organizational effort', and it showed that local and occupational solidarities were capable of building a formidable working-class movement in spite of all the obstacles.[7]

But this was the high point of the weavers' success; and the terms of trade continued to shift inexorably against them. They persisted in petitioning Parliament, but with scant hope of success, for they were swimming against a strongly flowing tide of *laissez-faire* economic orthodoxy; and their organisation and activity became fitful and despairing. The last county-wide strike took place in 1818, on the crest of a wave of similar activity in other trades; but again the wage rises achieved were patchy and short-lived. Already in 1812, weavers' societies had been involved in machine-breaking, as the threat of the power-loom became increasingly apparent; and a period of intensified hardship in 1826 led to a widespread outbreak of loom-smashing and other attacks on employers' property. There were similar episodes in 1829 in response to wage cuts; and by this time there seems to have been no effective weavers' organisation beyond the local level. The Rochdale flannel weavers were still capable of organising a sustained strike in 1830, and skilled and specialised branches like the quilting weavers could still defend their interests against their employers; but for the hand-loom weavers in general, 1818 was the last milestone in a prolonged rearguard action. We shall see that petitioning for legal protection of wages and of apprenticeship continued into the 1830s; but by that time the weavers' unions had long lost what limited credibility they had ever possessed as industrial bargainers.[8]

The mule-spinners in the new steam-powered factories are often presented as the antithesis of the hand-loom weavers: a well-organised élite group of well-paid skilled and supervisory workers who were able to carry the fight to their employers in good times, and to defend themselves more effectively than most during industrial depression, and who benefited from the same economic forces that drove the weavers into penury and violent radicalism. Such a portrayal is misleading on several counts, and becomes increasingly inaccurate during the years of transitional insecurity and disturbance which spanned the 1830s and 1840s.

Mule-spinning required skill, stamina and experience, although recruitment to the trade was never controlled by formal apprenticeship; and it also involved the exercise of authority over subordinate workers called piecers, usually children or adolescents, who repaired broken threads, cleaned machinery and generally helped to maintain continuity of production. The spinners were relatively well paid, although their true circumstances were obscured, and their affluence was exaggerated, by the prevalent practice of paying the piecers out of the total income of the machine, a form of subcontracting which was common in other industries. Mule-spinners clearly had some pretensions to the status of a 'labour aristocracy', and it was fitting that they began to organise in trade unions from the earliest days of their transfer into the factory. Unions were formed in Stockport and Manchester in 1792, and other places soon followed suit. We lack hard evidence for subsequent continuity of organisation, but it seems likely that it was achieved at the local level in most Lancashire towns from the 1790s onwards.[9] As the demand for their services increased, moreover, the spinners asserted their industrial muscle, and in 1795 we find them striking successfully in pursuit of a substantial wage claim in Manchester. Further disputes followed at regular intervals, and in 1803 the Manchester masters combined to raise a fighting fund of £20,000 to defend themselves against 'this dangerous and unjust combination'. Despite their illegal status, however, seven years later the spinners went a stage further in their organisation, as they federated across the whole of Lancashire in an attempt to standardise wage-rates by bringing the 'country' districts up to the level of the Manchester area. They used the innovatory tactic of the 'rolling strike', tackling a single area at a time and supporting its strikers with the resources of the whole county; but the employers responded with a county-wide look-out, and the spinners were vanquished after a long and bitter struggle.[10]

This was a portentous defeat. Henceforth the spinners were to be on the defensive, fighting against wage cuts, dilution and disruptive technological innovation; and despite increasing organisational sophistication, and attempts to build mutually supportive links with other trades, the spinners' record in set-piece confrontations was dismayingly unsuccessful. In 1818 a strike, which sought the restoration of wages to the level which had existed before the wage cuts of 1816, was broken in spite of attempts to gain support from other trades and areas, and several leaders were imprisoned or blacklisted, while an attempt at bringing together a wide range of trades into a general union was stillborn. Further attempts to build a federation of mule-spinners across and beyond Lancashire followed in 1824–5 and 1829–31, when John Doherty's National Association for the Protection of Labour revived a more ambitious plan for mutual assistance between trades; but in all these cases internal dissension, sectional jealousies, impatience, lack of resources, government repression and trade depression combined to make the spinners' position untenable.[11]

Three themes stand out: the spinners' eagerness to collaborate with other trades; their ability to mobilise support from other groups of factory workers who lacked their power to organise, and whose wages and conditions were effectively determined by those secured by the spinners; and their inability to defend their interests effectively against the employers, even after the repeal of the Combination Laws, for which they had campaigned assiduously. They were not the aloof, complacent labour aristocrats of frequent stereotype; and their campaigns were increasingly defensive rather than aggressive in character. As mules grew larger and the threat of the self-acting mule, operated by women or unskilled labour, became more plausible in the later 1820s, the demand for spinners began to contract, and a pool of blackleg labour became available to masters who were only too willing to resort to the industry-wide lock-out in order to drain the spinners' resources as rapidly as possible. The spinners knew themselves to be vulnerable, and feared the fate of the hand-loom weavers: hence their eagerness to federate and to build bridges to other trades. But they experienced a succession of defeats in 1830–1, which left Doherty's Manchester spinners, who had been the prime movers in attempts at wider organisation, bereft of funds and members. The National Association for the Protection of Labour also collapsed, and the Bolton spinners were 'badly mauled'. It took several years for the spinners throughout Lancashire to regain a measure of their strength, and we shall see that they remained weak and vulnerable throughout the Chartist period.[12]

Even in textiles, of course, the cotton spinners and hand-loom weavers were only part of the story. The spinners were the best-organised sector of a much larger factory labour force, which was numerically dominated by women and children; but outside the mule-room, attempts at organisation even among the men were occasional and ephemeral. But weaving and the finishing processes present a more complex picture. Power-loom weavers were already organising by 1818 in Stockport, where there were angry strikes in this sector during 1829–32, boosted by the leavening of the labour force with a substantial minority of adult males, including former hand-loom weavers who brought the traditions of their trade with them.[13] Alongside the cotton hand-loom weavers, moreover, were strong concentrations of domestic silk and flannel weavers, several thousand in number. The former were numerous in Middleton and parts of Manchester and became predominant in the Leigh area during the 1820s, while the latter were much in evidence around Rochdale. The power-loom came late to these industries, although they began to suffer overstocked labour markets in the 1830s as cotton hand-loom weavers moved across in search of work, while competition from the Spitalfields silk weavers in London intensified. But the silk weavers were still capable of winning a major set-piece strike against reductions to a recently agreed wage list in 1827, although their bargaining power declined thereafter; and the Rochdale flannel weavers contrived to maintain wage levels and trade customs through the 1820s, until they were disastrously embroiled in the collapse of the NAPL in 1831. The fustian cutters, another numerous outworker group, kept up their strength for a longer period, winning an industrial dispute even in the generally traumatic years of 1830 – 1. But the calico printers conformed more closely to the general experience in textiles. Like the spinners, they were undermined by technological innovation, and in 1831 their union was effectively smashed, and their wages and manning levels severely reduced, by a concerted initiative from the employers.[14]

As Sykes points out, too, jobs outside textiles accounted for most of the adult male workforce, even in the 'cotton towns' themselves. 'In 1841 ... there were almost certainly more shoemakers, and possibly more carpenters, in Manchester than there were working cotton spinners or hand-loom weavers.' The cotton district was 'an area of organised artisan strength', and we need to consider the fortunes of a wide range of trades, especially in building, clothing and coal mining.[15] In most cases, the non-textile sectors resisted pressure for wage cuts, dilution and piecework more successfully than the weavers and cotton factory workers, although we shall see that their position became more difficult during the troubled 1830s. Apart from the declining and demoralised Chowbent nail-makers, the metal trades of the cotton district were 'well paid [and] highly unionised' by the 1820s, as new and expanding occupations soon generated organisations to defend their interests. The building trades remained strongly organised in a period of high demand and minimal technological innovation, and even the clothing trades were not yet experiencing the pressures of sweated labour, slop work, systematic subcontracting and chamber-mastering which were beginning to affect their counterparts in London and the footwear trades of Northampton. The main struggles in these sectors came after the 1832 Reform Act rather than before it.[16]

For the miners as for the textile workers, however, 1829 – 31 were to be heady but ultimately disastrous years. Miners' friendly societies had spread rapidly in Lancashire during the later eighteenth century, but visible evidence of trade union activity as such was occasional and localised until 1818, although in 1792 Wigan coalmasters had called in the military to overawe several hundred colliers who 'threaten to destroy the Works by pulling up the Engines, throwing down the wheels and filling up the pits' if their demands were not met; and a coalowner observed that many colliers from distant works had 'come to observe the progress of our people' in their pursuit of increased wages, 'and had they succeeded it would certainly have spread far over this county'.[17] The miners of south-east Lancashire conducted a successful strike in 1818, in a manner which suggested that they were building on existing organisations; and the following year saw the first known strike on the St. Helens coalfield, where the miners held out for nine weeks before abandoning the struggle, after borrowing the spinners' 'rolling strike' technique and apparently organising through the local friendly societies.[18] In 1830 matters were taken a stage further, again in the manner of the spinners, when a federal Friendly Society of Coal Mining was founded in Bolton and spread its tentacles beyond Lancashire into Staffordshire, Wales and Derbyshire. At a time of high demand for coal, local wage increases of 25 and even 33 per cent were obtained in late 1830 in south-east Lancashire, and in early 1831 the strike spread to St. Helens. But the successes were short-lived, the masters combined against union 'dictation', and before the year was out the union had crumbled before lock-outs, imported blacklegs and legal repression. Like the spinners, the miners had to regroup and rebuild through their local trade societies.[19]

Sykes suggests that the miners were better organised in the cotton district than in Wigan and the west; and this probably holds good for trade unions generally.[20] Craftsmen in the building, clothing and other established trades had their local societies, here as elsewhere, and the new metalworking and engineering branches also developed unions of their own. The Liverpool shipwrights' society was alleged to be particularly effective at enforcing output quotas in the early 1820s. In the St. Helens area the alkali workers and glass bottle makers are known to have had friendly societies of their own by the 1820s, and these may have had trade union functions; but most Merseyside workers were unable to build lasting trade societies even at the local level, in an economy dominated by casual and unskilled labour, and the contrast with the widely sustained and sometimes ambitious and increasingly sophisticated trade unions of the cotton district is sharp and telling.[21]

Lancashire's trade unions remained small-scale, local and highly specialised throughout these years; and in most industries they kept these characteristics for long afterwards. These were face-to-face societies. Even the spinners, the archetypal factory workers, operated in production units containing remarkably small numbers of adult men: figures for 1838 show averages per firm ranging from 42.9 in Manchester to a mere 13.1 in Rochdale. In the building trades, too, the numbers in specific skilled occupations were few enough for towns to retain genuine occupational communities.[22] This made for local strength, solidarity and attachment to trade customs. All the unions kept the friendly society functions of conviviality and mutual insurance, and the burgeoning new societies, even in cotton factories and engineering workshops, organised themselves along traditional lines. But the divisions between trades and towns also made for sectional suspicions, jealousies and even antipathies, as in the running conflict between Bolton and Manchester which bedevilled the spinners' attempts to federate beyond the local level; and when legal and administrative difficulties are also considered, it is remarkable that attempts to build wider federations and general unions should have been sustained as often and for as long as they were. This was a harsh environment, and most of the unions were on the defensive most of the time. Indeed, in several trades the dilution of apprenticeship, reductions of earnings and loss of workplace authority and autonomy were beginning to bite deeply during the 1820s as the masters, who could combine with impunity, gained the upper hand. The defeats of 1831 marked a further stage in this process, and no doubt gave additional vigour and bitterness to the working-class campaign for parliamentary reform.[23]

Under all the circumstances, it is hardly surprising that trade disputes sometimes gave rise to collective violence and riot. As well as the occasional attacks on factories and weaving-sheds, as in 1779, 1792, 1812, 1826 and 1829, strikes routinely engendered violence associated with picketing and (in the case of hand-loom weavers) the confiscation of shuttles or destruction of cloth; and there were occasional attacks on millowners. Industrial violence was not confined to the cotton industry, of course: it was endemic to disputes in mining and the building trades, for example, as Manchester brickmakers destroyed bricks made with new machinery, and Liverpool ropemakers and sawyers resorted to arson and murder.[24] For a long time, too, industrial conflicts over wages and conditions overlapped with older forms of protest over food prices and the regulation of markets. The deficient harvests, food shortages and high prices of 1795 – 6 and 1799 – 1800 brought widespread food rioting in urban Lancashire, as grain and potatoes were seized and sold at what the rioters deemed to be 'fair' prices, and magistrates were urged to interfere against profiteers and monopolists. Bohstedt argues that the food riot as calculated demonstration, subject to its own internal controls and appealing to a tradition of 'moral economy' with which magistrates retained at least a residual sympathy, remained important in the lesser manufacturing centres; but in Manchester itself increasing social dislocation, and lack of contact and empathy between the divergent cultures of the magistrates and the populace, ensured a greater propensity to random violence and wanton destruction, put down with increasing firmness by the strong arm of the law.[25] Whatever the truth of this contention, food riots rapidly declined in incidence and importance during the early nineteenth century. The last widespread outbreak in Lancashire formed part of the wider industrial and political crisis of 1812; and here and there alternative ways of protecting living standards against rising food prices emerged. In Manchester a Union of Friendly Societies collected donations and distributed food cheaply to the poor during the crisis of 1800, alongside the more orthodox provision of soup kitchens organised by the town's élite; and in 1829 a 'milk and butter strike' was organised in several towns to boycott dairy goods unless they were sold at reduced 'fair' prices decided by mass meetings.[26] But this 'strike' was the brainchild of hand-loom weavers of politically radical bent, and linked to the need for parliamentary reform and the repeal of the Corn Laws; and this reflected an increasing tendency for food riots, like trade union activities, to merge with radical politics. The decline of the food riot owed something to improvement in the supply system, and to the visibly widening gap between distant suppliers and urban consumers, which destroyed the rationale of the old-style food riot; but in a sense this form of protest and negotiation was displaced by the growing primacy of new foci of conflict based on wages and the pursuit of political reform. These patterns of conflict overlapped and reinforced each other; and in both cases an explicit class dimension, a visible and systematic conflict between employers and employees, became increasingly important.

From the mid-1790s onwards, the relationship between political and industrial grievances became apparent to ever-widening circles of hard-pressed wage-earners, as they suffered from wartime trade disruption and high taxation. In 1799 magistrates and employers saw political radicals and perhaps insurrectionaries behind the sudden appearance of the Association of Weavers, and they also saw a connection between a campaign by several Manchester trade societies against a new Combination Act, and wider political issues. Their fears may have been exaggerated, but they were probably not entirely without foundation. As the weavers and other trades felt the weight of the laws against combinations and oath-taking in the early nineteenth century, and saw Parliament consistently ignore their petitions for minimum wages and other protective legislation, it was not surprising that their thoughts should turn to a radical reform of the political system. Those who were sufficiently aware and committed to organise illegal trade unions were likely also to be radical politicians; and the evidence of overlap becomes stronger as time passes. The combination of war, dearth, industrial depression and repression ensured that the Luddite year of 1812, with its heady combination of food riots, machine-breaking and radical reform campaigns, would link economic and political grievances directly and vividly in many minds. However shadowy the actual evidence of revolutionary plotting may be, Dinwiddy may be right to argue that it was at this point, in Lancashire at least, that a radical political programme gained mass support for the first time; and Booth argues for a similar turning point rather earlier, at the turn of the century.[27] By the 1820s, as campaigns for factory reform and the repeal of the Combination Acts made the relationship between industrial and political campaigns even more explicit, the workers' leaders were developing an 'alternative political economy' to set against the doctrinaire *laissez-faire* outlook of their employers and political masters. They sought shorter hours, restraints on excessive competition, wages boards to protect the weavers' living standards, and higher general wage levels to stimulate domestic consumption and demand. A reform of Parliament was an essential prerequisite for the adoption of this heretical economic policy; so it is no surprise to find that in the late 1820s the leaders of the Manchester spinners, and of the National Association for the Protection of Labour, were also committed advocates of parliamentary reform. The rank and file were, of course, less consistent; but the evidence for a sustained connection between trade union concerns and wider political activity among the emergent working class of early-nineteenth-century Lancashire is substantial, unsurprising, and impossible to ignore.[28]

Political radicalism at working-class level appeared in Lancashire in early 1792, some time after the emergence of the middle-class reform societies. Booth suggests that their immediate inspiration was the appearance of a sixpenny edition of Paine's *Rights of Man*, which was avidly bought and read throughout the cotton district, especially the second part with its proposals for social reform. The Patriotic Society was founded in Manchester in late May, followed by the

Reformation Society in the same town, and similar bodies at Stockport, Warrington and Liverpool. But formal organisations were the tip of an iceberg of uncertain size, and every town and village in the cotton district, as well as other places further north such as Ulverston, soon had a coterie of radical reformers. Where the membership of popular societies can be traced in any detail, weavers were much in evidence, along with factory workers and labourers as well as artisans and petty tradesmen. In contrast with the middle-class societies, with which they generally had little or no contact (except in Manchester), the working-class reformers set more store by Paine's appeal to the natural rights of man and to pure reason than by appeals to history in the form of a lost democratic Saxon constitution or of more recently subverted rights of represen-tation. They stressed popular sovereignty, freedom of speech and conscience, and equality before the law; and their proposals for manhood suffrage and annual parliaments assumed that these reforms would provide a panacea for social and economic as well as political ills. The moral superiority of the poor was often assumed, and the rhetoric of the popular societies had strong overtones of class conflict; but as Booth remarks, 'Rhetoric was not solution, and the lack of an economic programme did undermine support for the movement'. At this stage, however, the popular societies had neither the resources nor the opportunity to build a lasting platform of mass support. They convinced an articulate minority, but the advent of repression and war, and the successful arousal of violent constitutional loyalism by supporters of the existing political system, ensured that they were driven underground within months of their first appearance. But the apparent suppression of the movement was misleading. To quote Booth again, 'Paineite principles had driven deep into the soil of the industrial north. Here they lay dormant for several years awaiting the stimulus of economic privation which would give them both a wider relevance and a mass base.'[29]

When the middle-class reformers retired from the fray in the mid-1790s, indeed, it was left to the artisan radicals to keep the flame of reform alight through the repression at the turn of the century. In 1796 the 'mechanics' among the Manchester reformers set up a Corresponding Society, with little or no effective help from their social superiors. They found an outlet in the recently founded *Manchester Gazette*, and gave particular emphasis to the struggle against the war and the heavy tax burden that it engendered. But the society became increasingly isolated and uneasy in the face of intimidatory interference with its meetings and correspondence, and many of its more committed members soon went under-ground, joining the secret Society of United Englishmen which was beginning to recruit in small but significant numbers before the end of 1796. This move-ment borrowed the ideology and organisation of the United Irishmen, with their eagerness to contemplate insurrection and collaboration with a French invasion. Its basic goal remained 'a complete and radical REFORM of the REPRESEN-TATION of the PEOPLE in PARLIAMENT', but there were also strong republican and even atheistic overtones. Cells of United Englishmen multiplied rapidly and spread outwards from Manchester through the cotton district during 1797, with outposts in Liverpool and Wigan. The Manchester Irish were important among the organisers and promoters, but local recruitment was buoyant. By the end of 1797 there were probably several hundred members in Manchester alone, and several hundred more in the surrounding district. Weavers were especially prominent in the movement, alongside other artisans and factory spinners; and the authorities were acutely alarmed at the reports of their informers, especially where evidence appeared of attempts to infiltrate the military.[30]

The United Englishmen were severely disrupted by the arrest of several Manchester leaders early in 1798; and in the following year they and the Corresponding Societies were formally proscribed. But cells of local radicals continued to meet, during this period of repression as during previous ones; and the severe depression and soaring food prices of 1799 – 1800 brought a new upsurge of popular support, alongside an epidemic of food riots and desperate thefts, and with a further stimulus from the overlapping campaign against the new Combination Acts. All this came to a head in the spring of 1801, when a series of pamphlets and open-air meetings featured established radicals and made explicit the links between political and economic grievances. Again, the combination of repression and trade revival nipped the threat of insurrection, which was always remote, in the bud; but the balance of popular sentiment had shifted from Church and King towards covert or overt radicalism, after several years of war and pressure on living standards, and the language of class conflict was beginning to appear. Henceforth, most Lancashire towns and industrial villages contained a coterie of advanced radicals, many of whom also had trade union interests; and in every industrial depression or period of rising prices they were able to mobilise the support of thousands of neighbours who clearly felt, at such times, that they had little to lose. The Lancashire radicals had developed widespread, if tenuous, contacts with allies in the neighbouring counties and in London, as well as in Ireland; and although they were always most vulnerable to internal dissension and penetration by spies and informers when at their most ambitious and active, local magistrates and central government had reason to be alarmed. For the next half-century, each succeeding depression brought a popular political response, and Lancashire became a national centre, and sometimes the national core, of a series of assertive and sometimes numerously supported movements for extensive political and economic reform.[31]

The closing years of the war, and the economically unstable years after Waterloo, were particularly turbulent. As well as the food riots, machine-breaking and insurrectionary delegate meetings, 1812 saw the symbolically significant sacking of the Exchange Hall, the opulent temple of Manchester capitalism, by rioters who had gathered to oppose a vote of thanks to the Prince Regent for retaining his father's ministers and continuing the war. This provided startling confirmation of popular immunity to Church-and-King propaganda, even when it equated the radical reformers with a monstrous conflation of Bonapartism and Popery; and the popularity of radical sentiments among the 'lower orders' became even more widespread and evident when hard times returned after 1815.[32] The weavers were especially active, as their petitions went unheard and their existing protective statutes were repealed. The Hampden Clubs of 1816 – 17, pressing for universal suffrage and annual parliaments but stopping short of the secret ballot and making no explicit economic demands, attracted widespread support among Lancashire artisans. By March 1817 there were forty clubs in the cotton district, with perhaps 8000 members, deriving much of their support from the smaller towns and weaving villages around Manchester. Some of their members undoubtedly sought more violent and far-reaching solutions than were envisaged by the traditionalist, constitutional mind of Major Cartwright, the originator of the clubs; and early in 1817 delegates were going forth from Lancashire to evangelise the West Riding and the Potteries. The crisis came in March, when the so-called Blanketeers set out for London to petition the Regent for reform, with their constitutional rhetoric masking plans for intimidation and insurrection. But the machinery of repression was already in motion: the Blanketeers' launching meeting was broken up, and few of them travelled far beyond Stockport before being arrested and forced to return home. Rumours of plans to 'make a Moscow of Manchester' came to nothing, and a series of arrests followed. Several Lancashire radicals were taken to London and threatened with a charge of high treason, although the evidence was insufficient to proceed. The movement was already breaking up under its own internal dissensions, and these events brought about a temporary collapse; but not for long.[33]

The improved economic circumstances of 1818 gave renewed hope of successful trade union activity; but political activists tried, with some success, to link economic and political issues during the strike campaigns, and as the weavers' strike declined in a series of defiant nocturnal meetings, a Stockport employer asserted that, 'They want a *Revolution*'.[34] By the end of the year, the radical reformers were already regrouping. Stockport became a particular stronghold, and in October the Stockport Union for the Promotion of Human Happiness was founded by a Presbyterian minister called Joseph Harrison. It inaugurated a widespread revival of radical organisation, the Union Societies, which spread through the cotton district as rapidly as the Hampden Clubs in the renewed economic depression of 1819, and probably reached a far greater number of people. Stockport's society was unusual in the degree of attention it paid to religious issues and education. Its radical Sunday school had up to 2000 members at its peak, and the society as a whole may well have recruited as many as 5000. Other societies followed suit, drawing scholars away from the established loyalist Sunday schools; and for a time the radical reformers, who had added the secret ballot, the repeal of the Corn Laws and the redress of various fiscal, financial and religious grievances to their programme, could call on a genuine mass following among the distressed and disaffected. Their new mouthpiece, the *Manchester Observer*, claimed a circulation of up to 4000 in the middle of 1819, with a readership of several times that figure. Here was an exciting opportunity for the Radicals. How were they to make use of it?[35]

The early months of 1819 saw a series of mass meetings to petition and remonstrate against political corruption, economic depression, low wages and high prices. These themes were increasingly seen to be related, as when a Manchester weavers' meeting to protest against industrial grievances and advocate assisted emigration 'was won over by the Radicals Saxton and Walker to the cause of Radical Reform'.[36] During the spring, reform meetings with thousands of attenders were occurring regularly in all the towns around Manchester, and at Stockport on 28 June the local magistrates and yeomanry were unable to suppress a gathering of up to 20,000 which proposed national delegate meetings and a national subscription to enforce the law against the Home Secretary, who had declined to forward petitions to the Regent.[37] The authorities were increasingly alarmed by reports of nocturnal drilling using pikes and firearms. Whether the aim of this was to present an impressive and disciplined appearance in processions and demonstrations, as Samuel Bamford asserted, or whether there was widespread and genuine insurrectionary intent, may never be known, though some of the angrier radicals certainly hoped that a mass meeting might provide the spark for a general rising. The climax of this accelerating tempo of events was the Manchester meeting of August 16, known to posterity as the Peterloo Massacre. A galaxy of famous Reform orators, led by Henry Hunt himself, attracted between 50,000 and 150,000 people, many of them marching proudly in orderly procession behind specially made banners from the surrounding towns and villages, to a monster reform meeting which was supposed to speak for the whole of Lancashire. Samuel Bamford's account conveys the spirit of carnival and community in which the radical silk weaver and dialect poet set out from Middleton with his band of supporters; and the presence of large numbers of women and children, along with the complete absence of the pikes and firearms which the authorities feared, attests to the peaceful intentions of the vast majority of the marchers. But the meeting had hardly begun when it was broken up by the drawn sabres of the Manchester and the Cheshire yeomanry cavalry, the local ruling class in arms, and the Hussars. At least eleven died and several hundred were wounded or otherwise injured in the ensuing crush and panic. Whether or not the massacre was in some sense provoked by stone-throwing, perhaps from the volatile Stockport contingent, it was the prelude to a period of coercion and severe legal repression, and it generated widespread hatred and anger against the magistrates who ordered the military intervention, and the government which hastened to provide a public endorsement of their actions.[38]

The immediate aftermath of Peterloo saw preparations for revenge, as arms were made and gathered and secret meetings proliferated. The authorities called for government support against an imminent rising, and the popularity of Reform was illustrated by the enthusiastic reception for Hunt and other arrested Radical leaders on their return from having bail fixed at Lancaster Castle. Tens of thousands of supporters lined the roadsides from Preston to Manchester, and the event became a triumphal procession.[39] Popular anger and commitment was sustained for several months. In December, the superintendent of Haslingden's Wesleyan Methodist circuit gave an anguished description of the state of his district:

The country for a few miles round here may with propriety be called the hotbed of radicalism. I believe I shall be in compass in saying that two-thirds of the population in this circuit are reformers, and having no magistrate or chief constable within 8 miles, every man seems as if left to do that which is right in his own eyes. We have had them parading the streets almost every night by 200 or 300 together, singing their favourite songs of Hunt and Liberty, with lighted torches, flags and a Cap of Liberty hoisted upon a high pole with a lanthorn suspended with it. At the houses of the Radicals they stop and salute them with three cheers, and at the houses of the *marked kings-men* they give three horrible groans. They make no hesitation at calling by name the *marked* ones, who are to be killed the first day the orders come for them to break out ...[40]

'Great numbers' of pikes had been made, and he himself had been threatened with one in his own garden. But on the whole, the advocates of armed rising remained a minority of the radical leadership, and by this time a gap was widening between the ultra-radicals and the mainstream followers of Hunt, who pursued a peaceful campaign within the due processes of law. As the Six Acts limited the range of legally acceptable activities anyway, and the reform movement became internally divided and visibly lacking in attainable goals, it was unable to sustain its mass support as economic recovery began in 1820. J. B. Holroyd, the Haslingden circuit superintendent, still feared the 'sullen silence' and continuing conspiracies of the reformers in late January; but by this time a return to normality was already well advanced over much of Lancashire. The committed radicals had lost their wider constituency, and it was to be a decade before they were able to accumulate a mass following again.[41]

The campaigns of 1816–19 were national in scope, and Lancashire took a leading part only intermittently, most obviously at the time of Peterloo. The charismatic figures in the movement, such as Cartwright, Cobbett and Hunt, came from outside the county; and most, though not all, of the radical pamphlets and periodicals, which sold so well in Lancashire, were produced in London. Moreover, despite the dark murmurings of Spencean and other plotters who had their Lancashire adherents, there was no attempt at insurrection on the lines of Pentrich in Derbyshire or Folley Hall in the West Riding. Within Lancashire, too, radical reform was almost completely confined within the cotton district. It was always weak in Liverpool: significantly, the printer Joseph Mitchell left the town in 1816, disgusted by the empty posturings of the inward-looking middle-class Concentric Society, to make his career as a 'political missionary' in south-east Lancashire.[42] In 1819 a lively reform meeting was held in Clayton Square in the aftermath of Peterloo, and Cobbett was greeted by an enthusiastic crowd on his return from America; but more significant for the future were the riotous confrontations between Orangemen and Irish Catholics on July 12.[43] There is little evidence of radical activity elsewhere in the county. Within the cotton district, too, the centre of gravity was shifting away from Manchester itself, towards the smaller manufacturing communities around it: a process which was perhaps accentuated by the unwillingness of Manchester's Benthamite middle-class reformers to link up with the more plebeian and outspoken Huntite radicals. Above all, this was a movement of hand-loom weavers and artisans, with a leavening of factory spinners and tradesmen and a leadership which included prosperous maverick gentry and near-gentry who acted as necessary spokesmen and intermediaries with the governing class. The weavers' trade union leaders might sometimes seek to distance themselves from the radicals, as in Stockport; but their shared experience of unsuccessful petitioning and unredressed economic grievances, together with their sheer numbers, makes their predominance among the arrested Blanketeers and the Peterloo casualties less than surprising.[44] The only puzzle is that their importance has ever been doubted.[45] By 1819, whole communities were becoming radicalised. Women were participating actively alongside the men in places like Middleton, Blackburn and Stockport; and the older generation of Jacobin reformers from the 1790s was joined by younger blood, the 30-year-old Samuel Bamford and his peers.[46] Admittedly, most of the participants lacked the confidence, resilience and firmness of purpose to persist in the more difficult conditions of the early 1820s; but the return of hard times and political discord was to bring them out again in force in 1830.

The 1820s have been described as 'the formative decade' in the making of popular radicalism. So perhaps they were in the making of new ideologies; but in Lancashire, at least, the new currents of thought exacerbated existing divisions without providing widely attractive new alternatives.[47] The splits between the followers of Hunt and Richard Carlile, between republicans, freethinkers and a shifting variety of fringe religious sects, made it all the more difficult to build bridges between political principles and economic grievances. In the aftermath of the weavers' riots during the depression of 1826, there were reports of nocturnal meetings urging the pursuit of parliamentary reform through insurrection.[48] Trade union and radical concerns also overlapped in campaigns for the repeal of Combination Acts and Corn Laws, and perhaps in the spinners' pursuit of factory reform; but this was generally a period of political quiescence for the working-class radicals. The middle-class reformers in Manchester were making headway, and Liverpool's Whig reformers were vociferous if not so successful; but there was little evidence of the spirit of 1819. It was not dead, however, but only dormant. The ideas and principles of the reformers lived on in many hearts and minds, as the events of the 1830s were to show.

The parliamentary reform campaign of 1830–2 coincided, as we have seen, with a wave of unsuccessful strikes in several Lancashire industries, and with the renewal of attempts at collaboration between trades with a view to building general unions. Working-class leaders such as John Doherty were active in both the political and the industrial sphere, and as in 1819 it is no surprise to find relationships between middle-class and working-class reformers at best strained, at worst conflict-ridden and even vitriolic. The popular reform campaign, which demanded universal manhood suffrage, the secret ballot and annual parliaments, began in earnest with the foundation of the Manchester Political Union in July 1830. This had some middle-class support, including the journalist Archibald Prentice, the future hagiographer of the Anti-Corn Law League; but the Potter circle of wealthy moderate reformers held aloof, as the union's council became dominated by 'lower-middle-class shopkeepers and small masters'. The tone was set by Hunt's Peterloo anniversary meeting, which attracted up to 60,000 people; and political unions also appeared at Bolton and Oldham. At first, however, the bulk of working-class radical opinion was behind the Reform Bill as presented to Parliament, as an attainable first step. Despite Hunt's widespread popularity, and his victory in the Preston by-election in December 1830, his opposition to the Bill attracted little support when his Manchester followers set up a rival Political Union of the Working Classes in January. But when the Lords rejected the Bill for the first time in October 1831, opinions hardened quickly, and the PUWC was able to take the initiative, as it enrolled 4000 paying members in Manchester alone and began to spawn branches in the surrounding towns. As the crisis deepened, the language of radical reform became more violent, and there was new talk of drilling, arms and insurrection. But a strong groundswell of support for a moderate interim measure of reform persisted, and the various strains of radicalism were unable to agree on strategy, tactics or even principles. As Sykes remarks, 'Right to the end, the Reform Bill, by being a sufficiently extensive and plausible measure to split the radicals, inhibited the development of a consistent united working-class response throughout the district.'[49]

Sykes also makes the point that, 'The whole Reform Crisis and the resultant Reform Act permanently raised the level of local political activity.'[50] In the first place, of course, Lancashire had several additional parliamentary seats, which were concentrated in its new industrial towns. The county's total nearly doubled, from 14 to 26; and while Lancaster, Preston, Liverpool and Wigan retained their status as two-member constituencies under the new franchise, they were joined by Oldham, Blackburn, Bolton and Manchester itself, while Ashton, Bury, Rochdale, Salford and Warrington returned one MP each, along with Clitheroe which lost one of its seats. The working class, of course, formed a small minority of these urban electorates on the £10 householder franchise. The proportion of adult males with the vote varied between approximately one in four in Salford and one in twelve in Wigan, with the average being about one in six. But even Wigan had five times its number of pre-Reform voters. As late as 1865, however, after over thirty years of rising urban rents had widened the £10 franchise everywhere, the proportion of the electorate deemed by a parliamentary return to be working class ranged from only 13 per cent in Liverpool and 14 per cent in Oldham through 21 per cent in Bolton to 27 per cent in Manchester.[51] Another indication of the limited representativeness of the post-Reform electorate is that in Ashton-under-Lyne, a cotton town *par excellence*, only about one-sixth of the electorate was directly engaged in the cotton industry.[52] But Reform raised the expectations of the organised working class in Lancashire, generating angry reactions when the reformed parliament proved unresponsive to petitions for redress of grievances; and the regular parliamentary election campaigns helped to sustain a higher and more general level of political awareness than hitherto. The popular radicals sought to exert electoral influence through intimidation and exclusive dealing, a potentially potent weapon in electorates which contained a high proportion of shopkeepers; but in practice it was difficult to organise and carry out effectively, and Foster's arguments for its importance in Oldham during the 1830s have encountered sceptical reactions from other historians.[53]

For more than a decade after 1832, popular political activity in Lancashire remained intense, at least in the cotton district, as the campaign for radical parliamentary reform continued to simmer before boiling up again in the Chartist movement, while single-issue agitations for factory reform, trade union protection, minimum wages for hand-loom weavers, and in opposition to the New Poor Law and the Corn Laws, all sought parliamentary intervention and thus retained a political dimension. All this was set against a backcloth of persisting, and sometimes ambitious, trade union activity which often had its own political overtones; and in every case the nature and performance of the reformed parliament was such as to lend further fuel to the radical reformers.

The 1832 elections were strongly contested by the radicals in the cotton towns. Their only clear-cut success was in Oldham, where William Cobbett and the master manufacturer John Fielden shared a landslide victory; but their opponents were weak and tainted with attachment to the slave trade, and, crucially, there were no moderate Whig – Liberal reformers to split the vote.[54] Elsewhere the advocates of further reform might do well in the show of hands, but they had scant success at the polls, except perhaps at Ashton; but here the radical credentials of George Williams failed to stand the test of subsequent parliamentary voting. Whig reformers whose radicalism went little further than Free Trade and retrenchment dominated at the hustings in the rest of urban Lancashire, and six of the eight cotton constituencies returned a cotton employer in 1832, with Ashton following suit in 1835. It soon became apparent that the reformed parliament had little to offer to the working-class radicals; and its attitude to the popular issues of the 1830s confirmed this impression, as the hopes of the working class were dashed and their worst fears confirmed.[55]

Factory reform was already an issue at the 1832 election. The campaigns for shorter hours were dominated by the factory workers themselves, despite reservations in some quarters about the possible impact on family incomes. The spinners' unions and their leaders had a consistent record of activity in this field from 1814 onwards, with intermittent financial and moral support from a small minority of the employers. For the most part, too, the Tory paternalists and clergy who attracted so much attention in the West Riding were conspicuously absent from the Lancashire factory movement, and it was the operatives themselves who formed a committee in 1828 to seek the proper enforcement of the 1825 Factory Act. An Act restricting factory working hours to 10 per day was one of the hopes of the radical reformers; but the 1833 Factory Act fell far short of their expectations. The extent to which this Act was effectively enforced by the new inspectorate and the courts has recently become a matter for debate; but the perceived inadequacy of its restraints on the working hours of children and young people, and the obvious unwillingness of an entrenched parliamentary majority to consider further legislation, constituted one of the first demonstrations of the imperviousness of the reformed parliament to the concerns of the Lancashire working class.[56]

When industrial depression brought widespread short-time working to the cotton district, factory reform temporarily faded from the limelight; but its place was taken, with a vengeance, by the campaign against the introduction of the New Poor Law, which appeared to threaten workers and their families with incarceration in workhouses during every trade slump. There was widely effective passive resistance to the new legislation from employing and property-owning interests, too. They resented dictation from central government, and argued that the existing system, with its extensive use of outdoor relief and squalid but cheap poorhouses for the local infirm, was cheap, adequate and better suited to the circumstances of the Lancashire economy. The passive resistance of administrative inertia had the desired effect, and in many areas the administrative forms of the new system hid continuity of practice. The dreaded central workhouses or 'Bastilles', designed to deter the able-bodied applicant for relief, were neither as pervasive nor as daunting in practice as in theory; and their introduction was long delayed. Before the limited practical implications of the threat became apparent, however, the Lancashire cotton district, like the West Riding, saw an angry and sometimes violent working-class campaign against the new legislation. There is disagreement about the extent of this opposition, although there was successful intimidation at Oldham and riots against the new Poor Law Guardians occurred in 1838 at Todmorden. In the medium term, however, disorder was minimised by the unwillingness of local élites to risk confrontation even in places like Bolton, where there was some sympathy for the new Act among the leading citizens, but especially in Oldham or Rochdale where the prevailing middle-class opinion was itself hostile to the New Poor Law. As Sykes makes clear, however, there was a strong and distinct working-class campaign against the Poor Law Amendment Act and the Whig government which had introduced it; and its leaders included the radicals and trade unionists who were active in other causes at the same time; and as in the case of factory reform, the Tory paternalists and clergymen were of much less account west of the Pennines than they were in Yorkshire.[57]

These were not the only sources of anger and disillusionment in the early years of the reformed parliament. Despite the best efforts of John Fielden as MP for Oldham, the hand-loom weavers' campaign for the enforcement of minimum wages was treated dismissively, although successive parliamentary enquiries dragged on from 1834 to 1841.[58] Moreover, in many trades the defeats of 1829 – 31 were followed by a longer period of falling living standards and threats from new technology, as unions struggled to survive. The spinners recovered slowly and patchily, and a series of piecemeal wage reductions was imposed between 1837 and 1842. The calico printers, hatters, fustian cutters and tailors saw their unions broken or seriously undermined during the 1830s, although the power-loom weavers were beginning to organise wherever they included significant numbers of adult males. The builders and metalworkers were more successful, and the miners continued to organise locally and intermittently; but attempts to build wider federations and national unions still made little headway. The overall pattern of trade union experience was very dispiriting, and the case of the Tolpuddle Martyrs and the repression of the violent Glasgow cotton spinning strike in 1837 did not go unnoticed in Lancashire. Indeed, in 1837 – 8 a major campaign was launched in support of the Glasgow men, and the spinners' leader David M'Williams showed an awareness of the relationship between political and economic issues which may have been widely shared:

His opinion was, that the government and the manufacturing and commercial interests were determined to bring the working man down to the continental level in their wages. The unions amongst the working men were the great obstacles that stood in the way, and therefore had the determination gone forth to crush them ... The whigs intended to bring the working classes down to the level of the miserable pauper under the poor law amendment act.

When these interrelated grievances were coupled with the advent of new police forces and stronger forms of local government, dominated by employers who were beginning to control the magistrates' benches, the activities of the post-1832 parliaments, in terms of sins of omission and commission, could begin to look like a conspiracy by the political nation against the non-voting classes, or by capital against labour. It was under these conditions that Chartism acquired its mass following in the Lancashire cotton district, although it was to make a much less impressive showing elsewhere in the county.[59]

Parliamentary reform remained a live issue in Lancashire after the first Reform Act. In 1833, for example, a meeting at Padiham resolved in favour of four of what later became the Six Points of the Charter.[60] Chartism itself was imported into Lancashire from London and Birmingham in 1838, and the Northern Star, which became its most popular newspaper, was founded in Leeds in the previous year; but the combination of industrial depression and heightened political consciousness ensured that radical political activity would revive in strength in the cotton district during 1837 – 8, and that it would become a Chartist stronghold. The mass meetings at Kersal Moor and elsewhere in the later months of 1838 might attract tens of thousands of supporters, but the best indications of the movement's Lancashire importance come from its second phase, when it regrouped after the setbacks of 1839. At the end of 1841 Lancashire counted about one in six of the National Charter Association's branches, which put it on a par with the West Riding; and the national petition of 1842 claimed almost blanket coverage of the textile districts, although there was no doubt much exaggeration here. Chartism in Lancashire reached its peak with the great strike of August 1842, although there is heated dispute about the relationship between political and narrower trade union goals in the minds of many of the participants. After this, the movement's mass support faded rapidly, although the cadres of the committed were able to mobilise a limited and short-lived revival with the return of trade depression and national agitation in 1847 – 8. We need to ask questions about the nature of Lancashire Chartism, the identity of its supporters and the meaning of its rise and decline.[61]

At its peak, Chartism was perhaps strongest in the centres of the cotton spinning industry around Manchester, especially those where factories were small and surrounding settlements of hand-loom weavers were still capable of sustaining a radical culture which was already two generations old. It was also massively supported in the smaller weaving settlements of north-east Lancashire, such as Sabden, where at one time the *Northern Star* had 44 subscribers in a local population of perhaps 1500. Manchester itself, with its dispersed and cowed factory population, its paucity of hand-loom weavers and its growing commercial orientation, was less of a Chartist hotbed than is sometimes suggested, and in some of the spinning towns to the south of Manchester, such as Stockport and Staleybridge, the power of large employers was sufficient to reduce the movement to intermittent, if sometimes violent, bursts of angry activity. The western outposts of the cotton industry, Preston and Wigan, also proved to be infertile soil for large-scale and sustained Chartist organisation. Even the famous Preston massacre of 12 August 1842, when four alleged rioters were shot by the army, was part of a very short-lived display of support for a strike which was sustained for weeks together in other places. Outside the cotton district, Chartists were much thinner on the ground. There was a limited presence in Lancaster, and even in the little market town of Garstang; but in Liverpool and the mining and agricultural areas of south-west Lancashire there is very little evidence of Chartist support. There were Chartists among the Lancashire miners' leaders, but the Home Office was told that the country west of Wigan was 'entirely free from Taint' when insurrection was feared elsewhere in 1839, and the historians of St. Helens speak of a 'complete absence' of Chartism in that important mining district.[62] Significantly, the Chartist prisoners of 1842 were 'brought to

Liverpool for trial in order to be withdrawn from the disturbed districts', although one source suggests that up to 20,000 Liverpudlians signed the Chartist petition of that year, and there was certainly a late upsurge of support in 1848 when the call for the Charter was combined with a campaign for the repeal of the Act of Union with Ireland.[63]

Chartism attracted a broad cross-section of working-class support. Recent research has emphasised the strength of the links between Chartism and a comprehensive range of trade unions, especially in 1838–9 and above all in 1842, with only a few particularly 'aristocratic' trades remaining aloof.[64] As before, factory workers like the Preston power-loom weaver James Brown were active in the leadership alongside hand-loom weavers such as Richard Marsden and artisans like the chairmaker William Beesley. But Chartism was perhaps strongest where, and when, it could attract a good measure of support from shopkeepers, small tradesmen and even textile employers. In spite of John Foster's assertion of the proletarian character of Oldham Chartism, his own evidence lends credence to the suggestion that its success was based on a 'union of the productive classes' against the exploitation of the big employers and the corruption of central government. A similar pattern of support can be deduced for other Chartist strongholds.[65] But this kind of strength brought its own weaknesses. The divisions within Chartism over ideology and strategy are well known. They were not faithfully reflected in the social composition of the movement, but they acquired an extra dimension when mutually suspicious working-class and petty bourgeois radicals disagreed about such issues as how to proceed when a parliamentary petition was rejected, whether to compromise short of the Charter or pursue additional goals, and whether to promote political strikes or to threaten violent 'ulterior measures'. As hope receded, internal conflict sharpened, and the 'respectable' bases of Chartist support were the first to be severely eroded.

At first, Lancashire Chartism brought together several overlapping political traditions: the Paineite attack on 'old corruption' in Church and State; the political economists' critique of monopolies and other impediments to Free Trade, especially the Corn Laws; and the explicitly working-class attack on oppression and exploitation by government and employers, as exemplified by the Poor Law, the legal position of trade unions and the workings of the labour market. But believers in political economy were opponents of trade unions,[66] and these strands of reform had mutually incompatible expectations of the policies of a reformed parliament. Moreover, those who had loyalties to *laissez-faire* were open to persuasion by the Anti-Corn Law League that repeal was a more attainable, more efficacious and less risky panacea than the Charter. In any case, the radical Free-Traders were also often Nonconformists, whose priorities were directed more towards temperance, self-improvement and the battle against tithes and church-rates, which raged in several Lancashire towns during the 1830s, than towards remedies for more specifically working-class grievances. Those few reformers of this stamp who became involved in the early stages of Chartism – and Joseph Livesey in Preston, for example, held aloof – were quickly frightened off by the violent rhetoric and attempted insurrections of 1839. Many reformers in a broadly Paineite tradition were led away from Chartism as the threat of the New Poor Law receded and the prospect of piecemeal reform within the existing system beckoned in the 1840s. The Anti-Corn Law League, centred as it was in Manchester, was particularly seductive to moderate and petty bourgeois Chartists who drew back from violence and feared the resultant repression. Such developments proved especially damaging in early strongholds such as Oldham; and the political aspects of the attempted general strike of 1842 must have confirmed the apostacy of such people. There remained a convinced, committed and perhaps increasingly working-class core of principled Chartists, but after 1842 they had lost much of their petty bourgeois support and most of their capacity for mass mobilisation, in the face of widespread pessimism, fear and disillusionment.[67]

Chartism in Lancashire, perhaps more so than elsewhere, contained within itself a lively, aggressive, often vituperative vein of working-class consciousness. As might be expected from its genuinely close relationship with the trade unions, which was intermittent at a formal level but strong in terms of overlapping leadership and priorities, it was capable of generating an angry and increasingly sophisticated critique of local employers as well as national governments; and alliances with middle-class reformers were at best opportunistic, at worst mutually suspicious. This was, however, a set of perspectives *within* Chartism: it was *part* of the whole movement, and its ideas were the preserve of a committed minority. The Plug Plot strikers in 1842 voted to stay out until the Charter became the law of the land; but in practice, as events made clear, most of them would have been satisfied with the removal of the wage cuts which had prompted the strike in the first place. Even in Lancashire, Chartism was only partly a class-conscious working-class movement; and as we might expect, most of the participants had a very dim awareness of the relationship, as far as it went, between political exclusion and economic exploitation.[68]

If this interpretation is tenable, the decline of Chartism in Lancashire after 1842 becomes easier to understand; but the divisions in the movement, exacerbated as they were by judicious concessions from above, personal quarrels among the leadership, a carefully calibrated judicial repression in the aftermath of the major strikes and demonstrations, and the emergence of alternative panaceas, are only part of the story. Foster points out that in Oldham by 1847 the orthodox political parties were bidding successfully for radical support and working-class acquiescence, playing on religious and cultural divisions which had long been important; and this analysis has more than local importance, although Chartist candidates were still capable of winning the show of hands at Blackburn, for example, in that election. Foster also suggests that the employers conspired to divide the working class at the workplace by creating new labour aristocracies of pacemakers, supervisors and 'bosses' men', and that working-class anger was diverted away from the employers and the state towards the Irish immigrants whose numbers were swelling during the 1840s, in their role as religious and cultural deviants and suppliers of cheap labour. These ideas carry much less weight, for in so far as changes of this kind took place, they occurred in the 1850s and 1860s rather than the 1840s. They may have helped to sustain a new working-class political acquiescence, but they can have done little to *create* it.[69] The suggestion that the 1840s witnessed a revival and spread of employer paternalism, with schools, chapels, reading-rooms, excursions and sponsored entertainments aimed at bridging the cultural gap between capital and labour, may carry more conviction; but it would be hard to show that this trend was new or strongly marked, or that it was very effective, given the evidence of persisting employer authoritarianism, arbitrary actions and hostility to factory reform and trade unions.[70]

More important still, perhaps, was the upturn of the trade cycle after 1842, and the resultant retreat from the politics of despair, which lowered the political temperature until the repeal of the Corn Laws in 1846 and the 1847 Factory Act could show that central government was now capable of a positive response to pressure from without. One of the themes of this chapter, indeed, has been the close relationship between cyclical depression, trade union activity and mass radical political mobilisation; and although it would be crudely deterministic to make too much of this pattern, it is too boldly etched to be ignored. For a fuller understanding of working-class politics, and indeed of working-class lifestyles more generally, we need to look more closely not just at the trade cycle, but at broader trends in living standards, widely interpreted. These themes will introduce the next chapter.

9

STANDARDS AND EXPERIENCES: THE 'INDUSTRIAL REVOLUTION' AND THE LANCASHIRE WORKING CLASS

In this chapter I assess the impact of economic and cultural change on the living standards, broadly interpreted, of Lancashire's emergent wage-earning class between the late eighteenth century and the middle of the nineteenth. Trends in wages and prices, and in other aspects of the material standard of living, must form the basis of such an assessment. Housing and public health, for instance, cannot be ignored. But there is much more to the question than this. We must consider the ways in which working-class people protected themselves against the ever-present threats of cyclical and accidental poverty: short time, unemployment, a surfeit of dependent children, old age, illness, accident. Were these defences strengthened or weakened by changes in the wider economy and society? The informal institutions of family and neighbourhood must be at the centre of this discussion, alongside the role of Friendly Societies and other working-class voluntary organisations. We must also examine the extent and significance of cultural change. How far were existing modes of celebration and enjoyment, and ways of understanding the world, preserved in the face of extensive economic and social change? How far did they change autonomously, as the working class adapted to its new surroundings? How far was change imposed on them from above, through coercive restrictions or attempts by employers and others in authority to remake working-class culture in a more acceptable and less threatening image? We need to focus more generally on attempts by those in authority to mould working-class attitudes and expectations according to their own needs and preferences, whether their motives were mainly humanitarian or disciplinary. So we need to examine the impact of religious, educational and cultural institutions (not all of which were handed down or controlled from on high), and also to assess the implications for working-class living standards of the changing administrative bodies of the period, from the Poor Law to the Improvement Commission. How successful were these initiatives and organisations, and what was their impact on the working-class way of life? It will be clear that these themes are not only of vital importance in their own right: they will also add to our understanding of the developments which were analysed in the previous three chapters.

Few historical controversies have been more heated than the long-running dispute over trends in working-class living standards during this period. Much of the argument has centred on rival interpretations of the changing level of real wages, as pessimistic Marxists have confronted optimistic apologists for capitalism. Most contributions to the debate have been pitched at national level, although they have increasingly had to take account of regional studies. Unfortunately, no such study has yet made Lancashire its focus; but a tentative consensus seems to have emerged at national level, against which the complexities of the Lancashire experience can be set. Von Tunzelmann's sophisticated economic analysis of the available wage and price series leads to the conclusion that although the possible changes in real wage levels between 1750 and 1850 'range anywhere from an increase of 150 per cent ... down to no increase at all', the strongest evidence of improvement comes from the years between 1820 and 1850.[1] More recently, the work of Lindert and Williamson has been more confidently optimistic. Their 'best guess' from their range of evidence and equations is that 'real adult-male full-time earnings' increased between 1781 and 1851 by more than 60 per cent for farm workers, and more than doubled for artisans and for a 'middle group' which included urban labourers, coal miners and cotton spinners. Again, this improvement took place entirely between 1820 and 1850.[2] It is hard to see this kind of evidence, at national level, leading to significantly different results in the future.

As the participants are well aware, this does not mean that the argument is over. Pessimists can argue that these gains need to be counterbalanced by attention to the insecurity of health, employment and mortality in urban and industrial settings, and to overcrowding, appalling sanitation, adverse changes in work patterns and labour discipline, and the disruption of families, communities and cultures. Sceptics can point to the wide variations in regional experiences, which may vitiate attempts to make convincing generalisations at national level; and they can emphasise the difficulty of establishing agreed wage-rates for comparative purposes in conditions where there were wide and fluctuating variations in piecework rates and overall earnings within industries, and at the level of the locality and the firm as well as the region. Rents also varied considerably, as did housing types and practices, diets, and earning opportunities for women and children. In their anxiety to press home the optimistic case, Lindert and Williamson (especially the latter) have attempted to deal with some of these objections. The results are laughably unconvincing. The rent component of their cost of living index is based on 'a few dozen cottages in Trentham, Staffordshire'; optimistic claims for unemployment levels in the 1840s and earlier are made by extrapolating backwards from the experience of trade union members in engineering, metalworking and shipbuilding between 1851 and 1892; and claims about the limited extent of urban 'disamenity' are 'supported' by the use of Edwardian statistics as the basis for complex calculations about the 1840s. The mathematics may be sound, but the evidence is insufficient and inappropriate to bear the burden of the calculations. In terms of the broader range of arguments about the quality of life, the debate on working-class living standards in the 'Industrial Revolution' is still wide open; and in Lancashire at least, there is room for further discussion of the real wage question.[3]

Real wages in Lancashire, on the basis of the experience of building and road labourers, had fluctuated upwards from the 1720s to the late 1760s, with a severe setback in the mid-1750s; and from 1770 to the early 1790s they wavered around an average roughly half as much again as the figure for 1700.[4] But these figures are based on London prices, and they ignore, for example, the Lancashire propensity for consuming oatmeal rather than wheat as the staple cereal. Subsequently, the complexities increase. Spectacular increases in food prices occurred in 1795 and 1800–1, as oatmeal and potatoes rose to more than three times their 1791 price in Oldham, where the poor were reduced to eating dock leaves, while at one point nettles were on sale at twopence a pound. There were further price surges in the Manchester area in 1812–13 and (to a much lesser extent) in the mid-1820s; and in Lancashire at least, the price fall which provided the initial stimulus to the national rise in real wages was not yet in evidence by 1830. As T. S. Ashton, himself a declared optimist, remarked, 'In 1831 the standard diet of the poor can hardly have cost much less than in 1791. If ... so, it would seem that any improvement in the standard of living must have come either from a rise in money wages or from a fall in the prices of things not included in this index.'[5] Fleischman also points to high coal prices in the winter of 1800–1 and 1815–16, and finds evidence for substantial and sustained rent rises for cottages in the weaving village of Barrowford, of more than 50 per cent between the late 1790s and 1826.[6] There may have been a significant downturn in the prices of important elements in the Lancashire working-class budget, but if so it came after 1830, and we need more research to confirm it. In any case, generalisation about prices in Lancashire is overwhelmingly difficult, even if all were agreed on the consumption patterns which should be represented in a cost of living index. As basic an item as wheat flour was much more expensive in the early nineteenth century at Barrowford than at Bolton, and in 1817 the price at Manchester was 4s 6d for twelve pounds at one point when the Lancashire average was 2s 10½ d. Fuel prices also varied substantially, and Fleischman's research leads him to doubt the possibility of making effective general statements.[7] House rents at working-class level showed marked variation: in Stockport in the early 1830s working-class dwellings could be had for between £2 and

£8 per annum, and levels of overcrowding varied between streets and families, and fluctuated over time.[8] As Ashton said long ago, 'We require not a single index but many, each derived from retail prices, each confined to a short run of years, each relating to a single area, perhaps even to a single social or occupational group within an area.'[9]

In practice, the calculation of money wages is equally difficult, even for well-defined occupational groups or individual occupations. Lindert and Williamson offer a series of estimates of 'nominal annual earnings' for cotton spinners for selected years from 1755 to 1851. As Flinn remarked in a comment on their paper, it would be interesting to know who the cotton spinners in question were in 1755; but subsequently confusion becomes worse confounded.[10] Over this period the words 'cotton spinner' could refer to operatives working on jennies, throstles, hand-mules or self-acting mules, at varying speeds, with varying numbers of spindles and levels of productivity, and with wage tariffs also increasing according to the quality of the yarn spun. Wages also varied town by town, as trade union leaders knew only too well, as the low wages paid in Hyde, Preston or the country mills could be used by employers elsewhere as justification for competitive wage cuts of their own; and Foster, pointing out conservatively that 'within the Lancashire cotton industry there were variations in wages of up to 15 per cent for the same job', argues that wage-rates were highest in towns like Oldham where, he thinks, the labour movement was most effective in defending workers' interests.[11] Within individual towns, too, there was no uniformity in the wages paid by particular employers, as their apologist Harriet Martineau well knew; and even if such uniformity had been achieved on the basis of the Manchester spinning piece-rate list of 1829, there would still have been 540 different rates to consider, according to the size of the mule and the quality of the yarn produced.[12] Nor were such vagaries confined to the particularly difficult case of cotton spinning. They were equally applicable to hand-loom weaving, with its enormous range of cloth qualities and markets, to coal mining, and to agricultural labour, although here there seems to have been a tendency for wage-rates to level out as between the different areas of Lancashire during the first three decades of the nineteenth century.[13]

The only way forward is to eschew attempts to generalise about the living standards of 'the Lancashire working class' as a whole, and to concentrate on charting the changing fortunes of specific occupations or groups of occupations. Even this has its pitfalls, for the wage-rates of adult males are only part of the story in an economy where family incomes could be considerably augmented by the earnings of wives and children, where lodgers could provide a valuable buttress against the worst extremes of material poverty, and where many hand-loom weavers and town labourers continued to double as agricultural workers during the summer months, especially at harvest time, even after the demise (which was not yet universal in 1851) of the 'dual economy' of weaving and smallholder farming. In many families, too, the total income came from a mixture

[169]

of domestic industry and factory work. But a few comments about trends in wages can be made.

The most clear-cut case is that of the hand-loom weavers. Despite Lindert and Williamson's absurd assertion to the contrary ('Even the famous cotton hand-loom weavers may not have suffered any further net losses after 1820 ...'),[14] the evidence for a steady decline in piece-rate earnings during the first four decades of the nineteenth century is overwhelming. A brief revival in 1813 – 14 brought a passing reminder of the temporary prosperity of the early 1790s, but the downward trend accelerated in the late 1820s, with the slump of 1826 marking a turning point. It is impossible to shrug off the widespread evidence of distress among this declining but still numerous occupational group during the 1830s and 1840s. Here is an important and conspicuous sector for whom industrialisation brought short-term gains but long-term immiseration.[15]

The case of the mule-spinners, the best-documented and most controversial of the factory occupations, is much less straightforward. On the one hand, they were a relatively well-paid creation of the factory system, with a supervisory role and some claim to skilled status; and their real wages may well have risen considerably from an already favourable position between 1800 and 1830.[16] On the other hand, their privileged position was terribly vulnerable to cyclical unemployment and technological innovation, as we saw in Chapter 8; and in the light of this it comes as no surprise to find piece-rates falling by one-third between 1822 and 1832 for one grade of yarn, and to find a more general decline in spinners' wages during the 1830s, when increased productivity on larger mules did not compensate for falling piece-rates, and the growing numbers of self-actor minders were paid significantly less than most of the hand-mule operators.[17] The employers made much of the spinners' alleged ability to clear more than three pounds per week, after paying their assistants. This would have put them close to the top of the national wages league; but evidence from Manchester suggests that, even before 1829, this applied to only 25 or 30 of the most skilful of the town's 2500 spinners, and most cleared only about 16 shillings per week, a semi-skilled rate rather than an artisan wage.[18] In any case, spinners had a notoriously short working life, which was increasingly likely to be punctuated by illness and injury; and the innovations of the late 1820s and 1830s created a surplus labour pool of unemployed and underemployed. Their hot, dusty working conditions, and the stresses imposed by machine-minding, must also be taken into account. Even – and perhaps especially – after 1820, the experiences of the spinners do not fit in with optimistic assertions of rising working-class living standards.

Changing wage-rates in other adult male occupations are even harder to evaluate. Members of established or emergent labour aristocracies in printing, engineering and metalworking seem to have done well, but the disturbed industrial relations and frequent unsuccessful strikes in building and the clothing trades, in coal mining and calico printing, suggest that any increased purchasing power in these industries would have been heavily dependent on falling prices and regular work.[19] Agricultural wage-rates in Lancashire became relatively high in the late eighteenth century, and remained stable in the early decades of the nineteenth; but Marshall draws an important contrast between the position of 'well-established, mature or regular' farm labourers whose lot improved between 1813 and 1833, and a reserve supply of casual labour which ensured that there was 'always an element of stark poverty' in spite of the opportunities for migration to the towns.[20] In Liverpool, too, dock porters could earn from 21 to 24 shillings per week if in regular work; but this comfortable income was the preserve of a minority, and the casual and irregular nature of much of the work ensured that most did well to average 14 or 15 shillings per week throughout the year.[21]

These were far from being the worst-off among the Liverpool labour force, with its distressing predominance of the unskilled and casual; but these examples draw attention to the importance of considering actual incomes as well as nominal wage-rates. Here, the factory workers, with long hours but regular and predictable incomes, might be thought to have the edge; but in practice they suffered severely from the poverty and insecurity of cyclical unemployment and short-time working. Levels of unemployment are particularly difficult to calculate, but with all its imperfections, we cannot ignore the factory master Henry Ashworth's estimate that more than half of Bolton's millhands were unemployed in the trough of the 1842 depression, and nor can we set aside the abundant literary and descriptive evidence of widespread distress at every downturn of the trade cycle.[22] Not that Liverpool was immune from cyclical depression: in that same year of 1842, Finch's survey of Vauxhall Ward found that one-third of the population had no visible means of support, with the building and clothing trades suffering alongside general and dock labourers.[23] On the other hand, hand-loom weavers throughout the textile district, and casual workers of various kinds in central Manchester, suffered from chronic under-employment at most stages of the trade cycle.[24] It is difficult to tell whether these problems worsened in frequency or social range between the late eighteenth century and the 1840s; but at best they remained a serious drain on working-class living standards, or an ever-present threat to them; and their importance should not be underestimated or lightly dismissed.[25]

The most convincing evidence on working-class living standards towards mid-century comes from Foster and Anderson, who used the family and occupational listings in the 1851 census enumerators' books to calculate the incomes of a sample of families, in Oldham and Preston respectively, and compare them with the 'poverty lines' established by social researchers in the late nineteenth and early twentieth centuries. Their conclusions are revealing. In Oldham two-fifths of all families, and well over half of the wage-earning families, generated insufficient income to supply a barely adequate diet in the depressed year of 1847. Two years later, in better times, 15 per cent of all families were still in primary poverty, and a further 26 per cent had only a narrow and precarious margin above the very barest level of subsistence. On this measure, moreover, even in 1849 more than one-third of wage-earning families with young children were living in poverty, and when labourers' families were isolated the figure rose to 89 per cent.[26] Anderson's similar calculations for 1851, another good year for trade, find nearly 20 per cent of working-class families below an assessed poverty line; and more than half the families with children at home, but not in employment, were in this category or only just above it. These figures exclude hand-loom weavers, and are therefore likely to be biased towards optimism; and they also assume full employment, 'rational' spending patterns (nothing wasted on alcohol or entertainment, for example), and unadulterated food. These are all untenable assumptions for most families, of course; but even so, Foster and Anderson agree that poverty of the most basic and abject kind would come to all but perhaps one-seventh of all working-class families in an early Victorian cotton town at some stage in their career.[27] In Liverpool the predominance of unskilled labour, the high cost of housing and the lack of paid employment for women and children made matters worse. Taylor calculates that only constantly employed skilled workers could earn sufficient to keep a family above Foster's poverty line at mid-century; and 45 per cent of the household heads in 1851 were semi-skilled, unskilled and domestic servants.[28] If real wages had really soared to the extent asserted by Lindert and Williamson between 1820 and 1850, the situation before 1820 must have been appalling indeed; but it is more likely that their abstract mathematical calculations have no real bearing on the experience of the Lancashire working class in these difficult transitional years. It is a pity that the absence of comparable sources makes it impossible to replicate the Foster and Anderson analyses for the late eighteenth and early nineteenth centuries; but at very least they set a low ceiling on the extent of any real improvement in working-class living standards over the period.

Material on diet and housing corroborates these findings to a large extent. An analysis of nineteen working-class budgets collected in Manchester and Dukinfield in 1841 shows that the 'sober and industrious' in full employment might have a boring but adequate diet based on bread, potatoes and a little meat; but a group of labourers on short time were seriously deficient in protein and calories. A nutritionist thought it 'very likely that this diet would have some immediate effect on health and the ability to resist disease'. Moreover, none of the budgets made any allowance for tobacco, alcohol or entertainment, and foods were given their 1960 nutritional value without allowance for adulteration.[29] What of the less-disciplined workers, who might be vulnerable to Andrew Ure's strictures about the irrational preference for 'rank bacon' which he associated with 'vitiated palates accustomed to the fiery impressions of tobacco and gin'? The proliferation of beerhouses in Lancashire after the 1830 Act, and the discovery by Angus Reach in 1849 that the air of a Manchester music saloon was 'one rolling volume of tobacco smoke', suggest that such comments were not entirely misplaced, and there was ample scope, and every excuse, for falling into 'secondary poverty' in these ways.[30] As far as it goes, the evidence on working-class diet is certainly not encouraging.

At its worst, urban housing in industrial Lancashire could be notoriously bad; and it is difficult to argue for any real or sustained improvement before the 1840s at the earliest. Over much of the county, the quality of rural housing was comparatively good, and improving, especially where the use of stone and slate came early, in Bowland, the Lune valley and Furness. Hand-loom weaving villages like Middleton were capable of earning praise from visitors, too, even in the 1840s. Only in Garstang, the Fylde and the Leyland area, where mud and thatch persisted as building materials, were there persistent complaints in the countryside.[31] But by far the worst housing conditions emerged not in the factory towns, nor even in Manchester or the mining districts, but in Liverpool. Here, a combination of expensive land and a desperate need for accommodation close to the docks helped to ensure very high levels of overcrowding in squalid cellars and back-to-back courts long before the end of the eighteenth century. The number of persons per house was high, standing at more than six throughout the first half of the nineteenth century; and many of the 'houses' were one-room tenements. In 1790 and still in 1840, about one-eighth of Liverpool's population lived in cellars, some of which were dug into soil saturated with chemical refuse or 'super-saturated' with sewage. Courts increased from one-fifth of the town's housing stock in 1803, to one-third in 1850. The average working-class cottage occupied a mere 16 square yards of land, but prices – and rents – were substantially higher than in Bolton, Bury or even Manchester. When one adds a chronic shortage of sewers, water and basic amenities to this tale of woe, and points to the failure of sanitary reform initiatives in the 1840s, coinciding with the great Irish influx of that decade, the picture is complete. Environmental conditions undoubtedly deteriorated considerably in Lancashire's largest and fastest-growing town, and there is little wonder that by the 1840s it was notorious as the unhealthiest town in Britain.[32]

The pattern of housing provision in the cotton towns themselves was far from uniform. Manchester itself was scarifyingly described by Engels in 1844, but his most horrifying examples of the tumbledown, the insanitary and the grossly overcrowded were drawn from the older parts of the town, where former middle-class houses were subdivided and the pressures on the land and labour markets were not dissimilar to those of central Liverpool. Ancoats, with its sweatshops, textile outworkers and labourers, was already a notorious slum by the time of Peterloo, and its incidence of cellar dwellings, overcrowding and poverty remained on a par with the worst Liverpool conditions.[33] But Angus Reach in 1849 found nothing quite so bad as the worst of London or Glasgow; and he emphasised that the newer districts of Chorlton, and especially Hulme, were much airier, better planned and, as a result, better maintained. Even here, water supply and sanitation were still very imperfect indeed; but overcrowding levels, and the standard of new housing, were visibly improving during the 1830s and 1840s.[34] In the cotton towns of Manchester's hinterland, a similar pattern can frequently be seen, with housing supply beginning to catch up with demand after the peak years of rapid urbanisation in the 1820s, although older centres, such as Bolton, suffered severely from their extensive residue of decayed and over-crowded central tenements. Municipal improvements were just beginning to make headway in the 1840s. But Reach's general impression of Oldham should remind us of the limits to optimism: 'A mean-looking straggling town ... the whole place has a shabby underdone look. The general appearance of the operatives' houses is filthy and smouldering. Airless little back streets and close nasty courts are common'.[35] Some factory towns did benefit from the provision of a higher standard of housing by substantial factory owners, as in Hyde and Ashton-under-Lyne; and this was particularly frequent in the outlying factory villages, where motives of profit and control, and the need to assure a labour supply, jostled with the humanitarian impulse in the minds of the investors.[36] But a higher quality of employer-provided housing was usually the preserve of skilled and supervisory workers, and it accounted for only a small proportion of the total housing stock, most of which was built in haste by small speculative builders and tradesmen. Even so, the evidence suggests that factory industry was not, in itself, the villain of the piece here: conditions in the cotton towns may have been worse than in the countryside, but they were beginning to improve towards mid-century, and it was the low-wage, casual labour economy of Liver-pool which generated the worst living conditions of all from the late eighteenth century onwards.

On the crude measure of the ratio of persons per house, Lancashire as a whole remained second only to Middlesex as Britain's most overcrowded county in 1841. More to the point, perhaps, its death-rates were also consistently high throughout the period, when compared with the national average. Here again, the Liverpool figures were particularly arresting. They were high in the late eighteenth century, but declined between 1800 and 1820. Subsequently, how-ever, they rose disastrously, and between 1831 and 1849 the rate was always over 30 per thousand, reaching 45 per thousand in 1837 and a calamitous 71 per thousand in 1847, when the average for England and Wales was in the low twenties. Here was a telling index of falling living standards and environmental catastrophe.[37] Fleischman's tables of life expectancy at birth suggest that the cotton district fared rather better than this, with Manchester's figures fluctuating upwards from 18.7 years in 1782–91 to 21.5 years in 1792–1812, and holding firm at 21.4 in 1838–44. There was little change in Preston, too; but at Chorley and Burnley there were substantial falls between the late eighteenth century and the years around 1840; and the figures were always significantly worse than the totals for England and Wales as a whole. A similar pattern held good for life expectancy at the age of 5, although here the gap was narrower as a result of the high infant mortality rates in the cotton district. In Manchester itself, the death-rate for children under 1 year old was 244 per thousand in 1841, compared with 218 for England and Wales; and for the under-5s it was 527 as against 405. But we must not assume that the high infant mortality rates were purely the result of the social pathology of factory industry. Liverpool's infant mortality rates were even higher, although St. Helens seems to have been on a par with the national total; and the figures for Lancashire as a whole were little better than Manchester's. But the rural areas were much healthier, as evidence from Furness makes clear, and the really high and rising death-rates were concentrated in the industrial and commercial towns, with their polluted rivers and atmosphere, bad housing, and industrial accidents and disease.[38]

The available evidence strongly suggests that, in terms of material living standards, working-class people in the cotton towns fared much better than in Liverpool, and perhaps on Merseyside more generally. In large measure this was due to the boost to family incomes which was provided by the job opportunities for women and children in the cotton factories. We must not overstate this contrast. In Liverpool itself, the 1851 census found that 36 per cent of adult females were in employment, against a national figure of 45 per cent; but 71 per cent of these were in domestic service or dressmaking, which paid particularly low wages. The part-time charwomen, prostitutes and others who were likely to be missed by the census taker, were in similarly disadvantaged circumstances, and the lack of regular work for children was perceived as being a major cause of high levels of juvenile crime.[39] Agriculture, especially at harvest, and domestic manufacture continued to generate demand for women's and children's work, although this was not such a tangible increment to a family economy as a factory wage.[40] Women and children also worked in coal mining, in the Wigan and St. Helens districts but not, apparently, further east. The number of women involved by the early 1840s was only seven or eight hundred, but the total had probably been larger in earlier times; and there were still hundreds of children, perhaps two-thirds of whom had started work before the age of 9. Many of these people were employed by husbands and fathers on a subcontracting basis, and they made what was perceived to be a vital contribution to the family economy; but they were banished from underground by the 1842 Mines Act, although it was several years before it could be effectively enforced in south-west Lancashire. Reformers thought that the costs of female and child labour in mines, in terms of cruelty, danger and immorality, far outweighed the benefits in material living standards to the families concerned, in so far as this issue was considered at all; and similar arguments are even more important when we consider the relationship between female and child labour and the standard of living in the cotton industry.[41]

The extensive use of female and child labour in the cotton factories was a source of angry contemporary polemic. Humanitarians and moral reformers were horrified by the imposition of long hours of unrelenting, disciplined toil on young children, and by the implications of women, especially wives and above all mothers, working outside the home and away from the protection and supervision of their menfolk. Fears were expressed for the future of the family as a basic unit of social cohesion, discipline and morality, and the position of the man as breadwinner was thought to be threatened by technological innovations which facilitated the extended use of female and child labour. Engels was at one with the Evangelical factory reformers on this issue: 'The employment of women at once breaks up the family; for when the wife spends 12 or 13 hours every day in the mill, and the husband works the same length of time there or elsewhere, the children grow up like wild weeds; they are put out to nurse for a shilling or eighteenpence per week, and how they are treated may be imagined ... The children who grow up under such conditions are utterly ruined for later family life ... A similar dissolution of the family is brought about by the employment of the children. When they get on far enough ... they begin to pay the parents a fixed sum for board and lodging, and keep the rest for themselves ... and regard the paternal dwelling as a lodging-house, which they often exchange for another, as suits them.'[42] Aspersions were also cast on the sexual morality of factory girls, and on their suitability as future wives and mothers in the absence of appropriate domestic training.

These allegations are very important to an evaluation of working-class living standards in the 'Industrial Revolution'. To test their validity, we must begin by looking at the extent and nature of women's and children's factory employment, before assessing its implications for the families in question. Child labour was used extensively from the earliest days of water-powered factory industry, and the problems of obtaining a labour force in rural areas led entrepreneurs to import pauper children as 'apprentices' from as far away as London and the Home Counties. These children were worked for very long hours and paid little more than their keep, and although some employers, like the Gregs at Styal, provided adequate food, accommodation, medical care and moral supervision, others starved and neglected their apprentices, leading to occasional scandals. As a result, magistrates and Poor Law authorities began to keep a closer eye on the conditions of apprentice labour, and the first Factory Act of 1802 was intended specifically for their protection. By this time, however, the importance of the pauper apprentice system was already beginning to decline, largely owing to problems of cost and discipline, and to the readier availability of 'free' labour in the more thickly populated settings of the steam-age factories. The system survived into the 1830s in some places, but it was mainly a device of the earliest phases of factory industry.[43] In the early nineteenth century the demand for cheap, agile, nimble, subordinate labour in the cotton factories was being met overwhelmingly by the employment of local children from the age of 5 or 6 upwards. Numbers are impossible to obtain for the heyday of effectively unregulated child labour, but stray pieces of evidence suggest the magnitude of its importance. In 1819, for example, 40 per cent of McConnel and Kennedy's labour force in Manchester was aged between 8 and 15.[44] Even in 1835, after the formal (but ill-enforced) abolition of factory work for children under 8 in 1833, one in seven of the cotton factory labour force was under 13 years old, although the proportion subsided to around 5 per cent in the late 1830s and 1840s.[45] The incidence of child labour, and still more the better-paid labour of adolescents, made a very significant difference to the living standards and way of life of many thousands of families in the cotton district.

Women's factory work grew in importance as child labour declined. The same figures for 1835 show females over 13 as forming nearly half of the cotton factory labour force, and over 55 per cent of a total half as large again (331,000 instead of 218,000) in 1850. Above all the number of women in their twenties and early thirties was increasing. In 1835 and 1841 just over 40 per cent of female cotton operatives were over 20 years old, while in 1851 they were 57.4 per cent of the much larger total.[46] By 1851, too, the proportion of married women in the factories had increased considerably, standing at about 26 per cent. In Stockport in 1841 only 18 per cent of female factory workers were married, as against 28 per cent in 1851, and other evidence confirms that they were growing rapidly in importance during the 1830s and 1840s.[47] However, evidence from Preston suggests that even in 1851 only about half the wives engaged in factory work had dependent children, and this accounted for only one in nine or ten of the town's children under 10 years old.[48] As Anderson remarks, it was 'above all the younger wives and those with few or no children who were in employment at all'. All this sets the extent of wives' and mothers' factory work in perspective; and it should remind us of the extent to which factory work in Lancashire, for men and women alike, was for most people a life-cycle stage rather than a permanent career. As we saw in Chapter 6, in 1851, 15 per cent of the county's adult women, and nearly 38 per cent of its employed women, worked in cotton: but cotton accounted for nearly 40 per cent of girls aged between 15 and 19, and about 25 per cent of boys of that age. In the cotton towns themselves, factory work had become almost a universal experience for female teenagers, although this was probably quite a recent development; but for both sexes the age participation rate fell steadily through the twenties and thirties, as men who' failed to make the grade to the best-paid factory jobs moved to other industries, and women started families and – usually – left the factory.[49] But the incidence of female and child labour during the period as a whole was sufficient to cause considerable contemporary disquiet, and we must pursue its implications a little further.

Child labour in itself was nothing new, of course; and the systematic exploitation of children in domestic manufacture had long been an essential feature of the Lancashire textile economy. What aroused concern was the concentration of children in factories, working up to 14 hours a day, and sometimes even longer, shackled to the tireless rhythm of the machine, kept awake and alert by blows and threats, deprived of schooling or religious instruction, and removed from the control and affection of parental authority. How should one respond to this indictment? The physical realities are the most straightforward. The long hours, hot and dusty working conditions, injuries, deformities and illnesses are in-escapable, as is the evidence for the widespread use of corporal punishment. But the *extent* of the evil is impossible to gauge. At one extreme, apologists for the factory presented spirited children happy in their work, the 'lively elves' of Andrew Ure; at the other extreme, Engels and others provide us with the full catalogue of horrors, replete with horrifying examples.[50] But it is impossible to isolate the factory, as an influence on health, from the home and the general environment, apart from a few specifically industrial diseases, and it is difficult to chart a clearly defined path between the extremes. Angus Reach remarked in 1849, when hours were shorter and young children had been banished from the factories, that 'the labour cannot be said to exercise a seriously stunting or withering effect upon those subjected to it – that it does not, perhaps, make them actually ill, but that it does prevent the full development of form, and that it does keep under the highest development of health'.[51] This probably errs on the side of optimism, and it leaves out of account the mind-numbing tedium of a piecer's working day – 'the dull routine of a ceaseless drudgery, in which the same mechanical process is incessantly repeated', as J. P. Kay expressed it – but it remains impossible to assess the extent to which long hours in the factory were qualitatively worse than, perhaps, equally long hours in the domestic workshop.[52] What concerned the factory reformers at least as much – or rather the Tory paternalists who supported the cause – was the lack of educational and religious supervision, and the apparent dissolution of paternal authority. We shall look at schooling and religion shortly; but we need to discuss the relationship between the factory and the family here, because this contentious topic also has a bearing on the equally controversial issue of the social impact of women's factory work.

On the face of it, children's factory work would seem to break up the family as a working unit, divorcing authority at the workplace from authority in the home, and thereby diminishing the roles and responsibilities of parents. This is what contemporaries feared; and they expected children to break away from the family home at the earliest possible moment, asserting their status as inde-pendent wage-earners and undermining the stability of the family. The actual pattern of events was more complex in every way. In the first place, of course, there was nothing new about children working away from home, in service, apprenticeship or agriculture. The differences were that the factory took children out of the home at a younger age, and assigned a clear money value to their work. Moreover, in some cases, especially in mule-spinning, some of the children were hired as factory workers by their own fathers or other relatives, on a sub-contracting basis; and thus familial authority at the workplace was perpetuated in the factory. Smelser has argued that this was the norm in the early decades of the factory system, and that it was undermined only with the coming of larger mules requiring additional piecers and scavengers drawn from beyond the spinners' families, in the disturbed late 1820s and early 1830s. But this argument runs counter to much of the evidence. In the 1830s two-thirds of the under-18 male factory workers, and one-third of the females, were indeed hired by the operatives rather than directly by the masters; but Anderson has shown that only a small minority of spinners, who were mainly youngish men and often unmarried, can have had children of just the right ages to perform the required tasks at any given time, and evidence from the Preston area in 1816 confirms this. In the town itself, only about ten per cent of the factory children were employed by a parent, brother or sister, although in the surrounding rural area the figures rose to about a quarter.[53] The mule-spinners themselves might be able to employ their own relatives in the factory, but they employed other people's children as well; and most factory children had parents working outside the factory, especially during the great influx of hand-loom weavers' children in the 1820s. Children might often work under the supervision of more distant relatives, or of neighbours; and no doubt this often mitigated the harshness and strangeness of the factory régime.

Moreover, the family as an institution was strengthened rather than weakened by the transition to the factory. There is some evidence of teenage children leaving home to live in lodgings, but for many this option was enforced by the death of parents, rather than being chosen, and Anderson concludes that 'the vast majority of non-migrant children who had parents alive were ... living with them'.[54] Reach suggested in 1849 that the family's 'cohesive powers' were diminished by 'constant labour, and not unfrequent privation', and by the interests of individual wage-earners becoming stronger than the interests of the family as a whole, so that 'the factory system tends to a speedier recurring break-up, and a speedier recurring formation of families', than was usual among the lower classes. He contrasts this with the stronger and more lasting ties which he saw persisting among the Middleton hand-loom weavers.[55] But Anderson's work shows the persisting importance of the family, as relatives found jobs and lodgings for country cousins, children followed parents into the same workplace, and older relatives were on hand to mind children and provide other assistance while wives and mothers worked in factories. All this adds up to a stronger need for familial mutual assistance in the town than in the agricultural countryside, although Reach's contrast between the factory family and the hand-loom weaving family may not be entirely fanciful. The predominant pattern of short-distance migration enabled the family to adapt itself to reduce the trauma of adjustment to industrial society. Anderson thinks that the basis for familial mutual aid was calculative: that assistance was given in the expectation that it would be reciprocated in time of need. But there is no doubt that it was also vouchsafed for normative reasons: because people thought it their duty to help, often with little prospect of direct reciprocation, as with the domestic care of the aged and insane. If values are widely shared and enforced in a community, of course, the two sets of motives are mutually reinforcing.[56] We should remember that Anderson is describing a mature industrial town in which relationships had had time to cohere and expectations to develop and adjust; and it would be interesting to know more about the importance of the family during the difficult transitional decades of the 1820s and 1830s. What is clear is that the combined forces of urbanisation and factory industry did not destroy the working-class family, but forced it to adapt to changing circumstances.

Under these conditions, women's factory work was much less disruptive than it might have been. For the vast majority of married women, factory work was a necessary response to poverty, in the absence of a regular or sufficient income from a husband. It might be an alternative to, or sometimes a supplement to, the taking in of lodgers or sharing living space with relatives to economise on rent: 'huddling', as it was called.[57] Anderson's Preston findings put the imperatives for women's factory work in a nutshell: 'Over 60 per cent of the families of the wives who worked in factories would have been in difficulties had they not done so ... with the earnings of the wife, only one in six actually were.'[58] This, remember, in a good year. Contemporaries made much of the attendant evils: recourse to child-minders, systematic dosing of children with opiates and swelling infant mortality, and a lack of household amenities and hygiene which was calculated to drive the wretched husband to the ale-house. Examples can be found in support of most of these allegations, but they are not cumulatively convincing. Anderson concludes that almost all of the children in question were cared for by close relatives, friendly lodgers or neighbours, and he suggests that 'less than 2 per cent of all infant children ... were being left with professional child-minders' in industrial Lancashire at any given time.[59] This may be optimistic: Preston was not the whole of Lancashire, and the evidence of large-scale recourse to opiates in Manchester may reflect less well-developed family and neighbourhood ties where migrants came from longer distances and professional child-minding was more of an institution.[60] But infant mortality levels were no higher in the Lancashire cotton towns than in other areas where women did not work outside the home; and the indictment of factory girls as bad housewives is equally subjective and difficult to drive home. The allegation that factory work bred promiscuous sexual activity and teenage precocity is also impossible to confirm or deny; but illegitimacy was no higher in the cotton towns than elsewhere, and one suspects that middle-class observers, seeing scantily clad women working alongside men without supervision by husbands or fathers, assumed the worst automatically. In fact, the factory communities must have bred censorious gossip of a sort that must have inhibited sexual misdemeanour, and the organisation of the factory elevated the authority of men who were placed in supervisory positions which put them *in loco parentis* towards the young women in their charge. To this extent, the factory reinforced patriarchal authority, although there were undoubtedly cases where this was abused by individuals. On the whole, it seems clear that most of the attacks on women's factory work came from outside the culture within which it operated, and failed to understand the ways in which its impact was mitigated, or to sympathise with the real advantages it could bring. We shall return to these themes in Chapter 13.

Alongside the family, the factory towns in particular generated an increasingly wide-ranging and impressive system of working-class organisations, of varying degrees of formality, which further helped to ease the transition to large-scale urban living. By the 1840s, and probably much earlier, neighbourhoods were stabilising and mutual assistance networks were developing in the tightly packed streets. In Anderson's Preston almost 40 per cent of men aged 10 and over in 1861 were living within 200 yards of their 1851 address.[62] This was enough to form a substantial and influential core of shared experiences and norms, especially where neighbours shared the same workplace. Such neighbourhoods could be hostile to outsiders, but they looked after their own, sometimes against police or bailiffs as well as sickness or unemployment.[63] These defensive solidarities found more formal expression in the Friendly Societies which over-lapped with and sometimes acted as a cover for trade unions, insuring against sickness and injury and ensuring the provision of a proper funeral, while also offering a satisfying set of rituals and attainable goals in terms of offices and distinctions, and shoring it all up with conviviality at regular meetings in pubs and beerhouses. Cotton Lancashire became the great national stronghold of the Friendly Societies, which began as unsophisticated and vulnerable local organisations but federated under the banners of the Oddfellows, Foresters and Shepherds, especially after the French wars, although small local societies remained important alongside the proliferating lodges of the Affiliated Orders. By the 1830s saturation point had almost been reached, with enough Friendly Society members in Lancashire to provide one for each family.[64] At the very lowest level there were burial clubs which prevented the ultimate stigma of a pauper funeral. The pub was the main centre for this activity, although some Sunday schools and employers provided their own organisations; and the pub itself was, of course, an important social centre in its own right, offering warmth, gossip, information, entertainment, meeting-rooms and comradeship as well as disrupting family budgets, promoting fighting and rowdiness and, its critics alleged, nurturing most of the crime, vice and poverty in the county.[65]

There were also more specialised organisations, spontaneously generated within the working class. The pubs nurtured discussion groups and found room for choral societies as well as bawdy songs and clog hornpipes; and the hand-loom weavers, especially, included botanists, mathematicians and devotees of Handel as well as impassioned politicians. Owenite Halls of Science, secular Sunday schools and Co-operative ventures took root for a time in the 1830s, although the 'new model' Co-operatives on the Rochdale Pioneers pattern were still in their infancy in 1850. Owenism was, of course, a slightly exotic graft on to the existing radical culture, as were the atheist followers of Richard Carlile in the 1820s and the bearded Southcottians in Ashton-under-Lyne; but there was also a more traditional and popular culture of rough and genial excess which survived into the factory age with surprisingly little attrition or damage.[66]

The old popular culture of beer and boisterousness expressed itself in gambling, blood sports and calendar customs. Pigeon-flying, cock-fighting, foot-racing on the streets and highways, stone-bowling (a perilous pursuit which also took place on the highway), and many related activities survived and even flourished into the factory age, in spite of increasingly determined attempts to suppress them in the interests of morality, religion and labour discipline. Bull-baiting and the old-style mass football games, as at Bolton, were more conspicuous and easier to put down, although the new police were still struggling against the former in outlying hamlets like Gee Cross and Lydgate in the 1840s. But the strongest survivals of all were the wakes and pleasure fairs, whose popularity was such as to defy the constraints of limited space, lengthened working hours and the active disapproval of the growing Evangelical and Nonconformist middle class. The wakes, in particular, were a characteristic Lancashire institution, although they had parallels in other parts of the country. They were supposed to commemorate the anniversary of the dedication of the local church or chapel; but by the late eighteenth century they had become thoroughly secular festivals, dedicated to drink and hospitality rather than to religion. In many parishes, admittedly, rushes were ceremonially transported to strew the floor of the parish church, and by the early nineteenth century specially constructed rushcarts with elaborate decorations were being used for this purpose, accompanied by processions of morris dancers from the various outlying townships and hamlets. But this was more an expression of community pride and identity than a religious duty: the rushes were still brought even when the church floors were flagged and no longer needed them, and the fights between rival rushcarts which regularly enlivened the wakes at Oldham and elsewhere were obviously ends in themselves. The wakes went quiet during hard times, but picked up when trade revived. Employers were quite unable to suppress them, and publicans founded new ones to try to attract additional custom, with prizes for rustic sports such as donkey racing and chasing the greased pig. The flourishing survival of the wakes and allied institutions is a further reminder of the strength of traditions in the cotton district. Outside the workplace, the advocates of labour discipline did not have things all their own way; and popular attractions were still capable of emptying mills in the 1850s, even when they did not have the added legitimacy of tradition. A circus, a mountebank or even the passing of the local hunt could still disrupt production when the workers were willing to vote with their feet. We must not underrate the resilience of popular pleasures and customs in these tightly-knit communities.[67]

In all these respects the cotton district is much better documented than Merseyside or north Lancashire. Apart from the mines, the pinmaking industry of the Warrington area, and the St. Helens glassworks which in the early 1840s employed 'several hundred women and children' in grinding, smoothing and

Hornby Castle in 1840, when it was still a seat of the Duke of Leeds: the Fosters of Black Dyke Mills were aiming high. (See p. 224.) [*Below*] Lancashire socialists at play: a *Clarion* gathering enjoys tennis in the Ribble Valley just after the turn of the century. (See p. 275.)

Lancashire cheese for urban consumers: the Preston cheese market in Edwardian times. (See p. 218.) [*Below*] A mule-spinner at work. (See pp. 265–7.)

polishing plate glass, there was little industrial work outside the home for women and children on Merseyside or (outside the textile 'factory villages') in north Lancashire. In Liverpool, indeed, begging and petty crime were thought to be the main economic activities of the children of the poor.[68] Where migrants had come longer distances and identified with a wider range of sometimes mutually antagonistic cultures, the solidarities of neighbourhood and workplace may have been slower to develop. The numerous Irish presence in Liverpool is particularly relevant here. At mid-century about a quarter of Liverpool's population was Irish-born, many of them recent refugees from the famine of the later 1840s, and coming from the remotest western counties of Ireland. Taylor calculates the Irish Catholic population at little more than 6 per cent of the town's population in 1800, rising to just over one in nine in 1830; and in round numbers there were less than 5000 in 1800, nearly 20,000 in 1830 and 83,813 (including the Irish Protestants, who were always a significant minority) recorded in the 1851 census. It is worth remembering that, even apart from the (often bitter) Protestant/ Catholic divide, the Irish were far from homogeneous, and the men of different counties or provinces often fought against each other.[69] Only in central Manchester was there a similar concentration of the Irish in Lancashire, although Irish populations were growing rapidly in St. Helens, Wigan, Preston and some of the cotton towns further east by the 1840s.[70] The Irish were set apart from the population at large by religion (usually), language (often) and way of life, and their perceived willingness to accept low wages and undercut English labour was especially divisive. Moreover, although they were much thicker on the ground in some districts than in others, Papworth points out that even in the most concentrated districts of Irish settlement near the docks, the population street-by-street was rarely more than 50 per cent Irish.[71] So the Irish presence, with its own internal splits, was probably a widespread divisive factor inhibiting the formation of neighbourhood solidarities in Liverpool, especially given the competitive nature of access to the labour market, which would tend to exacerbate divisions of all kinds. There were also significant Scots and Welsh minorities, and on one calculation nearly half the town's 1851 adult population had come from 'Celtic' or foreign parts (including Cumbria!).[72] Although long-distance migrants tried to use family connections as far as possible, the prevalence of distant origins in Liverpool's population must also have made it difficult for the family to adapt and play the supportive role that it seems to have fulfilled in the cotton towns. There were similar symptoms of division and conflict in the St. Helens area, where the glassworks attracted migrants from France and distant parts of Britain and the Irish appeared in large numbers during the 1840s; and it could be argued that industrial Merseyside generally provided a less hospitable environment for the development of supportive working-class institutions. Friendly Societies, for example, were also thinner on the ground here, although they were expanding rapidly in St. Helens by the 1820s, and lower family incomes must have had a generally limiting effect.[73]

Evidence for the survival of traditional popular enjoyments outside the cotton district is also limited, although the surviving wakes in villages around Liverpool were becoming rowdy and violent affairs, invaded by drunken Liverpudlians, by the 1830s.[74] Migration over longer distances probably diluted the attachment to local customs on Merseyside in contrast with the very different pattern of population recruitment further east, although the rural and more stable north and west of the county saw fewer survivals than the cotton district, where industrialisation seems almost to have deepened the attachment to established customs.[75] It was in the cotton district, too, that beliefs in witchcraft, boggarts, fairies and other supernatural entities persisted most strongly into the railway age, in spite of sustained efforts by employers and Evangelicals to spread the influences of religion and calculative rationality among a recalcitrant population.[76]

We saw in earlier chapters, indeed, that the influence of organised religion on the Lancashire population at large had never been strong; and its difficulties were compounded by population growth and redistribution from the late eighteenth century onwards. Strenuous attempts were made to increase religious provision, especially during the second quarter of the nineteenth century; but the results in terms of actual attendance were disappointing. Only five English counties had lower levels of church and chapel attendance than Lancashire at the 1851 census of religious worship; and in only four counties was a lower level of Church of England attendance recorded.[77] The Irish presence, alongside the continuing survival of rural Catholicism, ensured that Lancashire would have the highest incidence of Roman Catholic worship, and on one calculation the Catholics accounted for almost one-sixth of all the county's worshippers, rising to more than one-third in Preston, almost one-third in Liverpool, more than a quarter in Wigan and nearly a quarter in Manchester. Nonconformist attendances were well below the national average, although there were pockets of Methodist and Congregationalist strength, in one or two rural areas and especially in Rochdale. But in general the urban figures were particularly disquieting, above all for the Church of England. Preston had the lowest overall attendance figure, and the lowest for the Church of England, of any English town in 1851; Oldham, Manchester, Salford, Bolton and Blackburn were all near the bottom of the table; and Lancashire had six of the 'worst' fourteen towns for religious attendance, and ten of the 'worst' thirty, not counting Stockport. Only in Warrington were attendances above the national urban average. In Rochdale, moreover, three-quarters of the actual attenders were Nonconformists; and more than half fell into this category in Oldham, Stockport, Ashton and Bury. On the formula adopted by the census compiler, fewer than one person in ten living in Liverpool, Manchester or the larger cotton towns went to church or chapel on census Sunday; and the figures for working-class attendance would, of course, be much lower than this.[78]

Disturbing though these figures were to contemporaries, they are probably a considerable improvement on the earlier part of the century; and the Church of England was still generally used for rites of passage, while attendances at the church's great festivals were probably less unimpressive, and we shall see that Sunday schools were flourishing. A major church-building programme was well under way by 1851, and the enormous and unwieldy Lancashire parishes were being subdivided into more manageable units. From 1847, too, Manchester had its own bishop. During the 1840s alone, 48 new churches were opened in Manchester deanery.[79] This was part of a belated response to competition from the Nonconformists, as the various subdivisions of Methodism proliferated as separate sects from the 1790s onwards, and the older Dissenting groups were revitalised and began to make converts, especially among the shopkeeping and trading lower middle classes of the towns.[80] Church provision was motivated by fear of social and political unrest, as well as by the desire to save souls. Church schools were seen as buttresses of the social order, and promoters of church expansion were eager to counter 'ignorance, barbarism, socialism and infidelity' as well as Nonconformity.[81] But even with the new breed of conscientious, self-sacrificing clergy, new churches with free seats were not automatically filled with eager hearers. 'Adam de Spotland' told readers of the *Manchester Courier* in 1846 that missions to the poor were needed: 'The people as a body are only partly civilized. It is idle to expect them rushing into churches as fast as you build them.'[82] Preston's appalling attendance figures in 1851 followed a decade and a half of busy church-building, fuelled by fears of Roman Catholic aggrandisement. Despite the importance of religion as a political litmus-paper at middle-class level, and the genuine commitment of active minorities, the churches and chapels were still a long way from winning the genuine allegiance of most of the working class at mid-century, although the Church of England had recovered a good deal of lost ground since the 1820s; but Foster's figures for Oldham, for example, suggest that Protestant Nonconformity in general, and the Wesleyans in particular, had put up a much more dynamic showing.[83] But only the Roman Catholics, as they began to supply churches and priests in the areas of Irish immigration, were able to command the loyalty of a major sector of working-class opinion; and here the strength of religious influences may have made up for the limited development of other aspects of cultural cohesion, especially in Liverpool.

The churches' educational role did become very important, however, although its wider significance is difficult to gauge. The expanding industries of Lancashire had little need of a literate labour force, but contemporaries saw a need for education to promote religion, morality and acceptance of the established order, including the tenets of orthodox political economy. Schooling would also be useful to keep children off the streets and out of mischief, and it would help to inculcate useful habits of order and discipline. Existing educational institutions in the late eighteenth and early nineteenth centuries were widely seen to be inadequate for these tasks. The endowed grammar and parish schools had failed to expand and multiply to keep pace with population change, and they were unable to reach the armies of factory children who worked long hours from Monday to Saturday. There were large and rapidly growing numbers of cheap private-venture schools for the poor, the so-called 'dame schools'; but educational reformers found them wanting on the grounds of inadequate discipline, lack of religious teaching, lack of acceptable books and other resources, overcrowding and unsuitable staff. Recent historians have queried this assessment, suggesting that the real problem was lack of élite and denominational control over schools which were run by the working class, for the working class; but whatever the truth of this, it is clear that literacy levels declined in industrial Lancashire in the late eighteenth and early nineteenth centuries.[84] Between about 1770 and 1815 the diffusion of basic literacy skills, as measured very imperfectly by the ability to sign the marriage register, declined sharply not only in Manchester and a cross-section of textile centres, but also in the St. Helens and (probably) Wigan, Warrington and Leigh areas. By the second quarter of the nineteenth century, matters were improving again, although there was a great gulf between Rochdale and Wigan at one extreme, where only 19 per cent of newly-weds could sign the register in the 1830s, and the rural areas of north Lancashire around Morecambe Bay and the Lune valley, where figures in the high sixties and seventies predominated.[85] We must not make too much of the evidence for improvement, for the marriage registers tell us nothing directly about reading ability, and nothing about the extent and fluency of an individual's literacy skills. They also tell us nothing, in themselves, about the values which were transmitted along with the skills. We shall see that these are important considerations. But the improvements after 1820 or so, which coincided with rapid urbanisation and recurrent social dislocation, clearly owed much to the increasing provision of mass schooling under religious auspices, in the form of day schools and Sunday schools.

Sunday schools began early in the Lancashire cotton district: they were being established in Manchester and some of the surrounding towns in the early 1780s, at the inception of the national movement. In several cases, as at Manchester and Stockport, their beginnings were interdenominational; but by the turn of the century sectarian divisions, sometimes exacerbated by the political controversies of the 1790s, were undermining the initial unity of purpose. But in the cotton towns above all, the Sunday school became an almost universal experience of working-class children and adolescents. As early as 1816 a parliamentary return suggested that 'almost all the children of the working class must have been on the books of some Sunday school or other' in Manchester, although in 1818 Lancashire as a whole ranked sixteenth among the English counties, with 5.2 per cent of its population enrolled in Sunday schools. The most dramatic expansion came in the 1820s, and by 1833 Lancashire ranked sixth, with one in seven of the population on the books; and by 1851 the figure was almost one in 6.[86] By this time the ratios in cotton towns ranged from one in 4.4 of the population in Stockport to one in 6.23 in Preston, with Salford and Manchester showing slightly higher figures which were nevertheless thrown into sharp relief by Warrington's one in 9.08 and Liverpool's one in 17. The national average was one in 7.45.[87]

The actual content of the education varied considerably, and changed over time. Initially the schools taught writing as well as reading; but by the early nineteenth century the Church of England and the Wesleyan Methodists, who between them provided most of the places, were concentrating more narrowly on teaching religious doctrine and the reading of the scriptures in the few hours available; but attempts to ban writing altogether, ostensibly on Sabbatarian grounds, were not universally pursued, as children were withdrawn in immense numbers from some of the schools which took this line. The Unitarians characteristically went to the other extreme, and taught arithmetic and even accounts. But this evidence suggests a divergence between the aims of the providers and the wishes of the consumers. The schools' patrons, by and large, wanted to propagate religion for social discipline as well as salvation; and Oldham's millowners significantly increased their contributions at times of social tension.[88] The children's parents, for their part, wanted them to acquire useful skills which cost too much in time and fees to be afforded at the day schools. This conflict of expectations must have reduced the impact of the Sunday schools as agencies of indoctrination; and significantly few of the children went on to become regular attenders at the churches and chapels in question. Almost everywhere, teachers were unpaid after the earliest years of the movement; and recruitment was often difficult. The third annual report of the Liverpool Sunday School Union in 1818 complained, 'How very small a proportion of the affluent professors of Christianity are to be found in the list of teachers', blaming snobbery and self-indulgence; and those who did agree to teach were often erratic in attendance. In practice, much of the teaching was performed by working-class teenagers, some of whom were felt to be too readily tempted by the attractions of fairgrounds and Saturday night singing saloons. Much of the teaching was mechanical, as the clergy eventually became aware. It was all very well for James M'Burney to win a prize at Bethesda Chapel, Liverpool in 1817 by memorising and reciting 3488 verses of the Bible; but the extent of his actual understanding might well have been very limited. For a minority who kept up regular attendance for three years or more, real progress in basic literacy could be made; but the extent of the Sunday schools' actual effectiveness as agencies of religious and social indoctrination is at best doubtful. As Poole remarks, the Sunday schools 'fitted all too smoothly into working-class life. For parents, the most popular thing about them, as well as the literacy they provided, was that they got the children out of the way on Sunday to allow, amongst other things, a little sexual privacy in overcrowded housing. For the children, the entertainments were the schools' best attraction ... as they grew up, they simply discarded them for more exciting activities.' This may be a little too cynical; but the Sunday schools certainly fell a long way short of achieving the ideals of their promoters.[89]

The Sunday schools were particularly important in the cotton towns, and the limited but real improvements in literacy levels here from the 1820s and 1830s must have owed something to their influence. Day schools were much thinner on the ground in the cotton district, and this was certainly connected with the high demand for child labour, and its essential contribution to many family economies. Church of England and Nonconformist day schools on the monitorial system began to supplement the old endowed schools after 1810, but local businessmen were unwilling to contribute, and Cruickshank comments that still in 1841 'on a generous estimate, many of the towns like Rochdale and Oldham, together with their surrounding areas, had less than 1 per cent of their population in day schools'.[90] The over-optimistic ideal, based on the assumption that all children between 5 and 12 or 14 years old should be in school, hoped for more than 16 per cent; and during the following decade the Anglicans, prompted by fears of competition, infidelity and social unrest, began a major school-building programme in the cotton district, although most of the money still had to come from London, landed and Southern sources. By this time, of course, more factory children were available for school, and in 1844 the existing factory school provision was augmented by the introduction of so-called half-time education for factory workers between 8 and 13 years old. In 1851, however, most of the larger cotton towns had between one-third and two-fifths of their 5 – 14-year-olds in day schools, and in Oldham the figure was only just over one-fifth; it was probably much lower in many smaller industrial settlements. The rural areas did much better, though here the existing facilities were often still adequate; and in Lancaster and Liverpool nearly half the age-group were in school on the day of the census.[91] How effective these schools were, and to what end, remains a more difficult question. By 1851 the average Lancashire child probably spent three or four years in day school, augmented by Sunday school attendance, but probably interrupted by spells of work or inability to afford the fees. The impact on basic literacy is measurable; but the wider cultural implications are open to debate. The schools may have helped to discipline children for the world of work, and their increasing Anglican domination and control may have helped to inculcate the working-class Tory and virulently Protestant attitudes which became so visible in the mid-Victorian cotton and mining districts of Lancashire as well as in Liverpool.[92] These are controversial issues, and we shall return to them. Meanwhile, it may be revealing to see what working-class people did with their literacy. Liverpool Domestic Mission's minister to the poor was relieved to find that the atheist and (by 1851, at least) the radical press were minority interests; but what did sell well among the poor were 'the exciting and pestilent weekly Romances of the poison and dagger school', with titles like 'Captain Hawk' and 'Death Grasp', which sold in their thousands at a penny a week. Abel Heywood, based in Manchester and the leading Lancashire supplier, confirmed the popularity of 'these weekly instalments of trash', but listed a large number of altogether more respectable penny weeklies, such as the *London Journal* and

Family Herald, which comfortably outsold them, while the most popular of all was the 'political and democratic' *Barker's People*.[93] But the heyday of the *Northern Star* and its antecedents of the radical unstamped press was apparently over by mid-century, although whether the spread of schooling under religious and employer auspices had a direct influence on this must remain an open question. The fact remains that much of the reading matter of the working class was not what the promoters of mass literacy had hoped for or envisaged, even though it erred on the side of immorality rather than insurrection.

For an earnest minority within the working class, of course, self-improvement beckoned through the Mechanics' Institutes and the many more or less formal mutual assistance societies which blossomed in conjunction with Owenism as well as with the Sunday schools. The Mechanics' Institutes were supposed to offer general adult education with a scientific and vocational bias, with a view to encouraging useful inventions and individual self-advancement; and they spread rapidly in Lancashire, with Manchester and Lancaster figuring among the first batch of foundations nationally in 1824. In practice, with a few exceptions, they were funded and dominated by the employers, their most popular classes taught basic literacy, and otherwise by the 1840s most had become the preserves of clerks and an aristocracy of skilled labour, and novels were becoming the most popular items in their libraries.[94] Political and religious discussions were banned, although this was sometimes contentious. No doubt the Mechanics' Institutes and similar bodies provided much of the reading public for journals like *Chambers' Information for the People*, of which Abel Heywood was distributing 1200 copies weekly in 1849.[95]

There were further important innovations in working-class leisure; but most of them were much less respectable than this. Pubs and (after 1830) beerhouses, which often operated on a shoestring in the front rooms of terraced houses, multiplied much faster than the urban populations, and they were supplemented by unlicensed 'hush shops' and illicit distilling, especially in the Irish areas. Some publicans in the larger towns began to specialise in spirits, especially after 1830, and as early as 1832 J. P. Kay thought there were 322 'gin shops' in Manchester alone, including several very opulent and well-patronised establishments in the town centre.[96] As competition intensified, publicans also diversified their attractions and became entertainment entrepreneurs, sometimes on an impressive scale. One of the most remarkable was William Sharples of Bolton, whose Star Inn concert room, which opened in 1832 and moved to larger premises in 1840, offered music, singing, dancing, clowns, acrobats and novelty shows such as an illuminated tableau of the Great Fire of London and 'Perkins' Patent Steam Gun'. The Star also included a museum containing waxworks, models and live exhibits, and there was a garden and ornamental pond. The concert hall could hold 1500 people, mostly but certainly not entirely young factory workers of both sexes, and in Whit Week 1849, 3600 bottles of ginger beer were sold in a day.[97] This was almost unique, although the Belle Vue and Pomona Gardens in

Manchester also offered an immense range of attractions, and Manchester also had its concert rooms and singing saloons with variety acts and regular attendances of a thousand or more. In some respects the cotton towns have a stronger claim than London to the invention of the Victorian music-hall. Here again, there was a numerous teenage presence; but much of the drink consumed was non-alcoholic, and the performances were over by ten o'clock even on a Saturday.[98] These activities were not confined to the cotton district: Liverpool in 1851 had forty concert saloons which opened every night, and were also attractive to teenagers, although the largest seems to have been less than half the size of its Manchester counterpart.[99] But the cotton towns, with their large numbers of young factory workers earning relatively good wages and as yet without responsibilities, led the way in the commercialisation of mass entertainment.[100]

These commercial initiatives, which grew out of existing working-class preferences and coexisted with established customs, alarmed contemporary reformers because their associations with drink, gambling and immorality seemed to threaten property, propriety and order. There was a genuinely high incidence of prostitution and violence in Liverpool, especially, and in Manchester during times of trade depression; and 'respectable' opinion was especially affronted by the increasingly general use of the streets as places of alfresco and informal entertainment, from gossiping and insulting passers-by to playing pitch and toss or organising races for wagers.[101] The widespread loss of footpaths and access to open spaces was beginning to contribute to this latter trend by the 1830s. Reformers, drawn mainly from the Evangelical (though not necessarily Nonconformist) wing of the trading and manufacturing middle class, tried to tackle the perceived problem of working-class leisure in two ways: through coercive prevention, and by providing or encouraging counter-attractions to wean the working man and his family away from the pub and its associated unregenerate pursuits. Counter-attractions took many forms, and increased rapidly in number and diversity during the 1830s and 1840s. Sunday schools offered tea parties, processions, field days and later railway excursions to remove their flocks from the temptations of wakes and fairs; and the temperance movement, which became particularly strong in cotton Lancashire, operated in a similar way. Preston was, of course, the cradle of the teetotal movement. Public parks and free libraries began to spread during the 1840s, and some of the larger employers began to provide reading-rooms and lectures for their workers. But these activities displaced the earthier enjoyments only for a minority of committed sectarians or teetotallers, or autodidacts, who remade their lives around the new institutions. For many people, the park and the pub, or even the Sunday school treat and the fairground, were complementary rather than mutually exclusive: most working-class people took what they wanted from the 'rational recreations' which the reformers provided, but rejected those parts of the message which they found unduly restrictive or demanding.[102]

Coercion was perhaps more effective, at least on the surface. The reform and expansion of police forces and local government, again especially in the 1830s and 1840s, provided scope for local as well as national legislation, and manpower for enforcement. The new police forces, especially those introduced or expanded in the boroughs under the Municipal Reform Act of 1835, were indeed used against working-class street enjoyments and public drunkenness: in Bolton, for example, 'the players and spectators of street games were prosecuted for obstruction, trespass, breaches of the peace, vagrancy and desecration of the sabbath'.[103] Popular blood sports, too, were eventually driven from the public eye. But there were narrow limits to the scope for effective legal coercion. Not all magistrates or other leading citizens were thoroughgoing supporters of restrictions, and the tory landowner – industrialists who remained important throughout Lancashire remained part of 'the hunting, shooting and cockfighting world of county society … they tended to favour drinking, prize-fighting, blood sports and all sorts of revels as ways of stiffening the national fibre, keeping a disorderly people happy, and bringing the upper and lower classes together in common enjoyment'.[104] This strand of ruling-class opinion was much more influential than the working-class lobby for rationality and reform which found expression in a combination of self-improvement, teetotalism and the pursuit of the Charter; and it was difficult to suppress cockfights when, as at Ashton-under-Lyne in the 1840s, magistrates might be prominent among the attenders.[105] Moreover, the 'reformed' police were not the most convincing instruments of moral and recreational reform. They were recruited largely from the ranks of unskilled labour, and they were vulnerable to the same temptations as the working-class population at large, as well as being badly paid for long hours, with little job security. Scandals were frequent. The whole of the first Wigan force was sacked in little more than a year, for offences among which drunkenness and sexual misdemeanours while on duty featured prominently, and in 1838 there were 282 cases of punishment for inebriation in the Liverpool force. Examples could be multiplied, and the borough forces were often run on a shoestring with a minimum of men, while the county police force which was introduced in 1839 was widely resented as an external imposition by civic leaders in the smaller towns.[106] Moreover, the police often had difficulty gaining access to pubs in working-class areas, and in finding evidence for prosecutions; and even when disreputable activities were banished from the streets, they often found a secure haven in the beerhouses.[107] In practice, neither coercion nor counter-attractions were making much difference to patterns of working-class enjoyment by the mid nineteenth century: the crucial changes were to come later.

The new police forces of the 1830s were at least more numerous than their precursors, especially in Liverpool and Manchester; and they had some pre-tensions to order and discipline, although a large proportion of their number came from the ranks of the old town watchmen. But it is difficult to assess their impact on crime prevention and punishment. The crime statistics are full of inescapable ambiguities, and can never provide a profile of crimes committed, as opposed to crimes reported and prosecuted. Lancashire's crime-rate, measured in committals for trial per 100,000 population, was substantially higher than the national average, and very much higher than the neighbouring counties of Cumberland and Westmorland, throughout the first half of the nineteenth century, reaching a peak in the economically and politically disturbed year of 1842. The vast majority of these recorded crimes were thefts: 89 per cent in 1838. A straw-hat salesman told a parliamentary commission at this time that travellers saw the upland roads in the Manchester area as particularly unsafe, as 'some ferocious highway robberies have been committed', while the inhabitants around Blackstone Edge and Todmorden were 'barbarous to an unusual degree'. There were wreckers on the Wirral coast, and there was widespread fear of Irish navvies. The existence of these fears is important in itself, although they were not sufficient to inhibit the growth of trade in portable and valuable articles; but Midwinter is probably right to argue that the steady attrition and irritation of sustained petty theft was the most important influence on the growing willingness of ratepayers to shoulder the financial burden and accept the political risk of introducing more numerous and better-organised police forces. Violence was endemic in some sectors of the working class: the Irish were notorious brawlers, and miners, especially, were infamous for no-holds-barred fighting with a liberal use of teeth and iron-tipped clogs. J. P. Kay in Manchester also expressed widely held fears of political violence: 'The civic force of the town is totally inadequate to main-tain the peace, and to defend property from the attacks of lawless depredators; and *a more efficient and more numerous corps ought to be immediately organized*, to give power to the law, so often mocked by the daring front of sedition, and outraged by the frantic violence of an ignorant and deluded rabble.' But strikers and Chartists came and went, and the more mundane pressure of small regular robberies was more influential, alongside the concern to regulate working-class enjoyments and public morality. Many remained unconvinced of the value of the new police – perhaps understandably – and there were regular manpower cuts and economy drives at municipal level, even though resources were con-centrated into protecting the central commercial and suburban residential property of the shopkeepers, manufacturers and tradesmen. As yet the effective impact of the police on working-class life, for good or ill, was limited by the grudging funding and experimental nature of the new forces.[108]

Similar inhibitions and uncertainties bedevilled the introduction of public health reform. A recent historian has criticised the 'failure of local government' in Liverpool and Manchester to deploy available resources which were 'sufficient to have averted the abominable living conditions of the new urban lower class'.[109] The evils of overcrowding, lack of sanitation, completely inadequate water supplies, and so on, were real enough; but this critique gives insufficient weight to the powerful ideological, technological and administrative obstacles to reform. The burden of the rates fell disproportionately, especially in the second-rank and smaller towns, on small property-owners who were acutely conscious of the precarious state of their finances. They were also deeply committed to the prevailing orthodoxies of *laissez-faire* and economic individualism, and shared the comforting and convenient belief that bad living conditions arose from the improvidence and intemperance of individuals rather than any deficiencies in the wider organisation of economy and society. Such perceptions helped to channel charitable help into educational and religious rather than material and practical solutions. The compulsory installation of drainage and water supplies, and the provision of services by local government instead of private enterprise, were seen as unwarranted interference with private property and the free play of market forces. Cholera and other epidemics sometimes modified these perceptions, but not permanently. Until the 1848 Public Health Act, moreover, powers for sanitary improvement were difficult and expensive to obtain, and rival local government bodies contended against each other or were riven with internal faction-fighting, as we saw in Chapter 7. Moreover, there was as yet no agreement about the appropriate technology for public health reform, and rival factions attached themselves to rival systems of water supply or sewage disposal. The divided élites were more concerned with their own struggles over power, patronage and religious issues than with sanitary improvement; but there was no working-class campaign on this issue either, as parliamentary reform and wages engrossed the attention of radicals and trade unionists. As it was, very little headway was made before the 1840s, when the national campaigns by physicians, statisticians and Benthamite reformers at last began to affect the outlook of well-intentioned but blinkered and ignorant local leaders. Manchester, whose doctors had included eager advocates of public health reform since the 1790s, and Liverpool were well to the fore in national terms, despite Vigier's strictures; but attempts to control smoke, to ban back-to-back housing and cellar dwellings, and to secure sufficient supplies of pure water from distant sources, all fell foul of vested interests and suffered obstruction and delay. The smaller towns, with fewer resources and less self-confident civic leaders, lagged considerably. We shall return to these issues in Chapter 13; but meanwhile it is worth noting that middle-class attempts to influence working-class living standards and ways of life were pursued with much more eagerness, if perhaps with little more effect, in the spheres of religious, educational and moral reform than in the field of public health.[110]

The better-off members of Lancashire society did not ignore the material needs of the poor altogether, however. Every sizeable town had a growing multiplicity of charities, aimed at providing succour and assistance for various categories of the apparently deserving poor; and every trade depression brought out soup kitchens and distributions of coal and clothing, in spite of the pervasive belief that working-class people had a duty to save during good times so as to provide for themselves when the inevitable depression came. Provision of this kind expanded considerably in Manchester during the 1790s, as the Strangers' Friend Society was established to succour the destitute, a 'soup charity' distributed potato soup (with a small admixture of onions and meat) at times of stress, a Lying-in Hospital for poor married women and a House of Recovery were opened to supplement the well-established Infirmary, and a series of *ad hoc* committees collected public subscriptions, especially during hard winters.[111] Liverpool developed a similar range of charities, with dispensaries, hospitals, a Ladies' Benevolent Society to provide relief in food and clothing accompanied by appropriate admonitions, a Dorcas Society to make clothes for the poor, and the inevitable Magdalen Asylum.[112] Such charities encountered frequent financial crises. Liverpool's Dispensary relieved 11,000 patients in 1809 and over 30,000 in 1824, but the level of annual subscriptions showed a slight decline during those years, and its Committee bitterly remarked that the Dispensary's supporters amounted to fewer than one in 200 of the town's population, 'whilst one-fifth of the whole town yearly receives its relief'.[113] Lower down the urban hierarchy, provision was much patchier, and in newly emerging industrial towns like St. Helens it might depend unduly on the whims of a few powerful individuals; but everywhere there was expansion, as the increasing visibility of social problems and deprivation aroused humanitarian feelings and fears of uprising and desperate crime.

Most charitable recipients were the 'deserving poor': those who were thought to be honest, industrious and in difficulties through no fault of their own. The patronage of an employer or clergyman could make the essential difference between relief and neglect. Even among the propertied, however, most held aloof from charitable activity, and a grudging attitude to the needs and problems of the poor was increasingly evident in the administration of the main avenue of relief, the Poor Law system. Certainly, the cost of poor relief in Lancashire remained relatively low under the Old Poor Law. The mid-century rise in pauperism continued in some places until the turn of the century, but in 1802 – 3 expenditure per head of population was only 4s 10d in Lancashire as a whole, compared with a national average of 8s 11d and figures of up to 16s 1d (Berkshire) and 22s 6d (Sussex) in Southern agricultural counties.[114] There were wide variations within the county: in rural Furness the figure was 6s 11d, suggesting that in the industrial districts it would be substantially lower than the county average. On the other hand, *rates* were much higher in Bolton and Manchester than in Furness, owing to the much greater population density and the relative paucity of substantial landholders. Again in 1831, when Lancashire's per capita Poor Law expenditure, at 4s 4½d, was the lowest in England and Wales, local variations ranged from 2s 1d just outside Liverpool to 17s 2d in Ulverston. Rates, too, were as low as 10½d in the pound in West Derby and as high as 6s in Padiham, where there was a numerous population of distressed hand-loom weavers.[115]

What did these figures mean in practice? Should we take them as an index of parsimony or of relative prosperity? Should we assume that charity and thrift shouldered the burden during cyclical depressions, and left the Poor Law to deal only with the 'permanent poor', the sick, aged, illegitimates and their mothers, and orphans? Suggestions of obsessive care of ratepayers' money have increasing substance in some places. In the agricultural areas of Furness, and no doubt elsewhere, the depression of the 1820s brought retrenchment on rents and pensions, and closer attention to the settlement laws.[116] At the other extreme, Liverpool also began to adopt a tougher attitude to its poor in the early decades of the nineteenth century. In 1814 a parish committee complained bitterly of lax administration, as rates went uncollected, embezzlement undiscovered, and the workhouse inmates lacked employment and discipline. By the early 1830s, however, the Poor Law Commission's investigator found it to be a model authority, reducing expenditure sharply by 'a thorough examination of all the cases' and deterring potential paupers from its workhouse by a strict régime of oakum-picking. A similar transformation had occurred in Manchester. Throughout Lancashire, moreover, wages were rarely made up out of the poor-rates, except in the case of hand-loom weavers in some areas; and the evils complained of in the Southern counties, with their overstocked agricultural labour markets, were not applicable here. Under these conditions, parsimony could be tempered by humanity; and the tough stance adopted in Liverpool may have been unusual. Throughout industrial Lancashire there was a general reluctance to test indigence by threatening relief applicants with the workhouse; and the workhouses themselves were small and undisciplined. They were often insanitary, rowdy and even dangerous places, as lunatics and people with infectious diseases were herded together indiscriminately; but they carried neither the stigma nor the threat which later came to be associated with the workhouse. The day book of Spotland Workhouse, Rochdale, with its evidence of concern about diet and clothing and of the ease with which paupers came and went, gives strong support to these impressions.[117] In most of Lancashire, too, the New Poor Law made little real difference to the existing pattern. Even where the new official administrative machinery was set up at once, the Guardians themselves were rarely eager to inaugurate a new harsh régime of less-eligibility, the abolition of outdoor relief and the compulsory incarceration of paupers in new, large, purpose-built workhouses. In general, established officials and existing practices continued. Apart from anything else, they were seen to be cheaper; and the workhouse was obviously no solution to the intermittent poverty of industrial workers who were obliged to seek relief in vast numbers through no fault of their own in the regular cyclical slumps.

It would be difficult to demonstrate that Lancashire's Poor Law administrators were more parsimonious or discriminating in their allocation of relief than their counterparts elsewhere; and the explanation for the low per capita relief payments probably lies in the relatively high family incomes of the cotton district (coupled with the undeniably harsh régime which emerged in Liverpool), along with the strength of family ties and voluntary institutions, and the spirit of independence which contemporaries were so eager to praise. But we must not forget the widespread dependence on charity during trade depressions, which should make us qualify too eager an endorsement of generalisations about the stubborn independence of the Lancastrian character. As we have seen, anyway, there was a lot of poverty in Lancashire; and the low levels of poor relief expenditure do not invalidate that conclusion. What this evidence emphasises is the availability of alternative familial and communal ways of dealing with the threat of poverty, which made recourse to the Poor Law less necessary than in many other parts of the country, and thereby reduced the pressure on it, enabling it in turn to present a more human face to those who needed its services.

Any assessment of trends in working-class living standards in Lancashire must be tentative and qualified, because so many variables and value-judgements are involved, and it is not at all clear what the basis for comparisons should be. If we compare the agricultural labourer of the late eighteenth century with the cotton spinner of the 1840s, we give a very different impression from that conveyed by comparing the lot of a late eighteenth-century hand-loom weaver with his counterpart sixty years on. Changes in occupational structure and population distribution also complicate the picture. One or two tentative generalisations may be attempted, however. In most occupations, there is little evidence for rising real wages before the late 1840s, and we should bear in mind the frequency of industrial depression and distress in the cotton district, and the debilitating effects of the casual labour market in Liverpool. Environmental conditions undoubtedly deteriorated, and Lindert and Williamson's argument that workers sought and expected a 'wages premium' to compensate for this makes remarkable assumptions about the rationality of the labour market.[118] There was, however, surprisingly little cultural dislocation, especially in the cotton towns themselves, where the family and other institutions adapted success-fully to the new industrial setting. Moreover, working-class culture and attitudes were remarkably impervious to attempts to mould and shape them from above: the Sunday schools, for example, were a great success in attracting children, but their impact on wider lifestyles and behaviour was probably quite limited. The major social problems arose more from urbanisation than from the advent of factory industry, and the clearest evidence of falling living standards, on all counts, comes from Liverpool with its long-distance migrants, ethnic divisions, casual labour and appalling housing, although we should remember that many of the Irish, especially in the 1840s, were fleeing from actual starvation in their homeland. Conditions in the cotton towns were made tolerable by the supple-ment to family incomes which came from female and child labour, although this imposed high social costs on some families, and a very basic standard of living in good times was in some senses dearly bought. The real beneficiaries of economic change were the substantial factory masters, coalowners, landowners and Liverpool merchants, whose opulent houses and ornamental estates, foreign tours and art collections put the debate about the working class into its true perspective.[119] Below this level was an extensive, shifting, insecure stratum of small employers, shopkeepers and professionals, for whom the threat of bankruptcy and penury was ever-present. Under these conditions, the political volatility of much of Lancashire was not surprising. What is most remarkable of all, however, is the speed with which the picture changed after mid-century; and we shall explore the advent of mid-Victorian stability and more widely diffused prosperity, and assess its limitations, in Chapters 10 to 13.

10

A MATURE INDUSTRIAL ECONOMY:
TRIUMPH AND INSECURITY, 1850 – 1914

The heyday of industrial Lancashire spanned the years between the mid nineteenth century and the First World War. The cotton industry continued its
remarkable growth. It was inevitably unable to sustain the spectacular percentage
output increases of earlier days, but it was still capable of generating enormous
cumulative expansion in absolute terms, and the mill-building boom of 1904 – 7
stood comparison with the most dramatic of earlier episodes. Worries about
foreign competition were becoming increasingly disturbing in some sectors
towards the turn of the century, but on the eve of the war Lancashire's world-
wide supremacy remained intact. In 1913 Britain exported 'an all-time, all-
country record of almost 7.1 billion yards of cotton cloth', and although the
British share of world cotton goods exports peaked at 82 per cent in 1882 – 4,
it was still an impressive 58˙per cent in 1910 – 13.[1] To most contemporaries,
without the benefit of hindsight, Lancashire's position seemed unassailable,
despite a widespread failure to keep abreast of technological innovation and an
inability to sustain sales in the protected markets of developing rival nations.
Moreover, engineering, papermaking and a range of other industries continued
to prosper, new manufactures such as rubber and electrical goods began to
develop, and continuing population growth and urbanisation in the cotton district
generated plenty of work for building and related trades. The labour force in
the late Victorian cotton towns developed a rapidly growing appetite for consumer goods as living standards rose, and this in turn boosted employment in
distribution, entertainment and other service trades. There were losses to set
against these gains, as we shall see; and the upward trends were regularly
punctuated by cyclical depressions. Fortunes varied within the cotton industry,

too, and in Rossendale it was already in retreat by the turn of the century. Overall, however, these were good years for the cotton industry and the cotton district.

The rest of Lancashire also saw the substantial consolidation of existing industries and towns. The port of Liverpool continued to prosper. The net registered tonnage of shipping using Liverpool doubled between 1890 and 1914, and although Liverpool's share of the British export trade, by value, fell significantly over the half-century after 1857, it was still 34 per cent on the eve of the war, while the share of imports amounted to nearly 25 per cent.[2] Coal mining and some sectors of the chemical industry (which had experienced a dramatic mid-Victorian expansion, especially in the booming new town of Widnes) were running into difficulties by the 1890s, admittedly, and further north the mid-Victorian promise of Barrow was not sustained, while Lancaster's surge of prosperity after mid-century was also quite short-lived. The late Victorian agricultural depression made its mark in some areas, too, although the extent and nature of its impact in Lancashire is a matter of debate. But we should not make too much of these qualifications. Most of the setbacks involved falling or interrupted growth-rates rather than actual decline, and the long-run economic indicators for the county as a whole remained decidedly favourable. A significant symptom of widespread economic well-being was the rapid growth of seaside resorts (especially Blackpool, which pioneered the working-class seaside holiday as a mass experience) and residential suburbs in the county and adjoining areas. To develop these themes further, we must again begin with the cotton industry.

Lancashire already had nearly 60 per cent of Britain's cotton workers in 1838, and adjoining parts of Cheshire, Derbyshire and Yorkshire brought the cotton district's total to well over 80 per cent. The corresponding figures for 1898–9 were nearly 76 per cent and over 91 per cent of a much higher total.[3] This concentration into Lancashire was already accompanied at mid-century by a recognisable element of specialisation within the county, and this became much more marked during the second half of the century, as new firms concentrated on either spinning or weaving rather than combining the processes in a single enterprise. Spinning increasingly dominated in south-east Lancashire, north-east Cheshire and Rossendale, while power-loom weaving migrated northwards to leave its distinctive imprint on an arc of towns running eastward from Preston and Blackburn through Burnley to the late-developing and highly specialised centres at Nelson and Colne. This pattern was never a perfect fit, for there were always significant numbers of weavers in the 'spinning area' and (to a lesser extent) vice versa. Bury, Radcliffe and Farnworth, for example, were outposts of weaving in the Manchester area, and weaving remained important in Rossendale, while Preston kept a leading position in spinning as well as weaving. But weaving centres such as Blackburn and Burnley (where spinning had still been expanding in the 1860s) lost almost all their spindles in the late nineteenth century, and north Lancashire came to specialise mainly in plain cloths, while the fancier work was still performed on the numerous surviving looms in the south-east. Even so, a basic north/south divide between weaving and spinning provides an increasingly workable approximation to reality.[4]

To complicate the picture further, town-by-town specialisations were also emerging before mid-century, and they became increasingly pronounced. In spinning, for example, Manchester itself spun the finest yarns, while Bolton concentrated on medium and medium-fine grades and Oldham confirmed its reputation as the main centre for the coarsest yarns. In weaving, Blackburn depended increasingly on basic cloths for the Indian and Chinese markets, as well as becoming the commercial capital of the weaving district, while Preston manufactured high-class cloths for the home, European and United States markets and Nelson's sateens and coloured goods fell between the extremes.[5] Local variations in products and markets engendered differences in wage-rates, industrial relations and the age/sex composition of the labour force, and even in the phasing and impact of the trade cycle, as demand fluctuated according to different influences in different areas of the world.

These local idiosyncracies were by-products of the Lancashire cotton industry's world-wide search for markets to sustain its continuing growth. Britain's average annual consumption of raw cotton nearly trebled from 426 million pounds in 1839–41 to 1211 million in 1871–3, and over the next forty years it nearly doubled again, to 2132 million. These were much less spectatular growth-rates than those of the 'heroic age' between 1780 and 1840, but they were cumulatively much weightier; and they were conditional on the continuing expansion of exports.[6] On Deane and Cole's calculations, exports already accounted for half the value of the industry's 'final product' in the second quarter of the nineteenth century; by the mid-1870s they had reached 70 per cent, and at the turn of the century the figure was almost 79 per cent.[7] But the export distribution pattern changed beyond all recognition during the nineteenth century, as successive countries and regions of the world acquired cotton industries of their own or alternative sources of supply. Exports to Europe and the United States made up nearly 70 per cent of the volume, and three-quarters of the value, of British cotton exports in 1820. Already in 1850 the corresponding figures were 26 per cent and 43 per cent, and by 1896 they were 8 per cent and 22½ per cent. The percentages are a little misleading: export growth was so enormous that Europe actually received a greater volume and value of British cotton goods in 1896 than in 1850, and growth in some markets continued into Edwardian times. But the growth that mattered was elsewhere. Latin America and the Middle East provided buoyant markets for much of the nineteenth century, but what really counted was Asia. In 1820 it accounted for 5.7 per cent of the volume, and 5.15 per cent of the value; the 1850 figures were 31 per cent and 24 per cent; and by 1896 they had reached 58 per cent and 43 per cent. India dominated this inexorable shift in emphasis, which continued into the new century: by 1913,

45 per cent of the total yardage of British cotton exports went to the sub-continent.[8] A vast and ever-growing sector of the Lancashire cotton economy, especially in plain weaving, thus came to depend not only on the United States, which remained overwhelmingly the dominant source of raw cotton, but also on the captive, and increasingly restive, markets of India. This led to successful Lancashire interference in Imperial politics, in opposition to Indian protective tariffs and to the rise of the Bombay coarse spinning industry; and attempts were made to promote cotton growing in India, to consummate a symbiotic relation-ship between British manufacture and colonial agriculture. It was, above all, the growth of the Indian market that freed the cotton industry from the spectre of mid-century stagnation, and allowed continuing expansion on the grand scale in face of competition from the United States, Europe and, later, Brazil and Japan. This dependence on India and on long sea routes no doubt helped to push Lancashire politics into a Palmerstonian and later an imperialist mould, en-couraging the rise of a flag-waving, Navy-loving, jingoistic popular Toryism in some of the late Victorian cotton towns.

The continuing expansion of the Lancashire cotton industry was neither serene nor straightforward. In the first place, we should set it in perspective. The 'Cotton Famine' of the early 1860s exposed the myth that the industry was essen-tial to the well-being of the British economy, and its share of the value of British exports fell from 40 per cent in 1850 to 30 per cent in 1873, although it was still 29 per cent in 1896. These were still impressive figures, though; and although in 1893 the number of factory spindles in the rest of the world overtook the British total for the first time, Lancashire still dominated world output and trade in cotton twenty years later.[9] But growth was punctuated by severe depressions. The 'Cotton Famine' itself was really a cyclical slump whose causes were disguised by the American Civil War blockade, and there were 'major cyclical depressions' in 1877 – 9, 1884 – 5 and 1891 – 3, as well as less dramatic setbacks later. But the impact of the trade cycle was mitigated increasingly by the tendency for trends in India to be counter-cyclical, and by the late nineteenth century employees were beginning to experience slumps in the form of short time and wage cuts rather than lay-offs, although there were several long and bitter strikes in response to attempted wage reductions. The employers were the main sufferers from pressure on margins and the rate of profit in the later nineteenth and early twentieth cen-turies, as the price of cotton goods fell steadily and competition sharpened. There continued to be a high mortality rate, among the new limited companies as well as the smaller and increasingly the older private firms. Even so, and despite a suc-cession of very lean years between 1892 and 1896, the cotton industry remained attractive to entrepreneurs, investors and lenders almost throughout its estab-lished territory.[10] Between 1884 and 1914, Kenny calculates, Lancashire in-creased its number of spindles by 45.5 per cent, and of looms by 51.3 per cent, with particularly rapid growth in the coarse spinning capital of Oldham, where spindleage increased by 75 per cent, and in Burnley, where the number of looms more than doubled.[11]

The cotton industry's growth was neither linear nor uncomplicated, then; but the results were ultimately impressive. They were achieved without major changes in the overall composition of the labour force or in the predominant technology, although the organisation of the firm began to alter in significant ways during the later nineteenth century.

According to the factory inspectors' returns, the number of 'operatives employed in cotton factories' in Britain rose from 331,000 in 1850 to well over half a million in the early twentieth century. But the age/sex composition of the workforce across the whole industry remained remarkably stable. Women and girls over the age of 13 made up between 54 and 56 per cent of the employees throughout the second half of the nineteenth century, rising to just over 60 per cent in Edwardian times; men over 18 were consistently about or just over a quarter of the total; boys between 13 and 18 hovered around 7 or 8 per cent; and younger children actually increased from less than 5 per cent in 1850 to 14 per cent in 1874, before falling away in face of changing school attendance regulations and practices to a mere 3.2 per cent in 1907.[12] In some respects, this striking overall consistency is misleading. It hides much wider fluctuations in weaving, where the use of children increased from 0.5 per cent of the workforce in 1850 to 13.5 per cent in 1874, while weaving firms increased their share of the industry's child labour from 1 per cent in 1850 to 43 per cent in 1890. The figures also mask some astonishing variations from town to town. In 1901 the number of females per hundred males in the industry ranged from 61 in Royton and 85 and 95 in the late-developing weaving centres of Nelson and Colne, where there was little alternative work for men, to 261 in the north Cheshire weaving outpost of Hyde and 295 and 340 in the mixed urban economies of Manchester/Salford and Accrington. The specialised spinning towns had ratios between 140 and 170. Local labour markets thus affected the supply of factory labour, just as detailed differences in specialisation and technology affected the demand; and these variations had implications for labour relations and family incomes. Generalisations in these fields should therefore be made with caution and awareness of complexity. Even so, Farnie's comment that 'Lancashire ... retained the highest proportion of half-timers, working girls, and working women in the whole country', is indisputable; but the nature, extent and significance of cotton factory work as a male occupation varied considerably from town to town. We shall return to these issues.[13]

Despite these complications, the continuity in the overall structure of the workforce probably reflects the limited extent of technological innovation in the cotton industry during these years, in sharp contrast with the flux and conflict of the generation before 1850. This is not a straightforward matter, however, and we shall return to it shortly. First, we should point to the changes that did take place in factory size and the organisation of the firm.

The size of factories grew slowly, except in spinning in the late nineteenth and early twentieth centuries. Problems of definition remain, and we should remember that one factory could contain several firms, while one firm could own or operate several factories. Vertically integrated, combined spinning and weaving firms remained a minority, and new firms specialised in one process or the other, with little amalgamation or consolidation. In 1914 the industry was still dominated by medium-sized firms, and there were still about two thousand of them, with a core of well-established concerns and a very large number of insecure and fluctuating businesses, especially in weaving. The average number of employees per spinning factory was little more than a hundred in 1850, increasing gradually to about half as many again by 1890, and no doubt rising further in the next generation as new mills were built on a much grander scale, while older, smaller concerns continued to fall out of use through obsolescence and fire. The rise in productive capacity was much greater, as average spindleage more than trebled between 1850 and 1890, and subsequent new factories were larger still. Employees per factory in weaving averaged about a hundred in 1850, still fewer than 150 in 1878, and 173 on one calculation in 1890. The details are hard to disentangle, but the overall pattern is clear enough: as Farnie says, 'Only in the closing decades of the century and only within the spinning sector did the large mill become typical of the industry.' The experiences of individual towns still varied. In the 1850s, for example, most Oldham mills still employed fewer than a hundred people, while 53 of Bolton's 81 mills averaged 174; but the picture changed rapidly in Oldham from the 1870s with the advent of large limited companies. The high capital cost of mills and equipment made spinning more and more difficult for the small entrepreneur to enter, although mill management for the new limited companies provided a new kind of career structure; but weaving remained relatively accessible, as companies and partnerships built premises and continued to rent them out in small units. Even in spinning, however, changes in the size of production units over the period were gradual and cumulative rather than revolutionary.[14]

The most important transformation involved the organisation of the industry, as family ownership and private partnerships gave way to limited companies after 1860. This was a long process, and it went further, faster, in spinning than in weaving. Producer co-operatives in the 1850s, in Oldham and Rochdale especially, offered a false promise of industrial democracy and profit-sharing on the road to the Owenite millenium; but the first great boom in joint-stock company promotion came in Rossendale during the boom of 1860-1. The later nineteenth century saw further surges of company flotation in 1873-5, 1880-4 and 1889-92, and Oldham, in particular, became famous for its large number of aggressively competitive limited companies in coarse spinning. The experience of other towns varied: Rochdale was quick to follow the Oldham precedent, and so was Ashton-under-Lyne, but the centres of fine spinning in Bolton and Manchester were much slower in beginning and proceeding with the transition. By the turn of the century, however, the limited company was the dominant mode of organisation in most of the Lancashire spinning industry. The change started later and took longer in weaving, but it proceeded apace in the early years of the twentieth century. On the eve of the First World War the limited company, with its board of directors and salaried manager responsible to the shareholders, dominated the cotton industry as a whole.[15]

The implications of this important change are not straightforward. Joyce argues that it undermined an existing social and political order based on a personal, paternalist relationship between master and operative, replacing a stable system with 'a history of bitterness and suspicion' as the 'Limiteds' substituted the cash nexus for the individual industrialist's sense of *noblesse oblige*.[16] We shall return to this contentious set of issues. Meanwhile, we should remember that the implications varied in practice according to the nature of the 'Limiteds' that were established. Only 155 of the 1046 companies floated before 1896 were established specifically to build new mills, and one-third of the total were private limited companies which effectively extended the benefits of limited liability and corporate organisation to existing family firms and partnerships, with no necessary change in the power structure or even the ethos of the concern. Where existing firms did open themselves out to a wider shareholding public, the new companies were often short-lived, as vendors over-valued their assets and left their successors to struggle. We must therefore be careful not to overstate the importance of the coming of the 'Limiteds' as such; and in Oldham, where their impact was most obvious, the existing tradition of employer paternalism was particularly weak. Outside Oldham, moreover, the 'working-class' limited company, with its £5 shares, democratic constitution and shareholders drawn from the labour aristocracy and shopkeeping classes, was most unusual, and it soon declined in importance in Oldham itself. A more usual pattern involved shares of high denomination, or hefty minimum shareholdings, and a smaller number of higher-status investors. This suggests that the more optimistic argument that the 'Limiteds' democratised the cotton industry by giving the workforce the opportunity to become investing participants in the capitalist process, should also be taken with a pinch of salt, although many companies did raise additional capital by accumulating loans from small investors and paying competitive rates of interest. Again, we shall return to these matters in a later chapter.[17]

Increases in factory size and changes in the organisation of the firm were not accompanied by extensive technological changes in either spinning or weaving. The mid-Victorian years saw the working out of existing trends. The transition from hand-mule to self-acting mule took much longer on the finer yarns, and the hand-mule was still important in Bolton in the early 1880s. The decline of the hand-loom weavers had been further advanced by 1850 than that of the hand-mule, but it took the 'Cotton Famine' to finish them off in several former strongholds, including Todmorden, Samlesbury and Colne. They lasted longer still on certain fancy fabrics, and in 1866 there were still 1500 in Manchester and a similar number in Bolton. Most gave up when a new tariff pushed them out of the United States fancy goods market in the late 1870s, and the last survivors of all were the Bolton counterpane weavers, who kept going into the 1890s.[18] More important, however, was the Lancashire cotton industry's resistance to two important innovations which were widely adopted elsewhere: ring-spinning and the automatic loom. Ring-spinning offered greater productivity with the opportunity to employ cheaper female labour, although the mule produced a softer yarn. This new technology originated in the United States, where it already predominated in 1870; and it was adopted eagerly in the new Asian cotton industries, though more slowly in continental Europe. Britain was last of all, and as late as 1913 British factories contained 45.2 million mule spindles but only 10.4 ring spindles. Most of the latter were used for the coarsest yarns, although American experience showed that ring-spinning was actually much more versatile than this suggested.[19] The automatic loom, introduced in the United States in 1894, and already accounting for nearly half of all American looms in 1914, was even slower to make headway in Lancashire. The Northrop or Draper loom, as it was called, was available in England from 1903 onwards, but at most 10,000 of Lancashire's 805,000 looms were automatic by 1914, despite the higher productivity promised by the manufacturers.[20]

Some historians have blamed Lancashire employers severely for their neglect of these innovations, alleging that it fits into a general pattern of late Victorian entrepreneurial failure in Britain, and that it helps to explain the collapse of the cotton industry between the wars. More recently, however, Sandberg and Lazonick have argued that under prevailing British conditions the decision to persist with established technologies was economically rational, while no amount of re-equipment could have prevented the post-war disasters, which arose from circumstances beyond the employers' control. The cost savings to be made from ring-spinning were only attractive in the manufacture of coarse yarns, and for the installation of new plant rather than the replacement of existing mules; and under these conditions Lancashire spinners were willing to introduce the new technology. The opposition of the mule-spinners themselves may have helped to inhibit management, as strikes and disruption were likely to bedevil any piecemeal transition to a system that threatened established livelihoods and workplace authority; but despite the strength of their organisation, the Lancashire mule-spinners were less well-paid than their American counterparts, a point which was itself contributory to the limited returns on prospective investment in ring-spinning. Indeed, the spinners' willingness to co-operate with management in raising productivity on the existing system, was itself a major buttress against technological change. Burgess points out that between the 1830s and the early 1890s the number of spindles per mule more than doubled, as did the speed of mule operation; and Sandberg and White agree that the intensity of work in the spinning processes continued to increase, with a corresponding rise in output per worker, between 1890 and 1914. Why run the risks associated with a wholesale shift to a new technology and a new kind of workforce, when the existing system is already delivering impressive improvements in output and productivity? In weaving, the improvements which increased the ratio of looms per operative from one to nearly four between the 1830s and the 1890s, and doubled average loom speeds, were not sustained, and productivity stagnated; but the automatic loom involved high capital and (probably) maintenance costs, was unsuitable for high-quality fabrics, and required ring-spun yarn whose supply was still uncertain in Edwardian Lancashire. As Lazonick suggests, a vertically integrated cotton industry, with spinning and weaving co-ordinated by the same firms, would have made both sets of innovations easier to adopt; and the limited capital of most weaving firms made them unlikely purchasers of expensive automatic looms. Under prevailing circumstances, at any rate, Lancashire's lukewarm response to ring-spinning, and its general rejection of the automatic loom, seem entirely understandable.[21]

On the whole, indeed, this was a period of unparalleled prosperity for the Lancashire cotton industry, despite interludes of depression and industrial conflict and tightening pressure on overseas markets and profit margins. The experiences of spinning and weaving might diverge increasingly in many respects, as we have seen, but they shared a remarkably consistent experience of continuing growth. In many ways, however, the happiest beneficiaries of these years were those who serviced the cotton industry. Builders and businessmen in allied trades not only did well out of the continuing rise in housing demand, at least until the early twentieth century; they also made fat profits out of mill-building, to such an extent that many became involved in company promotion more with a view to creating business for themselves than to setting up concerns which would be profitable to their shareholders in the long run. Accountants, solicitors and other professionals also did well out of the continuing expansion and growing financial complexity of the cotton industry.[22] Above all the textile engineering industry did well out of these years of consolidation, and we need to examine the fortunes of this major employer of adult male labour in most of the cotton towns.

The growth of textile engineering alongside the cotton industry itself provided major advantages for the Lancashire economy in the short and medium terms, although the policies of the firms eventually played their part in the dethronement of 'King Cotton'. The needs of the cotton industry ensured a ready market for spinning and preparatory machinery, for steam engines, and later for power-looms. In the early days, much of the demand was met from the larger firms' own workshops, but specialist engineering concerns soon emerged. Already in 1841 a survey found 115 'mechanical establishments' in Lancashire, employing over 17,000 people, more than 5000 of them in Manchester. They included almost all of the major firms of the later nineteenth century, and the subsequent growth of the industry was rapid. In Oldham, Hibbert and Platt became the largest machine-making works in the world during the 1860s, and between 1859 and 1871 they doubled their labour force to 7000. By 1910 their successors, Platt

Brothers, had over 10,000 employees, and at least four other firms had over 2000 each. Textile machine making gained a firm foothold in almost all of the cotton towns, catering for the particular needs of local economies in coarse or fine spinning, or weaving; and only the 'late developers', Nelson and Colne, failed to acquire substantial firms. But the spinning side of the industry nurtured the real giants, because here there was the greatest scope for capturing export markets, especially after the formal lifting of restrictions in this field in 1843. Loom-making was less varied, innovative and sophisticated, and most of the firms here were much smaller and more localised in their markets. The Lancashire mill-building boom of the 1870s generated enormous windfall profits: Platts averaged 34 per cent per annum during 1872–7, five times the profits of the spinning mills they supplied. But long-term expansion to a peak on the eve of the First World War was based on exports: in 1913 the United Kingdom had 87.1 per cent of world trade in spinning machinery, and the figure for weaving was 64 per cent. Ring-frames were exported as well as mules and carding machines: Farnie comments that by the 1880s Lancashire was making improved ring-frames at half the transatlantic price, and overcoming freight charges and tariff barriers to sell them in the United States. The development of export markets was largely the preserve of the giant firms that dominated the industry: it was easy to begin in a small way, and many often short-lived small concerns did specialised work on commission for their larger neighbours, or did repairs and jobbing work, but they lacked the capital and expertise to make it into the big time. This was a prosperous industry of national importance. In 1907 textile machinery still produced a higher gross output than the railway locomotive builders, and accounted for more than one-third of all mechanical engineering production. The availability of machinery supplies on the doorstep cut capital costs and overheads by up to one-third for Lancashire cotton firms compared with overseas rivals, and the engineering firms' well-paid workforce helped to balance and stabilise the local labour market. The price of this prosperity was the nurturing of foreign competition through the export of Lancashire's machinery and expertise; but in 1914 this was still a problem for the future.[23]

Engineering of other kinds also flourished. The demand for mill steam engines, increasingly of large standard types which were also exported, shifted the main centre of stationary steam engine manufacture from Birmingham to Bolton by the 1840s, and in Manchester firms like Galloways developed to build the classic 'Lancashire boiler' and the largest stationary engines. Nor was the cradle of the modern railway system without its locomotive-building plants, as Manchester acquired the enormous Beyer Peacock works at Gorton, the Vulcan Foundry became established at Newton-le-Willows and the building of the Lancashire and Yorkshire Railway's central locomotive and rolling stock plant transformed the ailing economy of the textile finishing centre of Horwich.[24] Lancashire also became an important centre for the manufacture of machine tools; throughout the period 1870–1914 it was second only to the North-East in its number of active firms, and the Lancashire industry included famous names such as James Nasmyth. An official history described the county as 'the early home of the machine tool trade, and at one time had the reputation of producing the best quality tools'. The Lancashire firms began to suffer from American competition in the 1890s, but their reputation for solid construction (which, as in textile engineering, meant that they had to wait a long time for repeat orders) and openness to innovation kept them a secure share of established markets.[25] Cotton Lancashire was also, and importantly, engineering Lancashire.

But this concentration on two industries must not be allowed to obscure the diversity and scale of 'cotton Lancashire's' economic development in this period. Until 1883, when it was narrowly overtaken by South Wales, Lancashire was the most productive British coalfield outside the North-East, although it lost ground rapidly thereafter as its output stagnated in the 1890s and declined after 1907. Most of this coal was mined around Wigan and at points south and west, but much of it was consumed in the cotton district, and various estimates for the 1860s suggest that steam engines in cotton factories devoured between 2.5 and 4.5 million tons per year, up to one-third of the coalfield's output.[26] A few less-important industries were more directly tied to cotton: paper-making used cotton rags and also supplied the industry, and bobbin-making, which had migrated from the Lake District to Todmorden by 1890, was dependent on the spinners' requirements, while some aspects of the chemical industry were also cotton-dominated. But Farnie long ago provided an extensive list of other manufactures in which Lancashire held a leading position in late Victorian times. They included glass, soap, chemicals and candles, which were concentrated on Merseyside rather than the cotton towns as such, but also coaches, wagons, felt hats, india rubber manufacture and sawmilling. Lancashire was second only to London in gasmaking, to Kent in bricks and tiles, to Warwick and London in furniture (a Lancaster preserve), and to London in food processing and tobacco (both mainly Liverpool activities), and paper. The manufacture of clocks, watches, wire and beer, on Merseyside especially, was also of national importance; and the inventory of the textile district itself still included wool and silk manufacture, as well as a growing late Victorian slipper industry in Rossendale and garment manufacture in Manchester itself.[27] Cotton predominated in Lancashire, and especially in its Manchester-centred heartland, but this was far from being a monolithic economy.

Within the cotton district itself, the distinction between Manchester and its manufacturing satellites widened. Fine spinning remained important, but it was swamped by growth in the commercial and service sectors as well as engineering and transport, as Manchester's metropolitan functions became ever more pronounced. As the cotton industry grew, so did the scope for merchants and agents to find outlets for the goods produced by a myriad of firms with insufficient resources to do their own marketing. Manchester commercial men sold yarn overseas or (increasingly in the later nineteenth century) to the weaving firms of north Lancashire; they organised the distribution of 'Manchester goods' in the home market; and most importantly, they consigned Lancashire cloths overseas. Manchester became cosmopolitan: already at mid-century it had a well-established population of German and other overseas merchants, and an increasingly prosperous Jewish community. As the merchants, bankers, agents and dealers colonised the burgeoning suburbs, so their tall, palatial warehouses dominated much of the old town centre; and they provided relatively secure, if far from opulent, employment for a growing army of clerks and warehousemen. By the 1860s the literate products of Ancoats slum schools were finding their way into the warehouses, and forty years on a marine insurance firm provided a congenial and undemanding refuge for the young Neville Cardus on the early steps of his journey from dubious back-street origins to journalistic fame as music critic and cricket writer. Alongside these opportunities for the literate but impecunious, Manchester's casual and sweated labour markets provided conditions as painful and poverty-stricken as anywhere, and a further distinctive twist to its social structure arose from the unusually high level of demand for domestic servants, who were as numerous in Moss Side or Withington as anywhere in England in 1901, in sharp contrast with their unimportance in the cotton and mining towns of Manchester's hinterland. Manchester already presented a distinctive, specialised and sophisticated economic and social profile at mid-century: by Edwardian times these features were considerably accentuated.[28]

Manchester's distinctiveness was given an additional dimension when the opening of the Manchester Ship Canal in 1894, based on Corporation sponsorship and capital coupled with the investments of 39,000 shareholders, gave it the potential to become a port of international standing, emancipating it from the Liverpool dock dues and monopolistic railway rates which had long been a source of complaint. In practice, this epic of engineering and investment took time to make its mark in terms of attracting trade, although its mere existence was sufficient to bring down the freight rates of its rivals. Resistance from railway companies and Liverpool shipping lines was persistent and determined. But by 1914 it was firmly established, with nearly 5 per cent of Britain's import trade by value, and 4.4 per cent of domestic exports. A strong trading relationship with Canada had been established, and Manchester had taken a significant share of the grain, cotton and timber trades. The growth of imports, especially foodstuffs, confirmed Manchester's position as regional distribution as well as merchandising centre, and reinforced its commercial specialisation still further.[29]

Despite this powerful new rival, and the loss of much of its coal trade to railway docks in the Mersey estuary, especially Garston, Liverpool continued to prosper as the port and commercial centre for Lancashire and a much wider area. Between 1850 and 1913 its imports trebled in value at current prices and increased more than threefold in volume; its exports grew nearly fourfold in value and nearly fivefold in volume. On top of this was the flourishing passenger traffic, including for most of the period a substantial contingent of emigrants to the United States. The extraordinary expansion of the docks continued, south of the river in Birkenhead as well as in Liverpool itself. More than fifty acres of docks were added during the 1840s, and this rate of growth continued in the next decade despite incipient financial strain. After 1858 the new Mersey Docks and Harbour Board continued the process, retrieving the fortunes of the Birkenhead docks and further extending the Liverpool system. In the forty years or so after 1870, Merseyside dock expenditure stayed at just over 20 per cent of the national total, in spite of rapid expansion from smaller beginnings elsewhere. Annual dock revenues at current prices rose from £457,299 in 1858 to £1,685,176 in 1913. There was a tendency for growth-rates to slow down in the early twentieth century, and the removal of the White Star Line express passenger terminal to Southampton in 1907 was a threatening straw in the wind; but the overall picture was still healthy. When Hyde remarks that, 'By 1914, the high peak of achievement had been reached and passed; the lean years were about to begin', his perception is convincing; but his gloomier comment that, 'Within this prosperity, the seeds of decline had already been sown', may owe more to hindsight than to an objective appraisal of Liverpool's remarkably sustained long-term growth from what was already a commanding position.[30]

Within the general picture of expansion there were significant changes in the pattern and organisation of trade. As Hyde says, 'In the latter half of the nineteenth century, King Cotton reigned supreme in Liverpool'. This applied especially to exports, but raw cotton imports stood at 360,000 tons in 1850 and 690,000 tons in 1913. Even so, the growth of other imported commodities surpassed that of cotton, whose share of import values fell from just over 40 per cent in the early 1850s to 30 per cent in 1913. Sugar and tobacco also grew in volume but declined in relative importance, while the main growth sectors were grain (especially wheat), rubber, wool and copper. Cotton goods accounted for half the value of Liverpool exports in 1901, and 41.6 per cent in 1913; and a major secondary role was played by heavy engineering and railway equipment, which expanded rapidly in Edwardian times. But Liverpool's export hinterland extended beyond Lancashire, and woollen and worsted goods were also increasing in importance after 1900. Much more marked were the changes in technology and organisation. The transition from sail to steam was gathering momentum irrevocably between the 1850s and 1870s, as Lairds of Birkenhead rose to prominence as builders of iron steamships and Alfred Holt pioneered the application of steam power to the long-distance cargo traffic. The late 1860s and early 1870s saw a spectacular steamship investment boom in Liverpool, and at the end of the 1870s the Liverpool Steam Ship Owners' Association claimed to represent 30 per cent of British steam tonnage. Sail survived much longer on some of the most distant routes, but the dominant trend was to ever-increasing investment in the most sophisticated steam technology. Between 1870 and 1914 the employed capital of six leading steamship lines rose ninefold (allowing for inflation) to over fourteen million pounds, as Liverpool's shipowners spread their tentacles across the world's trade-routes, monopolising the West Africa trade and competing effectively and successfully elsewhere, including Australian and Pacific routes where the interests of the cotton industry were of little importance. Cotton had convincing pretensions to involvement in a world market, but Liverpool's range of geographical interests was capable of making the leading Lancashire manufacturing industry seem almost parochial by comparison.[31]

International commerce provided Liverpool with its dynamism and unique character, and the port's social structure reflected the needs of trade and services rather than manufacturing industry. The older Liverpool manufactures, such as pottery and watchmaking, had disappeared by the late nineteenth century, although a variety of new ones arose in their place. The shipyards on the Liverpool side of the Mersey dealt with repairs rather than shipbuilding, but engineering and foundries were major employers, and import processing activities such as flour milling, sugar refining, rice and spice milling, seed crushing and tobacco manufacture combined to find work for several thousand Liverpudlians on the eve of the First World War. But the main employer in manufacturing was the building industry, and the dominant sectors of adult male employment were dock labouring, the mercantile marine, railways and carting on the waterfront. Female job opportunities remained very limited, with domestic service over-whelmingly predominating. Otherwise, sweated labour in the clothing trades was important, as in Manchester, and a few manufactures, especially jam-making and tobacco, provided employment for a small minority. Children's employment was still in short supply in the early twentieth century, and much of it took the form of 'dead-end' jobs of the street-trading or messenger-boy variety. But the range of employment across the board had increased greatly since the mid-Victorian years, and dockers and seamen no longer dominated the town's labour market to the same extent. Railway and municipal labour offered more security than hitherto to an important section of the labour force, and the growth of white-collar employment was also changing the social structure. By 1914 there were nearly 12,000 male commercial clerks, about as many as there were seamen, and insurance workers, bankers, stockbrokers, accountants and the law accounted for several thousand others. This was also an expanding sphere of women's work, to the alarm of the male clerks and their unions; and much clerical work was indeed insecure and ill-paid. Even so, prosperity or at least relative security and comfort were much more widely diffused through Liverpool society in 1914 than in 1850, although we shall see that substantial pockets of abject poverty and appalling living conditions remained, and the gap between capital and labour widened considerably on the waterfront. Above all, though, Liverpool remained essentially a commercial port whose economy was still dominated by unskilled and casual or sweated labour, and its social structure and employment patterns remained quite sharply differentiated from those of the cotton towns.[32]

The industries of Liverpool's immediate hinterland also continued to develop in a way which suggested variations on a theme or consolidation accompanied by changes of emphasis. Coal and chemicals expanded very rapidly in mid-Victorian times but failed to sustain their growth subsequently, the plate glass industry at St. Helens became a great Victorian success story, and the older metalworking industries generally continued their decline. We need to examine the fortunes of these distinctive manufacturing economies in more detail.

We have seen that the Lancashire coalfield's growth lost momentum, both relatively and absolutely, in the late nineteenth and early twentieth centuries; but more must be said about the context and implications of this trend. Employment and investment followed a similar pattern to output. The rapid increase in coal-mining employees, which was already apparent in the 1840s, was continued in mid-Victorian times: the 31,000 mineworkers of 1851 had doubled temporarily by 1874 and permanently by 1879, and trebled by 1901, reaching a peak at 108,000 in 1913. Capital investment similarly slackened from the 1890s and declined in real terms after 1906, as smaller pits began to close, especially in the eastern part of the county. Productivity, measured in output per man-year or per man-shift, stagnated from the 1860s and declined from the turn of the century, especially after 1906. This was due more to the increasing age of the largest pits, which meant that more time was absorbed in travelling to the coal-face and maintaining underground communications, than to technological backwardness: Lancashire's record in introducing coal-cutting machinery and electrical equipment, for example, was on a par with most coalfields and better than several. There were also innovations in the size and organisation of the firm. The small firms and pits, which were still much in evidence at mid-century, declined in importance; and the predominance of a few large and old-established concerns, such as the Knowleses and Fletchers and the Wigan Coal and Iron Company, if anything increased. In coal as in cotton, too, there was a rapid transition from the later nineteenth century from individual firms and partnerships (owning 56 per cent of collieries in 1873 and 38 per cent in 1890, and employing only 11 per cent of the coalfield's miners by 1913) to limited companies. This seems to have widened the distance between masters and men, and exacerbated the disputes which were inevitable as geological difficulties and deeper shafts increased investment commitments and threatened continuity of output. Profits in Lancashire coal mining were still no worse than average on the eve of the First World War, however, and the royalties demanded by landowners, although on the high side, were less onerous than in Cumberland or Scotland. In general, too, the economic situation was probably better in the south-west and central parts of the coalfield than in the east; and the Lancashire coal industry as a whole was still in reasonable health, if no longer actually flourishing, when the war came.[33]

The alkali industry on Merseyside grew even faster than coal mining in mid-Victorian times, as it diversified its products and markets beyond the needs of local industries and consumers, and competed successfully against rival centres, especially on Tyneside. Within south-west Lancashire, the high transport costs imposed by the local railway and canal monopoly after 1848, and especially after 1854, undermined the locational advantages of St. Helens and removed the main focus of growth a few miles southwards to Widnes, although new firms were still being established in St. Helens in the mid-1870s, and the chemical industry retained a foothold there until beyond the First World War. But Widnes was the alkali industry's mid-Victorian boom town, ideally situated as it was for Cheshire salt, Lancashire coal and access to the Mersey estuary and the rapidly expanding markets of Western Europe and the United States. Between the late 1840s and the early 1870s the population of Widnes grew tenfold to top 20,000, and its rateable value grew twelvefold. In 1872 24 of its 35 industrial plants were chemical works, and several others supplied machinery or equipment to the chemical firms or processed their by-products, although a large iron foundry also made such items as seaside piers and water supply pipes. The Leblanc process could be operated on a small scale, and was still not difficult to enter. It spread rapidly on the other side of the Mersey in Runcorn, too, during these years, and there were several small factories in the cotton district, meeting the local needs of the textile finishing processes, and in Liverpool itself. Two of the leading firms in Widnes each employed 500 men in 1870, and ten years later half the town's industrial workforce was making its living from alkali manufacture.[34]

Widnes soon acquired a reputation to match its unique and vulnerable industrial structure. Contemporaries noted its perpetual pall of smoke and chemical pollution, and it was dubbed, 'The dirtiest, ugliest town in England'. Vegetation withered and died, and mounds of chemical waste covered the landscape, while their seepings polluted the brooks and rivers. St. Helens experienced similar problems, including a pervasive 'rotten eggs' odour where hydrogen sulphide was generated by chemcial reactions in the watercourses. A crescendo of complaint from farmers and landowners led to the Alkali Act of 1863, which was directed against air pollution from hydrochloric acid gas. Enforcement was difficult, but the legislation encouraged and intensified the search for saleable by-products from the lengthy and complicated Leblanc process. By the 1870s soda ash was only one of several important products of a ramifying Merseyside chemical industry.[35]

The remarkable growth of the chemical industry imposed severe social and environmental costs, in the form of dingy streets and appalling working conditions as well as pollution. During the 1870s, moreover, the Merseyside success story began to be threatened by developments elsewhere. The successful introduction of the cheaper, brine-using Solvay ammonia process, which was also less environmentally damaging, by Brunner Mond at Winnington on the Cheshire saltfield soon ate into the Leblanc producers' markets, while the German and other West European alkali industries began to ally cheapness to quality and expertise, and the Americans entered the field. The Leblanc manufacturers had set little store by scientific research, despite their employment of German chemists and their mid-Victorian innovations in the development of by-products; and they were caught wrong-footed by the challenge, with extensive capital tied up in suddenly obsolescent plant, as soda prices fell by 50 per cent between 1875 and 1890. After several attempts at inter-firm collaboration to fix prices and output levels, almost all the British Leblanc firms amalgamated in 1890 to form the United Alkali Company. This unwieldly conglomerate presided over a rearguard action for the next quarter of a century, as American competition intensified, the introduction of electrolysis added a further rival process, and the Leblanc producers became increasingly dependent on sulphuric acid and other sulphur-related by-products of their process. The Lancashire plants did relatively well, with most of the inevitable closures coming in Scotland and the North-East; and the UAC itself ventured into ammonia soda production at Fleetwood, using newly discovered brine deposits at Preesall. But this was a depressed and difficult period, especially in the late 1890s, and (except for Winnington, where Brunner Mond made spectacular profits) the Merseyside chemical industry was visibly ailing by the turn of the century.[36]

The glass and soap industries, which had helped to call the alkali industry into being, sustained their prosperity much more convincingly. The demand for household soap grew impressively in Britain, and increasingly overseas, and Merseyside firms such as Gossage's of Widnes, Crosfield's of Warrington and, spectacularly after a late entry in 1885, Lever Brothers of Port Sunlight expanded their output, employment and range of markets in response, while giving demand a further boost through fiercely competitive advertising in late Victorian and Edwardian times. Crosfield's labour force was 120 in 1871, about 250 in the mid-1880s, over 800 in 1896 and nearly 2500, including about 500 women and girls, in July 1913. Output and profits remained buoyant, and the range of products diversified to include Portland cement, glycerine, 'vegetable butter', caustic soda and other chemicals. W. H. Lever enjoyed an even more magnificent success story: by 1914, after absorbing several competitors, his firm controlled over 60 per cent of Britain's soap output. His humble origins and brashly innovative promotion and marketing methods did not endear him to his rivals, but he provided a tremendous stimulus to further growth in an already prospering industry. Indeed, the vast late Victorian and Edwardian expansion of the Merseyside soap industry, which opened out new markets, especially but not exclusively in India and the colonies, was punctuated throughout by bitter competition between the leading firms, which was only just beginning to moderate on the eve of the First World War when Crosfield's and Gossage's were brought together under the capacious umbrella of Brunner Mond.[37]

The Merseyside soap industry thus confounds a persistent stereotype of the late nineteenth and early twentieth centuries as a period of incipient decline, business complacency and entrepreneurial failure. In the glass industry, the rise of Pilkingtons of St. Helens to world dominance in face of potentially crippling

Two images of female factory workers at the turn of the century. (See p. 288.)

The living-room of a fish-and-chip shop proprietor in Edwardian Salford: a carefully-posed self-portrait on a time-exposure. (See p. 293.)   [*Below*] Prosperous and respectable working men: the committee of Rawtenstall Conservative Co-operative Society. (See p. 301.)

competition from Belgium and the United States, provides even stronger evidence of the persistence of entrepreneurial vitality. The demise of most of Pilkingtons' British rivals in the crown and sheet glass industries at mid-century enabled them to treble their workforce from 450 to 1350 between 1849 and 1854. A period of consolidation followed, but from the mid-1860s Pilkingtons were at the forefront in adopting a series of important innovations: the Siemens gas furnace in 1864; the introduction in the early 1870s of lehrs to accelerate the cooling process, and tank furnaces to enable continuous production; the opening of a plate glass factory in 1876; and the early adoption of the most sophisticated polishing and grinding machinery. These developments, watched over by a rising generation of Pilkingtons (including William Windle Pilkington, a genius at adapting and improving the inventions of others), help to explain the almost uninterrupted expansion and prosperity of the firm, while its remaining British competitors languished and collapsed during the difficult 1890s. Pilkingtons operated their own coal mines and saltcake plant, to assure a constant cheap supply of adequate raw materials; and they began to invest overseas, in Canada and France, while by the turn of the century their markets were genuinely world-wide. There were few traces of entrepreneurial failure here, and the overwhelming local influence of the company helped to make St. Helens into an island of grimy but genuine relative prosperity by the early twentieth century.[38]

St. Helens was also the home of important iron foundries and of Beecham's Pills, another tribute to the power of mass advertising in late Victorian England. Explosive growth in the 1880s enabled Beecham's labour force to grow from 19 to 88 in five years, with an output of nine million pills per day in 1890; and these were early days for the patent medicine firm. Coal mining, however, remained the major employer alongside the glassworks.[39] Elsewhere on Merseyside, too, there were prospering sectors of manufacturing. Warrington retained its economic diversity, as textiles and brewing continued to flourish, and wiremaking and other metalworking industries produced a diverse range of products, to complement the success of Crosfield's. On the Cheshire side of the Mersey, Ellesmere Port became a thriving little industrial town after the advent of the Manchester Ship Canal, with flour milling and a galvanised iron factory which had migrated from Wolverhampton in pursuit of cheaper imported raw materials and fewer municipal restraints. Lever's model settlement at Port Sunlight and the less famous Price's Patent Candle Company village at Bromborough provided further expressions of the long-term buoyancy of much of Merseyside's industry during this period.[40]

The contrasts between the cotton district and Merseyside, or between industrial Lancashire east and west of Wigan, were accentuated by the developments of this period; and apart from the continuing importance of the port of Liverpool, and its commercial services and expertise, to the cotton industry, the links between the two economies became less significant. Chemicals, glass, engineering and metalworking, like mining, dock work and the building trades, offered few economic opportunities for women and adolescents. In terms of paid labour, industrial Merseyside was very much a man's world; and this exacerbated the problems arising from low wages, irregular employment, illness and injury. The vast majority of jobs in chemicals and glass were for unskilled labourers, and well-paid labour aristocrats like the glassblowers were themselves becoming vulnerable to technological change. Merseyside was also becoming an area of large, capital-hungry firms, especially at the turn of the century. This applied to shipping and especially to soap, chemicals and glass, where the dominant positions of Lever, Brunner Mond and Pilkingtons were strengthened further by take-overs and mergers between 1890 and 1914. The gulf between capital and labour was widening in all the major Merseyside industries, and only the coastal shipping and fishing trades of Runcorn,[41] the ubiquitous small retailers (themselves meeting competition from the Co-op and the new multiples), the building trades and the commercial services of central Liverpool were major exceptions to the trend. In all these respects, Merseyside was significantly different from the cotton district, and especially from the smaller weaving towns; and we shall see that these differences had wider implications for living standards, labour relations and politics.

Industrial development north of the Ribble remained patchy, and heavily concentrated into Lancaster and the Barrow area, with a lesser outpost at Carnforth, where the railway traffic in iron ore from Furness met the coke trains from Durham and encouraged a steelworks to develop. Lancaster itself entered a new lease of industrial life, despite the collapse of its port and the failure of shipbuilding to respond to attempts at resuscitation. Its ailing cotton industry was largely replaced by the manufacture of oilcloth and table baize, which captured an immensely expanding home market for floor-coverings and made enormous fortunes for the two leading and rival entrepreneurial families, the Williamsons and the Storeys, whose firms dominated local employment and politics at the turn of the century and beyond.[42] Developments in Furness were more impressive in the short run, although they failed to fulfil their early promise or to match the grandiose hopes of their promoters. Barrow was a mid-Victorian mushroom town, as an alliance of landowners and capitalists, with the Duke of Devonshire playing a more than ornamental role, developed iron ore mines, docks, railways, and (from 1859) a steelworks, while providing the necessary housing and services (eventually) for a labour force which arrived from districts as distant as Staffordshire, Cornwall and the Clyde. The rich local haematite iron ore was a scarce resource, and its purity made it essential to the Bessemer steelmaking process which was introduced in 1856; and during the third quarter of the nineteenth century the newly created town and its surrounding ore-mining settlements expanded at a rate almost unparalleled in Victorian England. But the later years of the century saw depression, reduced dividends, unsuccessful new ventures and blighted hopes. Iron ore output peaked in the early 1880s at over 1¼ million tons per year, but it fell to less than one-third of that figure in the early twentieth century. The ore deposits were worked out all too quickly, and the Gilchrist – Thomas steelmaking process, which was less fastidious than Bessemer in its iron ore needs, robbed Furness haematite of its special value from the 1880s onwards. Attempts to challenge Liverpool as a passenger port, and to develop Barrow as a cargo-handling port of world importance, made little headway; and by the 1890s the limited population growth of a stagnating Barrow was based on natural increase rather than migration. A new basis for economic well-being was emerging at this time, however, as shipbuilding recovered under new management from its shaky origins, and Barrow's shipyards began to concentrate on warship contracts. Under the able management of Vickers, a specialisation in submarines alongside a proven ability to build the largest surface vessels ensured Edwardian prosperity, despite inevitable fluctuations in Admiralty orders and the uncertainty of custom from foreign navies. Barrow's economy remained unhealthily dependent on adult male employment in a narrow range of industries, and it was very much a 'company town', with little work for women after the failure of a jute factory in the 1870s. On the whole, indeed, the experience of Barrow and Lancaster over the period probably had closer parallels on Merseyside than in the cotton district, although the two towns differed widely from each other in several important respects.[43]

The nearest rival to Barrow for sheer rapidity and scale of growth, however, was Blackpool, although here the fastest expansion came in the 1890s rather than the 1860s, as the resort's spring population doubled to over 47,000 in response to the rise of the working-class seaside holiday habit in cotton Lancashire, the West Riding and parts of the West Midlands, and to a widening of the market for seaside residence and retirement. Morecambe, further north, provided another island of urban growth in response to similar opportunities, although here the sources of demand were less overwhelming and more localised, and the results were correspondingly less impressive.[44]

But over most of north Lancashire agriculture remained predominant; and it retained enough importance, even in industrial Lancashire, to warrant attention. The county contained extensive areas of arable farming and market gardening in the south-west, although the existing orientation to pasture and especially dairying was intensifying elsewhere; and the south-west was largely responsible for Lancashire containing, in 1870, the third largest potato acreage after Lincolnshire and Yorkshire, and generating, in 1905, a much higher potato yield per acre even than Lincolnshire. More generally, this was a period of impressive – and expensive – innovation, and of significant and sometimes traumatic change, especially for landowners and farmers. The third quarter of the nineteenth century saw widespread heavy investment by landowners in drainage on the inhospitable clay soils, in response to the availability of cheap finance and the railways' opening out of more general access to urban markets for dairy produce. This drainage investment was accompanied by improvements in farm buildings, and stricter supervision of farming practices. But the land-owners' returns were disappointingly meagre; and worse still, they were short-lived. It now seems clear that Lancashire, despite its urban markets and predominantly livestock farming, was not spared by the agricultural depression of the late nineteenth century; and landowners complained of rent arrears, rebates and reductions in response to falling agricultural prices, which cut their incomes at the very time when they might have expected to collect a healthy return on their investment. Land values fell, too, and landowners' borrowing powers were correspondingly reduced. By the turn of the century, the finances of several estates were in terminal crisis. For these people, the mid-Victorian improvements in output and efficiency had been dearly bought. The size of farms, meanwhile, had been increased on many of the larger estates, although the small family farm continued to predominate on the uplands, and especially in north-east Lancashire, where tiny pastoral holdings supplied fresh milk to nearby towns. But farming capital seems generally to have been in short supply, except among a few dynasties of prosperous, substantial farmers; and when the depression came, the largest farms proved most difficult to let. The wealthiest farmers were eager to adopt labour-saving innovations, but the majority preferred to (or were obliged to) intensify their exploitation of family labour, as agricultural wages maintained their upward trend. In 1892 the Lancashire average was 19s 8d per week, compared with 14s 9d in Wiltshire; and the police and the railways provided accessible alternative occupations for the young. Significantly, the employed workforce in Lancashire agriculture declined from 36,000 in 1851 to just over 20,000 in 1911. The safety-valves of migration and alternative employment were continuing to operate effectively, creating labour shortages on the land and giving a further stimulus to the transition to permanent pasture. The sufferers from these long-term trends were the landed estates, especially those which had invested too enthusiastically or too late, and the families of hard-pressed small farmers who were finding it difficult to cope with the falling prices of the late nineteenth century. Lancashire agriculture in general followed the pattern of several of the county's older industries: a mid-Victorian investment boom (although the profits were never up to much) and a depressing aftermath of unrealised ambitions, falling returns and occasional crises.[45]

The persisting importance of agriculture in absolute terms must not be allowed to mask the dominant trends of continuing population growth and urbanisation on a massive scale; and the visible results of this were all the more arresting because they were concentrated into a relatively small area of the south and east. Lancashire's population had nearly trebled to just over 2 million during the first half of the nineteenth century. During the second half it more than doubled: an additional 2.37 million to set against the increment of 1.36 million in the previous half-century, posing even greater problems of housing, sanitation and the provision of goods and services. By 1911 Lancashire contained 4.8 million people. Nearly one-third of them lived in Liverpool and Manchester, each of which housed over 700,000 within their recently expanded boundaries. Salford (with over 230,000), Bolton (over 180,000), Burnley, Blackburn, Oldham and Preston each had well over 100,000, with Rochdale, St. Helens and Wigan not far behind. Five other towns had more than 50,000, leaving the likes of Darwen, Accrington, Eccles, Leigh, Lancaster or Nelson, which with their 40,000 or so inhabitants would have been important regional centres in most counties, reduced to comparatively inferior stature. About half of Lancashire's population in 1911 lived in large towns and cities of more than 100,000 people; about three-fifths lived in centres with more than 50,000; and more than five-sixths lived in towns whose populations exceeded 10,000. Nine of the sixteen largest towns were in the cotton district, and Wigan was on its fringe. The others included Bootle, still administratively separate from Liverpool, and St. Helens, as well as Liverpool itself, on Merseyside; Barrow; and two other Victorian mushroom towns, the contrasting resorts of Blackpool and Southport.[46]

All this amounted to a sustained and remarkable increase in the scale of urban living, as towns spread their tentacles along the east Lancashire valleys and sprawled inelegantly across the south Lancashire plain. Suburbs merged with suburbs and each town blended imperceptibly into the next, as south Lancashire gave grimy and unlovely substance to the concept of conurbation. Population concentration was made possible by improved transport, and in turn encouraged the proliferation and intensification of the network. South Lancashire acquired the most comprehensive rail and (later) tramway systems in the country (with the possible exception of Greater London), and most of the Lancashire and Yorkshire Railway's passenger traffic involved very short distances, usually, no doubt, journeys to work in the next town or industrial village. Without the transport capacity provided by the railways, indeed, it is difficult to imagine the continuing development of Victorian urban society on such an enormous scale. But we must not forget that even the biggest towns contained within themselves smaller, more manageable, districts and neighbourhoods, which preserved a more intimate scale of living and a more immediate sense of collective identity. The largest towns were becoming much more difficult to escape from, despite the railway excursion (which tended increasingly to link one kind of town with another) and (from the 1890s) the cheap electric tram; but they were still far from being impersonal anthills. A sense of stability and continuity was enhanced in the later nineteenth century, as migration flows slackened and towns began to recruit by natural increase, as families put down roots and improved living standards widened the gap between birth- and death-rates.[47]

Smaller settlements remained important in their own right, despite the demise of old hand-loom weaving communities, the decline of some isolated factory 'colonies' after the 'Cotton Famine', and the extension of urban built-up areas to engulf others. Industrial villages like Sabden, in the hills between Burnley and Clitheroe, or Trawden, near Colne, could prosper modestly as textile centres despite their lack of canal or railway connection, while Colne itself is a good example of a medium-sized cotton town whose by-law terraces terminate suddenly in breezy countryside. The Rossendale towns similarly had hilly pastures at their back, and even in Burnley or Bolton the moors were clearly visible and readily accessible to the determined. Even Manchester had its cheap trains to the Peak District on summer weekends. Much of this countryside was sooty and bleak, but its existence and accessibility should remind us that even in the heart of the cotton district, the urban sprawl of the nineteenth century never completely dominated landscapes and lives, except for the poorest and the exhausted, and the slum-dwellers of inner Manchester and Liverpool.

The relationship between the nature of Lancashire urbanisation and the living standards of the working-class town-dweller will form one of the themes of Chapter 13. Meanwhile, the importance of the novel and unique scale of urban development in south Lancashire should be reiterated. Not all of the towns were enormous, and urban influences were rarely all-pervading; but this was, in many ways, a new social system, which was itself continually changing. The continuing growth and intensification of the Lancashire urban network had implications for all levels of local society, as had the other changes examined in this chapter. Our next step is to explore these implications, beginning with an analysis of the governing groups in Lancashire society, and the changes and continuities in their attitudes, culture and policies.

11

LANCASHIRE'S RULERS, 1850 – 1914: PROPERTY, AUTHORITY AND CULTURE

The Victorian and Edwardian heyday of industrial Lancashire saw important changes in the nature of the county's governing classes and the institutions through which they sought to rule. This was a period of growing responsibility coupled with extensive independence for local government, especially at municipal level. It was a period of steadily widening democratic participation in almost all levels of local government – the Duchy of Lancaster was even nominating working-class magistrates from 1885 onwards[1] – as well as in parliamentary elections; and this was reflected in styles of electioneering, policy formation, and ultimately in the social composition of elected assemblies. A third important theme is the continuing change in the balance of power between rural and urban élites, between the landed gentry and the newer influences of industry and commerce. As towns grew, spread and acquired sophisticated and increasingly independent and exclusive local government institutions of their own, so the area and range of county government's powers and responsibilities declined. In county government itself, too, the swamping of the established landed gentry by the representatives of industry and commerce continued. These trends were already apparent in the 1830s and 1840s, as we saw in Chapter 7; and the cross-currents and complexities of those years remained. The divisions between landed and industrial wealth were already artificial in some cases, and they were blurred still further by the passage of time and the growing complexity of the Lancashire economy. Aristocrats and gentry continued to involve themselves in a widening range of industrial activities, while manufacturers and merchants continued to acquire landed estates without necessarily severing their connections with the original sources of their wealth. The middle classes, too, continued to be internally divided on religious, political and broader cultural lines, as well as embracing an enormous range of lifestyles and experiences in economic terms, from the merchant prince to the struggling and vulnerable small employer or insecure professional man. All this necessarily complicates our attempts at analysis; but we can begin by looking at the changing fortunes of the gentry, and at the steady augmentation of the ranks of landed society by recruits from commerce and industry. The most opulent and cultivated of these were being assimilated with increasing ease into county society by the early twentieth century, when a new plutocracy was beginning to cohere, bringing together the old wealth and the new in the top public schools, on the hunting field, in the London season and through marriage alliances.

The wider influence of the older landed gentry continued to decline. Their financial circumstances varied, and in several cases the worsening problems of agriculture were counterbalanced by urban ground-rents, mineral royalties, industrial activity and the sale of land to railways, although these sources of revenue were probably healthiest in the mid-Victorian years when agricultural rents were also buoyant. The Earl of Derby was still, by common consent, Lancashire's leading citizen in Edwardian times; but his effective influence hardly extended beyond his own estates, and it was waning even there. In 1910 the seventeenth Earl denied any intention of requiring his tenants to vote for the Conservative candidate: 'I should be ashamed of myself if I ever tried to do such a thing, as I should be ashamed of them if they were influenced by any attempt that I made.'[2] Not all of his contemporaries were so self-effacing, but the power of most landlords was declining along with (in many if not most cases) their economic position. Many Lancashire gentry were becoming absentees by the turn of the century, repudiating their responsibilities and going off in search of congenial company and enjoyment. John Talbot Clifton was an early example. After succeeding to the estate in 1851, he 'immediately instructed his agent to scale down the costs of his own charitable subscriptions as far as possible', and he became 'a stranger on his own estate, preferring to divide his time between a country retreat in Northamptonshire, his London homes and the fashionable high-spots of the Mediterranean'. His grandson, another John Talbot, succeeding in 1889, was even more elusive and extravagant, travelling extensively in South America, Africa, the Himalayas and the Arctic, and ruining the estate's finances during his long absences.[3] Most absentees headed for less exotic places: the Heskeths of Rufford and Lord Lilford joined the exodus to Northamptonshire, for example, where the hunting was good and access to London was easier.[4] Major Montague Joseph Feilden ensconced himself in near-solitary splendour on the island of Herm, near Guernsey, while Sir Humphrey de Trafford found Berkeley Square more congenial as Trafford Park became transformed into an industrial estate.[5]

These refugees were a minority; but those who stayed behind found themselves a dwindling minority on the county bench. By 1886 there were 727 county magistrates, the vast majority of whom were industrialists, merchants, bankers and professionals. By 1903 the total number of magistrates was rather smaller, and in 1889 their administrative functions had been taken over by the new elected county council. Here, the 'old' gentry were in a small minority from the beginning, although their handful of representatives put in long service, often as committee chairmen, and the Fitzherbert-Brockholes family, of Claughton Hall near Garstang, sent three generations into office on the county council. But the old close relationship between the established landed élite of the county and its government was already outmoded by 1850, and at the turn of the century it was long gone.[6] The landowners – or their agents – were left to rule their estates and try to retain the loyalty of tenants and villagers through ostentatious paternalism. Even this local influence became more difficult to sustain, as the economic climate worsened and the Poor Law Guardians extended their responsibilities into areas which had hitherto been the landowner's prerogative, while in 1894 the coming of elective parish councils provided a further potential challenge to his authority at the most local level of all. As it turned out, Thomas Fair's expectation that, 'If parish councils were elected instead of having leading men on them they would be presided over by some liberal shoemaker surrounded by all the pot-house ruffians', was not borne out. In 1894 the Speke estate actually tried to secure the election of a token agricultural labourer alongside the farmers, but to no avail; and the parish councils' limited powers ensured that apathy soon supervened, as at Glasson Dock, with a preponderance of uncontested elections and control vested in the safe hands of large farmers and substantial tradesmen.[7] Only where a resident landowner or his agent took a sustained interest in the farmers' economic circumstances and political allegiance did strong local landed influence survive into the twentieth century, however; and this was most likely to occur where the estate itself was a major employer and consumer. No other establishment could match the Earls of Derby at Knowsley, who had actually contrived to increase their Lancashire acreage considerably between 1873 and 1908, and in the latter year employed, at Knowsley itself, 39 gardeners, 20 men to look after the 40 horses, a butler, two chefs, several under-butlers and more than a score of maidservants. The Earls of Sefton at Croxteth were almost in the same league, but patronage networks of this kind were rare and becoming rarer.[8] Under all the circumstances, it is not surprising to find that the older landed families continued to decline in number and importance as Lancashire MPs, nor that the Edwardian survivors were drawn from the Stanley and Cavendish families, together with the powerful and extremely wealthy coal-owning Lindsay family whose head was the Earl of Crawford and Balcarres at Haigh Hall.

The Lancashire aristocracy, in particular, kept a good measure of prestige as figureheads and patrons of high culture. The Earls of Derby kept up their residual urban connections, and the sixteenth Earl was Mayor of Liverpool in 1895 and Guild Mayor of Preston in 1901–2. The older families continued to be in demand to head subscription lists, provide officers in the Volunteers and preside over charities and learned societies. The Vice-Presidents of the Historic Society of Lancashire and Cheshire in 1892 included the Duke of Devonshire and the Earls of Derby, Sefton and Lathom.[9] In all these spheres, however, Lancashire's old gentry families were being augmented, and in some senses challenged, by successful industrial dynasties who sought to legitimise and enjoy their wealth in the time-honoured way, by investing in a landed estate and the lifestyle that went with it.

Commerce and industry had long supplied recruits to the Lancashire gentry, of course, while younger sons of established landed families had often gone into business, with the result that gentry and industrialists were often closely related, and there were many families with a foot in each camp. The recruitment of industrialists into the gentry was greatly accelerated in the nineteenth century, however, though some sought the transition more eagerly and achieved it more rapidly and completely than others. By 1873 the Fosters of Hornby Castle were among the eight largest landowners in Lancashire, and by 1900 the sitting incumbent, Colonel W. H. Foster, could project the image of 'the complete country gentleman', with his interest in horse-breeding and his attention to 'philanthropic work and social amenities' in the surrounding Lune valley countryside. But the Fosters' fortune came from the famous Black Dyke worsted mills at Queensbury in Yorkshire, and they only acquired the Hornby Castle estate in 1861. For many years, too, they combined a role as improving land-owners and county magistrates with the active supervision of their firm.[10] The only unusual feature of the Fosters was their origin east of the Pennines. On R. O. Knapp's definition, 'over 20 per cent of those families existing in Lancashire's [landed] élite society by 1870, had derived their wealth from the great textile expansion of the Industrial Revolution period'.[11] The proportion probably increased in the late nineteenth century, and the case of George Kemp provides a useful illustration of the assimilation process in action. In 1903 Kemp was still managing director of the Rochdale textile firm of Kelsall and Kemp, and he had a Rochdale address alongside his others near Keswick and at Portland Place. He was Rochdale-born, but educated at Shrewsbury and Trinity College, Cambridge; he was an officer in the Duke of Lancaster's Own Yeomanry Cavalry; he was MP for Heywood; his recreations were tennis, golf, hunting and cricket, at which he had played for Cambridge University and Lancashire; he was a member of White's; and most impressive of all, his wife was the third daughter of the Earl of Ellesmere. He was soon to be knighted, and eventually became Lord Rochdale.[12] The Lancashire cotton and related industries had produced a considerable number of men of Kemp's stamp and status by the turn of the century: members of the second and third generations of industrial dynasties, educated at public schools and mixing with apparent ease in high society. Some had disengaged themselves from their firms completely by this time, and even those who retained an interest had often acquired country seats in more socially desirable settings than Lancashire could provide. Thus Frederick Cawley was a calico printer, bleacher and dyer, a Lancashire JP, and MP for Prestwich, where he lived; but he was also the owner of Berrington Hall in Herefordshire, where he had a substantial estate. E. B. Fielden had gone further down the same road: he was still chairman of Fielden Brothers of Todmorden, and a director of the Lancashire and Yorkshire Railway, but he lived at Condover Hall, 'the grandest Elizabethan house in Shropshire' according to Pevsner, and was a JP for Oxfordshire as well as Shropshire.[13] Examples could be multiplied, and not just from the cotton district. The second Sir Gilbert Greenall, of the Warrington brewing dynasty, bred horses, had herds of pedigree cattle and pigs, and became Master of the Belvoir Hounds. Liverpool merchants ventured into Lancashire and Cheshire county society, and also into Wales, where the banker John Naylor built an enormous mansion at Leighton, near Welshpool, at a cost of £275,000, between 1850 and 1856, with amazingly elaborate decoration, landscape gardening and a home farm with extensive waterworks and a funicular railway, along with many other remarkable gadgets.[14] This was unusually ostentatious, and the estate was broken up before the First World War; but it is one example among many of the export of capital and capitalists from industrial and commercial south Lancashire into the neighbouring agricultural counties during this period.

Not all the Lancashire industrialists and merchants chose to invest in land and status at this level. Only a successful minority even had the resources. Some preferred to build up extensive industrial investment portfolios. Thomas Barnes of Farnworth was in the 1880s and 1890s a major shareholder and office-holder in concerns as diverse as the Bank of Bolton, the Wrexham, Mold and Connah's Quay Railway, the Lancashire and Yorkshire Railway, the Provincial Insurance Company, the Farnworth and Kearsley Gas Company, the Assam Railways and Trading Company, the Royal Sardinian Railways and a Welsh slate quarry.[15] Whether or not they spread their investments in this way, many industrialists preferred to acquire smaller, ornamental and recreational rather than territorial estates on the fringes of the main urban areas, or in Cheshire or the Lake District. Lancaster's linoleum king, James Williamson II, who became Lord Ashton in 1895 and left £9½ million when he eventually died in 1930, leaving other Lancashire plutocrats straggling in his wake, acquired Ashton Hall with several hundred acres on the outskirts of Lancaster, and several other residences, but never sought to become a territorial magnate; and in this he was far from being alone.[16] Lower down the scale of resources or pretensions, other merchants and industrialists moved out to opulent new villas in the seaside resorts, especially Southport, Lytham and later St. Annes, or settled for Cheshire suburbia along the rail routes south of Manchester, or escaped across the Mersey from Liverpool to the Wirral, or came to roost in the mansions which appeared at the western edge of most of the industrial towns, upwind of the smoke, such as the colony on the Chorley New Road in Bolton.

Each of these alternatives made its own social statements and contained its own social pecking order. Katharine Chorley, whose father was the managing director of the large Manchester engineering firm Mather and Platt, recalled the pattern of life in the big houses of Edwardian Alderley Edge, in Manchester's southern outer suburbia. The village was socially sharply differentiated from more exclusive Cheshire retreats to the south and south-west, and from less opulent Manchester suburbs to the north, while containing complex social and cultural gradations of its own. 'Snobbery was also geographical; it was almost an axiom for instance that, socially speaking, no good thing would be likely to come out of Wilmslow, the neighbouring village nearer Manchester. On the other hand, Peover, a village deeper in Cheshire than Alderley Edge, where the manager of the Manchester branch of the Bank of England lived in semi-county state, was regarded with equal though different scorn as the preserve of people who liked to be ''in with'' the county.' But within Alderley Edge itself, the question of who called on whom, enmeshed in elaborate rituals with visiting cards, reflected labyrinthine problems of status as expressed through occupation, income, place of residence and awareness of cultural niceties. 'The complications were endless.'[17]

Manchester, of course, was an early generator of specialised suburbs in complex patterns and gradations. Thus Engels in 1844, describing a system which had been in the making for a generation and more: 'Outside, beyond this girdle, lives the upper and middle bourgeoisie, the middle bourgeoisie in regularly laid out streets in the vicinity of the working quarters, especially in Chorlton and the lower lying portions of Cheetham Hill; the upper bourgeoisie in remoter villas with gardens in Chorlton and Ardwick, or on the breezy heights of Cheetham Hill, Broughton, and Pendleton, in free, wholesome country air, in fine, comfortable homes ...'[18] The new suburb of Victoria Park, protected by its gates and gentility, was already beginning to attract its distinctive population of German merchants, and over the next two decades Manchester's prospering Jewish community began to crystallise in Strangeways and part of Cheetham Hill.[19] Suburban status and residential patterns changed during the second half of the nineteenth century, as outer suburbs became more accessible and inner residential areas were engulfed by trams, lower-quality housing and industry. Victoria Park, with its 'massive turreted stone houses, at the base of them broad steps leading up to the portals, flanked by lions *couchant*', remained as an anomalous island of Edwardian gentility: a fitting survival for one of the earliest exemplars of the finely-tuned system of residential zoning which Victorian Manchester had developed to an almost metropolitan extent.[20]

Liverpool's middle-class suburbs were less finely graded, but they, too, spread outwards with increasing rapidity after mid-century, as merchants retreated from the old city centre and working-class terraces advanced to engulf their interim staging-posts at Everton and Bootle.[21] At all levels of the propertied and professional classes across Lancashire, indeed, the flight from the city centres accelerated and the most desirable goals became more geographically remote. Among the industrial élite, the exodus to distant landed estates became accentuated in the late nineteenth century, encouraged by falling land prices. The lists of official residences of Lancashire county magistrates are suggestive in this context. In 1886, 68 out of 727, or 9.3 per cent, gave addresses beyond Lancashire and the adjoining counties, while in 1903 the corresponding figure was 76 out of 697, or nearly 11 per cent.[22] This is less than spectacular, and the figures include older gentry families as well as industrialists, while some of the addresses were clearly town houses in places like Leamington (a favourite, for some reason), Hove and especially the West End of London; but it suggests that the drift of industrial as well as established gentry families away from Lancashire, which was being pioneered at or before mid-century by Oldham manufacturers as well as by the merchant princes of Liverpool and Manchester, was gradually becoming more apparent even among those who identified sufficiently with their county to undertake judicial and administrative office in it. When James Edward Platt gave his address as Howbury Hall, near Bedford, or Peter Stubs as Blaisdon Hall, Newnham, Gloucestershire, it suggests the landed metamorphosis or apotheosis of a successful manufacturing family, with a definite hint of the repudiation of roots. This phenomenon would repay sustained study. Most refugees from industry came to rest closer to home, like Sir John Hibbert, who became a barrister and politician instead of following his father in textile engineering, and settled in the Furness countryside rather than at Oldham, ending his career in 1908 after nearly twenty years as the first chairman of Lancashire County Council.[23] Some industrialists still identified staunchly with the sources of their wealth in Edwardian times, like W. M. Musgrave, whose official address in the magistrates' list of 1903 was 'Globe Iron Works, Bolton'. But widely though the distances might vary, in both geographical and social terms, the separation of home and business rapidly became the norm after the middle years of the nineteenth century. The implications were various and profound, as we shall see.

The newer industrial and commercial wealth crowded the established landed families out of predominance at almost all levels of the Lancashire power structure. We have seen that the county magistracy was already a lost cause by mid-century; and as Howe remarks, 'cotton lords, whether landed or not, became eligible for ... the deputy lieutenancy, and the shrievalty' as well as the county bench. Only the Lord Lieutenant, the highest county officer, continued to be drawn solely from 'the premier aristocratic families' before 1860, and long afterwards. The Deputy Lieutenancy was supposedly a military office, but it usually carried more status than real responsibility, and by the 1860s its incumbent usually came from the 'manufacturers of the top rank'. The office of High Sheriff, 'essentially decorative', and expensive in money and time, was opened out to industrial wealth after 1850, but only if the candidate satisfied his aristocratic neighbours of his suitability in manners and demeanour, criteria which favoured the second- or third-generation industrialist with a public school education and some acquaintance with 'high culture'.[24]

Parliamentary elections were also dominated by industrial and commercial candidates. Joyce calculates that of the 250 candidates between 1860 and 1886 in his 'North-West Region', which includes Barrow and four industrial constituencies in north Cheshire, but excludes Liverpool, 90 were from 'industrial' and 52 from 'commercial' backgrounds, while only 47 were 'landed'. Shipowners and merchants seem to have prevailed in Liverpool, and here as elsewhere, most aspirants to Westminster were local men. Joyce defines 165 of his 250 as 'local', and emphasises the hostility which often confronted the carpet-bagging candidate. Most outsiders were professional men, usually barristers, or career politicians. Landed society still accounted for more than half of the candidates for the county seats, although industrial influence here had to be courted by party managers, and most of the landowner politicians were Conservatives. Commerce, on the other hand, was Liberal by 40 to 12 in Joyce's sample, while the industrialists divided much more evenly, with a small Liberal majority. Again, this evidence shows a continuation and accentuation of trends which were already becoming apparent in the 1830s and 1840s.[25] The pattern described by Joyce still remained strongly marked at the turn of the century: the ideal candidate was a patriarchal local figure, a substantial employer and contributor to local charities, a man of known influence and reputation. Only in Edwardian times, and especially after 1906, did this picture begin to change, as a generation of Tory paternalists was wiped out on the Tariff Reform issue, and national politics and imported politicians came to the fore. So, at least, argues P. F. Clarke, although he may have exaggerated the extent and suddenness of the process in the interests of a more general argument about the nature of political change in Lancashire.[26] Lancashire's industrial and commercial élites were undoubtedly social leaders in their local communities, especially where they were large employers; and this led them inexorably into becoming public persons in the political arena. For a small but growing minority, such activity began to reap status rewards on the national stage, as the early trickle of knighthoods was augmented in the late nineteenth century and swollen by baronetcies and eventually the occasional peerage.[27] This indicates a measure of genuine acceptance into a national élite for some, though not for all, Lord Ashton being a telling exception. But for most of Lancashire's industrial and commercial leaders, the exercise of power, patronage and charity was locally based, and the most obvious channel for expressing status and accepting responsibility was through municipal government.

The municipal corporations which proliferated in Lancashire throughout the period offered attainable glory as well as visible power to urban capitalists. The office of alderman, and still more that of mayor, carried a special mystique, an impression of special citizenship reinforced by allusions to antiquity. When Liverpool and Manchester acquired *Lord* Mayors, of course, the magic was intensified. Moreover, the field of action for municipal government expanded steadily, moving beyond law and order to encompass street lighting and maintenance, drains and sewers, gas and water, parks and libraries, building regulations and eventually municipal housing, tramways and electricity. The larger Lancashire towns became pioneers of what became known as municipal socialism, especially in the vital spheres of gas and water supply, where local government control was a commonplace in the county long before the much-publicised activities of Joseph Chamberlain and his cohorts in the Birmingham of the 1870s. These responsibilities, so obviously expensive and so obviously important to the health and comfort of individuals and businesses, were generally believed to require the attention of substantial businessmen, accustomed to economical and efficient administration on a large scale, and to the taking of important decisions. For a variety of reasons, for two crucial generations after the mid-1830s this big business commitment to municipal government was precisely what occurred. Apart from power, glory and a sense of *noblesse oblige*, what Howe calls 'the fear of the penalty of refusal [of office], to be governed by someone worse than themselves' must have played its part at this level as at others; but there was clearly a widespread and lasting positive commitment to municipal service among the employer élites, which drew in Tories and Liberals, Anglicans and Dissenters, old wealth and new; and indeed, political rivalry, the desire to score electoral points (although votes in the council chambers were seldom cast on party lines) provided a further motivation for involvement. The civic institutions of mid and late Victorian Lancashire, with their impressive and growing powers to influence the daily lives of ordinary people, were dominated by the leading local capitalists.[28]

This assertion can be supported by examining the membership of municipal corporations. Garrard's occupational analysis of three councils for large towns in the cotton district shows that at Salford manufacturers and merchants, classed together as 'large proprietors', accounted for between 40 and 60 per cent of all council members in seven 5-year periods covering 1845–80, with 'gentlemen' (most of whom had retired from business) and professionals making up a substantial proportion of the rest. The range of 'large proprietor' representation at Bolton was only slightly less impressive, and at Rochdale they never fell below 52 per cent of the council, and provided over 60 per cent of its members between 1856 and 1865.[29] Howe's more impressionistic snapshots for various places and dates between 1835 and 1870 suggest that Oldham was not dissimilar to Rochdale in this respect, while Blackburn and Preston marched roughly in step with Salford and Bolton. But the pattern of 'large proprietor' dominance was not universal in the cotton district: at Ashton in 1847 and 1857 they were outnumbered by dealers and shopkeepers, and at Wigan in 1836 the retailers had an overall majority.[30] In the late-developing north Lancashire weaving towns Burnley's large employers still dominated recruitment to the Corporation in the 1870s, although at nearby Accrington civic leadership was already mainly in the hands of shopkeepers.[31] For most places, though, this evidence confirms the political pre-eminence of big business in Lancashire's Victorian industrial towns; and the 'large proprietors'' strategic influence was much greater than these figures would suggest, for they were disproportionately well represented among the aldermen, committee chairman and especially the successful aspirants to the mayoralty.

Even in Liverpool and Manchester, where the lure of outer suburbia and country estates began to draw large numbers of economic giants away at a relatively early stage, big business dominated council membership for a long time. The 64 Liverpool councillors and aldermen of 1857 included 35 merchants and shipowners and 11 substantial manufacturers, and the 4 shopkeepers were themselves in specialised, up-market trades requiring considerable capital.[32] Manchester's new Corporation began life in 1838 with 34 merchants and large manufacturers, and several of the town's leading citizens at their head; and although by 1853 their number had fallen to 22 out of 64, their eclipse by the small shopkeeper and brewing interests was a long and gradual process.[33] Municipal office was never closed to the lesser shopkeepers and tradesmen, although stringent property qualifications often limited the pool of eligible talent; and all councils contained men of this stamp, often pressing their claims as defenders of the small ratepayer against extravagance. Sometimes an assiduous municipal career might be crowned by honours and public celebrity, as office conferred status rather than expressing or reinforcing it, for a hard-working petty tradesman. But for most of the nineteenth century this was unusual, and the glittering municipal prizes usually went to those who had already 'arrived' in an economic sense.[34]

The lesser lights among the urban middle ranks found outlets at less prestigious levels of local government. In the smaller towns the Local Boards of Health and Improvement Commissions which were established in large numbers around mid-century were often dominated by petty tradesmen and owners of house property. These more specialised bodies lacked the glamour and spending power of a full-scale Corporation, and their proceedings were often vituperative and undignified. Even at this level, however, élite participation was sometimes impressive. At Darwen a group of leading employers, with Eccles Shorrock, representing one of the town's two most conspicuously wealthy families, taking command, controlled the Local Board from its formation in 1854 until the early 1870s; and at Chorley before 1880 the cotton masters usually supplied at least 40 per cent of the Improvement Commission, and more than half of the long-serving core of 27 who dominated proceedings were large manufacturers or coalowners.[35] The Poor Law administration was not widely attractive to the 'large proprietors', except where they became *ex officio* Guardians as Justices of the Peace. In Salford and Rochdale, for example, shopkeepers and tradesmen took control from the 1850s and 1860s, while Accrington's manu-facturers were very heavily outnumbered by shopkeepers and builders after

1880.[36] This was another unglamorous realm of activity which was more likely to attract odium and wrath than prestige and appreciation, and the wealthiest citizens of the Lancashire industrial towns preferred to keep their distance.

How did the social composition of urban governing bodies affect the quality of their administration? Big business representatives might be expected to bring wider vision and understanding to their municipal work than their less opulent colleagues, and to be proportionately less burdened by the fear of rate increases and municipal bankruptcy. Such an argument has been advanced for Manchester, where major improvements were pushed through at the behest of an urban patriciate. Howe's preliminary soundings suggest that a simple correlation between the strength of 'large proprietor' representation and the level of municipal expenditure is unconvincing, as shopkeeper-dominated Wigan put up a poor show in terms of per capita municipal expenditure at mid-century and in 1867, but Blackburn's figure was considerably worse and Oldham's little better.[37] But we need more systematic evidence before we can argue confidently for or against the contention that a strong big business presence made for an active, innovatory municipality in mid-Victorian Lancashire, for business leaders themselves ran the gamut from the open-handed and socially concerned to the tight-fisted and narrowly economistic, as we shall see.

From the 1880s onwards, however, the social composition of Lancashire's borough councils began to change, as the influence of big business went into a patchy but cumulative decline. The speed and extent of this process varied from place to place and according to the angle of vision. The Liverpool Trades Council in 1894 denounced the Corporation as dominated by 'rich merchants and rack-renting slum property owners'. The merchants had shrunk in number from 35 to 18 since 1857, with tradesmen and professionals filling the vacant spaces; and a similar trend was apparent in Manchester. Shena Simon notes the gradual mid-Victorian infiltration of brewers, house property owners and shopkeepers, anxious to defend their vested interests against Corporation initiatives; and by 1899 Beatrice Webb was unimpressed with the predominant social status of the councillors, and disparaging about their administrative efficiency: 'The social status is predominantly lower middle class, a Tory solicitor and an ILP journalist being the only men with any pretension to culture. The abler administrators have no pretension to ideas, hardly any to grammar – they are merely hard-headed shopkeepers divided in their mind between their desire to keep the rates down and their ambition to magnify the importance of Manchester as against other cities.'[38] Lower down the scale of urban development, in town after town the numerical importance and effective influence of the large employers declined in the late nineteenth and early twentieth century. In Blackburn 27 per cent of the council were cotton masters in 1880, and 19.5 per cent in 1900; in Burnley the figures were 40.5 per cent and 23 per cent; in Oldham the percentage of 'manufacturers' fell from 58 in 1888–9 to 29 in 1908–9; in Bolton from 62.5 in 1869 (including merchants) to 31 (on a fairly generous definition) in 1890;

and in Accrington new entrants to the council included 16 large manufacturers out of 56 (28.6 per cent) in 1878–87 and 2 out of 21 (9.5 per cent) in 1907–13. In these towns, too, the vacuum was filled mainly by tradesmen and professionals, with a sprinkling of salaried managers and working-class representatives which gradually increased in importance in the early twentieth century.[39]

Occupational labels tell only part of the story, of course; but other indicators of wealth and standing confirm the impression that members of the local plutocracies were moving out of municipal government at this time. Why was this? The responsibilities of local government continued to increase, and the growing financial importance of central government loans was as yet having little or no impact on local autonomy. Local office of this kind still confirmed or conveyed prestige and power. A growing patrician distaste for the rough and tumble of contested elections may have helped to deter a new generation of the wealthy, secure in their status, from entering the municipal arena, especially where new opponents were emerging in the form of articulate and angry working-class representatives. The rise of the limited company and the widening distances between home, preferred lifestyle and factory or counting-house certainly played their part. Katharine Chorley expresses the consequences well as they affected Manchester:

But when the sons of these nineteenth-century citizens moved out they could no longer carry on the tradition. The city became the place they worked in by day and abandoned in the evening as quickly as might be. Their leisure interests and recreations were elsewhere and the time they gave to civic duties dwindled. The city was no longer the centre of their cultural lives and ... they tended to withdraw their services from the city council ... My grandfather was proud to be an alderman and mayor, but not one of his sons sat on the council.[40]

The old urban governing class was giving up its post from choice rather than necessity: it abdicated civic authority before there was any serious threat of its being ousted. But this was, to reiterate, a long process, fuelled more by failure to recruit than by the premature departure of existing stalwarts. The towns of Edwardian Lancashire still had their share of aldermen and committee chairmen, exercising disproportionate influence, drawn from the manufacturing and mercantile élites; and it was under these auspices that the continuing expansion of municipal services and improvement in working-class living conditions took place around the turn of the century.

Over these same years, however, the solid middle class of the Lancashire towns became more internally cohesive. The bitter struggles over Free Trade and the civil rights of religious Dissenters were fading from the limelight by the 1870s; and by this time an incipient drift to the Conservatives was already noticeable enough to have attracted the attention of such diverse commentators as Marx and Engels, Cobden and Bright and the future (as at 1853) fifteenth Earl of Derby. It was accompanied by a shift from Dissent to Anglicanism among the established plutocracy, and was inseparable from the acquisition of landed estates and the pursuit of acceptance into an overwhelmingly and increasingly Tory county society. The Liberal divisions over Home Rule for Ireland accentuated the process in 1886, and the changing nature of the main political parties provided a further impetus, as late Gladstonian and post-Gladstonian Liberalism appeared to threaten the sanctity of property and inheritance, and presented unacceptably interventionist programmes of radical social legislation. By contrast, the Edwardian Tory infatuation with Tariff Reform, which in attacking Free Trade posed a challenge to a policy which many saw as the central pillar of Lancashire's prosperity, was almost acceptable. Edwardian Toryism in most of Lancashire inherited the hard-faced *laissez-faire* characteristics of the political economy of so-called Manchester School Liberalism, with appropriate hostility to trade unions and welfare measures, but without the Manchester School's belief in Free Trade as a millennial promoter of international harmony and world peace. Millowner Conservatism had never been eclipsed, of course; and Liverpool and some of its satellites remained as strongly Conservative as ever in their idiosyncratic sectarian way; but the shift in allegiance among the propertied classes in the cotton towns; though gradual, was inexorable. It was a matter of emphasis, and its full extent was disguised by the Liberal landslide in the Tariff Reform election of 1906; but Lancashire's urban élites, and especially the well-established millowning dynasties, were becoming predominantly Tory in their politics by the turn of the century.[41]

This shift in the political spectrum of the upper strata of the Lancashire middle classes, which left Liberalism and Dissent increasingly though never exclusively the preserve of the smaller and newer employers, the shopkeepers, traders and artisans, and the politically articulate segments of the working class, was matched by a growing tendency towards cultural homogeneity among the late Victorian and Edwardian urban élites. As with the change in the political atmosphere, this trend fell a long way short of being complete or all-embracing, but it was tangible enough nevertheless. At mid-century, the employing class in most Lancashire towns was still deeply divided between Church and Dissent, Tory and Reformer. In Bolton, for example, 'The Mechanics' Institute of 1825 was completely boycotted by many conservatives, while a plan for an Athenaeum in 1846 was effectively sabotaged by the conservative faction led by the vicar, who refused to accept any form of education which did not conform to Church of England doctrine.' Similar divisions 'split and destroyed ... a whole string of choral societies and glee clubs'. The members of the rival élites had attended different schools, supported rival churches, and turned their backs on each other's cultural institutions.[42] The strong survival of a Tory employer culture which found room for beer, blood sports and bonhomie was anathema to the militant Nonconformists, who preached teetotalism and distrusted most forms of traditional or commercial enjoyment. A minority of moderate Anglican Liberals and heterodox Dissenters uneasily held the middle ground, enjoying field sports and mixing cautiously with county society; but there was much mutual hostility between the contending cultures, expressed, for example, in mutually exclusive patterns of marriage alliances.[43]

Changes were already in the wind by the 1860s. In Bolton new scientific and choral societies began to bridge the gap between the élites, and although a unifying scheme for a Gentlemen's Club to 'keep the social machinery running smoothly' was unsuccessful, and the political divide remained, Poole suggests that 'a social network similar on both sides was emerging'.[44] But it was not until the 1880s and 1890s that the enmities began to fade and the local grandees began to share their preoccupations and enjoyments with any appearance of amity, as the experience of boarding school, Oxbridge and a rural lifestyle began to forge a recognisably shared élite culture, as Nonconformist taboos relaxed and allowed a new generation into the world of the golf club and the Volunteers. But Haslam Mills's reminiscences of a Congregationalist childhood in Ashton-under-Lyne in the 1880s should remind us that for most of the townbound, middling and lower middle class, and for some intransigent families among the élite, the old social divisions continued to bite deeply. In the declining years of the patriarchal millowner Hugh Mason, whose disapproval of drink, immorality and popular enjoyment of all kinds set a severe standard for his workpeople and for the members of 'his' chapel, social life for the congregation revolved around the sermon, the tea meeting, the Whit walk and the Anniversary. The *Manchester Guardian* was hidden in a drawer for the duration of Sunday, as a dangerous temptation to secular thought, and Sanger's Circus and the theatre were beyond the pale. The Church of England was a different world.[45]

Even in this restricted setting, however, a thaw was beginning towards the turn of the century. A few members of the congregation might admit to visiting the theatre, in London or Manchester rather than in Ashton; and a son experiencing University could tentatively sing the praises of beer in moderation. More generally acceptable, of course, were the Hallé concerts; and these were one of the institutions that brought together, temporarily but importantly, the various strands of the Lancashire ruling class, and reminded them of the common elements of their culture. The railways ran 'Hallé trains' on Thursday evenings from Cheshire suburbs and industrial towns, catering for an enthusiasm which transcended political boundaries. But, as Katherine Chorley points out, this was exceptional. It was also occasional, and metropolitan. Even so, it was in important ways symptomatic.[46]

It is arguable that, in most of urban Lancashire, the vertical divisions between Tory and Liberal, Anglican and Nonconformist, within the middle classes became less important in the later nineteenth century while the horizontal distinctions of wealth and status became magnified and harder to overcome. The increasing relative importance of large firms and dynastic wealth would lend weight to such a conclusion. Blackburn's landed large employers consumed increasingly conspicuously, displaying the paraphernalia of matching horses, carriages and liveried servants, and later turning their stables over to Rolls

Royces and Daimlers. Below them stretched the denizens of the various categories of salubrious villa along the carefully protected Preston New Road, ranging from cotton employers to high-class town-centre tradesmen such as wine merchants and glovers; and on a lower rung still were further middle-class outposts at Queen's Park and Witton. This residential hierarchy was reproduced and reinforced in, for example, church and chapel attendance patterns.[47] The nature of the hierarchies varied town by town, of course: in Burnley, for example, the resident landed gentry were more visible and more powerful, and wealthy professional men found it easier to move in the same circles than did the cotton masters, whose firms were generally smaller and of more recent foundation than those of Blackburn. Even in Liverpool, where the sectarian divide continued to dominate popular electoral politics, the prevailing tone of polite society was hierarchical. At the top were 'our old families', some of whom mixed freely with county society, aided by similarities of education, taste, and political outlook; and the Liverpool centre of élite social life was the Wellington Rooms, with strictly controlled membership and a five-guinea annual subscription, where Unitarian Liberals and vehement Tories mingled socially on polite and friendly terms, and the carriages arriving for the balls revealed 'ladies dressed with gorgeousness such as befits the wives and daughters of the wealthiest men in Great Britain's greatest seaport, and wearing jewellery more costly in its entirety than all that our best shops have on show at Christmas'. Below this level came overlapping circles of merchants, shipowners, professionals and tradesmen, in a complex hierarchy of suburbs, out-of-town residences, societies and congregations; but the upper reaches became progressively harder to enter as firms amalgamated and the capital needed to set up in business at an appropriate competitive level soared beyond the reach of aspiring newcomers.[48] At the top, here as elsewhere, sports clubs, debating and cultural societies, charities and social events provided a common social round, reinforced by ties of friendship and marriage; but even in cosmopolitan Liverpool, the top was becoming less accessible with the passage of time.

Most of the leading families, and many of the less eminent ones, looked outwards at the wider society as well as inwards at their own social whirl and pecking order; and they did so not only through the formal institutions of municipal and other local government, but also through the exercise of charity and patronage, and through the oversight and sometimes the attempted control of aspects of the lives of employees and poorer neighbours. Charitable provision took increasingly permanent and sophisticated forms. Liverpool and Manchester already had a range of voluntary hospitals, and several towns had Dispensaries; but the later nineteenth century saw the spread of charity hospitals in most of the larger industrial centres, drawing on middle-class endowments supported increasingly by organised weekly payments collected from employees at workplaces. Private donations on a large scale also fuelled denominational school provision, provided parks and libraries which were then administered by local authorities, distributed religious books and teaching in slum areas, and provided premises like the famous Ancoats Settlement to act as centres for the 'civilising' of the urban poor. John Pickstone argues plausibly that these capital-hungry schemes flourished most readily in older-established towns with traditional élites of Tory paternalist bent, with secure wealth, a sense of *noblesse oblige* and the supportive activity of surrounding county gentry. A sustained commitment, whether in financial terms or through active involvement in the numerous visiting and teaching schemes, was certainly the preserve of a minority of the affluent and leisured. In 1854 the Revd A. Hume found that half of the contributions to the principal Liverpool charities came from fewer than 700 subscribers, out of the 9760 who gave anything at all. This produced a horrified response, and for a time ostentatious charitable activity became the fashion in Liverpool, reviving with every bad winter and trade depression, but rarely offering more than immediate palliatives. Above all, visiting, teaching and sewing for the poor provided outlets for the energies of middle-class women, deprived of an active commercial role by the separation of business and home and by changing attitudes to the proper sphere of respectable female activity. They became workhouse visitors, sanitary advisers, and in a few cases nurses and pioneer social workers, especially in Liverpool. In the two regional capitals, especially, the sheer scale of the problems of poverty and squalor, and the impossibility of detecting impostors, led to the early adoption of co-ordinating committees and societies to direct relief towards the 'deserving' and to prevent individuals and families from obtaining aid from several charities at once. Liverpool's Central Relief Society was a national pioneer in pursuing this approach, although the inevitable heavy expenditure on administration did not escape censure in hard times. Serious and sustained commitment to work of this sort was the preserve of a small minority, disproportionately composed of Unitarians and High Church Anglicans: for most of the middle class, involvement stopped short at attending the annual balls and other fund-raising events, where it was possible, as contemporary satirists grimly noted, to be seen rubbing shoulders with social superiors while being ostentatiously identified with a good cause. Alongside these ignoble motives, we must not forget genuine philanthropic and religious concern, and the urge to defuse social tensions, build bridges between the classes and remould the urban poor in a moral and quiescent guise; and despite an often narrow social base, which became painfully apparent in the cotton towns during the 'Cotton Famine', when outside aid dwarfed local contributions, we must not ignore the extent to which middle-class charitable activity brought a genuine measure of social amelioration to the most deprived sectors of Lancashire society in these years.[49]

Cultural patronage was also patchy and unduly dependent on individuals. The Hallé and the Whitworth Art Gallery in Manchester were isolated successes, although the John Rylands Library was an inspired individual benefaction, and the county's two new universities depended heavily on donations and bequests from leading citizens. But sport counted for more than the arts, despite music's immense popular following, while too much of Nonconformity was indeed engrossed in its private round of tea meetings and fund-raising sermons, leavened only (but importantly) by the well-attested enthusiasm for choral music in general and Handel in particular. Where employers reached out successfully to gain the respect and acclaim of their workforces, however, the safest route lay through an appeal to sporting prowess and the endorsement of a popular culture of beer, gambling and hedonism. We shall explore this theme further in the next chapter.[50]

Lancashire industry and commerce generated considerable fortunes for thousands of fortunate individuals, and immense wealth for a favoured few. Rubinstein has argued that the great Victorian fortunes were made in finance and commerce rather than in manufacturing, and in the City of London rather than the provinces. He produces figures to suggest that Lancashire was well down the scale of fortune-generators in the nineteenth century, accounting for only 12 of the 54 millionaires dying between 1880 and 1899, and 26 of the 141 half-millionaires. The corresponding figures for 1900–14 were 4 out of 70, and 29 out of 170. Most were merchants, and Liverpool featured more prominently than Manchester.[51] One or two comments are in order, to set the status of Lancashire wealth-holders more clearly in national perspective. In the first place, these figures are really quite impressive: they only seem disappointing if set against an unrealistically high expectation of Lancashire's place in the national league table of wealth-holders. Secondly, Lancashire's position becomes much more impressive if we look at the distribution of individual income tax payers on profits of more than £3000 per annum in 1879–80, which Rubinstein also provides. Here, Lancashire was second only to London, and far ahead of any other non-metropolitan county. Liverpool alone had more taxpayers in all of the higher brackets than the whole of Yorkshire, and Manchester was far ahead of Warwickshire and Staffordshire combined.[52] This picture is reinforced if we remember than 159 Liverpool magistrates appointed between 1835 and 1885 left an *average* of £160,000 at death: a formidable concentration of provincial wealth, and it leaves the town's wealthier and more influential Tories out of account.[53] Moreover, Rubinstein's calculations from probate returns suffer from several problems of distortion and interpretation, some of which he discusses; but he plays down the under-representation of landed wealth, which is entirely omitted for deaths before 1898 and largely omitted between then and 1925. The large number of Lancashire industrialists and merchants who bought their way into landed estates will therefore be severely under-valued in Rubinstein's sources. Despite Rubinstein's low estimate of the Lancashire economy as a generator of large fortunes, it emerges comfortably at the top of the provincial list, and its position would be further enhanced if full account could be taken of the numerous band of landowner–industrialists. We must give due weight to the impressive scale of the industrial and commercial fortunes created by the 'Industrial Revolution' in Lancashire, and to the large number of beneficiaries. The wealth of the Lancashire middle classes had no parallel in England outside the metropolis itself.

The emphasis on landowner – industrialists leads into a further argument. Does the evidence for wealthy Lancastrians' propensity to move away from the sources of their wealth, and especially to acquire landed estates, send sons to public schools and seek assimilation into county society, leave them vulnerable to Martin Wiener's arguments about an alleged 'decline of the industrial spirit'? Were they betraying the capitalist values which had created their fortunes, and settling comfortably into the leisurely and cultivated lifestyle of the landed gentleman, retreating from competition and profit maximisation and abandoning the work ethic? It is too early to say. We need to know more about the changing pattern of management as families moved out to seaside resorts and country estates, and sons went into the professions or pursued gentility in other ways. As B. G. Orchard remarked in 1892, 'The superior opportunities to penetrate [county society] are by no means the least reason why so many sons of prosperous traders adopt the less lucrative pursuits of barrister or clergyman.'[54] But was the quality of the replacement management significantly or demonstrably inferior to supervision by the family itself? We do not know: we lack the detailed case studies which would answer a question posed in this particular form. Moreover, the entrepreneurial talents of the Lancashire aristocracy and gentry, or their agents, were themselves far from contemptible. The Earls of Crawford and Balcarres, for example, continued to do well out of their coal mines and iron-works. Admittedly, they had many other interests. The Earl himself was, in 1903, a Fellow of the Royal Society, and of the Royal Astronomical Society, President of the Camden Society, and a Trustee of the British Museum. His son held office in the National Trust and the Society for the Protection of Ancient Buildings.[55] No doubt Wiener would sneer at these activities, and at the many similar pre-occupations of industrialists of more recent emergence. They show an unhealthy preoccupation with the past, with pure science, and with activities which do not make profits. No doubt the Rathbones' Liverpool charitable work was similarly reprehensible. When set against Wiener's view of the ideal industrialist, it must be admitted that most Lancashire industrialists fall surprisingly short on sheer greed and the single-minded accumulation of profit for the sake of profit. But, as we saw when looking at the cotton industry in Chapter 10, there is no con-vincing evidence that their businesses suffered thereby. Lancashire's economy continued to grow with remarkable speed in most of its sectors right up to the First World War. It did so in an environment of remarkable social stability, which certainly owed something to a pervasive brand of employer paternalism which had some of its roots in an older style of landed society and aristocratic hegemony. Lancashire's success, in other words, probably owed something to a style of industrial relations which had as much to do with 'feudal' survival as with capitalism red in tooth and claw. But we need to say much more about the peculiar nature of Lancashire politics and industrial relations in this period; and employer paternalism is only part of the story. We shall pick up these themes in the next chapter.

12

FROM CHARTISM TO LABOURISM? WORKING-CLASS ATTITUDES AND POPULAR POLITICS, 1850 – 1914

Chartism as a mass movement wilted miserably in Lancashire after 1848, even in the cotton district where it had flourished most luxuriantly; and no subsequent movement mobilised the economic and political grievances of the working class in such a threatening – or promising – way. Trade union disputes were often hard-fought, geographically wide-ranging and angry with the rhetoric of class conflict, but they consistently lacked an overt or sustained political dimension; and the Lancashire working class became firmly assimilated into the orthodox two-party political system which crystallised nationally in mid-Victorian times. The strong allegiance of Lancashire working men – and women – to Liberals or Tories (especially the latter), was demonstrated after the 1867 Reform Act by the high level of enthusiastic popular participation in election campaigns. So deeply were these political allegiances internalised, indeed, that in much of the county the emergent labour movement of the late nineteenth and early twentieth centuries found it difficult to make headway. How and why did the post-Chartist transition take place? What were the roots of the general acceptance of the two-party system among the Lancashire working class? How successfully, and where, was the established political structure being challenged by mass trade unionism and the rise of the Labour Party in the early twentieth century? These questions lead us into fundamental and controversial questions about the nature of Lancashire society as well as politics in this important period of consolidation and continuing change.

Chartism did not disappear overnight, of course, and local activists and cells persisted into the 1850s and even the 1860s, linking up with the campaign for the second Reform Act. The career of Thomas Livsey in Rochdale shows that it was possible for a 'life-long Chartist' to become a vitally important mediator between the working class and the local élite, a power broker and office-holder, and a revered figure at whose funeral in 1864 the Corporation attended in a body, while a silent crowd of 40,000 lined the streets.[1] But it is highly significant that Livsey was very much a 'moral force' Chartist, a small manufacturer rather than an employee, and an activist for the Anti-Corn Law League, factory reform, the campaign against the New Poor Law and the opposition to Church Rate as well as for the Charter itself. He was, in fact, part of that serious-minded and self-consciously respectable wing of Chartism which became attached to the radical Nonconformist section of the emergent Liberal Party. Parliamentary reform in general, and the Charter itself in particular, were not high priorities on his political agenda from the early 1850s, and this made his views acceptable to a wide range of employer and property-owning opinion during the mid-Victorian years. Livsey's political trajectory was followed, less successfully or dramatically, by many ex-Chartists who took some of their reforming principles under the restraining wing of one or other of the mainstream parties in these years.

The Lancashire working class as an organised, independent political force was practically extinguished after 1848. Chartism was never a mass movement again, and in Preston, for example, the last Chartist meeting to be reported was in October 1849.[2] Elsewhere, and especially perhaps in south-east Lancashire and north-east Cheshire, the movement was more resilient. In 1852 differences on the Manchester Chartist executive between moderate advocates of an alliance with middle-class reformers, and the proto-socialist group led by Ernest Jones, were resolved in favour of the latter; and a measure of renewed activity followed. In 1853 R. G. Gammage could call to mind 58 provincial branches of the reconstituted National Charter Association, of which 10 were in cotton Lancashire and adjoining areas of Cheshire and Derbyshire. They included Ashton, Oldham, Rochdale, Manchester and Bacup.[3] In other centres, such as Burnley, there were also surviving knots of committed Chartist support. A south Lancashire delegate meeting was still being held every few weeks, although it was chronically short of cash. In 1854, 2000 people attended a Chartist rally on Blackstone Edge, and as late as 1858, 800 crammed into the Chartist Institute at Stalybridge to hear Ernest Jones and W. P. Roberts. The same year saw the foundation of the Manchester Manhood Suffrage Association, a working-class response to Bright's more moderate campaign to widen the borough franchise and redistribute seats away from the smaller boroughs, with the large towns to be the main beneficiaries.[4] This marked a narrowing of the emphasis of reform campaigns, however, and the initiative had already shifted to the London artisans. The Manchester Association eventually became the Northern Department of the London-based Reform League as the campaign for moderate reform hotted up again in the mid-1860s; and Chartism itself was effectively dead by 1860. Throughout the decade, the pursuit of independent working-class politics in Lancashire had been a discouraging uphill struggle for a small minority of principled enthusiasts. As they admitted with varying degrees of disappointment and dismay, there was no longer any support from the rank and file. A major political transformation had taken place, not overnight, but in a remarkably short time. As Kirk remarks, it amounted to a 'stabilisation, as opposed to harmonisation, of overall class relations' after 1850: as we shall see, industrial conflict was still endemic and sometimes violent and sustained, but it no longer linked up overtly with the political sphere.[5]

Contemporaries were well aware of the changed atmosphere. It was in this context, after all, that Engels made his celebrated remark in 1858 about England's acquisition of a 'bourgeois proletariat', tainted with reformism and the pursuit of material gain within the existing system. To many observers, the new stability was confirmed and emphasised by the workforce's response to the 'Cotton Famine'. As we shall see, this brought mass unemployment and severe deprivation to the cotton towns, which had seethed with such threatening industrial and political unrest under the less apocalyptic circumstances of 1842. In December 1862, 49 per cent of *all* operatives, not merely those employed in the cotton industry itself, were workless in the 28 Poor Law unions of the cotton district, and only 16 per cent were working full-time. Unemployment remained over 30 per cent all through 1863 and 1864, and it was much higher in black spots like Ashton where a particularly strong specialisation in cotton spinning was allied with particularly heavy dependence on American rather than Egyptian cotton.[6] But, to the bafflement of Karl Marx and the surprise of the local propertied classes, the crisis was met more with resignation and fortitude than with anger and conflict. The Honorary Secretary of the Darwen Relief Committee distilled the perceptions of many observers:

Now began a state of affairs in Lancashire which must redound to the everlasting honour of the working classes of the county, and of the whole cotton district. Never in the history of the world did any class bear such a calamity ... with the exemplary fortitude, patience and forbearance, manifested by the whole population, or almost unanimously ... [they] bore without a murmur, and with unexampled patience, the pangs of poverty, hunger and extreme destitution ...[7]

Historians have endorsed these responses. Ellison, for example, mentions the riots of March 1863 in the Ashton area, but uses them 'to highlight the preference for restraint and orderly protest that otherwise prevailed during the cotton famine'. Farnie remarks, rather strangely, that 'the unemployed bore their affliction with the phlegm of the Saxon and the stoicism of the peasant', earning 'lavish praise from their social superiors for their pacific and law-abiding disposition'. Rose offers an excusable over-simplification when he suggests that the Lancashire working man's reward for this evidence of 'moral and political maturity' was to be 'the award of the franchise in 1867'.[8]

Two comments should be made. In the first place, the 'Cotton Famine' was not endured as passively as these comments suggest, although resistance to authority on specific issues never threatened to broaden out into a general political critique. More generally, the reasons presented for the quiescence of the cotton towns' working class during these traumatic years are closely related to some of the explanations which have been offered for the decline of Chartism and the more general and long-term 'transition to order'.

Retrospective congratulation of the Lancashire workforce came easier than any expectation of stability at the time. There were widespread fears of pauperisation, loss of morale and self-respect, and of a consequent spread of rioting and social and political unrest. As well as the riots at Ashton and Stalybridge, there were further disturbances in north Lancashire, and at one point the possibility of a full-scale uprising was being seriously discussed by alarmed magistrates in the Burnley area. There were angry disputes over the terms and conditions on which relief was offered, over low relief scales, over the application of labour and school attendance tests, over the treatment of 'deserving' unemployed operatives as if they were undeserving idlers, and over the failure of some of the well-to-do to contribute adequately to relief funds. At Burnley, and perhaps elsewhere, the distribution of relief was biased against trade unionists and Co-op members. Here, and elsewhere, there were operatives' relief committees operating alongside those run by the local élites. A strong spirit of independence brought a much-praised unwillingness to apply for help and to receive charity, and savings and trade union and Friendly Society relief were exhausted before applications were made; but this pride and resourcefulness should not be confused with passivity. The Lancashire workers were not as supine in adversity as their social superiors subsequently preferred to believe, although their resistance seldom took overtly political form; but the praise which was subsequently showered upon the unemployed operatives owed as much to relief as to reality, while the resolution of Lord Derby's Committee in December 1862 that unparalleled destitution was being borne with 'a patient submission and resolution entitling [the operatives] to the warmest sympathy of their fellow-countrymen' was part of a campaign to sustain external relief contributions, and an expression of hope for the future as well as a comment on present circumstances.[9]

The perceived quiescence of the distressed workers was attributed to the widespread adoption of habits of thrift and discipline. Thus Dr John Watts, erstwhile Owenite lecturer and now a propagandist for the millowners, in 1866: 'The discipline of the cotton mill has spread its influences beyond the workshop, and regularity and punctuality have become essential parts of Lancashire life ... the effects of manufacturing discipline have not been less upon the workpeople than upon their employers. The habit of working together has taught them to associate for other purposes, and the necessity of submission to strict rules within the mill has led them to make rules for their own guidance in matters which seem to concern themselves more immediately.' Where this took the form of trade union activity, Watts was very dubious about the results; but where it took the form of saving through banks, building societies, Friendly Societies and the

Co-op, he was very enthusiastic, as he itemised the savings of the Lancashire working class and asserted that they showed 'an amount of prudent forethought and practical frugality for which few people give the working classes credit; and which must be productive of important results'.[10] The spread of Sunday schools and popular adult education, and of a general ethos of 'respectability', were widely seen as being conducive to stability in time of hardship; and all these cultural developments need to be evaluated as part of an explanation for the remarkable transformation of working-class political attitudes in mid-Victorian cotton Lancashire. In the context of the 'Cotton Famine' itself, however, two concluding points are worth making. The institutions of working-class thrift, which Watts and others praised so highly, did not *prevent* destitution and dependence: they merely delayed it, although the habits of mind which encouraged the grim, dogged accumulation of ultimately substantial savings from inadequate wages may well have been conducive to the silent endurance of a deeper adversity. Secondly, the 'Cotton Famine' was less likely than previous depressions to generate systematic class hostility, because its causes were perceived to be external, indeed remote, and employers were more likely to be praised for keeping their mills open than blamed for wage cuts and short-time working. The nature of the crisis also ensured a generous supply of aid from outside the district, and although there were inevitable disputes about the manner of its distribution, it took some of the pressure off the local social system, and helped to defuse conflict. If the spectacular over-production of the boom of 1859–60 had been allowed to issue in the straightforward cyclical depression whose onset was masked by the American Civil War and the cotton blockade, a more demanding test of Lancashire's 'transition to stability' would have been posed.[11]

But we do need to try to explain the real and lasting political changes of the 1850s and 1860s. We saw in Chapter 8 that the decline of Chartism after 1842 is probably best explained in terms of short-term fluctuations in the trade cycle, the effective use of carefully calibrated repression on the part of the authorities, the loss of much middle-class support, the inability of Chartist ideology to cope with legislative concessions from a State which was supposed to be totally and irredeemably corrupt, and the related successes of the established parties in adjusting their programmes to provide encouragement for working-class reformers.[12] But the longer-term transition to relative political stability or equipoise, the failure of Chartism or some analogous mass movement to appear in the next generation, needs to be accounted for in terms of an enduring and substantial shift in working-class attitudes and experiences. Several potentially complementary and overlapping components of such a shift have been identified by historians. Rising living standards, it has been argued, provided not only increasing comfort and security, but also spread confidence in the ability of the existing economic system to deliver the goods, and confirmed its claims to be 'right' and 'natural'. This trend was enhanced by improved opportunities for upward social mobility, and by the successful growth of working-class institutions of thrift, self-help and mutual assistance, especially the Friendly Societies and the Co-op. The legitimacy of the State was enhanced by the passing of legislation to make life easier for these organisations, and even, in the early 1870s, for trade unions themselves. Local initiatives from above, in the form of educational and religious provision by ostentatiously paternalistic employers, and sometimes in the form of employer patronage of less 'improving' and reputable activities, also helped to anchor working-class people and organisations to the established social and political order. Divisions also widened within the working class itself, as some historians argue for the emergence of a 'labour aristocracy' of a new kind, with 'respectable', thrifty, abstinent, Nonconformist values, working through the new, well-organised, conciliatory trade unions and attaching themselves to the Liberal Party. Meanwhile, an alternative strand of working-class opinion attached itself to the pub, the beerhouse and militant Protestantism, or rather angry anti-Catholicism, which found expression in attacks, usually verbal but sometimes physical, on Irish immigrants whose culture was visibly different and whose alleged competition in the labour market exacerbated the anger of these vituperative working-class Tories. So, a composite picture could be assembled to suggest that the working class was bought off by rising real wages, assimilated by political concessions, propaganda and the lure of 'respectability', and internally divided both horizontally, between the 'labour aristocracy' and the rest, and vertically, between the Liberal improvers and the Tory hedonists and bigots. How far does this explanation carry conviction?[13]

To begin with, the argument for rising living standards after 1848 has limited substance. Substantial increases in cotton workers' money wages are not in evidence until after the 'Cotton Famine'. G. H. Wood finds a rise in his general cotton wage index from 54 in 1850 to 67 in 1860 (with 1900 counting as 100), but these gains were eaten into by inflation, especially during 1855 – 7, and any sustained gain in real wages must have been precarious at best before the late 1860s. Collier argues that the evidence for Rochdale, Bury, Bacup and Todmorden is consistent with stagnation in real wages between 1844 and 1871.[14] This scepticism about rising living standards in cotton merely emphasises in a particular context the more general doubts on this score which had been expressed by Church and Perkin.[15] The stabilisation which was already apparent by 1860 had taken place before we can identify any clear upward trend in real wages. The best that can be said is that cyclical depressions had become less devastating and apocalyptic, and that conditions and opportunities may have been improving faster for the most vociferous and articulate strata of the working class.

Did the channels towards upward social mobility widen significantly around mid-century? In terms of the availability of opportunities for setting up in business with limited resources, it is impossible to answer this question, except to comment that the rapid development of small firms in power-loom weaving was a feature of this period which might have some significance. In terms of the spread of opportunities to save and accumulate capital and resources, however, we are on firmer ground. Most obvious among these was the rise of the Co-operative movement on the new pattern established by the Rochdale Pioneers in 1844. Once the Co-op put the building of an alternative society, free of competition and exploitation, on to the back burner, and began to concentrate on offering short-term satisfactions and opportunities within the existing social system, it began to flourish mightily. It encouraged the accumulation of working-class savings through the acquisition of shares and the division of profits among the shareholding members according to the amount of their purchases. By refusing to offer credit it also encouraged planned budgeting, thrift and frugality. This version of the Co-op, which offered tangible and predictable rewards, spread rapidly in the cotton district during the 1850s, and again after being interrupted by the 'Cotton Famine'. Its earliest successes were in the spinning district around Manchester, and it spread into the weaving areas to the north and west a few years later, especially after 1860. As a democratic organisation which still paid lip service to an ideal of opposition to untrammelled competition, it was attractive to ex-Chartists, and many used it to achieve positions of relative comfort. Many, indeed, became office-holders and paid officials in the movement. Twenty-one societies founded in Lancashire between 1845 and 1854 were still extant in 1912; and for 1855 – 64 the figure was 67, with a spectacular peak in 1860 – 1. Growth in membership and turnover was also impressive, and ventures into manufacturing and housing were beginning. Rochdale-style Co-operation looked like a splendid way of promoting the material and moral improvement of the working class through the advancement of individuals within the existing social system; and as such it must have played its part in diverting energies away from radical political and social reform.[16]

The development of Co-operation shows a marked discontinuity at mid-century, in a way which cannot be demonstrated for Friendly Societies, savings banks, building societies and other institutions which enabled or assisted working-class people to protect themselves against contingencies or accumulate resources. So the argument from upward social mobility and working-class thrift institutions lacks power and substance beyond the interesting case of the Co-op. But these organisations did help to spread an ethos of 'respectability' which brought together thrift, self-reliance, independence, a respect for education and religious practice, an abstinent lifestyle and a willingness to deter gratifications; and this ethos, or aspects of it, proved attractive and fulfilling to many former Chartists who were pulled in a Liberal direction during the 1850s. We shall see that this culture of 'respectability' had autonomous roots within the working class itself, and that it permeated the trade unions; but aspects of it were also encouraged by sections of employer and wider middle-class opinion.

The increased provision of churches, chapels, Sunday schools, day schools and adult education, which was widespread by the 1820s and accelerating in the

1840s, continued apace. Sunday school attendance was genuinely a mass experience, for adolescents as well as children, by the 1850s, and the rising generation of the mid-century was, perhaps significantly, the first to have been exposed in large numbers to the pressures for religious and social conformity which were applied by most of these organisations. A boom in church and chapel building was also carried over from the 1840s into the next two decades. J. S. Leatherbarrow tells us that the first Bishop of Manchester, Prince Lee, consecrated 110 new churches between 1848 and 1869, at a cost of at least £450,000, while 20 existing churches were rebuilt. Between 1870 and 1885 Bishop Fraser consecrated a further 105. The bishop's role was 'to tap [the] vast sources of new industrial wealth, and to encourage the middle classes in providing spiritual and social amenities in the ... towns where their wealth was made'. Whether or not directly prompted by the bishop, the result was, as Pevsner comments, 'an impressive record of local church building activity', and an equally impressive list of industrialist patrons can be supplied. Contributions also came from 'the *little people*', in Leatherbarrow's phrase, and working-class congregations certainly increased substantially in mid-Victorian times; but the initiative and essential financial and practical support came, time after time, from the large employers.[17] Anglican school-building marched in step with the new churches, parishes and clergy; and the Nonconformists and Roman Catholics also expanded their provision. Indeed, this golden age of church and school building was motivated partly by competition between the denominations and fear of losing influence, as well as by a more general desire to stabilise and 'civilise' the 'masses' and by a genuine concern for the saving of souls. The overall impact of this alliance of religion and paternalism is hard to assess; but one result was undoubtedly to point up the importance of sectarian issues and divisions in popular politics, and thereby to distract from the pursuit of radical political remedies for secular problems. As the day school took over from the Sunday school as the most important formal educational influence, even on factory children, the superior resources of the Church of England enabled it to consolidate its influence in this sphere, and we shall see that the widespread dominance of Church schools in the mid-Victorian cotton district has been held to have pushed the working-class voters of the later nineteenth century in a Tory direction.[18] But the Nonconformist contribution was far from negligible, and it is significant that Nonconformists predominated strongly among the sample of post-Chartist labour leaders analysed by Neville Kirk, although the leading part played by Unitarians in this group brings out the extent to which they were unrepresentative of the working class as a whole.[19]

Nevertheless, we cannot ignore the growing influence of religion and its institutions on the Lancashire working class; and it may well have made a major contribution to the new mid-Victorian climate of opinion. The growth and changing nature of adult education played a related role. The Mechanics' Institutes, Working Men's Colleges, Lyceums and similar institutions, which had spread rapidly during the second quarter of the nineteenth century, had failed to provide the genuinely popular scientific education envisaged by their founders; but in several towns they recovered some of the lost ground in the 1850s and 1860s, recruiting well among skilled workers and even factory labour as they provided a form of secondary education monitored by annual examinations. In 1864–5 the Lancashire and Cheshire Union of Mechanics' Institutes claimed that half its members were 'operatives on weekly wages', and during 1867–71, 1224 of the 3229 examinees for this organisation were cotton workers. The aims of the patrons of these bodies were often quite explicitly stated. The Oldham Lyceum, founded in 1839 but not firmly established in its own building until 1856, was intended to propagate 'some of the graces and refinements of intellectual cultivation' among the 'labouring population'; to 'raise the moral and intellectual standard of the people'; and (quoting Sir Robert Peel with approval) to reduce popular dissatisfaction by 'proving ... that avenues to distinction are open to which merit alone, whatever be the lot and condition of men, can secure access and gain the prize'. Lord Stanley, the future fifteenth Earl of Derby, went further as a successful visiting speaker. In 1855 he hoped to see the Lyceum's patrons 'establish a new connection, worthier and freer than that of ancient feudalism, more elevating and more noble than that of a mere pecuniary tie', between employers and workpeople. He also stressed, in 1856, the importance of spreading the teachings of political economy, which was also calculated to win the assent of an educated working class to the existing social system.[20] The prospect of individual self-advancement may well have dominated the motivation of most of the working-class consumers of adult education; but the fact that they were being taught under overtly paternalist auspices, and in a setting where the employers' version of 'political economy' was unchallenged orthodoxy, relegating strikes to the outer darkness of economic irrationality and prescribing laissez-faire as dogma, must have had a cumulative impact on many of the working-class attenders.

Education as a route to upward social mobility, however, was more a comforting illusion than a widespread reality. More to the point was the emphasis on employer paternalism and patronage, which was increasingly pervasive after mid-century in cotton Lancashire as a whole, and not just at the Oldham Lyceum. Factory paternalism could take the form of supervised model housing, parks, libraries and institutes, chapels and temperance societies, aiming at the improvement of morals and the encouragement of controlled and limited social advancement and acculturation to an approved pattern of attitudes and standard of behaviour. This was the Liberal, Nonconformist, 'Manchester School' model, exemplified in extreme form by Hugh Mason of Ashton-under-Lyne, who sought to impose his numerous hatreds ('drink in any quantity or colour, gambling, racing, trotting ..., the theatre, and even tobacco ...') on his workforce and 'his' town.[21] On the other hand, the Hornby family of Blackburn exemplified mill-owner feudalism in a more populist form, patronising working-class sport and endorsing a popular culture revolving around blood sports and beerhouses. There were many staging-posts between these extremes, and there was a general eagerness among employer paternalists to identify the workforce with celebrations within the family, especially the coming-of-age or marriage of the heir, and to encourage active participation at election times in ostentatious support of the millowner's favoured candidate. The sponsored railway excursion to seaside or beauty spot, sometimes accompanied by a church or chapel sermon and supervised by managers and overlookers, was a favourite way of demonstrating benevolence and rewarding good behaviour, as was the works dinner and dance. Patrick Joyce argues that this millowner feudalism, which followed the advice of social commentators as diverse as Dickens and Disraeli, was an effective control on working-class behaviour. He suggests that as work dominated the lives and defined the horizons and expectations of factory operatives, so they came to identify their interests with those of their masters, and to accept the deferential values which were passed down the hierarchy of the factory through the overlookers and other supervisory workers. On this argument, the culture of the factory was dominated by the employer, and was powerful enough to pervade and dominate the wider society beyond the factory gate, acting as a potent explanation for working-class political quiescence.[22]

This explanation has many attractions, and it appears to be supported by voting patterns in the 1868 election, the first after the Second Reform Act, when evidence from Blackburn and Bury, especially, shows that voters in streets adjoining mills with Liberal owners voted strongly and sometimes overwhelmingly Liberal, and voters near Tory mills similarly supported the Conservatives. It must be allotted a contributory influence on the post-Chartist political transition. But it is certainly far from being the whole story. In the first place, it depends very heavily on evidence from Blackburn, where paternalist employers with enclaves of dependent housing around their mills were particularly numerous. Urban industrial colonies of this kind existed in several towns, but they usually accounted for a much smaller proportion of both labour force and housing stock, and in Oldham (where on some accounts the mid-century transition is particularly difficult to explain) and Manchester, for example, they were of little moment.[23] Secondly, there is the problem of how far the paternalist régimes described by Joyce were new at mid-century, although Kirk agrees that there were many new initiatives of this kind in the 1850s in south-east Lancashire and north-east Cheshire, and the will to build bridges and defuse social tensions at this time may have been widespread enough to make a difference. We do not yet know.[24] Thirdly, we need to remember that not all adult males in cotton towns worked in cotton mills: indeed, in most places they were in a clear minority, and any large employer influence must have been exercised through the contributions of wives and children to family economies where paterfamilias was a building worker or a labourer. This may help to account for the often substantial minorities in most streets who voted *against* the politics of the millowner in

1868.[25] As Joyce is well aware, moreover, deference is not a straightforward concept. An unknown number of employees may have paid lip service to the preferences of their employers, without actually internalising the loyalty to the firm, its patriarchs and its politics which was demanded both by employers and management, and by vociferous and sometimes violent elements within the workforce who demanded overt conformity to the politics of the mill, with a public display of ribbons and favours in the appropriate political colours on the machines in the factory as well as on the hustings. Again, we cannot know; but deference was particularly likely to be assumed or skin-deep where rival cultures to the factory, formal or informal, were stronger than Joyce allows; and we need to know more about this, too. Two further problems with Joyce's analysis are relevant here, and lead us into additional important issues. The influences for deference and the culture of the factory may have worked particularly strongly on those skilled and supervisory workers who reaped the most lucrative rewards, put down the deepest roots in their local communities and were most likely to qualify for the vote; and the evidence for persisting trade union activity and endemic industrial conflict is embarrassing to an interpretation which stresses the identification of interests between employers and workpeople and the defusing of industrial conflict.

Joyce's analysis of voting patterns in 1868 was performed by tracing voters listed in the poll-books to the 1871 census, from which their occupations could be obtained. This biases his occupational voting figures towards people who put down deep roots in their locality, staying in one place for at least the four years between qualifying for the vote in 1867 and being enumerated in 1871. In so far as these men actually worked at the nearest factory (which is a matter of assumption rather than direct and convincing evidence), they were part of the settled, long-serving minority of the workforce, who identified with the ethos of the employer and the local institutions. Indeed, they may well have brought their political and religious loyalties to a congenial place of employment, rather than taking on the coloration of their employer.[26] Those who did not fit in, were likely to move elsewhere; and Savage's work on Preston, admittedly for the 1890s, suggests that this was a common phenomenon even among spinners.[27] It is perhaps significant that in Park Ward, Blackburn, for 1868, Joyce was able to trace 70 per cent of the Conservative voters in the 'Conservative area', but only 50 per cent of the Liberal voters in that area.[28] Even if acceptance of (or congruence with) employer politics and values were confined to a (substantial) minority of firmly-rooted and relatively secure and comfortable workers, this would still be an important contribution to our understanding of the achievement of political stability, and these comments question aspects of Joyce's evidence and assumptions about the nature and direction of causation, without denying the value of his overall approach.

The argument of the previous paragraph is consistent with the notion that political quiescence and acceptance of employer values can be associated particularly with a 'labour aristocracy' of skilled and supervisory workers, who were the most obvious gainers from the mid-Victorian upturn in the economy. As we saw in Chapter 8, Foster ascribed the decline of Oldham's working-class movement of the 1840s in large part to the creation of new worker élites of supervisors and pacemakers, who became separated out from the working class as a whole, living in slightly superior housing and hiding in a 'cocoon' of defensive and exclusive institutions, religious, economic and educational. We also saw that Foster's attempts to tie such changes down to the 1840s were completely unsuccessful; and the evidence for the emergence of new kinds of labour aristocracy as sources of working-class division in subsequent decades is no more convincing. Roger Penn has recently confirmed the widespread suspicion that Foster's statistical evidence for the increasing residential separateness of skilled craftsmen between 1841 and 1851 is completely misconceived.[29] In cotton, the transition between the hand-mule and the self-acting mule did not transform a craft occupation into a supervisory one. Cotton spinning continued to require skill as well as supervisory functions, and it would be difficult to show that the nature and implications of the spinner's authority changed significantly. In any case, the displacement of the hand-mule by the self-actor spanned several decades, from the 1820s to the 1870s and even beyond, and it does not seem to have been particularly divisive at mid-century.[30] In engineering, there was indeed an increased recourse to systematic piecework, especially after the defeat of the new Amalgamated Society of Engineers in the great lock-out of 1852. The subcontracting of tasks to leading hands, the so-called 'piecemaster' system which converted a few favoured men into pacemakers with a 'driving' managerial function, was particularly prevalent in south Lancashire. But even here only 16 per cent of the ASE's membership was employed on piecework of any kind in 1861, with a maximum of 25 per cent in 'the large-scale textile machinery and stationary engine centres of Manchester and Oldham, Rochdale [and] Bolton'. As Burgess remarks, 'Piece-work required a degree of standardization and repetition production that remained absent in a large part of the industry.' Thus, there is no convincing evidence of a mid-century watershed in the internal structure of the working class at the workplace in either cotton or engineering; and the evidence for coal mining is even shakier. If a new 'labour aristocracy' played an important part in the stabilisation of politics and society in cotton Lancashire after mid-century, its novelty was not based on the organisation of authority at the workplace.[31]

We cannot provide systematic evidence of the dominance of the agencies of thrift, mutual insurance, self-improving education or religion by an 'aristocracy' of the skilled and supervisory workers, either. The Co-op should logically have attracted the skilled and regularly employed, because it charged slightly higher prices and rarely offered credit; but we lack hard evidence on the social structure of its rank and file, although its *leaders* were drawn mainly from skilled and supervisory workers.[32] The strongest of the Friendly Societies, the Affiliated

Orders such as the Oddfellows and Foresters, probably recruited mainly from the upper working class; but as early as 1840 nearly 1000 of the 2164 Oddfellows in the Stockport District were labourers, weavers and 'other hands' in cotton mills, and over 700 of the rest were shopkeepers, tradesmen and employers.[33] Even at their best, too, the Mechanics' Institutes reached only a tiny minority of Lancashire's working-class population, and their occupational structure varied widely from town to town.[34] It is almost impossible to identify the social structure of the temperance movement, and the congregations of Nonconformity seem often to have recruited from all strata of the working class, as well as from the tradesmen who usually dominated their committees and positions of responsibility.[35] The importance of a 'respectable' stratum of thrifty, religious, earnest self-improvers within the Lancashire working class cannot be denied; but it is impossible to identify it with any specific occupational grouping. The great divide between 'rough' and 'respectable' ran vertically rather than horizontally across cotton town society; and if the growing influence of the latter was conducive to the new political stability, it arose from the role of particular institutions rather than the mass conversion and isolation of a 'labour aristocracy'.

This brings us to a seeming paradox, for another argument to explain the mid-century 'transition to order' concentrates on improved organisation and growing moderation and 'realism' on the part of the trade unions, which at this period were composed essentially of 'labour aristocrats' and have often been linked with the progress of 'respectability'. In fact, they conform more readily to the first part of the stereotype than to the second; and it is here that their record can be made to look embarrassing to Joyce's rather cosy picture of paternalism and class harmony. Among the leading industrial unions, the engineers come nearest to the expectation of mid-century remodelling; but their new centralised organisation in the form of the ASE brought no major changes of policy, as they continued to stress the protection of differentials through the enforcement of apprenticeship, along with opposition to piecework and defence of the status and customs of their trade. If they became less assertive after mid-century, this was due mainly to the need to recover from their disastrous and financially crippling defeat in the 1851–2 lock-out; and by the later 1850s they were defending their interests successfully again, which was itself likely to reduce class tensions in a generally buoyant market.[36] The cotton unions, in both spinning and weaving, remained well capable of federating beyond their basic local organisations to sustain bitter and sometimes violent strikes against wage reductions; and this pattern persisted through the mid-Victorian period alongside efforts to develop and spread the use of agreed piece-rate wage lists, and to establish conciliation procedures. The great set-piece confrontation of 1853–4, the Preston strike and lock-out which lasted for nearly a year and attracted the literary attentions of both Dickens and Mrs Gaskell, was only the longest and angriest of a series of struggles in south Lancashire, as the cotton workers tried to make up the wage cuts of the late 1840s. Financial support for the strikers came from London and beyond as well as from most of Lancashire; and the rhetoric of the strike leaders was often fierce and sometimes tinged with persisting Chartist aspirations. As Dutton and King remark, however, the contrast with 1842 was telling: only two minor riots, no military presence, no fatalities, a 'moderate and respectable leadership which commanded the grudging admiration of even the most hostile middle-class observers', and 'demands which never went beyond the narrowly economic'.[37] Significantly, however, the anger and hostility towards despotic employers remained; and it surfaced again at regular intervals thereafter, especially in the widespread strikes of the boom of 1859–60 and the 'stormy year' of 1867.[38] In 1878 Blackburn itself saw sustained violence as part of the wave of weaving strikes in that year, when the employers' spokesman had his house sacked and looted, and even Harry Hornby was not immune to the physical fury of the rioters.[39] The endemic mid-Victorian violence in the Manchester brickmaking trade is another reminder of the limits to 'respectability' among Lancashire trade unionists.[40] Trade unionists were no longer being driven into radical politics to defend their interests against the state; but industrial conflict remained endemic even where employers attempted to defuse it. This evidence makes it necessary to qualify Joyce's assertions about the pervasive influence of employer paternalism, and it should also remind us that trade unionists could be thrifty and pursue self-improvement without necessarily extending their adoption of 'respectability' to include the abjuration of industrial conflict.

The working class had been divided between skilled, supervisory and the rest, and between 'respectables' and others, during the Chartist years as well as afterwards, and it is not surprising to find that the causal influence of these divisions on mid-Victorian stability was not strong. More important, perhaps, was the corrosive influence of anti-Catholicism and militant antagonism towards the Irish immigrants who became so numerous during the 1840s, and could be presented as convenient scapegoats for a variety of social ills. The Irish presence in Liverpool and Manchester was already well established by the end of the eighteenth century, of course, and a steady flow of migrants continued during and especially after the Napoleonic Wars; but the mass exodus of the great famine during the later 1840s was nevertheless a watershed. The Irish-born population of Lancashire nearly doubled between 1841 and 1851 to reach over 191,000, about 10 per cent of the county's inhabitants; and growth was especially rapid in the second-rank and smaller cotton towns. By 1851 the Irish-born accounted for 17 per cent of the population of Manchester district, 7 per cent of Ashton-under-Lyne, and 10 per cent of Stockport borough, with similar orders of magnitude in places like Oldham and Preston. When we include the English-born but ethnically Irish, the Irish presence becomes still more impressive.[41]

It was, above all, around mid-century that hostility to the Irish became widespread and virulent among the working class at large: hitherto, relations had been mixed but often cordial, and the Irish had not been absent from Chartist and trade union activity.[42] From the late 1840s onwards, however, the picture darkens. The cost of relieving the Irish poor placed additional burdens on small ratepayers; and more generally, the Irish were perceived to be undercutting the locally-born at the lower end of the labour market, and their use as strike-breakers by employers, as in the Preston strike of 1853–4, attracted more attention than their resistance to wage cuts elsewhere. These economic grievances gained wide currency, although it is difficult to confirm their basis in reality. But Kirk's work makes clear that in Ashton, Stockport and Stalybridge, at least, there was a 'mass influx' of the Irish into the town-centre cotton factories from the late 1840s, which gathered momentum during the next decade, when Irishmen even became a sizeable and significant minority among the spinners and self-actor minders. At the same time, the Irish were colonising whole streets which had hitherto been occupied by the locals. We do not yet know how far this competition for work and housing was apparent elsewhere, though in Ancoats 36.8 per cent of Rushton's sample for 1851 were Irish-born, and there were Irish enclaves in all the cotton towns.[43] The Irish were also accused of being particularly filthy, drunken, violent and immoral, outraging the 'respectable'. Lowe confirms that the Irish-born were particularly likely to live in overcrowded housing, to become recipients of poor relief, and to be arrested for drunkenness, assaults (especially on the police), vagrancy and prostitution; but this probably had more to do with the Irish tendency to live in poor areas and to work in ill-paid and insecure occupations than with anything else, and the police may well have been disproportionately likely to arrest Irish people rather than locals, as they themselves became infected with anti-Irish attitudes.[44]

All of the dire prognostications about the Irish which had already been expressed by social commentators of the 1830s and 1840s, from J. P. Kay to Engels (whose views on this topic were nothing short of racist), were thus gaining wider currency at mid-century. But the main pretext for anti-Irish agitation was religious and political. Most of the migrants were Roman Catholic, at least nominally, although an important but often-forgotten minority were Protestants, especially from Ulster and especially in Liverpool. They thus fell foul of that popular strain of Low Church Protestantism which saw the Pope as a dire and immediate threat to the English crown and constitution, plotting ceaselessly to subvert the liberties of the free-born Englishman, while the Catholic priest was a dangerous and unnatural creature, professing celibacy while threatening the chastity of English wives and daughters with his conniving wiles. These issues generated particularly obsessive concern among some of the Church of England clergy, especially as Anglo-Catholicism made headway within the Church, and among activist groups within the middle classes. The Orange Order, an Irish Protestant import, made rapid headway in the cotton towns during the 1830s and 1840s. In the aftermath of the Pope's restoration of the Catholic hierarchy of archbishops and bishops in England, in September 1850, these groups were able to mobilise mass support, fuelled by the growing sense of economic grievance; and the anti-Irish riots in Stockport in 1852 were the first large-scale manifestation of antagonisms which were to simmer, and occasionally to erupt, in most if not all of the cotton towns at regular intervals until the late 1860s. These events may have had some of their origins in manipulation from above, but the adoption of the Irish as scapegoats for a variety of social and economic ills had deep roots in working-class experience. To some extent, they displaced the state and the employers from popular demonology as the prime cause of poverty and unemployment after mid-century; and by dividing the working class and diverting its attention from conflicts based on class and the political system, the Irish issue played its part in the political transition of the mid-Victorian cotton towns.[45]

The changes and realignments within the working class were accompanied by a strengthening of the forces of order. This perhaps owed more to the spread of barracks and the consequent increased military presence in the cotton towns, than to the strengthening of the new police forces. But the Manchester police force grew in number from 398 to 554 between 1842 and 1856; Salford's more than trebled from 31 to 95 between 1844 and 1856; and other forces were expanding rapidly from the mid-1840s, and especially in the mid-1850s. Police pay and quality were still extremely low, and there was a persistent high turnover among the officers, featuring many sackings for drunkenness and other mis-demeanours; but the increased visibility of the forces of order must have been discouraging to radicals of 'physical force' bent, even though the police usually had to be bailed out by the military when sustained rioting occurred in mid-Victorian times.[46] It may be significant that in 1851 Lancashire had 'by far the largest' county police force, with 509 of the country's 2749 county policemen, and a year later Lancashire boroughs employed more than one-third of the national total of borough police.[47] These statistics are certainly not irrelevant.

But the main function of the police was to protect property, order and morality against thieves, vagrants, prostitutes and perceived disreputable elements of all kinds, and they concentrated their attentions on the central urban areas where slums, entertainments and moveable property were in dangerously close mutual proximity. It is no coincidence that it was Liverpool rather than Manchester or the cotton towns which invested most heavily in policing during these years, as its force expanded from 290 to 886 men between 1836 and 1856. Liverpool's waterfront had formidable problems of crime, vice and drunkenness as well as filth and disease; and it experienced food riots in 1855. It also, of course, had the most numerous Irish population of all the Lancashire towns, and suffered from endemic sectarian violence as a result. But its dockers and seamen continued to lack formal or effective organisation, as well as being internally divided, and working-class radicalism as such was attenuated to the point of non-existence.[48] Similarly, in the mining, metalworking and chemical manufacturing towns of south-west Lancashire, and in the urban outposts north of the Ribble, the working class had remained politically quiescent even in the most tumultuous of the Chartist years, and there was no transition at mid-century to explain. But there were many common themes in the politics of the mid-Victorian cotton towns and the rest of Lancashire, despite their differing backgrounds in the 1840s and their contrasting industrial and social structures; and a further exploration of the nature of parliamentary electoral politics, and of the sources of support for the Conservatives and Liberals before and after the Second Reform Act of 1867, will shed further light on the nature of Lancashire society in these years.

The mid-Victorian electorate in Lancashire remained predominantly middle-class, with a strong tradesman and shopkeeper presence, until the Second Reform Act, although as rents and assessments increased in the boroughs, and as a growing proportion of new houses commanded the magic £10 rental, the number of working-class voters steadily increased. These processes were particularly advanced in Manchester, where in the 1840s, 17 per cent of adult males had the vote, and in 1865 the proportion had risen to 24 per cent in a much larger population. On one calculation 27 per cent of the Manchester electorate in 1866 was drawn from the working class, especially the 'highest class of operative', and the growing attainability of the franchise in this way must have made its own contribution to the changing political climate, as a thrifty, sober lifestyle could be seen to provide the vote along with modest prosperity and a measure of security.[49] In other boroughs the same trend was visible but its pace and extent varied, partly according to the housing market, although in Manchester at least it was noticeable by 1860 that large numbers of £10 householders were not bothering to claim their votes, perhaps an additional symptom of working-class detachment from the political process.[50] The survival of freeman voters in some of the older boroughs complicated the picture, too, as many of them were working-class and their numbers declined while the occupants of the cheaper £10 houses grew in numbers. At Lancaster as late as 1865 about 1000 of the 1339 actual voters qualified on the freeman franchise, although the Liverpool freemen had declined to under 10 per cent of the electorate as early as 1858.[51] But the 1866 return which gave 27 per cent of Manchester's voters a 'working-class' label produced comparable figures of 21 per cent for Bolton, 14 per cent for Oldham and only 13 per cent for Liverpool, putting the real but limited extent of potential working-class participation in perspective, although organised groups among the non-voters could try to influence events by publishing lists of 'black sheep' who had voted the 'wrong' way, and trying to organise consumer boycotts of errant shopkeepers and tradesmen.[52] It is difficult to know how effective this tactic was; but to work properly it would have required a degree of unanimity and commitment to one particular party among working-class consumers which was certainly not in evidence in 1868.

Evidence from poll-books provides interesting snapshots of borough electorates in particular places at particular times. Vincent analyses those who voted in Rochdale in 1857 thus: capitalists (mostly manufacturers) 9 per cent, 'respect-ables and dependants' (mostly wholesalers, agents and professionals) 18 per cent, retailers 26½ per cent, the drink interest 14 per cent, craftsmen (combining employers, employees and the self-employed) 23 per cent, and 'others' (including 5 labourers and only 4 farmers) 9½ per cent.[53] At Oldham in 1852 the drink interest accounted for perhaps one-sixth of the voters, and farmers were nearly as numerous. 'Gentry' and professionals were just over 10 per cent, and employers slightly outnumbered the publicans and beersellers. But here again, the shopkeepers and tradesmen were the dominant group, with nearly 30 per cent of the actual voters. Warrington in 1847 presents a broadly similar picture, with drink and farming slightly less in evidence and an identifiable working-class presence of well over 10 per cent.[54] We have here the mid-Victorian borough electorate in broad outline, although analysis is complicated by the elasticity of some of Vincent's categories, and in both Oldham and Warrington about 5 per cent of the voters are mysteriously unaccounted for in the published tables.

These borough electorates were dominated numerically by the lower middle class of shopkeepers, tradesmen and the self-employed: the social strata which were hardest hit by mid-Victorian taxation, especially local taxation, and which predominated among the active members of church and chapel congregations, especially mainstream Nonconformity in the form of Baptists, Congregationalists and the various Methodisms. It comes as no surprise to find that issues associated with these preoccupations maintained a high profile in parliamentary elections, with the demise of Chartism and the eclipse of the Corn Laws and factory reform as live political issues. Above all, sectarian matters were consistently of central concern. In the cotton towns this meant that the special constitutional position of the Church of England was much debated, as the Liberation Society, which crusaded for disestablishment, depended heavily on Lancashire money. The remaining legal disabilities of Dissenters, and the question of their liability to pay church-rates towards the upkeep of the parish church, were also political hot potatoes; and so were the moral concerns of earnest Nonconformity, especially the drink question. Struggles between capital and labour, and wider questions of the legitimacy of the political system, were now of little account in constituency politics. In cotton Lancashire, practically all active Conservatives were also Anglicans, while the vast majority of Nonconformists were Liberal supporters; and on this limited electorate, the most important influences were those of religious allegiance rather than class. Vincent's voting analyses support this judgement, showing that most occupations split their allegiance with remarkable evenhandedness, with occasional exceptions such as publicans when drink became an issue. As Neale has demonstrated in the very different setting of Bath, these occupational groupings could conceal class-based divisions, with master shoemakers, for example, voting Conservative while their work-people, in smaller houses and less prestigious districts, voted Radical; but in cotton Lancashire the circumstantial evidence on political preoccupations is in Vincent's favour.[55] With this electorate and this political agenda, the Liberals flourished in Manchester and the surrounding constituencies. As Hanham summarises, between 1832 and 1867 'Ashton, Bury, Salford and Manchester itself returned none but Liberals, Rochdale returned a Conservative only in the exceptional circumstances of 1857' (when the Liberal offended the drink interest) 'and Oldham and Stockport returned Liberals without exception after 1852'.[56] Within Liberalism, the emphasis shifted from the Free Trade idealism of Cobden, Bright and the Anti-Corn Law League to a more flag-waving Palmerstonian outlook; but in most of these constituencies the strings continued to be pulled by an inner caucus of wealthy merchants and manufacturers. There was little room for class conflict in this political environment.

To the north and west, the Conservatives put up a much better showing in the outlying cotton boroughs, where nearby gentry families and squirearchical millowners exerted influence in their favour, and the leading landed families continued to divide the spoils in the county constituencies. Corruption was also a consideration, and it persistently dominated elections in Lancaster, where a particularly spectacular display of competitive bribery led to the abolition of both the borough's seats after the 1865 election.[57] Liverpool was nearly as notorious as Lancaster, without suffering the same fate; and the politics of influence by large landlords and major employers may have affected its parliamentary politics, as they certainly attracted attention in some wards at municipal elections. Thus in 1857 Great George Ward could be described as 'the natural inheritance of the Lawrences', as 'the fragrant steam from their coppers and coolers confers a delight upon every nostril in it', while the power of this brewing family as employers was augmented by their tied houses and their ownership of ordinary house property. At the same time, 'The coal trade in St. Paul's Ward is what the timber trade is in the Toxteths, and the black diamonds have a lustre which dazzles and wins.'[58] Here as in cotton Lancashire, however, sectarianism provided the most reliable and emotive touchstone of political allegiance; but here Nonconformity was weak, and the great divide was between militant Low Church Anglicans and immigrant Irish Roman Catholics. Liverpool's Liberals were ambivalent on this issue, but its Conservatives entered the fray eagerly in defence of Church and Constitution, appealing also to fears of Irish competition in the port's crowded labour markets, and building a popular following which extended their dominance far beyond the Second Reform Act. Local history was against the Liberals, too: their aloof Unitarian patriciate had been prominent, and unpopular, as opponents of the slave trade and promoters of unsectarian education, and their support for the North in the American Civil War also went against the perceived economic interests and cultural attachments of many fellow townsmen. Even so, as Waller has noticed, the Liberals were strong enough to win 'a majority of councillors in six years and parity in three' in the municipal elections of the decade after 1858. But in terms of parliamentary politics, Hanham sums up a pattern which contrasted completely with the cotton heartland: 'The Liberals occasionally won parliamentary elections, although almost always for local reasons of a temporary nature ...' This pattern was to prevail for several generations to come, as the Liverpool Liberals lost ground to Irish Nationalists and then to Labour, while the town retained its reputation as a haven of working-class Toryism.[59]

The 1867 Reform Act reinforced the political peculiarities of Liverpool, while necessitating alterations in the manner of their expression. In cotton Lancashire, however, it made a major and lasting difference to the pattern of parliamentary politics, revealing the hitherto unsuspected strength of working-class Conservatism in the cotton district a generation after the Chartists. The Second Reform Act was, after all, an important and far-reaching measure. It brought household suffrage to the boroughs, increasing the electorate in the cotton town constituencies fivefold or sixfold, though 'only' doubling it in Manchester. It thus gave working-class voters a clear predominance in the manufacturing towns, although in several cases it was accompanied by boundary changes which diluted the urban working-class voters with an admixture of farmers and suburbanites. Eight more seats were added to the county's representation, three going to the county divisions, one to Liverpool, one to Manchester and three to cotton towns, to make up a total of 36. In the 1865 general election, Lancashire's 28 seats had been evenly divided; three years later, under the new rules, the Conservatives won 24 to the Liberals' 12. Manchester and its surrounding cotton towns had returned 11 Liberals and a solitary Tory in 1865, but now the score was 8 – 7 the other way. In the cotton seats overall, a 12 – 6 Liberal lead was reversed, and in 1868 the Conservatives prevailed by 13 – 7, as well as winning all 8 of the county seats. This was a remarkable reversal of fortunes, and it was recognised as such at the time. Moreover, it was no mere flash in the pan. The Conservatives held on to most of their gains in 1874, and the Liberals' recovery of lost ground in 1880 was only temporary. Under the wider county franchise of 1884, and the ensuing redistribution which increased the number of Lancashire seats to 58, the Conservatives won 38 seats in 1885, including 5 out of 6 in Manchester, and they continued to dominate the county's electoral map until the Liberal landslide of 1906. This pattern requires explanation.[60]

The Tory successes were achieved in a context of impressively high polls, although the electorate itself fell a long way short of manhood suffrage. In 1901 between 50 and 70 per cent of adult males had the vote in the vast majority of Lancashire constituencies, with Stretford's figure as high as 83.6 per cent and Liverpool Scotland as low as 42 per cent.[61] The polls themselves, which often exceeded 90 per cent on ageing registers, were no doubt inflated by personation and other sharp practices, and the apathetic or non-aligned were particularly likely to lose their votes when the registers were scrutinised, as they lacked partisan defenders when their eligibility was challenged before the revising barrister. But there is no doubt that elections were occasions of mass enthusiasm and lively popular participation, with crowded meetings, favours generally sported, and no lack of enthusiastic volunteer canvassers on either side.[62] No doubt this general excitement was fuelled by the likelihood of a close contest, and we should remember that most of the victories on either side were narrow ones. Most Lancashire constituencies were divided almost down the middle in political terms: so we are seeking to explain a prevalence of narrow Tory victories, rather than an overwhelming dominance. Vincent, indeed, argues that the Tory victories in 1868 were narrow enough to be explicable in terms of boundary changes and quirks in the electoral system, rather than an upsurge in popular Toryism; but there seems to be no convincing way of explaining away the Conservative victories of 1868 and afterwards, except in terms of a solid basis in working-class support.[63]

Why, then, were Lancashire's Conservatives so successful in attracting and retaining a high and electorally vital proportion of the urban working-class vote? Intimidation may have been part of the answer, but these voting patterns persisted after the Ballot Act of 1872, and Liberal employers were as willing to apply the pressure as their Tory counterparts. The evidence strongly suggests widespread positive, even enthusiastic attachment to the main political parties. This was made easier by the absence of working-class alternatives after the decline of Chartism; but we should note that when Ernest Jones stood as a Radical under the Liberal banner at Manchester in 1868, he was beaten into fifth place behind the two Tories and the other two Liberals, despite polling very well in Ancoats and Miles Platting, the old Chartist strongholds. In the newer working-class districts, however, he came nowhere.[64] When the new parties of the left appeared in late Victorian times, they were to find the established bipartisan structure very difficult to penetrate, perhaps especially on the Conservative side.

Tradition, a factor which should never be underestimated in Victorian Lancashire, played its part. The Church and King brand of popular Toryism, inherited from the constitutional loyalists and Pittites of the French wars, retained its own popular appeal, and resurfaced in the Operative Conservative Societies of the 1830s, with the support of Tory Radical reformers. These in turn disappeared from the historian's line of vision during the Chartist years, but they seem to have remained in existence, with patronage from local notables, in Wigan, Oldham, Bolton and perhaps elsewhere, until the revival of organised working-class Conservatism which coincided with Reform in the late 1860s. This almost subterranean tradition of working-class Toryism, which had a much more visible continuity in Liverpool in association with the Orange Order, perpetuated the opposition of many operatives to the harsh *laissez-faire* doctrines of leading Liberal employers, especially those who were identified with Nonconformity, the Anti-Corn Law League and the so-called 'Manchester School'. The support of prominent or vociferous Conservatives for factory reform, the retention of the relatively mild relief policies of the Old Poor Law, and other popular causes of the 1830s was still remembered and publicised thirty years on; and this helped to bolster the efforts of Lancashire Conservatives in Disraeli's time to present themselves as the working man's true friends.[65]

A widespread working-class predisposition towards the Conservatives was both reflected and reinforced by the rapid spread of working-class Conservative Clubs in all the Lancashire towns after 1867. By 1887 there were 31 such clubs in Bolton, with 3200 members; and this level of penetration was not unusual. The Liberals responded in kind, as their clubs proliferated in fierce competition; and in so far as Joyce's calculations in this respect are comprehensible, the political clubs appear to have contained something like one-sixth of the electorate by the late 1880s. Both parties used the clubs to reinforce the influence of the leading local politicians, and there were few protests on that score; but the Conservatives, with their generally readier toleration of drink and amusements, and the less didactic tone of their proceedings, were probably more effective at building bridges to a wider cross-section of the working class, although membership of a club is of course no guarantee of agreement with the political opinions of its sponsors.[66] On the other hand, apart from the overtly political clubs there were many other voluntary organisations developing in mid and late Victorian Lancashire which became identified with one political party or the other, including football clubs, churches and chapels, the Co-op (usually leaning heavily towards the Liberals), and of course the public houses, which became more and more committed to the Conservatives as the militant temperance movement, an embarrassing minority within the Liberal ranks, frightened brewers, publicans and drinkers alike. These phenomena provide further evidence, alongside the fervent election campaigns and high voting turn-outs, of the strength of entrenched loyalties to the established political parties at this time for a substantial proportion of the working-class electorate.[67] Nor should we ignore the political influence of religion and of the trade unions.

Joyce remarks on the paradox that 'for the great majority of the working class attachment to the institutions and dogmas of organised religion was informal, often vestigial, yet the conflict of religious denominations was as near the centre of political life as any other matter'.[68] Partly, this was due to entrenched attitudes and attachments, which engendered religious loyalties if not necessarily religious attendance. The almost universal experience of Sunday school attendance, which persisted into the new century and concentrated with increasing single-mindedness on denominational dogma, helped to create a climate of opinion which upheld and respected a range of basic if secularised Christian virtues, while perpetuating institutional loyalties which had been forged in childhood and reinforced in adolescence. Sunday school teachers, past and present, formed a particularly influential core of the committed.[69] Even more important, perhaps, was the uniquely strong position of the Church of England in the provision and control of day schools in Lancashire, which was consolidated in mid-Victorian times and sustained by an immense financial effort after the 1870 Education Act. In several large towns, including Wigan, Stalybridge, Warrington and Blackburn, Church of England schools taught at least half of the scholars even at the turn of the century, while at Preston, St. Helens and

Wigan the Anglicans and Roman Catholics together accounted for more than 75 per cent. By this time the Nonconformists had largely given up the unequal struggle. Clarke has shown that towns with high levels of Anglican school attendance were also likely to return Conservative MPs, although exactly what this means is difficult to decide. Many parents seem to have sent their children to the nearest school, regardless of denominational affiliation, while others were more concerned with other aspects of the education on offer. Many children, like Robert Roberts, must have been unmoved by the often mechanical religious teaching they received. There is evidence of attempts to use the church schools for political propaganda, but it is impossible to say how effective they were. No doubt such attempts at indoctrination only made headway when they went with the grain of family influences and the attitudes of friends; and the affinity between Anglican schools and Conservative politics in the Lancashire towns was probably more a symptom than a cause of prevailing political attachments.[70]

Sectarianism was as important an influence on the wider electorates of the later nineteenth century as it had been on the more socially homogeneous voters of the pre-1867 years, despite the difficulty we experience in unravelling the nature of its workings. It helped the Tories more than the Liberals, while setting an agenda which made it all the harder for class issues, as such, to make headway. Most Nonconformists voted Liberal (though many Wesleyan Methodists were Tory supporters), and most Anglicans were also Conservatives. But the Liberals were unable to attract support on religious and moral issues beyond a core of principled Dissenters, while the religious messages of Anglican Conservatives were capable of striking home outside the ranks of the churchgoers. There was widespread support for the idea of the Church as an essential pillar of the Constitution, and the Liberals also suffered from their association with restrictive legislation on drink, gambling and Sunday observance. Above all, though, the Tories gained from the campaigns against Popery, which of course overlapped with popular opposition to Irish immigrants, and brought an additional dimension of anger and violence to the election campaigns which followed the Second Reform Act. Throughout Lancashire, hostility to Roman Catholicism became identified with the Church of England, which was overwhelmingly Evangelical in the county, and fiercely hostile to anything which smacked of Ritualism. In the late 1860s, especially, working-class antipathy to the Catholic Irish was stoked up by the Orange Order, whose membership in cotton Lancashire was increasing, and by the vicious rhetoric of ultra-Protestant clergymen. It fed on the fear that the Liberals might disestablish the Irish Church, and on the activities of the Fenians, who were taken very seriously by the authorities in spite of the comic-opera failure of their attack on the Chester Castle armoury. The flames were fanned by itinerant anti-Catholic orators, above all William Murphy, who specialised in lurid descriptions of the alleged sexual depravities of priests and nuns, provoking violent clashes between his followers and the local Irish wherever he went, sometimes leading to full-scale riots and the sack and pillage of Irish streets and chapels. All this gave the Catholic issue pride of place in the 1868 election campaigns, making a major contribution to the Conservative victory in Salford and probably in several other constituencies. Although the Church of England was only one of the contributors to this episode, it became identified as the spearhead of anti-Catholicism, with the Nonconformists, themselves no friends to Popery, being obliged to keep a low profile, inhibited as they were by the ambiguities of the Liberals' Irish policies. Thus the alliance between the Church of England and the Conservatives, deprecated as it was by several moderate churchmen, subsequently including Bishop Fraser of Manchester himself, provided a vote-winning populist platform which helped to establish Tory predominance in the aftermath of Reform.[71]

This highly charged brand of sectarian conflict became much less important in cotton Lancashire after 1868, which was in many ways a 'one-off' election; but religious affiliation remained remarkably effective as a touchstone for political alignment, even among non-churchgoers, beyond the turn of the century, as conflicts between Church and Dissent continued to flare, especially on issues connected with education. In Liverpool, of course, the direct confrontation between ultra-Protestantism and the Irish Catholics remained firmly at the centre of local politics, and the issue remained very much alive at Widnes and Wigan. The Second Reform Act reinforced existing trends, in Birkenhead as well as Liverpool itself, and the Conservatives found that their surest route to success was to organise the working-class vote under the banners of sectarianism. The Working Men's Conservative Association, founded in 1868, had twelve branches by 1872, and obtained a genuine influence on the choice of candidates and policies. Unease was expressed from time to time by the local Tory plutocracy, and the populist leaders of the late nineteenth and early twentieth centuries, Arthur Forwood and Archibald Salvidge, had to adopt a conciliatory stance on trade union and labour issues as well as participating in the pungent and vulgar ultra-Protestant rhetoric of the Orange lodge and the hot-pot supper. Such was the price of popular support, and the merchant princes and their courtiers sometimes jibbed at paying it. Their hostility to Forwood's style and professions helped to lose him the by-election of 1882, a most unusual reverse for Liverpool Toryism. On the other hand, the Orange Order was frequently rebellious, and could not always be relied upon to deliver the goods. But the tensions within Liverpool Conservatism, though rarely far from the surface, were seldom fierce enough to give class antagonism priority over party attachment; and the Liberals had many more problems than their rivals. The wealthy Whigs had to make concessions to Irish Nationalism, this time on the Home Rule issue; and by the early 1880s an angry group of militant Nationalists contested Irish wards in municipal elections, seeking support from the 'working men' as opposed to the 'swells'. In 1885 the Nationalists won Liverpool Scotland after the redistribution of seats which followed the Third Reform Act, and T. P. O'Connor held it for them until 1929. Labour-related issues became nearly as contentious and internally divisive as the Irish question in the late nineteenth century, and a policy of reforming individuals, through temperance controls and the suppression of vice, rather than improving economic and material conditions, won few supporters from the ranks of the uncommitted. The Liberals controlled the Corporation between 1892 and 1895; but this was a brief interlude, and the pattern of Liverpool politics continued to be dominated by a populist sectarianism which almost invariably issued in Conservative dominance.[72]

Just as Liverpool's politics were strongly influenced by a traditional attachment to causes which the Tories made their own, and which the high-minded, largely Unitarian Whig élite angrily repudiated, so the town's social structure also made life difficult for the Liberals. The old craft unions and the new industrial unions alike were thin on the ground in this commercial metropolis, and at a national level these were thought to be generally sympathetic to the Liberals. Casual and unskilled workers who depended heavily on the goodwill of employers and foremen for their livelihood were perceived to be especially vulnerable to coercion and undue influence; and most of Liverpool's large employers were Conservatives. Two more general points arise from this. One is that contemporaries gave some credence to the importance of employer influence, and perhaps even of deferential voting, among the working-class electorate of Liverpool as well as in the cotton towns. It was, of course, a ubiquitous possibility; but Joyce's case rests on the assumption that the factory and its institutions were peculiarly suited to the formation of relationships of dominance and dependence which could be translated into the political sphere. But this was, at best, only part of the story. We have seen that Liverpool's working-class voters, whether Protestant or Irish Catholic, were able to wring concessions from their 'betters' as the price of their support; and this should remind us that these were generally two-way relationships, and that employers and politicians were expected to express and respond to the interests of the workpeople, rather than merely imposing on them or dictating to them. We should also remember some of the earlier interpretations of the social roots of popular politics in later nineteenth-century Lancashire, which are diametrically opposed to Joyce's thesis. Hanham clearly suggests that working-class Lancastrians voted Conservative in large numbers *in opposition* to Liberal millowners and their unpalatable doctrines; while Clarke finds supporting evidence for such a thesis in the politics of Ashton-under-Lyne and Stalybridge.[73] It is indeed noticeable that in most constituencies the new voters after 1867 seem to have tipped the balance away from the established incumbents, whatever their party affiliation. All this suggests that important though employer paternalism may have been, it was a matter of negotiation rather than divine right, and some of the electorate may have voted against rather than for their employers. This drives home the complexity of the situation. Some of the new voters followed their employers, for a variety of motives; some voted with the political orthodoxy of their mill or other workplace communities; some defined themselves against the politics and personalities of large employers, of whatever political complexion; many were swayed more significantly by other loyalties or antipathies, whether based on pub or place of worship; and many voting decisions were the product of a tangle of countervailing attitudes and attachments. Monocausal explanations, whether based on the workplace or the economy, on religion or personality, are bound to distort as well as stimulate; but the persisting problem remains: how does one go beyond the provision of a shopping-list of possible influences, and weight the various factors according to the relative importance of their impact? Under present conditions it is difficult to go beyond the mere unsatisfactory assertion and description of complexity.

What is clear is that at a political level, the divisions within the Lancashire working class were more important than the forces which tended to pull it together; and this brings us to a second general point. Class conflict in this period was expressed in terms of economic rather than political issues: it was endemic in the workplace but deflected from the hustings, until the end of the nineteenth century. As part of this process, the trade unions moved out of the political arena; and as they developed and changed in mid-Victorian times, they became acutely aware that their membership in Lancashire was divided between the two established political parties. Throughout urban Lancashire, therefore, the correspondence between trade unionism and Liberalism was much less pronounced than some of the stereotypes would lead us to expect. This was particularly true of cotton and coal. Clarke's suggestion that 'the Weavers were predominantly Liberal but the Spinners were, at least to a large degree, Conservative' is an over-simplification with some basis in fact, and was expressed at the turn of the century in the respective political leanings of the Spinners' leader James Mawdsley, who stood for parliament as a Tory in 1899, and the Weavers' David Holmes. But, as Clarke also points out, since Chartist days the cotton unions, as such, 'had sought to avoid involvement in party politics'. The dangers of too obvious a breach of this principle were exemplified by the events in Blackburn in 1885, when 'the radical inclinations of the original weavers' leadership spurred on the creation of a powerful and Tory-inclined rival organisation'.[74] The cotton unions' prime political concerns involved lobbying for specific reforms on issues relating to such topics as hours and working conditions, and this form of pressure-group activity had little to do with wider party divisions.[75] The Lancashire miners' leaders flirted with the Liberals from time to time, especially when labour representation was a real possibility; but the county had 'large numbers of miners with Conservative convictions' in late Victorian times, and this continued to inhibit wholehearted political commitment.[76] Again, their more sustained involvement was with pressure-group tactics for protective legislation. More generally, as Joyce remarks, the Trades Councils which emerged in most Lancashire towns in the mid-Victorian decades tended to avoid party political issues, and 'individual unions almost always declared that they were above politics'. The Liberals probably attracted the support of the majority of articulate, independent trade unionists, but here as elsewhere, the power of the

Conservatives could not be ignored or neglected.[77] Lancashire's trade unions were steadily gaining in strength and industrial muscle during the second half of the nineteenth century; but until the turn of the century and afterwards they were unable or unwilling to convert their influence into effective independent political clout. Before examining the rise of organised labour as a separate political force, and its relationship with the emerging late Victorian socialist movements, we need to look more closely at the development, organisation and policies of the trade unions after 1850.

Much of Lancashire's trade unionism in these years was highly idiosyncratic. This was especially true of the cotton unions, which were very much a law unto themselves; but the spinning and weaving sides of the industry followed separate and contrasting paths of development, and had little contact one with another. The Lancashire miners also developed their unions in distinctive ways, and the peculiarities of the Liverpool waterfront ensured that the dockers and transport workers of Merseyside would also have unique features of their own. This array of regional idiosyncracies should not be allowed to overwhelm or distort the overall picture: the engineers and many craft unions, with considerable Lancashire memberships, conformed much more closely to more general ex-periences and patterns of development, and have therefore attracted less attention in a purely Lancashire context. But the cotton unions were so important, and so distinctive in so many ways, that we must nevertheless begin by examining their activities.

The spinners' organisations continued to dominate the spinning and preparatory branches of the cotton industry. They retained their privileged supervisory role despite the protracted transition from hand-mule to self-actor, and each spinner, or minder, continued to oversee the labour of two or more piecers. Technological change had made this pattern of working unnecessary in theory, and in some places other arrangements were made, sometimes in-volving female labour on mules as well as the alternative systems of ring- and throstle-spinning. But the spinners' unions set their faces against any dilution of their supervisory role, and in the main centres of the industry they were able to retain their status and, in large measure, keep up their differentials. In theory, they were vulnerable to being undermined or superseded by their piecers, many of whom were perfectly capable of operating the machines, and all of whom were paid a fraction of the spinner's wage, which left the young adult 'big piecers' receiving less than many unskilled labourers. The spinners' position was pre-served by a combination of influences. Many piecers hoped to be promoted to the higher grade, and therefore had a vested interest in maintaining the status quo. Many others were relatives and neighbours of spinners, which inhibited independent action. Moreover, the spinner's role was partly disciplinary and authoritarian, and it was thought to require the strength and presence of a grown man with authority vested in him. Increasingly, too, the spinners showed a telling willingness to support employers' initiatives for higher productivity, through the speeding up of machinery and the covert extension of working hours: for the spinners were paid on piece-rates, and reaped the benefits of harder work, while their subordinates were paid by time and made no gains from this intensified exploitation. Alongside these important influences, however, we should also set the growing strength and bargaining power of the spinners' unions.[78]

By the mid-1840s the spinners were already retreating from radical politics, and distancing themselves from other occupations within their factories, and from other trades beyond the factory gate. Their attitudes and policies were beginning to justify allegations of aloofness and sectionalism. This seems to have applied both to the embattled older aristocrats of the hand-mule, and the new self-actor minders who were still striving to define their position and establish their status. But they were also divided geographically, with much mutual suspicion between areas specialising in coarse, medium and fine spinning. Renewed attempts at a permanent county-wide federation of the local unions took place in 1853 and 1860, but both disintegrated after a short time. A permanent (though at first unstable) Spinners' Amalgamation was at last put together in 1870, and consolidated with a reformed constitution in 1884. The unions had already been successful in defining and defending the spinner's distinctive status at the workplace, and they now became more effective at defending wages and conditions. This was increasingly important, as falling prices and overseas competition began to cut into millowners' margins, and wages were the most tempting sector for attempts at economies. But the spinners were strong enough to deflect this pressure from themselves, although not to widen their differentials or secure sustained large increases in money wages. They achieved very high membership levels: in 1891 the Spinners' Amalgamation included over 93 per cent of Lancashire's minders, although local figures ranged from 99 per cent in the Bolton fine-spinning district to 77 per cent in the Oldham district. They employed expert negotiators to cope with the complex mathematical calculations of the piece-rate wage lists which were being agreed with growing numbers of employers across widening areas of the county. They levied high subscriptions: a basic rate of 1s 2d per week in the 1880s, which was matched only by the Amalgamated Society of Engineers, and which was considerably augmented by local and factory dues. In exchange, they offered 'luxurious' benefits, including payments for lock-out, breakdown, victimisation, emigration and leaving the industry, as well as strike pay. This drives home the extent to which the spinners' unions were 'closed' and élitist; and their treatment of their assistants reinforces this point. The piecers were ignored, as a body, by the spinners except when they began to organise on their own account, when the threat – for such it was – was defused by threats or blandishments, with growing numbers of piecers being admitted to associate membership of the spinners' unions, but without real power or enhanced status. The piecers bore the brunt of the increased productivity by which the spinners augmented their earnings and bought the goodwill of their employers in late Victorian and Edwardian times, but they were not allowed to share in the increased incomes. The spinners' privileged position was maintained at the expense, in part, of the piecers.[79]

As the spinners' organisation became more sophisticated, so their employers began to federate, despite internecine jealousies of their own; and an industry-wide system of collective bargaining began to emerge, despite the widely differing economic circumstances and industrial organisational arrangements which came to prevail, in the fiercely competitive Oldham coarse-spinning trade at one extreme, with its abrasively managed limited companies, and the family-run, prosperous fine-spinning Bolton firms at the other. Spinning remained a strike-prone occupation, but the growing power of the full-time officials was used to discourage the continuance and spread of disputes, and, as White argues, to further 'the routinization of conflict', confining it to 'technical rather than ideological issues' and seeking 'accommodation with the other side as opposed to one-sided victory'.[80] These trends culminated in the Brooklands Agreement of 1893, which settled a six-month lock-out in south-east Lancashire by elaborate compromise while establishing a complex system of formal conciliation procedures, and limiting annual wage adjustments to a maximum of 5 per cent each way. Brooklands remained in force until 1913, and succeeded in preventing the escalation of the endemic local disputes over pay and conditions into industry-wide confrontations. Its wage provisions probably benefited the employers rather than the workforce, but by stabilising industrial relations it helped to perpetuate the existing manning practices and patterns of workplace authority, in which the spinners had an entrenched vested interest.[81]

The spinners were a small fraction of the workforce on their side of the industry, and they showed little interest in organising the numerous card- and blowing-room workers or the other employees in the preparatory processes. The card-room workers were beginning to organise separately on their own account in the late 1850s, but they did not make substantial headway until the mid-1880s. Sustained organisation began in the strife-torn limited companies of Oldham, and was spearheaded by the strippers and grinders, who looked after the servicing of the carding machines. These men succeeded in enhancing the status and wages of their occupation systematically over the next generation, in pursuit of the élite status of the spinners. They dominated the leadership and policies of the Card-room Amalgamation which was formed in 1886, and the large number of women, including many ring-spinners, who came under the Cardroom umbrella at the turn of the century had no real voice in the union's councils despite forming the vast majority of its membership. Here again, conciliation and the localisation of conflict increasingly prevailed.[82]

The weavers' unions likewise came to be numerically dominated by women and administratively led by men. The power-loom weavers' societies which proliferated during the 1850s spawned a partial amalgamation in 1858, centred in north-east Lancashire; but there was no county-wide federation until 1884, when the 'Second Amalgamation' was founded at a delegates' conference, and gradually superseded its more localised precursor. Membership grew rapidly in the late nineteenth century, as the Second Amalgamation rose from 34,000 members in 1889 to 84,000 in 1895, though this was still less than half of Lancashire's weaving population. Further Edwardian gains brought the total to more than 137,000 in 1911, by which time the union was pushing for a closed shop in some of its north-east Lancashire strongholds, and by the eve of the First World War nearly 200,000 weavers were in the Amalgamation. Like the Card-room Amalgamation, the Weavers charged low subscriptions: about 1 ½ d per week in the 1880s, although at Nelson in the nineties most paid a penny per loom. Some insurance benefits were paid out of this, but the main concern was to build up a contingency fund to sustain strikes when necessary, for the Weavers' main concern was the protection and enhancement of wages, and the general adoption of standard piece-rate wage lists so as to prevent undercutting and unfair competition between areas and firms. As an 'open' union, with little differentiation between members' incomes and no privileged position to protect, the Weavers lacked the Spinners' concern to maintain authority and differentials. Like the Spinners, however, they put their trust increasingly in expert paid officials, especially from the 1870s onwards, and the officials concentrated their energies on defusing and containing endemic local conflicts. Whereas the Spinners complained persistently about their employers' attempts to enhance their competitiveness by cost-cutting in the quality of raw materials, causing frequent loss of production through yarn breakages, the Weavers objected to 'driving', whereby overlookers who were paid on a commission basis put undue pressure on weavers to maximise output, and 'steaming', the creation of artificially humid and unhealthy conditions to facilitate the production of low-grade, adulterated cloth. Disputes over wages and conditions reached a peak in the 1880s, in weaving as in spinning, but local battles over particular issues remained a permanent feature of the industry, in spite of a long respite from major confrontations which lasted from the early 1890s to the years immediately preceding the First World War.[83]

These were not the only unions in the cotton industry: its complex processes led to the emergence and survival of many small organisations which looked after the interests of people with particular skills, in the weaving and finishing processes especially. But they were absolutely dominant numerically and (usually) strategically, and their late Victorian and Edwardian development reveals an interesting and significant common trend towards the employment of skilled officials, the minimisation and containment of conflict and the acceptance of wage cuts in the short term in order to protect the status quo. Despite their varying membership patterns, the cotton unions had come to accept the employers' version of how the economy worked, and to operate within the system in a sophisticated way, participating in a collective bargaining system which aroused the amazed admiration of the Webbs and other contemporary observers. This required the co-operation of the employers, of course, and this was made easier

when unions could be seen to deliver the goods, and when the employers themselves began to federate in earnest, not always with altruistic motives, in the
1890s. Who gained and who lost by these strategies is open to debate; but what
is remarkable is the broad similarity of approach between the various unions.
The Spinners, after all, were jealous, suspicious aristocrats of labour, while the
Weavers have some claim to be described as the first of the 'New Unions' of the
unskilled, with their distinctive problems and strategies, which proliferated after
1889. They had little contact with each other until Edwardian times. Under the
circumstances, the extent to which their leaders shared values and expectations,
and the rank and file accepted their policies, reveals a great deal about the extent
to which the cotton workers came to accept and internalise the political economy
of their employers in the decades after 1850 and especially after 1870.[84]

The cotton unions do not fit cosily into the national generalisations about
mid and late Victorian trade unionism which feature in most textbooks. The
complexity of the coal miners' experience also inhibits ready generalisations, and
the Lancashire miners were more idiosyncratic than most. Above all, they shared
the persistent localism of the cotton unions; but whereas the latter turned this
into a strength, it weakened the miners' organisations systematically until almost
the end of the century. The basic unit of organisation was the district union,
whose lodges were based on pubs rather than pits, and whose boundaries were
hazy: indeed, they competed furiously with each other for members. Miners at
a particular pit might be divided among several lodges, making it impossible
to produce a coherent, controlled response to the most local matter of dispute;
and the lack of central control even within the districts meant that many miners
slipped through the net of union membership. Beyond the local level, delegate
meetings lacked accountability and credibility, and it was easier for the districts
to affiliate to national unions than to form an effective federation at the level of
the coalfield. Membership levels fluctuated according to the state of trade and
the current credibility of unions and their leaders; but most of the time the unions
were dominated by a 'labour aristocracy' of hewers, coalface workers on piecework wages, with transport workers and other daywagemen forming a despised
minority. The unions recruited best in the Wigan area, but encountered particular difficulty in north-east Lancashire, where a mixture of very small pits
and intransigent substantial coalowners provided inhospitable territory. Leading
employers such as Andrew Knowles and Son refused to recognise trade unions
until the 1890s, and responded to union infiltration of their labour force by
sackings, evictions, lock-outs and the importation of blacklegs from Staffordshire
and as far away as Cornwall. All this was made easier by the wide variations
in wages and employment patterns in the different mining areas of Britain, and
indeed within Lancashire itself: in April 1873, on Challinor's calculations,
'average daily pay' ranged from 6s 9d in the Wigan and St. Helens coalfield to
4s 0d in Burnley. It was all too easy, additionally, for Lancashire to be supplied
with coal by rail from other coalfields, especially when a dispute took place on

the downswing of the trade cycle when surplus stocks were readily available. All these factors made effective organisation all the more difficult, while increasing the need for it. For many years federations of the local unions were short-lived and strife-torn, as cautious leaders trying to husband modest resources were regularly overwhelmed by angry militants, and strikes were called under unpropitious conditions only to be defeated with ignominy, confusion and recrimination. The long, violent strike in the bitterly cold January and February of 1881 exemplified all these themes, and when it ended with no clear-cut overall result a new attempt at a county-wide federation was made. This time it held together through the ensuing depression, and when trade picked up at the end of the eighties it was able to win impressive wage increases. This success in turn encouraged successful negotiations for a wider organisation to challenge the timid leadership of the existing Miners' National Union, and the resultant Miners' Federation of Great Britain was able to resist a new attempt at wage cuts in the 1893 lock-out. But the Lancashire miners were only kept afloat through the dispute by enormous donations from other coalfields, and the Lancashire Federation's weaknesses were still manifest even in the moment of victory. It was not until 1897, when a new centralised structure removed the autonomy of the district unions within the county, that the Lancashire miners were able to deploy the full potential of their industrial muscle, and a drive to extend recruitment among the daywagemen began at once.[85]

For most of the nineteenth century, and in important respects beyond it, the Lancashire miners, like the cotton workers, were divided geographically, politically and hierarchically; and these divisions had to be transcended if any semblance of working-class political unity was to be established. The great national unions in building and engineering had a much less distinctive pattern of development in Lancashire, although their nominally centralised organisations always had to take account of local peculiarities and concerns. They were, of course, particularly anxious to protect the sectional interests of skilled and supervisory workers against dilution from piecework, the spread of new technology and unapprenticed labour; and these preoccupations, which were similar to those of the Spinners, also limited the scope for wider labour solidarity. Even among the 'New Unions' of the dockers and transport workers on the Liverpool waterfront, however, divisions based on employment, sectarianism, ethnicity and location all conspired both to inhibit organisation and then to reduce its wider impact.

Liverpool's dockers and seamen were no strangers to trade union activity long before the famous London dock strike of 1889. Strikes occurred in 1853 and 1866, with some success in the latter year, and some sections of the labour force, especially the coalheavers, had long been organised. The problem was to build a lasting organisation to protect the interests of dockers in general; and the circumstances of economic change on the Liverpool waterfront made this both pressing and difficult. The vast majority of dockers, in Liverpool as elsewhere, were casual workers. This did not mean that the work was unskilled: it was open to all-comers, but experienced men were much more efficient and less dangerous to themselves and others. Daily wage-rates, moreover, were relatively high, and this attracted a steady flow of migrants to the port; but in practice, chronic underemployment prevailed, exacerbated by this swelling of the surplus labour pool, and men were lucky if they averaged three days' work a week. The dock labour force doubled in numbers between 1861 and 1890, and this ready labour supply enabled the employers to neglect the opportunities to mechanise cargo handling which were being embraced in rival ports. The employment structure was changing in these years, as the shift to steam operation brought the concentration of capital into fewer hands, and limited companies displaced family firms. This trend was especially marked at the north end of the long waterfront, where the transition to steam came first and most fully. But the system of employment was itself extremely complicated. The work was divided basically into stevedorage, involving loading ships and stowing cargoes, and porterage, which involved unloading, sorting and packing imports on the quayside. Taplin tells us that employers were of four kinds: 'master stevedores and master porters who either belonged to a firm of shipowners or worked under contract; shipowners responsible for their own stevedoring and porterage; merchants who undertook their own porterage; and [much less important] the Mersey Docks and Harbour Board' as direct employer. So there was, in effect, a lot of subcontracting, and there were many stands at which dockers could offer themselves for hire. This made for division in the labour force, which was exacerbated by the existence of a multitude of specialisms in different cargo types and handling techniques, and by the great divide between the regular hands who were known to the employers and their representatives, and who could expect a reasonable share of what work there was, and the true casuals. Moreover, certain occupations were the preserve of particular religious or ethnic groups, and the better-organised workers at the south end were predominantly Protestant, while the north end was dominated by Catholics. The sectarian atmosphere of working-class Liverpool, indeed, was a particularly daunting barrier to organisation beyond the most local and specific of occupational groups within the astonishingly complex economy of dockland.[86]

Apart from a small minority of the regularly employed, who had adequate and predictable wages, Liverpool's dockers suffered from irregularity of work and income, which encouraged heavy drinking while waiting for the chance of work, while making systematic thrift almost impossible, and making union subscriptions harder to collect. Wage-rates were consistently higher than in most other ports, London included; but working conditions were deteriorating in the later nineteenth century, and there were long periods of trade depression and sustained severe poverty. The port's numerous merchant seamen were in a similar situation. This helps to account for the regular outbreaks of labour unrest in the 1870s and 1880s, which culminated in the establishment of the waterfront unions. The boom of 1872 – 3 saw a series of agitations for wage increases, which achieved some success despite the absence of co-ordination and the lack of permanent organisations in most sectors; and in 1879 – 80 three trade unions emerged as dockers and seamen struck against wage cuts, with some eventual success in the former case after arbitration in which the Earl of Derby acted as referee. The new unions failed to survive the ensuing depression, however, and it was not until 1889 that a lasting trade union structure was established across the waterfront as a whole. Successive strikes by seamen and dockers, welling up from the rank and file in pursuit of wage demands, were orchestrated by unions which had been formed in Sunderland and Glasgow, and had only recently secured a foothold in the port. The unions, indeed, sought conciliation rather than conflict, aware of their limited funds and difficult bargaining position. Concessions were made on wages, but to ensure a settlement of lasting value, the unions sought the introduction of a closed shop which would enable them to regulate the supply of labour and end the insecurity of the casual labour market. Here, the employers dug in their heels. They imported blackleg labour and starved the strikers back to work. But the unions survived, though their membership levels were much depleted during the 1890s, and it was to be twenty years before the next major strike took place, and the casual labour problem remained intractable for a much longer period. However, from 1889 onwards the Liverpool waterfront workers were organising behind their own leaders, and forcing their employers to take notice of their demands.[87]

The years around 1889 also saw the emergence of similar trade unions of the 'unskilled' elsewhere in Lancashire, most notably in the Merseyside glass and chemical industries.[88] Liverpool itself, indeed, saw a spate of activity of this kind, alongside the dockers' and seamen's initiatives. It is no coincidence that the emergence of organised labour as a political force dates from these years, although we must not over-simplify the connections. The dockers and seamen, after all, were at loggerheads in 1890 after the latter had helped to break the former's strike, and Waller suggests that the dockers' union had become too firmly attached to the Irish Catholics and therefore to the Irish Nationalists to become the focus for wider activity. Moreover, socialism as such had not been a force in the Liverpool strikes, however important it may have been as a formative influence on similar developments elsewhere. In the cotton district, too, and even more so further north, the existing moulds of Lancashire politics were to prove their resilience in the face of new working-class political initiatives. But such there were; and we need to analyse their emergence and development.[89]

In the early summer of 1867 Lancashire trade unions massed behind the banners of parliamentary reform. The Manchester demonstration of the Reform League and Reform Union, for example, attracted a long roll-call of unions, including the cotton spinners and several engineering trades as well as building workers and a variety of skilled craftsmen.[90] However, fear of the possible divisive consequences of involvement in party political terms was sufficient to deter the Trades Council from participating as a body; and as we have suggested, these attitudes remained predominant for many years, especially among the older-established craft and supervisory unions. But the potential scope of trade unions as a focus of resistance to the dominant political cultures of the employers and their allies remained immense. It was they who defended the interests of their working-class members in what was recognised to be a relationship based on endemic conflict, usually latent but sometimes overt and even violent, over the distribution of the product of industry. This might be disguised by conciliation machinery, by 'official' discouragement of local strikes and other forms of rank-and-file 'indiscipline', and by the employers' use of the unions (as in Preston in the early 1890s) to enforce fair competition by threatening strike action at particular mills to equalise wage-rates and working agreements. It might even coexist with a sense of interdependence between employer and employee, and an acceptance of wage cuts in time of depression out of fear of competition in foreign markets and an admission of the employer's right to a conventionally acceptable rate of profit. Beyond this acceptable level, however, wage cuts were fiercely opposed; and workplace relationships between master and employee remained potential, and sometimes actual, bases for class conflict at the point of production. The problem for the socialists who were beginning to appear in the 1880s was to bring the nature of the relationship into the open, and to extend a generalised consciousness of systematically conflicting interests from the workplace into the wider political arena.[91]

The range and strength of trade union influence increased enormously throughout industrial Lancashire at and after the turn of the century. The Spinners sustained their strength; the Weavers' growing confidence was reflected in membership figures which rose from 50 per cent of their labour force in 1880 to nearly 90 per cent by 1914 in Blackburn, and from 30 per cent to over 90 per cent in Burnley.[92] In 1910, admittedly, only 44 per cent of the cotton workers were in unions, but this was due to the later and slower spread of organisation to the card-room workers, and even this industry-wide figure was exceeded nationally only by miners and shipbuilding workers.[93] Moreover, the overlookers and other supervisory workers moved over during this period to identification with the interests of fellow workers rather than bosses, reducing the impact of an important source of division and potential strike-breaking at the workplace.[94] Miners' union membership increased from 6000 (at most) in 1881 to perhaps 40,000, about two-fifths of the workforce, in 1900; in 1910 it stood at between 50,000 and 60,000, after briefly topping 70,000 in 1907–8.[95] The position in Liverpool was more complicated, but clear advances were being made. Already in 1891 the Trades Council, recently reinforced by the affiliation of the National Union of Dock Labourers alongside its core of artisan unions, was the largest outside London, representing 47 trades and 46,168 individual members. Subsequent progress on the waterfront, and among porters, carters and transport workers, was chequered but cumulatively significant. It culminated in the great transport strike of 1911, when union membership briefly flared from 24,500 (itself an impressive figure, in context) to 91,000. This was evanescent, but the dockers' and seamen's unions were forces to be reckoned with in the longer term as well.[96] But the other 'new unions' of the 'unskilled', such as the gasworkers and tramwaymen, were much less well organised in Liverpool; and the clerks, too, were weak in numbers and retiring in policy, despite a small socialist presence in their ranks.[97] The situation in Manchester was not dissimilar, although the newer unions had deeper roots and the clerks were more active. Everywhere, the engineers were strong and active, despite their defeat in the lock-out of 1897–8 and the problematic relationship between the apprenticed men and the rest; and even outside the cotton district, the trade union movement was growing rapidly in numbers and influence in Edwardian times. Only in the smaller and more isolated towns, without skilled labour forces affiliated to national unions, and with autocratic employers persisting in a patriarchal role, was expansion held back. Lancaster and some of the smaller Rossendale towns are cases in point, and the contrast between the cowed, divided and deferential Lancaster labour movement and the increasingly confident militancy of the engineers and shipyard workers of Barrow is particularly telling in this context.[98] Even the agricultural workers were beginning to stir in south-west Lancashire on the eve of the First World War, with help from Liverpool and from the railwaymen; and their new-found militancy in this area of advanced agrarian capitalism was expressed in a lengthy and angry strike in 1913.[99]

The growing strength and self-confidence of trade unionsm in Lancashire from the 1880s onwards soon began to make an impact on parliamentary and municipal politics, as recognisably working-class political movements began to cohere. There were three main strands to this development, which were sometimes interrelated in a positive way and sometimes locked in internecine conflict. These were the Social Democratic Federation, the Independent Labour Party and the trade union campaign for labour representation. The first two strands were strongly influenced by various socialist doctrines, but the third treated socialism with suspicion and reserve.

The SDF began life in the mid-1880s as an overtly Marxist organisation, aiming at the rousing of the unemployed and looking to a revolutionary transformation of English society. Many of its members subsequently retreated from this posture, becoming actively involved in the established trade union movement and in the pursuit of labour representation. By the mid-1890s the SDF was stronger in Lancashire than anywhere else outside London, with perhaps one-third of the national membership. Its adherents were concentrated in the cotton district, with particular strongholds in Salford and Burnley, where the movement's leader, the idiosyncratic businessman H. M. Hyndman, came very close to winning the parliamentary seat in 1906. Burnley was unique, and the SDF's special position there owed much to the town's late development and lack of paternalist employers and established labour institutions, and to the personal involvement of Hyndman himself. In its early years the SDF specialised in demonstrations, direct action and the formation of new unions of the 'unskilled', and it never lost this distinctive physiognomy; but in practice its branches showed a growing willingness to act alongside the ILP and other organisations of the left in pursuit of limited and short-term goals. Criticisms of the SDF's sectarianism and dogmatism seem ill-founded in Lancashire, where it became very much a part of the wider labour movement.[100]

The ILP was a more widely diffused and more numerously supported body. It was founded nationally in 1893, but its emergence had been anticipated in Manchester, where it was involved in the 'cascade' of new unions which appeared at about this time, embracing a remarkable spectrum of occupations from navvies to hairdressers. At the inaugural conference, indeed, 32 of the 120 delegates came from Lancashire and Cheshire. Some of the nearby branches owed their origins to Manchester missionary work, and at the time Manchester had pretensions to rival Bradford as the true begetter of the new party. From the beginning, the ILP in Lancashire had distinctive characteristics of its own, and was perhaps a broader 'church' than in other areas. It recruited not only from serious-minded Nonconformity and ethical, evolutionary socialism, but also from SDF pioneers of decidedly secular bent. One of the Manchester founding fathers, too, was Robert Blatchford, whose ill-defined but lively socialist rhetoric was combined with an aggressive, militaristic patriotism and a relish for the good things of life which contrasted sharply with the Temperance wing of the new party. Blatchford soon severed his official connections with the ILP, but his *Clarion* newspaper and its associated cycling clubs provided a further umbrella under which many Lancashire socialists found shelter and friendship. The socialism of the ILP meant many things to many people, and this was both advantage and problem. Above all, as Ainsworth remarks, ILP socialism in Lancashire recoiled from the idea of class struggle, and stressed instead the inevitable evolution of socialism as the product of progress towards human brotherhood. Hence attempts to invade the suburbs and evangelise the rich did not seem incongruous; and ILP activists became immersed in practical, immediate reforms which would assist the advancement of their anticipated millennium.[101]

The SDF and ILP seldom achieved much electoral success on their own. Socialism, as such, remained a minority creed, the butt of hecklers on Blackpool beach and in the market place. The attachments of the old 'cultural' politics, the divisions within the working class on religious, ethnic, occupational and workplace lines, were too deeply engrained, and the identification of the existing state of things with 'common sense' was too firmly established, to allow a mass following for even the ILP's eclectic socialisms. Indeed, socialist branches themselves took on some of the trappings of other voluntary organisations in the society around them, weaving a cocoon of collective and comradely activities which looked inwards and became ends in themselves. To achieve a wider electoral influence, and to stand a chance of undermining the bipartisan division of Lancashire society, they had to appeal to the narrower solidarities of trade unionism, and to seek to build outwards from an uneasy alliance with those who sought the representation of interest-groups within the working class, and the defence of trade union interests within the existing system, rather than the remaking of society. Some trade unionists were also socialists, of course; but most were not. The evolution of the Labour Party in the early twentieth century, in Lancashire as elsewhere, bore witness to that enduring truth.

The Lancashire miners led the pursuit of labour representation in Parliament, following precedents which had been set elsewhere since 1874. Their members were too dispersed to dominate any constituency, but they were very numerous among the electorate in Wigan and nearby Ince, and they had a particular interest in the mass of mining legislation, actual and possible, which affected such issues as safety, working hours and employers' liability in what had become a notoriously dangerous coalfield. In 1892 two miners' leaders stood at Ince and Wigan, which had effectively been pocket boroughs of the Wigan Coal and Iron Company, and at Ince Sam Woods defeated the sitting Conservative to become Lancashire's first working-class MP. But uproar ensued. The contests had been based on an electoral deal with the Liberals, and Woods's own Liberal sympathies were well known. Disaffected Tories among the miners complained bitterly, and some seceded to form the Conservative Labour Union, the so-called 'blue button union'. At the other end of the spectrum, socialists – and there was a significant leavening of SDF members among the miners – were equally disenchanted by Woods's unwillingness to back key labour issues such as the Eight Hour Day. Thomas Ashton, the miners' Tory secretary, defended Woods as a labour representative first and foremost; but many were unconvinced. This was the first of many such arguments.[102]

Woods failed to retain Ince in 1895; but the Lancashire Miners' Federation was not deterred for long, as it gained strength at the end of the century. Alone among the miners' unions nationally, it showed strong interest in the national Labour Representation Committee from the very beginning, and in 1903 it became affiliated, five years before the national union followed suit. In 1906 the miners' candidates were elected as Labour MPs at Ince and St. Helens, gaining from the electoral pact between the LRC and the Liberals but fighting as Labour candidates pure and simple. Despite a persisting strong Tory presence among the rank and file, which owed much to Orange influence, the miners became enthusiastic supporters not only of labour representation, but also of nationalisation of the mines, although for most of them the attractions of socialism extended no further.[103] In the cotton industry, there were similar obstacles to overcome. Here again, labour representatives needed somehow to be detached from established party politics without offending the partisans; and despite the importance of parliamentary regulation of the industry, this was not easy. A ballot of the major cotton unions in 1894 resulted indecisively, with a very small majority in support; and again, the cotton unions did not affiliate to the LRC at its inception. They waited until 1902, when it had become clear that the Taff Vale judgement would threaten the finances of cotton unions as well as railwaymen, and that a parliamentary presence would help to reverse it. But the first MP to emerge, David Shackleton of the Weavers at Clitheroe, was emphatically a Liberal sailing under Labour colours, and the cotton unions were no more eager than the miners to run overtly socialist candidates. Socialist commitments might be written into union constitutions from time to time, but they were soon expunged; and even in Burnley, where the SDF was particularly strong, the socialist weavers seceded from the main union for several years after a backlash against their policies.[104]

Labour candidates made headway in parliamentary elections in 1906, when on Howell's calculation 'almost half of the successful LRC candidates' nationally came from 'Lancastria'. There were thirteen in all: but it is highly significant that no Labour candidate succeeded before 1914 without explicit trade union backing, that in 1906 only two MPs were sponsored by the ILP and none by the SDF, and that all of the Labour victors were given a clear run by the Liberals, who usually ran a candidate of their own in harness with Labour under the banner of the 'Progressive Alliance'. Where socialists joined forces without trade union backing, as at Rochdale, they did well to poll twenty per cent of the vote in a three-cornered contest. This was not to be sniffed at; but it showed the limits of a purely socialist appeal. Between 1906 and the First World War, too, Labour was struggling to hold its ground as a separate political force, as its electoral fortunes became more closely entangled with the Liberal Party, which in turn did much to estrange the socialists. The ILP had tapped the funds and influence of the trade union movement, but at the cost of losing its distinctive ideological and electoral identity, while the SDF and its successor bodies went their own way into the political wilderness.[105]

At the time, of course, the more salient feature of the 1906 election was the demolition of Lancashire's Conservative majority as the Liberals swept to a landslide victory, with a political agenda dominated by Free Trade, education and the Irish question rather than labour issues. P. F. Clarke has argued that this transformation of the parliamentary electoral map marked a transition to the politics of class, from which the Liberals rather than Labour were the beneficiaries, and that but for the war the Liberal reformers would have retained the loyalty of the working-class vote and continued to dominate, engrossing and subsuming what he calls the 'most powerful of all the sectional groups', organised labour.[106]

There is much to be said for the suggestion that the political ground-rules were being transformed in Edwardian Lancashire; but Clarke's view of the implications and consequences has been hotly challenged. The old 'cultural' politics were indeed in decline. Employer influences were waning, as local plutocrats retreated to suburbs and seaside resorts, the Lake District and the shires, and family firms gave way to limited companies. The sectarian spirit and the Nonconformist conscience were also losing their electoral magic, except in Liverpool, which significantly continued to offer no political comfort to either Labour or the Liberals. Carpet-bagging imports replaced local candidates, as national political issues overrode established local loyalties. These were gradual, patchy and cumulative changes, and the sudden Liberal landslide in 1906 was misleading in this context, depending very heavily on the Free Trade issue, which was especially emotive in a Lancashire which saw the threatened shibboleth as the cornerstone of its prosperity. But should we see the Liberals as the lasting beneficiaries of these changes? Critics of Clarke point to the continuing tensions in the relationship between the Liberals and Labour at constituency level, except in those mining constituencies where the Liberal party machine was already moribund. They point to the unease of propertied Liberals when faced with trade union issues and working-class candidates, and to the growing pressure on Labour to challenge sitting Liberals after 1910. In the short run, this merely split the anti-Tory vote; in the longer term, its consequences might have been more profound. There was impressive overlap between the Liberal and Labour votes where candidates ran in harness in 1910 (much less so in 1906); but this may have been a passing phase rather than a permanent realignment. J. L. White points out that in a special poll in 1913 clear majorities of those who voted in all three main cotton unions declared in favour of using trade union funds for political purposes; and he argues quite convincingly that 'the workers who voted yes must be considered hard-core Labourites'. Freed from the distractions of parliamentary election campaigns, where loyalties were confused by the adoption of issues which cut across class lines, the level of support for Labour (but not necessarily socialism) in this long-resistant cluster of unions appears to have been strong and growing on the eve of the war.[107]

This general comment masks considerable local variations. White notes, for instance, that the Oldham spinners were out of step, showing strong opposition to the Labour levy. Oldham had a tradition of abrasive labour relations, but this was combined with widespread working-class investment in local companies, and the unusually close (and paradoxical) relationship between labour, capital and property ownership in this peculiar town may well have affected attitudes to the Labour Party.[108] It is probably significant that Oldham failed to elect a single Labour or socialist member to its municipal council chamber until 1910, and he remained a lone voice in 1914.[109] Elsewhere, the municipal record of Labour was chequered. At the opposite extreme to Oldham stood Nelson, where the local Weavers' Association was prominent in the emergence of Lancashire's first Labour-controlled local authority in 1905, and St. Helens, which soon emulated this success.[110] At Barrow, in yet another different industrial setting, Labour took effective control of the Poor Law Guardians as early as 1904, although this was not a sustained victory and town council successes came more slowly.[111] A more usual pattern in the industrial towns of Edwardian

Lancashire saw a small minority of Labour members on most local authorities, but consistently outvoted when it mattered by Liberals, Tories or both in unison. This was the case in Blackburn (where a peak of 12 representatives, evenly split between SDF, ILP and Trades Council, was reached in 1905), Burnley (where the SDF never had more than 2 local councillors out of 48), Bolton and, less surprisingly, Lancaster.[112] Radical Liberals long retained a strong presence on local Trades Councils, and labour representatives often had difficulty in formulating distinctive municipal programmes, although they were always conspicuous advocates of mild workhouse régimes and special schemes for the unemployed when they stood for the Guardians. The cotton unions often favoured distinctive policies of another kind in School Board elections, as they defended the notorious 'half-time' system and resolutely opposed all attempts to raise the minimum school-leaving age. But the forward march of Labour was ragged and halting in all but a few of the larger Lancashire towns, and in Manchester and Liverpool working-class representation also made slow progress. Manchester's Labour Party, which kept unusually strong socialist influences, was able to build on the pioneering work of the ILP in the 1890s, and by 1910 the city had 15 Labour councillors: an impressive presence, but a long way short of control. In sectarian Liverpool, faced with accusations that Labour meant Socialism meant Atheism, Labour started later and made slower headway. Two councillors, including James Sexton the dockers' leader, were elected in 1905, and a wave of Labour victories followed the brutal repression of the local transport strike in 1911, when 7 councillors were elected. But they joined 81 Tories, 34 Liberals, 14 Irish Nationalists and a Protestant, and they were condemned to 'make a noise, [but] not the millennium'.[113]

This was an interim judgement rather than an epitaph. Some headway was being made everywhere: even Blackpool acquired its first socialist local councillor in 1906.[114] Voting percentages and elected representatives are imperfect guides to Labour's progress and independence, too. The political agenda was defined in terms of the concerns of the two established parties, and the first results of Labour intervention in local elections, where there was seldom any electoral compact with the Liberals, was to split the anti-Tory vote. Where Labour became stronger, on the other hand, its opponents often developed electoral compacts of their own to keep the 'socialists' out. The bitter struggles in local elections provide a better guide to the future relationship between Labour and the Liberals than the uneasy alliance at parliamentary level; and even in 1910, endorsement of Labour candidates by the Liberals was not always reciprocated. There was ample scope for future conflict, and for the continuing rise of Labour as a separate political force. The transition to class politics, after all, was far from complete, as was indicated by the persisting and renewed discrepancy between angry industrial conflict and traditional voting behaviour. The cotton and engineering unions, among others, participated to the full in the so-called 'great unrest' of 1910–13, and the Liverpool general transport strike of 1911 frightened the authorities into importing battleships as well as troops and additional police.[115] But the Liverpool strike, despite its syndicalist pretensions, did not transcend the established political and sectarian divisions within Liverpool's working class completely, or for long, while plenty of cotton workers continued to vote for employers and their mouthpieces in spite of their industrial grievances. In the light of this evidence, Clarke's analysis is open to question on both counts: the transition to class politics had a long way to go in the Lancashire of 1914, and the Liberals may well have been only the short-term beneficiaries of the important changes which had already taken place. The intervention of the war, of course, puts really confident conclusions out of reach. What is clear is that, even in its north-east Lancashire weaving strongholds of Burnley, Nelson and Colne, socialism remained the often ill-defined creed of a small if eager minority, although it was cheerfully brandished as a bugbear by Labour's opponents throughout these years, even against candidates who repudiated the label with indignation.

The north-east Lancashire weaving district had another claim to fame in Edwardian times. It became the heartland of the working-class women's suffrage campaign whose remarkable history has only recently been rescued from obscurity by Jill Liddington and Jill Norris, and whose development reveals a great deal about the distinctive nature of trade unionism, society and politics in the cotton district.[116]

We shall see that the weaving districts of north and north-east Lancashire were the main national centres of women's factory work. The cotton unions as a whole accounted for five-sixths of all organised women workers in Britain in 1896, and women predominated numerically both in the weavers' and (especially) the card-room amalgamations by this time. Admittedly, these high membership levels were seldom translated into activism. White finds a handful of women on weavers' branch committees in towns from Preston to Glossop in 1914, but considers that most branches had all-male executives, while women were completely excluded from office among the card-room workers. Liddington and Norris find a little more evidence of female participation, including the Wigan branch which was 'virtually run by women', though this was largely due to the paucity of male weavers in the town. In Salford, a separate women's union of power-loom weavers was founded in 1902, and survived attempts by the Weavers' Amalgamation to assimilate it after bitter arguments on both sides. There was also a Manchester and Salford Women's Trade Union Council, founded in 1895 under Liberal and Trades Council auspices, which organised a small minority of the towns' female workforce in a heterogeneous variety of trades. But most women's trade union activity was passive rather than active, despite the occasional appearances of female Lancastrians as delegates to the TUC in the early twentieth century. Nevertheless, the unusually high level of working-class women's paid employment, the scope that employment gave for the exchange of ideas (especially among winders, but also among weavers, and less so in the card-room), and the widespread experience of organisation, made parts of the cotton district particularly fertile ground for women's suffrage campaigners.[117]

The initiative came from Manchester, where the flagging Suffrage Society, which had been founded in 1867 and remained very much a middle-class organisation, was revitalised in 1893 under the secretaryship of Esther Roper, a graduate of Manchester University and an enthusiast for a variety of women's causes. She set out to attract the support of working-class women, especially in the cotton towns, and she recruited organisers and propagandists from their own ranks. From these beginnings a lasting campaign resulted, gaining devoted support from women whose aspirations were already being stimulated by the Women's Co-operative Guild and its popular discussion groups, by the labour movement (especially the ILP, which was sometimes ambivalent on the suffrage issue but admitted women as members on equal terms), by Blatchford's *Clarion* (despite the editor's traditionalist views), and even by University Extension classes and other forms of adult education. The peak of the working-class suffrage movement's visibility came in March 1901, when a deputation of fifteen Lancashire cotton workers travelled to Westminster to present a petition signed by nearly 30,000 women from the industry. The campaign continued thereafter, as persistent and eventually successful efforts were made to gain and retain the support of the ILP, the Labour Party, the cotton unions and the labour movement in general for an immediate and attainable measure of women's suffrage. Increasingly, however, this work was obscured and compromised by the antics of the Pankhursts and their Women's Social and Political Union. At its peak, however, the 'radical suffragist' movement commanded genuine mass support, despite the opposition of husbands and the divisions over tactics and principles within its ranks. Moreover, it produced activists like Selina Cooper whose commitment to women's suffrage coexisted with a wide range of other political activities, especially in local government, and led them into a more general concern for women's health and welfare and for child care. Even in Nelson and Colne, however, there were narrow limits to the effective impact of such campaigns, and it is difficult to assess the breadth and depth of the movement's real impact on the lives of working women, beyond the impressive cadres of local activists. For the vast majority of women, the signing of the petition was probably the full extent of their commitment; and the pervasive social expectations of marriage and family remained generally unruffled by the suffragists' endeavours. But the campaign revealed and strengthened a general pride in the contribution of women textile workers to the economy and, indeed, to the funds of trade unions and the Labour Party. By keeping their necessary sharp focus on the committed and their campaigns, Liddington and Norris may have incidentally given the impression that the suffragists attracted more general and sustained positive support than they actually did; but their efforts nevertheless make an important and revealing contribution to the social and political history of the cotton district.[118]

The unique political importance of Lancashire's working women was based on their equally distinctive contribution to the family economy of the working class in the cotton towns. The social implications of women's factory work were much debated at the time, and are still controversial now. They will be discussed at length in the next chapter, which assesses the evidence for improvement in working-class living standards between the Chartist period and the First World War, and compares the experience of working people in the cotton towns with the very different conditions which prevailed in other parts of the county.

13

WAYS OF LIFE AND STANDARDS OF
LIVING: THE LANCASHIRE WORKING
CLASS, 1850 – 1914

The previous chapter depicted a working class which was remarkably thoroughly assimilated into the economic and political systems of industrial Lancashire. This process was undoubtedly assisted by improvements in material living standards, and perhaps by optimistic perceptions of the opportunities for cultural self-improvement and upward social mobility. A great deal of evidence can indeed be marshalled in support of a steady (though not uninterrupted) upward trend in most aspects of living standards, especially (and perhaps paradoxically) after 1870. But this evidence will need careful assessment and qualification. It is more convincing for some parts of Lancashire than for others, and it does not preclude the persistence of a substratum of the chronically impoverished which was impervious to most of the benign influences of the period. Even in the cotton district, where working-class family incomes were often relatively high and the indicators of a trend to better times are most compelling, there are darker sides to the picture. The substantial family incomes which permitted the emergence of a working-class consumer society in the late Victorian and Edwardian cotton towns, except in time of strike, lock-out or severe depression, depended on contributions from married women and children which had potentially disturbing implications for the quality of family relationships, hygiene, health and comfort: implications which have exercised the minds of historians as well as contemporaries. At the very least, they help to explain the paradox whereby female factory workers were at once particularly receptive to the arguments of suffrage campaigners, while finding it particularly difficult to respond to them in a positive and sustained manner, given the burden of the twin responsibilities of domestic work and wage-labour. The problematic implications of women's factory work will recur in this chapter.

Our analysis must begin with wages, difficult though it is to allow for short time and unemployment, to translate piece-rates into incomes, to allow for multiple incomes within families and to work out the implications of changes and variations in spending patterns. In terms of broad, general, long-run trends, the years between the Chartists and the First World War can be subdivided into three fairly distinctive periods. A mid-Victorian span covers the years from mid-century to the end of the 1860s, and sees limited gains in real wages, punctuated by severe economic crises and accompanied by persisting low standards of health and hygiene. The strongest evidence for widespread improvement comes during the long fall in basic commodity prices which followed the money wages boom of the early 1870s, although the extent and implications of both cyclical unemployment and structural underemployment remain difficult to evaluate. However, these years saw significant improvements in housing and municipal amenities, and a falling incidence of disease and premature death, as well as the emergence of a mass consumer market which extended to sport, seaside holidays and entertainment. Soon after the turn of the century, however, a brake was put on these encouraging trends, as inflation reappeared and the rise in real wages was checked. It is certainly no coincidence that this Edwardian change in trend was accompanied by a renewed surge of conflict at the workplace, and it may also have played its part in the limited and patchy but genuine progress made by Lancashire's political labour movement in these years. Further examination of these trends will reveal important variations between occupational groups and between places and areas within Lancashire, and some reaped far more benefits than others from the late Victorian influences for improvement. These qualifications are borne out by what can be discerned of trends in real wages.

As we saw in Chapter 12, the widespread contemporary belief that living standards were rising in the cotton district is hard to substantiate until after the end of the 'Cotton Famine', although a marked improvement in real wages is apparent in the later 1860s. This was, no doubt, particularly clear-cut in the case of skilled and supervisory workers, and money wage increases of more than one-third were common to several occupations, with the strippers and grinders, who were improving their status as aristocrats of the card-room, doing especially well. Kirk suggests that the spinning towns fared better than the weaving centres, with their abundant supplies of cheap labour; and Bolton, with its specialisation in fine spinning and its extensive engineering works, stood at the top of the Lancashire wages league. But the cotton towns offered relatively high wages to most craft and labouring occupations, and Manchester itself was similarly a high-wage economy by contemporary standards. Even in Ancoats, there is evidence that poverty became less pressing between 1851 and 1871. Less use was being made of strategies for minimising or ameliorating poverty in the latter year: fewer families shared accommodation with kin, lodgers or landlords, and the proportion of working-class wives in paid employment while the children were young declined from nearly two-fifths to just over one-quarter.[1] The 'considerable improvement' in Preston school attendance over the same period, especially at very young ages and among the Irish, may reflect a similar reduction of stress.[2]

But this limited and sometimes inferential evidence must not obscure the persistence of an enormous abyss of poverty, insecurity and even abject want, especially in old age and when children were too young to work. Social surveys in the 1860s found at least 25 per cent of the inhabitants of working-class areas of Manchester and Salford to be in primary poverty; and though definitions might vary, and casual and sweated labour was particularly in evidence here, the specialised cotton towns were far from being exempt.[3] Whatever progress had been made, through painfully accumulated savings and improved furnishings, was set at naught even for many thrifty families by the disastrous impact of the 'Cotton Famine'. As the crisis deepened in late 1862 and early 1863, clothes and furniture were sold, savings were withdrawn, houses were given up and destitution beckoned before relief was sought. Expenditure on food was cut sharply, with an increasing concentration on bread and oatmeal and the near-abandonment of meat. Even potatoes became a luxury. Reduced diets (from levels which had previously been relatively lavish in working-class terms) and overcrowding (to reduce rent and heating costs) brought disease. Scurvy, typhus and dry inflammation of the eyes were all in evidence, as were a variety of other diseases which were encouraged by the conditions. Women were particularly vulnerable, and the most recent analyst of these desperate years believes that 'circumstantial evidence ... suggests that the population was affected by a nutritional famine', with 'nutritional deficiency diseases and lowered resistance to infectious disease'.[4] The 'Famine' strained new working-class self-help and mutual assistance organisations, especially the Co-op, almost to breaking point, although the rapidity of their recovery from the mid-1860s is remarkable testimony to better times.

The 'Cotton Famine' also brought added misery to the Liverpool waterfront. The cotton porters and lumpers were among the first to lose employment, with knock-on effects for others in the dock labour force. At the same time, great speculative fortunes were being made in the port's cotton exchange, although two banks and many merchants failed when the price of cotton collapsed at the end of the war.[5] But this was merely a passing exacerbation of the endemic poverty of the Liverpool working class. McCabe is pessimistic about their wages and purchasing power in mid-Victorian times. On his calculations, real wages for printers and engineers fluctuated around three-quarters and four-fifths of their 1850–1 levels for most of the 1850s and 1860s, with only a modest allowance for unemployment; and the fortunes of these labour aristocrats were probably less precarious than those of the predominant dockers, seamen and building workers. All suffered from the rising cost of food. It rose by 40 per cent between 1851 and 1854, and remained closer to the higher than to the lower level thereafter. McCabe doubts whether there was any rise in real wages on Merseyside before the 1870s; and this meant that widespread destitution remained the norm in the teeming courts which huddled around the docks, especially in the slumps of 1857 – 8 and 1866 – 7, as well as the more localised distress of the 'Cotton Famine' itself.[6]

Evidence on wage trends elsewhere in Lancashire is even less satisfactory. Experiences in the mid-Victorian boom towns seem to have varied. Skilled glassblowers at St. Helens, who vied with ironfounders and the cream of the engineers as the highest-paid industrial workers of the time, saw their wages fail to keep pace with inflation during the 1850s and 1860s, and Pilkingtons made all-round wage cuts in 1869 – 70 which provoked a long strike by the sheet glass blowers.[7] In Barrow, which was growing with astonishing speed during these decades, wages were comparatively high in ironworking and building, but they were said to be more than counterbalanced by the very high rents and over-crowding of these years, and by dear food in the local market.[8] Further complications are raised by the rising agricultural wages of these years, from what was already a favourable position in national terms. This trend was accompanied by a rapid transition from living-in farm service to 'outdoor' recipients of money wages in south-west Lancashire. This gave the labourer more independence but less security, and perhaps a lower standard of diet. It also encouraged the widening distinction between skilled 'teamsmen' who were hired on a regular basis, and 'datallers' whose employment was less regular. At peak periods in the agricultural year, recourse was had to casual labour of various kinds, especially women and (in summer) migrant Irishmen. At the other end of the county, farm service was much more resilient in Furness and Cartmel, where the growth of Barrow and the rise of haematite iron mining led to considerable wage increases between 1850 and 1870.[9] The perceived gaps in wages and opportunities between industry and agriculture, town and country were sufficient to ensure a steady flow of migration off the land, however; and this suggests that trends in non-agricultural wages may have been rather better overall than the very limited and one-dimensional direct evidence may suggest. Wages were not the only consideration, of course, and we shall look at other aspects of the migration equation, and at contrasts between differing urban and industrial environments, later in the chapter. Meanwhile, we should remember that throughout these years Lancashire as a whole was a relatively high-wage economy, in industry as well as agriculture: its money wages were consistently exceeded only by London, job for job. Nor was this advantage demonstrably vitiated by a higher cost of living: urban rents were sometimes high, but they were counterbalanced in most towns, most of the time, by relatively low food prices. Whatever we may conclude about trends in real wages during these years, the Lancashire experience stood favourable comparison with the rest of England and Wales, although it will be clear that such optimism looks much more convincing for the cotton district than for Liverpool.[10]

These patterns are etched more sharply if we take the earnings of women and children into account, and examine the family incomes which form a more realistic basis from which to assess living standards. According to the 1851 census, Lancashire's 'female activity rate', the proportion of women over 15 years old in paid employment, was exceeded only by Bedfordshire and Buckinghamshire. It stood at 47 per cent for the county as a whole; and in the cotton district itself the proportion must have been much higher. The corresponding figure for children between 10 and 15 years old was also well above average, at 39 per cent: only three counties clearly exceeded the Lancashire score.[11] These categories of work remained relatively very important in the following decades, although the balance tilted increasingly from children to women, and especially towards married women. Not only were women and children numerous among the wage-earners: they were also relatively well paid. This was especially true of the cotton industry, and above all of power-loom weaving, where women could theoretically earn as much as men on the piecework wage lists. In practice, this was rarely the case; but jobs in weaving paid at or near the top of the range of women's industrial wages throughout the second half of the nineteenth century, making up to some extent for the low level of the male weaver's wage compared with other male occupations. The mid-Victorian persistence of women's and children's seasonal earnings opportunities in agriculture will have been under-estimated by the census, and women's work at the pit top remained locally important in the Wigan area, although it was becoming controversial by the 1860s.[12] Liverpool and Manchester generated more characteristic and worse-paid work for women in the sweated clothing trades; and domestic service, although negligible as a full-time employer in the cotton towns, was in great demand in the growing suburbs of Lancashire's great commercial cities and in the emergent seaside resorts. In the cotton towns, part-time, non-resident servants, charwomen and the like, were much in evidence; and women's factory work itself generated a demand for laundry workers and child-minders as well as cleaners, spreading factory earnings more widely through the community, as working wives paid their neighbours to perform basic household chores.[13] The net effect, in the cotton towns at least, was to shorten the phase of the poverty cycle when children were too young to contribute to the family budget, to ameliorate (without extinguishing) the poverty engendered by inadequate adult male wages, and to permit a growing measure of consumer spending, thrift and insurance investment in good times. There were costs of other kinds to set against the material benefits of high family earning capacity, of course, and cotton families probably received low total earnings per hour; but the scope for additional family incomes undoubtedly redounded to the benefit of working-class people in the cotton towns in visible and tangible ways.

These themes were given added emphasis by the economic changes of the later nineteenth century, as wages in most occupations increased in cotton Lancashire while the cost of basic foodstuffs, which accounted for more than 50 per cent of most working-class expenditure, fell steadily. Meanwhile, the importance of married women's work to domestic economies continued to increase, and in

Preston, Burnley and other north Lancashire weaving centres over 30 per cent of married women worked, along with as many as three-quarters of the un-married.[14] Factory work was the norm for female teenagers in the cotton towns. Younger children also remained numerous in the mills: as late as the mid-1890s there were still nearly 100,000 'half-timers' in Lancashire, although their numbers were falling steadily by this time.[15] A sample from the census manu-scripts suggests that 'three out of ten households in Burnley, four out of ten in Blackburn, contained a working wife' as early as 1871; and only a minority of households in these towns, headed usually by skilled or white-collar workers, depended on a single wage.[16] The general recourse to industrial work which took women and children out of the home for long hours, while substantially augmenting family incomes, set the cotton district apart from the rest of Lancashire as from almost the whole of Britain. What does this pattern of family employment reveal about basic standards of living and material comfort? Was married women's work in the 1880s and 1890s still a defensive response to abject poverty, as it had been at mid-century? Or was it aimed at financing a more opulent lifestyle than hitherto, with cheap consumer durables, little luxuries and seaside holidays? This was much debated at the time; and our interpretation of this issue will colour our wider attitudes to the nature of working-class society in the late Victorian cotton towns.

The socialist journalist Allen Clarke, commenting on Bolton in the mid-1890s, brought out the value-judgements which are associated with this question: 'Many married women are compelled to work in the factory because the husband's wage is not sufficient to keep the house going; though there are also many women, in comparatively good circumstances, who work out of sheer greed, or in order to spend their earnings in fine feathers for themselves.'[17] Elizabeth Roberts, assessing her oral history findings for Preston in the early twentieth century, stresses the driving force of need, and claims that adult male wages were particularly low in the cotton towns, partly because of the expectation that women's wages would eke out the household budget.[18] No doubt wives and mothers were strongly encouraged to continue in the factory when their husbands were ill-paid piecers, four-loom weavers or card-room hands, or labourers outside the factory; but Roberts does not succeed in showing that male wages in unskilled occupations were higher in towns where fewer women worked. Even within Lancashire, any differences must have been so small as to be negligible, and the distinctive household earning pattern of the cotton towns was not caused by unusually large numbers of men being so badly paid as to make it impossible to subsist without additional sources of income.[19] Adult male incomes in the lower strata of the cotton industry's workforce at the turn of the century were no worse than those of labourers, dockers or chemical workers elsewhere. They were more reliable and predictable than most, and they rose noticeably as the cost of living fell between the mid-1870s and the early twentieth century. Weekly earnings, as opposed to piece-rates, showed a particularly pronounced upward trend after the setbacks of the 1878 depression. In spinning, admittedly, the improvements were bought with increased productivity and intensity of work, while the declining output per worker in weaving was accompanied by an increased use of child labour (especially where six-loom weaving was introduced with the aid of assistants) and the introduction of artificial humidity into weaving-sheds. The wage evidence suggests that by the late nineteenth century most wives, and the vast majority of adolescents and unmarried women, went into or stayed on in the mills to augment a barely adequate standard of living, or to enhance the family's enjoyment of a brief crest of the poverty cycle, rather than as a desperate remedy for dire poverty. Whatever else may be said of women's work in the cotton industry, it provided a genuine boost to family incomes in time of need: Roberts exaggerates the proportion of wages swallowed up in child-minding and other expenses by comparing a low wage earned during short-time working with a very high price for child-minding and meals. When times were good and dependants not too pressing, on the other hand, women's work allowed well-earned indulgences in cheap finery and entertainment. At the other extreme from Roberts's pessimism, too much has been made of the alleged working-class opulence, with incomes of up to £5 per week when a labourer's wage was about £1, furnished by multiple incomes within families whose prosperity was always transitory and vulnerable to short-time working and cyclical unemployment. The cotton towns had their seamy side, as we shall see; but the availability of factory work for women gave their inhabitants a marked material advantage over the denizens of areas where women's work was neither so plentiful nor so relatively well paid.[20]

The contrast with Liverpool was especially striking. Marriner's optimism about the opportunities for women here is difficult to endorse: 'Openings for women, especially in domestic service, were good ... again in ports prostitutes were in demand. There were, therefore, fewer unemployed women than men.'[21] Admittedly, Liverpool had a higher proportion of women (married or not) recorded as working than Glasgow, according to the 1911 census; but most of the work was sweated or otherwise ill-paid, and there was little scope for wives or daughters to augment the low and unpredictable incomes of well over 40,000 casual labourers, carters and dockers. There remained an extensive stratum of the poverty-stricken, despite the evidence that Liverpool shared in the great price fall of the later nineteenth century, as the price of bread, tea and sugar halved between 1874 and 1894, while cheap meat became increasingly available. Not all dockers faced primary poverty, of course. Perhaps a quarter of Liverpool's dockers were so regularly employed as to reap the full benefits of the port's comparatively high hourly wage-rates, generating a very respectable average weekly wage of thirty shillings or so throughout the year, although even at this level weekly fluctuations were often so wide as to make domestic budgeting very difficult. On the other hand more than half the workforce probably averaged less than a pound per week, as the casual labour system, the fluctuating demand for labour and the employers' concern to spread the work among a large number of men, providing sufficient labour for peak periods and keeping a surplus labour pool for the rest of the time, combined to reduce the average working week to three days or so. It was alleged that some men, especially among the considerable minority who averaged 15 shillings a week or less, preferred this pattern of irregular work, knocking off to drink and loaf after earning a basic subsistence; but contemporaries found it difficult to apportion the causes of poverty between irregular wages and irregular habits, and they seem to have been mutually reinforcing. Some dockers divided their time between dock labour and other sources of income, which complicates the picture further. But an Edwardian survey of casual labour in Liverpool found an average *family* income of just under 22 shillings per week, which sets the generally low income levels and lack of earning power for women and children in perspective. We shall see that the endemic poverty of much of Liverpool's labour force was exacerbated by other aspects of the town's economic arrangements and social organisation.[22]

Many Liverpool labouring families were thus in primary poverty at the turn of the century: unable to sustain an adequate diet even if all the household income were spent to the best advantage. In practice, of course, men who hung around waiting for work were liable to consume considerable quantities of alcohol, and irregular incomes made thrift and forward planning impossible. Under these conditions, moneylenders flourished, and gambling acquired a rationale of its own, offering the plausible hope of funding an otherwise unattainable binge. All this made the problems of the slums even more intractable. Higher up the scale, skilled labourers and those in regular employment, such as railwaymen and some categories of municipal employee, were in a position to benefit from the falling cost of living; but the numerous white-collar labour force had problems of its own. The growing army of routine clerical workers on between £60 and £100 per year faced increasing insecurity and competition from female clerks and typists at the turn of the century, while trying to keep up a respectable lifestyle in the by-law suburbs on an income which did not match such aspirations. The underlying trends to improvement were strong even in Liverpool during the later nineteenth and early twentieth centuries, but their impact was less than it might have been among the numerous uneasy and vulnerable strata of the maritime metropolis.[23]

Elsewhere in Lancashire experiences varied, but nowhere matched the scope for expanded family incomes which the textile towns provided, or the miserable poverty of inner Liverpool. Women's full-time paid employment was in short supply everywhere outside the cotton district, and this reinforced the importance of the gap in income and regularity of earnings between the skilled and supervisory workers and their unskilled assistants and labourers. This was true of building and engineering work at Barrow, where the skilled men were better able to seek work outside the town in time of depression, and of the Lancaster economy, where the well-paid craftsmen at the Waring and Gillow furniture works were much better placed than the legions of labourers at Williamson's and Storey's linoleum and table baize factories, where the wages were just over £1 per week and there was a compulsory lay-off of several weeks every summer. As Elizabeth Roberts points out, though, there were compensations for workers in these northern industrial outposts which helped to keep the worst manifestations of poverty at bay. Fishing, especially at Barrow, allotments and a general propensity for 'living off the land' which was simply not available in the same manner in Preston, Bolton or Liverpool, provided additional sources of protein and income. No doubt petty thieving and other more disreputable activities constituted the Liverpool equivalent, while the miners of south Lancashire at least had ready access to cheap fuel.[24] Everywhere, however, the key trend of the late Victorian years was the sustained fall in essential commodity prices, and it would have taken a rare and unfortunate combination of short time and regular unemployment to counterbalance the almost universal tendency to improved choice and purchasing power.

For the last few years before the First World War, however, these favourable influences were threatened and checked by rising inflation and trade depression which gave rise to widespread industrial conflict. This change of fortune was more pronounced in some sectors than in others. The evidence for cotton, where wages had been rising faster than in any other textile industry between the mid-1880s and mid-1900s, is inconclusive, although 1908 and 1909 were very bad years. The cost of basic commodities rose sharply in Blackburn and Burnley between 1905 and 1912, with coal, flour, butter, bacon, eggs, potatoes and rent all showing sharp upturns, and similar trends were in evidence elsewhere in the county. The wage-rates of spinners in the Oldham coarse spinning factories were being outpaced by inflation between 1908 and 1913, although it is not clear that actual earnings followed the same trajectory. However, White's figures are less pessimistic, suggesting that for the cotton industry as a whole earnings more or less kept pace with prices for most of these years.[25] Apart from the 1908–9 depression, too, White is correct in stressing the relatively low levels of unemployment in cotton, where demand for labour was buoyant after 1910; and even in bad times, short-time working or a reduction in the number of looms per weaver had already become standard alternatives to laying workers off, as the fullest contemporary analysis of Edwardian unemployment makes clear.[26]

Other industries were less fortunate. Liverpool dockers, shipyard workers at Barrow and on Merseyside, glassworkers at St. Helens, railwaymen in Liverpool and elsewhere, were among many groups of workers who saw their wages being eroded by inflation. Lancaster's economy was in sustained depression between 1905 and the First World War, and there was little scope for wage increases to counterbalance the new inflationary trends. Much the same could be said of the ailing chemical industries of Widnes and Runcorn. Even Blackpool, with the hazards of its seasonally fluctuating resort economy, saw nearly one in six of its population receiving relief from the Chief Constable's fund in the worst of these years. At its lowest point, in November 1908, the worst industrial slump for a generation had put perhaps one in seven or eight trade unionists out of work in the engineering trades of Liverpool, Manchester and the cotton towns; one in five in Merseyside shipbuilding; one in five in Lancashire ironfounding; and (less reliably) one in three of the county's unionised general labourers.[27]

This painful dose of unemployment and short time no doubt threatened the always precarious security of many, as well as eating into the resources and reserves of the worst sufferers; but the overall impact of the pre-war setbacks was to challenge rising expectations without cancelling out the real material gains of the late Victorian years. Most of the unemployment analysed by Chapman and Hallsworth in 1909 was short-term, merging imperceptibly into the normal workings of casual and seasonal labour markets; and where other things were equal, material living standards were substantially better in the early 1910s than the early 1880s for the vast majority of the Lancashire working class. But the most thorough and thoughtful contemporary survey, that by Bowley and Burnett-Hurst for Warrington in 1913, is a useful antidote to complacency. At a time of 'normal' trade in most of Warrington's many industries, perhaps one in eight of all households, and one in seven of the sample population studied, were 'below the [income] level necessary to keep them in physical health, except at the sacrifice of clothing and other necessary intermittent expenditure'. The calculations, moreover, were based on 'rational' patterns of expenditure and full-time employment. The vast majority of impoverished families depended entirely on the wages of one adult male breadwinner in a low-paid occupation; and five-sixths of the cases analysed owed their deprivation to low wages, dependent children or a combination of the two. Poverty at this level was more widespread in Warrington than in Northampton, where women's work in the boot, shoe and clothing industries offered nearly as much employment to the unmarried (though at lower wages) as the cotton industry, or in Stanley, County Durham, where coal mining was almost the only industrial employment. But Warrington did better than Reading, with its high proportion of unskilled labourers in biscuit factories and its surrounding reserve army of ill-paid agricultural labourers.[28] It is unfortunate that we lack similar surveys of other Lancashire towns at this time.

Warrington was, of course, in no sense a representative Lancashire town. It was part of the Merseyside economy of coal, chemicals and heavy industry, but its economy embraced a much wider range of trades than its neighbours, with brewing, ironworking, wire manufacture, soap, fustian cutting and an outlying cotton mill. This diversity of trades meant that sectoral depressions bit less deeply, and there was a significant amount of waged work for women, especially in soap and textiles. Its working-class inhabitants were much better off, on average, than those of inner Liverpool or the main centres of the chemical industry, where there was little work for women and working lives were shortened by particularly unhealthy working conditions. Lancaster, too, had more pockets of severe poverty and perhaps a lower proportion of skilled and supervisory workers, while Barrow was more vulnerable to the trade cycle. But the key comparison is with the cotton towns, and it was here above all that the scope for augmenting family incomes through women's and children's factory work, and the spin-off in demand for laundry, cleaning and child-minding, brought a clear boost to material living standards. If Warrington's experience was middling, that of Bolton, Ashton or even (by Edwardian times, at least) Burnley must have been, in important respects, relatively good.

This optimism about the cotton towns in the 1890s and beyond is, of course, guarded. The living standards enjoyed were good only by comparison with contemporary working-class conditions elsewhere. Judged by more demanding yardsticks they were still, at best, severely lacking. Elizabeth Roberts even argues that, taking wages and lifestyles into account, working-class families of similar status were actually better off in Barrow and Lancaster than in Preston, and by extension than in the cotton towns more generally. As regards wages, this assertion is quite simply wrong. If we look beyond wage levels to assess the quality of life in a broader sense, however, there is much more to discuss. Roberts argues, for example, that culinary standards were higher in the north Lancashire towns than in the cotton district. Women in Barrow and Lancaster made their money go further by baking their own bread, and cooking nourishing stews and vegetable dishes, whereas cotton workers' families subsisted largely on shop bread, shop-made pies and cakes, fry-ups and fish and chips, more expensive and less nutritious. Margaret Hewitt alleges more emphatically that millworkers made poor household managers, and Robert Roberts's memories of Edwardian Salford, for example, provide some circumstantial support for such a view.[29] All this is plausible enough in principle; but there are complications. Not all of Roberts's Preston interviewees conformed to stereotype, and Walter Greenwood's Salford reminiscences involve Sunday roasts and the systematic theft by young lads of vegetables from the greengrocers' barrows: a reminder that greengrocers' shops proliferated alongside the confectioners' in late Victorian cotton towns.[30] We have quite a lot of subjective impressions, but not enough evidence to underpin confident generalisations about working-class diet; and we should bear in mind that many of the strictures about the eating habits of cotton workers and their families came from outsiders (even Robert Roberts and Walter Greenwood were shopkeepers' sons) while some of the comments made by Elizabeth Roberts's interviewees were prompted by leading questions. Elizabeth Roberts's interview sample is in any case insufficient to form a numerical basis for quantitative statements (such as 'The majority of working-class women in Barrow and Lancaster were enthusiastic bakers'), especially as we are not told the principles on which the interviewees were selected, and we are unable to judge how socially representative they are, and of what. It is likely that women working the 'double shift' of mill work and housekeeping would have more recourse to 'convenience foods' than full-time housewives; but we cannot know how common such practices were, nor how far these was a pattern of food consumption in the cotton towns which deserves a distinctive label. In any case, the suggestion that the Barrow and Lancaster diets were somehow 'better' than those attributed to the cotton towns is itself based on retrospective and subjective value-judgements which take no account of the possible preferences of contemporaries.

Similar problems recur throughout Elizabeth Roberts's influential portrayal of women, families, neighbouring and living standards in Barrow, Lancaster and Preston between the 1890s and 1940; and a further difficulty is that she frequently neglects possible changes over time during these difficult and some-times turbulent years. Her published work, enthralling though it often is, must therefore be used with caution. Her use of oral history can put enticing flesh on dry statistical bones, and direct shafts of illumination into the darkest inner workings of families and the cultures of street and neighbourhood. Without her research, the potential importance of petty trading and part-time, home-based employment for women, which helped to eke out family budgets for hard-pressed households in Barrow and Lancaster, might have remained hidden from historians just as it was invisible to census enumerators and other official and commercial sources. The sheer diversity of other expedients, from fishing and 'living off the land' to the ingenious use of workplace perquisites, might also have remained obscure. But there are limits to the historical uses of evidence of this kind. Oral history shows us what was possible, and what some people thought about their lives, rather than what was necessarily 'normal' or 'typical'. Inter-views supply wonderful and seductive vignettes which can all too easily be accorded more explanatory and descriptive weight than they really deserve. They supply illustrations and cautionary examples; but we generalise from them at our peril.[31]

We shall need to bear these issues in mind when we look at other aspects of working-class living standards, especially those connected with changes and variations in values and the quality of family relationships. I shall argue that we can contrast a nascent consumer society in the late Victorian and Edwardian cotton towns, with high family incomes but also high expectations and expen-diture and a distinctive predominant system of values, with a lower-income, lower-pressure social system in other parts of manufacturing Lancashire, and with the pathological poverty of much of working-class Liverpool. But we shall see that the pattern of change was much more complex than this bald introductory summary suggests.

The symptoms of widespread (though of course far from universal) working-class prosperity were being expressed with increasing clarity in the late Victorian cotton towns. Prominent among the most visible and distinctive were the rise of the working-class seaside holiday as a mass experience, and the early develop-ment of commercially organised spectator sport on a large scale; but in many other ways contemporaries were impressed by the precocious growth of com-mercial leisure and consumer spending in cotton Lancashire.

The working-class seaside holiday as an extended visit lasting several days, as opposed to the cheaper and more easily organised day excursion, was almost a Lancashire invention, the only rival claimants being the London artisans who visited the Kent coast on the cheap steamers of the 1830s. Already at mid-century the surviving summer holidays at Whitsuntide or the Wakes were being used for long weekends at Blackpool or Southport by skilled and supervisory workers who took advantage of the scope for cheap fares and block bookings on the rapidly extending railway network, whose tendrils brought all but the remotest industrial villages into easy reach of the coast during the 1850s. By the 1870s many cotton towns enjoyed agreed (though unpaid) summer holidays of three days beyond the weekend, and twenty years later further extensions brought about a full-scale 'Wakes Week', although a few towns, such as Bolton and Preston, had to wait into the new century for this concession. By 1914, however, some weaving centres in north and north-east Lancashire were getting ten days in the summer, and short September holidays were beginning to appear. By the 1890s towns like Burnley and Blackburn were deserted during their holiday weeks, as shops closed and churches and chapels held combined services for a remnant of their congregations. Such general observance was not universal: Rochdale, for example, seems to have kept most of its inhabitants at home during Rushbearing week as late as 1902. Nearby Oldham, on the other hand, was in the forefront of the rush to the sea; and in most Edwardian cotton towns only those most disadvantaged by low wages and large families were unable to share in the delights of the seaside. The main beneficiary of these developments was Blackpool, which adjusted its facilities and expectations to cope with and encourage the late Victorian surge of working-class demand, and became the world's first specialised working-class seaside resort. It continued to cater for the 'better classes' at either extremity of its long promenade, and on the other hand working-class Lancastrians were to be found in large numbers in the North Wales coast resorts, at Scarborough and Cleethorpes, and on the Isle of Man, as well as venturing to the more up-market Lancashire resorts, especially Southport and Morecambe. In the early twentieth century some of the most affluent and adventurous were beginning to discover Torquay, Bournemouth and even the Continent.[32]

How did this happen, and what did it mean? Above all, it was a distinctive cotton town phenomenon; and it predated similar developments elsewhere by twenty years and more. Even the superficially similar West Riding textile district lagged a long way behind. Significantly, family incomes were much lower east of the Pennines; and the relatively strong financial position of many cotton workers and their families must form the core of an explanation. Labour discipline in this mature factory society was strong enough to ensure a sustained income through the year, and this made it easier to save regularly in the anticipation of enjoyment as well as insuring against harder times. Established traditions could be harnessed in support of the seaside holiday, too. Lancashire had a popular pre-industrial tradition of therapeutic sea-bathing, which was perpetuated and encouraged by cheap rail fares; and the Wakes and other summer holidays were zealously defended against encroachments by employers, and extended in good times: a reminder that labour discipline was demanding week in, week out, but it could occasionally be defied systematically by a determined and unanimous workforce with custom at its back. The habit of saving for specific goals was widespread and well established, and existing institutions provided models for the development of holiday savings clubs, which proliferated remarkably in the late Victorian cotton towns and disbursed hundreds of thousands of pounds annually in some places in the early twentieth century. The Co-op was another effective repository for holiday savings, especially in Rochdale and Burnley. The close-knit urban neighbourhoods provided additional resources, as a variety of institutions, from streets to chapels to pubs, promoted excursions and organised cheap fares, while neighbours provided advice and recommended accommodation to apprentice holidaymakers. Ultimately, an annual holiday seems almost to have become a social obligation in all but the poorest districts of the cotton towns.[33]

For most working-class Lancastrians, the seaside holiday meant Blackpool, or somewhere similar. A few enthusiasts headed off into the wilds with the Co-operative Holiday Association, or made for Devonshire under their own steam in search of natural beauty and relaxation.[34] But the vast majority bustled their way through the bewildering array of artificial attractions and shows which late Victorian Blackpool's entrepreneurs were assembling, as the Tower, the Winter Gardens and a host of lesser entertainment centres competed for the trippers' sixpences. There were further sources of delight, of course: a boisterous sea, a fairground on the beach, to which many of the showmen from the Lancashire Wakes fairs migrated in the late nineteenth century, and a free and easy atmosphere, with plenty of pubs, which was made possible by the lack of a restrictive dominant landowner and the emergence of a local government system whose representatives generally identified their interests with the encouragement of working-class visitors with few pretensions. Blackpool's landladies, too, developed an early specialisation in cheap, homely, crowded accommodation for an undemanding clientele; and all these aspects of Blackpool, which made it unique among the large English resorts, provided further encouragement for the growth of the seaside holiday habit. Within Lancashire, indeed, it stood in sharp contrast with Southport or Lytham, where restrictive landowners and local government bodies had created inhospitable environments for all but the quietest and most aspiring of working-class visitors.[35]

Blackpool's visitors notoriously played hard and spent freely. They were alleged to observe factory hours, leaving the promenade empty at the standard mealtimes, and to spend all their holiday money as a point of honour. Some saw all this as irrational, and even as a manifestation of secondary poverty. Allen Clarke claimed that the factory worker's seaside holiday was not a source of pleasure, but a necessity to the recuperation of health; but he also alleged that a week in 'stifling, jostling' Blackpool was worse than useless, as 'the factory folks work harder than at their daily toil, rushing to and fro in order to see everything in their brief sojourn, and they generally go home more weary and jaded than they are after a week's work'.[36] Clarke, of course, was making polemical points about the awfulness of the factory worker's lot; but we cannot ignore the suggestion that the seaside holiday was a misapplication of resources which could have been better spent or saved. There is something in it, especially when we remember that many family holidays depended on the premature drudgery of young children through the rest of the year. But it may be significant that the rise in working-class holidaymaking coincided with an improvement in working-class spending power which affected the housewife's purse rather than the husband's wage packet, as it came from falling commodity prices. Holidays were a family affair: wives enjoyed them as well as husbands, and the initiative for saving may well have come from this quarter. No doubt many seaside holidays were in some sense an alternative to additional drinking, rather than a drain on basic essentials through the rest of the year; and it will soon become clear that most families had sufficient resources by the 1890s to invest in commercial enjoyment at home as well as going to the coast, and to afford improvements in diet and furniture, while continuing to save for a rainy day and insure against contingencies.[37]

Cotton Lancashire, along with Sheffield (which was also a pacesetter in the development of working-class seaside holidays, though under very different economic circumstances), was also one of the earliest centres of commercialised professional football, which developed rapidly in the 1880s in the enthusiastic environment of Blackburn, Darwen, Bolton, Preston and the surrounding industrial villages. The spread of the Saturday half-holiday from cotton to other industries after 1850 left time available in which muscular clergymen and employers' sons from the public schools could spread the gospel of football as a healthy, character-building 'rational recreation' to those young working men who came under their influence; and in Lancashire as elsewhere, churches and employers were prominent among the early patrons of the game. With its inexpensive equipment and competitive sociability, football spread very quickly after 1870. No fewer than 25 of the hundred clubs who went into the draw for the second round of the FA Cup in April 1883 were from the cotton district, including at least three teams from Darwen, two from Blackburn, three from Bolton and an amazing array of village sides, including factory settlements like Low Moor near Clitheroe, Eagley and Turton. By this time professionalism was already firmly established in Lancashire. Darwen and Blackburn Rovers were almost certainly playing imported professionals in the late 1870s, and Scots players arrived in large numbers in the early 1880s. Publicans and tradesmen were becoming more widely involved in the running of clubs, and rivalries were fuelled by the presence of large crowds of supporters whose threepences and later sixpences made professionalism both possible and difficult to avoid. Under these conditions, the village teams like Turton and Astley Bridge soon faded from the limelight, and the successful sides were those who could command regular attendances of several thousand paying spectators. Five of the twelve founder members of the Football League in 1888 were from the cotton towns, and even in 1913, with ten out of forty (including Stockport County and Glossop from just beyond the Lancashire boundary), the cotton district had the heaviest concentration of League clubs in England. The larger clubs were already investing in grandstands and earthworks during the 1880s, and crowds continued to grow, and to become more working-class in composition, thereafter. We know nothing in detail about the social composition of football crowds – or indeed of the members of the very large number of amateur sides – but the rapid growth of football as a business (though never a very profitable one) provides further evidence of the growth of disposable working-class income, this time in the pockets of youths and men. Ladies were quite numerous among the spectators in the early stages, but their presence soon became residual, and working-class wives can seldom have been able to attend. There are, here again, debatable side-effects, and contemporaries worried about the encouragement to gambling (especially when primitive football pools began to circulate in the late 1880s) and perhaps to drinking after the match; but the overall impact of this evidence reinforces the suggestion that working-class spending power was growing and the outlets for it were diversifying. Significantly, perhaps, the West Riding woollen districts, which were not short of local patriotism, interested clergy, employers and publicans, again lagged a long way behind cotton Lancashire in the development of an important aspect of working-class leisure spending.[38]

Plenty of other illustrations of the growth of a mass market in leisure and consumer goods in the late Victorian and Edwardian cotton towns can be supplied. Club cricket also began to organise itself into leagues, with an increasing concentration on gate receipts and employment of professionals; and although it never matched the extent of the movement of Association football in these directions, it may be significant that here, too, the Bolton area with its particularly high wages saw unusually intensive development.[39] Similar trends were no doubt present in other sports. Less reputably in the eyes of many contemporaries, cotton Lancashire also spawned a great efflorescence of music-hall and popular theatre during the second half of the nineteenth century. Many towns acquired palatial new or rebuilt premises in the 1880s and 1890s, some of which seated several thousand people; and Saturday evening performances, in particular, attracted married couples as well as younger people of both sexes. Below this level of opulence, at which proprietors had to be very careful not to offend magistrates with increasingly strict licensing powers and propensities, there was a further layer of cheap back-street music-halls and singing saloons, charging threepence rather than sixpence or a shilling, and catering for an unequivocally working-class audience, with no leavening of clerks or tradesmen. Here, entertainment was more participatory and makeshift; but two Oxford observers from the Christian Social Union in the 1890s found it less objectionable than in the more sophisticated halls. The entertainments were strongly-flavoured, conventional, and undemanding in depth and length of individual performance, reinforcing a widely deplored preference for 'tit-bits' and 'snippets'; but they were rarely prurient, and they lacked the systematic innuendo and suggestive gestures by which the slicker performers at the more expensive halls evaded censorship. C. E. B. Russell agreed, arguing that the music-hall was a lesser evil than the pub or the street corner, especially for the young people who were so numerous among the audiences; and in many cases it was cheap enough to enable whole families to attend. Russell was less happy about the cheap dancing saloons which were also a distinctive feature of working-class leisure in the cotton towns, blaming them for immorality among the young; but what emerges most clearly from all this is the sheer extent and range of commercial entertainment provision in the late Victorian and Edwardian cotton towns, building on and expanding from firm mid-Victorian foundations, and reaching almost all levels of working-class society. The cinema in the early twentieth century provided an additional alternative alongside the other leisure outlets, and seems to have been especially popular with the wage-earning young who formed a distinctive and even unique market for entertainment entrepreneurs in the cotton towns.[40]

The importance of these commercialised entertainments is undeniable, and Lancashire's cotton towns seem to have been particularly rich in them, especially from the 1870s onwards. But it is difficult to demonstrate in a really convincing way that these institutions were thicker on the ground than in other urban and industrial areas. It seems likely, but it is impossible to prove without a great deal of additional research. Much the same applies to the social importance of the public house, which retained its central position in masculine working-class leisure despite the emergence and growth of so many potential competitors. In terms of sheer numbers, the availability of pubs in cotton Lancashire was less than spectacular. Although some towns consistently had fewer people per pub than the national average, there were considerable variations. The county boroughs were better endowed than the smaller towns. A return of 1895 showed Manchester itself close to the top of the list of county boroughs, with 600 licensed houses per 100,000 inhabitants, with Rochdale and Salford not far behind. On the other hand, Oldham, Bury and Burnley were relatively short of pubs. The smaller boroughs all had fewer drink outlets per 100,000 people than the national average for this category of town. Nelson was particularly 'dry', with a figure of only 123, and Accrington, Mossley and Darwen were on a par with Burnley towards the drier end of the spectrum.[41] The variations clearly reflect differences in licensing policy, and it is certainly significant that some late-developing towns were particularly lacking in drink outlets. Much of the growth of Nelson and Burnley, for example, had taken place after the tightening up of licensing regulations in 1869 and 1872, which had given the growing number of Dissenting and 'Temperance' magistrates additional power to refuse new licenses and even to suppress existing ones. The figures may well be misleading as a basis for wider comparisons, because it is likely that pubs in the cotton towns included a high proportion of large and opulent premises with a high turnover and correspondingly inflated social influence. There were marked trends in this direction during the 1850s and 1860s, as a continuing proliferation of beerhouses was accompanied by the extension and embellishment of existing pubs, as the brewers who were controlling an increasing proportion of the drink outlets continued to adopt the innovations of the 1830s and 1840s. But the social influence of drink and the pub reached a peak in the 1870s. After 1876 alcohol consumption levels were in decline nationally, and no doubt locally, while restrictive licensing policies reduced the availability of pubs in the new artisan areas of by-law housing on the urban fringe. Publicans had to take more care to keep on the right side of police and magistrates, too, and the larger pubs perforce became more respectable. The publican continued to act as entertainment entrepreneur, sponsoring bowls tournaments and investing in football clubs as well as supplying music and dancing; and pubs remained important as meeting-places for some organisations, although they were being challenged by a variety of school and church halls and other meeting-rooms. But the importance of drink became diluted by a widening range of alternatives, and the extent of the change was witnessed by the declining Edwardian levels of prosecution for drunkenness. By 1914 gambling had displaced drink in the minds of many concerned observers as the most dangerous source of working-class misery. The pub was still of central significance in working-class life, and in Lancashire its frequenters included women as well as men; but its influence was much less pervasive in the Edwardian years than it had been in mid-Victorian times. As temperance reformers pointed out, this was itself an important contribution to rising living standards. It was perhaps also an indicator of an improved ability to cope with industrial life.[42]

The new commercialised leisure outlets which augmented the pub, and to some extent competed with it, formed only part of the story. We shall see that the efforts of philanthropists, religious bodies and municipalities to provide 'rational recreations' for the working class were unceasing and not altogether fruitless: indeed, professional sport had many of its roots in endeavours of this kind. Moreover, the traditional enjoyments associated with Wakes and other festivals did not simply wither away at the touch of the railway and the music-hall. But to complete the picture of a rising working-class consumer society in cotton Lancashire, a word about retailing is necessary. The late Victorian price fall was accompanied by a remarkable increase in the number of shops selling specialised lines or non-essential goods to what must have been, at least partly, a working-class market, given the distinctively bottom-heavy social structure of the cotton towns. This suggests a widening range of choice, and a growing concern for the accumulation of domestic comforts which reflects the improvement in women's spending power and in housing and public health conditions. Barrett's 1894 directory for Blackburn lists, among other things, 6 artists and a further 12 photographers; 20 specialist baby linen and underclothing dealers; 12 carvers, gilders and picture frame makers; 12 cycle dealers (a reminder of another rapidly expanding working-class leisure activity); 72 fishmongers and 162 fruiterers and greengrocers alongside the 103 fish and chip shops and 49 tripe dressers and dealers (undermining easy generalisations about cotton town diets); 108 'hairdressers' (all male); 201 milliners and dressmakers; 13 music and musical instrument dealers, and 40 'music professors'; 43 'watch and clock makers' and a watercress salesman. Exactly what all this means is, of course, open to dispute, and it would take a major research project to establish exact trends and make really informed guesses about spending patterns; but the overall picture of an amazing diversity of retail outlets, most of which must have depended mainly or entirely on working-class custom, gives strong support to the argument of this section. Alongside these private fixed retail outlets, markets remained important (and their premises were improved), itinerant traders continued to make their rounds (especially the so-called 'Scotch drapers' who sold cloth on credit), and above all the retail Co-operative movement put down deep roots. Its rapid spread through the spinning towns around Manchester in the 1850s and 1860s was interrupted only temporarily by the 'Cotton Famine', and it was extending very quickly in the weaving towns and villages to the north and west by 1870. During the price fall it gained a real mass membership in towns like Bolton and Burnley, where its libraries, educational facilities and entertainments also became important. So a growing portion of the working class, including by the 1890s a clear majority of families in many towns, had access to unadulterated foods and to a means of saving while they spent. Despite its competition, however, the private traders also continued to proliferate, even if they did not always flourish. All this adds up to really convincing evidence of a widespread and major improvement in living standards and purchasing power.[43]

The obvious supplementary questions are: *how* widespread were these improvements, and how deep did they go? Allen Clarke, in relatively prosperous Bolton, admitted to important improvements over the fifty years since the 1840s; but as well as emphasising the persistence of general ill-health, bad housing conditions and insecurity, to which we shall have to return, he also attacked outsiders' portrayals of high material living standards. An optimistic German, von Schulze-Gävernitz, came under heavy fire for suggesting that pianos were common items of working-class furniture. Clarke retaliated equally polemically: there was 'one piano in about every hundred of the operatives' houses, and then only got when all the children are growing up and working, and generally on the hire system'. Although a few operatives received good wages and obtained parlours and pianos, 'the majority live in small cottages, shabbily furnished, unblest by literature or music'.[44] It is remarkably difficult to establish levels of domestic comfort across the working class as a whole, but one suspects that the rival authors, like many others, were generalising from the experience of unrepresentative groups within the working class; and Clarke had much higher hopes and expectations than most of his contemporaries. But there was, quite clearly, a residue of severe poverty even in the late Victorian and Edwardian cotton towns, into which many families might be pushed by the poverty cycle, illness, injury or trade depression. The problem is to assess its extent. Poor relief figures, as far as they go, remain relatively optimistic. Only in Wigan Poor Law Union did pauperism in the cotton district stand higher than the national average at the beginning of 1911, and in the main spinning and weaving centres it was almost always well below. Pauperism in Manchester, admittedly, ran at well over twice the national incidence, but this was a metropolitan population with a lot of casual employment and a high incidence of long-distance migrants who were isolated from kin and other sources of informal assistance.[45]

Formal pauperism was only part of the story, of course: it remained the last resort of the near-destitute, as the 'Cotton Famine' showed. To avoid the stigma of poor relief from the Guardians, families would pawn their possessions down to the last stick of furniture; and this was still the case in Manchester during the severe winter of 1894–5, which disrupted employment in several trades. This should remind us that there was much intermittent, half-hidden, but severe poverty which had particularly sad implications for wives and female children, who were expected to bear the brunt of the privations. As late as 1911 a survey of 10,000 schoolchildren in Blackburn found 16 per cent to be showing signs of malnutrition; and when the children were small there were still a significant number who lived on 'a miserable round of tea and bread and butter and bread and butter and tea', with pie and peas sometimes from the hot pea saloon. But the point is that these were a smaller minority in cotton Lancashire (excepting parts of inner Manchester and Salford) than in other industrial towns. Even the numerous pawnshops were used more as savings banks, suppliers of short-term capital and places of safe keeping for possessions whose value lay partly in their use as security for loans, than as last resources for the destitute or depraved. *Justice*, the SDF journal, gave the most plausible picture of the lifestyle of the mainstream working-class family in a turn-of-the-century cotton town: 'A one pair back in a dull street, comfortable shoddy, for literature the evening paper, pictures out of the illustrated weekly, a run into the country or to the seaside once a year in the fine weather, a shilling or two a week for the "public", the football match or the music halls ...' For a brief span, young women could dress fashionably and enjoy cheap finery, and for a few years later in life, mature families could acquire consumer durables and live in moderate comfort. It was not much, perhaps, but it was a great improvement on earlier times and other places.[46]

Clarke believed that this limited measure of comfort and enjoyment was accompanied by a cultural impoverishment which he found depressing. Factory work in particular numbed the intellect and restricted the capacity for sustained thought, inducing a craving for 'light and sensational reading' and the 'noisy pleasures of stimulants and singing-rooms'. The most popular papers in Bolton were *Comic Cuts, Tit-Bits, Answers, Pearson's Weekly* and the sporting and betting papers. Sales of the *Clarion* were insignificant by comparison.[47] Thoroughgoing dissent from this proposition would be hard to sustain. But we should qualify it in several ways. Basic literacy, as measured by the ability to sign the marriage register, was already improving rapidly in the 1850s and 1860s, and by the 1880s the cotton towns had caught up with the nation at large. Some working-class people did use their literacy for more demanding material than *Tit-Bits*, too. The Socialist Sunday Schools of the 1890s provided particularly stimulating fare. Alice Foley's sister in Bolton read and discussed William Morris's *Dream of John Ball*, and Selina Cooper in Brierfield, never the most confident or grammatical of writers, was tackling a variety of socialist authors while naming her first child after John Ruskin. Some of these autodidacts and mutual assistance groups were even trying to come to terms with *Das Kapital*, and Bolton had an enthusiastic group of disciples of Walt Whitman.[48] A more orthodox stimulus to serious reading was the public library movement, which developed early in some of the cotton towns. Manchester, Bolton and Blackburn were among the first handful of municipalities to take up the Act of 1850 which empowered the levying of a penny rate for library purposes, and by 1890 – 1 sixteen other towns in the cotton district had established public libraries. By this time Manchester claimed over 40,000 borrowers in its population of half a million, while Bolton had nearly 7000 out of 115,000 and Rochdale 5000 out of 70,000. These were relatively good figures, as were the estimates of 60 per cent of issues being 'fiction and juvenile books' in the two former cases. Libraries clearly did not languish unused, but as with the Mechanics' Institutes, which declined in their original guise as the public libraries rose, the number of serious and systematic working-class readers was a very small proportion of the population. In Bolton it was 'a self-improving, status-conscious artisan élite', some of whom complained that 'the books in the lending library were not of a sufficiently high character'; but these were people who brought developed tastes and interests to the library, rather than allowing it to form them from the beginning.[49]

A similar pattern was generally sustained in most of the other 'rational rec-reations' to be sponsored by philanthropists, religious bodies and municipalities. Association football and seaside excursions had been sponsored and promoted from above, but were adapted to more secular and less 'improving' uses by the recipients; and in the same way the Working Men's Club movement, founded as a harmless (at least) and sociable counter-attraction to the pub, was taken over by its members, in Bolton and elsewhere, freed from patronage and opened out to the sale of beer. The brass bands which became perhaps the most famous element in a flourishing popular musical culture, attracting packed and knowledgeable crowds to their regular competitive concerts at Manchester's Belle Vue and elsewhere, were often similar assertions of independence from church or employer sponsorship and control, although evidence from the West Riding suggests that this may have been less common than is sometimes thought.[50] The municipal parks which were opened in many mid-Victorian cotton towns, boosted by relief work schemes during the 'Cotton Famine', were used as an additional resource by working-class families in search of free if restricted outdoor enjoyment, rather than displacing the pub or the music-hall in their affections.[51] Many 'improving' recreational initiatives, of course, came under religious auspices, especially the enormous variety of sewing circles, discussion groups, Pleasant Sunday Afternoon assemblies and other groups which cohered around each church and chapel congregation. They seem to have been more successful the less they concerned themselves explicitly with sectarian doctrine; and the influence of organised, formal religion on most working-class people seems to have been very limited. Sunday school attendance remained the norm for working-class children and teenagers, but regular church or chapel attendance was the preserve of a small minority of adults. The worried comments of clergy and ministers suggest that it was declining sharply in the early twentieth century. There was, of course, a pervasive ethic of 'do-as-you-would-be-done-by' among working-class communities, and a widespread strong attachment to sexual respectability; but this was congruent with religious teachings, and no doubt partly fostered by Sunday school experience, without necessarily being associated with the conscious or committed acceptance of religious dogma. Elizabeth Roberts's assertions about the all-pervading influence of religious bodies on the Edwardian working class fly in the face of other evidence, and are probably strongly influenced by unrepresentative aspects of her interview sample.[52]

For the most part, efforts on the part of concerned elements within the middle classes to act as cultural missionaries were still being rejected by the vast majority of the working class, or accepted partially and on the recipients' own terms. There remained a vigorous and impermeable independent working-class culture, which guarded its traditions and adapted them to new circumstances, and which was strengthened by the increasing stability of the late Victorian cotton towns, as migrants became fewer and less significant, towns recruited mainly by natural increase, and an established body of shared values and expectations developed and sustained itself. These comments apply most strongly to the older-established cotton towns, such as Bolton or Oldham, and least convincingly to the late-developing north Lancashire weaving centres around Nelson and Colne, where migrants from Cornwall and southern England were rubbing shoulders with new arrivals from Yorkshire villages at the turn of the century. But they have some force everywhere. The heyday of the Wakes holidays as celebrations of neighbourliness and occasions for family reunion came in mid-Victorian times, as the railways made convivial visits easier and cheaper: it was only when the extended seaside holiday became more popular from the 1870s onwards that the local customs really declined. Even then, rushcarting persisted in Saddleworth and a few other places into the 1890s, in spite of adverse economic conditions; and in some respects the old ways of celebrating were transferred to the seaside along with the fairgrounds, as visits were exchanged between relatives and neighbours in adjacent boarding-houses and the local newspapers of the holiday-making towns dominated the news-stands in the popular resorts of Northern England. Dialect poetry and stories also continued to flourish, and a pride was retained in the distinctive customs and modes of speech of individual towns and even hamlets. Traditions could still be manufactured as well as being perpetuated or adapted: the Bacup Easter coconut dancers seem to have created their own custom in mid-Victorian times. People from the cotton towns famously valued their outspoken independence, humour and lack of pretension; and an increasingly inward-looking, egalitarian system of working-class values was enforced by informal sanctions against those who stepped out of line. Alice Foley was soon called to order by her workmates in the mill when she discarded her shawl for a 'shabby sailor hat': the offending headgear was paraded around the workplace on a sweeping brush, with much giggling, and after meeting the procession she took the hint. As we have seen, the working class contained its own hierarchies of status and respectability, as well as divisions based on politics and religion; but most of it was also united by a common culture which blended a strong work ethic with a sense of the importance of kinship and neighbouring and an expectation that common standards would be maintained and mutual assistance provided. Social bonds were further expressed and reinforced by the use of nick-names: Alice Foley, again, worked with 'Owd Sweat', 'Hell-fire Jack', 'Owd Dawdler' and 'Bill Custard' in her Edwardian weaving-shed, while watercress was hawked from door to door by 'Owd Sally'.[53] These were, increasingly, close-knit and self-regulating communities.

But we must not romanticise this social system. It could be oppressive as well as supportive, and it could reject as well as embrace. Beatrice Webb noticed that the Bacup of the 1880s had no place for idlers or social misfits: they were pushed out by the concerted disapproval of their neighbours, perhaps swelling the ranks of casual labour or prostitution in Manchester and helping to explain the limited extent of these problems in the cotton towns themselves.[54] On the other hand, although indirect evidence suggests that the cotton district was more likely to keep its 'lunatics' at home and out of the asylum at mid-century, the enormous growth in asylum capacity in Lancashire thereafter suggests that, at this extreme level, the willingness to support the slow-witted and the mentally incapacitated may have declined over the generations.[55] Moreover, it was not a closed system: there were opportunities for mobility out of the ranks of the working class, as well as from one rung to another within it. The prevailing value system also sanctioned, indeed almost required, that children should go into factory work at the earliest possible moment; and it perpetuated unhealthy practices which helped to inflate the high rates of accident, sickness and infant mortality which prevailed in the cotton towns, and which must be considered in any comparative and cross-cultural assessment of living standards. Bad housing and working conditions, and environmental conditions more generally, were at the root of these problems, of course: but the stoical passivity and conservatism of late Victorian factory society helped to perpetuate the evils.

The extent of upward mobility from the manual working class into the ranks of employers, shopkeepers, managers, teachers or white-collar workers is very difficult to document, and almost impossible to compare convincingly over time and between places. In most of cotton Lancashire it was probably becoming more difficult to move securely upward from the factory floor to become a substantial employer by the late nineteenth century, as firms became larger and more capital-intensive; but small trading and lesser professional and white-collar opportunities were becoming more widespread. Opportunities for the enterprising operative to advance into and through the employing class were much more widespread in weaving than in spinning, even at mid-century; and by the 1880s the continuing proliferation of small firms renting room and power and using borrowed money and second-hand equipment in the newest centres of Burnley and Nelson made them the last major spawning ground of self-made cotton manufacturers. Already, too, this was in sharp contrast with Preston and Blackburn, where the average size of firm was growing rapidly and established dynasties already ruled the roost. Forty per cent of a sample of Burnley cotton employers in the late nineteenth century sprang directly from manual working or shopkeeping back-grounds, often involving hand-loom weaving. This was double the Blackburn proportion; but by the early twentieth century Burnley, too, was going the same way, as the renting of weaving-sheds declined and limited companies encroached. When Chapman and Marquis claimed in 1912 that a high proportion of cotton employers were recruited from the ranks of the operatives, however, they based their assertions on a sample of millowners drawn from Burnley, which was still the town best suited to support their case; and the questionnaire on which their figures depended was loaded so as to be likely to generate the answers they sought. Even in Burnley, the idea that there was plenty of scope for operatives to become employers, and to succeed and prosper as such, was largely mythical. It was important, however, because it was widely believed, and because it could always be supported by reference to a highly visible handful of exceptional men who had successfully made the transition. The belief that the cotton industry was wide open to Smilesian upward social mobility may well have played its part in legitimising and stabilising the social and political arrangements of the late Victorian and Edwardian cotton towns, for it transferred the blame for failure squarely on to the shoulders of individual operatives. It was a convenient myth; but a myth it was, all the same.[56]

The limited companies provided less scope for advancement into salaried management then might be expected. They recruited their managers from 'insurance brokers, shopkeepers and clerical workers' to a large extent, or appointed substantial shareholders to the post. Recruitment from the ranks of the labour force, where it occurred, involved the intermediate supervisory grades which were increasingly becoming hereditary within families or open only to those whose relatives could afford substantial premiums. Only in Oldham, moreover (where there was a great deal), was there much working-class investment in limited companies, and then it came almost entirely from the well-paid ranks of the skilled and supervisory, who invariably invested in firms other than those in which they worked. The number of shares necessary to become a director was increasing in many mills in the early twentieth century, and for the overwhelming majority of factory workers the hurdles which barred the way to management were impossibly high. Upward social mobility was much more likely to occur on a less ambitious scale, as men and some women from working-class families found their way into clerical work, schoolteaching and the marginal professions. Shopkeeping was above all the most likely recourse for the ambitious manual worker, and the publican's lifestyle might also beckon. Spinners, especially, with their truncated working lives, were likely to end up precariously perched among the petty bourgeoisie. The opportunities for such transitions were undoubtedly growing, and even that shopkeepers' bugbear, the Co-op, offered some scope for managerial and clerical employment; but this whole area needs a great deal more research. At present it seems likely that, even if the routes upwards out of the working class were becoming more accessible in the late nineteenth and early twentieth centuries, they were not yet undermining the shared values and cultural expectations which characterised and unified the vast majority of the cotton towns' working class, and in some senses and contexts transcended the occupational, religious and political influences which divided them.[57] More important than all these things, perhaps, was the scope for thrift within the working class, as building societies recruited well alongside the Co-op and the savings banks, and Friendly Society membership approached saturation point. Here again, there were important variations between towns. In Oldham, despite the apparent popularity of building societies, only 8.3 per cent of the houses were owner-occupied in 1906, a similar figure to that for Blackburn; while in Burnley the percentage of owner-occupiers was variously estimated at between one-third and one-half. The Burnley Building Society already had investments of half a million pounds in the 1880s, with a largely working-class membership. We need to know more about these indices of relative security and prosperity among an important section of the labour force.[58] It was at this level of the relatively prosperous and secure, no doubt, that the alert interest in technical education noted by von Schulze-Gävernitz was most in evidence, although here this German observer was interestingly, and perhaps revealingly, at variance with English critics of the technical education system, who were prone to making adverse comparisons with what they thought to happen in Germany.[59] But in general terms, the scope for long-range and permanent social mobility beyond the working-class was, and remained, very limited in the cotton towns.

Working-class society in the cotton towns was thus perhaps becoming increasingly insular and inward-looking, although there are enough cross-currents to make such an assertion extremely hard to prove. Opportunities for long-range upward social mobility were declining, although at a more immediate and less demanding level the growth of the service and the tertiary sectors meant expanding opportunities for movement into the petty bourgeoisie and into white-collar occupations. Above all, though, this was a relatively well-off working class in material terms. International comparisons seem to bear this out. On Gibson's calculations the gap in real wages which opened out between British and American cotton workers in the later nineteenth century had been narrowed but remained considerable in 1914, and von Schulze-Gävernitz was confident that Lancashire's cotton workers were much better off than their German counterparts in the early 1890s.[60] But, as Allen Clarke argued, there were costs to set against these benefits. We must examine the arguments on this score.

In the first place, this relative material well-being depended heavily on the expectation that children should go to work in the mill at the earliest opportunity; and cotton Lancashire, along with the West Riding textile districts and, interestingly, Blackpool, became one of the last bastions of the half-time system in education. Indeed, from the mid-1850s to the mid-1890s child labour had steadily increased in importance, and it was sturdily defended by some factory inspectors as well as by trade unionists and civic dignitaries. It was said to promote alertness and dexterity, and to be an essential preparation for the world of work. The cotton trade unions endorsed these views, and campaigned consistently against successive raisings of the minimum working age, with full support from ballots of their members (although most half-timers came from families whose heads were not employed in cotton). But it is highly significant that the National Union of Teachers led the campaign against children's factory work within the trade union movement from 1890 onwards, with strong medical support. Half-timers were said to lose all their aptitude for study, and to retard the progress of the rest of the class. Their growth was stunted, and they fell victim to a variety of physical ills, many of which persisted into adult life. They suffered from accidents and fear of machinery, and were exposed to indecent talk and 'Phallic ceremonies'. Allen Clarke was particularly angry, exposing the absurdity of the Bolton spinners' campaign for shorter hours owing to bad working conditions, when juxtaposed with their support for the continuance of 'half-time'. He saw the system as symptomatic of a more general cupidity and moral degeneracy: 'The majority of parents in Lancashire regard children only as commercial speculations to be turned into wage-earning machines as soon as the child's age and the law will permit.' At least the work was regulated, unlike surviving outposts of child labour elsewhere, and the factory surgeons often discovered existing ailments which might otherwise have gone untreated; but on balance the implications of persisting child labour and the 'half-time' system are gloomy. They were a major cost of relative material affluence, a cost which must be considered in psychic as well as physical and educational terms, although the intemperate nature of Clarke's comments reveals the social distance which separated him from the mainstream of the Bolton working class.[61]

Factory children were not the only sufferers from chronic if not always spectacular ill-health. The factory system nurtured occupational diseases of its own, as well as accidents and increasing stress, which affected adults and their families, although it is often difficult to disentangle the causes of diseases, as the home and the wider urban environment had their own interrelated contributions to make. Spinners were vulnerable to cancer of the scrotum, which arose from contact with carcinogenic oils, and the atmosphere of the card-room was particularly conducive to byssinosis and, no doubt, to less specifically industrial lung diseases including the greatest scourge of all, tuberculosis. This and other illnesses were spread by the almost universal custom of 'kissing the shuttle' to draw the weft through quickly in the weaving-sheds; and this also hastened the early decay of teeth, which was anyway almost universal among the working class in general. Clarke argued that less specific ill-health was endemic among factory workers, who 'hardly ever feel quite well; they are always hanging between moderately bad health and serious illness, mostly troubles of indigestion and chest complaints'. Hence, he thought, the immense sales of herbal remedies, quack medicines, and also pickles and vinegar to stimulate jaded palates. Women suffered especially, said Clarke, becoming old at 30: 'they seem to collapse, in one shrinking, wrinkling fall, from girls to old women'. This subjective evidence is harder to evaluate, especially as part of a political polemic; but there is certainly something in it. The persistence of frequent accidents, often fatal or disabling, is easier to document, and attempts to cut corners and maintain output played their part in this, especially when children were ordered to clean machinery while it was still running. Where cotton factories figured in a notional league table of hazardous employments is much harder to assess, especially when we bear in mind that the Lancashire coalfield was more dangerous than its rivals, that the chemical industry also promoted bad teeth, lung disease and sudden as well as less spectacular premature death, and that dock work involved hazards of its own which made their mark indelibly on the disfigured features of the dockers' union leader James Sexton. But there is no doubt that high family incomes in cotton were often paid for by ill-health, disease and industrial injury, and that textile workers often had to retire in their forties rather than their sixties, which made an accumulation of savings during the good years a necessity rather than a luxury.[62]

The cotton towns also became notorious for high rates of infant mortality, often more than 200 per 1000 children dying before their first birthday, and sometimes over 250 per 1000. Many contemporaries blamed working mothers and inadequate child-minding arrangements, and this mode of explanation was orthodox among the local Medical Officers of Health. It is easy to see how these ideas gained currency. Working mothers stayed on at work until the last possible minute: weavers, especially, sometimes gave birth at the loom. They returned to work at the earliest opportunity, long before the children were weaned. This meant the widespread employment of child-minders, often but not always elderly relatives; and it meant either that infants were exposed to the cold air when taken to their mothers to be fed, or that they were unhygienically bottle-fed on cows' milk from often suspect sources. The importance of older relatives as child-minders probably helped to perpetuate child-rearing practices which were increasingly viewed with horror by doctors and the Lady Health Visitors who were growing in numbers in the early twentieth century. But in practice matters were not so simple, as contemporaries like the suffrage campaigner Ada Nield Chew were well aware. Some cotton towns, like Burnley and Preston, had very high infant mortality rates; others, like Nelson, were close to the opposite end of the spectrum. There was no overall positive statistical correlation between the proportion of working wives in a town's population and the level of infant mortality. Within Lancashire, Liverpool's infant mortality rate consistently stood comparison with the worst of the cotton towns; and among the smaller places, the sixteen centres with rates of 200 or more per 1000 in 1904 included mining settlements like Abram, Skelmersdale and Ince-in-Makerfield, the nascent resort of Bispham-with-Norbreck and the port of Heysham as well as textile centres like Padiham and Farnworth. The rates were beginning to fall significantly in many places during the Edwardian years, without any necessary decline in women's factory work. The real reasons for high infant mortality rates were clearly very complex, and may elude analysis. They probably include child-rearing practices (especially feeding patterns), ignorance, general environmental conditions (including age and quality of housing stock and extent of over-crowding), and, indeed, sheer poverty. But there is no convincing evidence that a high level of infant mortality was, in itself, a necessary concomitant of the high family incomes in the cotton towns.[63]

From the 1860s onwards, it became increasingly apparent that cotton workers had lower fertility levels and smaller completed families than other groups within the working class, apart from certain other textile industries. This applied both to male and female fertility, and it was particularly marked in weaving, where women's wages and employment after marriage were both far above the average. The statistical evidence poses some problems, but the pattern seems clear; and the trend became strong enough to affect the birth-rates for whole towns by the turn of the century, with the odd exception like Preston, where the decline in fertility merely kept pace with the average for England and Wales as a whole. In most of the cotton district, fertility fell much faster than this; and by the early twentieth century the birth-rate for Lancashire as a whole was considerably below the national average, in sharp contrast with the position half a century earlier. Factory work must have provided scope for passing on advice about family limitation and the spacing of children, and may also have encouraged women to be more forthcoming about their needs, fears and expectations in discussing sex and family planning with their spouses. The evidence is fragmentary,

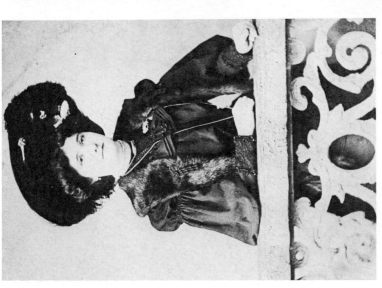

A Lancashire weaver in her Edwardian finery, posing for a studio photograph. (See Chapter 13.) [*Right*] Faces of child labour: a factory girl and two 'pit-brow lasses' in 1916. (See p. 309.)

The magnificent Edwardian flagship building of St Helens Co-op. (See p. 320.)
[*Below*] Widnes celebrates its smoke: a postcard from the late nineteenth century. (See p. 322.)

however, and we remain unsure how far family size was regulated by contraception, by abortion and even by abstinence. Some contemporaries were convinced that abortion was widespread, especially in weaving centres like Burnley and Nelson; and obvious abortifacients were prominently advertised in local newspapers. The shortage of direct evidence on abortion in oral interview evidence (although it is not altogether absent) is hardly surprising in the context, and should not be taken too seriously. But the evidence is also insufficient to sustain arguments that abortion was so widespread as to constitute the most important control on fertility in cotton Lancashire. Nevertheless, it does seem to have been, all too often, the first line of defence against an unwanted pregnancy. Where practised, it must often have undermined the health of mothers and perhaps of subsequent children; and it was so dangerous and unpleasant that its prevalence suggests the pressures under which many women in the cotton towns were living. The 'double shift' of factory work and housework, especially when the husband's contribution stopped at a portion of his wage packet, created intolerable burdens for some working mothers, and made the prospect of an additional child even more threatening than the risks and social stigma of abortion. This is only part of the story, but it is a significant part; and it reminds us that women as well as children suffered in the cause of higher material living standards in cotton Lancashire.[64]

High levels of infant mortality, and perhaps low fertility, were also affected by wider environmental conditions and by housing standards. The cotton district had particularly pressing problems of environmental pollution at mid-century, and it was not until the 1870s that remedial measures began to make any impact at all. The rivers of the Mersey basin were grossly polluted long before the chemical industry of Widnes and St. Helens heaped the final indignity on them. Town sewage and industrial pollution combined to turn rivers into health hazards within a few miles of their headwaters. The Irwell was a classic case. It rises two and a half miles above Bacup, and in that short distance, in 1870, it received the effluent from nineteen cotton factories, two dyeworks, two flour mills, a sawmill and a printing works. There were further sources of pollution on its tributaries, and at Bacup it received the town's untreated sewage. After this, what happened at Ramsbottom, Bury and further downstream was almost irrelevant. This was sadly typical, and very little was done to improve matters between the 1870s and the First World War, despite the formation of a Mersey and Irwell River Authority in 1891.[65] Too many vested interests with economic muscle were at stake. Much the same applied to air pollution. Contemporary diatribes about the appallingly grimy output of factory chimneys and domestic hearths were given retrospective substance by the remarkable adaptive behaviour of the peppered moth, which developed a much darker form to cope with industrial atmospheres. In 1848 the first black specimen of the peppered moth was caught in Manchester; by 1898, 98 per cent of the moths in the Manchester area took this form, 'an extremely rapid change given that the peppered moth breeds just once a year'.[66] Local legislation was already appearing before mid-century, but the will to enforce it effectively was lacking. In 1904, for example, only 29 prosecutions were undertaken in Lancashire outside the county boroughs (which admittedly excluded the largest towns) against emitters of 'black smoke', and the Medical Officer of Health complained that efforts in this direction were still 'inadequate'. Manchester was making 'serious though unsuccessful attempts ... to check atmospheric pollution' by the turn of the century, but in the mid-1930s it could still be estimated that 'the cost of household washing in Manchester would be reduced by about £250,000 a year if Manchester were as clean as Harrogate'.[67]

These general environmental influences affected amenity and comfort as well as health, and their impact on death and disease rates was impossible to disentangle from other factors. Despite the intractable nature of these problems, however, death and disease rates in the cotton district did begin to show a marked decline from the 1870s onwards; and the explanations must be sought in improved housing, water supply and perhaps health care, with a further contribution no doubt coming from rising material living standards.

Between 1840 and 1860 the death-rate for Lancashire as a whole, adjusted for changes in the age/sex composition of the population, fell by 4 per thousand to a level about 25 per cent above the national figure; but there were sharp fluctuations in the intervening years, and setbacks followed in the 1860s. Only after 1870 did a sustained downward trend begin in earnest; and over the last quarter of the century a national fall of more than one-third in the overall death-rate was matched in Lancashire, although the county's mortality remained comparatively worse than the nation as a whole. The cotton district shared in the improvement, although the high death-rates in the older housing around the central business districts remained intractable, and improvement was concentrated in the by-law terraces which were proliferating on the fringes of the old built-up area. For Manchester, Marilyn Pooley has calculated that 'between 1851 – 60 and 1891 – 1900 almost 88 per cent of the total reduction in mortality was due to a decline in mortality from the specified infectious diseases', and more than 60 per cent of the lives saved were those of children under 5 years old. Before 1880, the main reductions came from a decline in water-borne and food-borne infections, but subsequently inroads began to be made into tuberculosis mortality. Cotton Lancashire shared in the sharp national fall in deaths from smallpox, scarlet fever and diphtheria, although the hazily defined 'diarrhoea and dysentery' category was more intractable. The evidence is riddled with problems of definition and interpretation, but the late Victorian decline in mortality from environmentally related diseases (including, of course, the dreaded Asiatic cholera itself) is abundantly clear. This is, in itself, a strong indicator of improved living standards, in the form of life expectancy and personal security, although it was not as visible to contemporaries as it is to statistically minded historians. It is also easier to demonstrate than to explain; but we can point to environmental improvements which must have had some effect on the patchy and fluctuating but ultimately substantial fall in the death and disease rates.[68]

Better housing certainly made its contribution, although the story is far from simple. New houses for the working class were built to steadily more exacting standards, as building by-laws forbidding back-to-backs and cellar dwellings, prescribing minimum room heights and air space, and eventually requiring the provision of water-closets, were gradually adopted, first in some towns, then in others, from the 1860s onwards. Over most of the cotton district, substantial additions to the housing stock came under the new régime of wider streets and drier foundations, especially during the building booms of the mid-1870s and especially the late 1890s. But these new houses on the urban fringe remained the preserve of a privileged minority, and their nature and importance varied from town to town. In Oldham, new housing provision for the working class declined sharply in Edwardian times, and in several places it collapsed completely after 1911, as speculative investors sought richer pickings in other sectors. In Preston, a full range of by-laws was not introduced until 1880, in the teeth of obtuse but determined opposition from builders and property-owners, and new houses were still being built to pre-1880 specifications for many years afterwards in areas where plans had been rushed through just in time to beat the legis-lation.[69] Practically all the housing was left to private enterprise and the profit motive. Only in Manchester and Salford were municipal housing schemes significantly in evidence; but Manchester's slum clearance tenement blocks in Ancoats were spartan, unpopular and too expensive, in the absence of any conception of subsidised rents, for those who needed them most; while the 200 low-density houses on the Corporation's 'garden suburb' estate at Blackley were inaccessible as well as dear. A few Co-operative ventures provided a superior standard of housing for those who aspired to owner-occupancy, especially in Oldham.[70] But for the vast majority of working-class town-dwellers, any hope of improvements that went deeper than the obsessive scrubbing of flagstones and donkey-stoning of doorsteps depended on the imposition of amendments to the sanitary arrangements of older houses by the local authority. Manchester was particularly active in this respect. An Act of 1867 empowered the Corporation to enforce the closure of houses deemed unfit for human habitation, unless the landlord made repairs and improvements as required. After 1885 this Act was systematically enforced, and by 1914 about 27,000 houses had been demolished or altered under local government compulsion. Back-to-back houses were almost abolished, water-closets became nearly universal in place of ashpits and middens, and proper piped water supplies were installed. Chronic overcrowding persisted, especially in the numerous one- and two-bedroomed inner-city slums; but this was real, if unglamorous, progress. The smaller cotton towns followed more slowly; but even Preston was making headway by the turn of the century. A local working-class campaign against the remarkably high death and infant mortality rates, supported by vigorous prodding from central government, brought a sustained campaign for the replacement of privies by water-closets, and of insanitary ashpits by dustbins, so that people were no longer living among their own excrement (which had, in many cases, been cleared only once a year, leaving a permanent stench in many back streets). Extensive slum clearance programmes were also introduced.[71] Such measures were almost universal in the cotton towns by the 1890s; and the improved sanitary arrangements, coupled with the widespread closer supervision of milk supplies and the spread of health education, must have made an important contribution to the eventual fall in death and disease rates, including infant mortality. The spread of public parks after the 'Cotton Famine' can only have reinforced the trend, although it was the improvements to homes, streets and yards that really counted. To complete the picture, the quality and accessibility of piped water supplies was also improving rapidly in the later nineteenth century.

A constant water supply at adequate pressure was necessary if sewers were to operate efficiently, as well as enabling residents to escape from the constraints, dangers and expense of dependence on wells (increasingly polluted by the percolation of sewage from ashpits and cesspools), ponds, itinerant water vendors or the appalling rivers. Here again, Manchester led the way, with its enormous borrowing resources, active and educated élites, and access to expertise. Its water supply came under municipal control in 1851, as the Corporation replaced an 'outstandingly incompetent' private company. Between 1847 and 1878 the number of customers increased from nearly 35,000 to over 155,000, and consumption per house went up from 50 gallons per day in 1841 to 130 in 1878. By this time about four-fifths of Manchester's houses had an internal water supply, while almost every house at least had 'access to water fittings'. Soft Pennine water from Longdendale was available from 1851, with corresponding benefits to industry (especially textile finishing); and the controversial Thirlmere water scheme ensured that the expansion of services and consumption could continue into the new century. Perhaps significantly, the opening of the first Thirlmere pipeline in 1894 coincided with the initiation of the city's new main drainage system. It also gave many of Manchester's neighbours access to Lake District water, improving the quality and flexibility of their own supplies. But they, too, had not been idle. Moorland reservoirs were coming into use at the backs of most of the cotton towns during the 1850s and 1860s, though there were endless debates about the relative merits of private and municipal operation, and about technology and, above all, cost. Towns like Preston, Bolton, Oldham, Ashton, Rochdale and Wigan were getting municipal water, making it possible to supply their poorer districts properly. But even in 1870, supply often failed to meet demand in time of drought, and reserve supplies were sometimes suspect, as Accrington had recourse to a coal mine, Oldham to polluted wells and Stockport to river water which was contaminated with arsenic. But matters were improving rapidly in the late nineteenth century, and by the Edwardian years only the outlying industrial villages were still posing serious problems. Within the towns, of course, there remained slum areas with completely inadequate supplies, and fitted baths remained a rare luxury in working-class homes. As John Hassan points out, too, it is impossible to *prove* that the vast improvements in water supply, from appalling beginnings at mid-century, in themselves made a significant impact on the people's health. But the burden of proof must lie with the sceptics, and on grounds of amenity and comfort alone, these developments constituted a major improvement in the living standards of most working-class town-dwellers in the cotton district.[72]

The municipalities of the cotton district were increasingly active in other spheres, besides water supply, which ultimately enhanced the quality of life of most of their inhabitants. The mid-Victorian years saw extensive municipal involvement in gas as well as water supply, and on both counts the cotton towns were a long way ahead of Birmingham, which has become misleadingly famous in this respect. Contemporaries were well aware that municipal control meant better quality and cheaper supplies, when the alternative was a monopolistic private concern which siphoned off its profits to often distant shareholders. Tramways and electricity also came under Town Hall control later in the century in most of urban Lancashire, as of course did parks and libraries; and all this helped to channel the prosperity of industry and property speculation in ways which benefited the workforce at large. With all its limitations – and contemporary socialists were quick to point to them, especially in the field of housing subsidies and municipal wage-rates – urban government in cotton Lancashire played an increasingly prominent, and perhaps a distinctive, part in boosting working-class living standards in the late nineteenth and early twentieth centuries.[73]

The second half of the nineteenth century, and again especially the years after 1870, also saw the expanded formal provision of medical aid to working-class people in the cotton towns. As Pickstone says, 'between 1857 and 1887, new or larger voluntary hospitals were built in all the major towns of the [Manchester] Region'; and many are still in use in the 1980s. They were funded partly by local notables, but increasingly they depended on regular collections and subscriptions from churches and workplaces, and many working-class people assured themselves of a hospital bed at need by making regular payments. The belated spurt of new workhouse building in the mid-Victorian years included infirmary provision, sometimes in separate, purpose-built premises, and the county lunatic asylums also continued to expand their capacity. Isolation hospitals for infectious diseases developed rapidly in the late nineteenth century under local government auspices, as did sanatoria for tuberculosis. Free medical treatment became more widely available for those in need, and even when it came under the Poor Law umbrella it involved less of a stigma after 1885, when receipt of medical relief alone no longer carried the penalty of disfranchisement. Aspects of this extension of institutional care have debatable implications, of course, especially in the case of lunatic asylums; but the overall and predominant effect was to reduce stress, insecurity and the risk of spreading infection in crowded working-class districts. This was truer of the years after about 1870, as trained nursing care became more frequent and hospital environments became safer and more controlled, than in the mid-Victorian years, and the exact nature and extent of hospitals' contribution to falling death and disease rates can never be known. A great deal of reliance was still placed on home treatment and herbal remedies, and working-class families still ran up doctors' bills which they could never hope to pay; but at least we can point to the steady expansion of an improving system of care and treatment in cases of acute and chronic sickness, and also in dealing with the industrial accidents which remained such an endemic feature of working-class life.[74]

The drawbacks to life in the cotton towns were real and numerous. They included pollution, ugliness, high mortality and some of the implications of the employment of whole families outside the home. More visible and tangible to most of the inhabitants, however, were the relatively high levels of material living standards, basic comfort and security which could increasingly be attained, the scope for unpretentious and inexpensive enjoyment outside clearly defined working hours, and the supportive ties of close-knit neighbourhoods. Many of the drawbacks were themselves being cut down to size by the turn of the century, and some existed more in the minds of outside observers than in those of the inhabitants themselves. This is not to deny that the Edwardian cotton towns were unlovely places; nor is it to wish away the poverty (material, mental and spiritual), the pain, the insecurity and the exploitation which remained. There is an important kind of truth in Allen Clarke's denunciation of the Bolton of the 1890s:

... a terrible heap of houses and buildings, with blackened church spires standing here and there, and hundreds of high chimneys belching forth, like huge fiery dragons, till the whole place looks like a city sunk in a sea of smoke. Amidst that sickening jerry-jumble of cheap bricks and cheaper British industry, over a hundred thousand men, women and children toil and exist, sweating in the vast, hot, stuffy mills and sweltering forges ... growing up stunted, breeding thoughtlessly, dying prematurely, knowing not, nor dreaming, ... of aught better than this shrieking, steamy sphere of slime and sorrow.[75]

But Clarke admitted that the inhabitants 'see nothing very hideous or sad in their town; they have been used to nothing better'. They may also have been aware that they might have been much worse off elsewhere; for the evidence from Merseyside suggests that its towns had most of the disadvantages of the cotton towns, without compensating for them in other ways. For other areas of Lancashire, the evidence is more ambivalent, and conclusions are affected more obviously by the values and personal preferences of the observer; but on most criteria, and perhaps especially on those used by most contemporary working-class people themselves, the late Victorian improvement in living standards was much more general and pronounced in the cotton towns than in the rest of this first industrial county.

Liverpool is the most clear-cut case, although it is much less well-researched than the cotton towns. Leisure, for example, seems to have been dominated by the pub, with fewer refinements and alternatives than in the larger cotton towns, at least. Dock labourers and carters drank while waiting for work, and again while waiting to be paid, or picking up their wages on the Saturday. Hugh Shimmin, in 1857, portrayed a Liverpool underworld of crime, vice, obscenity, vulgarity, gaming, pugilism and dog-fighting which, with all his exaggerations and propagandist intent, has no counterpart in the literature on the Manchester region.[76] The centrality of drink was slow to be eroded by alternative enjoyments. 'Rational recreations' made little headway, and even the Working Men's Clubs saw more members at the 'gaming tables' than in the reading-rooms. Saving for deferred gratifications such as seaside holidays was at best a minority preoccupation: the half-day ferry trip to the disreputable attractions of New Brighton was the summit of most people's ambitions. The parks were largely given over to the sports of clerks, shopkeepers and the middle class. Such were the assertions of contemporaries, and it is difficult to contradict the overall picture they present. Only in the 1890s, as licensing controls were tightened and the city's professional football teams gained mass followings which drew many working-class men away from the pub on Saturday afternoons, did minor changes begin to be noticed. From small and belated beginnings in the mid-1880s, Liverpool by 1894 had acquired two of the nation's leading football teams, had housed the FA Cup Final and held the national attendance and gate receipts records. Everton, indeed, was the most prosperous of the founder members of the Football League. Much of the support for these ventures was middle-class, however, and intensity of attachment to the game was probably less than in the smaller cotton towns. The low and irregular incomes of the Liverpool working class were reflected in the persisting predominance of drink and gambling at the expense of other enjoyments, and the rapid development of professional football was exceptional in this regard.[77]

Liverpool's economy and social structure also stunted the growth of the thrift and mutual assistance organisations which were so numerous and effective in the cotton towns. Joan Smith observes that 'the great friendly societies simply didn't have a Liverpool membership' in 1910: 'their 6072 Liverpool members and 2154 Cheshire members were less than the number of skilled workers in Liverpool'. Co-operation on the Rochdale model was a late developer, being imported by railway workers in the 1890s and remaining the preserve of a small minority before the First World War. Liverpool men joined tontines or dividing societies in large numbers, but the only widespread subscriptions to insurance schemes involved burial societies which paid funeral benefits and nothing else. It is probably significant that most of the national 'collecting societies', seven of the largest eleven in 1872, including the giant Royal Liver and Liverpool

Victoria, were Liverpool-based. These bodies were run despotically by central committees or individual entrepreneurs, and up to half their income in mid-Victorian times might go on administration, mainly managers' and collectors' salaries and bonuses. They depended for their success on members failing to keep up their payments, and their main purpose seems to have been financial exploitation rather than the encouragement of thrift. Many of those insured were young children, and the Liverpool coroner in 1874 believed that many parents deliberately neglected or even murdered their offspring to gain the death benefit. The societies were made to reform themselves to some extent in the late nineteenth century, but they still compared very unfavourably with the ordinary Friendly Societies as agencies of thrift and providers of genuine insurance.[78] Moneylending at exorbitant rates of interest was also rife, to tide the irregularly paid through short-term crises; and the prevalence of long-distance migration and sectarian divisions probably made for less mutual support and assistance between neighbours than was the case in the cotton towns. This was altogether a less secure society, in the short run as well as in the longer term.[79]

Housing problems were particularly severe in Liverpool, both in terms of the quality of the housing stock and of the level of overcrowding. The disastrous mid-century inheritance of courts and back-to-backs left a task of unique magnitude for sanitary reformers, who also had to contend with vociferous opposition from the slum property owners' defence organisations. Despite a persistent doctrinaire unwillingness to build cheap housing unless private enterprise refused to make the attempt, Liverpool Corporation was a surprising pioneer of municipal housing, starting in 1869, and of slum clearance. The populist Toryism of Sir Arthur Forwood stimulated a great expansion of the slum demolition and rehousing programme from 1898 onwards, and by 1915 the council had built 2895 dwellings, almost all of them flats. It housed a higher proportion of its population than any other British city, although the figure was only 1.31 per cent. More impressively, nearly 20,000 'insanitary' houses had been demolished between 1864 and 1913, more than half of them by the Corporation, and only 2771 court and back-to-back houses remained. Only a small proportion of the displaced slum-dwellers were rehoused by the Corporation, despite promises to that effect: they were deterred by high rents and strict tenancy conditions, and Pooley and Irish show that even with tenants drawn mainly from skilled labour, there was a disturbingly high rate of turnover. Moreover, although death-rates were beginning to fall by the turn of the century, the slums retained their reputation for unusual squalor and endemic violence. Associated problems of prostitution and disease also remained intractable. All this was much worse than anything Manchester had to offer, and even the almost-parallel development of the municipal water supply, with Welsh water supplementing the Rivington reservoirs from 1892 onwards, failed to produce real parity in public health and environmental conditions. Despite the energetic but belated and incomplete efforts of its municipality, Liverpool was unable to recover from its mid-Victorian position as the 'black spot on the Mersey', and in 1911 it still had 'the unenviable reputation of possessing the worst slums of any English city'.[80]

This was not the whole story, and many of Liverpool's better-off working-class families by 1914 lived in by-law terraces at a distance from the festering slums of dockland. But in general, conditions were clearly worse here than in the cotton towns, except for the most secure of skilled labourers or well-established, regular dock and railway workers. Moreover, the scope for upward social mobility was probably more limited, as the major industries and commercial activities became more capital-intensive. Admittedly, the Liverpool shipowners who emerged as really substantial wealth-holders at the turn of the century were remarkable for their humble origins as well as their surprising acceptability in high society; but this perhaps reflected the ease of entering the trade and profiting from the early days of ocean-going steamers at the start of their careers, and they were certainly the exceptions that proved the rule.[81] For most people, there was little or no hope of advancement; and most of the legion of commercial clerks were as ill-paid and insecure as the manual workers. The gulf between capital and labour was similarly widening in the mining and heavy industrial centres of south-west Lancashire. Coal and glass had always been more demanding than the cotton industry in their entry requirements, although the chemical industry offered more scope for enterprising men of limited resources in mid-Victorian Widnes; and the size of the optimum enterprise increased dauntingly as technology became more sophisticated after the mid-Victorian boom. W. H. Lever's triumphs in the soap trade and Beecham's patent medicine success were triumphs of the unorthodox from which it would be rash to generalise. At a more mundane and accessible level, there were fewer skilled, supervisory or junior management positions to provide a ladder of opportunity in industries whose working conditions imposed more than their fair share of hardship, discomfort and danger.

The towns and industrial villages of Merseyside, with their concentration on coal, chemicals, glass and heavy engineering and metalworking, offered relatively good and sometimes excellent wages to skilled men and to those in dangerous trades; but the structure of employment left few options for women and young children, leaving family incomes often precariously dependent on a single bread-winner in a risky or unemployment-prone job. Under these conditions a distinctive working-class culture seems to have developed, although as yet we know relatively little about it. One important strand was an ideal of masculinity which was hard and sometimes violent, and often associated with heavy drinking. 'Purring', or no-holds-barred fighting which featured systematic kicking with heavy clogs, was a frequent occurrence in the mining district in the 1870s and beyond, and it sometimes gave an additional dimension of horror to domestic violence. More orthodox pugilism and blood sports also survived strongly; and as the older ways eventually began to decline in the late nineteenth century, it may well be significant that it was in this area of Lancashire, in contrast with the rest of the county, that what became Rugby League attracted a mass following and became the predominant code of organised professional sport: for the violence of this game is well attested by the high casualty rates of the 1880s and 1890s. Above all, hard drinking remained general and intractable, among the skilled as well as the unskilled. Glassblowing was a thirsty occupation, and the banning of beer-drinking from Pilkington's works at St. Helens led to frequent truancy in search of beer during working hours, which sometimes provoked the works manager into angry visits to local pubs. Widnes saltcake workers, and chemical yard workers generally, also had a spectacular reputation for beer consumption and drunkenness, and the problem was endemic in the area.[82]

This was not the whole story. Miners, especially their union leaders, included advocates of thrift, temperance and self-improvement, and agencies promoting these ideals were not absent from the area. Some made considerable headway in the late nineteenth century. Even Widnes was acquiring an array of more 'rational' recreations: a theatre was established in the late 1870s, the brass band movement became popular, a well-used public library was given new premises, shared with the municipal technical school, in 1896, and by this time there was an annual Widnes Eisteddfod, though it must have been a pale shadow of similar events in Liverpool, with its flourishing Welsh community. St. Helens, too, was developing libraries, lecture courses and a popular musical culture: in 1899 a visit from the Hallé Orchestra was the occasion of one of the future Sir Thomas Beecham's first appearances as a conductor. The extent of working-class interest here is hard to gauge, as is the nature of working-class responses to the mid-Victorian growth in church and chapel provision, which was still being consolidated at the turn of the century. Friendly Society membership was much healthier than in Liverpool, but the great late Victorian success story in these towns was the dramatic rise of the Co-operative movement. The St. Helens Industrial society, founded by workers at a bottle factory in 1883, topped 3000 members in 1892 and reached 6833 by 1900, thus accounting for nearly half the houholds in the town. By this time there were nine branch shops. The Runcorn and Widnes society grew more slowly from earlier origins. It was founded in 1862 but trebled its membership to over 6000 between 1880 and 1902, continuing to grow steadily thereafter.[83]

All this suggests that civilising influences were spreading and living standards were improving on a broad front by the late nineteenth century, despite severe trade depressions in 1878–9 and 1894–5, and despite the late Victorian problems of the chemical industry. By this time, too, stable working-class neighbourhoods were cohering as population increase came from local births rather than migration. But housing and working conditions were often very poor, and environmental pollution created extra hazards for those whose wages and working hours obliged them to live close to their work. The housing crises of the 1850s and 1860s, especially in St. Helens and Widnes, had given rise to severe overcrowding in the short term; but matters were gradually improving thereafter, although many streets remained ill-planned, crowded and cheerless, and there were persisting high numbers of persons per inhabited house, especially in Widnes. Contemporaries admitted that urban slums still existed in the early twentieth century, although by 1911 Warrington's Medical Officer of Health could claim that, on his definition, only 1175 of the borough's 72,375 inhabitants lived in them. The smaller mining villages fared worst for longest. Skelmersdale in 1874 was described thus in *The Lancet*: 'The houses, many of the most miserable construction, are almost buried in the filth of the inhabitants; the privies so foul as to repel even those most familiarised with them; the drainage accumulated in horrible puddles, fed also by the liquid abominations of pig sties and midden-steads.' Thirty years later, Skelmersdale had caught up with improvements elsewhere: it had a main sewerage system, two outfall treatment works, and scavenging undertaken by an urban district council, although its death-rate was still the highest in Lancashire outside the major towns. This was a representative, if belated, improvement; but in general, throughout the area sewering, constant piped water and other basic public health improvements arrived later and less effectively than in the cotton district. The pollution of the Widnes Gas and Water Company's supply with caustic soda in the early 1860s was unusual; but even under normal circumstances the company's water was heavily impregnated with salt. Long after this problem had been resolved, the Widnes of 1898 still had no proper sewering, with the overwhelming majority of its houses still depending on open privies and ashpits. St. Helens was similarly dilatory. In public health provision, and in general quality of local government, the cotton towns had the edge.[84]

Much the same could be said about private and charitable welfare measures. Pilkington's of St. Helens were unusual in combining authoritarian labour relations with providing sporting facilities, lectures and a works canteen, and contributing to their employees' sick and burial society. Most firms did little or nothing. Despite a high industrial accident rate, Widnes had no accident hospital until 1878, and no further provision until 1893, while St. Helens's Cottage Hospital had to be rescued from financial collapse in 1875 by a workpeople's penny-a-week fund.[85] But industrial disease and injury were rampant, and the long hours worked in the chemical industry made matters worse. Exposure to acid and chlorine gas posed terrible hazards, and those who escaped death or disfigurement all too often ended their lives prematurely in Whiston workhouse. The accident rate in Lancashire's coal mines was also high in relation to output and labour force, and deaths from respiratory diseases among Lancashire miners were 75 per cent above the national average.[86] Air and water pollution from the chemical industry also depressed living standards in general around Widnes and St. Helens. Even when controls on hydrochloric acid gas emissions began to make a difference in the last quarter of the nineteenth century, there remained a legacy of dead trees and blasted hedgerows; and pollution levels remained depressing to health, even if they were not more positively injurious. The stench from polluted becks which had recently been trout streams added to the discomfort. Outsiders were horrified: Matthew Arnold called St. Helens 'a hell hole', and Robert Blatchford described its atmosphere in 1899 as 'a blend of railway tunnel, hospital ward, gas works and open sewer'. Hundreds of acres of land were given over to chemical waste tips. To the locals, of course, smoke meant prosperity, and some defended their town against the sneers of visitors. Widnes mothers praised the fumes from the saltcake plant as a sovereign cure for the children's whooping cough, and a local schoolmaster replied to the criticisms of Edwardian journalists in lame but heartfelt verse. Postcards could be bought, celebrating the smoky pall of Widnes with a kind of inverted pride. We cannot ignore these responses, but it is difficult to escape the conclusion that lives were materially impoverished by these conditions, even more so than in the cotton towns; and it is surely significant that death-rates in the area began to fall later and more slowly than in the Manchester region.[87] More generally, this was an area in which families headed by fit men in the prime of life could achieve a measure of material comfort, if the temptations of drink were resisted; but despite the impressive rise of the Co-op late in the century, living standards were less secure than they had become in the cotton towns, family spending power was less, and living, working and environmental conditions for most people were considerably worse. There were real improvements, especially in the late nineteenth century; but they cannot compare with the stronger and more general evidence of rising living standards east of Wigan.

In the far north of the county, Barrow had much in common with the mid-Victorian boom-towns of greater Merseyside. Wages for skilled men were high, and there was buoyant demand for skilled labour except in time of depression. A mid-Victorian housing shortage was overcome in the last quarter of the century, although many families lived in bleak Scottish-style tenements on Barrow Island. On the debit side, too, rents and prices remained high, and there was little waged work for women. Where Barrow scored, however, was in its ready accessibility to countryside and seashore which were useful, in terms of Nature's bounty, as well as beautiful; and it was a planned town, uninspiring though its gridiron layout was, with better housing standards than most of Lancashire's industrial centres. Less optimism is in order for the surrounding industrial villages, where iron ore mining, dirty and unreliably paid, was already beginning to decline sharply in the 1890s; although here, too, the late Victorian growth of the Co-op suggests a widespread capacity for cash trading and indirect saving. The other major northern outpost of Lancashire industry, Lancaster itself, was more problematic. Its rapidly growing oilcloth and table baize industries employed large numbers of labourers who were paid the classic 'round about a pound a week', it had some waged work for women, but not very much, and it contained crowded and insanitary slums around the old town centre. Here again, however, a clean river and unspoiled countryside provided additional resources. Elizabeth Roberts argues, from her oral evidence, that the household management skills of wives who were happy in their domestic sphere of activity, made for a healthy diet and gave both Barrow and Lancaster better real standards of living than the usual indicators might suggest. This is an interesting argument, but it does not convince. The interviewees are drawn from those who were contented enough to stay put, and sufficiently competently reared to survive into a coherent old age. Their memories of home baking and nourishing stews, of mothers' part-time work and home dressmaking, of marriages as consensual partnerships (except where husbands drank), are fascinating and revealing, but we cannot know how far they were 'typical', and of what. On the evidence as a whole, it seems plausible that Barrow might have provided better all-round living conditions for its workers than the superficially similar heavy industrial towns of Merseyside; but it is altogether more difficult to be optimistic about Lancaster, despite its advantages in some respects. The stunted growth of its organised working class is a telling symptom here. There were ways of alleviating the grinding poverty which prevailed in much of Lancaster; but they were less effective, though less stressful (especially for wives and mothers) than the factory-centred family economies of the cotton towns.[88]

The towns of industrial Merseyside and north Lancashire sent very few working-class people to the seaside, except as occasional day-trippers; and this is a further comment on the contrast in resources and, no doubt, values when we compare them with the cotton towns. Demand from the cotton district was sufficient to prompt, and in large part to sustain, the development of the world's first working-class seaside resort at Blackpool, although even here the North Shore and parts of the residential south remained socially select. But life was precarious for the landladies and small business people, usually from working-class backgrounds, who strove to make ends meet during the short summer season; and the many unskilled labourers were regularly plunged into winter poverty. Even in this most successful of seaside resorts, and more so at Morecambe and in the working-class quarters of Southport and Lytham, prosperity was elusive and making ends meet was often a difficult and complex process. Many seaside entrepreneurs soon returned defeated to the grimier but more prosperous environments of the cotton towns which had spawned them and generated their investment capital. The seaside provided lively holidays and, increasingly, comfortable retirement, but it posed problems of its own for its hard-pressed working-class residents.[89]

Patterns of working-class experience varied remarkably within Lancashire during these years of generally increasing prosperity. On most criteria, the cotton towns fared best, especially during the late Victorian price fall; but there were clear improvements everywhere from the late 1860s and early 1870s onwards, despite recurrent and sometimes major setbacks. As it turned out, however, the First World War marked a great watershed in the fortunes of the cotton industry in particular, and of most of industrial Lancashire.

After 1920, at any rate, things were never quite the same again; and much of the county experienced severe industrial depression and decline through the years between the wars. It remains for us to describe and explain this salutary reversal, and to assess its implications for living standards, social relations and politics in the economically troubled and sometimes disastrous 1920s and 1930s.

14

THE LOSS OF INDUSTRIAL PRIMACY: DEPRESSION, DECLINE AND ADJUSTMENT, 1914 – 39

The year 1913 was the high water mark of the Lancashire cotton industry. The First World War brought disruption to raw material supplies, production and marketing; its aftermath saw a short-lived but disastrous investment boom, fuelled by false expectations of returning prosperity; and this in turn worsened the impact of the sustained slump which followed, as established markets were irrevocably lost to overseas competitors. Some semblance of stability was emerging by the mid-1930s, but it was to be short-lived. Coal and chemicals also experienced sustained hard times between the wars, and the depressed state of Liverpool reflected the reduced circumstances of its hinterland. But the picture was not uniformly gloomy. New industries were developing in parts of the county, especially on a Liverpool – Manchester axis, and there were pockets of prosperity further north in the 1930s. Lancashire's economy was more diverse, and its new initiatives more numerous and successful, than in the other depressed industrial areas, such as South Wales and the North-East. The complexity of the pattern will need further elucidation. But the predominant elements are clear enough. The relative prosperity and world economic importance of Lancashire were evaporating at alarming speed during the inter-war years, and attempts to arrest the decline of the Victorian and Edwardian staple industries were never more than palliatives. The changes of these years put at risk a whole way of life, and challenged the basis of an established culture and political system. The full implications took a long time to work through, and it took the final demise of cotton and its communities in the 1950s and 1960s to make them explicit, in a climate of general rapid transformation in culture, attitudes and material living standards. Responses to change in the 1920s and 1930s, indeed, were low-key and, perhaps, surprisingly passive. But the transitional nature of these years is evident, although hindsight has sharpened our perceptions; and the economic, social and political currents of the inter-war years in Lancashire require sustained explanation.

The economic effects of the First World War as such were patchy, and few of the changes within Lancashire had long-term implications. The initial impact on the cotton industry seemed to threaten catastrophe, as 'the Liverpool Cotton Exchange closed down, and unemployment among the cotton workers soared to enormous proportions'.[1] But adjustments were soon made, and the problems of wartime working were eased by government intervention. Many cotton workers volunteered for the armed forces, especially when height requirements were eased for the 'Bantam' battalions, and many more were later conscripted. Already in 1915 there were complaints from Bolton that mules were being run short-handed, because of the loss of piecers to the war; and female piecers were having to be introduced. The local spinners' union complained of the intolerable pressure of work on their remaining members. Bolton, as a centre of fine spinning using Egyptian cotton, was less affected by supply problems than the sectors of the industry which relied on American imports. After 1916 short-time working 'increased progressively' until the war ended, as transatlantic cotton shipments had a relatively low priority. In 1917 a Cotton Control Board was established to control raw cotton prices and organise work-sharing between the different firms, with groups of workers standing down in turn on a rota system, and receiving unemployment pay. This system broke down before the war ended, but it lasted long enough to prevent serious dislocation.[2] While the Lancashire cotton industry was marking time in this way, with no innovations or new investment, important developments were occurring in the Indian and Far Eastern markets which were crucial to the industry's future. Exports to India were cut by 'the curtailment of British production, especially of coarse goods, and the shortage of shipping capacity', enabling the emergent Indian cotton factories to increase their output, aided by the introduction of a protective tariff on cotton imports in 1917. The Japanese moved in, too, co-ordinating mercantile, banking and shipping initiatives to remarkable effect, and they also stepped in to fill the export vacuum to China, which likewise began to develop manufacturing capacity of its own. The war acted as a forcing-house for growth which was already taking place, and the results were to be disastrous for Lancashire in the 1920s and 1930s.[3]

The other distinctive manufacturing industry of the cotton district, engineering, was less affected by the war than in most places. Textile engineering was less involved in munitions work than any other branch of the industry. The largest arms firm in the Manchester area, Armstrong-Whitworth at Openshaw, had 7000 workers by 1917, but this was 'small by the standards of other areas'. Ordinary commercial work remained important alongside arms contracts, and this brought industrial strife when firms attempted to extend the 'dilution' of skilled labour by the admixture of women and unapprenticed men from war work to civilian contracts. Action of this sort in Rochdale precipitated a strike in May 1917 which soon spread through Lancashire and into other areas, and the engineering unions were anxious to remove the women from the workplaces as soon as possible after the war.[4] Outside the cotton district, Barrow's shipyards saw an enormous wartime boom, with endemic labour unrest and appalling overcrowding; and here and in Lancaster, among other places, munitions factories provided unaccustomed high wages and independence for women workers, although this situation, profoundly disturbing as it was to contemporary moralists, did not survive the ending of hostilities.[5]

Like Barrow, the heavy industrial towns of the south-west Lancashire coalfield experienced boom conditions during the war. At Widnes the ailing United Alkali Company increased its labour force from 3500 men in 1914 to 4800 men and 700 women in 1918. New processes were introduced, and new plant was installed. Crosfield's of Warrington made very large wartime profits, not all of which were due to inflation, on both the soap and chemicals sides of the business, and again there was extensive investment in new plant. Pilkington's of St. Helens also coped well with the war, although here the temporary cessation of competition in the home market has to be set against the collapse of export markets, into some of which United States glass manufacturers moved with alacrity.[6]

Both Pilkington's and Crosfield's had strong Territorial Army links, fostered by leading members of the firms; and this meant that large numbers of their workers departed for the front at the first opportunity. Many never returned. Waller's calculation that 'the war claimed 13,500 Liverpudlians' is a telling reminder that, throughout the county as throughout the nation, this aspect of hostilities dominated the experience and formed the perceptions of a very large number of families, especially where lonely or grieving women were left struggling to make ends meet on inadequate allowances. In this respect as in others, the experience of Liverpool was particularly complex. The number of ships using the port in 1918 was less than half the 1914 total, although the tonnage held up rather better. Even so, the port was permanently congested, as several thousand dockers enlisted in the early months of the war, and the limited level of investment in basic technology like cranes and dock railways was cruelly exposed. Attempts to introduce women to portering duties on the waterfront were successfully resisted by the dock labourers' union in 1916, after which investment in such items as locomotives and electric cranes was increased. But the Mersey Docks and Harbour Board suffered financially, as the government paid for war-related work at three-quarters of the standard rate, while dockers' pay was increased as they were brought under the same conditions as munitions workers. A Dockers' Battalion, formed in 1915, brought 1200 dockers under quasi-military discipline at higher rates of pay. The shipping lines suffered unevenly from government requisitions and enemy action. Fat profits could be made in the early war years on the more distant routes, and in some cases they were reinvested;

but competitors were emerging during these years, especially for the Pacific, South African and Central and South American routes, while 1.5 million tons of Liverpool-registered shipping were being lost. The port of Liverpool actually achieved its highest post-Victorian proportional share of the United Kingdom's domestic exports (38.8 per cent in 1917) and imports (36.8 per cent in 1918) during the war years, and it must have seemed busy and prosperous; but the balance of world trade was beginning to tilt against it.[7]

The war advanced the cause of industrial militants, especially in the engineering industry, and propelled women into new kinds of economic activity. It also split the labour movement, in centres as diverse as Liverpool and Nelson, on questions involving the legitimacy of the conflict and the ethics of conscription. Nevertheless, the war and its aftermath helped to create the conditions for a reconstituted Labour Party to increase its local influence and representation. The wartime innovations in women's employment, however, whether in munitions, the tramways or the postal service, evaporated with the signing of the Armistice. In the economy more generally, the end of the war brought new beginnings and, before very long, uneasy or even disastrous outcomes.[8]

The cotton industry welcomed the coming of peace with a brief and spectacular boom during 1918 – 20. The average dividend paid by 150 spinning companies was 16¼ per cent in 1918, 21¼ in 1919 and 40.21 in 1920, compared with a maximum of nearly 16 per cent at the crest of the 1905 – 7 boom, and more normal figures of between 5 and 7 per cent.[9] These figures were misleading: output never approached its 1913 peak, and the pressure on capacity depended on the need to catch up with domestic demand: cloth exports in 1920 stood at less than two – thirds of the 1913 figure, and yarn exports at less than one-third. Inflation also contributed to high profits, and Sandberg argues that they 'were in large part due to a failure of wages to adjust rapidly to the labor shortage', while potential over-capacity was disguised by the reduction of the working week from 57½ to 48 hours in July 1919. At the time, however, the impressive returns generated ludicrous optimism. Many firms were reconstructed and recapitalised: 'about one-third of [the spinning industry] was reconstructed, the original concerns selling out to new ones at about eight times the old value'. Speculation was rife, and London capitalists moved in, amid forecasts of sustained high profits for at least five years. All this activity merely exacerbated the problems in the spinning industry when the boom collapsed in 1921, as over-capitalisation crippled dividends and discouraged investment, while loans had to be repaid and creditors pacified. The post-war future of the cotton industry would have been perilous at the best of times: as it was, the legacy of the frenzied financial activity of 1918 – 20 was as a millstone round its neck. Sandberg comments that, 'Perhaps the best thing that can be said about this brief spurt is that it did not last long enough to result in any major investments in new capacity.' Paul Harris is more outspoken: 'The attitude of the cottonocracy to the boom was one of unadulterated greed, unsubstantiatable optimism, wild speculation, short-sightedness, incompetence and negligence.' We shall return to these allegations.[10]

The post-war bubble burst disastrously in 1921, and the cotton industry was never to be the same again. This was not immediately apparent to contemporaries, who watched hopefully, indeed expectantly, but in vain for the revival of orders from India and the Far East. A steady fall in the price of raw cotton brought no response, and it slowly became apparent that the wartime increase in coarse yarn and cheap cloth output in India, China and Japan was accelerating, and was squeezing English cotton out of its most important markets. The granting of fiscal autonomy to India in 1921 was followed by rising tariffs on British cotton cloth imports, reaching 25 per cent in 1931, soon after the Congress Party began its campaign for a nationwide boycott of British cloth. By this time, much of the damage had already been done. Exports to India hovered around half the 1909–13 average throughout the 1920s, and by 1937 they had fallen to about one-tenth of the pre-war peak. Exports to China, the Middle East and Egypt followed a similar trajectory, with a sharp fall sustained through the 1920s and, as Sandberg says, 'total disaster' in the 1930s. Other parts of the world presented a less catastrophic picture, and exports to Canada, Australia, New Zealand and sub-Saharan Africa held up particularly well, fostered by close political links and favourable trading arrangements. This was the top end of the market in quality terms; and the lost markets were concentrated at the coarser and cheaper end of the industry's output inventory. The magnitude of the impact of these changes on the industry as a whole is inescapable, however. In 1929 British cotton cloth exports were little more than half the 1913 level. The collapse of 1930–1 halved the export yardage again, and in 1938–9 cotton exports fell below their mid nineteenth century level. The home market remained intact, but the picture remained deeply gloomy. We shall assess the implications of all this for employment and living standards shortly. In the meantime, we need to explore the reasons for this remarkable transformation, and evaluate the industry's response to a novel and alarming situation.[11]

The high degree of local specialisation within the cotton industry meant that the timing and impact of the slump was not uniform; and this is itself suggestive about the likeliest explanations for the disaster. On the spinning side, the producers of fine yarns from Egyptian cotton shared the general suffering in 1921, but then remained 'moderately successful' until 1925, and did not really begin to feel the pinch until 1929; while towns specialising in the coarse yarns which were most vulnerable to emergent competitors experienced sustained depression through almost all of the inter-war years. Oldham thus had a rougher passage than Bolton, despite attempts to go up-market and compete with the established spinners of the finer yarns. In weaving, too, the worst sufferers were the manufacturers of cheap shirtings and dhotis for the Indian and Far Eastern markets, and Blackburn and Darwen endured slump conditions longer and more severely than Nelson and Colne, which produced high-quality fancy and coloured fabrics and were 'least affected by the Depression' until its second and more severe phase arrived in 1929.[12]

All this reinforces the suggestion that the basic cause of Lancashire's cotton's problems was the competitive power of rival cotton industries developing behind tariff walls in Lancashire's former markets, while more established industrial nations were themselves seeking export orders with increasing determination. The initial setbacks came from the former kind of development, especially in India, cutting export demand for the cheaper fabrics; but the world depression of 1929–31 exacerbated the situation, and export competition from Japan (especially), the United States and Italy, among others, made life more difficult for a wider range of manufacturers. Why was Lancashire unable to meet this competition? The employers' organisations blamed high wages and taxes, and sought a remedy in wage cuts, municipal economy and a longer standard working week (ironically, in view of the endemic prevalence of short-time working). But real wages in cotton, on Gibson's calculations, rose faster in the United States than in Great Britain during the inter-war years, and the same writer calculates that during the 1930s cotton workers in the United States had a standard of living 24 per cent higher than in Britain.[13] The cheap labour argument may apply to India or Japan, but not to the United States; and it is therefore only part of the story. The Lancashire cotton industry was clearly beginning to suffer for its failure to keep up with technological innovation, understandable though that may have been in the pre-war years. Gibson, again, argues that the United States' cotton industry saw a much greater increase in productivity per 'man hour' between 1909 and 1935 than Lancashire; and he ascribes this partly to the readier American adoption of new kinds of machinery, and partly to more effective organisation in large, vertically linked firms making a limited range of standard products and selling through a small number of merchant houses, most of which were closely connected with the manufacturing companies.[14] Lancashire's alleged deficiencies in these respects have been much discussed by recent historians, and we need to assess their extent and significance.

There was indeed remarkably little innovation in the Lancashire cotton industry between the wars, whether in technology or organisation. The changeover from mules and Lancashire plain looms to rings and automatic looms went on at a snail's pace, and ring-spinning equipment was being junked alongside the mules when reductions in the industry's capacity began in earnest in the 1930s. Nor was new, faster machinery for the preparatory and intermediate processes, such as winding and warping, being adopted. We shall see that attempts to boost productivity by changing working practices, and especially by increasing the number of looms per weaver, were sternly resisted by the trade unions, despite the difficult economic circumstances. But, as Lazonick argues, the root of the trouble lay in the way in which the industry was organised, and the near-impossibility of changing it to meet new needs and problems. The 'vertical disintegration' of the industry into sharply demarcated spinning and weaving sectors during the second half of the nineteenth century made it administratively difficult to adopt the new technologies, as costs would have been greatly increased due to the incompatibility of ring-spun yarn with plain looms and mule yarn with automatic looms. In the short run, it was much less risky to persist with tried, trusted, established systems which had been successful in the past, and which were fully understood by a proud and experienced workforce. The persisting dominance of small firms with limited horizons and resources, unable to look beyond the fierce local competition of their immediate environment, and living from hand to mouth from one week's specialised production to the next, made the likelihood of a coherent transition from one system to another even more improbable. One of the key virtues of the existing technology was its versatility: mules and plain looms could readily be adapted from one kind of product to another. This was invaluable in a context of small quantities being produced to order, rather than the standard products made for stock which predominated elsewhere. The existing technology was also better able to cope with poor-quality cotton and yarn, the use of which was an established aspect of the Lancashire system. In any case, most firms lacked the resources to invest in the expensive new technology, especially where spinning firms had become over-capitalised in the post-war boom; and the small, often family-run weaving firms could not afford the capital cost of automatic looms, especially as their premises were often old and difficult to adapt. Moreover, the need for urgent action was slow to become apparent, as what appeared to be an ordinary cyclical depression refused to lift; and by the late 1920s, in the hardest-hit Far Eastern sector, it was arguably already too late. Attempts at amalgamation and reconstruction, and efforts from the industry's leaders to impose reductions in capacity and drive inefficient firms out of business, made little headway; and bankruptcy was a blunt and unselective instrument of contraction. Only after 1930, as the banks began to fear for their investments and helped to drive the reluctant owners and directors of ailing firms into a long-overdue surrender of the autonomy and independence which they had prized more than profits and dividends, did the industry begin to contract significantly; and even then, the crippling division between spinning and weaving remained sacrosanct. An industrial structure which had served Lancashire cotton well during its years of prosperity, proved quite unable to adjust to the stark new realities of the 1920s and 1930s.[15]

Lancashire cotton clearly suffered severely from its pioneer industrial role, which left a legacy of outdated plant, organisation, attitudes and values. But the failure to innovate and adjust probably mattered more in the longer term than in the inter-war years themselves. The cheaper, coarser products of the cotton towns were terribly vulnerable to competition from developing economies overseas, using cheap labour and more appropriate technologies. It is hard to see how any amount of innovation, reorganisation or wage-cutting could have coped with the rise of India, China, Japan and Brazil. There was no prospect of cutting labour or transport costs to a competitive level, especially in the face of tariffs and political hostility. At the upper levels of the market, however, competition was slower to make a serious impact. Lancashire's skills and expertise might have been harnessed to better effect if new machinery, working practices and forms of organisation had been introduced in time: and the final collapse of what remained of the industry in the post-war decades might have been avoided. From this perspective, the inter-war decades, and especially the 1930s, might be regarded as a period of lost opportunities as well as inevitable disaster. To this extent, the suggestion that the cotton bosses of inter-war Lancashire were adequate managers on a day-to-day basis, using established criteria, but entrepreneurial failures, because they failed to make the necessary adjustments to visibly changing circumstances, carries conviction.

Cotton's troubles had knock-on effects on engineering. The textile machine making firms suffered from the collapse of the home market after the end of the post-war boom, and even the replacement rate for old machinery was low. The Victorian mules and plain looms had been built to last, and a very large number of them remained in use through the 1930s. Export markets held up much better, and firms like Platt Brothers were not slow to develop ring-spinning machinery for overseas markets despite the limited demand at home. In the late 1930s, indeed, Platt Brothers claimed to be exporting 95 per cent of their output. Overall, exports generally accounted for rather more than half of total output during the 1920s and 1930s, despite the growing volume of second-hand machinery which was being reconditioned and exported from bankrupt factories. But the overall picture was gloomy. Home demand fell to little more than half its 1924 figure during 1929–37, while world demand fell by nearly 30 per cent during the 1930s. Textile machinery exports declined by 6.2 per cent a year between 1921 and 1938. It is no surprise to find that this industry, like cotton itself, had a shrinking labour force and a propensity to short-time working.[16]

The twin pillars of the cotton towns' economy were thus crumbling between the wars; and coal mining was also in decline in this area. The losses in these sectors must be set against the emergence and growth of new products and industries, but their impact was patchy. New developments were most in evidence in and around Manchester itself, and in the Preston area; and they were most obviously lacking in the stricken heartland of the weaving district. In Manchester and Salford the decline in general engineering as a employer between 1923 and 1937 was cancelled out by the growth of electrical engineering, especially on the Trafford Park industrial estate; and losses in dressmaking and millinery were more than counterbalanced by increased employment in other branches of the clothing trades. Cotton itself declined less sharply here than elsewhere, and the insured labour force actually grew by 19 per cent during these years. Manchester's heavy engineering sector was beginning to do well out of rearmament by 1937, too. The Preston area saw particularly successful industrial restructuring, with motor vehicle building and electrical engineering well to the fore. Preston's official handbook for 1937 could state that the town did not have 'all its eggs in one basket', citing the rubber and wood pulp industries as well as the growing importance of rayon, and listing an enormous range of manufactures, from asphalt to chocolates to neon signs and refrigerating machinery. Parts of the cotton district were coming to terms with the new trends in the wider economy.[17]

The Preston area was uniquely fortunate; but all parts of the spinning district had additional manufacturing industries besides the old staples. Rayon and electrical engineering were especially widespread, even in Oldham, and Rochdale's textile industries had adapted themselves especially well to new conditions. In the Rossendale valley, too, the early decline of coarse spinning had freed factories to house a modestly successful cheap footwear industry, supported by the implausible-sounding growth sector of cardboard box manufacture. Most of the spinning district was capable of reaching 'a certain modest prosperity at the peak of the trade cycle' even in the 1930s. The weaving area, as a whole, seems to have been much less successful at attracting and keeping new industries, although they were not altogether absent, and on one calculation new factories in the Blackburn and Burnley area offered employment to over 10,000 people between 1933 and 1938.[18]

These isolated gleams of usually uncertain optimism do little to lighten the general gloom. Town centres became run-down and seedy, bankrupt shopkeepers left empty and derelict premises, and by the late 1930s 'the generally drab appearance ... and poor quality of housing and social amenities' in many cotton towns appeared to be deterring industrial investors. Population trends reflected the general malaise. Although the Manchester area saw very limited population growth in the 1920s and an almost imperceptible increase during 1931–8, the weaving area lost people steadily throughout the inter-war years, and so, more slowly, did the spinning centres. Preston in the 1930s was the only exception. Fertility rates were consistently low, and there was a steady trickle of out-migration in search of better things, although it was held in check by the prevalence of working-class home-ownership, investment in local industry and the complexities of family incomes.[19]

To the west, the very different economies based on coal mining and heavy industry around Wigan and St. Helens experienced mixed fortunes. Coal mining declined: in Lancashire as a whole it employed over 110,000 insured workers in 1923 and fewer than 70,000 in 1937. Despite relatively high levels of mechanisation in terms of coal-cutting machinery and conveyor systems, geological difficulties and worked-out seams ensured low productivity per man, and overall output fell sharply during the 1920s, though it stabilised after 1930. The price of Lancashire coal held up comparatively well, and most of the county's output was consumed locally, so Lancashire suffered less than other coalfields from the loss of export markets. Wages were low, and the pit villages around Wigan were particularly depressed during the 1930s as the coalfield's main centre of operations shifted southwards, while few alternative sources of employment were appearing.[20]

The heavy chemical industry resumed its decline after the war. It disappeared from St. Helens, and the Widnes district, reorganised after 1926 under the new régime of ICI, stagnated until almost the eve of the Second World War, with continuing factory closures and a high rate of unemployment, although the important and environmentally desirable transition to the use of electrolysis for chlorine and caustic soda manufacture was effectively made.[21] A more strongly marked – and clearly favourable – trend was the growth of the glass industry which now dominated the economy of St. Helens. Pilkington's had trouble in their export markets, but their plate glass output responded to the rapid expansion in home demand from the buoyant inter-war housebuilding industry, and from the rise of motor-car manufacturing with its growing need for glass windows. The performance of the glass industry considerably mitigated the impact of the inter-war depression in St. Helens, although Pilkington's had to shed labour in the worst years of the early 1930s; but at its peak the firm employed up to one-third of the town's workforce.[22] Warrington also came off relatively well, although the experience of Crosfield's and its labour force illustrates more general complexities and cross-currents. Crosfield's, now part of Unilever, did well in the inter-war years: a fall in the sale of hard soap was more than counterbalanced by the rise of 'Persil' and the scouring powder 'Glitto', and by diversification in several fields. Plant extensions on a large scale went ahead in the 1920s, and after the 1921 slump trading profits remained healthy, with the firm suffering 'comparatively little' in the slump of 1929 – 33. But this achievement had its social costs: wages were cut, and there was 'a good deal of weeding-out' of so-called 'inefficient labour' in the 1920s, while the labour force declined from over 3000 in 1924 to 2309 in 1931 and 1647 in 1939. Labour-saving innovations, reduced demand for female labour in the hard-soap sector, and a decline in new construction after 1930 accounted for much of this; and it forms a reminder of the probable results of any similar policy of innovation in adversity in the cotton industry. At the same time, Warrington's wiremaking, non-ferrous metalworking and brewing industries were in a healthy state, and it was spared the worst traumas of the inter-war years.[23]

The main focus of new industrial growth in inter-war Lancashire was the Manchester Ship Canal, on the Cheshire boundary, which accentuated the southward and south-eastward migration of investment and jobs within and just beyond the county. The Port of Manchester was consistently the fourth or fifth customs port in the United Kingdom by import and export value between 1919 and 1938, except in 1920 and 1925, when it was third. Along with the development of Trafford Park at the Manchester end, the Canal attracted soap, steel and chemical works, flour and paper mills and above all oil refineries, though most of the associated urban growth was on the Cheshire side of the county boundary, at Runcorn and especially Ellesmere Port. Farnie comments that 'By the 1930s ... a "Ship Canal Zone" had emerged as a new industrial complex distinct from the older world of "Cottonia", benefiting the south of Lancashire at the expense of the north and bringing industry into the rural borderland of Lancashire and Cheshire.'[24]

Even here, the inter-war years were not all plain sailing. Ellesmere Port had its own problems of unemployment and adjustment, with the decline of the Shropshire Union Canal and the galvanised iron and sheet steel works which had been its original staples. Between 1929 and 1937 its unemployment levels were above the national average. But they remained substantially less than those recorded for Merseyside as a whole, and especially for Liverpool, which had a difficult time between the early 1920s and the late 1930s.[25]

The Board of Trade survey of Merseyside in 1930–1 summarised the 'industrial picture' for Liverpool and Birkenhead thus: 'As the limitless porcupine array of cranes along its network of docks bears witness, more than half the working activity of the area is concerned with the shipping and handling of goods.' This apart, the economy was dominated by building, assorted services and 'innumerable' but generally small import processing industries.[26] This persisting profile meant that the declining importance of the port had serious repercussions for the local economy. Although the annual tonnage of shipping using the Liverpool and Birkenhead dock system showed a slight but sharply fluctuating upward trend, and the annual number of vessels varied around a figure somewhat below the 1921 post-war peak, the port's economy fared worse than this evidence might suggest.[27] Liverpool was losing ground when compared with other ports: her share of United Kingdom trade fell from 31 per cent on the eve of the First World War to 20.8 per cent in 1938. In absolute terms, exports fell particularly seriously, from £480 million in 1920 to £234 million in 1922 and £103 million in 1932, recovering to £155 million in 1937. Even if allowance is made for falling prices during most of this period, these are arresting statistics. Cotton goods exports were hit especially hard, of course, and this led in turn to a fall in raw cotton imports. Across the board, the pattern was complex and fluctuating; but the shipping lines found it difficult to adjust to new trade flows and barriers, competition intensified, and the financial scandals surrounding Lord Kylsant and his Royal Mail Group made matters worse. Southampton took over Liverpool's long-established role as Britain's premier passenger port, and we shall see that unemployment levels in dock and shipping work were high and intractable. World trade depression and the problems of Lancashire's industries played the major parts in all this, and Hyde suggests that Liverpool's shipping entrepreneurs did well to keep afloat in adversity; but these were generally difficult years.[28]

Attempts to counterbalance the economic and social pathology of the port by creating a broader and more stable industrial base, achieved limited success. Shipbuilding and ship repairing were chronically depressed for most of the inter-war years, and new industries were slow to appear, despite the Corporation's attempts to lure them to a new industrial estate at Speke, most of whose firms had merely relocated from elsewhere on Merseyside. The shortage of skilled and disciplined local labour was an endemic problem, although the rayon industry, which employed 2600 people, mostly women, by 1930, was able to overcome this by training its workforce from scratch. Aircraft building also grew, but only when the rearmament campaign prior to the Second World War got into full swing. Otherwise, the difficulty in finding optimistic industrial indicators is suggested by the prominence given by the Board of Trade report to a firm which had diversified beyond polish manufacture into making toy tea sets. Liverpool was also, of course, the home of Meccano sets and football pools. Building remained a major employer, although its workers were at the mercy of changes in municipal housing finance and government housing policy; and projects like the Mersey Tunnel and East Lancashire Road made important contributions. The established import processing industries generally held their own, but the pressure on the local economy was exacerbated by uniquely high birth-rates and natural increase levels, which were only partly offset by out-migration. the prospects in the late 1930s were still unpromising, despite a recent economic upturn.[29]

Barrow was classed, rather oddly, with Merseyside for the purposes of the Board of Trade survey; but its inter-war problems were of a different order. Apart from the traumas of post-war adjustment and depression, and the generally disastrous slump of the early 1930s, the local shipbuilding industry came off relatively lightly, and general engineering diversified into a variety of new products. The iron and steel industry was less successful in highly competitive markets, and nearby Dalton's economy was blighted by the final demise of iron ore mining. Barrow's economic base remained narrow and vulnerable, and in contrast with Liverpool, women's employment opportunities failed to expand. But for most of the inter-war years Barrow did better than most centres of heavy industry, despite its geographical isolation and the alleged neglect of the docks by the LMS Railway.[30] Elsewhere in Lancashire north of the Ribble, the inter-war years brought a generous measure of economic prosperity. Lancaster did especially well: its oilcloth and linoleum industry was flourishing by 1931, and additional employment was provided by the advent of artificial silk manufacturers in the late 1920s. Hospitals also provided relatively secure employment.[31] The resorts of Blackpool (especially) and Morecambe experienced a rapid rise in population (masked by the taking of the 1921 census in June), at a time of stagnation and decline in the industrial districts (and, indeed, in Southport). This growth was fuelled entirely by migration, as the retired and residential population increased; but Blackpool had over 3000 registered workers in 'entertainment and sport' by 1939. Together with the agricultural and suburban areas of west Lancashire (around Ormskirk) and the Fylde, this 'Lancashire coast area' formed an outpost of uncomplicated prosperity and economic growth, clouded only by the decline of the Fleetwood fishing industry. This was the only part of Lancashire to see sustained population growth at a faster rate than the national average.[32]

It will be clear that Lancashire's experience of the inter-war years was not all gloom and doom. There was little to compare with the sustained mass unemployment and hopeless, humiliating poverty of parts of the North-East, South Wales or west Cumberland; and because of this, special assistance from central government was much less in evidence. Even the worst-hit area, the weaving district around Blackburn and Burnley, did not qualify for Special Area status, although its omission was controversial at the time. New houses, new roads and expanding service industries appeared here and there, although wealth was visibly being redistributed away from the older industrial centres. The new industries of the South and Midlands were little in evidence, electrical engineering apart. In any case, the mitigating features of the inter-war economy should not obscure the extent of poverty, insecurity and suffering among the Lancashire working class in these difficult years, especially in the old centres of cotton and coal and in the remaining slums of inner Liverpool and Manchester – though every industrial town had its miserably insanitary and overcrowded districts throughout these years. How did Lancashire's working class experience the economic changes of the inter-war decades?

A recent trend towards optimism about inter-war living standards, with emphasis on new industries, better working conditions, housing improvements and declining disease and mortality rates (especially infant mortality), and stress on the development of state medical provision for the poor, has even more recently been hotly challenged by critics who seek to bring the experience of the disadvantaged areas back to the centre of the stage, and cast doubt on the validity of the official statistics on which the optimists rely. The anger of the novelist Nigel Gray (the optimists' verdict is 'so glib that it is an insult to millions whose experience of living at that time ran quite counter to this rosy analysis') has a validity of its own, but it is now being underpinned by the research of Charles Webster and others at a national level. Webster has suggested that, 'The depression must be regarded as a significant exacerbating factor, tending to worsen still further prevailing low levels of health, and so contributing towards a crisis of subsistence and health different in kind but similar in gravity to the crises known to students of pre-industrial societies.'[33] This is a highly charged contention, especially to those who have read about the horrors of the first half of the seventeenth century in Lancashire. Clearly, on the national stage it is more applicable to Merthyr than to Luton or Coventry, and within Lancashire it is more likely to carry weight in Blackburn than Blackpool, in Liverpool rather than Lancaster. Contemporary commentators, admittedly with their own axes to grind, offer colourful endorsement. George Orwell's portrayal of life on the dole in Wigan is the most famous, and the chapter on Lancashire in Allen Hutt's *The Condition of the Working Class in Britain* is perhaps the most scholarly, with its footnotes and its self-conscious evocation of Engels. At times it transcends its purpose as Communist Party propaganda.[34] *Love on the Dole*, too, conveys a savage truth which has to be confronted, despite the literary devices by which Walter Greenwood sought to defuse his explosive material and make it tolerable for a middle-class reading public.[35] I shall pursue the contentious question of working-class living standards further through an examination of unemployment levels, wages and lifestyles in different Lancashire settings, beginning with the hardest-hit sectors of the cotton industry and its associated economy.

The specialised weaving towns and industrial villages of north and north-east Lancashire suffered the most sustained and widespread unemployment and insecurity (and the two are inseparable) during the inter-war years. Within this area, however, fortunes varied. Great Harwood, dominated by a handful of vulnerable large employers, and Darwen consistently did worst; Blackburn and Padiham were little better; Burnley occupied an intermediate position, and Nelson and Colne, with their concentration on the home market, were least affected. The official figures consistently under-record unemployment levels, and the figures were progressively massaged by the removal of certain categories from entitlement to assistance. Moreover, much of the reduction in actual employment levels was hidden by the general practice of cutting individual workloads to two or three instead of four looms (with a corresponding reduction in wages) rather than working short time or laying people off. Even so, the figures are striking. The slump of the early 1920s saw employment levels in cotton running at about half their 1920 peak throughout 1921 and 1922 and into 1923. In Great Harwood unemployment averaged over 50 per cent in both 1930 and 1931, with a dire return of 72.5 per cent in August 1931. In Darwen unemployment never fell below 49 per cent throughout the 16 months beginning in July 1930. Blackburn's experience was nearly as bad; and even when matters began to improve in 1932–3, official figures revealed an intractable core of unemployment which stayed at more than 20 per cent in some towns even in the relatively reasonable year of 1937. After this, a renewed burst of severe depression began. At the other extreme, Burnley in 1929 and Nelson and Colne in 1936 recorded unemployment rates which were actually better than the national average. But even this short-term and localised silver lining turns out to be an optical illusion if we allow for underemployment. This half-submerged stratum of reduced income and productivity was sufficiently widespread after 1926 to increase the 'real' level of unemployment by at least half: so even in 1936, with a temporary recovery well under way, unemployment and underemployment taken together meant that 'half the insured labour force in the weaving industry was either unemployed or on reduced earnings' in Blackburn and Darwen. Only in 1937 was there a brief respite. Other areas were less badly hit, but this evidence drives home the point that, at their worst, conditions in the weaving towns could be as bad as anywhere. At best, there was widespread severe poverty.[36]

Unemployment was particularly concentrated in certain categories. Contemporaries were disturbed by high levels of adolescent unemployment in the worst years of the early 1930s; but in the longer run women, especially married women, and the over-45s were particularly likely to suffer long periods without work. The position regarding married women was complicated. Critics ascribed their prominence among the long-term unemployed in 1929–31 to a tendency to remain registered when no longer genuinely seeking work, to augment depleted family incomes, and to a reluctance to give up the possibility of work in hard times. Any such 'players of the system' were removed by the so-called 'Anomalies Act' of 1931, which made it much more difficult for married women to continue to receive unemployment benefit. It also discriminated successfully against many of the genuine long-term unemployed. Married women suffered also from local and occasional pressure to discriminate against them when selective redundancies were declared; and there were fewer alternatives to the cotton industry for women than for men in the highly specialised economies of the weaving towns. Attempts were made in the early 1930s, with central government prompting, to withdraw benefits from single women who refused to offer themselves as resident domestic servants or army canteen workers in distant places; but these ran into a gale of angry opposition, and were abandoned. By the time the Pilgrim Trust investigated Blackburn in 1936, some married women were coming to terms with domesticity on a pittance, and some were resigned to being unable to adjust from plain weaving to the more difficult fancy products into which the Blackburn industry was attempting to diversify. Many, however, missed the social life of the mill and the independence of a wage of their own; and this loss of opportunity, self-respect and sociability must be counted as one of the social costs of the Depression.[37]

Long-term unemployment was the experience of a minority of cotton workers in the weaving district, however, whether men or women. On the other hand, the vast majority spent some time out of employment: in Blackburn, Burnley and Darwen, and indeed in the spinning centre of Oldham, 77 or 78 per cent of the insured population claimed benefit at some point during 1930, with the figure for women reaching 92 per cent in Darwen.[38] Few working-class families can have gone through the Depression without some loss of income through unemployment or underemployment, and the threat of being laid off or 'playing for warps' was ever-present. For those in work, moreover, wages and working conditions were deteriorating. Pope's figures suggest a 25 per cent fall in earnings for a weaver in full employment between 1924 and 1937, a fall which outpaced the slight price reductions over the period, and left the weaver's wage lagging far behind other male occupations in which income held firm or even increased over the same period. These calculations apply to a Burnley four-loom weaver of ordinary grey cloth; and they left even fully employed weavers firmly anchored at the bottom of the wages league. Admittedly, in one respect they are anomalous. By 1936 most Burnley weavers seem to have been working six looms rather than four, on the controversial 'more-looms system'; and their earnings were boosted disproportionately by special piece-rates which had been agreed in 1935, with the intention of increasing the cost of the new system and restricting its introduction. But Burnley was unusual, and the 1937 weaving census suggested that in Lancashire as a whole only about 15 per cent of weavers, and perhaps a quarter of adult men, were working six looms, with a handful operating even more. A small minority of weavers ran the new automatic looms; and here wages for men were comparatively good, but women fared much less well. Gray argues that men were employed where a two-shift system was introduced, enabling employers to pay higher rates in response to determined wage-bargaining, while women predominated where single-shift working persisted, forcing employers to set low wate-rates in order to ensure a return on their investment. In general, however, weaving was becoming a notoriously ill-paid occupation, to the extent that it was increasingly difficult to recruit male school-leavers. As the Pilgrim Trust pointed out, too, weaving was no longer a comparatively well-paid occupation for women by 1936; its wages compared very unfavourably with the hosiery and footwear industries in Leicester, for example.[39]

Any real improvement in wages had to be paid for, moreover, by increased productivity (although the minders of extra looms had some of their workload transferred to specialist assistants) or a departure from the long-established tradition of single-shift working. Employers cut corners at every opportunity, supplying poorer-quality yarn while insisting on higher standards of output, manipulating the piece-rate regulations with allegedly novel cynicism, trying to push employees into working for less than the agreed rate, and digging in their heels in opposition to innovations like paid holidays which were spreading rapidly in other industries by the 1930s. Working conditions remained squalid, and little or nothing was done to improve them. If anything, matters must have worsened as plant and premises aged.[40]

All this adds up to a more complex picture than prevailed in the depressed areas of mining and heavy industry. Most families endured severely reduced family incomes, with intermittent employment and underemployment, and steadily eroded wages; but the impact is harder to quantify than in a setting where a single adult male breadwinner was the norm. The psychological damage must have been all the worse because once-prosperous households were seeing their savings evaporate (especially where they had been used to buy shares in the mills), their possessions deteriorate and their pride undermined. Soup kitchens and free school meals had a high take-up rate during the worst of the depressed years, and for the very large numbers of really hard-pressed the 'Means Test' was enforced with almost gleeful savagery outside the county boroughs, where there was more understanding and resistance to central government pressure. On the other hand, established traditions of enjoyment were not forgone without a struggle. In the early 1930s a common practice developed in Blackburn of unemployed holidaymakers returning from Blackpool twice during the holiday, to sign on and to collect benefit. This was, no doubt, the result of special efforts to retain something to look forward to, akin to the determined enjoyment of the Wakes in bad years in the early nineteenth century; and the regular grind of endemic poverty was indicated by shop closures and declining takings in public houses. Most telling of all was the failure of infant mortality and disease rates to fall as rapidly as in the nation at large. Indeed, during the worst years of the Depression they rose quite sharply in some towns, and the differential between middle-class and working-class experience probably widened. Some impoverished urban wards still exhibited Victorian rates of infant mortality. The maternal mortality rate, too, was high and remained intractable. Evidence on undernourishment or malnutrition is difficult to evaluate, because of the subjective criteria for assessment; but the comments of some of the local Medical Officers of Health suggest that official complacency on this score was probably ill-founded. Webster's apocalyptic comparison with seventeenth-century famine conditions does not hold water in the Lancashire weaving district, but there was a general grim and creeping impoverishment which sapped the will and vitality and undermined the pride and self-sufficiency of once-flourishing communities, and there was clearly a lot of abject and enduring poverty by any Western standards.[41]

The cotton spinning district was less severely affected than the weaving area. Oldham was the worst-hit: Hartley Bateson's local history calls the twenties 'the Heartbreak Years', and stresses the sad stories told by thrifty but impoverished rate defaulters and the 10,527 pairs of clogs distributed to 'necessitous children' by the Clog Fund Committee by February 1928, when there was worse to follow. Conditions here matched those in the weaving area, and in 1931 the spinning district as a whole saw nearly one-third of its insured labour force out of work. As in weaving, the picture is complicated by family earnings; but it is clear that alongside the ever-present threat of mill closures, unemployment and short-time working, the wage-rates of workers in the card-room and in spinning itself were being reduced. The established mule-spinners suffered least, financially, when they were able to keep in work: in 1932 their weekly earnings, reduced as they were, still matched those of bricklayers or engine drivers. The big piecer, however, by 1933 earned little more than an agricultural labourer, and far less than an unskilled urban worker. The path of promotion to spinner was blocked, and piecers were increasingly likely to be married men in their twenties. As in weaving, higher productivity and higher standards were being demanded from substandard raw materials; and the appallingly filthy condition of much of the raw cotton worsened the discomfort and unhealthiness of card-room work. Unemployment in Manchester was consistently much lower than in the surrounding spinning towns, however, and there were more alternative and additional sources of employment than in the weaving area, although wages in engineering also came under sustained pressure. The erosion of living standards and the prevalence of poverty may have been less serious in degree than in Blackburn or Darwen, but they were similar in kind.[42]

Elsewhere in Lancashire, Wigan and the mining villages and small towns around it probably saw the worst suffering. Some of Orwell's comments, based partly on his experiences here, have wider applicability: 'In one way, things ... are not so bad as they might be. Life is still fairly normal, more normal than one really has the right to expect. Families are impoverished, but the family-system has not broken up. The people are in effect living a reduced version of their former lives. Instead of raging against their destiny they have made things tolerable by lowering their standards.'[43] This version of normality embraced the break-up of some families under the pressure of the 'Means Test'; the desperately dangerous scramble for fragments of waste coal on the spoil-heaps; the sodden and insanitary encampments of makeshift dwellings along the canal bank at Wigan; and a permanent state of not quite chronic undernourishment which coexisted with addiction to cheap luxuries like the cinema (for warmth as well as entertainment) and cigarettes. But at least, he suggests, the unemployed were no longer ashamed of their unemployment. Whatever one may think about Orwell's writings in general, there is a ring of dour plausibility about some of these comments, which convey gloom and monotony rather than approaching apocalypse.

Barrow experienced sharp bursts of poverty and unemployment on two occasions between the wars, but relatively briefly; and Lancashire's other industrial areas seem not to have been so badly hit, although the St. Helens miners knew very hard times, especially in 1926. But the other main centre of inter-war depression and unemployment in Lancashire was Liverpool, which had a distinctive experience of its own.

Officially recorded unemployment on Merseyside (including Bootle, Birken-head and Wallasey) never scaled the heights reached in the cotton towns; but it only briefly fell below one in six of the insured labour force, and during 1930–5 it remained above one in four. At its worst in the early thirties it accounted for one-third of insured adult males. Shipbuilding was particularly badly affected during the 1930s, but across the board unemployment on Merseyside declined more slowly after 1932 than in Britain as a whole, and in 1939 the area's unem-ployment rate was double the national figure.[44] As the Pilgrim Trust was aware, however, the experience of short-term unemployment was built into the culture of the waterfront casual labour market, whose organisation and ethos persisted between the wars; and it is difficult to assess the extent to which, if at all, the situation in the early 1930s was worse than what had gone before in the inner-city slums. But by this time a substantial core of long-term unemployed was developing, with a much higher proportion of young men in their teens and twenties than could be found elsewhere: a disturbing phenomenon for social observers. Matters were exacerbated by a persisting pattern of early marriages, high birth-rates and large families, which worsened overcrowding as well as putting pressure on resources more generally. Women's work opportunities were expanding, however, among a rising generation, especially in retailing

Ostentation at the top in the cotton industry: the manager's office at Horrockses, Preston. (See pp. 328–32.) [*Below*] Part of Preston's diversifying inter-war economy: the foundry at the Dick, Kerr engineering works. (See pp. 332–3.)

Sheep graze on a former industrial landscape: these distinctive hillocks, formed by limestone 'Flashings', are at Thursden, close to the Yorkshire border in the hills above Nelson. (See Chapter 15.)   [*Left*] A view from just behind Colne's main shopping street, showing the abrupt transition from terraced housing and factories to pastures and surprisingly leafy countryside. (See pp. 219–20.)

and clerical work. By 1921, indeed, the level of women's employment in Liverpool was already above the national average, although there was an increasing tendency for women to give up work on marriage. This may have nurtured tensions in working-class marriages, as women found difficulty in sustaining their prescribed role as household managers on low and unreliable incomes, and resorted to the pawnbroker, the moneylender and the bookmaker, or found themselves part-time jobs, all of which had to be hidden from husbands whose threatened masculinity sometimes issued in domestic violence. These suggestions, drawn from oral interview evidence, are interestingly at variance with Elizabeth Roberts's more optimistic findings about the domestic partnership as fulfilling norm for women in Barrow and Lancaster. We are left wondering how far the differences reflect contrasting social realities, and how far they express the contrasting expectations and interview styles of the investigators.[45]

At the core of these problems, of course, was poverty; and the Pilgrim Trust found that on their preferred definition 30 per cent of unemployed Liverpool men in their sample were living in 'deep poverty', as compared with 17 per cent in the total sample, while 48 per cent were living below the trust's poverty standard, compared with 30 per cent overall. On the waterfront, casual labour and its associated undisciplined lifestyle persisted in a shrinking labour market, and Caradog Jones calculated that 24 per cent of the dockers were living below his, rather different, chosen poverty line in the early 1930s. At this time, too, the proportion of Liverpool's population in receipt of poor relief was running at up to twice the national figure. Secondary poverty, expressed through drink and especially gambling, above all on the football pools, was apparently genuinely widespread, although it did provide a measure of limited autonomy, hope and interest for the participants. The general urban malaise of Merseyside was manifested in persistently high, though slowly falling, infant and child mortality rates. Poverty was so endemic in Liverpool that for some families unemployment assistance may actually have made household budgeting easier, providing as it did a guaranteed and predictable weekly sum, however small. More promisingly optimistic was the growth of the Co-op, whose 155 branches attracted membership from up to 29.2 per cent of Merseyside householders in 1924, while 280 branches provided for up to 48.5 per cent of households in 1929. But even this limited measure of the spread of improved security and perhaps higher living standards below the level of the 'labour aristocracy' met with a reversal during 1929–32; and we do not know what use the members made of their membership. Most hopeful of all is the suggestion that by the early 1930s fierce competition had turned central Liverpool into a popular low-price area, reversing the Victorian position; but we do not know how far this applied to the corner shop. In many respects, indeed, the distinctive cocktail of urban problems, already endemic in Victorian and Edwardian times, remained almost unaltered in the inter-war years. It is hard to find really convincing evidence of improvement among the inner-city poor, and once-prosperous groups like the shipyard workers were sharing some of their misery. At best, the Depression restricted or vitiated attempts to bring about improvements in the living standards of the lower strata of the Liverpool working class. This is particularly apparent when we look at housing.[46]

The Pilgrim Trust commented that, 'Housing conditions are the most obvious of these environmental influences which help to shape the life and mind of the unemployed man in Liverpool.' Their investigators visited 'an almost unending series of houses falling to pieces, long ago condemned as unfit for human habitation, and of families living under conditions such as to make any attempt at a respectable family life a heroic struggle'. They identified prevalent low standards of furniture and diet, with shop white bread (severely criticised by Orwell, too) and tinned condensed milk much in evidence, and 'definite signs of mismanagement' in 14 per cent of houses. These are subjective and value-laden judgements, but they contain an important residue of plausibility. Certainly, many of the worst housing conditions of pre-war inner Liverpool persisted intractably. Indeed, the housing problem actually worsened after the war, 'from a situation where only the poor were in acute housing need to one where there was a shortage of houses of all types, with families on relatively good incomes being forced into overcrowded and insanitary rooms'. The proportion of the population in Liverpool itself living at more than two per room rose from 10.1 per cent in 1911 to 12.1 per cent in 1921, and fell back only to 10.9 per cent in 1931; and on one definition nearly one child in four among the under-13s lived in overcrowded housing in 1930. The persisting pressure on the housing market helped to ensure that the Corporation's slum clearance programme ground to a halt. Over 1600 of the insanitary court and back-to-back houses which had escaped demolition before 1914, were still providing tumbledown, bug-infested accommodation in 1931, although the clearance rate improved in the 1930s. The building of new council houses and flats was pursued energetically, however, as private investors preferred to put their money elsewhere. Between 1920 and 1929 nearly 19,000 municipal dwellings were built in Liverpool, and between 1930 and 1945 over 20,000 were added, almost all before 1939. Between 1919 and 1931 the Corporation built 75 per cent of Liverpool's new houses, compared with 8.7 per cent between 1900 and 1918.

All this activity was precipitated by dire housing shortage and encouraged intermittently by the policies of central government. It was partly due to government pressure that the vast majority of the council housing of the 1920s was built in low-density suburbs at the edge of the built-up area, requiring a level of expenditure on rents and fares which was enough to deter most potential refugees from the convivial squalor of slumdom. Most of the tenants came from the ranks of skilled labour and even white-collar occupations, and it was only when political pressures were brought to bear within the council that cheap tenement accommodation was made available on a substantial scale on the expensive cleared land of the inner city during the 1930s. But the poorest were generally excluded by rents beyond their means, although Caradog Jones thought that a significant proportion of slum-dwellers could have afforded better accommodation had they chosen to budget for it; and the strict rules and management policies by which the Corporation sought to protect its property also had a deterrent effect. It was hoped that deserving tenants would filter upwards from the poorest housing by stages to the best; but most of Liverpool's municipal housing did surprisingly little, in itself, to relieve the insanitary horrors of the central slums, to which many of their inhabitants had become remarkably attached. With all their virtues, too, the suburban estates suffered from lack of shopping, pubs and other amenities, and it took time to build up a sense of community on green-field sites. On the eve of the war, despite all these efforts, an enormous waiting list for municipal housing remained. This is not to decry a remarkable effort of invest-ment, management and planning, in response to an appalling and unique legacy of overcrowded slumdom. Liverpool failed to deliver all of the goods, to the people who were felt by many to need them most; but the rise of municipal housing, especially in the complete absence of any interest in low-rent housing supply by private enterprise, brought space, cleanliness, bathrooms and gardens to many who would otherwise have had to do without. It was far from perfect, but it was a major achievement.[47]

Manchester, too, was running hard in a desperate attempt to keep pace with what seemed to be an ever-growing problem, as family formation in the 1920s made a mockery of the civic policy-makers' expectations. The Corporation built more than 27,000 houses between 1920 and 1938, and assisted private enterprise in supplying over 8000 more, in addition to nearly 16,000 from private builders acting alone. There was a higher proportion of suburban houses than in Liver-pool, and the Corporation's pride and joy, the full-scale satellite town of Wythenshawe in the Cheshire countryside, took shape during these years, with its parkways, extensive open spaces, and express bus service to the city centre. Here again, prosperous artisans and clerks predominated, and tenants per-sistently sought permission to build garages for their cars. But the problem of the slums remained. Sir Ernest Simon though that 80,000 of the city's 180,000 houses were in the 'slum belt' in 1935. On the credit side, the reconditioning campaign had abolished back-to-backs and cellar dwellings, and supplied nearly every house with 'a separate paved backyard, a water-closet, and water laid on inside the house'. But 'most of the houses in the slum belt are now dilapidated, verminous, damp and worn out', and the need for complete re-planning for space, air and sunlight meant that demolition was the only answer. It is easy to criticise these remarks with hindsight, in the knowledge of some of the great planning disasters which were to follow. Perhaps Simon's view of some of this housing was too gloomy, and too much was eventually done too quickly. But the evidence of the time suggests that the faults were to lie with the replacement housing, and that the overcrowding and built-in filth of the Victorian slums and subdivided Georgian terraces required drastic surgery. For the time being, ambition outran resources, as government policy moved towards austerity in the early 1930s. As it was, the provision of vastly improved housing for the better-off workers coexisted with the continuing decay of the slums, which Simon thought in 1935 to be 'in a much worse condition now than they were at the end of the War'.[48]

The smaller industrial towns had less spectacular problems, but responded to them with more limited ambition and imagination. Oldham's proposal for 500 houses in 1919 was rejected by the Minister of Health as inadequate, and by 1942 only 2573 municipal houses had been built in 21 years: fewer than the 2616 back-to-backs which existed in 1919. Widnes did proportionately much better, building 2092. Admittedly, as the Liverpool experience made abundantly clear, not everyone appreciated the new estates. Alice Foley was delighted to 'expand and spread our wings in cleaner air and quietude'; but her mother missed the inner-city life of Bolton, complaining, 'Eh, Alice, what did thi' fotch me here for; there's nowt but cocks an' hens'. But Allen Hutt, in a scarifying catalogue of ashpits, infestations, overcrowding, stench and indignity embracing Bolton and a representative range of other Lancashire towns, reminds us of what she was also missing; and all this makes clear that throughout urban Lancashire, the improved housing standards of the inter-war years brought benefits only to the better-off among the working class, usually offering little or nothing at affordable rents or in accessible places to the unemployed and disadvantaged, and leaving a dismaying number of them in the deteriorating back-to-backs and cramped terraces which survived from the heroic years of the classic 'Industrial Revolution'.[49]

Amid this enduring legacy of squalor, some local authorities pursued civic improvement schemes whose main impact was cosmetic and imposing, in a revealing echo of the great Victorian town hall projects at Bolton, Rochdale and Manchester, or the building of St. George's Hall at Liverpool.[50] Bolton's city centre development of the 1930s is a case in point, and an ambitious scheme at Oldham, floated in 1936, was thwarted only by the Second World War.[51] But usually the dominant concern of local government was to keep the rates as low as possible: a preoccupation which was reinforced by the haemorrhage of rateable value from factory closures, and the parlous finances of many ratepayers and their representatives. This obsession with economy extended to the relief of the poor and unemployed; and central government kept an inquisitorial eye and ultimately a controlling hand on local committees who tried to bend the regulations in favour of claimants. Controls were tightened from 1930 onwards, as the Poor Law Guardians were replaced by Public Assistance Committees which drew their members mainly from local or county councillors, without direct elections, and were administered through the County Council or the County Boroughs. From 1935 onwards a new, fully centralised Unemployment Assistance Board took over responsibility for the long-term unemployed.

Prevailing attitudes among Guardians and PAC members varied interestingly. In Bolton, the Conservatives were dominant for most of the inter-war years. They were not drawn from the established manufacturing and landowning élite, but from a lower stratum of professionals and shopkeepers; and Harris describes their prevailing ideology as 'tough laissez-faire combined with repressive paternalism'. They endorsed cuts in benefits with enthusiasm, while professing benevolence and sympathy towards claimants; and in 1926 they cut off all relief to the families of striking miners. Their Labour opponents on the Board of Guardians, always in a small minority, sought to mitigate the operation of the system in practice without overtly challenging its principles: apart from a bitter conflict over miners' relief, their anger was often dissipated on minor, though perhaps symbolic, issues like the provision of butter rather than margarine for the children at the Cottage Homes. The early 1930s sharpened conflict, however, and in 1932 the Labour Party withdrew from the administration of the 'Means Test', leaving a Conservative majority to maintain its policy of low relief scales and to perpetuate a rate of refusals of benefit which ran at 43 per cent during 1931 – 5, compared with a rate of 33 per cent for Lancashire as a whole which was itself suggestive of comparative parsimony in the face of need.[52]

Nelson stood at the opposite end of the scale. Here, every effort was made by authorities with a strong Labour representation to provide relief as of right and as generously as possible to claimants who were regarded as unfortunate rather than feckless or workshy. In 1922 Nelson was already out of step with its neighbours, providing only 11 per cent of its poor relief in kind compared with 17 per cent in Colne and between 38 and 65 per cent for other districts in the Burnley Union. Relief in kind was much resented by the recipients, for obvious reasons, and the Nelson committee was responding to their preferences. The Nelson approach led to a battle with the Ministry of Health in 1929; and from the beginning of the new Public Assistance régime in 1930 the Nelson local committee was locked in conflict with its overlords at the Lancashire County Council offices in Preston over such issues as the need to assist weavers who were working only one or two looms, the need to adjust scales to allow for high local rents, and (in 1930) the right of locked-out weavers to receive relief. Many individual decisions made in Nelson and district were revoked by the Conservative-dominated Central Relief Sub-Committee and its officials in Preston, and much resentment was generated. The 'Means Test' was the final blow, and after the failure of an attempt to resist the requirement that all household income should be considered before a decision about relief was made, the Nelson committee dissolved itself in August 1932. The alternative to opting out, in an impossible dilemma for Labour representatives, was to stay in office and try to mitigate the working of the system as far as possible. But, as Salford's committee found, there was little room for manoeuvre, and the odium of enforcing national policy devolved onto its local opponents. By the later 1930s, as the national economic crisis waned, and the PAC lost responsibility for the unemployed, more 'liberal' interpretations of rules and needs emerged at county level; but during the worst years of the Depression local government had very limited scope (even where it had the will) to protect the living standards of the unemployed, or to lift them above a very basic level of subsistence. Even in Nelson, too, little could be done about the brusque treatment of respectable claimants, who felt the humiliation of their circumstances severely, by harsh and hard-pressed officials.[53]

The personnel, and perhaps the policies, of local government were affected by continuing changes in the governing class, both at county level and in individual towns. The decline of the old industrial ruling class as a dominant and cohesive force in urban society is exemplified by developments in Bolton. In 1919, despite an established pattern of out-migration to the Lancashire coast, the Lake District and socially salubrious areas of the South, Bolton's social leadership was dominated by 'the old owner-managers of redoubtable character, independent opinions and large resources', linked by 'kinship ties, by industrial and financial interests, by political affiliations, by common educational and military background and experience'. This élite, whose common interests and culture largely transcended the increasingly irrelevant distinction between Conservative and Liberal, Anglican and Nonconformist, did not disappear in the inter-war years. However, it was severely undermined by defections in the aftermath of the cotton boom of 1918–20, as millowners sold up, took their profit and left the town in droves, sometimes leaving their homes for use as hospitals and maternity homes, but invariably withdrawing their capital, spending power and expertise from the town in which their money had been made. The remaining established capitalists, coalowners, engineers and landowners as well as cotton men, were joined by a rising group of shopkeepers and self-made cotton speculators, to form a more complex and less cohesive élite; and the older families were further weakened by the defensive mergers which formed an important response to the slump in all the established industries, and by an associated persisting drift away from Bolton suburbia and the mansions on the urban fringe to the affluent irresponsibility of life as a *rentier*. Local charities and cultural institutions lost their patrons and figureheads, and borough politics lost many of its paternalistic and sometimes far-sighted advocates of investment rather than retrenchment. The social structure of the Corporation changed less radically than this might suggest, but there was a distinct switch from old wealth to new affluence, and from the cotton industry to the provision trades. The cotton interest itself was also becoming less distinctive, as its members diversified their investments and moved into growth industries like advertising and entertainment.[54]

Bolton may well have been unusual in the continuing vitality of its old élite at the end of the First World War, in the persistence of the family firm, and in the (perhaps related) continuing strength of the Conservative Party in the inter-war years; and we have seen that the post-war speculative mania was much less prevalent in weaving than in spinning. But these trends were widespread in urban Lancashire at this time; and not just in the cotton district. Waller notes the extinction of the distinctive patrician culture of Liverpool's Liberal Unitarians between the wars, and mergers in the soap and chemical industries, and in the coal mines, of greater Merseyside were similarly destructive of an older hierarchical order, replacing patriarchal employers by managers who represented an impersonal and sometimes distant board of directors. In Lancaster, too, the hegemony of the Williamson and Storey families was being undermined by new firms, deaths and departures. The paternalist industrialist as civic leader was becoming an endangered species; and his municipal habitat was itself suffering from a loss of power and autonomy as the influence of central government waxed. These were interrelated phenomena.[55]

County society ceased to function as a distinctive social system during the 1920s, as many of the great estates were broken up and the drift to fairer climes continued. Agricultural depression hastened the process, with poultry-keeping the only growth sector; and the ideals of *noblesse oblige* crumbled before the pursuit of individual pleasures. The Earl of Derby remained a name to conjure with, especially in Conservative Party circles in south-west Lancashire. A conscientious core of landed gentry and gentleman industrialists continued to manage the affairs of the County Council, but they were fighting a rearguard action. Here again, the established Victorian system of social leadership was steadily being eroded.[56]

The politics of the County Council were quite low-key until the elections of 1931, when the transfer of poor relief functions to the council gave a new impetus and concern to the Labour Party. Labour's representation at County Hall had grown from 11 in 1919 to 20 in 1928, a small minority of the total. In 1931, despite the poor relief issue, the national collapse of the Labour Party was reflected in a fall to 18 seats; but by 1937 Labour accounted for 30 of the 120 elected councillors. This was a long way from the exercise of any real power, of course, but Labour suffered from a shortage of candidates with sufficient time and resources to make the regular journeys to Preston. Support was heavily concentrated in a few localities, especially the Wigan area, Manchester and Salford, and the weaving centres around 'Red Nelson'. But the limited headway made by Labour on this admittedly inhospitable terrain, and the persistence of a Conservative régime described by Sydney Silverman, MP for Nelson, in 1937 as 'notorious throughout the land for its meanness, its cheese-paring, its grim selfishness', were indicative of the general lack of a sustained or organised radical response to the troubles of the Depression. In parliamentary elections, Labour did make considerable inroads during the 1920s against the Conservatives who were fast becoming their only serious opponents. In 1929, 41 of Lancashire's 66 parliamentary seats went to Labour, with the Conservatives driven back to their strongholds of Liverpool, the Manchester suburbs, the seaside resorts and (for inscrutable reasons which require investigation) Bury. But the antics of MacDonald and Snowden turned the tide in 1931, when the Conservatives almost swept the board, winning all the Salford seats, all the weaving seats (even Nelson itself, to the despair of the local Labour movement) and taking St. Helens at the heart of the mining area, leaving Labour clinging precariously to Leigh and Liverpool Scotland. Recovery in 1935 was incomplete; and the 1931 disaster, which was even more strongly marked in Lancashire than elsewhere, points to inadequacies in the Labour approach which stemmed from an attachment to consensus politics and received economic ideas, and prevented the party from presenting a distinctive profile at municipal as well as parliamentary elections.[57]

Labour's municipal fortunes varied widely from town to town, as did the party's showing on the Poor Law Guardians. There were strongholds, such as Nelson (where Labour regained municipal control in 1927 and kept it thereafter) or St. Helens; places where a considerable Labour presence was not translated into effective power, such as Preston (where only the Aldermen kept Labour out of office in 1929, and a repudiation of the existing conventions about aldermanic elections would have tipped the scales); and places where the lack of Labour penetration might seem surprising in the light of industrial and social structure, such as Oldham and Lancaster. Beyond this, however, the policies and social profile of local Labour parties varied significantly. Here again, Nelson lies revealingly at one extreme. It spent remarkably heavily on education, maternity and child welfare and parks, baths and libraries. It provided nursery schools, clinics, municipal midwives, and post-natal care, as well as a municipal maternity home. It provided feeding centres and free entertainment for locked-out weavers, and refused to allow the national anthem to be played at public events, or to celebrate George V's Jubilee. The heavy spending was achieved without a serious impact on the rates, and its origins predated Labour control of the council. This reflected the importance of political pressure from the Weavers' Union, and especially from women's organisations, whose strength in Nelson owed much to the pattern of employment in weaving, in which men and women worked side by side for the same wage-rates and respected each other as skilled workers. The ILP was also a force in Nelson long after it had gone into terminal decline elsewhere. Here, Labour justified itself by providing a clear-cut and distinctive set of policy alternatives, and, in the particular and perhaps peculiar context of this late-developing weaving town, political and social success were mutually reinforcing.[58]

This was exceptional. In many places Labour councillors merely played along with the existing system. Hannah Mitchell remarked that her party members in Manchester wanted 'lower rates and more social services, and would not be convinced that both were not possible at one and the same time'. In Preston in the 1920s the party was dominated by the older craft unions, had little time for the issues which were so important in Nelson, and seemed at times strongly to *prefer* lower rates to improved municipal services of all kinds, although matters improved as a broader social base was built. But it was often alleged that Labour councillors were easily seduced by honours and the illusion of influence.

They were unwilling to break out of the constraints imposed by central government, and although they could be angrily vociferous in opposition, they had no alternative strategy. Socialism, as such, was beyond most of them: a more usual perception was that of Joe Toole, twice MP for Salford South, Lord Mayor of Manchester and assiduous womaniser and campaigner for the unemployed, who 'saw Socialism as a matter of improving the lives of the masses, bringing them a little nearer the level of the middle men, not as a matter of lopping at the highest level and distributing the benefits from the bottom upwards'. He was an admirer of Lord Derby and a flag-waving patriot. Toole was unusually flamboyant and idiosyncratic, but his ideology was in line with much of the Labour movement, especially the rank-and-file voters. Even more idiosyncratic was the Liverpool Labour Party, with its furious feuding between left and right, class-conscious 'crypto-Communists' and Irish ex-Nationalists who put Catholicism before labour issues. It split fatally in 1930 on the double reefs of sectarian education and the disputed sale of the old workhouse site to the Catholic Church for its new cathedral, and surrendered all hope of a local government majority in a city whose religious and ethnic divisions continued to pull its working class apart.[59]

During Labour's first surge in the early 1920s, it dented but did not destroy the established two-party dominance; but by 1929 it had seen off the Liberals almost everywhere. The worst of the slump, however, saw the unemployed and other sufferers voting in droves for the National Government in parliamentary elections; and the collapse of Labour in Lancashire did not lead to any sustained or effective mass extra-parliamentary or quasi-revolutionary activity. Neither the Communists nor the British Union of Fascists recruited very well in Lancashire. The Fascists attempted a Lancashire recruiting campaign in 1935, but with very little apparent success; and the Communists' efforts to work through the National Unemployed Workers' Movement, which had several branches in Lancashire, achieved some intermittent mobilisation of the unemployed in demonstrations and hunger marches, but this was more effective at eliciting violent reactions from the police than at wringing concessions from the authorities. Demonstrations against the 'Means Test' took place in towns as diverse in character as Great Harwood and Liverpool, and in some places, especially Manchester and Nelson, there was some sympathy and common action from Labour Party members and trade unions for the NUWM and the numerically tiny Communist Party at times during the 1930s, despite official hostility within the mainstream labour movement. On the whole, what stands out is the generally passive working-class response to the politics of the Depression; and Brenda Crosby is probably correct to suggest that, 'The majority of the Lancashire working class remained stolidly politically apathetic and conservative in all senses of the word, which made them as impervious to the forces of the radical right as to those of the left'.[60]

The trade unions fared badly in this difficult setting. This was especially true of the cotton unions, which had been advancing so confidently on the eve of the

First World War. Some had invested heavily in the mills in which their members worked: the Bolton Spinners had 'committed £151,500 of [the] £260,000 General and Superannuation funds to mill investments by 1925'. This itself brought additional financial weakness when the slump cut dividends and share values. Even the Spinners, indeed, were quite unable to protect their members from wage cuts and arbitrary dismissal when the Depression began to bite, and potential replacements and strike-breakers queued at every mill gate seeking employment. The tone was set by the refusal of the owners of the Ena mill in Bolton to consider re-employing 41 spinners, 22 of whom had invested £3460 as individuals in its shares, when the factory reopened after a shutdown. The sacking of Albert Law, a union leader and Bolton's Labour parliamentary candidate, in 1923 for alleged immoral conversations with his piecer, was another indicator of the tone of the times. The collective bargaining machinery rapidly degenerated into a vehicle for autocratic employers to assert their right to manage as they saw fit; and the masters in general were improving their organisation and going on to the offensive against their workforces, despite their inability to put together effective initiatives against the crippling effects of untrammelled competition among themselves. The pressures of the time hit weavers even harder, as trade union membership fell steadily; and in the depressed years of the early 1920s, before trade union unemployment pay was abandoned, the unions' reserve funds collapsed under the unprecedented burden of maintenance payments. The great wave of labour disputes in weaving in 1929–32, culminating in the epic struggle against the working of additional looms without adequate safeguards on wages and working conditions, expressed the anger of rank-and-file unionists in opposition to the more cautious approach of trade union leaders who knew that the terms of trade were hopelessly against them. The pride of the cotton unions was humbled with the inexorable decline of their industry, and their loss of the ability to protect their members against wage cuts and the stigma of state welfare benefits had its parallels in other industries. The miners were hit particularly hard by the failure of the General Strike and of the extended coal dispute which followed it, and the bargaining power of the engineers was severely reduced by the slumps of the early 1920s and early 1930s, although they were recovering towards the end of the decade. The inter-war years saw the carefully nurtured protective mutual assistance institutions of the working class steadily losing power and influence over much of Lancashire, as the living standards of most of their members declined or stagnated; and the one exception, the Co-operative movement, which continued to expand in membership and services, is a particularly attractive candidate for further research.[61]

Lancashire's economy was far from collapsing in the inter-war years, and we must not ignore the bright spots and growth sectors; but it lost its proud reputation for world leadership and working-class prosperity, and living standards fell decisively for many workers in key industries. Much of cotton Lancashire became custom-bound, ageing, inward-looking and defeatist, as the rising generation failed to respond to new stresses and new needs. Urban populations fell, birth-rates declined, in-migration almost ceased, and the mills themselves became dominated by the middle-aged and elderly. Opportunities for upward mobility from the shop floor declined almost into non-existence, as a small and contracting élite reserved positions of authority for relatives and friends. But values did not change to match the economic and social circumstances. Migration in search of work was inhibited by the cushioning effect on family economies when some members continued to earn, by resources tied up in depreciating and unrealisable share and property ownership, and by attachment to unmarketable skills and the reassurance of neighbourhood, familiarity and routine. The cotton industry's past successes militated against effective adaptation, as managers stuck to trusted formulae and unions resisted labour-saving innovation. The power of custom was strong enough to curb the introduction of new practices, and the myth of the open society remained a powerful palliative even under the grimmest of economic conditions. The old cultural politics of sectarianism and paternalism retained their hold after the dissolution of the institutions which had sustained them, and the Depression exacerbated divisions within the working class between skilled and less-skilled, and between one trade and another, while adding new sources of suspicion between the unemployed and their more fortunate neighbours. But the ties of community remained strong, and the new cheap pleasures of cigarettes, the cinema and greyhound racing, along with the more established enjoyments of football, the seaside, the football pools and other forms of gambling, added spice and hope to dreary lives. All this coexisted with a persisting attachment to thrift and the values of sturdy independence. The pioneer industrial society of cotton Lancashire had evolved a set of attitudes and allegiances which blended individualistic opportunism and collectivist mutual assistance, thrift and hedonism, earnestness and scepticism, independence and deference, hard work and ostentatious leisure. Change was inhibited by the importance of grandparents and other elderly child-minders as formative influences on the new generation, and it took a second war and a renewed assault on the established certainties to precipitate major changes in lifestyles and attitudes. Even then, the process was far from sudden, though cumulatively traumatic.[62]

The culture of the cotton towns was not the only distinctive Lancastrian way of life. Inner Liverpool also stands out, this time as a society which had long ago learned to live with chronic poverty and day-to-day insecurity. Here, the pub and the workplace were almost interchangeable for many of the men, while the pawnshop and the moneylender provided essential, if expensive, relief for the cash-flow problems of harassed housewives. Gambling became all-pervading in the Depression years, but it had always had a rationale of its own as the only hope for a brief flaring of opulence, popularity and fame. Some moralising outsiders were simply horrified, others tried to understand. Violence was never far from the surface, sometimes channelled into sectarian or racial hatred, sometimes directed at the police. The Liverpool police strike of 1919 – a remarkable event in itself – saw, it was said, 'serious rioting and looting ... without any reason but opportunity'. When unemployment riots in September 1921 led to allegations of police brutality, a worried Chief Constable set the situation in perspective: 'it is only in recent years that the Police in parts of Liverpool have been safe in working in less than fours together, and it was such an accusation against the Police of unnecessary violence which led to the feud which resulted in riots almost weekly for years'. He feared the possible consequences of left-wing and Irish extremists stirring up the unemployed, and urged that 'whether right or wrong, the Police as a whole should be exonerated by some means'. But disturbances remained endemic, just as they had been before the war, although Liverpool's dangerous classes never produced the full-scale uprising that their uneasy masters feared. Here too, however, in very different vein from the cotton towns, was a distinctive, and disreputable, working-class culture which proved to have remarkable resilience.[63]

Attachments to established Victorian ways of life and habits of thought were less pervasive and impenetrable in the relatively cosmopolitan environs of Manchester, and perhaps in the mining and heavy industry district of greater Merseyside and the distinctive urban economy of Barrow, where the social constraints on migration and adaptation seem to have been much less obtrusive. But most of urban Lancashire was by-passed by the changes of the inter-war years, and left in a time-warp from which it was occasionally retrieved by music-hall jokes and horrified social reporting. The lessons of the nineteenth-century formative years were learned too well by the workforce, who were unable or unwilling to unlearn them at the behest of economic change and political exhortation. Their masters, on the other hand, took the earliest opportunity to take their money and run when the going became really tough after the collapse of the post-war boom. The words of the popular proverb about industrial success, 'clogs to clogs in three generations', with their wrily comforting connotations of the ultimate humbling of the upstart mighty, and of pride coming before a fall, had come to pass; but the victims were the working class of the original industrial Lancashire, rather than those who had pocketed the surplus value of their labours. The wheel had almost turned full circle, and Lancashire was fast reverting to the relative poverty and provincial backwardness of its pre-industrial past.

15

LANCASHIRE IN PERSPECTIVE:
SOME THOUGHTS IN CONCLUSION

Donald Read's *The English Provinces*, which analyses the rise of provincial economic, social and cultural influences on England as a whole during the eighteenth and nineteenth centuries, ends with a sad catalogue of decline. Standardisation, centralisation and the rise of new, powerful and pervasive mass media in the twentieth century have cumulatively undermined local autonomy and distinctiveness, and some of the consequences are suggested by three consecutive sectional subheadings in Read's final chapter: 'The Decline of Interest in Politics', 'The Decline of the Provincial Great Towns', 'The Decline of Local Government'.[1] The book was published in 1964, and one or two countervailing trends might have been detected by optimists later in that lively and prosperous decade; but Read's perspective has been vindicated by the continuing trend of subsequent developments.

As part of this pattern, the years since the First World War have seen Lancashire return to the peripheral obscurity with which this book began. The Lancashire of Elizabeth II is much more accessible from without than that of Elizabeth I, of course; and events in the county can become public property almost instantly in London and over much of the world. But recent transport innovations have been more important in allowing travellers to pass through or over Lancashire than in encouraging them to make the county their destination, and the instant coverage of the new mass media is so selective and distorted as to give most people little more real understanding than was available, more slowly and tortuously, to Elizabeth I's governments. The Lancashire which is presented on the national stage is largely a matter of the doings of football teams in Manchester and Liverpool, and the allegedly subversive activities of the 'revolutionary' left in the financially beleaguered Merseyside metropolis. This is not so far removed from the obsessive interest of the rulers of late Tudor and early Stuart England in Lancashire's association with Sunday sports and Roman Catholic plots. The intervening centuries saw Lancashire achieve a very different position, as Manchester and Liverpool rose to national prominence, and then to fame throughout the Western world, as controversial emblems of a new society and a new way of life, while the towns around them gained a less circumstantial and more intermittent notoriety as the dingy satellites of these blemished but refulgent rising stars. This period of maximum visibility and success, between the late eighteenth century and the First World War, has been the central focus of this book. I have sought to analyse, explain and evaluate the transition of economy and society in south Lancashire from its long hibernation, through a tentative pre-industrial thaw, into Georgian springtime (if that is not too romantic a metaphor), Victorian heyday, Edwardian Indian summer (in more senses than one) and post-Edwardian gloom. With hindsight, this succession of phased changes can be made to seem as inevitable as the seasons. Perhaps this was indeed the case. But an attempt at an explanation for the meteoric passage of south Lancashire across the world historical stage, flaring briefly but spectacularly as it did in transit from one kind of obscurity to another, is inescapable.

The duty to explain, and to convey the complexity of the events and processes themselves as well as of their causes and implications, is reinforced by the existence of a simple and satisfying popular potted view of the rise of industrial Lancashire. Here is a representative rendering, from the *Alka-Seltzer Pub Guide* to the North-West: 'The whole of the North-West is a living record of the history and onward march of industrial and social progress ... It *was*, literally, here that people flocked from the fields to the factories and the birth of the Industrial Revolution was witnessed ... Lancashire's damp climate made it ideal for the spinning and weaving of cotton, while Liverpool provided the transport, and Manchester the commercial centre ... Sir Richard Arkwright was born [in Preston], and *thus* [my italics] Preston was one of the main cotton mill centres.'[2] This would, incidentally, be news to any seeker after information who depended on the borough's official guide for material on its industrial history: it has written cotton out of Preston's historical record.[3] But the Alka-Seltzer parade of unexamined assumptions, wilful illogicality and inspired near-misses provides a version of Lancashire history which many people would recognise. I have tried to provide an accessible alternative rendering which questions received assumptions about history as progress, reduces the importance accorded to the personalities of individual inventors and entrepreneurs, or to the collective personality of Lancastrians more generally, and downgrades the importance of religious peculiarities and rainfall statistics (although it must be admitted that cotton did benefit from a damp climate: the question is whether Lancashire was significantly damper than other possible places). Liverpool did, of course, in a sense 'provide the transport', but I have also tried to bring out the difficulties involved in assessing how its contribution to the wider Lancashire economy developed and changed over time. I give more causal weight, on the other hand, to patterns of landownership and agriculture, sources of capital, and the nature of the existing textile industries on the eve of the enormous upsurge in supply of and demand for cotton and cotton goods in the late eighteenth and early nineteenth centuries.

There is a less clear-cut popular perception of the reasons for Lancashire's precipitate decline after 1920: it is a less glamorous story, and it lacks heroes or monuments. Masters and workpeople blamed each other, and both sides combined to blame government policies and overseas competition, especially behind tariff barriers. I give more weight to the notion that Lancashire's competitiveness was undermined by aspects of the structure of the cotton industry which inhibited innovation and impeded increased productivity; but this was only one of Lancashire's industries, and we must not neglect the other explanations. Above all, of course, the collapse of overseas markets was at the core of Lancashire's problems; and this offers a reminder that the action of this book was played out in a much wider context than that of Lancashire, Britain or even Western Europe. I have chosen to concentrate on industrial development as it affected Lancashire society, and on the ways in which the nature of Lancashire society in turn affected responses to industrial development. I have not sought to explain in any sustained or systematic way the shifting patterns of trading and diplomatic relations, and the economic fortunes of distant nations, which helped to determine the nature of the Lancashire experience, dependent as its major industries were on export markets and on far-flung sources of supply. A formal focus on Lancashire and the world economy would have made a very interesting and important book, but not the one I wanted to write. A full explanation of the rise and decline of Lancashire's economic staples would require a detailed analysis of the relationships between world trade, markets and politics, embracing theories of imperial and colonial exploitation. My concerns have been narrower and deeper. I have generally taken events in the wider world as given, and concentrated my attention on the internal dynamics of Lancashire, and especially on the social impact of industrial change. There is room for a complementary volume to supply the missing dimension, and I hope someone will write it.[4]

The outstanding characteristic of Lancashire itself is the social stability which underpinned the economic changes of this long and often hectic period. When we consider the near-famine conditions which prevailed for much of the late sixteenth and early seventeenth centuries, the misery, insecurity and palpable political unfairness which propelled so many into Chartism and allied movements, and the widespread deprivation of the inter-war years, the stolid, stoical response and the limited recourse to violent or unconstitutional behaviour should give pause for thought. The years between the Chartists and the early twentieth century were particularly stable politically, as increasingly well-organised trade unions took what they could for their members within the existing economic and political framework, and the divisions within the working class more than outweighed the possible influences for unity, as economic issues remained outside the accepted agenda of political debate. But this frame of mind was always predominant. It was reinforced, rather than being undermined,by the cultural continuities and adaptability to changing needs and circumstances which were so marked in Lancashire society, especially in the cotton towns. Short-distance migration, the continuing vitality of the family and its supplementation by a variety of more formal mutual assistance groups, and the associated persistence of customs in common, perpetuated a strong sense of local cultural identity which bordered on insularity. This common culture expressed itself in ways which changed over time and varied between places; but its overriding characteristics were conservative and defensive, and its attachments were to the immediate, the tangible and the traditional, rather than to the abstract or the external. Even Liverpool, with its cosmopolitan seafaring economy and its Irish, Scots, Welsh and other more exotic minority communities, developed characteristics of this kind. Lancashire was capable of nurturing radicals, whether in religion, politics or a combination of the two, from the Puritans of the Manchester area and the Quakers to the Social Democratic Federation in Burnley, the Independent Labour Party in Nelson and elsewhere and the Liverpool syndicalists, by way of the United Englishmen, the Peterloo marchers and the Chartists. It was capable of generating outbreaks of sporadic but purposeful violence, from the Pilgrimage of Grace through the food riots and machine-breaking of the late eighteenth and early nineteenth centuries to the angry mid-Victorian strikes and the marches against the 'Means Test' in the early 1930s. But above all, the vast majority of its people were firmly rooted in their culture, sceptical of innovations and slow to rouse. It is a paradox that these characteristics should be so prominent in the cradle of the first 'Industrial Revolution'; but it says a great deal about the nature and limitations of the changes that took place. Without these underlying continuities, indeed, Lancashire might never have sustained the breakthrough into a new system of social relations; and its decline, when it came, would certainly not have been met with such passive fatalism. The secret of Lancashire's distinctive pattern of economic development lay in the persisting blend of tradition and innovation in its society, which infused a sense of identity while defusing or limiting conflict.

In spite of the sustained economic decline and centripetal cultural and governmental tendencies of the recent past, Lancashire retains a strong flavour of regional distinctiveness. The pride and separateness of localities, with their long tradition of resisting interference from outsiders, whether from London or from the next parish, has yet to evaporate. The traditions of the 'Industrial Revolution' and before are now being self-consciously nurtured by museums and tourist boards, and a process of creeping romanticisation has been set in motion. Perhaps this is a necessary evil. But there is survival as well as revival here, and a genuine attachment to a proud history and cultural tradition, as well as a desire to turn a fast buck or two in the tourist trade. It would be a tragedy if Lancashire's past should be turned to account solely to build a museum and playground economy in a degenerate present. But under current circumstances, what other future is there? Nostalgia for a hard and grimy past is a dangerous peril for a professional historian, and my analysis of the circumstances of earlier generations of Lancastrians should dispel any temptation to wallow uncritically in past glories. But it may be that J. B. Priestley, looking sourly ahead from the depressed depths of 1933 in Blackburn, had Lancashire's long-term future in an all too plausible perspective. 'Probably', he suggested, 'by the time the North of England is an industrial ruin, we shall be able to beat the world at table tennis.'[5] This is still not quite an appropriate epitaph; but far though it may be from literal accuracy, it is dangerously close to an important spiritual truth. From subsistence farming to the spinning jenny and the mule was a long journey: from the mule to the museum is a shorter one, and none the less traumatic for that.

Notes

Introduction

1 I fail to see the point of A. D. King's apparent objection to the use of terms like 'the cotton district' (A. D. King, *The Bungalow: the Production of a Global Culture* (1984), 262). Such terminology is convenient shorthand, and carries no implication whatever of any lack of awareness of Lancashire's relationships with a wider world economy.

2 J. Langton, 'The Industrial Revolution and the Regional Geography of England', *Transactions of the Institute of British Geographers* N.S. 9 (1984), 145–7, 164, and *passim*; W. C. Sellar and R. J. Yeatman, *And Now All This* (1932), 31–2, 43–4.

3 B. Trinder, *The Industrial Revolution in Shropshire* (Chichester, 1973), 1.

4 E. Williams, *Capitalism and Slavery* (1964 edn.; first published 1944).

5 A. Redford, *Labour Migration in England, 1800–50* (1926).

6 C. H. Lee, 'The Service Sector, Regional Specialization, and Economic Growth in the Victorian Economy', *Journal of Historical Geography* 10 (1984), 139–55.

7 T. Wyke, 'Nineteenth Century Manchester: a Preliminary Bilbiography', in A. J. Kidd and K. W. Roberts (eds.), *City, Class and Culture* (Manchester, 1985), 218–71; D. A. Farnie, *The English Cotton Industry and the World Market, 1815–1896* (Oxford, 1979), 340–84. The Joint Committee on the Lancashire Bibliography, based in Manchester, is performing Herculean (and Sisyphean) labours for the county as a whole.

8 J. D. Marshall, *Lancashire* (Newton Abbot, 1974); P. Gooderson, *A History of Lancashire* (1980); C. Aspin, *Lancashire: the First Industrial Society* (Helmshore, Lancs., 1969); J. J. Bagley, *A History of Lancashire with Maps and Pictures* (Beaconsfield, five editions, the first in 1956).

9 T. W. Freeman, H. B. Rodgers and R. H. Kinvig, *Lancashire, Cheshire and the Isle of Man* (1966).

10 J. Aikin, *A Description of the Country from Thirty to Forty Miles round Manchester* (1795; reprinted Newton Abbot, 1968); E. Baines, *History, Directory and Gazetteer of the County Palatine of Lancaster* (2 vols., Liverpool, 1824; reprinted Newton Abbot, 1968).

Chapter 1

1 C. Haigh, *Reformation and Resistance in Tudor Lancashire* (Cambridge, 1975), especially Chapter 7.

2 W. Camden, *Britannia* (1610).

3 Haigh, *Reformation*, especially Chapters 1, 6, 11.

4 B.W. Beckingsale, 'The Characteristics of the Tudor North', *Northern History* 4 (1969), 67–83; see also L. Stone, *The Crisis of the Aristocracy, 1558–1641* (abridged edn., Oxford, 1967), Chapter 5, sections 1–3.

5 E.J. Buckatzsch, 'The Geographical Distribution of Wealth in England, 1086–1843, *Economic History Review* 2nd ser., 3 (1950–1), 180–202; R.S. Schofield, 'The geographical distribution of wealth in England, 1334–1649', *idem*, 18 (1965), 483–510; cf. Haigh, *Reformation*, 20, 22.

6 G.H. Tupling, *The Economic History of Rossendale* (Manchester, 1927), 165; J. Thirsk (ed.), *The Agrarian History of England and Wales*, IV (1967), 86; N. Lowe, *The Lancashire Textile Industry in the Sixteenth Century* (Manchester, 1972), 7–8.

7 H.B. Rodgers, 'Land use in Tudor Lancashire', *Transactions of the Institute of British Geographers* 27 (1955), 79–98; but cf. Freeman, Rodgers and Kinvig, *Lancashire ...*, 47.

8 Thirsk, *Agrarian History*, 87; the suggestion in E. Kerridge, *The Agricultural Revolution* (1967), 144–6, that herds were rather larger seems to apply to a later period.

9 Tupling, *Rossendale*, Chapters 2–3 and 165–6; J. Porter, 'Waste Land Reclamation in the Sixteenth and Seventeenth Centuries: the case of South-East Bowland, 1550–1630', *Historic Society of Lancashire and Cheshire* 127 (1978), 1–24; *idem*, 'A Forest in Transition: Bowland 1500–1650', *idem* 125 (1974), 40–60; Lowe, *Textile Industry*, 7–8, 25.

10 W.G. Howson, 'Plague, Poverty and Population in Parts of North-West England, 1580–1720', *Historic Society of Lancashire and Cheshire* 112 (1960), 29–56.

11 F. Walker, *The Historical Geography of South-West Lancashire before the Industrial Revolution* (Manchester, 1939), 54–8; Thirsk, *Agrarian History*, 87–9.

12 Walker, *South-West Lancashire*, 52–3.

13 G. Youd, 'The Common Fields of Lancashire', *Historic Society of Lancashire and Cheshire* 113 (1962) 1–42.

14 Kerridge, *Agricultural Revolution*, 146, 316.

15 J. Thirsk, 'Industries in the Countryside', in F.J. Fisher (ed.), *Essays in the Economic and Social History of Tudor and Stuart England* (1961); Tupling, *Rossendale*.

16 *Victoria County History: Lancashire*, Vol. II (1908), 272; cf. Haigh, *Reformation*, 81.

17 Lowe, *Textile Industry*, especially 10–11, 58–64; Haigh, *Reformation*, 159–60.

18 John Leland, *The Itinerary in or about the years 1535–43* (5 vols., ed. L. Toulmin Smith, 1964), V, 41, 43; *V.C.H.* II, 291–2, 357; J.U. Nef, *The Rise of the British Coal Industry, 1550–1700*, I (1932), 60–2.

19 *V.C.H.* II, 364–5, 393; R.J.A. Shelley, 'Wigan and Liverpool Pewterers', *Historic Society of Lancashire and Cheshire* 97 (1945), 1–26.

20 G.H. Tupling, 'The early metal trades and the beginnings of engineering in Lancashire', *Lancashire and Cheshire Antiquarian Society* 61 (1949), 1–5.

21 P. Corfield, in D.C. Coleman and A.H. John (eds.), *Trade, Government and Economy in Pre-Industrial England* (1976), 241 n. 22; T.S. Willan, *Elizabethan Manchester* (Manchester, 1980), 38–9; cf. J. Watson, 'The Lancashire Gentry, 1529–58, with special reference to their public services', MA thesis, Univ. of London, 1959.

22 Corfield, in Coleman and John; and see also Haigh, *Reformation*, 159, although the mid-sixteenth-century population figures suggested there come from a most unreliable source.

23 Leland, *Itinerary*, V, 41.

24 Haigh, *Reformation*, 92.

25 A. Everitt, in Thirsk, *Agrarian History*, 497; G.H. Tupling, 'An Alphabetical List of the Markets and Fairs of Lancashire Recorded before the Year 1701', *Lancashire and Cheshire Antiquarian Society* 51 (1936), 86–110.

26 P. Clark (ed.), *The Early Modern Town* (1976), 93–4.
27 Haigh, *Reformation*, 22, 160.
28 Willan, *Elizabethan Manchester*, Chapter 3.
29 For the Stanleys see now B. Coward, *The Stanleys, Lords Stanley and Earls of Derby, 1385–1672* (Manchester, 1983); also Haigh, *Reformation*, 104–5; Stone, *Crisis*, 123.
30 Haigh, *Reformation*, 105; F. R. Raines (ed.), *Stanley Papers* (Manchester, 1853), 1–12.
31 B. Coward, 'A "Crisis of the Aristocracy" in the sixteenth and early seventeenth centuries? The case of the Stanleys earls of Derby, 1504–1642', *Northern History* 18 (1982), 54.
32 Watson, thesis, Chapters 3–5.
33 Haigh, *Reformation*, 107; cf. P. R. Long, 'The Wealth of the Magisterial Class in Lancashire, *c*. 1590–1640', MA thesis, Univ. of Manchester, 1968, 9.
34 Stone, *Crisis*, 38–9.
35 P. Laslett, *The World We Have Lost* (1971 edn.), Chapter 2; K. Wrightson, *English Society 1580–1680* (1982), 23–6; J. S. Morrill, 'The Northern Gentry and the Great Rebellion', *Northern History* 15 (1979) 70–4.
36 B. G. Blackwood, *The Lancashire Gentry and the Great Rebellion, 1640–60* (Manchester, 1978), 4–5. His criteria for gentility may well be misleadingly generous.
37 Haigh, *Reformation*, 90, 106; Long, thesis, 2–3 says that there were 36 in 1561.
38 Watson, thesis.
39 Haigh, *Reformation*, 161–8, and 'Slander and the Church Courts in the Sixteenth Century', *Lancashire and Cheshire Antiquarian Society* 78 (1975), 3–7, 11–12.
40 Watson, thesis.
41 Watson, thesis, 29–30; N. Pevsner, *The Buildings of England: North Lancashire* (1968), 20–3.
42 Pevsner, *North Lancashire*, 18; *idem*, *South Lancashire*, 15–16.
43 O. Ashmore, 'Household Inventories of the Lancashire Gentry, 1550–1700', *Historic Society of Lancashire and Cheshire* 110 (1958), 65–89.
44 Ibid., 99–100.
45 Thirsk, *Agrarian History*, 84–8; Tupling, *Rossendale*, Chapter 3; Porter, 'South-East Bowland', 3.
46 Thirsk, *Agrarian History*, 752.
47 Haigh, *Reformation*, 92–4; A. Charlesworth, *An Atlas of Rural Protest in Britain, 1549–1900* (1982).
48 *V.C.H.* II, 289–90, 294; Haigh, *Reformation*, 59–61, 118–19.
49 Haigh, *Reformation*, 250–1; Tupling, *Rossendale*; J. Porter, 'The Reclamation and Settlement of Bowland with special reference to the period 1500–1650', Ph.D. thesis, Univ. of London, 1974.
50 W. Bennett, *The History of Marsden and Nelson* (Nelson, 1957), 59, 85.
51 Thirsk, *Agrarian History*, 401–4, 446, 610; Haigh, *Reformation*, 82.
52 Lowe, *Textile Industry*, Chapters 3–4; Willan, *Elizabethan Manchester*, Chapter 4.
53 Watson, thesis, 106–31.
54 Ibid., 2, 39.
55 Haigh, *Reformation*, 161.
56 Ibid., Chapters 2–3.
57 Ibid., 65–7, 71–2.
58 Lowe, *Textile Industry*, Chapter 6, and see below, Chapter 2. For the Pilgrimage of Grace, C. Haigh, *The Last Days of the Lancashire Monasteries and the Pilgrimage of Grace* (Manchester, 1969).

59 Camden, *Britannia* (rev. E. Gibson, *c.* 1700), II, 978.
60 C. Hill, 'Puritans and the "Dark Corners of the Land"', *Royal Historical Society Transactions* 5th ser., 13 (1962), 77–102.
61 J.A. Twemlow (ed.), *Liverpool Town Books*, I, 1550–1571 (Liverpool, 1918).
62 P. Clark and P. Slack (eds.), *Crisis and Order in English Towns* (1972), 126.
63 Haigh, *Reformation*, 82.

Chapter 2

1 Cf. J. Thirsk, *Economic Policy and Projects* (1978); and for the demand for textile goods see also M. Spufford, *The Great Reclothing of Rural England* (1984).
2 Tupling, *Rossendale*, 167.
3 Willan, *Elizabethan Manchester*, Chapter 4; Lowe, *Textile Industry*, 98; A.P. Wadsworth and J. de L. Mann, *The Cotton Trade and Industrial Lancashire, 1600–1780* (Manchester, 1931), 12.
4 Cf. Spufford, *Great Reclothing*.
5 Wadsworth and Mann, *Cotton Trade*, 11–23.
6 Lowe, *Textile Industry*, 99.
7 Wadsworth and Mann, *Cotton Trade*, 21.
8 Willan, *Elizabethan Manchester*, 63; Wadsworth and Mann, *Cotton Trade*, 29–53; cf. Lowe, *Textile Industry*, 42, 55.
9 Lowe, *Textile Industry*, Chapter 3.
10 Wadsworth and Mann, *Cotton Trade*, 9, 33–5; Willan, *Elizabethan Manchester*, 9–16; Long, thesis, 6–7; Blackwood, *Great Rebellion*, 18.
11 Willan, *Elizabethan Manchester*, 60.
12 Tupling, *Rossendale*, 163; and see also W. King, 'The Economic and Demographic Development of Rossendale, *c.* 1650–*c.* 1795', Ph.D. thesis, Univ. of Leicester, 1979, Chapter 6.
13 Wadsworth and Mann, *Cotton Trade*, 52.
14 M. Brigg, 'The Forest of Pendle in the Seventeenth Century', *Historic Society of Lancashire and Cheshire* 113 (1961), 88–93.
15 Porter, 'South-East Bowland'; J. Porter, *The Making of the Central Pennines* (Ashbourne, Derby, 1980), Chapter 3; Lowe, *Textile Industry*, Chapter 4; Wadsworth and Mann, *Cotton Trade*, 10.
16 Blackwood, *Great Rebellion*, 1–3.
17 Nef, *Coal Industry*, I, 64; J. Langton, *Geographical Change and Industrial Revolution* (Cambridge, 1980), 43.
18 Nef, *Coal Industry*, I, 63–4; Long, thesis, 97–103.
19 Langton, *Geographical Change*, Chapters 2–3.
20 Ibid., 50–4.
21 Porter, 'South-East Bowland', 8–18; *idem*, 'Forest in Transition', 45.
22 Porter, *Central Pennines*, 29–31; Brigg, 'Forest of Pendle', 72; Tupling, *Rossendale*, 162.
23 Thirsk, *Agrarian History*, 83, 88; Walker, *South-West Lancashire*, 54–8, 145–8; Long, thesis, 78–9.
24 Freeman, Rodgers and Kinvig, *Lancashire ...*, 46–9; Blackwood, *Great Rebellion*, 144–5.
25 Thirsk, *Agrarian History*, 80–9; Tupling, *Rossendale*, 165–6; but cf. King, 'Rossendale', Chapter 8, for a different view on sheep. 'Backward' may be an unfair word to use: Lancashire's agriculture was well adapted in contemporary terms to the county's

climate and soils, and there is some unpublished evidence of innovation in the south-west. My thanks to Professor Hennock's seminar at Liverpool University for these comments.

26 See note attached to Table 1, and J. Swain, *Industry and Economy in North-east Lancashire, c. 1500–1640* (Manchester, 1986).

27 Langton, *Geographical Change*, 46–8; Blackwood, *Great Rebellion*, 7–8; Marshall, *Lancashire*, 40.

28 P. Clark and P. Slack, *English Towns in Transition, 1500–1700* (1976), 11.

29 Willan, *Elizabethan Manchester*, Chapters 4–5.

30 C. N. Parkinson, *The Rise of the Port of Liverpool* (Liverpool, 1952), 36–51.

31 Wadsworth and Mann, *Cotton Trade*, 58; and see also T. S. Willan, 'Plague in Perspective: the case of Manchester in 1605', *Historic Society of Lancashire and Cheshire* 132 (1983), 32–3.

32 Blackwood, *Great Rebellion*, 3–4; Willan, *Elizabethan Manchester*, 82–3; Wadsworth and Mann, *Cotton Trade*, 68.

33 For the urban crisis theme, cf. Clark and Slack, *Crisis and Order*.

34 Willan, *Elizabethan Manchester*, 84–5.

35 Long, thesis, 188–90; Brigg, 'Forest of Pendle', 65; Porter, 'Forest in Transition', 41. See also now Sarah Pearson, *Rural Houses of the Lancashire Pennines, 1560–1760* (1985), a splendid production by the Royal Commission on the Historical Monuments of England. Nigel Morgan kindly told me about this book, and took me to some of the houses.

36 Long, thesis, 32–3, 142–4, 174, 182–3, 201, 210–14; Ashmore, 'Household Inventories', 68, 71, 77–8, 103.

37 Brigg, 'Forest of Pendle', 66–7; see also Pearson, *Rural Houses*.

38 B. W. Quintrell, 'Government in Perspective: Lancashire and the Privy Council, 1570–1640', *Historic Society of Lancashire and Cheshire* 131 (1982), 36–7, 55; Blackwood, *Great Rebellion*, 20.

39 Long, thesis, 28–31, 69; Blackwood, *Great Rebellion*, 11–18. But cf. Morrill, 'Northern Gentry', for a different emphasis.

40 Blackwood, *Great Rebellion*, 18–21, 95–100, and Chapter 4.

41 K. Wrightson, 'The Puritan Reformation of Manners, with special reference to the Counties of Lancashire and Essex', Ph.D. thesis, Univ. of Cambridge, 1974, 180.

42 Tupling, *Rossendale*, 163–5.

43 Wadsworth and Mann, *Cotton Trade*, 60, n. 4.

44 Thirsk, *Agrarian History*, 88; Langton, *Geographical Change*, 43, 71.

45 Marshall, *Lancashire*, 45–6.

46 C. D. Rogers, *The Lancashire Population Crisis of 1623* (Manchester, 1975).

47 A. B. Appleby, *Famine in Tudor and Stuart England* (Liverpool, 1978).

48 Wrightson, thesis, 180–9.

49 G. Ormerod (ed.), *Tracts relating to Military Proceedings in Lancashire during the Great Civil War* (Manchester, 1864), 277–8.

50 J. Walter and K. Wrightson, 'Dearth and the Social Order in Early Modern England', *Past and Present* 71 (1976), 38–40; M. James, *Social Problems and Policy during the Puritan Revolution* (1930), 54–5, 244–5. See also W. King, 'Illegal Behavior in Seventeenth-Century Lancashire', Ph.D. thesis, Univ. of Michigan, Chapter 2, for evidence of famine or near-famine in 1644. King also stresses the continuing importance of informal almsgiving alongside the Poor Law; but this also came under pressure in the 1640s.

51 Wrightson, thesis, 183, 189. King, 'Illegal Behavior', notes that oats were in good supply in south-west Lancashire in 1654, and that the crisis in the south-east probably had much to do with the 'decay of trade' which was noted in 1653.

52 Compare D. M. Palliser, 'Tawney's Century: Brave New World or Malthusian Trap', *Economic History Review* 2nd ser., 35 (1982), with Appleby, *Famine*.

53 Walter and Wrightson, 'Dearth', 24, 27.

54 Long, thesis, 109–13; N. N. Foster, 'The Peasantry and Aristocracy: a study of the peasant–gentry relations in peace and war, 1600–1715, with special reference to Lancashire', MA thesis, Univ. of Manchester, 1977, 26–7, 35–6; Coward, 'Crisis', 58.

55 B. G. Blackwood, 'The Lancashire Cavaliers and their Tenants', *Historic Society of Lancashire and Cheshire* 117 (1965), 24–31.

56 Long, thesis, 113–18.

57 A. B. Appleby, 'Agrarian Capitalism or Seigneurial Reaction? The North-West of England, 1500–1700', *American Historical Review* 80 (1975); Long, thesis, 127.

58 Tupling, *Rossendale*, Chapter 5, and 'The Causes of the Civil War in Lancashire', *Lancashire and Cheshire Antiquarian Society* 65 (1955), 1–32.

59 Ormerod, *Tracts*, 65; Foster, 'Peasantry', 67–8; B. Manning, *The English People and the English Revolution* (pbk. edn., 1978), 238–9.

60 'Disloyal', that is, to their landlords rather than to the Crown: Foster, 'Peasantry', 64–76. See also Blackwood, *Great Rebellion*, 51–2.

61 Quintrell, 'Government', 36; Blackwood, *Great Rebellion*, 26; Brigg, 'Forest of Pendle', 75.

62 Long, thesis, 198; C. D. Rogers, 'The Development of a Teaching Profession in England, 1547–1700', Ph.D. thesis, Univ. of Manchester, 1975, 31–2. Cf. Quintrell, 'Government', 38.

63 W. K. Jordan, *The Social Institutions of Lancashire* (Manchester, 1962), 71.

64 Rogers, thesis, 30.

65 Blackwood, *Great Rebellion*, 26.

66 Jordan, *Social Institutions*, 29–75.

67 Wrightson, thesis, 119–20. This is based on an admittedly small sample. To put it in wider perspective see especially R. A. Houston, 'The Development of Literacy: Northern England, 1640–1750', *Economic History Review* 2nd ser., 35 (1982).

68 Rogers, thesis, 32, 65, 69.

69 Long, thesis, 10; Blackwood, *Great Rebellion*, 26.

70 W. I. Williams, 'Some Aspects of Nonconformity in the North-West of England, 1650–1750', MA thesis, Univ. of Wales (Bangor), 1973, 55–6.

71 Wadsworth and Mann, *Cotton Trade, passim*.

72 Haigh and Blackwood both provide supporting evidence for these contentions; and see Willan, *Elizabethan Manchester*, 127–8, and R. C. Richardson, *Puritanism in North–West England* (Manchester, 1972).

Chapter 3

1 Richardson, *Puritanism*, 15–17; Haigh, *Reformation*, 22–3.

2 H. Fishwick (ed.), *Lancashire and Cheshire Church Surveys, 1649–55*, Lancashire and Cheshire Record Society, 1 (1879), 110–11.

3 Haigh, *Reformation*, 31, 66–7; Fishwick, *Church Surveys*, xx; cf. Tupling, quoted by Jordan, *Social Institutions*, 75–6, for alternative figures of 62 churches and 128 chapels.

4 Haigh, *Reformation*, Chapters 2, 3, 15; Richardson, *Puritanism*, 3; D. Lambert, 'The Lower Clergy of the Anglican Church of Lancashire, 1558–1642', MA thesis, Univ. of Liverpool, 1964, Chapter 1.

5 Haigh, *Reformation*, 240–1.

6 Wrightson, thesis, Chapter 11, and especially 231–8, 274.

7 Richardson, *Puritanism*, 3–5; Haigh, *Reformation*, 233–6, 321; Wrightson, thesis, 110–15, 264; R. A. Marchant, *The Church under the Law* (1969), 211–12.

8 K. Thomas, *Religion and the Decline of Magic* (1971), 195 and Chapter 6, *passim*.

9 Quintrell, 'Government', 37–54.

10 Blackwood, *Great Rebellion*, 130–3.

11 Coward, 'Crisis'; Richardson, *Puritanism*, 117–18.

12 Long, thesis, 2–3, 22–3; Haigh, *Reformation*, 106. A full analysis of Lancashire JPs between 1603 and 1642 is now provided by D. J. Wilkinson, 'The Commission of the Peace in Lancashire, 1603–1642', *Historic Society of Lancashire and Cheshire* 132 (1983), 41–66.

13 Long, thesis, 5–7, 22–4, 41–2; Wilkinson, 'Commission'.

14 K. Wrightson, 'Two Concepts of Order: Justices, Constables and Jurymen in Seventeenth-Century England', in J. Brewer and J. Styles (eds.), *An Ungovernable People* (1980).

15 King, 'Illegal Behavior', Chapter 3; and for intermediate officials, A. Hodge, paper presented to the Economic History Conference, Univ. of York, 1985.

16 Wrightson, 'Two Concepts of Order', 26–34, and thesis, Chapter 9; King, 'Illegal Behavior'; J. Kent, 'The English Village Constable, 1580–1642', *Journal of British Studies* 20 (1981), 26–49.

17 G. W. Oxley, 'The Permanent Poor in South-West Lancashire', in J. R. Harris (ed.), *Liverpool and Merseyside* (1969), 17–19, 22–4.

18 Jordan, *Social Institutions*, 12–13.

19 Ibid., 18–21, 25.

20 Oxley, 'Permanent Poor', 22.

21 King, 'Illegal Behavior', Chapter 6, and 'The Regulation of Alehouses in Stuart Lancashire', *Historic Society of Lancashire and Cheshire* 128 (1979); Wrightson, thesis, Chapter 5; and for context see P. Clark, *The English Alehouse: a social history, 1200–1830* (1983).

22 Haigh, 'Slander'.

23 E. Peel and P. Southern, *The Trials of the Lancashire Witches* (1969); J. Crossley (ed.), *Pott's Discovery of Witchcraft in the County of Lancaster* (Manchester, 1845). There remains a great deal of potential mileage in this topic.

24 A. Macfarlane, *Witchcraft in Tudor and Stuart England* (1970), Chapters 10–16. Macfarlane has since repudiated the interpretation given here, but I find Macfarlane Mark I much more convincing than any of the later models.

25 King, 'Illegal Behavior', Chapter 9.

26 Peel and Southern, *Trials*, 31–2; Haigh, *Reformation*, 321–3; Richardson, *Puritanism*, 164.

27 For what follows see especially Haigh, *Reformation*, Part III; J. Bossy, *The English Catholic Community, 1570–1850* (1975), especially Chapters 5–6; and see also R. G. Dottie, 'The Recusant Riots at Childwall in May 1600: a reappraisal', *Historic Society of Lancashire and Cheshire* 132 (1983), 1–28.

28 J. S. Leatherbarrow, *The Lancashire Elizabethan Recusants* (Manchester, 1947), 22, 65; Haigh, *Reformation*, 287.

29 Haigh, *Reformation*, 316–18; Walker, *South-West Lancashire*, 78–82.

30 Haigh, *Reformation*, 277.

31 C. Haigh, 'From Monopoly to Minority: Catholicism in Early Modern England', *Royal Historical Society*, 5th ser., 31 (1981), 129–48.

32 Bossy, *Catholic Community*, 86.

33 Haigh, *Reformation*, 281; cf. Leatherbarrow, *Recusants*, Chapter 4, and Walker, *South-West Lancashire*, 66.

34 Haigh, *Reformation*, 86, 285 and *passim*; R. B. Manning, 'The Making of a Protestant Aristocracy: the Ecclesiastical Commissioners of the Diocese of Chester', *Bulletin of the Institute of Historical Research* 49 (1976), 69.

35 Richardson, *Puritanism*, Chapter 1; Haigh, *Reformation*, Chapter 18; Tupling, 'Civil War', 4–6; R. Halley, *Lancashire: its Puritanism and Nonconformity* (1867), Chapter 3; F. R. Raines (ed.), *The Journal of Nicholas Assheton of Downham* (Manchester, 1848); Morrill, 'Northern Gentry', 76–7.

36 F. R. Raines (ed.), 'State Civil and Ecclesiastical of the County of Lancaster', *Chetham Miscellanies*, Old Series, V (1875), 3–4.

37 See especially Haigh, *Reformation*, Chapter 18.

38 E. Axon (ed.), Oliver Heywood's *Life of John Angier of Denton* (Manchester, 1937), 142.

39 Ibid., 148; also 141, 149–51; cf. Wrightson, thesis, 276.

40 Halley, *Lancashire* ..., II, 146–52.

41 C. Haigh, 'Puritan Evangelism in the Reign of Elizabeth I', *English Historical Review* 92 (1977), 30–58.

42 But cf. P. Collinson, *The Religion of Protestants* (Oxford, 1982).

43 Morrill, 'Northern Gentry', 87; Blackwood, *Great Rebellion*, Chapter 2, for much of what follows; and see also his most recent statement in 'Parties and Issues in the Civil War in Lancashire', *Historic Society of Lancashire and Cheshire* 132 (1983), 103–26.

44 Morrill, 'Northern Gentry', 77.

45 P. R. Newman, 'Catholic Royalists of Northern England', *Northern History* 15 (1979), 88–95; Newman, 'Aspects of the Civil War in Lancashire', *Lancashire and Cheshire Antiquarian Society* 1983; cf. K. J. Lindley, 'The Part Played by the Catholics', in B. Manning (ed.), *Politics, Religion and the English Civil War* (1973), 127–76.

46 Manning, *English People*, 8–9.

47 Ibid., 225–30, 235, 237–40, 267–9; Morrill, 'Northern Gentry', 84–5.

48 Cf. Tupling, 'Civil War'; R. C. Richardson, 'Puritanism and the Ecclesiastical Authorities: the Case of the Diocese of Chester', in Manning, *Politics* ..., 16–25.

49 E. Broxap, *The Great Civil War in Lancashire* (Manchester, 1910, reprinted 1973); Blackwood, *Great Rebellion*, 50–3.

50 Blackwood, *Great Rebellion*, 60–2; Morrill, 'Northern Gentry', 81–4.

51 Blackwood, *Great Rebellion*, 77–88.

52 Ibid., Chapters 3–4.

53 Ibid., 75–6; Halley, *Lancashire* ..., II, 93–104.

54 Halley, *Lancashire* ..., I, 432, 436–8.

55 Ibid., II, 45–90; Wrightson, thesis, Chapter 12.

56 King, 'Alehouses'; Wrightson, thesis, 91; Clark, *English Alehouse*, 48–50.

57 Wrightson, thesis, Chapters 4–5 and 133–5, 220–5; Clark, *English Alehouse*, Chapters 7–8; and cf. Halley, *Lancashire* ..., II, 34, for the equivocations of Major-General Worsley.

58 Wrightson, thesis, 209–13, 224–7; Halley, *Lancashire* ..., I, 206–16, II, 33–4, 72–3.

59 Halley, *Lancashire* ..., II, 128–31.

60 Wrightson, thesis, 14, 215; and see King, 'Illegal Behavior', Chapter 7.
61 K. Wrightson, 'The Nadir of English Ilegitimacy in the Seventeenth Century', in P. Laslett, K. Oosterveen and R. M. Smith (eds.), *Bastardy and its Comparative History* (1980), 180 – 1, 185 – 6.
62 Wrightson, thesis, 48 – 9.

Chapter 4

1 See especially Wadsworth and Mann, *Cotton Trade*; also G. W. Daniels, *The Early English Cotton Industry* (1920) L. W. Moffitt, *England on the Eve of the Industrial Revolution* (1925), is sadly of very little value.
2 Wadsworth and Mann, *Cotton Trade*, 88 – 90, 277 – 8; Tupling, *Rossendale*, 183 – 4; King, 'Rossendale'.
3 Aikin, *Thirty ... Miles Round Manchester*, 302 – 3; F. Singleton, 'The Flax Merchants of Kirkham', *Historic Society of Lancashire and Cheshire* 126 (1977), 73 – 108.
4 Wadsworth and Mann, *Cotton Trade*, Chapter 8.
5 Ibid., 170 – 1, 520 – 1.
6 Ibid., 314 – 5, 326; King, 'Rossendale', Chapter 13; Tupling, *Rossendale*, 183 – 5; D. Hey, 'Northern England: Lancashire and Yorkshire', in J. Thirsk (ed.), *Agrarian History of England and Wales*, V (1985).
7 Wadsworth and Mann, *Cotton Trade*, 78 – 90, 278; King, 'Rossendale', Chapter 9.
8 Wadsworth and Mann, *Cotton Trade*, 72 – 8, 241 – 8, 278 – 83; Aikin, *Thirty ... Miles Round Manchester*, 182 – 4.
9 Daniels, *Cotton Industry*, 36 – 9; Tupling, *Rossendale*, 189 – 90; B. L. Anderson in W. H. Chaloner and B. Ratcliffe (eds.), *Trade and Transport* (Manchester, 1980).
10 King, 'Rossendale', Chapters 11, 13, 15; Wadsworth and Mann, *Cotton Trade*, 314 – 23; Aikin, *Thirty ... Miles Round Manchester*.
11 Wadsworth and Mann, *Cotton Trade*, Chapters 5, 15.
12 Ibid., 306 – 8; (James Ogden), *A Description of Manchester, by a Native of the Town* (1783), 83 – 6.
13 Wadsworth and Mann, *Cotton Trade*, 452 – 5, 468, 471.
14 Aikin, *Thirty ... Miles Round Manchester*, 155 – 6, 228, 261, 266; Wadsworth and Mann, *Cotton Trade*, 509 – 11; T. Percival, *Observation on the state of Populations in Manchester and adjacent places* (1778); P. Corfield, *The Impact of English Towns, 1700 – 1800* (Oxford, 1982), 1 – 16 and *passim*.
15 Wadsworth and Mann, *Cotton Trade*, 277.
16 For an introduction to the now extensive literature on this issue, see L. Clarkson, *Proto-industrialization* (1985).
17 For the complexities of the West Riding, see P. Hudson, 'Proto-industrialization: the West Riding wool textile industry', *History Workshop Journal* 1983.
18 D. Farnie, *The English Cotton Industry and the World Market, 1815 – 96* (Oxford, 1979), 47 – 51, puts a strong case for the importance of humidity and 'implacable grey skies'.
19 See above, Chapter 2, and cf. Wadsworth and Mann, *Cotton Trade*, 279.
20 All of the sources concur on this point; and for the importance of linen, Wadsworth and Mann, *Cotton Trade*, 171.
21 Ogden, *Description*, 93 – 4.
22 Wadsworth and Mann, *Cotton Trade*, 98 – 106.
23 Ibid., Chapter 6.

24 Ibid., 72, 78, 187–9, 232–3; Anderson, in Chaloner and Ratcliffe, *Trade*, 64–5; W. Enfield, *An Essay towards the History of Leverpool* (Warrington, 1773), 80–7; and see S. Engerman, 'The Slave Trade and British Capital Formation in the Eighteenth Century', *Business History Review* 46 (1972), 430–43.

25 Williams, *Capitalism and Slavery*, 63, 68.

26 Blackwood, *Great Rebellion*, 8; Enfield, *Leverpool*, 25–6; Aikin, *Thirty ... Miles Round Manchester*, 335.

27 P. G. E. Clemens, 'The Rise of Liverpool, 1665–1750', *Economic History Review* 2nd ser., 29 (1976), 212, Table 1; F. E. Hyde, *Liverpool and the Mersey* (Newton Abbot, 1971), 28, 30.

28 Hyde, *Liverpool*, 14–15, 19–21; S. Marriner, *The Economic and Social Development of Merseyside* (1982), Chapter 4.

29 Clemens, 'Rise', 212, Table 1; Hyde, *Liverpool*, 34.

30 D. P. Lamb, 'Volume and Tonnage of the Liverpool Slave Trade, 1772–1807', in R. Anstey and P. E. H. Hair (eds.), *Liverpool, the African Slave Trade, and Abolition* (Liverpool, 1976), 91.

31 R. Anstey, 'The Historical Debate on the Abolition of the British Slave Trade', and D. Richardson, 'Profits in the Slave Trade: the Accounts of William Davenport, 1757–1784', in Anstey and Hair, *Slave Trade*; F. E. Hyde, B. B. Parkinson and S. Marriner, 'The Nature and Profitability of the Liverpool Slave Trade', *Economic History Review* 2nd ser., 5 (1952–3), 368–77; Hyde, *Liverpool*, 3–4; Marriner, *Merseyside*, 37. The profitability debate continues in the *Journal of Economic History* in 1985–6, but I see no reason to alter the argument of this paragraph.

32 Clemens, 'Rise', 217–18, 225.

33 Enfield, *Leverpool*, 73–9.

34 Corfield, *Impact*, 35–7, comments usefully on this theme; and see Aikin, *Thirty ... Miles Round Manchester*, 383.

35 Hyde, *Liverpool*, 13–15.

36 Clemens, 'Rise', 214–15; T. Heywood, *The Norris Papers* (Manchester, 1846).

37 Hyde, *Liverpool*, 15–17.

38 *A Trip to Leverpoole, by two of Fate's Children in Search of Fortunatus's Purse ... by a Gentleman of Lincoln's-Inn* (1706), 3–4.

39 James Boardman, *Liverpool Table Talk a Hundred Years Ago* (Liverpool, 1871), 11, 13, 16, 21, 24, 36, 47–8.

40 T. C. Barker and J. R. Harris, *A Merseyside Town in the Industrial Revolution: St Helens, 1750–1900* (Liverpool, 1954), 13–15; F. A. Bailey, 'The minutes of the trustees of the turnpike roads from Liverpool to Prescot, St Helens, Warrington and Ashton-in-Makerfield, 1726–89', *Historic Society of Lancashire and Cheshire* 88 (1936), 159–200; 89 (1937), 31–76; Marriner, *Merseyside*, 16.

41 C. Hadfield and G. Biddle, *The Canals of North-West England* (Newton Abbot, 1970), I, Chapters 1–3; J. R. Ward, *The Finance of Canal Building in Eighteenth-Century England* (Oxford, 1974), 26–7; Barker and Harris, *St Helens*, 15–22; D. Anderson, *The Orrell Coalfield, Lancashire, 1740–1850* (Hartington, 1975), 27–39; R. G. Dottie, 'Transport and the Rise of Liverpool', in E. Sigsworth (ed.), *Ports and Resorts in the Regions* (Hull, 1980), 30.

42 W. Albert, *The Turnpike Road System in England, 1663–1840* (1971), 34, 4–50, 107; Dottie, 'Transport', 29; Hadfield and Biddle, *Canals*, I, 18–19; Langton, *Geographical Change*, 107; Freeman, Rodgers and Kinvig, *Lancashire ...*, 58–62.

43 Hadfield and Biddle, *Canals*, I, Chapters 1–3; Ward, *Finance*, 27–9, 33–4; J. R.

Harris, 'Liverpool Canal Controversies', in Harris (ed.), *Liverpool and Merseyside* (1969).

44 Langton, *Geographical Change*, Chapters 4 – 7; Barker and Harris, *St Helens*, Chapters 3 – 4.

45 Langton, *Geographical Change*, 96 – 101, 176 – 81; Tupling, 'Early Metal Trades'; Shelley, 'Pewterers', 12 – 13; J. R. Harris, 'Origins of the St Helens Glass Industry', *Northern History* 3 (1968), 105 – 17.

46 J. Holt, *General View of the Agriculture of the County of Lancaster* (1795, reprinted 1969), 5 – 7, 127 – 8, 149 – 50.

47 Aikin, *Thirty ... Miles Round Manchester*, 204, 235, 303.

48 J. D. Marshall, *Furness and the Industrial Revolution* (Barrow, 1958; reprinted Beckermet, Cumbria, 1981), 58.

49 Hey, 'Lancashire and Yorkshire'.

50 Ibid.; Holt, *Agriculture*, 57 – 63; Aikin, *Thirty ... Miles Round Manchester*, 306.

51 Holt, *Agriculture*, 54 – 5; Hey, 'Lancashire and Yorkshire'.

52 Holt, *Agriculture*, 166 – 8; King, 'Rossendale', Chapter 15; Marshall, *Furness*, 58 – 9.

53 Hey, 'Lancashire and Yorkshire'; Holt, *Agriculture*, 143 – 5; King, 'Rossendale', Chapter 15.

54 Hey, 'Lancashire and Yorkshire'; Holt, *Agriculture*, 14, 21 – 3, 26, 34, 179 – 82.

55 D. Defoe, *A Tour Through the Whole Island of Great Britain* (Everyman's Library edn.), II, 268; J. D. Marshall (ed.), *The Autobiography of William Stout* (Manchester, 1967), 30 – 63; M. Schofield, *Outlines of an Economic History of Lancaster*, I (Lancaster, 1946); Marshall, *Furness*, 39 – 41, 126.

56 Based on a comparison between Blackwood, *Great Rebellion*, 7, and the first census in 1801.

57 R. S. Schofield and E. A. Wrigley, *The Population History of England, 1541 – 1871* (1981); cf. the figures given in P. Deane and W. A. Cole, *British Economic Growth 1688 – 1959* (Cambridge, 1962), where the county estimates for the eighteenth century are completely unconvincing.

58 The returns for Bishop Gastrell's 1717 survey are printed in F. R. Raines (ed.), *Notitia Cestrensis*, Chetham Society, Old Series, Vols. 19, 21, 22. The year 1717 seems a more plausible date than the 1722 suggested by John Addy: see Vol. 19, 9, n. 2. An interesting additional dimension to the pattern of population change comes from the Hearth-Tax-based figures for the number of houses in Lancashire in 1690, amassed by Davenant and Houghton and set out in D. V. Glass and D. E. C. Eversley (eds.), *Population in History* (pbk. edn., 1974), 216 – 20. These contemporary investigators failed to agree, and Davenant's figures almost certainly err on the high side: but his evidence suggests a 40 per cent increase in Lancashire's population between 1664 and 1690, while Houghton's suggest a 20 per cent rise. If we give any credence at all to this material, it suggests even more strongly that population stagnated or even fell between 1690 and 1717. Local evidence from parish registers bears this out for the textile district, and it seems even more probable that saturation point had been reached within the existing economic system by the 1690s, and it took a new upsurge in the employing power of the textile industries to stimulate renewed population growth after 1717. More research is clearly needed here.

59 The returns are in Chester County Record Office, series EDV/7. Jenny Smith kindly helped with the gathering of the evidence.

60 King, 'Rossendale', Chapter 3; Marshall, *Furness*, 98 – 103; R. Speake, 'The Demographic and Social History of Carnforth and District since 1700', M. Litt. thesis, Univ. of Lancaster, 1969.

61 Wadsworth and Mann, *Cotton Trade*, 311; Corfield, *Impact*, 129, 183; Marshall, *Furness*, 102. The 1778 visitation suggests populations of 6460 for Preston and 8550 for Warrington.

62 E.A. Wrigley, 'The Growth of Population in Eighteenth-Century England: a Conundrum Resolved', *Past and Present* 98 (1983); Langton, *Geographical Change*, 119–20, 210–11.

63 H. Medick, 'The Proto-industrial Family Economy', *Social History* 1 (1976).

64 King, 'Rossendale', Chapter 10.

65 Ibid., Chapters 3, 10.

66 Cf. Wrigley and Schofield, *Population History*.

67 See above, no. 60, for Marshall and Speake.

68 Blackwood, *Great Rebellion*, 164.

69 Ibid., Chapter 4; M.J. Galgano, 'Restoration Recusancy in the Northwest of England: a social history 1658–1673', Ph.D. thesis, Vanderbilt Univ., 1971, 80 and *passim*; but cf. Langton, *Geographical Change*.

70 P.N. Borsay, 'The English Urban Renaissance: Landscape and Leisure in the Provincial Town, *c.* 1660–1760', Ph.D. thesis, Univ. of Lancaster, 1981, 47, 76–9, 82–5, 304–5, 312–14, 318–19, 327–8; A. Hodge, *History of Preston: an Introduction* (Preston, 1984), 14–16.

71 Borsay, thesis, 88–90; C.W. Chalklin, *The Provincial Towns of Georgian England* (1974), 100–2.

72 Aikin, *Thirty … Miles Round Manchester*, 184–90; J.A. Picton, *Memorials of Liverpool*, I (2nd edn., 1875), 182, 196–8; Enfield, *Leverpool*, 62; Boardman, *Liverpool Table Talk*, 9–12.

73 Borsay, thesis, 275 n. 57.

74 J.D. Marshall, 'Agrarian Wealth and Social Structure in Pre-industrial Cumbria', *Economic History Review* 2nd ser., 33 (1980), 509, 519 and *passim*; J.V. Beckett, 'The Pattern of Landownership in England and Wales, 1660–1880', *Economic History Review* 2nd ser., 37 (1984), 17, n. 71.

75 Hey, 'Lancashire and Yorkshire'.

76 King, 'Rossendale', Chapter 12; see also W. Bennett, *The History of Burnley*, III (Burnley, 1949), 45–6.

77 Wadsworth and Mann, *Cotton Trade*, 386–95; King, 'Rossendale', Chapter 12.

78 Langton, *Geographical Change*, 113–20, 194–212; Wadsworth and Mann, *Cotton Trade*, 390.

79 Aikin, *Thirty … Miles Round Manchester*, 192 ff.; Enfield, *Leverpool*; T. Percival, *Further Observations on the State of Population in Manchester, and other Adjacent Places* (1774), 5, 7.

80 Langton, *Geographical Change*, 200.

81 Ibid., 195–9; King, 'Rossendale', Chapter 10; Marshall, *Furness*, 14–15, 104–9.

Chapter 5

1 B. Coward, 'The Social and Political Position of the Earls of Derby in Later Seventeenth-Century Lancashire', *Historic Society of Lancashire and Cheshire* 132 (1983), 127–54; L.K.J. Glassey, *Politics and the Appointment of Justices of the Peace, 1675–1720* (Oxford, 1979), 277–8, 284.

2 Coward, 'Earls of Derby', 150; Glassey, *Justices*, 286–90.

3 D.P. Carter, 'The Lancashire Militia, 1660–1688', *Historic Society of Lancashire and Cheshire* 132 (1983), 162, 171.

4 R.C. Jarvis, *Collected Papers on the Jacobite Risings*, I (Liverpool, 1971), Chapter 6, especially 126–7; J.R. Western, *The English Militia in the Eighteenth Century* (1965), 57, 73.

5 Carter, 'Lancashire Militia', 180–1.

6 Wilkinson, 'Commission of the Peace', 43–4; Glassey, *Justices*, 272.

7 Glassey, *Justices*, Chapter 10.

8 Ibid., 274–5, 282–3.

9 Wadsworth and Mann, *Cotton Trade*, 362–3; D. Foster, 'The Changing Social Origins and Political Allegiances of Lancashire J.P.s, 1821–51', Ph.D. thesis, Univ. of Lancaster, 1972; Barker and Harris, *St Helens*, 146.

10 W.R. Ward, *The English Land Tax* (1953), 7–10.

11 See Corfield, *Impact*, 146–52.

12 M. Mullett, 'Conflict, Politics and Elections in Lancaster, 1660–1688', *Northern History* 19 (1983), 61.

13 M. Mullett, 'The Politics of Liverpool, 1660–1688', *Historic Society of Lancashire and Cheshire* 124 (1972), 31–56; Picton, *Memorials*, I, 156, 174–5, 183, 198–203; Wadsworth and Mann, *Cotton Trade*, 67.

14 M. Mullett, ' "To Dwell Together in Unity": the Search for Agreement in Preston Politics, 1660–90', *Historic Society of Lancashire and Cheshire* 125 (1974), 61–81; *idem*, 'Lancaster', 61–86.

15 Cf. A. Redford and I.S. Russell, *The History of Local Government in Manchester*, I (1939).

16 Bennett, *Burnley*, III, 29, 46–7.

17 Barker and Harris, *St Helens*, 147.

18 Ibid.

19 A. Fessler, 'The Official Attitude towards the Sick Poor in Seventeenth-Century Lancashire', *Historic Society of Lancashire and Cheshire* 102 (1951), 107, 101–11; Bennett, *Burnley*, III, 58; M. Gray, *The History of Bury, Lancashire, from 1660 to 1876* (Bury, 1970), 22–5, 36–40.

20 Barker and Harris, *St Helens*, 146–7; King, 'Rossendale', Chapters 5, 10, 12; Bennett, *Burnley*, III, 60–1; Marshall, *Furness*, 133.

21 Oxley, 'Permanent Poor'.

22 Ibid.; Marshall, *Furness*, 137; Barker and Harris, *St Helens*, 132–7; Bennett, *Burnley*, III, 60–1; King, 'Rossendale', Chapter 12; H. Bateson, *A History of Oldham* (Oldham, 1949), 69.

23 Fessler, 'Sick Poor', 112.

24 Barker and Harris, *St Helens*, 135–6, 141–2, 148.

25 W.L. Blease, 'The Poor Law in Liverpool 1681–1834', *Historic Society of Lancashire and Cheshire* 61 (1909), 97–122.

26 G.B. Hindle, *Provision for the Relief of the Poor in Manchester, 1754–1826* (Manchester, 1975), Chapters 1–2; Redford and Russell, *Local government*, I, Chapter 8; Wadsworth and Mann, *Cotton Trade*, 406; British Library, *A Case in Relation to an Act of Parliament, Humbly Desired for the Erecting a Work-House in the Town of Manchester* (1730).

27 *Manchester Vindicated: being a Compleat Collection of the papers lately Published in defence of that town, in the Chester Courant* (Chester, 1749), 6; Chester County Record Office, EDV/7.

28 Bossy, *Catholic Community*, 186–7; J. Addy, 'Bishop Porteous' Visitation of the Diocese of Chester, 1778', *Northern History* 13 (1977), 175–94.

29 Bossy, *Catholic Community*, 406–7.

30 Galgano, 'Restoration Recusancy', 97.

31 J. Miller, *Popery and Politics in England, 1660–1688* (1973), 60–2, 167–8, 192–3; Galgano, 'Restoration Recusancy', 334 and *passim*; Langton, *Geographical Change*; T. Ellison Gibson (ed.), *A Cavalier's Note Book* (1880), 131–2.

32 E.A. Rose, 'Methodism in South Lancashire to 1800', *Lancashire and Cheshire Antiquarian Society* 81 (1982), 67.

33 Williams, thesis, 32.

34 Halley, *Lancashire ...*, Chapter 6; and see list in Williams, thesis, 30–1.

35 Halley, *Lancashire ...*, Chapter 7; N.N. Foster, thesis, 67.

36 Halley, *Lancashire ...*, II, 294–5; M. Watts, *The Dissenters*, I (Oxford, 1978).

37 Raines (ed.), Gastrell survey.

38 Halley, *Lancashire ...*, II, 295; Williams, thesis, 42, 108–10.

39 Halley, *Lancashire ...*, II, 325; Marshall, *William Stout*; Marshall, *Furness*, 103; Raines (ed.), Gastrell survey, Chetham Society 19, 147–8.

40 M. Mullett (ed.), *Early Lancaster Friends* (Lancaster, 1978), 12, 23–5; Marshall, *Furness*, 21, 25, 103.

41 Halley, *Lancashire ...*, II, 378–9; Addy, 'Visitation', 189.

42 Halley, *Lancashire ...*, II, 379–90, 430–5; W.T. Whitley, *Baptists of North-West England, 1649–1913* (1913), Chapter 8; Rose, 'Methodism', 67–8.

43 Rose, 'Methodism', 67–76; Addy, 'Visitation', 189–90; and see also Wesley's *Journals*.

44 Williams, thesis, 52; Addy, 'Visitation', 177, 183, 187.

45 Raines (ed.), Gastrell survey, Chetham Society 19, 151; Addy, 'Visitation', 180, 183.

46 Wesley, *Journals*.

47 Halley, *Lancashire ...*, II, 363.

48 Ibid., II, 257–8.

49 Wesley's *Journals* (Everyman edn.), IV, 9, 71.

50 Addy, 'Visitation', 180–2.

51 M. Sanderson, 'Literacy and Social Mobility in the Industrial Revolution in England', *Past and Present* 56 (1972), 76–7, 82–3.

52 Mrs Raffald, *Manchester Directory* (Manchester, 1773).

53 Wadsworth and Mann, *Cotton Trade*, 386–91.

54 *A Serious Disswasive from an Intended Subscription, for Continuing the Races upon Kersal Moor* (Manchester, 1733).

55 Langton, 'Regional Geography', 159–62, has much of interest here. See also R. Poole, 'The Lancashire Wakes', Ph.D. thesis, Univ. of Lancaster, 1985, which concentrates revealingly on a later period; and a wide range of local histories, such as T. Newbigging, *History of the Forest of Rossendale* (2nd edn., Rawtenstall, 1893), 271–7. The collections of 'traditions' and 'folk-lore' by Roby, Harland and Wilkinson and their successors would repay further investigation.

56 Halley, *Lancashire ...*, has revealing evidence on this theme.

57 W.L. Sachse (ed.), *The Diary of Roger Lowe of Ashton-in-Makerfield, 1663–74* (1938); Halley, *Lancashire ...*, II, 338–9, 408–9.

58 Wadsworth and Mann, *Cotton Trade*, Chapter 19.

59 Ibid., Chapter 20.

60 Ibid., 356–61; Charlesworth, *Riots*, 80–94.

61 E.L. Lonsdale, 'John Lunt and the Lancashire Plot, 1694', *Historic Society of Lancashire and Cheshire* 115 (1963), 91–106.

62 F. McLynn, 'The Regional Distribution of Jacobite Support in England before 1745', *Journal of Regional and Local Studies* 3 (1983–4), 23; Halley, *Lancashire ...*, Chapter 8; B. Lenman, *The Jacobite Risings in Britain, 1689–1746* (1980).

63 Lenman, *Jacobites*, 273, 275; Jarvis, *Jacobite Risings*, II (1962), Chapters 21–3; *Manchester Vindicated* ...

64 Jarvis, *Jacobite Risings*, I, 239–49.

65 *An Account of a Dreadful Mob at Manchester, and in other Places in England* (Edinburgh, 1715); Halley, *Lancashire* ..., II, 318–9, 337–41, 345–6.

66 Picton, *Memorials*, I, 180.

67 A. Macfarlane, *The Justice and the Mare's Ale* (Oxford, 1981); J. Styles, ' "Our Traitorous Money Makers": the Yorkshire Coiners and the Law, 1760–83', in Brewer and Styles, *Ungovernable People*, 172–249.

Chapter 6

1 See especially O. Ashmore, *The Industrial Archaeology of North-West England* (Manchester, 1982).

2 Farnie, *Cotton Industry*, 52–4, provides a brief, sharp summary.

3 M. M. Edwards, *The Growth of the British Cotton Trade, 1780–1815* (Manchester, 1967), 110–11.

4 J. G. Timmins, *Hand-loom Weavers' Cottages in Central Lancashire* (Lancaster, 1977), is more convincing on this point than D. Bythell, *The Hand-loom Weavers* (Oxford, 1969).

5 P. Mathias, *The First Industrial Nation* (1969), 486.

6 Edwards, *Cotton Trade*, Chapter 5.

7 H. Catling, *The Spinning Mule* (Newton Abbot, 1970); Wadsworth and Mann, *Cotton Trade*, 476–80 (including material on the riots against spinning jennies in 1768), 486–8, 492–3, 502.

8 Edwards, *Cotton Trade*, 8, 182–3, 186–7; S. D. Chapman, in J. P. P. Higgins and S. Pollard (eds.), *Aspects of Capital Investment in Great Britain, 1750–1850* (1971).

9 Edwards, *Cotton Trade*, 8; Catling, *Spinning Mule*.

10 Wadsworth and Mann, *Cotton Trade*, Book V; and for a compact introduction to all this, S. D. Chapman, *The Cotton Industry in the Industrial Revolution* (1972).

11 Bythell, *Hand-loom Weavers*.

12 Edwards, *Cotton Trade*, 183, 186; V. A. C. Gatrell, 'Labour, Power and the Size of Firms in Lancashire Cotton in the Second Quarter of the Nineteenth Century', *Economic History Review* 2nd ser., 30 (1977), 126–7.

13 A. J. Bailey, 'The Instability of Growth in a Leading Sector: the Economics of Cotton Firms during the British Industrial Revolution', paper presented at the Economic History Conference, Glasgow, 1984. It is important to remember that a single factory could, and often did, contain several firms.

14 Calculated from Gatrell, 'Size of Firms', 98, 127.

15 O. Ashmore, *The Industrial Archaeology of Lancashire* (Newton Abbot, 1969), 241–2.

16 Calculated from A. E. Musson, 'Industrial Motive Power in the United Kingdom, 1800–70', *Economic History Review* 2nd ser., 29 (1976).

17 Catling, *Spinning Mule*, 53–4; Gatrell, 'Size of Firms', 112.

18 Gatrell, 'Size of Firms'; R. Lloyd-Jones and A. A. Le Roux, 'The Size of Firms in the Cotton Industry: Manchester, 1815–41', *Economic History Review* 2nd ser., 33 (1980), 72–82.

19 P. Joyce, *Work, Society and Politics* (Hassocks, Sussex, 1980), 20 and *passim*; see also the much inferior book by K. Honeyman, *Origins of Enterprise* (Manchester, 1983).

20 Edwards, *Cotton Trade*, Chapters 9–10; Chapman, in Higgins and Pollard, *Capital Investment*.

21 S. D. Chapman, 'Financial Restraints on the Growth of Firms in the Cotton Industry, 1790–1850', *Economic History Review* 2nd ser., 32 (1979), 50–69.

22 Medick, 'Proto-Industrial Family Economy'; Bythell, *Hand-loom Weavers*.

23 The information for this passage comes from unpublished research by J. G. Timmins for his Lancaster Ph.D. thesis on the Lancashire hand-loom weavers. I am most grateful to him for allowing me to use this material before the completion of this important thesis. Any errors in transmission or interpretation are, of course, my responsibility.

24 J. S. Lyons, 'The Lancashire Cotton Industry and the Introduction of the Power Loom, 1815–50', Ph.D. thesis, Univ. of California, Berkeley, 1977, 34–99; Timmins, *Cottages*, 51; Farnie, *Cotton Industry*, 276–84; evidence from the Ribchester area, supplied by J. Wardman.

25 Lyons, 'Power Loom'; Farnie, *Cotton Industry*; Gatrell, 'Size of Firms', 98.

26 Farnie, *Cotton Industry*, 24.

27 P. Rushton, 'Housing Conditions and the Family Economy in the Victorian Slum: a Study of a Manchester District (Ancoats), 1790–1871', Ph.D. thesis, Univ. of Manchester, 1977, 198; Lyons, thesis, 147–51; R. K. Fleischman, Jr., 'Conditions of Life among the Cotton Workers of Southeastern Lancashire during the Industrial Revolution', Ph.D. thesis, State Univ. of New York, Buffalo, 1973, 29.

28 See especially R. S. Fitton and A. P. Wadsworth, *The Strutts and the Arkwrights, 1758–1830* (Manchester, 1958).

29 Wadsworth and Mann, *Cotton Trade*, 476–85; A. E. Musson and E. Robinson, *Science and Technology in the Industrial Revolution* (1969).

30 See above, n. 3.

31 E. Butterworth, *A Statistical Sketch of the County Palatine of Lancaster* (1841; reprinted Manchester, 1968), 56.

32 Marriner, *Merseyside*, 31.

33 Hyde, *Liverpool*.

34 Ibid.; Farnie, *Cotton Industry*, 58; Marriner, *Merseyside*, 30, 39.

35 Lamb, 'Volume and Tonnage'.

36 H. S. Klein and S. Engerman, 'Slave Mortality on British Ships, 1791–7', in Anstey and Hair, *Slave Trade*, 115.

37 S. Drescher, 'Capitalism and Abolition', in Anstey and Hair, *Slave Trade*, 189–90.

38 Hyde, *Liverpool*; Butteworth, *Sketch*, 56; Marriner, *Merseyside*, 40.

39 Marriner, *Merseyside*, 31–3; Butterworth, *Sketch*, 57.

40 Hyde, *Liverpool*; Marriner, *Merseyside*, 53–6; Aikin, *Thirty ... Miles Round Manchester*, 372; Barker and Harris, *St Helens*, 223.

41 Marriner, *Merseyside*, 65–6.

42 Butterworth, *Sketch*, 57; Marriner, *Merseyside*, 58; Barker and Harris, *St Helens*, 223–8.

43 I. C. Taylor, '"Black Spot on the Mersey": a study of environment and society in eighteenth and nineteenth-century Liverpool', Ph.D. thesis, Univ. of Liverpool, 1976, Tabel 5.11.

44 Quoted by Edwards, *Cotton Trade*, 191.

45 See above, Chapter 4, n. 24, 31.

46 Farnie, *Cotton Industry*, 58; Marriner, *Merseyside*, 40.

47 Hadfield and Biddle, *Canals*, I, Chapter 3.

48 Ibid., 164, 176, 267, 279–80; Ward, *Finance*; Farnie, *Cotton Industry*, 67–8; Musson,

'Motive Power', 431 n. 31. For a general reappraisal of transport before the railways, see D. H. Aldcroft and M. J. Freeman (eds.), *Transport in the Industrial Revolution* (Manchester, pbk. edn., 1986).

49 Ashmore, *Lancashire*, 185.

50 See especially G. S. Veitch, *The Struggle for the Liverpool and Manchester Railway* (1930); R. E. Carlson, *The Liverpool and Manchester Railway Project* (Newton Abbot, 1969). The suggested traffic pattern is confirmed in Hadfield and Biddle, *Canals*, 103.

51 S. Broadbridge, 'The Sources of Railway Share Capital', in M. C. Reed (ed.), *Railways in the Victorian Economy* (Newton Abbot, 1969), 184–211.

52 Farnie, *Cotton Industry*, 59, 68–70.

53 F. C. Mather, *After the Canal Duke* (Oxford, 1970), especially Chapter 10; Hadfield and Biddle, *Canals*, 170, 353, 399 and *passim*.

54 Langton, *Geographical Change*, especially 154–5, 212–24; Barker and Harris, *St Helens*, Chapters 3–5; Anderson, *Orrell Coalfield*, Chapter 4.

55 Langton, *Geographical Change*, 148–55, 238; A. J. Taylor, 'The Wigan Coalfield in 1851', *Historic Society of Lancashire and Cheshire* 106 (1954), 117–26.

56 Barker and Harris, *St Helens*, 193–6.

57 S. Pollard, 'A New Estimate of British Coal Production, 1750–1850', *Economic History Review* 2nd ser., 33 (1980), 229–30.

58 Langton, *Geographical Change*, 176–9; T. S. Ashton, *An Eighteenth-Century Industrialist: Peter Stubs of Warrington, 1756–1806* (Manchester, 1939); E. S. Dane, *Peter Stubs and the Lancashire Hand Tool Industry* (Altrincham, Ches., 1973).

59 Barker and Harris, *St Helens*, Chapter 7, and 239–44.

60 Ibid., Chapters 9, 16; T. C. Barker, *The Glassmakers* (1977), Chapters 1–7.

61 Barker and Harris, *St Helens*, 223–35; A. E. Musson, *Enterprise in Soap and Chemicals* (Manchester, 1965), Chapters 2–4; L. Gittins in *Journal of Historical Geography* 8 (1982).

62 J. T. Danson and T. A. Welton, 'On the Population of Lancashire and Cheshire and its Local Distribution during the Fifty Years 1801–51', *Historic Society of Lancashire and Cheshire* 1859, 50–2. This is one of a remarkable series of articles, which for methodological sophistication put some recent contributions to shame.

63 T. W. Fletcher, 'The Agrarian Revolution in Arable Lancashire', *Lancashire and Cheshire Antiquarian Society* 72 (1965), 93–122; J. P. Dodd, 'South Lancashire in Transition: a Study of the Crop Returns for 1795–1801', *Historic Society of Lancashire and Cheshire* 117 (1965), 89–107; G. Rogers, 'Social and Economic Change on Lancashire Landed Estates during the Nineteenth Century, with Special Reference to the Clifton Estate, 1832–1916', Ph.D. thesis, Univ. of Lancaster, 1981, Chapter 4; Holt, *Agriculture*.

64 P. J. Gooderson, 'The Social and Economic History of Lancaster, 1780–1914', Ph.D. thesis, Univ. of Lancaster, 1975; Schofield, *Outline*; Marshall, *Furness*; D. M. Clark, 'The Economic and Social Geography of Rural Lonsdale', MA thesis, Univ. of Liverpool, 1968.

65 Danson and Welton, 'Population', 31–2.

66 Ibid.; R. Lawton, 'Population Trends in Lancashire and Cheshire from 1801', *Historic Society of Lancashire and Cheshire* 114 (1962), 189–213.

67 See especially Fleischman, 'Cotton Workers', 260–346.

Chapter 7

1 D. Fraser, *Urban Politics in Victorian England* (Leicester, 1976), 22.
2 V. A. C. Gatrell, in D. Fraser (ed.), *Municipal Reform in the Victorian City* (Leicester, 1981), 17 – 18.
3 Rogers, 'Lancashire Landed Estates'; R. Boyson, *The Ashworth Cotton Enterprise* (Oxford, 1970).
4 F. M. L. Thompson, *English Landed Society in the Nineteenth Century* (1963), Chapter 5; J. Bateman, *Great Landowners of Great Britain* (1878 edn.); R. O. Knapp, 'Social Mobility in Lancashire Society, with special reference to the Social Origins of Landowners in the "Modern Domesday" Returns, 1873 – 6', Ph.D. thesis, Univ. of Lancaster, 1970, xxv.
5 Gatrell, in Fraser, *Municipal Reform*, 22 – 3.
6 Rogers, 'Lancashire Landed Estates', Chapter 1; and material from Bateman, *Great Landowners*.
7 Rogers, 'Lancashire Landed Estates', 22.
8 J. Liddle, 'Estate Management and Land Reform Politics: the Hesketh and Scarisbrick Families and the Making of Southport, 1842 to 1914', in D. Cannadine (ed.), *Patricians, Power and Politics in Nineteenth-Century Towns* (Leicester, 1982), 140 – 2.
9 Mather, *After the Canal Duke*, 320 – 33.
10 Rogers, 'Lancashire Landed Estates'.
11 Barker and Harris, *St Helens*, 120 – 2.
12 Joyce, *Work*, 6 – 10; Honeyman, *Enterprise*, 15 and Chapters 5 – 6; Gatrell, in Fraser, *Municipal Reform*, 29 – 32.
13 F. S. Stancliffe, *John Shaw's, 1738 – 1938* (Manchester, 1938), 123 – 49.
14 S. A. L. Gunn, 'Insiders and Outsiders: Urban Elites and the struggle for Municipal Power in Liverpool, 1800 – 35', MA dissertation, Univ. of Lancaster, 1982.
15 Gatrell, in Fraser, *Municipal Reform*, 24 – 9; J. Seed on Manchester Unitarians, *Social History* 7 (1982); I. Sellers, 'William Roscoe, the Roscoe Circle, and Radical Politics in Liverpool, 1787 – 1807', *Historic Society of Lancashire and Cheshire* 120 (1968), 45 – 62.
16 V. A. C. Gatrell, 'The Commercial Middle Class in Manchester, *c.* 1820 – 57', Ph.D. thesis, Univ. of Cambridge, 1972, 154.
17 A. C. Howe, 'The Lancashire Textile Masters, 1830 – 1860: a Social and Political Study', D.Phil. thesis, Univ. of Oxford, 1980, Chapters 1 – 2; W. D. Rubinstein, 'The Victorian Middle Classes: Wealth, Occupation and Geography', *Economic History Review* 2nd ser., 30 (1977), 602 – 23.
18 Howe, thesis.
19 J. O. Foster, *Class Struggle and the Industrial Revolution* (1974), 177 – 80.
20 W. E. Brown, *Robert Heywood of Bolton, 1786 – 1868* (Wakefield, 1970).
21 Boyson, *Ashworth*, 243, 247 – 8.
22 Joyce, *Work*, 154 and Chapter 4; S. Bamford, *Walks in South Lancashire* (1844; reprinted Hassocks, Sussex, 1972, with an introduction by J. D. Marshall), 174 – 201; W. H. Elliot, *The Story of the 'Cheeryble' Grants* (Manchester, 1906).
23 Foster, *Class Struggle*, Chapter 6.
24 Gatrell, thesis.
25 Boyson, *Ashworth*, 251 – 3.
26 D. Foster, thesis; Howe, thesis, 108 – 20.
27 Redord and Russell, *Local Government*; A. Hewitson, *Preston Court Leet Records* (Preston, 1905).

28 Gunn, dissertation; Gatrell, thesis; J. Garrard, *Leadership and Power in Victorian Industrial Towns* (Manchester, 1983), Chapters 2–3 and *passim*.

29 Rogers, 'Lancashire Landed Families', 33.

30 J. Bohstedt, *Riots and Community Politics in England and Wales, 1790–1810* (Cambridge, Mass., 1983), 102–3.

31 Bohstedt, *Riots*, 104–6; F. Knight, *The Strange Case of Thomas Walker* (1957), Chapters 1–4; A. Booth, 'Reform, Repression and Revolution: Radicalism and Loyalism in the North-West of England, 1789–1803', Ph.D. thesis, Univ. of Lancaster, 1979, 25–8.

32 Bohstedt, *Riots*, 106–25; Knight, *Thomas Walker*; Booth, thesis, Chapters 2–3; A. Prentice, *Historical Sketches and Personal Recollections of Manchester* (1850), Chapter 1.

33 Gatrell, in Fraser, *Municipal Reform*, 32–5.

34 Prentice, *Historical Sketches*, Chapters 2, 5, 8, 11–12; Gatrell, in Fraser, *Municipal Reform*, 35. See also D. Read, *Peterloo* (Manchester, 1958), Chapter 6, for divisions between 'Ultras' (mainly merchants and landed men) and 'Pittites' (mainly manufacturers) within the Manchester Tories.

35 Gatrell, thesis; Prentice, *Historical Sketches*.

36 Booth, thesis; Sellers, 'William Roscoe'; B. D. White, *A History of the Corporation of Liverpool* (Liverpool, 1951); Gunn, dissertation; F. E. Sanderson, 'The Liverpool Abolitionists', in Anstey and Hair, *Slave Trade*, 196–238.

37 Booth, thesis, Chapter 3; M. B. S. Doyle, 'Social Control in Over Darwen, 1839–78', MA dissertation, Univ. of Lancaster, 1972; Joyce, *Work*, 13 and *passim*; and cf. Garrard, *Leadership and Power*.

38 D. A. Gowland, *Methodist Secessions* (Manchester, 1979).

39 Cf. P. T. Phillips, *The Sectarian Spirit* (Toronto, 1982), which pursues this theme in a Lancashire urban setting.

Chapter 8

1 J. R. Cuca, 'Industrial Change and Progress of Labour in the Lancashire Cotton Industry', *International Review of Social History* 22 (1977), 241–55, provides a useful though simplistic introduction.

2 H. A. Turner, *Trade Union Growth, Structure and Policy* (1962), 106–7.

3 Foster, *Class Struggle*, Chapter 3; Wadsworth and Mann, *Cotton Trade*, Chapter 9.

4 Bohstedt, *Riots*; Bythell, *Hand-loom Weavers*.

5 Turner, *Trade Union Growth*, 50–62; R. Glen, *Urban Workers in the Early Industrial Revolution* (1984), 146; Bohstedt, *Riots*, 131.

6 Booth, thesis, 299.

7 Bohstedt, *Riots*, 156 and Chapter 6; Turner, *Trade Union Growth*, 63–5; Glen, *Urban Workers*, 153–63; Bythell, *Hand-loom Weavers*, Chapter 7.

8 R. G. Kirby and A. E. Musson, *The Voice of the People* (Manchester, 1975), 67–8, 178–80; Turner, *Trade Union Growth*, 68–71; Glen, *Urban Workers*, Chapter 8 and 201–4; Bohstedt, *Riots*, Chapter 6; Bythell, *Hand-loom Weavers*, Chapter 7.

9 See above, n. 5.

10 Turner, *Trade Union Growth*, 63–4, 66–7; Bohstedt, *Riots*, 129–31.

11 Kirby and Musson, *Voice*.

12 R. Sykes, 'Popular Politics and Trade Unionism in South-East Lancashire, 1829–42', Ph.D. thesis, Univ. of Manchester, 1982, Chapter 3.

13 Sykes, thesis, 173–5, in convincing opposition to Glen.

14 Sykes, thesis, 200–9 and Chapter 5.

15 Ibid., iv.

16 Ibid., 281–338.

17 Barker and Harris, *St Helens*, 258–9, 262–3; Anderson, *Orrell Coalfield*, 128.

18 R. Challinor, *The Lancashire and Cheshire Miners* (Newcastle upon Tyne, 1972), 23–5; Barker and Harris, *St Helens*, 159–64.

19 Barker and Harris, *St Helens*, 263–6; Challinor, *Miners*, 25–8.

20 Sykes, thesis, 338–42.

21 Marriner, *Merseyside*, 83; Barker and Harris, *St Helens*, 261–2.

22 Sykes, thesis, 81–2, 315–31.

23 Ibid.; Kirby and Musson, *Voice*.

24 Sykes, thesis, 331ff.; Picton, *Memorials*, I, 386.

25 Bohstedt, *Riots*, Chapter 4; A. Booth, 'Food-riots in North-West England', *Past and Present* 1977.

26 Bohstedt, *Riots*, 91; Sykes, thesis, 355–6.

27 J. Dinwiddy, 'Luddism and Politics in the Northern Counties', *Social History* 4 (1979); cf. Bohstedt, 160; Booth, thesis, Chapter 7.

28 Sykes, thesis, 345, 355; cf. Glen, *Urban Workers*, and Bythell, *Hand-loom Weavers*.

29 Booth, thesis, 40–58, 66–102.

30 Booth, thesis, 190–247, 278–84. I find Booth's well-researched and careful account altogether more convincing than alternative interpretations of this controversial episode.

31 Booth, thesis, Chapter 7.

32 Bohstedt, *Riots*, Chapter 7.

33 S. Bamford, *Passages in the Life of a Radical* (Oxford, pbk. edn., 1984), Chapters 2–26; E. P. Thompson, *The Making of the English Working Class* (Harmondsworth, pbk. edn., 1968), Chapter 15; Read, *Peterloo*, 97–102.

34 Glen, *Urban Workers*, 224.

35 Read, *Peterloo*, 40–56; Glen, *Urban Workers*, 225–30.

36 Read, *Peterloo*, 109.

37 Glen, *Urban Workers*, 240–1.

38 Read, *Peterloo*, Chapter 8; Bamford, *Passages*, Chapters 30–6; R. Walmsley, *Peterloo: the Case Reopened* (Manchester, 1969); Glen, *Urban Workers*, 244–7; Foster, *Class Struggle*, 144; Thompson, *Making*, 745–80.

39 Read, *Peterloo*, 140–6; Bamford, *Passages*, 214–15.

40 W. R. Ward (ed.), *The Early Correspondence of Jabez Bunting, 1820–9* (1972), 24–5.

41 Read, *Peterloo*, 147–51; Glen, *Urban Workers*, 247–53; Ward, *Bunting*, 24–8, 62–3.

42 Thompson, *Making*, 705.

43 Picton, *Memorials*, I, 354–8.

44 Thompson, *Making*, 709n; Read, *Peterloo*, 24.

45 Bythell, *Hand-loom Weavers*.

46 Bamford, *Passages*, Chapter 28; Glen, *Urban Workers*, 231–3, 243, 245–6.

47 E. Royle and J. Walvin, *English Radicals and Reformers, 1760–1848* (Brighton, 1982), Chapter 8; Glen, *Urban Workers*, Chapter 11.

48 Kirby and Musson, *Voice*, 42; J. M. Wiener, *Richard Carlile* (1983), 143–6.

49 Sykes, thesis, Chapter 8; Kirby and Musson, *Voice*, Chapter 11.

50 Sykes, thesis, 362.

51 Fraser, *Urban Politics*, 223.

52 J. Vincent, *Poll-books: How Victorians Voted* (Cambridge, 1967).
53 Foster, *Class Struggle*, and critiques by D. Gadian, *Historical Journal* 1978; R. Sykes, *Historical Journal* 1980.
54 Sykes, thesis, 388 – 92.
55 Ibid., 379 – 88.
56 Kirby and Musson, *Voice*, Chapter 10; Sykes, thesis, 428 – 38; A. Peacock on the enforcement of the Factory Acts, *Economic History Review* 2nd ser., 37 (1984), and discussion in *idem*, 38 (1985).
57 Sykes, thesis, 426, 441 – 9; N. C. Edsall, *The Anti-Poor Law Movement, 1834 – 44* (Manchester, 1971); E. C. Midwinter, *Social Administration in Lancashire 1830 – 60* (Manchester, 1969), 22 – 4, and *passim*; Garrard, *Leadership and Power*, 150 – 4, 183 – 7.
58 Bythell, *Hand-loom Weavers*, Chapter 7; P. Richards, 'The State and Early Industrial Capitalism: the Case of the Handloom Weavers', *Past and Present* 83 (1979).
59 Sykes, thesis, Chapters 4 – 6, and 'Early Chartism and Trade Unionism in South-East Lancashire', in J. Epstein and D. Thompson (eds.), *The Chartist Experience* (1982), 157 and *passim*.
60 Bythell, *Hand-loom Weavers*, Chapter 9.
61 Gatrell, 'Commercial Middle Class' (which supersedes D. Read, 'Chartism in Manchester', in A. Briggs (ed.), *Chartist Studies* (1959), as the most plausible account of Manchester Chartism); Foster, *Class Struggle*; M. Jenkins, *The General Strike of 1842* (1980); the discussion between Foster and A. E. Musson in *Social History* 1 (1976); J. King, *Richard Marsden and the Preston Chartists* (Lancaster, 1981); C. Calhoun, *The Question of Class Struggle* (1982); Sykes, thesis; D. Gadian, 'A Comparative Study of Popular Movements in North-West Industrial Towns 1830 – 50', Ph.D. thesis, Univ. of Lancaster, 1977.
62 King, *Richard Marsden*, 17; Challinor, *Miners*, 41 – 3; Barker and Harris, *St Helens*, 297, 323.
63 Picton, *Memorials*, I. 496; J. Belchem, 'English Working-Class Radicalism and the Irish, 1815 – 50', *North-West Labour History Society Bulletin* 8 (1982 – 3), 5 – 18.
64 Sykes, 'Early Chartism'.
65 Foster, *Class Struggle*, Chapter 5; Gadian, thesis and *Historical Journal*, 1978.
66 I. Kovacevic, *Fact into Fiction* (Leicester, 1975), 225 – 301 ('A Manchester Strike', by Harriet Martineau) contains some arresting expressions of this theme.
67 See especially King, *Richard Marsden*; N. McCord, *The Anti-Corn Law League* (1958); Gatrell, thesis; Phillips, *Sectarian Spirit*; Garrard, *Leadership and Power*; and for a stimulating general interpretation, G. Stedman Jones, 'The Language of Chartism', in Epstein and Thompson, *Chartist Experience*, 3 – 58.
68 Foster, *Class Struggle*, and Jenkins, *General Strike*, argue differently. See also Mather in J. Stevenson and R. Quinault (eds.), *Popular Protest and Public Order* (1975); A. G. Rose, 'The Plug Riots of 1842 in Lancashire and Cheshire', *Lancashire and Cheshire Antiquarian Society* 67 (1958), 75 – 112.
69 Foster, *Class Struggle*, Chapter 7; N. Kirk, *The Growth of Working-Class Reformism in Mid-Victorian England* (1985).
70 Joyce, *Work*; cf. the critique (directed mainly at a slightly earlier period, but still relevant) by H. I. Dutton and J. King, 'The Limits of Paternalism: the Cotton Tyrants of North Lancashire, 1836 – 54', *Social History* 7 (1982), 59 – 74.

Chapter 9

1 G. N. von Tunzelmann, 'Trends in Real Wages, 1750–1850, Revisited', *Economic History Review* 2nd ser., 32 (1979), 48.

2 P. Lindert and J. G. Williamson, 'English Workers' Living Standards during the Industrial Revolution: a New Look', *Economic History Review* 2nd ser., 36 (1983), 4, 13 and *passim*.

3 Ibid., 9, 14–16. See also Williamson's article in *Journal of Economic History* 1981, and the reply by S. Pollard; Williamson's tactical retreat in 'Was the Industrial Revolution Worth It? Disamenities and Death in Nineteenth-Century British Towns', *Explorations in Economic History* 19 (1982); and the coruscating attack by R. S. Neale, *Writing Marxist History* (1985).

4 E. Gilboy, in A. J. Taylor (ed.), *The Standard of Living in the Industrial Revolution* (1975), 10–14.

5 T. S. Ashton, in Taylor (ed.), *Standard of Living*, 52–6; Fleischman, thesis, 107, 122.

6 Fleischman, thesis, 132, 142.

7 Ibid., 105, 137. Cf., more optimistically, N. F. R. Crafts in *Explorations in Economic History* 19 (1982).

8 Glen, *Urban Workers*, 28; Rushton, thesis, 35, 95–7.

9 Ashton, in Taylor (ed.), *Standard of Living*, 52.

10 Lindert and Williamson, 'Living Standards', 4; M. W. Flinn, 'English Workers' Living Standards during the Industrial Revolution: a Comment', *Economic History Review* 2nd ser., 37 (1984), 91.

11 Foster, *Class Struggle*, 49; and this is a theme of Kirby and Musson, *Voice*.

12 Kovacevic, *Fact into Fiction*, 243 and *passim*; Kirby and Musson, *Voice*, 462–3; Sykes, thesis, 107.

13 Bythell, *Hand-loom Weavers*, Chapter 5; J. Benson, *British Coalminers in the Nineteenth Century* (Dublin, 1980), Chapter 3; J. D. Marshall, 'The Lancashire Rural Labourer in the Early Nineteenth Century', *Lancashire and Cheshire Antiquarian Society* 71 (1961), 90–128.

14 Lindert and Williamson, 'Living Standards', 10–11, n. 35.

15 Bythell, *Hand-loom Weavers*, Chapter 5 and Appendix; Fleischman, thesis, 102; Richards, 'Handloom Weavers'; and see above, Chapter 6.

16 Glen, *Urban Workers*, 82; Fleischman, thesis, 103.

17 Fleischman, thesis, 160; Sykes, thesis, Chapter 3.

18 Sykes, thesis, Table 3.3.

19 See above, Chapter 8. Benson, *Coalminers*, Chapter 3, is sceptical about generalisations on the miners, though ultimately optimistic. He emphasises the importance of regional and local variations.

20 Marshall, 'Lancashire Rural Labourer', 117.

21 Taylor, thesis, 87.

22 E. J. Hobsbawm, in Taylor (ed.), *Standard of Living*, 70–1; cf. Lindert and Williamson, 'Living Standards', 13, n. 38. See Manchester Central Library, Archives Dept., MSF 310/6/M5/115–16, for a survey of Ancoats unemployment at the start of the 1837 depression.

23 Taylor, thesis, 88–90.

24 Rushton, thesis, 167 and *passim*.

25 Cf. Lindert and Williamson, 'Living Standards', 12–16.

26 Foster, *Class Struggle*, 95–9.

27 M. Anderson, *Family Structure in Nineteenth-Century Lancashire* (Cambridge, pbk. edn., 1974), 29–32.
28 Taylor, thesis, 87–8, and Table 5.11.
29 J.C. McKenzie, 'The Composition and Nutritional Value of Diets in Manchester and Dukinfield, 1841', *Lancashire and Cheshire Antiquarian Society* 72 (1962).
30 A.B. Reach, *Manchester and the Textile Districts in 1849* (Helmshore, Lancs., 1972), 58.
31 Marshall, 'Lancashire Rural Labourer', 121; Reach, *Manchester*, 103–4, 109–10; Marshall, *Furness*, 121–3.
32 Taylor, thesis.
33 F. Engels, *The Condition of the Working Class in England* (1969 edn., ed. E.J. Hobsbawm), 75–99 (but cf. the critical comments of W.H. Chaloner and W.O. Henderson in their alternative edition). See also Rushton, thesis, and J.P. Kay, *The Moral and Physical Condition of the Working Classes* (Didsbury, Ches., 1969).
34 Reach, *Manchester*, 17–25.
35 Glen, *Urban Workers*, 22–30; Reach, *Manchester*, 84–5, 93; N. Morgan, *An Introduction to the Social History of Housing in Victorian Preston* (Preston, n.d.), Part I.
36 Compare L.D.W. Smith, 'Textile Factory Settlements in the Early Industrial Revolution', Ph.D. thesis, Univ. of Aston, 1976, with S.M. Gaskell, 'Housing Estate Development 1840–1918, with Special Reference to the Pennine Towns', Ph.D. thesis, Univ. of Sheffield, 1974, Chapter 2.
37 Fleischman, thesis, 274, 306–9; Taylor, thesis, 196–7 and Table 9.1.
38 Fleischman, thesis, 274–80; cf. M. Cruickshank, *Children in Industry* (Manchester, 1981), 62–4; Barker and Harris, *St Helens*, 317, 480; Marshall, *Furness*, 115–21. M. Pooley, 'Geographical and Demographic Approaches to Medical History', in J.V. Pickstone (ed.), *Health, Disease and Medicine in Lancashire, 1750–1950* (Manchester, 1980), 52–65, discusses the problems involved in analysing this material.
39 Taylor, thesis, 84.
40 Marshall, 'Lancashire Rural Labourer', 108.
41 A.V. John, *By the Sweat of their Brow* (1980), Chapters 1–2; Challinor, *Miners*, 252–3; Barker and Harris, *St Helens*, 270–4; D. Anderson, *Orrell Coalfield*, 133–7. Children also worked at pinmaking in Warrington: W.B. Stephens, *Adult Education and Society in an Industrial Town* (Exeter, 1980), 9–10.
42 Engels, *Condition*, 170–3.
43 B.L. Hutchins and B. Harrison, *A History of Factory Legislation* (1911), Chapters 1–2; Cruickshank, *Children*, 13–17; N.J. Smelser, *Social Change in the Industrial Revolution* (1959), 103–5, 186–7.
44 Cruickshank, *Children*, 19.
45 Smelser, *Social Change*, 202.
46 M. Hewitt, *Wives and Mothers in Victorian Industry* (1958), 17.
47 R. Burr-Litchfield, 'The Family and the Mill', in A.S. Wohl (ed.), *The Victorian Family* (1978), 183; Hewitt, *Wives*, 9–18.
48 Anderson, *Family Structure*, 71–2.
49 Ibid., 22–3, 72; and calculations from 1851 census.
50 A. Ure, *The Philosophy of Manufactures* (1835); Engels, *Condition*, 163–215.
51 Reach, *Manchester*, 16.
52 Key, *Condition*, 22.
53 Smelser, *Social Change*; Fleischman, thesis, 245; M.M. Edwards and R. Lloyd-Jones, in N.B. Harte and K. Ponting (eds.), *Textile History and Economic History* (1973); M. Anderson, 'Smelser Revisited', *Social History* 1 (1976).

54 Anderson, *Family Structure*, 54.

55 Reach, *Manchester*, 29–33, 110.

56 Anderson, *Family Structure*; cf. J. K. Walton, 'Lunacy in the Industrial Revolution', *Journal of Social History* 13 (1979–80), 1–22.

57 Foster, *Class Struggle*, 97.

58 Anderson, *Family Structure*, 72.

59 Ibid., 74.

60 Reach, *Manchester*, 47–56.

61 Hewitt, *Wives*. See also G. N. Gandy, 'Illegitimacy in a Hand-loom Weaving Community: Fertility Patterns in Culcheth, Lancs., 1780–1861', D.Phil. thesis, Univ. of Oxford, 1978, for high illegitimacy rates among hand-loom weaving families and the problem of what they might mean.

62 Anderson, *Family Structure*, 41–2

63 Ibid., 103–6; King, *Richard Marsden*, 1.

64 P. H. J. H. Gosden, *The Friendly Societies in England, 1815–75* (1961).

65 See especially R. Poole, *Popular Leisure and the Music-Hall in Nineteenth-Century Bolton* (Lancaster, 1982); P. Bailey, *Leisure and Class in Victorian England* (1978); B. Harrison, *Drink and the Victorians* (1971), Chapter 2; and the annual reports of the Revd John Clay, Chaplain to the Preston House of Correction, in the Lancashire Record Office.

66 R. Elbourne, *Music and Tradition in Early Industrial Lancashire* (1980); J. F. C. Harrison, *Robert Owen and the Owenites in Britain and America* (1969), and *The Second Coming* (1979); Wiener, *Carlile*.

67 Bailey, *Leisure*, Chapter 1; Poole, *Bolton*; Poole, thesis, Poole, 'Oldham Wakes', in J. K. Walton and J. Walvin (eds.), *Leisure in Britain, 1780–1939* (Manchester, 1983); J. K. Walton and R. Poole, 'The Lancashire Wakes in the Nineteenth Century', in R. Storch (ed.), *Popular Culture and Custom in Nineteenth-Century England* (1982); M. B. Smith, 'The Growth and Development of Popular Entertainments and Pastimes in the Lancashire Cotton Towns, 1830–70', M. Litt. thesis, Univ. of Lancaster, 1970; and information on stone-bowling in the Burnley area from Margaret Jones.

68 Barker and Harris, *St Helens*, 285; W. R. Cockcroft, 'The Liverpool Police Force, 1836–1902', in S. P. Bell (ed.), *Victorian Lancashire* (Newton Abbot, 1974); Annual Reports of the Liverpool Domestic Missionary.

69 Taylor, thesis, Table 1.3; and see C. G. Pooley, 'The Residential Segregation of Migrant Communities in mid-Victorian Liverpool', *Institute of Brtish Geographers* N.S. 2 (1977), 364–82.

70 W. J. Lowe, 'The Irish in Lancashire, 1846–71: a Social History', Ph.D. thesis, Trinity College, Dublin, 1975; A. Granath, 'The Irish in mid-Nineteenth Century Lancashire', MA dissertation, Univ. of Lancaster, 1975.

71 J. Papworth, 'The Irish in Liverpool 1835–71: Segregation and Dispersal' (Ph.D. thesis, Univ. of Liverpool, 1981).

72 Taylor, thesis, Table 3.5.

73 Barker and Harris, *St Helens*, 258–63 and Chapter 19.

74 Bailey, *Leisure and Class*, 15.

75 Walton and Poole, 'Lancashire Wakes', 124.

76 S. Bamford, *Early Days* (2nd edn., 1859), 159–69.

77 B. I. Coleman, *The Church of England in the Mid-Nineteenth Century* (1980), 40–1.

78 Joyce, *Work*, 244–5; cf. K. S. Inglis, 'Patterns of Religious Worship in 1851', *Journal of Ecclesiastical History* 11 (1960), 80–5.

79 M. Cruickshank, 'The Anglican Revival and Education', *Northern History* 15 (1979), 176–90; Manchester Central Library, MS.f 942.72 R121/33.
80 W. R. Ward, *Religion and Society in England 1790–1850* (1972); Gowland, *Methodist Secessions*; J. Lea, 'Baptists and the Working Classes in mid-Victorian Lancashire', in Bell, *Victorian Lancashire*, 59–82.
81 Cruickshank, 'Anglican Revival', 184.
82 Manchester Central Library, MS.f 942.72 R121/63.
83 Foster, *Class Struggle*, 214.
84 Cruickshank, *Children*, 56, perpetuates the contemporary reformers' views quite uncritically.
85 Sanderson, 'Literacy'.
86 S. E. Maltby, *Manchester and the Movement for National Elementary Education, 1800–70* (1918), 36–8; T. W. Laqueur, *Religion and Respectability* (1976), 49 and *passim*.
87 W. B. Stephens, *Regional Variations in Education during the Industrial Revolution* (1973), 31–2, Appendix IV.
88 C. Ward, 'Education as Social Control: Sunday Schools in Oldham, *c.* 1780–1850', MA Dissertation, Univ. of Lancaster, 1975.
89 Laqueur, *Religion*; Maltby, *Elementary Education*; Third Report of the Liverpool Sunday School Union, 1817, 18; Poole, *Bolton*, 20.
90 Cruickshank, 'Anglican Revival', 178.
91 Ibid.; Stephens, *Regional Variations*, and in D. Reeder, *Urban Education in the Nineteenth Century* (1977).
92 See below, Chapter 12.
93 Fourteenth Report to the Liverpool Domestic Mission Society, 1851, 18–19; Reach, *Manchester*, 61–4.
94 M. Tylecote, *The Mechanics' Institutes of Lancashire and Yorkshire before 1851* (Manchester, 1956).
95 Reach, *Manchester*, 63.
96 Kay, *Condition*, 57–8.
97 Poole, *Bolton*, 51–5; Bailey, *Leisure and Class*.
98 Reach, *Manchester*, 80–3, is especially interesting.
99 Fourteenth Report to the Liverpool Domestic Mission Society, 1851, 31–3.
100 Smith, thesis.
101 D. J. V. Jones, *Crime, Protest, Community and Police in Nineteenth-Century Britain*, 164–5; Cockcroft, in Bell, *Victorian Lancashire*.
102 Bailey, *Leisure and Class*; Poole, *Bolton*; Walton and Poole, 'Lancashire Wakes'; Harrison, *Drink*; A. Gallagher, 'The Social Control of Working-Class Leisure in Preston, *c.* 1850 – *c.* 1875', MA dissertation, Univ. of Lancaster.
103 Bailey, *Leisure and Class*, 21.
104 Poole, *Bolton*, 16.
105 W. Bowman, *England in Ashton-under-Lyne* (1960).
106 Midwinter, *Social Administration*, 157–60.
107 Poole, *Bolton*, 40.
108 J. D. Marshall, 'Some Aspects of the Social History of Nineteenth-Century Cumbria: Crime, Police, Morals and the Countryman', *Cumberland and Westmorland Archaeological and Antiquarian Society* N.S. 70 (1970); Midwinter, *Social Administration*, Chapter 4; Cockcroft, in Bell, *Victorian Lancashire*; Jones, *Crime*; C. De Motte, 'The Dark Side of Town: Crime in Manchester and Salford, 1815–75', Ph.D. thesis, Univ. of Kansas, 1977; T. Franklin on the Lancaster police force, MA dissertation, Univ. of Lancaster, 1982; Kay, *Condition*, 42–3.

109 F. Vigier, *Change and Apathy* (1970), Chapter 10.

110 Ibid.; Midwinter, *Social Administration*, Chapter 3; Garrard, *Leadership and Power*.

111 Hindle, *Provision*, Chapters 6–8.

112 The Annual Reports of these societies make interesting reading from a variety of perspectives.

113 Report of the Committee of the Liverpool Dispensaries for the year 1825, 4.

114 Marshall, *Furness*, 136; J.D. Marshall, *The Old Poor Law, 1795–1834* (1968), 26–7, 34.

115 Marshall, *Furness*, 136; Midwinter, *Social Administration*, 11–12.

116 Marshall, *Furness*, 138.

117 Midwinter, *Social Administration*; R. Boyson, 'The New Poor Law in North-East Lancashire, 1834–71', *Lancashire and Cheshire Antiquarian Society* 70 (1960), 35–56; Hindle, *Provision*; Oxley, 'Permanent Poor'; J. Cole, *Down Poorhouse Lane: the Diary of a Rochdale Workhouse* (Littleborough, Lancs., 1984); An Address to all who are Assessed to the Poor's Rate for the Parish of Liverpool (1814), 3–5, 16–19, 21–30, 33–4.

118 Lindert and Williamson, 'Living Standards'.

119 C.P. Darcy, *The Encouragement of the Fine Arts in Lancashire, 1760–1860* (Manchester, 1976).

Chapter 10

1 L. Sandberg, *Lancashire in Decline* (1974), 141. 'Billion' is used in the US sense of thousand million.

2 Hyde, *Liverpool*, 96–7; D. Farnie, *The Manchester Ship Canal and the Rise of the Port of Manchester* (Manchester, 1980), 26.

3 S.J. Chapman, *The Lancashire Cotton Industry: a Study in Economic Development* (Manchester, 1904), 148–50.

4 A.J. Taylor, 'Concentration and Specialization in the Lancashire Cotton Industry', *Economic History Review* 2nd ser., 1 (1948–9), 114–22; Farnie, *Cotton Industry*, 301–8; S. Kenny, 'Sub-regional Specialization in the Lancashire Cotton Industry, 1884–1914', *Journal of Historical Geography* 8 (1982), 41–67.

5 Farnie, *Cotton Industry*, 308–12; Chapman, *Lancashire Cotton*, 156–7.

6 Farnie, *Cotton Industry*, 7–8; Chapman, *Lancashire Cotton*, 144.

7 Deane and Cole, *British Economic Growth*, 187, Table 43.

8 Farnie, *Cotton Industry*, 91, Table 5, and Chapter 3, *passim*; Sandberg, *Lancashire in Decline*, Chapter 8.

9 Farnie, *Cotton Industry*, 186.

10 Farnie, *Cotton Industry*, 171; Sandberg, *Lancashire in Decline*, 105.

11 Kenny, 'Specialization', 45–8.

12 Chapman, *Lancashire Cotton*, 112; Deane and Cole, *British Economic Growth*, 190, Table 44.

13 Chapman, *Lancashire Cotton*, 160; Farnie, *Cotton Industry*, 300–1.

14 Farnie, *Cotton Industry*, 215, 286, and *passim*; K. Burgess, *The Origins of British Industrial Relations* (1975), 235–6; cf. C.H. Lee, 'The Cotton Textile Industry', in R.A. Church (ed.), *The Dynamics of Victorian Business*, (1980), 161–80.

15 Farnie, *Cotton Industry*, Chapters 6–7; Joyce, *Work*, 340; P.F. Clarke, *Lancashire and the New Liberalism* (Cambridge, 1971), 78–9.

16 Joyce, *Work*, 339–40.

17 Farnie, *Cotton Industry*, Chapters 6–7.

18 Lee, 'Cotton Textile Industry', 172–4; D. Farnie, 'The English Cotton Industry, 1850–96', MA thesis, Univ. of Manchester, 1953, 46–51.

19 Sandberg, *Lancashire in Decline*, 20–8.

20 Ibid., 68–9.

21 Ibid., Chapters 2–4; J. L. White, *The Limits of Trade Union Militancy* (Westport, Conn., 1978), 15–20; Burgess, *Origins*, 234; W. Lazonick, in *Cambridge Journal of Economics* 1979 and *Quarterly Journal of Economics* 1981.

22 Farnie, *Cotton Industry*, 223–4.

23 Ibid., 54–7, 159–60, 186–7, 246; Farnie, thesis, Chapter 4; R. M. Kirk, 'The Economic Development of the British Textile Engineering Industry, *c.* 1850–1939', Ph.D. thesis, Univ. of Salford, 1983, 4–21, 114–32, and *passim*.

24 Farnie, thesis, 70–2; B. J. Turton on Horwich and the Lancashire and Yorkshire Railway, *Lancashire and Cheshire Antiquarian Society* 72 (1962); L. Smith on Newton-le-Willows, *Historic Society of Lancashire and Cheshire* 129 (1980); J. Marshall, *The Lancashire and Yorkshire Railway* (3 vols., Newton Abbot, 1969–72).

25 R. Floud, *The British Machine-Tool Industry, 1850–1914* (Cambridge, 1976), 41, 54, 63 and *passim*; and see A. E. Musson, 'The Engineering Industry', in R. A. Church (ed.), *The Dynamics of Victorian Business* (1980), with its stress on the importance of developments in Lancashire.

26 B. R. Mitchell, *The British Coal Industry, 1800–1914* (Cambridge, 1983), 7, 30–1; Farnie, thesis, 184.

27 Farnie, thesis, Chapter 15; and see D. Whalley's MA dissertation on the Rossendale slipper industry, Univ. of Lancaster, 1984.

28 Farnie, *Cotton Industry*, 61, 64, 130–1; Rushton, thesis, 183; N. Cardus, *Autobiography* (1947), 37–42; G. Anderson, *Victorian Clerks* (Manchester, 1976).

29 Farnie, *Manchester Ship Canal*, Chapters 1–5.

30 Hyde, *Liverpool*, 100, 139–41, and Chapters 5–7, *passim*; S. Mountfield, *Western Gateway* (Liverpool, 1965), 203–5.

31 Hyde, *Liverpool*, Chapters 4,6.

32 F. J. Marquis, *Handbook of Employments … in Liverpool* (1915); Marriner, *Merseyside*, 120; Anderson, *Victorian Clerks*.

33 Mitchell, *Coal Industry*, 51, 62, 83, 94–5, 300, 314, 317, 322; Challinor, *Miners*, 49–50, 257–63.

34 K. Warren, *Chemical Foundations* (Oxford, 1980), Chapters 5,8; D. W. F. Hardie, *A History of the Chemical Industry in Widnes* (1950), Chapters 3–5; Barker and Harris, *St Helens*, 342–8, 436.

35 Warren, *Chemical Foundations*, 99–102; Barker and Harris, *St Helens*, 349–56; G. W. Diggle, *A History of Widnes* (Widnes, 1961); A. S. Wohl, *Endangered Lives* (pbk. edn., 1984), 224–32; and see also A. E. Dingle, ' "The Monster Nuisance of All" ', *Economic History Review* 36 (1983).

36 Warren, *Chemical Foundations*, Chapters 9–10, 13–16; Hardie, *Chemical Industry*, Chapters 7–11; Barker and Harris, *St Helens*, 437–47.

37 Musson, *Soap and Chemicals*, 88, 149 and *passim*; Marriner, *Merseyside*, 114–17; and see also the mammoth company histories by C. H. Wilson, *The History of Unilever* (2 vols., 1954), and W. J. Reader, *Imperial Chemical Industries: a History* (2 vols., Oxford, 1975).

38 Barker, *Glassmakers*, Chapters 8–9, 11–13.

39 Barker and Harris, *St Helens*, 378–9 and Chapters 24–5, *passim*.
40 P.J. Aspinall and D. Hudson, *Ellesmere Port: the Making of an Industrial Borough* (Didsbury, Ches., 1982), Chapters 2–4; Marriner, *Merseyside*, 10, 113.
41 H.F. Starkey, *Schooner Port* (1983), Chapters 10–11.
42 Schofield, *Outline*; Gooderson, thesis.
43 Marshall, *Furness*, Part II; J.D. Marshall and J.K. Walton, *The Lake Counties from 1830 to the mid-twentieth century* (Manchester, 1981), 29–31, 38–40, 45–50; and C. Trebilcock's history of Vickers.
44 J.K. Walton, *The English Seaside Resort: a Social History, 1750–1914* (Leicester, 1983), Chapter 3; J.K. Walton, *The Blackpool Landlady* (Manchester, 1978).
45 Rogers, 'Lancashire Landed Society', Chapters 3–5; A. Mutch, 'Rural Society in Lancashire, 1840–1914', Ph.D. thesis, Univ. of Manchester, 1980; T.W. Fletcher, 'Lancashire Livestock Farming during the Great Depression', in P.J. Perry (ed.), *British Agriculture, 1873–1914* (1973).
46 Calculated from the printed census returns.
47 R. Lawton, 'Population Trends'.

Chapter 11

1 J. Shepherd, 'James Bryce and the Recruitment of Working-Class Magistrates in Lancashire, 1892–4', *Bulletin of the Institute for Historical Research* 1979, 155–69.
2 Clarke, *Lancashire and the New Liberalism*, 250.
3 Rogers, 'Lancashire Landed Society', 78–81, 350–2; V. Clifton, *The Book of Talbot* (1932).
4 Rogers, 'Lancashire Landed Society', 351; Mutch, thesis, 103–4.
5 Lancashire County Council, Treasurer's Accounts, 1886, 97; 1903, 166.
6 J.D. Marshall (ed.), *The History of Lancashire County Council, 1889–1914* (1977), 9.
7 Rogers, 'Lancashire Landed Society', 371–5; Mutch, thesis, 115; and see the Lancaster M.Phil. thesis by J. Hayhurst, 'An Economic and Social History of Glasson Dock', 1984, for the workings of a parish council.
8 Mutch, thesis, 101–2, 107–10.
9 R. Burnett Tracy, *Lancashire at the Opening of the Twentieth Century* (Brighton, 1903), 115; B.G. Orchard, *Liverpool's Legion of Honour* (Birkenhead, 1893), 56.
10 Mutch, thesis, 94–5; Clarke, *Lancashire and the New Liberalism*, 229; Knapp, thesis, 342–5.
11 Knapp, thesis, 303, and Chapter 4, *passim*.
12 Burnett Tracy, *Lancashire …*, 127.
13 Ibid., 121, 123; N. Pevsner, *The Buildings of England: Shropshire* (1958), 112–13.
14 Burnett Tracy, *Lancashire …*, 153; Orchard, *Legion of Honour*, 64; R. Haslam, *The Buildings of Wales: Powys* (1979), 117–19.
15 Farnie, thesis, 160, and Chapter 12, *passim*.
16 Gooderson, thesis, 420–3.
17 K. Chorley, *Manchester Made Them* (1950), 155–6, and Chapter 9, *passim*.
18 Engels, *Condition*, 79.
19 M. Spiers, *Victoria Park* (Manchester, 1975); B. Williams, *The Making of Manchester Jewry* (Manchester, 1976), 80–1, 85–6, 125–6, 321, 364–9; J.R. Kellett, *The Impact of Railways on Victorian Cities* (1964).
20 N. Cardus, *Second Innings* (1950), 8–9.

21 P.J. Waller, *Democracy and Sectarianism* (Liverpool, 1981), 15; R. Lawton, 'The Population of Liverpool in the Mid-Nineteenth Century', *Historic Society of Lancashire and Cheshire* 107 (1955), 89–120; Kellett, *Railways*; M. Greatbatch on Bootle and Liverpool suburbia, MA dissertation, Univ. of Lancaster, 1983.

22 Lancashire Treasurer's Accounts, 1886 and 1903.

23 Marshall, *Lancashire County Council*, viii–ix, 7–8.

24 A.C. Howe, *The Cotton Masters* (Oxford, 1984), Chapter 7.

25 P. Joyce, 'Popular Toryism in Lancashire, 1860–90', D.Phil. thesis, Univ. of Oxford, 1975, 7–9; Joyce, *Work*, 274; Howe, *Cotton Masters*, 95–126; Waller, *Democracy*, Biographical Appendix.

26 Clarke, *Lancashire and the New Liberalism*, 243–5.

27 Howe, *Cotton Masters*, 266–9; Clarke, *Lancashire and the New Liberalism*, 213–22.

28 Garrard, *Leadership and Power*, 23–6, 31–2; Howe, *Cotton Masters*, 142; Fraser, *Urban Politics*.

29 Garrard, *Leadership and Power*, 14–21.

30 Howe, *Cotton Masters*, 144–5.

31 A. Russell, 'Elites at the Local Level of Society: Social Leadership in Burnley, 1870–1900', MA dissertation, Univ. of Lancaster, 1976, Appendix, Table 4; W.H.H. Wale, 'Politics and Society in Accrington, 1878–1914', MA dissertation, Univ. of Lancaster, 1975, 75.

32 [H. Shimmin], *Pen and Ink Sketches of Liverpool Town Councillors* (Liverpool, 1866).

33 S. Simon, *A Century of City Government* (Manchester, 1938), 395–400; Howe, *Cotton Masters*, 144–5.

34 Garrard, *Leadership and Power*, 31–5.

35 M.B.S. Doyle, 'Social Control in Over Darwen, 1839–78', MA dissertation, Univ. of Lancaster, 1972, 39–41; L.B. Nattrass, 'The Governing Elite in Chorley, 1854–1914', MA dissertation, Univ. of Lancaster, 1974, 25, 51; Midwinter, *Social Administration*; Howe, *Cotton Masters*, 137–42.

36 Garrard, *Leadership and Power*, 19–20; Howe, *Cotton Masters*, 137; Wale, 'Accrington', 78.

37 Simon, *Century*, 399; Howe, *Cotton Masters*, 152–3; cf. E.P. Hennock, *Fit and Proper Persons* (1973).

38 Waller, *Democracy*, 151–2; Simon, *Century*, 399–401.

39 G. Trodd, 'Political Change and the Working Class in Blackburn and Burnley, 1880–1914', Ph.D. thesis, Univ. of Lancaster, 1978, 132, 134; D.J. Ganley, 'The Social and Political Composition of Oldham Town Council, 1888–1939', MA dissertation, Univ. of Lancaster, 1976, 20; G. Evans, 'Social Leadership and Social Control: Bolton, 1870–98', MA dissertation, Univ. of Lancaster, 1974, Appendix B; Wale, 'Accrington', 75.

40 Chorley, *Manchester Made Them*, 139–40.

41 Clarke, *Lancashire and the New Liberalism*, Part II; Trodd, thesis, Chapters 2–3; Joyce, *Work*, 38–40.

42 Poole, *Bolton*, 17.

43 Joyce, *Work*, 6–29.

44 Poole, *Bolton*, 22.

45 W.H. Mills, *Grey Pastures* (1924); cf. Trodd, thesis, 74–5.

46 Chorley, *Manchester Made Them*, 143.

47 Trodd, thesis, 65–73.

48 Orchard, *Legion of Honour*, 3–76; Waller, *Democracy*, 13–14.

49 J. V. Pickstone, *Medicine and Industrial Society* (Manchester, 1985); A. J. Kidd, 'Out-cast Manchester', in A. J. Kidd and K. W. Roberts (eds.), *City, Class and Culture* (Manchester, 1985), 48 – 73; M. Simey, *Charitable Effort in Liverpool in the Nineteenth Century* (1951).

50 M. E. Rose, 'Culture, Philanthropy and the Manchester Middle Classes', in Kidd and Roberts, *City*, 103 – 19, is more optimistic about Manchester.

51 Rubinstein, 'Victorian Middle Classes', 605 – 6, 109 – 12. Rubinstein doubts whether the lesser landholdings of Lancashire industrialists can have amounted to very much, although he agrees that detailed (perhaps impossibly detailed) local studies would be necessary to prove the point one way or the other: conversation in bar at Social History Conference, Loughborough, January 1986. Also relevant to this discussion are Rubinstein, 'Wealth, Elites and the Class Structure of Modern Britain', *Past and Present* 76 (1977), and *Men of Property* (1981). Rubinstein's recent work on income tax returns suggests that middle-class incomes in Lancashire rose very rapidly indeed between the early nineteenth century and the 1860s, after which the rate of growth tailed off noticeably. The income tax evidence continues to suggest the persisting overwhelming preponderance of London, with Lancashire a distant second, and Rubinstein suggests that the growth of middle-class manufacturing wealth in Lancashire may have been held back from the 1860s onwards by falling profits of which a growing share went to labour. But, one might ask, what of Liverpool? There is plenty of scope for further discussion of this fascinating material. See Rubinstein's paper on 'The Geographical Distribution of Middle-Class Income in Britain, 1800 – 1914'. I am most grateful to him for sending me a copy.

52 Rubinstein, 'Victorian Middle Classes', 619.

53 Waller, *Democracy*, 14.

54 M. J. Wiener, *English Culture and the Decline of the Industrial Spirit* (Cambridge, 1981); Orchard, *Legion of Honour*, 31.

55 Burnett Tracy, 120, 151.

Chapter 12

1 Garrard, *Leadership and Power*, 35, 127 – 9.

2 H. I. Dutton and J. King, *Ten Per Cent and No Surrender* (Cambridge, 1981), 222 n. 65.

3 *People's Paper*, 26 March 1853.

4 Ibid., 5 Feb. 1853; Kirk, *Working-Class Reformism*, 68 – 9; F. B. Smith, *The Making of the Second Reform Bill* (Cambridge, 1966), Chapter 3, and 126 – 7; also A. B. Collier 'Some Aspects and some Determinations of Popular Politics in Bury, 1838 – 58', MA dissertation, Univ. of Lancaster, 1983.

5 Kirk, *Working-Class Reformism*, 24.

6 Ibid., 115 – 25.

7 *Darwen and the Cotton Famine* (Darwen, 1893), 18 – 19.

8 M. Ellison, *Support for Secession* (Chicago, 1972), 24; Farnie, *Cotton Industry*, 157; M. E. Rose, '"Rochdale Man" and the Stalybridge Riot', in A. P. Donajgrodzki (ed.), *Social Control in Nineteenth-Century Britain* (1977), 185.

9 Rose, in Donajgrodzki, *Social Control*, 186, 196 – 7, 201; Kirk, *Working-Class Reformism*, 258 – 67; *Darwen and the Cotton Famine*, 33 – 4; J. Watts, *The Facts of the Cotton Famine* (1866), 82; D. J. Oddy, 'Urban Famine in Nineteenth-Century Britain', *Economic History Review* 2nd ser., 36 (1983), 75; P. Augar, 'The Cotton Famine, 1861 – 5',

D. Phil thesis, Univ. of Oxford, 1979, Chapter 5; and discussions with Margaret and Eric Jones.

10 Watts, *Facts*, 63–4, 89.

11 For this view of the 'Cotton Famine', Farnie, *Cotton Industry*, 138–45.

12 See above, Chapter 8.

13 Kirk, *Working-Class Reformism*, provides by far the best discussion of all this.

14 Kirk, *Working-Class Reformism*, 91, 98–9, 102; Collier, dissertation, 45.

15 R. A. Church, *The Great Victorian Boom* (1975), 71–5; H. J. Perkin, *The Origins of Modern English Society* (pbk. edn., 1972), 413.

16 G. D. H. Cole, *A Century of Co-operation* (1944), 177–8 and map in endpapers; Kirk, *Working-Class Reformism*, 135–51.

17 J. S. Leatherbarrow, *Victorian Period Piece* (1954), 59, 123; D. Newsome, *Godliness and Good Learning* (1961), Chapter 2, for the administrative efficiency and difficult personal characteristics of Prince Lee; Pevsner, *South Lancashire*, 40–4; see also Phillips, *Sectarian Spirit*.

18 Clarke, *Lancashire and the New Liberalism*.

19 Kirk, *Working-Class Reformism*, 162.

20 Ibid., 190–8; A. Tait, *History of the Oldham Lyceum* (Oldham, 1897), 28, 35, 37, 40.

21 W. H. Mills, *The Manchester Reform Club, 1871–1921* (Manchester, 1922), 10–13; H. J. Hanham, *Elections and Party Management* (1959), 71–2.

22 Joyce, *Work*, Chapters 3–6; see also M. Savage, MA dissertation, Univ. of Lancaster, 1981, 52–3.

23 Gaskell, thesis.

24 Kirk, *Working-Class Reformism*, Chapter 1; Dutton and King, 'Cotton Tyrants'.

25 Joyce, *Work*, 202, 205, 210–11.

26 H. J. Perkin, 'The Development of Modern Glossop', in A. H. Birch, *Small Town Politics* (Oxford, 1959).

27 Savage, MA dissertation, 9–11.

28 Joyce, *Work*, 211.

29 R. Penn, *Skilled Workers in the Class Structure* (Cambridge, 1982), 28–30; Foster, *Class Struggle*, 125–8, 211, 263–6.

30 Lazonick, *Cambridge Journal of Economics*; M. Holbrook-Jones, *Supremacy and Subordination of Labour* (1982), 163–4.

31 Holbrook-Jones, *Supremacy*, 64–70; Burgess, *Origins*, 26.

32 Jenny Smith and J. K. Walton, 'Property, Employment and the Co-operative Movement: the Social Structure of Co-operation in Sabden, 1923', *Historic Society of Lancashire and Cheshire* 134 (1985), 129–49; Kirk, *Working-Class Reformism*, 199–200.

33 Phillips, *Sectarian Spirit*, Table XXI.

34 J. P. Hemming, 'The Mechanics' Institute Movement in the Textile Districts of Lancashire and Yorkshire in the Second Half of the Nineteenth Century', Ph.D. thesis, Univ. of Leeds, 1974, 92, 107.

35 Kirk, *Working-Class Reformism*, 204–5.

36 Burgess, *Origins*, Chapter 1; Holbrook-Jones, *Supremacy*, Chapter 3.

37 Dutton and King, *Ten Per Cent*, 54–5.

38 Kirk, *Working-Class Reformism*, Chapter 6.

39 J. King, '"We Could Eat the Police"', *Victorian Studies* 1985.

40 R. Price on the Manchester brickmakers, *Past and Present* 1975.

41 Granath, MA dissertation; Lowe, thesis, 54–63 (but some of the statistics, especially those involving 1 per cent samples or invoking the so-called 'Widnes factor', should

be taken with a generous measure of salt); N. Kirk, in K. Lunn (ed.), *Hosts, Immigrants and Minorities* (1980), 82 – 3.

42 D. Thompson, 'Ireland and the Irish in English Radicalism before 1850', in Epstein and Thompson, *Chartist Experience*, 120 – 51; Kirk, in Lunn, *Hosts*, 70 – 2.

43 Kirk, in Lunn, *Hosts*, 82 – 8, 96 – 8; Rushton, thesis, 356.

44 Lowe, thesis, Chapters 3 – 6.

45 Kirk, in Lunn, *Hosts*, 91 – 4; Foster, *Class Struggle*, 243 – 6.

46 Midwinter, *Social Administration*, 140 – 60; Jones, *Crime, Protest, Community and Police*; S. Davies, 'Classes and Police in Manchester, 1829 – 80', in Kidd and Roberts, *City, Class and Culture*, 26 – 47.

47 Midwinter, *Social Administration*, 155.

48 Midwinter, *Social Administration*, 141; Dutton and King, *Ten Per Cent*; Lowe, thesis, 232 – 3; Cockcroft, in Bell, *Victorian Lancashire*; R.M. Jones, 'The Liverpool Bread Riots, 1855', *North-West Labour History Society Bulletin* 6 (1979 – 80), 33 – 42.

49 Gatrell, thesis, 114 – 16.

50 Ibid., 117 – 19, 132.

51 Vincent, *Poll-books*, 121; Waller, *Democracy*, 364 n. 154.

52 Fraser, *Urban Politics*, 223; J. Vincent, *The Formation of the Liberal Party, 1857 – 68* (1966), 135 – 8. Despite Vincent's recent incarnation as a journalist on the *Sun* 'newspaper', this early work is quite respectable history.

53 Vincent, *Liberal Party*, 133; Vincent, *Poll-books*, 166.

54 Calculated from Vincent, *Poll-books*, 157, 187.

55 Vincent, *Liberal Party*, 131 – 53; Phillips, *Sectarian Spirit*; R.S. Neale, *Class and Ideology in the Nineteenth Century* (1972), Chapter 3.

56 Hanham, *Elections*, 286.

57 J.D. Marshall, 'Corrupt Practices at the Lancaster Election of 1865', *Lancashire and Cheshire Antiquarian Society* 63 (1952 – 3), 117 – 30.

58 *Pen and Ink Sketches*, 190, 192.

59 Waller, *Democracy*, 12 – 19; Hanham, *Elections*, 285 – 6.

60 Vincent in *Historical Journal*, 1968; Hanham, *Elections*, 289, 321 – 2; Clarke, *Lancashire and the New Liberalism*, 10.

61 Clarke, *Lancashire and the New Liberalism*, 427 – 8.

62 Joyce, *Work*, Chapter 8.

63 Vincent, *Historical Journal* 1968, challenged by Lowe, *Historical Journal* 1973.

64 Hanham, *Elections*, 320 – 1.

65 Joyce, *Work*, 269.

66 Hanham, *Elections*, 105 – 9; Joyce, *Work*, 269 – 72; J. Garrard, *Historical Journal* 1977.

67 Joyce, *Work*, 292 – 5; Clarke, *Lancashire and the New Liberalism*, 33 – 6.

68 Joyce, *Work*, 240.

69 A. Ainsworth, *Histoire Sociale* 1977.

70 Clarke, *Lancashire and the New Liberalism*, 64 – 9; E.C. Midwinter in *Northern History* 4 (1969); P.J. Dixon, 'Urban Environment, Socio-economic Condition, and School Attendance in a Lancashire Borough, 1850 – 76', M.Ed. thesis, Univ. of Liverpool, 1977; K.P.C. Thorne, 'The Development of Education in Chorley and District from 1800 to 1902', M.Litt. thesis, Univ. of Lancaster, 1970; R. Roberts, *A Ragged Schooling* (Manchester, 1976), especially Chapter 16.

71 Hanham, *Elections*, 303 – 8; Joyce, *Work*, 257 – 61; R. Greenall, 'Popular Conservatism in Salford, 1868 – 86', *Northern History* 9 (1974), 123 – 38; W. Arnstein on the Murphy riots, *Victorian Studies* 1975; Kirk, in Lunn, *Hosts*.

72 Clarke, *Lancashire and the New Liberalism*, 45–52; Waller, *Democracy*, Chapters 1–6.
73 Hanham, *Elections*, 308, 313–4; Clarke, *Lancashire and the New Liberalism*, 32; Trodd, thesis, 154–5.
74 Clarke, *Lancashire and the New Liberalism*, 84–5; Joyce, *Work*, 311.
75 H. A. Turner, *Trade Union Growth, Structure and Policy* (1962), 127; Clarke, *Lancashire and the New Liberalism*, 84–8; M. I. Watson, 'The Cotton Trade Unions and Labour Representation in the Late Nineteenth Century', *Northern History* 20 (1984), 207–16.
76 Challinor, *Miners*, 143, 201, 214–15.
77 Joyce, *Work*, 311–15.
78 Lazonick, *Cambridge Journal of Economics*; see also Catling, *Spinning Mule*, 149. R. Penn, 'Trade Union Organisation and Skill in the Cotton and Engineering Industries in Britain, 1850–1960', *Social History* 7 (1982), 37–56, is flawed by a failure to grasp the nature of the changes in spinning in the middle decades of the nineteenth century.
79 Turner, *Trade Union Growth*, Chapter 3; Burgess, *Origins*, Chapter 4; Holbrook-Jones, *Supremacy*, Chapter 5; R. Smith, 'A History of the Lancashire Cotton Industry between the Years 1873 and 1896', Ph.D. thesis, Univ. of Birmingham, 1954.
80 J. L. White, *The Limits of Trade Union Militancy* (Westport, Conn., 1978), 78–9.
81 Ibid., 79–80, 105–6; Burgess, *Origins*, 283–90; Holbrook-Jones, *Supremacy*, 176–7.
82 Turner, *Trade Union Growth*, 144–7, 161–5; White, *Limits*, 34, 109–10.
83 Turner, *Trade Union Growth*, 132–5 and *passim*; White, *Limits*, 77 and Chapter 8; Burgess, *Origins*, 258–9, 262–3, 273–8; A. and L. Fowler, *The History of the Nelson Weavers' Association* (Nelson, n.d.), 6–8; E. Hopwood, *The Lancashire Weavers Story* (Manchester, 1969).
84 A. J. McIvor, 'Employers' Associations and Industrial Relations in Lancashire, 1890–1939', Ph.D. thesis, Univ. of Manchester, 1983.
85 Challinor, *Miners*, Chapters 3–7, 9–12.
86 E. L. Taplin, *Liverpool Dockers and Seamen, 1870–90* (Hull, 1974), 7 and Chapter 1, *passim*; A. P. Stephens, 'Dock Labour in the Port of Liverpool, 1890–1914', M.Soc.Sc. thesis, Univ. of Birmingham, 1981, 57–77, 86; Waller, *Democracy*, 3–4.
87 Taplin, *Dockers*, Chapters 2–5; Stephens, thesis, 128–37; Waller, *Democracy*, 102–5.
88 Barker and Harris, *St Helens*, 457–9.
89 Waller, *Democracy*, 103–4; Taplin, *Dockers*, 78.
90 E. and R. Frow, *To Make that Future – Now!* (Didsbury, 1976), 14–15.
91 Savage, dissertation, Chapters 4–5; Trodd, thesis, 296.
92 Trodd, thesis, 291; cf. A. and L. Fowler, *Nelson Weavers*, 120.
93 White, *Limits*, 76.
94 Trodd, thesis, 300–3.
95 Challinor, *Miners*, 269–70; Clarke, *Lancashire and the New Liberalism*, 320.
96 Waller, *Democracy*, 105, 252, 259.
97 G. Anderson, *Victorian Clerks*, Chapter 7.
98 N. Todd, 'A History of Labour in Lancaster and Barrow-in-Furness, *c.* 1890–1920', M.Litt. thesis, Univ. of Lancaster, 1976.
99 Mutch, thesis.
100 Clarke, *Lancashire and the New Liberalism*, 329–30; Challinor, *Miners*, 219; D. Howell, *British Workers and the Independent Labour Party, 1888–1906* (Manchester, 1984); J. Hill, 'Social Democracy and the Labour Movement: the Social Democratic Federation in Lancashire', *North-West Labour History Society Bulletin* 8 (1982–3), 44–55.

101 Howell, *Independent Labour Party*; Clarke, *Lancashire and the New Liberalism*, 40 – 1; J. Hill, 'Manchester and Salford Politics and the Early Development of the I.L.P.', *International Review of Social History* 26 (1981), 171 – 201; N. Reid, 'Manchester and Salford I.L.P.', *North-West Labour History Society Bulletin*, 5, 25 – 31; A. Ainsworth, 'Aspects of Socialism at Branch Level, 1890 – 1900', and S. Carter, 'The I.L.P. in Ashton-under-Lyne, 1893 – 1900', both in *idem*, 4. It is worth remembering, however, that membership of the Conservative Primrose League far outnumbered the supporters of all the socialist societies put together, as Martin Pugh's recent book demonstrates.

102 Challinor, *Miners*, Chapter 13.

103 Ibid., Chapter 14; J. Hill, 'The Lancashire Miners, Thomas Greenall and the Labour Party, 1900 – 1906', *Historic Society of Lancashire and Cheshire* 130 (1981), 115 – 30.

104 Howell, *Independent Labour Party*; White, *Limits*, 157 – 61.

105 Clarke, *Lancashire and the New Liberalism*, Chapter 12; Howell, *Independent Labour Party*, Chapter 9.

106 Clarke, *Lancashire and the New Liberalism*, 311 and *passim*.

107 White, *Limits*, 152 – 5; J. L. White, 'A Panegyric on Edwardian Progressivism', *Journal of British Studies* 1976 – 7; and various contributions to *North-West Labour History Society Bulletin*.

108 Farnie, *Cotton Industry*.

109 Ganley, dissertation, 10.

110 A. and L. Fowler, *Nelson Weavers*, 16; Barker and Harris, *St Helens*, 461.

111 Todd, thesis, 147 – 50.

112 Trodd, thesis, 346 – 7; M. O'Leary on Labour in Edwardian Bolton, MA dissertation, Univ. of Lancaster, 1981, Chapter 3; Todd, thesis, Chapter 4.

113 J. Hill, in *International Review of Social History* 29 (1984), 198 – 9; Waller, *Democracy*, 214 – 9, 260 – 1.

114 J. K. Walton, 'The Social Development of Blackpool, 1788 – 1914', Ph.D. thesis, Univ. of Lancaster, 1974, 535.

115 White, *Limits*; Waller, *Democracy*, Chapter 15; H. R. Hikins, 'The Liverpool General Transport Strike, 1911', *Historic Society of Lancashire and Cheshire* 113 (1961), 169 – 95; and see now P. L. F. Garner on the policing of this strike, MA dissertation, Univ. of Lancaster, 1985.

116 J. Liddington and J. Norris, *One Hand Tied Behind Us* (1978).

117 White, *Limits*, 53 – 5; Liddington and Norris, *One Hand*, especially Chapters 3,5; E. and R. Frow, *Future*, Chapter 4.

118 Liddington and Norris, *One Hand*; B. Drake, *Women in Trade Unions* (1920, reprinted 1984), 31; J. Liddington, *The Life and Times of a Respectable Rebel: Selina Cooper, 1864 – 1946* (1984); Doris Chew, *The Life and Writings of Ada Nield Chew* (1982); G. Mitchell (ed.), *The Hard Way Up: the Autobiography of Hannah Mitchell, Suffragette and Rebel* (1968).

Chapter 13

1 Kirk, *Working-Class Reformism*, 82 – 96; Rushton, thesis, 213, 297, 318.

2 Dixon, thesis, 44 – 5, 59 – 64.

3 Kirk, *Working-Class Reformism*, 98 – 105.

4 Oddy, in *Economic History Review*, 1983, 72 – 86.

5 Lowe, thesis, 182; Picton, *Memorials*, I, 527–8, 530–1.
6 A. T. McCabe, 'The Standard of Living on Merseyside, 1850–75', in Bell, *Victorian Lancashire*, 127–49.
7 Barker, *Glassmakers*, 173–5.
8 Marshall, *Furness*, 307–22.
9 Mutch, thesis, 170–207; Marshall, *Furness*, 241–2, 422.
10 E. H. Hunt, *Regional Wage Variations in England 1850–1914* (1975), Chapters 1–2; and cf. generally Hunt, *British Labour History 1815–1914* (1981), Part I.
11 Hunt, *Wage Variations*, 118–19, 127–8.
12 Burr-Litchfield, 'The Family and the Mill'; Mutch, thesis, 207–8; John, *By the Sweat of their Brow*; D. Hudson, *Munby: Man of Two Worlds* (1972).
13 E. Higgs, in *Social History* 7 (1982).
14 Trodd, thesis, 217; Liddington and Norris, *One Hand*, 58. D. Gittins, *Fair Sex* (1982), 96, gives lower figures for 1911, but the discrepancy is explained by the different basis of the calculation.
15 A. Clarke, *The Effects of the Factory System* (1899; reprinted Littleborough, Lancs., 1985); Cruickshank, *Children*, 94.
16 Trodd, thesis, 207–8.
17 Clarke, *Effects*, 90.
18 E. Roberts, *A Woman's Place* (Oxford, 1984), 142–6.
19 Ibid., 206, Appendix 4.
20 E. Roberts, in *International Review of Social History*, 27 (1982); Trodd, thesis, 191–208; White, *Limits*, 16–18; R. Gibson, *Cotton Textile Wages in the United States and Great Britain* (New York, 1948), 30; J. Jewkes and E. M. Gray, *Wages and labour in the Lancashire Cotton Spinning Industry* (Manchester, 1935), 15–18.
21 Marriner, *Merseyside*, 153.
22 G. Phillips, and N. Whiteside, *Casual Labour* (Oxford, 1985), 26–35; R. Williams, *The First Year's Working of the Liverpool Docks Scheme* (Liverpool, 1913), Chapter IV; Marriner, *Merseyside*, 151–2; Stephens, thesis, 322; Joan Smith, 'Labour Tradition in Liverpool and Glasgow', *History Workshop Journal* 1984.
23 E. Rathbone, *How the Labourer Lives* (Liverpool, 1909); C. E. B. Russell, *Social Problems of the North* (1914), Chapter 9; G. Anderson, *Victorian Clerks*, 65–71.
24 Roberts, *Woman's Place*; Gooderson, thesis.
25 Trodd, thesis, 216–21; White, *Limits*, 22–4.
26 S. J. Chapman and H. M. Hallsworth, *Unemployment in Lancashire* (Manchester, 1909), Chapters 2–3.
27 Waller, *Democracy*, 251–4; Todd, thesis, Chapters 4–5; Barker, *Glassmakers*, 231–2; Walton, thesis, 167; Chapman and Hallsworth, *Unemployment*, 42–3.
28 A. L. Bowley and A. R. Burnett-Hurst, *Livelihood and Poverty* (1915).
29 Roberts, *Woman's Place*; Hewitt, *Wives*, Chapter 6; R. Roberts, *The Classic Slum* (1974 edn.).
30 W. Greenwood, *There Was a Time* (1967), 27; see also Cruickshank, *Children*, 108.
31 See also P. Thompson, *The Voice of the Past: Oral History* (1978).
32 Walton, thesis, Chapter 5; Walton, *Landlady*, Chapter 2; Walton, *Seaside Resort*, Chapter 2; P. Wild, 'Recreation in Rochdale, 1900–40', in J. Clarke, C. Critcher and R. Johnson (eds.), *Working Class Culture* (1979), 146–7, is rather more pessimistic about Rochdale.
33 J. K. Walton, 'The Demand for Working-Class Seaside Holidays in Victorian England', *Economic History Review* 2nd ser., 34 (1981), 249–65.

34 T. A. Leonard, *Adventures in Holiday Making* (1934); Liddington, *Respectable Rebel*, 81–7; Chew, *Ada Nield Chew*, 53–4, 188–9, 209–10.

35 Liddle, in Cannadine, *Patricians*; Rogers, 'Lancashire Landed Society', for the Clifton Estate and Lytham; P. S. Peers, 'The Development of St Annes-on-the-Sea as a residential town and watering-place', MA dissertation, Univ. of Lancaster, 1979.

36 Clarke, *Effects*, 32, 134–6. See also M. Tebbutt, *Making Ends Meet* (Leicester, 1983), 32; Cruickshank, *Children*, 98. For an optimistic contemporary view, Russell, *Social Problems*, 105.

37 A. E. Dingle, 'Drink and Working-Class Living Standards in Britain, 1870–1914', *Economic History Review* 2nd ser., 25 (1972), 608–22.

38 T. Mason, *Association Football and English Society, 1863–1915* (Brighton, 1980), Chapter 2, especially 61–2.

39 J. Williams of Liverpool Polytechnic is currently conducting research on cricket in Lancashire between the late nineteenth century and the Second World War.

40 Poole, *Bolton*, Chapter 7; Bailey, *Leisure and Class*, Chapter 7; C. E. B. Russell, *Social Problems*, Chapter 8; Wild, 'Rochdale'; Gallagher, dissertation, 19.

41 Parliamentary Papers 1895, lxxxi, 311 ff.

42 Gallagher, dissertation, Chapter 1; J. Parke, 'The Social Functions of Public Houses in Manchester and Preston, *c.* 1840–1900', MA dissertation, Univ. of Lancaster, 1977, Chapter 4; Poole, *Bolton*, Chapter 4; C. E. B. Russell, *Social Problems*, Chapter 9.

43 M. J. Winstanley, *The Shopkeeper's World* (Manchester, 1983); Tebbutt, *Making Ends Meet*, 169 and *passim*; Cole, *Century of Co-operation*, map; S. Pollard, 'From Community Building to Shopkeeping', in A. Briggs and J. Saville (eds.), *Essays in Labour History* (1960); Smith and Walton, 'Co-operation in Sabden'.

44 Clarke, *Effects*, 40, 43–4, 134–6.

45 White, *Limits*, 28–30.

46 Tebbutt, *Making Ends Meet*, Chapters 1–2; Trodd, thesis, 196, 241–2.

47 Clarke, *Effects*, 72, 80, 152–3.

48 A. Foley, *A Bolton Childhood* (Manchester, 1973), 46; Liddington, *Respectable Rebel*, 68, 76; my copy of Marx's *Capital* was originally awarded as an attendance prize by a Pleasant Sunday Afternoon meeting in Blackburn, as the bookplate shows.

49 J. Minto, MA dissertation on public health reform in Preston, Chorley and Newcastle, 'Local Governors – their Attitudes to Public Health, 1830–55', Univ. of Lancaster, 1984, 96–8; Poole, *Bolton*, 24–5; and information from Lyn Murfin.

50 Bailey, *Leisure and Class*, Chapter 5; Poole, *Bolton*, 27–8; D. Russell, 'The Popular Musical Societies of the Yorkshire Textile District, 1850–1914', D.Phil. thesis, Univ. of York, 1979.

51 Gallagher, dissertation, Chapter 2.

52 K. S. Inglis, *Churches and the Working Classes in Victorian England* (1963); Clarke, *Effects*, 142; Ainsworth, in *Histoire Sociale*, 1977; C. E. B. Russell, *Social Problems*, Chapter 11; E. Roberts, *Woman's Place*, 4–6; D. Pugh, in *Journal of Religious History*, 1983. Some fascinating evidence on Liverpool was compiled by the Liverpool Free Church Commission of Enquiry: W. J. Rowland, *The Free Churches and the People* (1908), especially 17–27. This documents a dramatic fall in attendances in Everton, where the middle-class exodus exposed the failure of the Free Churches 'to secure the wage-earning classes'. But there was also a noticeable decline between 1902 and 1908 in middle-class Wavertree and Sefton Park. It may be significant that more than one-third of the Everton congregations arrived late for morning service, and about 30 per cent did so in the evening. Cf. the optimistic view for an earlier period offered by J. Lea,

'Baptists and the Working Classes in Mid-Victorian Lancashire', in Bell, *Victorian Lancashire*, 59–82. For a thoughtful evaluation of the oral evidence, see now H. McLeod, 'Religion: the Oral Evidence', *Oral History* 14 (1986), 31–49.

53 Liddington, *Respectable Rebel*, Chapter 3; R. Dennis, *English Industrial Cities of the Nineteenth Century* (1984), 33, for late Victorian long-range migration to Bolton and Preston; Lawton, 'Population Trends'; Poole, thesis, and 'Oldham Wakes', in J. K. Walton and J. Walvin (eds.), *Leisure in Britain, 1780–1939* (Manchester, 1983), 71–98; Foley, *Bolton Childhood*, 17, 52, 58–9; and information from Tess Buckland on the coconut dancers.

54 B. Webb, *My Apprenticeship* (1926), chapter on Bacup.

55 Walton, 'Lunacy'.

56 Trodd, thesis, 90–103; White, *Limits*, Chapter 4; Farnie, *Cotton Industry*, 293–4. Trodd's figures are confusing: cf. p. 251 of his thesis.

57 Trodd, thesis, 251–6; White, *Limits*, Chapter 4; Farnie, *Cotton Industry*, Chapter 7.

58 C. Bedale, 'Property Relations and Housing Policy: Oldham in the Late Nineteenth and Early Twentieth Centuries', in J. Melling (ed.), *Housing, Social Policy and the State* (1980), 54; Trodd, thesis, 256–7.

59 G. von Schulze-Gävernitz, *The Cotton Trade in England and on the Continent* (1895 edn., trans. O. S. Hall), 146; G. Roderick and M. D. Stephens, *Scientific and Technical Education in Nineteenth-Century England* (Newton Abbot, 1972), and subsequent works by these authors in similar vein.

60 Gibson, *Wages*, 30; von Schulze-Gävernitz, *Cotton Trade*.

61 Cruickshank, *Children*, 93–101; White, *Limits*, 56–63; E. and R. Frow, *The Half Time System in Education* (Didsbury, Ches., 1970); Clarke, *Effects*, 84, 97–105.

62 Foley, *Bolton Childhood*, 52; Clarke, *Effects*, 43–4, 56–7, 64–70, 86–7; Challinor, *Miners*; Warren, *Chemical Foundations*; Waller, *Democracy*.

63 Cruickshank, *Children*, 104–8; Hewitt, *Wives*, Chapter 8, and 219–25; Roberts, *Woman's Place*, 164–8; Liddington and Norris, *One Hand Tied Behind Us*, 58–9; Chew, *Ada Nield Chew*, 212; Report of the County Medical Officer of Health, 1904, xix–xxiv.

64 Roberts, *Woman's Place*, 93–103; Hewitt, *Wives*, Chapter 7; Gittins, *Sex*, Chapter 4; and articles on abortion by A. McLaren and P. Knight in *History Workshop Journal* 4 (1977).

65 Royal Commission on River Pollution, Reports, 1869–72, and Minutes of Evidence; Marshall, *Lancashire County Council*, 88; Wohl, *Endangered Lives*, Chapter 9.

66 J. Cherfas, 'Clean Air Revives the Peppered Moth', *New Scientist* 1489, 2 January 1986, 17. I owe this reference to Jenny Smith.

67 County MOH Report, 1904, lix–lxi; Redford and Russell, *Local Government in Manchester*, III, 112; E. D. Simon and J. Inman, *The Rebuilding of Manchester* (1935), 134; Wohl, *Endangered Lives*, Chapter 8.

68 Cruickshank, *Children*, 101–26; M. Pooley, in Pickstone, *Health*; C. and M. Pooley, in R. Woods and J. Woodward (eds.), *Urban Disease and Mortality in Nineteenth-Century England* (1984); Annual Reports of the Registrar-General.

69 J. Parry Lewis, *Building Cycles and Britain's Growth* (1965), 314–15; Bedale, in Melling, *Housing*, 58; Morgan, *Housing in Victorian Preston*, 73–9.

70 Redford and Russell, *Local Government in Manchester*, III, Chapter 35; S. M. Gaskell, 'A Landscape of Small Houses', in A. Sutcliffe (ed.), *Multi-Storey Living* (1974), 88–121; Gaskell, thesis, Chapter 5.

71 Simon and Inman, *Rebuilding*, Chapter 3; Morgan, *Housing in Victorian Preston*, 102–8.

72 J. Hassan, 'The Impact and Development of Manchester's Water Supply', *Historic Society of Lancashire and Cheshire* 133 (1984), 29 – 42; Redford and Russell, *Local Government in Manchester*, III, 120 – 3; Midwinter, *Social Administration*, 84 – 5, 97 – 104; Royal Commission on River Pollution.

73 Walton, thesis, Tables 4.1, 4.2; and see above, Chapter 11.

74 Pickstone, *Medicine*, Chapters 6 – 11; E. Roberts, in Pickstone, *Health*; Cruickshank, *Children*, 126 – 45.

75 Clarke, *Effects*, 36 – 7.

76 T. Hull, 'The Social Significance of the Public House in the Liverpool Economic System, *c*. 1840 – 1900', MA dissertation, Univ. of Lancaster, 1979, 6 – 29; H. Shimmin, *Liverpool Life: its Pleasures, Practices and Pastimes* (Liverpool, 1857), *passim*.

77 Hull, dissertation, 32 – 48; P. Richardson, 'The Development of Professional Football in Merseyside, 1878 – 94', MA dissertation, Univ. of Lancaster, 1983; T. Mason on Liverpool and Everton, 'The Blues and the Reds', *Historic Society of Lancashire and Cheshire* 134 (1985); E. C. Midwinter, *Old Liverpool* (Newton Abbot, 1971), 131 – 48.

78 Smith, 'Labour Tradition'; P. H. J. H. Gosden, *Self-Help* (1973), 119 – 42.

79 Tebbutt, *Making Ends Meet*, 51.

80 I. C. Taylor, 'The Insanitary Housing Question and Tenement Dwellings in Nineteenth-Century Liverpool', in Sutcliffe, *Multi-Storey Living*, 41 – 87; B. D. White, *A History of the Corporation of Liverpool* (1951), Chapters 10 – 11; C. Pooley and S. Irish, *The Development of Corporation Housing in Liverpool, 1869 – 1945* (Lancaster, 1984), Chapter 3; Waller, *Democracy*, 163 – 4, 232.

81 Rubinstein, *Men of Property*, 97 – 101.

82 Barker and Harris, *St Helens*, Chapters 27 and 28; Challinor, *Miners*, Chapter 15; E. Dunning and K. Sheard, *Barbarians, Gentlemen and Players* (Oxford, 1979); Barker, *Glassmakers*, 94; Diggle, *Widnes*, 61, 75, 80, 90 – 1, 107 – 10. Women accounted for nearly 25 per cent of Widnes's drink prosecutions in 1892: Diggle, 90.

83 Diggle, *Widnes*, 94 – 5; Barker and Harris, *St Helens*, 463 – 4, 469 – 70, 477 – 9; W. Millington, *Jubilee History of the Runcorn and Widnes Industrial Co-operative Society Ltd.* (Manchester, 1912), Appendix.

84 Barker and Harris, *St Helens*, Chapter 26, and 465 – 7; Diggle, *Widnes*, 28 – 9, 89; Bowley and Burnett-Hurst, *Livelihood*, 99 – 100; Challinor, *Miners*, 244 – 5; County MOH Report, 1904, 169 – 70.

85 Barker, *Glassmakers*, 181 – 4; Diggle, *Widnes*, 48, 90; Barker and Harris, *St Helens*, 464 – 5; Warren, *Chemical Foundations*, 95 – 6.

86 Warren, *Chemical Foundations*, 98 – 9; Challinor, *Miners*, 158 – 9, 265; Wohl, *Endangered Lives*, 278; Barker and Harris, *St Helens*, 458 – 9.

87 Warren, *Chemical Foundations*, 99 – 102; Diggle, *Widnes*, 86, 104 – 6; Barker and Harris, *St Helens*, 454, 466.

88 Marshall, *Furness*, Chapters 13 – 19; Roberts, *Woman's Place*, Chapter 4; Schofield, *Outline*; Gooderson, thesis.

89 Walton, thesis, Chapter 3; Walton, *Landlady*.

Chapter 14

1 Hopwood, *Lancashire Weavers Story*, 81.

2 Jewkes and Gray, *Wages and Labour*, 20 – 2; S. Pollard, *The Development of the British Economy 1914 – 80* (pbk. edn, 1984), 28 – 30; Hopwood, *Lancashire Weavers Story*, 82.

3 Sandberg, *Lancashire in Decline*, 176–7, 184–6; W. Lazonick, 'Industrial Organization and Technological Change: the Decline of the British Cotton Industry', *Business History Review* 57 (1983), 226; N. K. Buxton and D. H. Aldcroft (eds.), *British Industry between the Wars* (1979), 30.

4 J. Hinton, *The First Shop Stewards' Movement* (1973), 198–200; J. B. Jefferys, *The Story of the Engineers* (1946), 183.

5 Todd, thesis, Chapter 7; E. Roberts, *Working-Class Barrow and Lancaster, 1890–1930* (Lancaster, 1977), 13.

6 Diggle, *Widnes*, 136–7; Musson, *Enterprise*, Chapter 17; Barker, *Glassmakers*, 242–5.

7 Waller, *Democracy*, 270; Hyde, *Liverpool*, 142–7; B. Humphreys on women's work in Liverpool in the First World War, MA dissertation, Univ. of Lancaster, 1983, 22–3; Mountfield, *Western Gateway*, Chapter 14; Farnie, *Manchester Ship Canal*, 26–8.

8 Waller, *Democracy*, 271–2; Liddington, *Respectable Rebel*, Chapters 15–16; A. and L. Fowler, *Nelson Weavers*, 32–3; Humphreys, dissertation; M. Savage, Ph.D. thesis on women, employment and the labour movement in Preston, *c.* 1890–1940, Univ. of Lancaster, 1984.

9 R. Robson, *The Cotton Industry in Britain* (1957), 7, 338–9; L. H. C. Tippett, *A Portrait of the Lancashire Textile Industry* (1969), 3.

10 Sandberg, *Lancashire in Decline*, 177–8; Robson, *Cotton Industry*, 7; P. Harris, 'Social Leadership and Social Attitudes in Bolton, 1919–39', Ph.D. thesis, Univ. of Lancaster, 148–56; B. Bowker, *Lancashire under the Hammer* (1928), 32–43.

11 Sandberg, *Lancashire in Decline*, Chapter 9; M. P. Fogarty, *Prospects of the Industrial Areas of Great Britain* (1945), 218.

12 Harris, thesis, 156–63; A. and L. Fowler, *Nelson Weavers*, 27.

13 Gibson, *Wages*, Chapter 3.

14 Ibid., Chapter 2; J. H. Porter, in Buxton and Aldcroft, *British Industry*, 33–4, gives comparative figures.

15 Lazonick, 'Industrial Organization'; M. W. Kirby, 'The Lancashire Cotton Industry in the Inter-War Years: a Study in Organizational Change', *Business History* 1974, 145–159; Porter, in Buxton and Aldcroft, *British Industry*, Chapter 1; Sandberg, *Lancashire in Decline*, Chapter 6.

16 T. R. Gourvish, 'Mechanical Engineering', in Buxton and Aldcroft, *British Industry*, 133–5, 151 n. 24; G. R. Saxonhouse and G. Wright, 'New Evidence on the Stubborn English Mule and the Cotton Industry, 1878–1920', *Economic History Review* 2nd ser., 37 (1984), 508, 513, 516–17; Bowker, *Lancashire under the Hammer*, 78–9.

17 Fogarty, *Prospects*, 229–32; Lancashire Industrial Development Association (LIDA), Reports on areas within the county: *The Spinning Area*, 19; Farnie, *Manchester Ship Canal*, Chapter 6; Preston Corporation, *Official Handbook* (1937), 29–34.

18 Fogarty, *Prospects*, 219–20; LIDA, *The Weaving Area*, 21; G. Rushton, 'A Geographical Study of the Changes in the Industrial Structure of Lancashire Towns since 1931', MA thesis, Univ. of Wales (Aberystwyth), 1962, 14–15.

19 Fogarty, *Prospects*, 210–12; LIDA, *Weaving*, 7–8, and *Spinning*, 6.

20 Fogarty, *Prospects*, 204, 227–8; N. K. Buxton, 'Coalmining', in Buxton and Aldcroft, *British Industry*, Chapter 2; LIDA, *The Coal and Chemical Area*.

21 Diggle, *Widnes*, 146; LIDA, *Coal and Chemical*, 48; Fogarty, *Prospects*, 225–6.

22 Barker, *Glassmakers*, Chapters 16–21.

23 Musson, *Enterprise*, Chapters 18–19; LIDA, *Coal and Chemical*, 25.

24 Farnie, *Manchester Ship Canal*, 153, 167–8 and *passim*.

25 Aspinall and Hudson, *Ellesmere Port*, Chapters 7–8.

26 Board of Trade, *An Industrial Survey of Merseyside* (1932), 14.

27 Hyde, *Liverpool*, 168–70, is confusing; see also Mountfield, *Western Gateway*, 205.

28 Hyde, *Liverpool*, Chapters 8–9; Board of Trade, *Merseyside*, 19.

29 Hyde, *Liverpool*, 171–7; Board of Trade, *Merseyside*, 158–9; LIDA, *Merseyside*, 12–13, 35–6, 52; Fogarty, *Prospects*, 232–9.

30 Board of Trade, *Merseyside*, 166–71; LIDA, Furness, 13–29; Fogarty, *Prospects*, 207–10.

31 A. Warde, 'The Changing Occupational Structure of Lancaster, 1901–51', Regionalism Group, Sociology Dept., Univ. of Lancaster, unpublished paper.

32 LIDA, *Lancashire Coastal Area*; Fogarty, *Prospects*, 214–15.

33 N. Gray, *The Worst of Times* (1985), 4; C. Webster, 'Healthy or Hungry Thirties?', *History Workshop Journal* 13 (1982), 125 and *passim*.

34 G. Orwell, *The Road to Wigan Pier* (1969 edn.); A. Hutt, *The Condition of the Working Class in Britain* (1933), Chapter 2.

35 W. Greenwood, *Love on the Dole*; S. Constantine, '"Love on the Dole" and its Reception in the 1930s', *Literature and History* (1981), 232–47.

36 R. Pope, 'The Unemployment Problem in North-East Lancashire, 1920–38', M. Litt. thesis, Univ. of Lancaster, 1975, Chapter 2; Board of Trade, *An Industrial Survey of the Lancashire Area* (1932), 104–8; E. M. Gray, *The Weaver's Wage* (Manchester, 1937), 28–30.

37 D. Martin, 'Women without Work: Textile Weavers in North-East Lancashire, 1919–39', MA dissertation, Univ. of Lancaster, 1985; Pope, thesis, Chapter 6; Board of Trade, *Lancashire*, 120–2; Pilgrim Trust, *Men Without Work* (1938), 235–43.

38 Board of Trade, *Lancashire*, 111.

39 Pope, thesis, 180, 185; E. M. Gray, *Weaver's Wage*, Chaptes 2–3; Pilgrim Trust, *Men Without Work*, 235–6.

40 Hutt, *Condition*, 60–6.

41 Pope, thesis, Chapter 5; Hutt, *Condition*, 81–8; Webster, 'Healthy or Hungry Thirties'.

42 Batson, *Oldham*, 204–5; Jewkes and Gray, *Wages and Labour*, Chapter 2; LIDA, *Spinning* and *South-East Lancashire*; N. Gray, *Worst of Times*, 76–89, 147–55.

43 Orwell, *Wigan Pier*, 88–9.

44 LIDA, *Merseyside*, 17–20; D. Caradog Jones, *The Social Survey of Merseyside* (1934), II, 6–7.

45 Pilgrim Trust, *Men Without Work*, 88–100; Caradog Jones, *Social Survey*, II, 14–24; J. Lambertz and P. Ayers, 'Marriage Relations, Money and Domestic Violence in Working-Class Liverpool, 1919–39', in J. Lewis (ed.), *Labour and Love: Women's Experience of Home and Family, 1850–1940* (Oxford, 1986), 194–219.

46 Pilgrim Trust, *Men Without Work*, 97–8; Caradog Jones, *Social Survey*, I, 227, 235, 238; II, 128, 134, 193–6; III, 35, 41. The Co-op membership figures cover Liverpool and Bootle only.

47 Pilgrim Trust, *Men Without Work*, 96–7; Pooley and Irish, *Corporation Housing*, 72–4 and *passim*; Caradog Jones, *Social Survey*, I, 107–43, 172, 181–97, 259–98; Waller, *Democracy*, 287–9.

48 Redford and Russell, *Local Government in Manchester*, III, Chapters 40–1; Simon and Inman, *Rebuilding*, 10–72. Cf. Salford, where very little was done: R. H. C. Hayburn, 'The Response to Unemployment in the 1930s, with particular reference to South-East Lancashire', Ph.D. thesis, Univ. of Hull, 1970, 96.

49 Bateson, *Oldham*, 198, 210; Diggle, *Widnes*, 151–2; Foley, *Bolton Childhood*, 79; Hutt, *Condition*, 70–8.

50 Cf. Vigier, *Change and Apathy*, 183–4.

51 Harris, thesis, 180–1; Bateson, *Oldham*, 210.

52 Harris, thesis, 230–62; cf. Mitchell, *Hard Way Up*, for a grim but less jaundiced view from a participant.

53 Pope, thesis, Chapter 4; Liddington, *Respectable Rebel*, 350–4, 360–1, 378–82; Marshall, *Lancashire County Council*, 121–4; Hayburn, thesis, 480–1. See also Waller, *Democracy*, 302–3. Again, Mitchell's Manchester memories are kinder to officialdom and suggest that *some* small concessions could be achieved.

54 Harris, thesis, Chapters 1,6.

55 Waller, *Democracy*, 274–80; Musson, *Enterprise*; Warren, *Chemical Foundations*.

56 Rogers, 'Lancashire Landed Society'; Liddle, in Cannadine, *Patricians*; Marshall, *Lancashire County Council*, 63–5, 225.

57 Marshall, *Lancashire County Council*, Chapters 4, 12.

58 J. Mark-Lawson, M. Savage and A. Warde, 'Gender and Local Politics: Struggles over Welfare Policies, 1918–39', in L. Murgatroyd (ed.), *Localities, Class and Gender* (1984); also Liddington, *Respectable Rebel*, Part III.

59 Mitchell, *Hard Way Up*, 205; Savage, thesis, P. Taylor, 'Preston Trades and Labour Council: its role in Preston politics and society, 1918–39', MA dissertation, Univ. of Lancaster, 1978; Harris, thesis, Chapter 7; M. Toole, *Our Old Man* (1948), 147–8; Waller, *Democracy*, 324–7; K. Wilson on the inter-war Liverpool Labour Party, MA dissertation, Univ. of Lancaster, 1985; Hayburn, thesis; A. Shallice, 'Liverpool Labourism and Irish Nationalism in the 1920s and 1930s', *North-West Labour History Society Bulletin* 8 (1982–3), 19–28.

60 Pope, thesis, 270–88; B. Crosby, 'The Lancashire Campaign of the British Union of Fascists, 1934–5', MA dissertation, Univ. of Lancaster, 1977, 38 and *passim*.

61 Pope, thesis, 247–65; Harris, thesis, 109–32, 147; McIvor, thesis; A. and L. Fowler, *Nelson Weavers*; Turner, *Trade Union Growth*; Hopwood, *Lancashire Weavers' Story*.

62 Cf. J. Seabrook, *City Close-up*, on Blackburn.

63 Public Record Office, HO.45/11032/423878. See also Waller, *Democracy*; Pilgrim Trust, *Men Without Work*, on Liverpool; R. Bean, 'Custom, Job Regulation and Dock Labour in Liverpool, 1911–39', *International Review of Social History* 1982, 271–89; Waller, *Democracy*; Tebbutt, *Making Ends Meet*.

Chapter 15

1 D. Read, *The English Provinces* (1964), Chapter 5.

2 R. M. Smith, *Alka-Seltzer Pub Guides: the North-West* (1979), 15–17. I owe this reference to Jenny Smith, who found it less useful than she expected.

3 Borough of Preston, *Official Guide* (n.d., c. 1982), 33–5.

4 Farnie, *Cotton Industry*, tells a lot of the story, and Sandberg, *Lancashire in Decline*, adds to it substantially.

5 J. B. Priestley, *English Journey* (1934), 283.

Index

[401]

INDEX

Furness 1, 2, 12, 18, 23, 29, 31, 34, 55, 74–7, 79, 81–2, 89, 94–5, 123–4, 173, 175, 194–5, 216–17, 227, 286
furniture manufacture 208, 290–1
fustian manufacture 21, 61, 147–8, 161
Fylde, the 1, 24, 41, 46, 61, 75, 91, 94, 97, 127, 173, 336

Galgano, M. J. 79, 92
Galgate 122–3
gambling 190, 290, 298, 300, 317, 343, 353
Gammage, R. G. 240
Garrard, John 229
Garstang 162, 173, 223
Garston 209
gas supply 229, 274, 315
Gaskell, Mrs 3, 251
Gatrell, V. A. C. 126, 133, 137–8
Gawthorpe 27
Gee Cross 182
gentry 7, 8, 13–19, 23, 27–8, 31–3, 34–5, 40, 45–7, 49–54, 56, 63, 79–81, 85–6, 88, 91–4, 98–101, 108, 118, 125–40, 157, 221–4, 235, 238, 256–7
geography 3
   geographical determinism 46–7
George III 135
German merchants 209, 214, 226
Gilbody, Mr 57
glass industry 23, 68, 74, 114, 119–21, 124, 182–3, 208, 212, 214–16, 272, 286, 291, 319–20
Glassey, L. K. J. 86
Glasson Dock 123, 223
Glossop 103, 280, 298
Gooderson, Philip 5
government 7, 12–14, 18, 26, 28, 34, 36, 39–43, 45–50, 55–9, 67, 80–91, 125–6, 132, 134–40, 150–65, 174, 191–6, 221, 227–33, 254–64, 274, 296, 304, 313–15, 320–1, 346–51
grain trade 114, 116–17, 122, 209–10
Grant brothers, of Ramsbottom 132
Gray, Nigel 337
Great Harwood 338, 351
Greenall, Peter 120
Greenall, Sir Gilbert 225
Greenland 70
Greenwood, Walter 3, 293, 338
guilds 34, 67

Haigh 11, 223
Haigh, Christopher 12–14, 16, 19, 25, 38–9, 46–8, 50
half-time system 202, 279, 288, 308
Halifax 102
Hallé concerts 234, 236, 320
Halley, R. 55, 57, 93, 96
Halsall 38
Halton-on-Lune 10
Hampden Clubs 154
Hanham, H. J. 256–7, 263
Hargreaves, James 112
Harrold, Thomas 99
Haslingden 62–3, 156
Hassan, John 315
hat manufacture 12, 129, 133, 161, 208
Hawkshead 82
Hearth Tax 24, 29
Hesketh 37
Hesketh, George 38
Heskeths, of Rufford 222
Heysham 310
Heywood, John and Robert 131–2
Hibbert, Sir John 227
Hill, Christopher 18
Historic Society of Lancashire and Cheshire 224
Holcombe 57
Holmes, David 264
Holt, Alfred 210
Hornby Castle 15, 224
Hornby family 129, 247–8, 252
Horner, Leonard 106–7
Horwich 94, 207
Hoskins, W. G. 12
hospitals 235, 315–16, 321, 336
houses, housing 15, 27, 80–2, 131–2, 172–5, 224–7, 229, 230, 250, 253, 284, 307, 313–14, 318–22, 344–6
Howe, A. C. 130–2, 227, 229, 231
Hulme 173
Hume, Revd A., 236
Hunt, Henry 155–8
Hutt, Allen 337–8, 346
Hyde 169, 174, 202
Hyde, F. E. 70, 210
Hyndman, H. M. 274–5

illegitimacy 43, 56, 58–9, 89, 180, 195
Ince-in-Makerfield 276, 310

Independent Labour Party 275–9, 281
India 61, 67, 114, 200–1, 326, 329–30, 332
inflation 16, 27–8, 31, 284, 291
Inns of Court 14, 32, 34
Ireland 11, 18, 26, 52, 61, 68–9, 118, 153, 233
Irish, in Lancashire 91, 100, 153, 157, 165, 183–5, 189, 192, 196, 244, 252–4, 258, 261–2, 272, 286
Irish Nationalism 262–3, 272, 351
iron industry 12, 23, 68, 74, 76, 114, 119, 123–4, 213, 215–17, 227, 286, 336
Ironbridge 3
Irwell, River 311

Jacobites 80, 85–6, 91, 95–6, 100–1, 135
James I 31, 45, 57
James II 86
Japan 201, 326, 329–30, 332
Jews, in Manchester, 209, 226
John Shaw's Club 129–30
Jones, Ernest 240, 259
Jordan, W. K. 33, 43
Joyce, Patrick 132–3, 204, 228, 248–9, 260, 263–4
Justices of the Peace 14, 27–9, 32–3, 39–42, 49, 53–4, 57–8, 85–6, 88–90, 93, 95, 98, 101, 134–5, 143, 150–3, 155–6, 161, 191, 221–5, 227, 230, 237, 298, 300
jute industry 217

Kay, James P. 178, 189, 192, 253
Kay, John 64
Kemp, George 224
Kenyon, Roger 86
kinship 83, 110, 129, 176–80, 183, 195–6, 248, 265, 282–3, 286–9, 294–7, 302, 304, 342
Kirk, Neville 241, 246, 248, 253, 284
Kirkham 61, 97, 129
Knapp, R. O. 224
Knowles, Andrew, and Son 269
Knowsley 223

labour aristocracies 164–5, 170, 216, 244, 249–51, 269, 285, 343
Labour party 239, 258, 276–81, 328, 347–51
Lancaster 12, 25, 27, 76, 87–8, 94, 101, 116, 123, 158, 162, 188, 199, 208, 216–17, 219, 225, 255, 257, 274, 279, 290–4, 322–3, 327, 336, 350
landowners, landownership 30–2, 34–5, 51–4, 63–4, 70–1, 75–7, 92, 116, 121–2, 127–8, 188, 213, 217–18, 223–8, 237–8, 296, 348–9
Langton, John 3, 23, 73, 78–9
Lathom, Earl of 224
Law, Albert 352
Lazonick, W. 205–6, 330–1
Leaf, Leigh 88
Lee, Prince, Bishop of Manchester 246
Leigh 2, 93, 116, 147, 186, 219, 350
Leighton Hall 31, 32
Leland, John 12
Lever Brothers 214–16, 319
Leyland 173
Leyland Hundred 10, 25
Liberals 137–9, 228–9, 233–5, 239–40, 244–5, 248–9, 255–64, 276–9, 348–9
libraries 190, 229, 236, 301, 303, 320
Lichfield, diocese of 8
Liddington, Jill, and Norris, Jill 280–1
Lilford, Lord 222
Lindert, P., and Williamson, J. G. 167–70, 196
linen industry 11, 16–17, 20–3, 26, 61–3, 106, 121
literacy 33, 94, 97–8, 185–6, 303
Literary and Philosophical Societies 129, 136–8
Little Crosby 31
Liverpool 1–4, 11, 12, 17–19, 23, 25, 26, 29–30, 34, 49, 56, 60, 67–74, 76–7, 80–3, 87–8, 90–1, 94–5, 100–1, 103–4, 112–24, 130, 134, 138–9, 149–50, 152–3, 156–9, 162–3, 171–5, 183–4, 185, 187–8, 190–6, 199, 208–12, 216–20, 223, 225–8, 230–1, 235–8, 252–5, 257–9, 262–3, 270–4, 278–80, 285–7, 289–92, 294, 310, 317–20, 325, 327–8, 335–6, 342–5, 350–1, 353–6
   docks 1, 70, 87, 114, 210, 335
Livesey, Joseph 164
Livsey, Thomas 239–40
lodgers 169, 180, 284
Lofthouse, Jessica 1
London 4, 11, 13, 19, 22, 31, 33, 34, 49, 56, 59, 63–4, 67, 81, 93, 112, 115–16, 119–20, 142, 147–8, 153–4, 156, 161, 168, 174, 176, 188, 208, 219, 227, 234, 237, 252, 274, 286, 295
Long, P. R. 27
Longdendale 314
Lonsdale 23, 31, 52, 76
Lowe, Roger 9, 33, 99
Lowry, L. S. 4
Luddism 145, 151

[403]

INDEX

Quakers 54, 92–4, 131–3, 139
quarter sessions 8, 41
Quintrell, B. W. 27

Radcliffe 22, 199
Radcliffe, Sir John 27
Raffald, Mrs 98
railways 112, 116–17, 128, 190, 207, 209, 211, 213, 216–20, 225, 234, 248, 269, 274, 290–1, 295–6, 304, 317
Ramsbottom 132, 311
Rathbone family 238
Ravenhead 120
rayon 333, 336
Reach, Angus 172–4, 178–9
Read, Donald 355
Redford, Arthur 4
reform of parliament 137, 141–2, 149–65, 188–9, 193, 240
 Reform Act (1832) 134, 137, 139, 158–60
 Reform Act (1867) 239, 241, 248, 255, 257–8, 261–2, 272
Reformation 17–18
rents 7, 31–2, 80, 127–9, 158, 167–9, 173, 180, 286, 291, 322
retainers 7, 8, 13, 14
Ribble, River 2, 25, 32, 46, 60, 76–7, 91, 103, 110–11, 121–3, 216, 254
Richardson, R. C. 38, 48
riots 88, 95, 100–2, 105, 136, 139, 141–2, 150–3, 157, 160, 241–2, 252–4, 351, 354
Rishton family 14–15
river navigations 71–2
roads 71–2, 116–17, 192, 336
Roberts 288–9, 291, 293–4, 304, 322–3, 343
Roberts, Elizabeth 288–9, 291, 293–4, 304, 322–3, 343
Roberts, Robert 261, 293
Rochdale 22, 25, 29, 49, 61–3, 65, 72, 75, 95, 110, 115–16, 139, 145, 147, 149, 158, 160, 181, 184, 186, 188, 195, 203, 224, 229–30, 239–40, 244–5, 255–6, 277, 295–6, 299, 314, 327, 333
Rogers, C. D. 25, 33
Rogers, Graham 128
Roman Catholics, see Catholics
Roper, Esther 281
Roscoe, William 138
Rossendale 9–12, 20, 24, 28–9, 32, 61–4, 75, 77–8, 82, 89, 107, 199, 203, 208, 220, 274, 333
Royle 88
Royton 86, 139, 202
rubber industry 198, 208, 210, 333
Rubinstein, W. 237
Rufford 15
rum imports 113–14
Runcorn 72, 120–1, 213, 216, 291, 320, 335
Ruskin, John 303
Russell, C. E. B. 299
Rylands, John 236

Sabbatarians 48, 56–7, 187, 234
Sabden 162, 219
Saddleworth 62, 78, 304
sailcloth manufacture 61, 121
St. Annes 225
St. Helens 23, 71–2, 74, 76, 78, 89–90, 97, 118–21, 124, 148–9, 162, 175, 182–3, 186, 194, 212–15, 219, 260, 269, 278, 286, 311, 320–2, 327, 333–4, 342, 350
'St. Monday' 82, 98
Salford 25, 65, 123, 158, 184, 186, 202, 219, 229–30, 254, 257, 262, 274, 280, 285, 293, 299, 302, 313, 332, 347, 347, 351
Salford Hundred 24–6, 41, 45, 49, 51, 57, 76
salt trade 68, 70, 113–14, 118, 121, 213
Salvidge, Archibald 262
Samlesbury 110, 204
Samlesbury Hall 15, 129
Sandberg, L. 205, 328–9
Sankey Brook 72, 118–20
sawmilling 208
Scarisbrick, Charles 128
schools 7, 17, 33, 49, 97–8, 130, 165, 185–8, 202, 209, 222, 224, 234–6, 245–6, 260–1, 279
 Sunday schools 154, 181, 185–8, 189–90, 196, 243, 245–6, 260, 303–4
Scotland 116–17, 132, 212, 214
seamen 115, 211, 254, 270–2, 274, 285
seaside holidays 295–7, 304, 317, 323, 340
Sefton 27, 58
Sefton, Earls of 127, 223–4
servants, domestic 94, 131–2, 175, 209, 211, 223, 287, 289
sewers 173, 192–3, 229, 311, 314, 321

sex 14, 38, 44, 56, 58–9, 180, 191, 253, 261, 304
Sexton, James 279, 309
Shackleton, David 277
Sharples, William 189
Shimmin, Hugh 317
Ship Money 52
shipbuilding 68, 114, 121, 149, 168, 211, 216–17, 273–4, 291, 335–6, 342
shopkeepers 26, 159, 163, 192, 198, 216, 229–33, 255–6, 293, 300–1, 306–7
Shorrock, Eccles 230
silk industry 121–3, 147, 155, 208
Simon, Shena 231
Simon, Sir Ernest 345–6
Skelmersdale 310, 321
slave trade 4, 63, 68–9, 76, 113, 115, 119, 138, 159, 257
slipper industry 208, 333
Smelser, N. J. 178–9
socialism 185, 274–80, 288, 303, 315, 350–1
 Social Democratic Federation 274–7, 279, 302
South America 114, 200
Southampton 11, 210
Southcottians 181
Southport 116, 121, 128, 219, 225, 295–6, 323, 336
Speke 223, 336
spinners, operative 142, 145–7, 149, 151–3, 157, 160–1, 167, 169–70, 196, 205, 244, 249, 251–3, 264–70, 273, 284, 288, 291, 307, 309, 326, 341–2, 352
spinning, cotton 64–5, 104–9, 199–206, 208, 329–33, 339–42
 spinning jenny 105–6
 water-frame 105–7, 133
 hand-mule 105–8, 111, 145–6, 169–70, 178–9, 204, 250, 265–6
 self-acting mule 108, 147, 170, 204–6, 250, 265–6, 330–1
 ring-spinning 205–7, 267, 330–1
Spring, Howard 3
Staffordshire 73, 148, 216, 237, 269
Stalybridge 162, 240, 242, 253, 260, 263
Standish 58
Stanley family, see Derby, Earls of
steam engines 73, 104–12, 207–8
steam ships 210–11
Steers, Thomas 71
Stockport 65, 103, 144, 146–8, 152, 154–5, 157, 162, 177, 184, 186, 251–4, 257, 298, 314
Stonyhurst 27
Storey Brothers 216, 291
Stretford 258
strikes 141, 143–8, 158, 164, 170, 192, 201, 205, 251–2, 267, 270, 272–4, 279–80, 326–8, 352, 358
Stubs, Peter 119, 227
suburbs 2, 192, 199, 209, 225–6, 258, 275, 277, 290
sugar trade 68–9, 76, 113–14, 210
Sykes, Robert 148–9, 158, 160
syndicalism 280

Tariff Reform 233
Tarleton 37
temperance movement 163–4, 190–1, 251, 256, 260, 263, 275, 299–300
tenants 13, 15–16, 24, 27, 30–2, 53, 75–6, 94, 101, 128
Test and Corporation Acts 134–5, 138
Thirlmere 314
Thirsk, Joan 10
Thomas, Keith 39
thrift 81–2, 194, 242–5, 250–2, 255, 271, 285, 296, 307, 317–18
timber trade 209
Timmins, J. G. 110–111
tobacco trade 68–70, 113–14, 208, 210
Tockholes 93
Todmorden 94–5, 160, 192, 204, 208, 225, 244
Toole, Joe 351
Tories 91, 95–6, 126, 129–30, 134–9, 160, 178, 188, 191, 201, 222, 228–9, 232–5, 239, 244, 246, 248–9, 255–65, 276–7, 279, 318, 347–50
Touchet, Samuel 63
Townley family 88
towns 7, 12, 17, 25–7, 56, 62, 65, 68, 77, 90, 106, 123–4, 126–8, 158–9, 184, 196, 218–20
Toxteth 49, 93
trade unions 99–100, 141–51, 153, 159, 161–3, 168, 239, 242, 245, 250–3, 263–81, 308, 350–2
Trades Councils 231, 264, 273, 279–80
Trafford Park 222, 332, 334
Trawden 219

[405]